Deleted

MILESTONE DOCUMENTS
OF AMERICAN LEADERS

Exploring the Primary Sources
of Notable Americans

MILESTONE DOCUMENTS
OF AMERICAN LEADERS

Exploring the Primary Sources
of Notable Americans

Volume 3
Jefferson – Polk

Paul Finkelman
Editor in Chief

James A. Percoco
Consulting Editor

The Wright Library
Westford Academy
30 Patten Rd.
Westford, MA 01886

Schlager Group

Contents

Volume 1: Abigail Adams to Frederick Douglass

Volume 2: W. E. B. Du Bois to John Jay

MILESTONE DOCUMENTS
OF AMERICAN LEADERS

Exploring the Primary Sources
of Notable Americans

Thomas Jefferson (Library of Congress)

THOMAS JEFFERSON   1743–1826

Third President of the United States

Featured Documents
- ◆ **Declaration of Independence (1776)**
- ◆ **The Virginia Act for Establishing Religious Freedom (1786)**
- ◆ **First Inaugural Address (1801)**
- ◆ **Second Inaugural Address (1805)**

Overview

Thomas Jefferson, the third president of the United States, was born into one of Virginia's most prominent families on April 13, 1743. He showed his intellectual curiosity at the College of William and Mary, where he studied Greek, the classics, philosophy, and science, practiced the violin, and perfected his French. From 1767 to 1773 he practiced law, and in 1769 he was elected as a representative to the Virginia House of Burgesses. He became involved in the movement for American independence in 1774 when he wrote "A Summary View of the Rights of British America" in opposition to Parliament's Coercive Acts, sometimes called the Intolerable Acts. He was elected as a delegate to the Second Continental Congress, where he was assigned to a five-member committee that drafted the Declaration of Independence, though Jefferson was the principal author.

In the years that followed, Jefferson served Virginia and the nation in numerous capacities. He returned to Virginia to serve in what was now called the Virginia House of Delegates. From 1779 to 1781 he was the governor of Virginia, and at one point he escaped just minutes from being captured during a British invasion of Virginia in the Revolutionary War. In 1783 he was elected to Congress. From 1785 to 1789 he served as the nation's minister to France, and he was in that post in 1786 when the Virginia Act for Establishing Religious Freedom, which he had drafted in 1779, was passed. From 1789 to 1793 he was President George Washington's first secretary of state. In 1796 he ran for the presidency but came in second to John Adams; under the provisions of the Constitution at that time, he became vice president as the second-place finisher in the electoral vote count. In 1800 he again ran for president; he was tied with Aaron Burr in the number of electoral votes, throwing the election to the House of Representatives, which elected Jefferson. He was sworn into office (and delivered his first inaugural address) in 1801. He was easily reelected in 1804, delivered his second inaugural address in 1805, and served as president until 1809. His chief accomplishment after leaving office was the establishment in 1819 of the University of Virginia, the nation's first institution of higher learning that did not have a religious component.

Jefferson often preferred intellectual pursuits over the political fray. In addition to the interests he cultivated in college, he was an ardent student of architecture, agriculture, horticulture, and the infant science of archeology. He died at his Monticello estate on July 4, 1826, exactly fifty years after the Declaration of Independence. Interestingly, the epitaph on his tombstone makes no reference to the presidency but rather identifies him as the "author of the Declaration of American Independence" and "of the statute of Virginia for religious freedom" and as "father of the University of Virginia."

Explanation and Analysis of Documents

Thomas Jefferson was a student of the eighteenth-century Enlightenment, with its emphasis on human reason and science and the rejection of outmoded traditions and social structures. At the foundation of his political philosophy was his admiration for the yeoman farmer and a distrust of financiers and big-city interests. He favored a limited federal government, strong states' rights, and the strict separation of church and state. Most of his political views are expressed in the Declaration of Independence, the Virginia Act for Establishing Religious Freedom, and his two inaugural addresses as president.

◆ Declaration of Independence

When the Seven Years' War between Britain and France ended in 1763, Britain was in deep debt. To alleviate this debt, Parliament passed legislation designed to increase tax revenues from Britain's American colonies. Among these measures were the Stamp Act of 1765 and the Townshend Revenue Act of 1767. Many colonists objected to these measures, arguing that because the colonies were not represented in Parliament, that body had no authority to tax them. They expressed their dissatisfaction through the well-known phrase "no taxation without representation." By the early 1770s numerous colonists, Jefferson among them, were beginning to believe that Parliament had no authority of any type over the colonies, each of which had its own legislature.

Matters came to a head in December 1773 with the Boston Tea Party. To restore order in the unruly colony of Massachusetts, Parliament imposed what came to be called the Intolerable Acts. In response to these laws, the colonists in 1774 held the First Continental Congress,

1743

- **April 13**
  Jefferson is born in Albemarle County, Virginia.

1760

- Jefferson enters the College of William and Mary, where he studies for two years.

1767

- Jefferson begins practicing law in Virginia.

1769

- Jefferson is elected to the Virginia House of Burgesses.

1776

- Jefferson drafts the Declaration of Independence as a delegate to the Second Continental Congress.

- Jefferson becomes a member of the Virginia House of Delegates, serving until 1779.

1779

- Jefferson becomes governor of Virginia, a post he holds until 1781.

1783

- Jefferson is elected to Congress.

1785

- Jefferson is named minister to France, a post in which he serves until 1789.

1786

- The Virginia Act for Establishing Religious Freedom passes.

1789

- Jefferson is named secretary of state under President George Washington and serves until 1793.

1797

- Jefferson becomes vice president of the United States under President John Adams, a post he holds until 1801.

which resulted in two measures. One was to petition the king of England, George III, asking him to repeal the acts. The other was to organize a boycott of British goods. Hope remained high among many Americans who were still loyal to the British Crown that some accommodation could be reached.

Those hopes were dashed when the king rejected the colonists' plea and the Revolutionary War began in April 1775 with the battles of Lexington and Concord. The Second Continental Congress convened in May 1775. Even then, most of the delegates to the Congress were unwilling to declare independence from Britain and continued to hope that the king would intervene. When the king refused and issued the Proclamation for Suppressing Rebellion and Sedition, the movement for American independence gained ground. It gathered more steam after Thomas Paine advocated independence and the formation of a republican government in his enormously popular pamphlet *Common Sense*.

On June 7, 1776, Richard Henry Lee, representing Virginia, submitted a resolution of independence. Some delegations opposed the resolution. Others had not yet been authorized by their colonies to support independence. Lee's resolution was tabled while the Congress formed a committee to draft a document that would be published to explain why the resolution of independence was approved, if in fact it later was. Accordingly, on June 11, Jefferson joined John Adams, Robert Livingston, Benjamin Franklin, and Roger Sherman on the "Committee of Five" assigned the task of drafting a declaration of independence. The committee in turn relied on Jefferson to write a draft of the declaration. Jefferson based the document on three primary sources: the preamble to the Virginia constitution, the Virginia Declaration of Rights, written by George Mason in May 1776, and the English Declaration of Rights, written in 1689 to end the reign of King James II. Ironically, the task was regarded as a routine assignment, not one that would produce a foundational document that would inspire Americans for generations.

After some discussion and revision the committee submitted the declaration to Congress on June 28. Debate continued until July 2, when Congress, with twelve affirmative votes and one abstention, voted to approve Lee's resolution. After two additional days of discussion and debate over the wording of Jefferson's declaration, Congress approved it for publication on July 4. In an interesting footnote, John Adams predicted that July 2, not July 4, would become a great holiday in the United States.

In the opening sentence Jefferson acknowledges that if the American colonies were going to break with Britain, the grounds for doing so must be reasonable and the colonists should explain them to the world. In this sentence Jefferson invokes the "Laws of Nature." In doing so he was bringing into the discussion the concept of natural rights, which represents a philosophical tradition from the eighteenth-century Enlightenment as articulated by such British philosophers as Thomas Hobbes and John Locke. The next paragraph begins with the most widely known words from the Declaration: "We hold these truths to be self-evident, that all men are created equal, that they are endowed by their Creator with certain unalienable Rights, that among these are Life, Liberty and the pursuit of Happiness." The word *unalienable* meant that these rights could not be alienated, or taken away. They were not granted by the state or a king, nor could the state or a king deny to citizens the full enjoyment of these rights. People possessed rights by virtue of being human.

Given these natural rights, Jefferson goes on to say that a government, because it is "instituted among Men," could have legitimacy only from the "consent of the governed." Accordingly, if a government deprived its citizens of "Life, Liberty and the pursuit of Happiness," citizens were justified in abolishing their government and forming a new one. Jefferson acknowledges that governments should not be abolished for "light and transient causes" and then goes on to say that the "abuses and usurpations" of the British government showed a clear desire to reduce the colonies under "absolute Despotism." Thus, colonists had not only the right but also the duty to "provide new Guards for their future security."

The bulk of the Declaration of Independence consists of a lengthy list of ways in which King George had violated the rights of the colonists. Many pertain to administrative and legislative matters: that he had "refused his Assent to Laws," that he had "forbidden his governors to pass Laws of immediate and pressing importance," that he had opposed laws "for the accommodation of large districts of people," that he had imposed taxes without the colonies' consent, that he had "dissolved Representative Houses," that he had obstructed trade, and that in general he had harassed the colonies with burdensome and "fatiguing" requirements. It is noteworthy that the document never refers directly to Parliament. The colonists regarded the British Empire as a compact of territories under the authority of the king; because colonies were not represented in Parliament, that body had no authority over them. Thus Jefferson refers to Parliament as a "jurisdiction foreign to our constitution."

Additionally, says Jefferson, the king had prevented efforts to populate the colonies by passing obstructive laws for migration and naturalization and, in matters of administration of justice, had submitted the courts and judges to his will alone, abolished colonial charters, transported criminals for trial, and deprived citizens of trial by jury. He had created "swarms" of administrators whose only purpose seemed to be to "harass our people, and eat out their substance." He had kept standing armies in the colonies without the consent of the legislatures, elevated the military over the civil authorities, required the colonies to "quarter" armed troops (that is, to provide food and housing for them), seized colonists on the seas and forced them to serve in the British military, and transported mercenary soldiers into the colonies for the purpose of fighting the war.

After listing these "usurpations," Jefferson notes that repeatedly the colonists had petitioned the king for "Redress" and had met with "repeated injury." This observation was included because still, even after the outbreak

Time Line

1801	
	■ Jefferson becomes president of the United States.
	■ **March 4** Jefferson delivers his first inaugural address.
1805	■ **March 4** Jefferson delivers his second inaugural address.
1819	■ Jefferson founds the University of Virginia.
1826	■ **July 4** Jefferson dies at his Monticello estate in Charlottesville, Virginia.

of hostilities, many Americans remained loyal to the British Crown. Jefferson adds that the colonists had tried to appeal to "our Brittish brethren" and their "native justice and magnanimity" but that the British had been "deaf to the voice of justice and of consanguinity"—that is, of ties of blood. Accordingly, while the British would be friends in peace, they were "Enemies in War." In the final paragraph, Jefferson incorporates the language of the resolution of independence adopted on July 2, 1776, in proclaiming that the colonies were now free and independent of Great Britain. It is generally believed that the delegates to the Second Continental Congress signed the Declaration of Independence on July 4, 1776. Even Jefferson himself later perpetuated this incorrect belief. The wording of the Declaration was approved on that date, but most of those who signed the Declaration did not do so until August 2, 1776, and some signed even later.

◆ **The Virginia Act for Establishing Religious Freedom**

Jefferson once summarized his religious views by saying that he belonged to a sect that had just one member. He was raised in the Church of England, which was the established church of Virginia and as such received tax money. Additionally, Virginia law made it an offense to deny the existence of God or the Trinity, punishable, on the third offense, with imprisonment. Anyone seeking to hold public office was required to swear that he rejected the Catholic doctrine of transubstantiation (the belief that the bread and wine of Holy Communion are transformed into the body and blood of Christ).

At the College of William and Mary, though, Jefferson studied the work of such Enlightenment philosophers and scientists as John Locke, Isaac Newton, and Francis Bacon, and under their influence he adopted the views of

The Committee of Five, including Thomas Jefferson, Roger Sherman, Benjamin Franklin, Robert R. Livingston, and John Adams (Library of Congress)

deism. Deism was more a religious philosophy than a religion. It posited the existence of one God, a set of moral laws, and an afterlife, but it rejected notions of ongoing spiritual revelation and the belief that Christ was an incarnation of God. A common metaphor for expressing the deist view was that God was a divine watchmaker who constructed the world and set it in motion and then withdrew from involvement in human affairs. In the Declaration of Independence, Jefferson incorporated some of the common terminology of deism when he used such words and phrases as *Creator* and *Nature's God*.

Jefferson was a firm believer in the separation of church and state, having come to the belief that an established religion was a form of tyranny that denied people freedom of conscience. He used the now-famous phrase "wall of separation between church and state" in an 1802 letter to the Danbury Baptists. After stating his belief that "religion is a matter which lies solely between man and his God, ... that the legislative powers of government reach actions only, and not opinions," Jefferson added: "I contemplate with sovereign reverence that act of the whole American people which declared that their legislature should 'make no law respecting an establishment of religion, or prohibiting the free exercise thereof,' thus building a wall of separation between church and State" (http://www.loc.gov/loc/lcib/9806/danpre.html). In his *Notes on the State of Virginia* he famously said: "The legitimate powers of government extend to such acts only as are injurious to others. But it does me no injury for my neighbour to say there are twenty gods, or no god. It neither picks my pocket nor breaks my leg" (qtd. in Peterson, 1993, p. 59). Two hundred years later the courts continue to struggle with the precise meaning of this "wall of separation."

Jefferson became a leader of reform in Virginia after the Revolution. In 1779 he drafted and submitted to the Virginia General Assembly the bill for establishing religious freedom. In 1786, while Jefferson was out of the country, James Madison guided a slightly revised version of the bill through the Virginia legislature. The bill is not easy reading, for the first sentence consists of 547 words. In clause upon clause Jefferson explains his justification for the bill and his opposition to any form of state-sponsored religion. He states that people have "free minds" and that efforts to make the holding of civil offices dependent on religious beliefs caused "hypocrisy and meanness." He calls civil and religious leaders who attempted to impose their religious beliefs on others "impious" because they themselves were "fallible and uninspired men" who propagated "false religions." He objects to any requirement that people's tax money be used to support a religion to which they did not belong and adds that even if they did belong to the religion, forcing them to contribute to religious institutions deprived them of their liberty and freedom of conscience. He asserts that people have natural civil rights and that to make such rights dependent on religious belief was to deny those rights. Jefferson continues by developing the theme of hypocrisy, stating that when the state provided privileges and salaries ("emoluments") to people based on their adherence to a particular form of religion, doing so constituted a form of "bribery" and encouraged people to make an external show of religion. He notes that the civil government should concern itself only with "overt acts" that are destructive of peace and order, not with private religious beliefs. And finally, as was typical with Jefferson, he argues that if anyone held mistaken religious beliefs, "free argument and debate," not civil law, would defeat the error.

The next sentence contains the essence of the bill:

> Be it therefore enacted by the General Assembly, That no man shall be compelled to frequent or support any religious worship, place, or ministry whatsoever, nor shall be enforced, restrained, molested, or burdened in his body or goods, nor shall otherwise suffer on account of his religious opinions or belief; but that all men shall be free to profess, and by argument to maintain, their opinions in matters of religion, and that the same shall in nowise diminish, enlarge, or affect their civil capacities.

Jefferson concludes the bill by once more citing the Enlightenment concept of "natural rights"; he asserts that any later law that infringed on religious liberty would violate a natural right.

◆ First Inaugural Address

The opening paragraph of the first inaugural address expresses goodwill, hope for the growing nation, Jefferson's humility at being called to such a high office, and his belief that the Constitution has provided him with effective counselors in the legislature and throughout government. Jefferson gets to the core of his message in the second paragraph when he alludes to the recent election ("contest of opinion") and to "the animation of discussions and of exertions" that had "sometimes worn an aspect which might impose on strangers unused to think freely and to speak and to write what they think." This statement is an almost comically understated reference to the bitter election that Jefferson had eventually won. He makes a call for unity—"We are all Republicans, we are all Federalists"—but this type of statement is common among new presidents, who express the hope that after the divisions of an election, legislators and citizens can come together for the common welfare.

Jefferson had good reason for wanting to appeal to national unity. In the election campaign of 1800 the Republican (or Democratic-Republican) Party he led was pitted against the Federalist Party led by the incumbent president,

John Adams. Jefferson's running mate, though, was the New York State assemblyman Aaron Burr, who was nominally a member of Jefferson's own party but held beliefs more like those of the Federalists and was, in fact, backed by many Federalists. These parties had widely differing visions of what America should be, with the Republicans favoring an agricultural nation with limited federal government and the Federalists envisioning a big-city manufacturing nation with a strong federal government. Throughout the campaign charges and countercharges flew. The Republicans claimed that the Federalists favored aristocratic values; the Federalists accused the Republicans of all manner of high crimes and warned that Republicans would usher in the kind of revolution that was in full swing in France. The campaign became personal, with slanders and smears on both sides. Jefferson's opponents characterized him as an "atheist" and an "infidel." Each party tried to manipulate the voting process in the states in its favor, and after the votes were cast, allegations of irregularities surfaced.

Although Jefferson won a strong majority of the popular vote, he and Aaron Burr were tied in the electoral vote count, throwing the election into the House of Representatives. Under the provisions of the Constitution in effect at that time, members of the Electoral College did not vote separately for president and vice president; they cast one vote, and the runner-up was to be vice president. From February 11 to February 17 the House conducted thirty-five ballots before electing Jefferson on the thirty-sixth. Jefferson's election marked a major realignment in the nation's political structure, essentially ending Federalist rule and bringing about the eventual demise of the Federalist Party.

The bulk of Jefferson's inaugural address, then, is an appeal for unity. He defends the Republican Party against the charge that it was not strong enough for the nation to survive. He notes that both parties had the same goals, such as a strong union based on representative government, where all citizens had the freedom and scope to pursue their own welfare, free from the despotism of monarchies. He appeals to the nation's "benign religion," practiced in "various forms" but united by "honesty, truth, temperance, gratitude, and the love of man." In the fourth paragraph, Jefferson outlines the principles that will shape his administration, including equal justice, no "entangling alliances" with other nations, support of the rights of the states, a "well-disciplined militia," frugality in public expenditures, the diffusion of knowledge, particularly through a free press, and the rights guaranteed by the Constitution. In the final two paragraphs he again expresses his humility in the face of the duties he has been called on to perform and asks for the blessing of an "Infinite Power."

◆ Second Inaugural Address

If Jefferson's first inaugural address was a general statement of principles and an appeal to national unity after the bitter election of 1800, the second inaugural address was a more specific summary of the accomplishments of the preceding four years. In 1805 Jefferson did not have to dwell on the 1804 election. During his first term his popularity grew, and he won almost 73 percent of the popular vote against his rival, the Federalist Charles Pinckney, who won just over 27 percent—still a record margin in a multiparty U.S. presidential election. The electoral vote count was 162 to fourteen in Jefferson's favor.

After two introductory paragraphs, Jefferson takes up the issue of foreign affairs. What is noteworthy is what Jefferson does *not* say: He does not directly refer to the Tripolitan War conducted against the Barbary Coast pirates in the Mediterranean Sea from 1801 to 1805—the first war that America fought on foreign soil and one that many Americans opposed. Dating back to the fifteenth century the Muslim states of Tripoli, Tunis, Morocco, and Algiers had increased their wealth by piracy and kidnapping directed against European Christians, and by the eighteenth century they were demanding payments of tribute. After American independence, Congress appropriated $80,000 for tribute to the Barbary states and later signed agreements with Morocco and Tripoli to make annual payments in return for the safety of American ships. Tripoli reneged on its agreement by raising its demands for tribute in May 1801 and declared war on the United States. Jefferson had long opposed payment of tribute, and in response to Tripoli's actions he sent a squadron of warships to the Barbary Coast, resulting in the defeat of the pirate states in 1805. It is possible that Jefferson is making a glancing reference to the war when he says that "history bears witness to the fact, that a just nation is taken on its word, when recourse is had to armaments and wars to bridle others."

Jefferson then turns to domestic affairs. He cites as a key accomplishment the discontinuation of "internal taxes" and the "domiciliary vexation" caused by hordes of tax collectors. He notes that the federal government's chief source of revenue was now tariffs collected on foreign luxury goods—and paid by the people who can most afford to do so, in contrast to the farmer, mechanic, and laborer, who never had to see a tax collector. He goes on to say that the nation was in the process of extinguishing its debt and could look forward to the day when revenues would be applied to internal improvements such as canals, roads, education, and projects undertaken by the states, and the federal government could meet its obligations without having to burden future generations with debt.

Jefferson next refers to the expansion of the country by the Louisiana Purchase. In 1803 the United States essentially doubled in size with the purchase from France of 828,000 square miles for $15 million—about four cents per acre. Many members of Congress and the public opposed the purchase. They argued that the Constitution did not give the president authority to purchase lands from foreign nations. They also balked at the expense, for $15 million was greater than the size of the entire federal budget. Nevertheless, the Senate ratified the purchase treaty on October 20, 1803, and settlement of the new lands, which included most of the territory between the Mississippi River and the Rocky Mountains, began immediately. Jefferson responds to the argument that expanding the size of the nation endangered its stability by saying, "The larger our association, the less will it be shaken by local passions; and in any view, is it not better that the opposite bank of the Mississippi should be settled by our own brethren and children, than by strangers of another family?"

After raising the issue of religion, noting that he has consistently opposed any effort to impose religious "exercises" such as days of fasting and thanksgiving, Jefferson turns to relations with American Indians. Like his attitude toward slaves, Jefferson's attitude toward the Indians was mixed. On the one hand he frequently said that the Indians were noble, and he took great interest in the archeology of Indian artifacts. On the other he believed that it would be impossible for the Indians to maintain their culture and way of life in the face of the onslaught of European settlers. He believed, as he expresses here, that the only hope for the Indians was to absorb them into the white culture and convert them from hunter-gatherers to settled agricultural people. He notes, however, obstacles to this goal, chiefly the "ignorance" and habits of mind of the Indians themselves, many of whom insisted on adhering to ancient ways and remained resistant to change. Although Jefferson expresses kindly feelings to the Indians, the policies of his administration began the process of forcing them off their ancestral lands and ever farther to the west, a policy that would gain full force during the administration of Andrew Jackson.

If Jefferson had mixed views regarding slaves and Indians, the same can be said about his relationship with the press. On the one hand he once famously wrote in a letter (January 16, 1787) to the Virginia statesman Edward Carrington, "Were it left to me to decide whether we should have a government without newspapers or newspapers without a government, I should not hesitate a moment to prefer the latter" (qtd. in Appleby and Ball, p. 153). On the other hand, he also said in a letter (January 2, 1814) to Walter Jones (a member of the Virginia House of Delegates and later the U.S House of Representatives), "I deplore… the putrid state into which our newspapers have passed and the malignity, the vulgarity, and mendacious spirit of those who write for them" (qtd. in Appleby and Ball, p. 38). In the second inaugural address, Jefferson is more tactful, but only marginally so, when he refers to the press's "licentiousness," "falsehood and defamation," and "false reasonings." In characteristic fashion, though, he expresses his faith that after a "full hearing" the "public judgment" will separate truth from falsehood. Jefferson concludes by reiterating some of the goals he enunciated in his first inaugural address: the public good, religious freedom, equality of rights, and the ascendancy of truth.

Impact and Legacy

Through his speeches, writings, and personal example Thomas Jefferson was one of the nation's most influential presidents—and perhaps the nation's most intellectual president, prompting President John F. Kennedy to remark to a gathering of forty-nine Nobel Prize winners in 1962, "I think this is the most extraordinary collection of talent and of human knowledge that has ever been gathered together at the White House—with the possible exception of when Thomas Jefferson dined alone" (qtd. in *Public Papers of the Presidents: Kennedy*, p. 347). Although he was a forceful president, he believed that the powers of the federal government should be limited. His vision of America was that of an agricultural utopia, so he maintained an inherent distrust of financiers, manufacturing interests, and big cities; he opposed, for example, the economic policies of Alexander Hamilton, George Washington's secretary of the treasury, which favored the interests of the moneyed classes to the detriment of farmers, artisans, and small-town citizens. He opposed the Alien and Sedition Acts passed during the administration of his predecessor, John Adams, regarding them as a threat to civil liberties. During his administration he practiced frugality, and his two terms as president were marked by the absence of any trappings of high office. He dressed simply, usually in a black suit, walked to his inaugurations, and greeted foreign dignitaries not with formal "levees" but with informal dinners where people were seated without regard to rank.

Jefferson believed that the young nation had already strayed from its republican roots and that if it was to survive, it had to return to those roots. In this context the term *republican* does not identify a political party. Rather, it refers to a philosophy of government that arose in opposition to eighteenth-century monarchies, viewing them as corrupt, tyrannical, and steeped in luxury. Republicanism at the time was based on the concept of egalitarianism, whereby independent, virtuous people worked the land and distinction and promotion were based on merit. It rejected the notion that only a strong, hereditary monarchy could maintain order over large and diverse populations. These concepts were at the core of what came to be known as Jeffersonian democracy.

These principles, products of the eighteenth-century Enlightenment and shared by most of the nation's founders, were enshrined in the Declaration of Independence and Constitution. Ironically, although the Declaration is now regarded as one of the nation's two most important foundational documents, in the years following July 4, 1776, it in some sense "disappeared," and political writers of the time rarely referred to it. It was rediscovered only in the 1790s with the rise of Jeffersonian democracy and its struggle with Federalists such as Hamilton and Adams.

The impact of Jefferson's views on religion, expressed in the Virginia Act for Establishing Religious Freedom, continue to resonate more than two centuries later. That Jefferson believed in Christian concepts of God is clear; that he regularly invoked the name of that God—in, for example, his inaugural addresses—is equally clear. But in raising the "wall of separation between church and state" he left it for later generations to determine where, and how high, that wall should be. Such issues as school prayer, the teaching of evolution versus creationism, religious displays on public property, and whether student prayer groups or religious clubs can meet in public schools continue to trouble Americans and the court system.

It remains to note Jefferson's views on slavery. In the minds of some Americans, Jefferson was guilty of an enormous hypocrisy as a slave owner in stating that "all men are created equal." Many historians now accept that he fathered children with one of his slaves, Sally Hemings, a claim first made in 1802. Although Jefferson owned slaves, he long advocated their emancipation, or at least the elimination of the slave trade; an early draft of the Declaration of Independence contained a clause condemning the British Crown for supporting the slave trade, but the clause was deleted during debates on the document's wording. Jefferson was often troubled by his conscience—on the one hand recognizing the evils of slavery and on the other having to contend with nearly lifelong extensive personal debt. He further believed, though he later repudiated this belief, that habit and custom would make it impossible for slaves to live as free men and women. In sum, he hoped to see the eradication of the slave trade with the hope that in future years the institution of slavery itself could be abolished.

Key Sources

Jefferson's papers and writings can be found in numerous sources. A handy one-volume edition is *Thomas Jefferson: Writings: Autobiography / Notes on the State of Virginia / Public and Private Papers / Letters* (1984). *Notes on the State of Virginia* was Jefferson's only book. Joyce Appleby and Terence Ball edited *Thomas Jefferson, Political Writings* (1999). Jefferson's letter to the Danbury Baptists can be found at the Library of Congress (http://www.loc.gov/loc/lcib/9806/danpre.html). An online collection of Jefferson's papers is provided by the Library of Congress at http://memory.loc.gov/ammem/collections/jefferson_papers/. The University of Virginia Library maintains an online collection of Jefferson's papers and letters at http://etext.virginia.edu/jefferson/texts/. Various of Jefferson's papers and speeches are available from the Avalon Project at Yale University, http://avalon.law.yale.edu/subject_menus/jeffpap.asp, and from Project Gutenberg at http://www.gutenberg.org/etext/16781. Two collections of letters are important: *The Adams-Jefferson Letters*, edited by Lester J. Cappon (1959), and *The Republic of Letters: The Correspondence between Thomas Jefferson and James Madison, 1776–1826* (1995). The chief collection of Jefferson's papers is *The Papers of Thomas Jefferson*, produced by a team of researchers at Princeton University. As of 2008 thirty-four volumes covering the period from 1760 to July 31, 1801, have been published.

Further Reading

■ Articles

Fatovic, Clement. "Constitutionalism and Presidential Prerogative: Jeffersonian and Hamiltonian Perspectives." *American Journal of Political Science* 48, no. 3 (2004): 429–444.

"We hold these truths to be self-evident, that all men are created equal, that they are endowed by their Creator with certain unalienable Rights, that among these are Life, Liberty and the pursuit of Happiness."

(Declaration of Independence)

"These United Colonies are, and of Right ought to be Free and Independent States."

(Declaration of Independence)

"No man shall be compelled to frequent or support any religious worship, place, or ministry whatsoever, nor shall be enforced, restrained, molested, or burdened in his body or goods, nor shall otherwise suffer on account of his religious opinions or belief."

(The Virginia Act for Establishing Religious Freedom)

"I believe this, on the contrary, the strongest Government on earth. I believe it the only one where every man, at the call of the law, would fly to the standard of the law, and would meet invasions of the public order as his own personal concern."

(First Inaugural Address)

"Nor was it uninteresting to the world, that an experiment should be fairly and fully made, whether freedom of discussion, unaided by power, is not sufficient for the propagation and protection of truth—whether a government, conducting itself in the true spirit of its constitution, with zeal and purity, and doing no act which it would be unwilling the whole world should witness, can be written down by falsehood and defamation."

(Second Inaugural Address)

"Since truth and reason have maintained their ground against false opinions in league with false facts, the press, confined to truth, needs no other legal restraint; the public judgment will correct false reasonings and opinions, on a full hearing of all parties; and no other definite line can be drawn between the inestimable liberty of the press and its demoralizing licentiousness."

(Second Inaugural Address)

Pasley, Jeffrey L. "Politics and the Misadventures of Thomas Jefferson's Modern Reputation: A Review Essay." *Journal of Southern History* 72, no. 4 (2006): 871–908.

Perry, Barbara A. "Jefferson's Legacy to the Supreme Court: Freedom of Religion." *Journal of Supreme Court History* 31, no. 2 (2006): 181–198.

■ **Books**

Ackerman, Bruce. *The Failure of the Founding Fathers: Jefferson, Marshall, and the Rise of Presidential Democracy.* Cambridge, Mass.: Harvard University Press, 2005.

Appleby, Joyce. *Thomas Jefferson.* New York: Henry Holt, 2003.

Questions for Further Study

1. The Declaration of Independence is a work of such brilliance and importance that, had it been his only achievement, it would have been enough to make Jefferson's name a household word for all time. But the Declaration did not spring simply from its author's brain; rather, it had its roots in developments stretching back half a millennium to the signing of the Magna Carta. Discuss the historical background of the Declaration with regard to relations between the English monarch and his subjects; the influence of the philosophers Thomas Hobbes and John Locke on its underlying principles; and its specific debt to the Virginia constitution, the Virginia Declaration of Rights, and the English Declaration of Right.

2. Consider the Declaration of Independence from the standpoint of subsequent history. Pay particular attention to its influence on American principles of government and views on freedom, especially as those later came to relate to groups not represented in the original document—that is, women and minorities. Also discuss the ironic fact that it was initially not even considered to be of great importance and would fall into relative obscurity in the quarter-century before Jefferson's election as president.

3. What were Jefferson's views on religion and its place in relation to government? Examine his deist beliefs and the impact they had on his thinking as well as his writings on church and state, particularly the Virginia Act for Establishing Religious Freedom. Then consider how he would have addressed later church-state issues, particularly those that have become part of the backdrop of modern life, such as the debate over Christmas displays on government property. What would Jefferson have to say about these issues if he were alive today?

4. People who think American politics in the twenty-first century is unusually rough and mean-spirited might be comforted (or not) by studying the history of past political conflicts, such as the brutal war between the Federalists, led by John Adams and Alexander Hamilton, and Jefferson's Democratic-Republicans. What were the principal areas of contention between the two philosophies? In what ways was the division of parties similar to that between the Democrats and Republicans today, and in what ways have the lines shifted? The fact that the two modern parties' names are drawn from that of Jefferson's party suggests that his side won, yet the federal principle is more alive today than ever, so who really had the victory in the end?

5. Unquestionably one of the greatest individuals in human, let alone American, history, Jefferson was a man of great strengths and abilities—but also of great contradictions. Discuss his achievements, not only in politics but also in other areas, such as scientific study, and consider his failings. Most notable among the latter, of course, was his attitude and relationship toward slavery. Why did he, the author of the words "all men are created equal," fail to apply this principle to an issue directly under his nose—or did he simply refuse to address a matter that had much to do with his livelihood as a Virginia plantation owner? To what extent can he be excused for this, as a mere mortal and a man of his time, and to what extent does his very genius and greatness make him all the more responsible for this and other shortcomings?

Banning, Lance. *The Jeffersonian Persuasion: Evolution of a Party Ideology*. Ithaca, N.Y.: Cornell University Press, 1978.

Bernstein, R. B. *Thomas Jefferson*. New York: Oxford University Press, 2003.

Cunningham, Noble E. *In Pursuit of Reason: The Life of Thomas Jefferson*. New York: Ballantine, 1988.

Dunn, Susan. *Jefferson's Second Revolution: The Election Crisis of 1800 and the Triumph of Republicanism*. Boston: Houghton Mifflin, 2004.

Ellis, Joseph J. *American Sphinx: The Character of Thomas Jefferson*. New York: Vintage, 1996.

Ferling, John. *Adams vs. Jefferson: The Tumultuous Election of 1800*. New York: Oxford University Press, 2004.

Finkelman, Paul. *Slavery and the Founders: Race and Liberty in the Age of Jefferson*. 2nd ed. Armonk, N.Y.: M.E. Sharpe, 2001.

Hitchens, Christopher. *Thomas Jefferson: Author of America*. New York: HarperCollins, 2005.

Jayne, Allen. *Jefferson's Declaration of Independence: Origins, Philosophy, and Theology*. Lexington: University Press of Kentucky, 1998.

Kennedy, Roger G. *Mr. Jefferson's Lost Cause: Land, Farmers, Slavery, and the Louisiana Purchase*. New York: Oxford University Press, 2003.

Malone, Dumas. *Jefferson and His Time*. 6 vols. Boston: Little, Brown, 1948–1982.

McDonald, Forrest. *The Presidency of Thomas Jefferson*. Lawrence: University Press of Kansas, 1987.

Peterson, Merrill D. *The Jefferson Image in the American Mind*. New York: Oxford University Press, 1960.

———. *Thomas Jefferson and the New Nation*. New York: Oxford University Press, 1975.

———, ed. *The Political Writings of Thomas Jefferson*. Chapel Hill: University of North Carolina Press, 1993.

Public Papers of the Presidents of the United States: John F. Kennedy, 1962. Washington, D.C.: U.S. Government Printing Office, 1963.

Sanford, Charles B. *The Religious Life of Thomas Jefferson*. Charlottesville: University Press of Virginia, 1984.

Schachner, Nathan. *Thomas Jefferson: A Biography*. 2 vols. New York: Appleton-Century-Crofts, 1951.

Sheridan, Eugene R. *Jefferson and Religion*. Chapel Hill: University of North Carolina Press, 2001.

Staloff, Darren. *Hamilton, Adams, Jefferson: The Politics of Enlightenment and the American Founding*. New York: Hill and Wang, 2005.

Tucker, Robert W., and David C. Hendrickson. *Empire of Liberty: The Statecraft of Thomas Jefferson*. New York: Oxford University Press, 1992.

—Michael J. O'Neal

DECLARATION OF INDEPENDENCE (1776)

When in the Course of human events, it becomes necessary for one people to dissolve the political bands which have connected them with another, and to assume among the powers of the earth, the separate and equal station to which the Laws of Nature and of Nature's God entitle them, a decent respect to the opinions of mankind requires that they should declare the causes which impel them to the separation.

We hold these truths to be self-evident, that all men are created equal, that they are endowed by their Creator with certain unalienable Rights, that among these are Life, Liberty and the pursuit of Happiness.—That to secure these rights, Governments are instituted among Men, deriving their just powers from the consent of the governed,—That whenever any Form of Government becomes destructive of these ends, it is the Right of the People to alter or to abolish it, and to institute new Government, laying its foundation on such principles and organizing its powers in such form, as to them shall seem most likely to effect their Safety and Happiness. Prudence, indeed, will dictate that Governments long established should not be changed for light and transient causes; and accordingly all experience hath shewn, that mankind are more disposed to suffer, while evils are sufferable, than to right themselves by abolishing the forms to which they are accustomed. But when a long train of abuses and usurpations, pursuing invariably the same Object evinces a design to reduce them under absolute Despotism, it is their right, it is their duty, to throw off such Government, and to provide new Guards for their future security.—Such has been the patient sufferance of these Colonies; and such is now the necessity which constrains them to alter their former Systems of Government. The history of the present King of Great Britain is a history of repeated injuries and usurpations, all having in direct object the establishment of an absolute Tyranny over these States. To prove this, let Facts be submitted to a candid world.

He has refused his Assent to Laws, the most wholesome and necessary for the public good.

He has forbidden his Governors to pass Laws of immediate and pressing importance, unless suspended in their operation till his Assent should be obtained; and when so suspended, he has utterly neglected to attend to them.

He has refused to pass other Laws for the accommodation of large districts of people, unless those people would relinquish the right of Representation in the Legislature, a right inestimable to them and formidable to tyrants only.

He has called together legislative bodies at places unusual, uncomfortable, and distant from the depository of their public Records, for the sole purpose of fatiguing them into compliance with his measures.

He has dissolved Representative Houses repeatedly, for opposing with manly firmness his invasions on the rights of the people.

He has refused for a long time, after such dissolutions, to cause others to be elected; whereby the Legislative powers, incapable of Annihilation, have returned to the People at large for their exercise; the State remaining in the mean time exposed to all the dangers of invasion from without, and convulsions within.

He has endeavoured to prevent the population of these States; for that purpose obstructing the Laws for Naturalization of Foreigners; refusing to pass others to encourage their migrations hither, and raising the conditions of new Appropriations of Lands.

He has obstructed the Administration of Justice, by refusing his Assent to Laws for establishing Judiciary powers.

He has made Judges dependent on his Will alone, for the tenure of their offices, and the amount and payment of their salaries.

He has erected a multitude of New Offices, and sent hither swarms of Officers to harrass our people, and eat out their substance.

He has kept among us, in times of peace, Standing Armies without the Consent of our legislatures.

He has affected to render the Military independent of and superior to the Civil power.

He has combined with others to subject us to a jurisdiction foreign to our constitution, and unacknowledged by our laws; giving his Assent to their Acts of pretended Legislation:

For Quartering large bodies of armed troops among us:

For protecting them, by a mock Trial, from punishment for any Murders which they should commit on the Inhabitants of these States:

For cutting off our Trade with all parts of the world:

For imposing Taxes on us without our Consent:

For depriving us in many cases, of the benefits of Trial by Jury:

For transporting us beyond Seas to be tried for pretended offences:

For abolishing the free System of English Laws in a neighbouring Province, establishing therein an Arbitrary government, and enlarging its Boundaries so as to render it at once an example and fit instrument for introducing the same absolute rule into these Colonies:

For taking away our Charters, abolishing our most valuable Laws, and altering fundamentally the Forms of our Governments:

For suspending our own Legislatures, and declaring themselves invested with power to legislate for us in all cases whatsoever.

He has abdicated Government here, by declaring us out of his Protection and waging War against us.

He has plundered our seas, ravaged our Coasts, burnt our towns, and destroyed the lives of our people.

He is at this time transporting large Armies of foreign Mercenaries to compleat the works of death, desolation and tyranny, already begun with circumstances of Cruelty & perfidy scarcely paralleled in the most barbarous ages, and totally unworthy the Head of a civilized nation.

He has constrained our fellow Citizens taken Captive on the high Seas to bear Arms against their Country, to become the executioners of their friends and Brethren, or to fall themselves by their Hands.

He has excited domestic insurrections amongst us, and has endeavoured to bring on the inhabitants of our frontiers, the merciless Indian Savages, whose known rule of warfare, is an undistinguished destruction of all ages, sexes and conditions.

In every stage of these Oppressions We have Petitioned for Redress in the most humble terms: Our repeated Petitions have been answered only by repeated injury. A Prince whose character is thus marked by every act which may define a Tyrant, is unfit to be the ruler of a free people.

Nor have We been wanting in attentions to our Brittish brethren. We have warned them from time to time of attempts by their legislature to extend an unwarrantable jurisdiction over us. We have reminded them of the circumstances of our emigration and settlement here. We have appealed to their native justice and magnanimity, and we have conjured them by the ties of our common kindred to disavow these usurpations, which, would inevitably interrupt our connections and correspondence. They too have been deaf to the voice of justice and of consanguinity. We must, therefore, acquiesce in the necessity, which denounces our Separation, and hold them, as we hold the rest of mankind, Enemies in War, in Peace Friends.

We, therefore, the Representatives of the united States of America, in General Congress, Assembled, appealing to the Supreme Judge of the world for the rectitude of our intentions, do, in the Name, and by Authority of the good People of these Colonies, solemnly publish and declare, That these United Colonies are, and of Right ought to be Free and Independent States; that they are Absolved from all Allegiance to the British Crown, and that all political connection between them and the State of Great Britain, is and ought to be totally dissolved; and that as Free and Independent States, they have full Power to levy War, conclude Peace, contract Alliances, establish Commerce, and to do all other Acts and Things which Independent States may of right do.

And for the support of this Declaration, with a firm reliance on the protection of divine Providence, we mutually pledge to each other our Lives, our Fortunes and our sacred Honor.

Glossary

affected to	taken steps to
compleat	complete
conjured	called upon
consanguinity	blood ties
contract Alliances	make treaties
a jurisdiction foreign to our constitution	a way of governing us that does not suit our personalities
Mercenaries	soldiers who will fight for anyone who pays them
Nor have We been wanting in attention to our Brittish brethren	we have not failed to inform the British people of our situation and feelings
obstructing the Laws for Naturalization... raising the conditions of new Appropriation of Lands	making it difficult for people to move to the region
out of his Protection	beyond the reach of his help
shewn	shown
Standing Armies	full-time professional armies, as opposed to militias composed of civilians called up in times of emergency

Jefferson, Thomas

THE VIRGINIA ACT FOR ESTABLISHING RELIGIOUS FREEDOM (1786)

Well aware that Almighty God hath created the mind free; that all attempts to influence it by temporal punishments or burdens, or by civil incapacitations, tend only to beget habits of hypocrisy and meanness, and are a departure from the plan of the Holy Author of our religion, who being Lord both of body and mind, yet chose not to propagate it by coercions on either, as was in his Almighty power to do; that the impious presumption of legislators and rulers, civil as well as ecclesiastical, who, being themselves but fallible and uninspired men, have assumed dominion over the faith of others, setting up their own opinions and modes of thinking as the only true and infallible, and as such endeavoring to impose them on others, hath established and maintained false religions over the greatest part of the world, and through all time; that to compel a man to furnish contributions of money for the propagation of opinions which he disbelieves, is sinful and tyrannical; that even the forcing him to support this or that teacher of his own religious persuasion, is depriving him of the comfortable liberty of giving his contributions to the particular pastor whose morals he would make his pattern, and whose powers he feels most persuasive to righteousness, and is withdrawing from the ministry those temporal rewards, which proceeding from an approbation of their personal conduct, are an additional incitement to earnest and unremitting labors for the instruction of mankind; that our civil rights have no dependence on our religious opinions, more than our opinions in physics or geometry; that, therefore, the proscribing any citizen as unworthy the public confidence by laying upon him an incapacity of being called to the offices of trust and emolument, unless he profess or renounce this or that religious opinion, is depriving him injuriously of those privileges and advantages to which in common with his fellow citizens he has a natural right; that it tends also to corrupt the principles of that very religion it is meant to encourage, by bribing, with a monopoly of worldly honors and emoluments, those who will externally profess and conform to it; that though indeed these are criminal who do not withstand such temptation, yet neither are those innocent who lay the bait in their way; that to suffer the civil magistrate to intrude his powers into the field of opinion and to restrain the profession or propagation of principles, on the supposition of their ill tendency, is a dangerous fallacy, which at once destroys all religious liberty, because he being of course judge of that tendency, will make his opinions the rule of judgment, and approve or condemn the sentiments of others only as they shall square with or differ from his own; that it is time enough for the rightful purposes of civil government, for its officers to interfere when principles break out into overt acts against peace and good order; and finally, that truth is great and will prevail if left to herself, that she is the proper and sufficient antagonist to error, and has nothing to fear from the conflict, unless by human interposition disarmed of her natural weapons, free argument and debate, errors ceasing to be dangerous when it is permitted freely to contradict them.

Be it therefore enacted by the General Assembly, That no man shall be compelled to frequent or support any religious worship, place, or ministry whatsoever, nor shall be enforced, restrained, molested, or burdened in his body or goods, nor shall otherwise suffer on account of his religious opinions or belief; but that all men shall be free to profess, and by argument to maintain, their opinions in matters of religion, and that the same shall in nowise diminish, enlarge, or affect their civil capacities.

And though we well know this Assembly, elected by the people for the ordinary purposes of legislation only, have no powers equal to our own and that therefore to declare this act irrevocable would be of no effect in law, yet we are free to declare, and do

Glossary

civil incapacitations	legal limitations
in nowise	in no way

declare, that the rights hereby asserted are of the natural rights of mankind, and that if any act shall be hereafter passed to repeal the present or to narrow its operation, such act will be an infringement of natural right.

FIRST INAUGURAL ADDRESS (1801)

Friends and fellow-citizens,

Called upon to undertake the duties of the first executive office of our country, I avail myself of the presence of that portion of my fellow-citizens which is here assembled to express my grateful thanks for the favor with which they have been pleased to look toward me, to declare a sincere consciousness that the task is above my talents, and that I approach it with those anxious and awful presentiments which the greatness of the charge and the weakness of my powers so justly inspire. A rising nation, spread over a wide and fruitful land, traversing all the seas with the rich productions of their industry, engaged in commerce with nations who feel power and forget right, advancing rapidly to destinies beyond the reach of mortal eye—when I contemplate these transcendent objects, and see the honor, the happiness, and the hopes of this beloved country committed to the issue and the auspices of this day, I shrink from the contemplation, and humble myself before the magnitude of the undertaking. Utterly, indeed, should I despair did not the presence of many whom I here see remind me that in the other high authorities provided by our Constitution I shall find resources of wisdom, of virtue, and of zeal on which to rely under all difficulties. To you, then, gentlemen, who are charged with the sovereign functions of legislation, and to those associated with you, I look with encouragement for that guidance and support which may enable us to steer with safety the vessel in which we are all embarked amidst the conflicting elements of a troubled world.

During the contest of opinion through which we have passed the animation of discussions and of exertions has sometimes worn an aspect which might impose on strangers unused to think freely and to speak and to write what they think; but this being now decided by the voice of the nation, announced according to the rules of the Constitution, all will, of course, arrange themselves under the will of the law, and unite in common efforts for the common good. All, too, will bear in mind this sacred principle, that though the will of the majority is in all cases to prevail, that will to be rightful must be reasonable; that the minority possess their equal rights, which equal law must protect, and to violate would be oppression. Let us, then, fellow-citizens, unite with one heart and one mind. Let us restore to social intercourse that harmony and affection without which liberty and even life itself are but dreary things. And let us reflect that, having banished from our land that religious intolerance under which mankind so long bled and suffered, we have yet gained little if we countenance a political intolerance as despotic, as wicked, and capable of as bitter and bloody persecutions. During the throes and convulsions of the ancient world, during the agonizing spasms of infuriated man, seeking through blood and slaughter his long-lost liberty, it was not wonderful that the agitation of the billows should reach even this distant and peaceful shore; that this should be more felt and feared by some and less by others, and should divide opinions as to measures of safety. But every difference of opinion is not a difference of principle. We have called by different names brethren of the same principle. We are all Republicans, we are all Federalists. If there be any among us who would wish to dissolve this Union or to change its republican form, let them stand undisturbed as monuments of the safety with which error of opinion may be tolerated where reason is left free to combat it. I know, indeed, that some honest men fear that a republican government can not be strong, that this Government is not strong enough; but would the honest patriot, in the full tide of successful experiment, abandon a government which has so far kept us free and firm on the theoretic and visionary fear that this Government, the world's best hope, may by possibility want energy to preserve itself? I trust not. I believe this, on the contrary, the strongest Government on earth. I believe it the only one where every man, at the call of the law, would fly to the standard of the law, and would meet invasions of the public order as his own personal concern. Sometimes it is said that man can not be trusted with the government of himself. Can he, then, be trusted with the government of others? Or have we found angels in the forms of kings to govern him? Let history answer this question.

Let us, then, with courage and confidence pursue our own Federal and Republican principles, our attachment to union and representative government. Kindly separated by nature and a wide ocean from the exterminating havoc of one quarter of the globe; too high-minded to endure the degradations of the others; possessing a chosen country, with room enough for our descendants to the thousandth and thousandth generation; entertaining a due sense of our equal right to the use of our own faculties, to the acquisitions of our own industry, to honor and confidence from our fellow-citizens, resulting not from birth, but from our actions and their sense of them; enlightened by a benign religion, professed, indeed, and practiced in various forms, yet all of them inculcating honesty, truth, temperance, gratitude, and the love of man; acknowledging and adoring an overruling Providence, which by all its dispensations proves that it delights in the happiness of man here and his greater happiness hereafter—with all these blessings, what more is necessary to make us a happy and a prosperous people? Still one thing more, fellow-citizens—a wise and frugal Government, which shall restrain men from injuring one another, shall leave them otherwise free to regulate their own pursuits of industry and improvement, and shall not take from the mouth of labor the bread it has earned. This is the sum of good government, and this is necessary to close the circle of our felicities.

About to enter, fellow-citizens, on the exercise of duties which comprehend everything dear and valuable to you, it is proper you should understand what I deem the essential principles of our Government, and consequently those which ought to shape its Administration. I will compress them within the narrowest compass they will bear, stating the general principle, but not all its limitations. Equal and exact justice to all men, of whatever state or persuasion, religious or political; peace, commerce, and honest friendship with all nations, entangling alliances with none; the support of the State governments in all their rights, as the most competent administrations for our domestic concerns and the surest bulwarks against antirepublican tendencies; the preservation of the General Government in its whole constitutional vigor, as the sheet anchor of our peace at home and safety abroad; a jealous care of the right of election by the people—a mild and safe corrective of abuses which are lopped by the sword of revolution where peaceable remedies are unprovided; absolute acquiescence in the decisions of the majority, the vital principle of republics, from which is no appeal but to force, the vital principle and immediate parent of despotism; a well-disciplined militia, our best reliance in peace and for the first moments of war till regulars may relieve them; the supremacy of the civil over the military authority; economy in the public

Glossary

agitation of the billows	shockwaves
at the call of the law, would fly to the standard of the law	if the situation demanded, would defend the law
the bar of the public reason	the court of public opinion
burthened	burdened
close the circle of our felicities	complete our happiness
the contest of opinion through which we have passed	the recent election
habeas corpus	a Latin expression, meaning "you shall have the body," referring to a principle whereby a government cannot imprison individuals without formally charging and trying them
jealous	watchful
militia	a military force composed of civilians, rather than full-time professional soldiers, called up on an emergency basis

expense, that labor may be lightly burthened; the honest payment of our debts and sacred preservation of the public faith; encouragement of agriculture, and of commerce as its handmaid; the diffusion of information and arraignment of all abuses at the bar of the public reason; freedom of religion; freedom of the press, and freedom of person under the protection of the habeas corpus, and trial by juries impartially selected. These principles form the bright constellation which has gone before us and guided our steps through an age of revolution and reformation. The wisdom of our sages and blood of our heroes have been devoted to their attainment. They should be the creed of our political faith, the text of civic instruction, the touchstone by which to try the services of those we trust; and should we wander from them in moments of error or of alarm, let us hasten to retrace our steps and to regain the road which alone leads to peace, liberty, and safety.

I repair, then, fellow-citizens, to the post you have assigned me. With experience enough in subordinate offices to have seen the difficulties of this the greatest of all, I have learnt to expect that it will rarely fall to the lot of imperfect man to retire from this station with the reputation and the favor which bring him into it. Without pretensions to that high confidence you reposed in our first and greatest revolutionary character, whose preeminent services had entitled him to the first place in his country's love and destined for him the fairest page in the volume of faithful history, I ask so much confidence only as may give firmness and effect to the legal administration of your affairs. I shall often go wrong through defect of judgment. When right, I shall often be thought wrong by those whose positions will not command a view of the whole ground. I ask your indulgence for my own errors, which will never be intentional, and your support against the errors of others, who may condemn what they would not if seen in all its parts. The approbation implied by your suffrage is a great consolation to me for the past, and my future solicitude will be to retain the good opinion of those who have bestowed it in advance, to conciliate that of others by doing them all the good in my power, and to be instrumental to the happiness and freedom of all.

Relying, then, on the patronage of your good will, I advance with obedience to the work, ready to retire from it whenever you become sensible how much better choice it is in your power to make. And may that Infinite Power which rules the destinies of the universe lead our councils to what is best, and give them a favorable issue for your peace and prosperity.

Glossary

our first and greatest revolutionary character	George Washington
regulars	full-time soldiers
sheet anchor	a source of help in an emergency, which is the reason that ships carry a large extra anchor
those whose positions will not command a view of the whole ground	those who opinions and biases prevent them from seeing the broader picture
traversing all the seas with the rich productions of their industry	sending our exports across the ocean
we are all Republicans, we are all Federalists	a reference to the Democratic-Republicans and the Federalists and to the fact that all Americans favored a free system of elected leaders (republicanism) in a nation composed of states loyal to a central government (federalism)
worn an aspect which might impose on	carried an appearance that might intimidate

Second Inaugural Address (1805)

Proceeding, fellow citizens, to that qualification which the constitution requires, before my entrance on the charge again conferred upon me, it is my duty to express the deep sense I entertain of this new proof of confidence from my fellow citizens at large, and the zeal with which it inspires me, so to conduct myself as may best satisfy their just expectations.

On taking this station on a former occasion, I declared the principles on which I believed it my duty to administer the affairs of our commonwealth. My conscience tells me that I have, on every occasion, acted up to that declaration, according to its obvious import, and to the understanding of every candid mind.

In the transaction of your foreign affairs, we have endeavored to cultivate the friendship of all nations, and especially of those with which we have the most important relations. We have done them justice on all occasions, favored where favor was lawful, and cherished mutual interests and intercourse on fair and equal terms. We are firmly convinced, and we act on that conviction, that with nations, as with individuals, our interests soundly calculated, will ever be found inseparable from our moral duties; and history bears witness to the fact, that a just nation is taken on its word, when recourse is had to armaments and wars to bridle others.

At home, fellow citizens, you best know whether we have done well or ill. The suppression of unnecessary offices, of useless establishments and expenses, enabled us to discontinue our internal taxes. These covering our land with officers, and opening our doors to their intrusions, had already begun that process of domiciliary vexation which, once entered, is scarcely to be restrained from reaching successively every article of produce and property. If among these taxes some minor ones fell which had not been inconvenient, it was because their amount would not have paid the officers who collected them, and because, if they had any merit, the state authorities might adopt them, instead of others less approved.

The remaining revenue on the consumption of foreign articles, is paid cheerfully by those who can afford to add foreign luxuries to domestic comforts, being collected on our seaboards and frontiers only, and incorporated with the transactions of our mercantile citizens, it may be the pleasure and pride of an American to ask, what farmer, what mechanic, what laborer, ever sees a tax-gatherer of the United States? These contributions enable us to support the current expenses of the government, to fulfil contracts with foreign nations, to extinguish the native right of soil within our limits, to extend those limits, and to apply such a surplus to our public debts, as places at a short day their final redemption, and that redemption once effected, the revenue thereby liberated may, by a just repartition among the states, and a corresponding amendment of the constitution, be applied, in time of peace, to rivers, canals, roads, arts, manufactures, education, and other great objects within each state. In time of war, if injustice, by ourselves or others, must sometimes produce war, increased as the same revenue will be increased by population and consumption, and aided by other resources reserved for that crisis, it may meet within the year all the expenses of the year, without encroaching on the rights of future generations, by burdening them with the debts of the past. War will then be but a suspension of useful works, and a return to a state of peace, a return to the progress of improvement.

I have said, fellow citizens, that the income reserved had enabled us to extend our limits; but that extension may possibly pay for itself before we are called on, and in the meantime, may keep down the accruing interest; in all events, it will repay the advances we have made. I know that the acquisition of Louisiana has been disapproved by some, from a candid apprehension that the enlargement of our territory would endanger its union. But who can limit the extent to which the federative principle may operate effectively? The larger our association, the less will it be shaken by local passions; and in any view, is it not better that the opposite bank of the Mississippi should be settled by our own brethren and children, than by strangers of another family? With which shall we be most likely to live in harmony and friendly intercourse?

In matters of religion, I have considered that its free exercise is placed by the constitution independent of the powers of the general government. I have therefore undertaken, on no occasion, to prescribe the religious exercises suited to it; but have left them, as the constitution found them, under the direction and discipline of state or church authorities acknowledged by the several religious societies.

The aboriginal inhabitants of these countries I have regarded with the commiseration their history inspires. Endowed with the faculties and the rights of men, breathing an ardent love of liberty and independence, and occupying a country which left them no desire but to be undisturbed, the stream of overflowing population from other regions directed itself on these shores; without power to divert, or habits to contend against, they have been overwhelmed by the current, or driven before it; now reduced within limits too narrow for the hunter's state, humanity enjoins us to teach them agriculture and the domestic arts; to encourage them to that industry which alone can enable them to maintain their place in existence, and to prepare them in time for that state of society, which to bodily comforts adds the improvement of the mind and morals. We have therefore liberally furnished them with the implements of husbandry and household use; we have placed among them instructors in the arts of first necessity; and they are covered with the aegis of the law against aggressors from among ourselves.

But the endeavors to enlighten them on the fate which awaits their present course of life, to induce them to exercise their reason, follow its dictates, and change their pursuits with the change of circumstances, have powerful obstacles to encounter; they are combated by the habits of their bodies, prejudice of their minds, ignorance, pride, and the influence of interested and crafty individuals among them, who feel themselves something in the present order of things, and fear to become nothing in any other. These persons inculcate a sanctimonious reverence for the customs of their ancestors; that whatsoever they did, must be done through all time; that reason is a false guide, and to advance under its counsel, in their physical, moral, or political condition, is perilous innovation; that their duty is to remain as their Creator made them, ignorance being safety, and knowledge full of danger; in short, my friends, among them is seen the action and counteraction of good sense and bigotry; they, too, have their anti-philosophers, who find an interest in keeping things in their present state, who dread reformation, and exert all their faculties to maintain the ascendency of habit over the duty of improving our reason, and obeying its mandates.

In giving these outlines, I do not mean, fellow citizens, to arrogate to myself the merit of the measures; that is due, in the first place, to the reflecting character of our citizens at large, who, by the weight of public opinion, influence and strengthen the public measures; it is due to the sound discretion with which they select from among themselves those to whom they confide the legislative duties; it is due to the zeal and wisdom of the characters thus selected, who lay the foundations of public happiness in wholesome laws, the execution of which alone remains for others; and it is due to the able and faithful auxiliaries, whose patriotism has associated with me in the executive functions.

During this course of administration, and in order to disturb it, the artillery of the press has been levelled against us, charged with whatsoever its licentiousness could devise or dare. These abuses of an institution so important to freedom and science, are deeply to be regretted, inasmuch as they tend to lessen its usefulness, and to sap its safety; they might, indeed, have been corrected by the wholesome punishments reserved and provided by the laws of the several States against falsehood and defamation; but public duties more urgent press on the time of public servants, and the offenders have therefore been left to find their punishment in the public indignation.

Nor was it uninteresting to the world, that an experiment should be fairly and fully made, whether freedom of discussion, unaided by power, is not sufficient for the propagation and protection of truth—whether a government, conducting itself in the true spirit of its constitution, with zeal and purity, and doing no act which it would be unwilling the whole world should witness, can be written down by falsehood and defamation. The experiment has been tried; you have witnessed the scene; our fellow citizens have looked on, cool and collected; they saw the latent source from which these outrages proceeded; they gathered around their public functionaries, and when the constitution called them to the decision by suffrage, they pronounced their verdict, honorable to those who had served them, and consolatory to the friend of man, who believes he may be intrusted with his own affairs.

No inference is here intended, that the laws, provided by the State against false and defamatory publications, should not be enforced; he who has time, renders a service to public morals and public tranquillity, in reforming these abuses by the salutary coercions of the law; but the experiment is noted, to prove that, since truth and reason have maintained their ground against false opinions in league with false facts, the press, confined to truth, needs no other legal restraint; the public judgment will correct false reasonings and opinions, on a full hearing of all parties; and no other definite line can be drawn between the inestimable liberty of the press and its demoralizing licentiousness. If there be still improprieties which this rule would not restrain, its supplement must be sought in the censorship of public opinion.

Contemplating the union of sentiment now manifested so generally, as auguring harmony and happiness to our future course, I offer to our country sincere congratulations. With those, too, not yet rallied to the same point, the disposition to do so is gaining strength; facts are piercing through the veil drawn over them; and our doubting brethren will at length see, that the mass of their fellow citizens, with whom they cannot yet resolve to act, as to principles and measures, think as they think, and desire what they desire; that our wish, as well as theirs, is, that the public efforts may be directed honestly to the public good, that peace be cultivated, civil and religious liberty unassailed, law and order preserved; equality of rights maintained, and that state of property, equal or unequal, which results to every man from his own industry, or that of his fathers. When satisfied of these views, it is not in human nature that they should not approve and support them; in the meantime, let us cherish them with patient affection; let us do them justice, and more than justice, in all competitions of interest; and we need not doubt that truth, reason, and their own interests, will at length prevail, will gather them into the fold of their country, and will complete their entire union of opinion, which gives to a nation the blessing of harmony, and the benefit of all its strength.

I shall now enter on the duties to which my fellow citizens have again called me, and shall proceed in the spirit of those principles which they have approved. I fear not that any motives of interest may lead me astray; I am sensible of no passion which could seduce me knowingly from the path of justice; but the weakness of human nature, and the limits of my own understanding, will produce errors of judgment sometimes injurious to your interests. I shall need, therefore, all the indulgence I have heretofore experienced — the want of it will certainly not lessen with increasing years. I shall need, too, the favor of that Being in whose hands we are, who led our forefathers, as Israel of old, from their native land, and planted them in a country flowing with all the necessaries and comforts of life; who has covered our infancy with his providence, and our riper years with his wisdom and power; and to whose goodness I ask you to join with me in supplications, that he will so enlighten the minds of your servants, guide their councils, and prosper their measures, that whatsoever they do, shall result in your good, and shall secure to you the peace, friendship, and approbation of all nations.

Glossary

aboriginal	native
acted up	lived up
advances we have made	debts we have incurred
anti-philosophers	opponents of thinking and reason
candid apprehension	honest fear
commonwealth	a state formed by the agreement of the people and for their common good
extinguish the native right of soil	remove the Indians
federative	referring to a federal system of government, in which states exercise a degree of independence on some issues yet submit to the rule of a central authority on matters of national importance
reduced within limits too narrow for the hunter's state	forced to occupy an area of land too small to sustain their survival by hunting
salutary coercions	beneficial applications of force or power

Andrew Johnson (Library of Congress)

ANDREW JOHNSON   1808-1875

Seventeenth President of the United States

Featured Documents
♦ First Annual Message to Congress (1865)
♦ Veto of the Freedmen's Bureau Bill (1866)
♦ Veto of the Civil Rights Act (1866)

Overview

Andrew Johnson, the nation's seventeenth president, was born in Raleigh, North Carolina, on December 29, 1808. He began his career as a tailor with no formal schooling, but he acquired a reputation as a forceful and effective orator, thanks in large part to his wife, who taught him reading, writing, and arithmetic. After moving to Greeneville, Tennessee, he was elected alderman in 1828, mayor in 1830, member of the Tennessee House of Representatives in 1835 and again in 1839, state senator in 1841, congressman in 1843, governor in 1853, and U.S. senator in 1857. When the Civil War broke out, Johnson was the only southern senator to remain loyal to the Union. He attracted the attention of Abraham Lincoln, who appointed him military governor of Tennessee in 1862 and selected him as his running mate in the 1864 presidential election. Johnson rose to the presidency on April 15, 1865, the day after Lincoln's assassination. After leaving the White House in 1869, he was elected to the U.S. Senate in 1875 and was the only former president ever to serve in the Senate. His tenure, though, was short-lived, for he died on July 31 that same year.

Johnson was at the center of Reconstruction of the Confederate states after the Civil War. In his early life he had developed an intense dislike for the South's monied slave-owning plantation class, and as vice president he gave every indication that the Reconstruction policies he would support with regard to southern "traitors" would be harsh. He believed, though, that blacks were inherently inferior and was a strong supporter of states' rights, a position he made clear in his 1865 annual message to Congress. Accordingly, his terms for readmitting the southern states to the Union were more lenient than had been anticipated. He granted a blanket amnesty to all but a few former Confederates and a pardon to the others on a case-by-case basis. He also installed provisional governors with the task of quickly assembling loyal state governments. In an effort to win back the loyalty of the South, in 1866 he vetoed the Freedmen's Bureau Bill (initiated under Lincoln in March 1865) and, just a month later, the bill that became the Civil Rights Act of 1866. His veto of the latter bill was the first piece of major legislation in U.S. history that Congress overrode.

Johnson found himself at odds with Congress, particularly with the so-called Radical Republicans led by Representative Thaddeus Stevens and Senator Charles Sumner. This loose political group favored sweeping changes in American politics and society after the Civil War. They sup-ported equality and voting rights for freed slaves and the harsh punishment of the South for the rebellion. At first the Radicals were pleased with Johnson's hard-line talk, but they grew dissatisfied with his actual policies. In 1868 the Senate, led by the Radical Republicans, impeached Johnson, charging him with deliberately violating the Tenure of Office Act by replacing Edwin Stanton as secretary of war. The article of impeachment failed by a single vote, and Johnson remained in office. Earlier, in 1867, the House of Representatives had voted against articles of impeachment.

Explanation and Analysis of Documents

Throughout his political career, Andrew Johnson was a strong supporter of states' rights, rendering it perhaps somewhat surprising that he did not join with the South and resign his Senate seat at the outbreak of the Civil War. Nevertheless, he was also a defender of the Union. In his first annual message to Congress and his veto messages for renewal of the Freedmen's Bureau and the 1866 Civil Rights Act, he consistently makes clear his desire to rein in the powers of the federal government over the states.

♦ First Annual Message to Congress

When Andrew Johnson delivered his first annual message to Congress on December 4, 1865, the nation was still reeling under the pressure of events. Johnson's predecessor, Abraham Lincoln, had been assassinated in April, just days after the Confederate army surrendered, bringing the Civil War largely to a close. The rebel states, though, had not yet been fully reabsorbed into the Union, and during the early months of his administration, Johnson was preoccupied with one task: reconstruction. Over time, attitudes about the Reconstruction period have undergone a marked shift. In the early part of the twentieth century, Reconstruction was viewed as sordid, a time when the Radical Republicans forced integration down the throats of the nation, particularly in the South. It was depicted as a time of corrupt state governments and of northern "carpetbaggers" (so called because they were seen as arriving, often by train, carrying luggage that looked as if it were made from carpeting material), who exploited the disarray of the postwar South for their own mercenary ends. Later historians, though, came to look on Reconstruction more favorably, as a time of attempted racial integration and reconciliation, a

1808
- **December 29**
  Johnson is born in Raleigh, North Carolina.

1843
- Johnson is elected to the U.S. House of Representatives for the Eastern District of Tennessee and serves until 1853.

1853
- Johnson becomes governor of Tennessee and serves until 1857.

1857
- Johnson is elected U.S. senator from Tennessee and serves until 1862.

1862
- Abraham Lincoln appoints Johnson as military governor of Tennessee.

1865
- **March 4**
  Johnson is sworn in as vice president.

1865
- **April 15**
  Johnson assumes the presidency after the assassination of Lincoln.
- **December 4**
  Johnson sends his first annual message to Congress.

1866
- **February 19**
  Johnson vetoes the Freedmen's Bureau Bill.
- **March 27**
  Johnson vetoes the Civil Rights Act, a veto later overridden by Congress.

1869
- Johnson's single term as president ends.

1875
- **March 4**
  Johnson takes office in the U.S. Senate.
- **July 31**
  Johnson dies near Elizabethton, Tennessee.

democratic experiment that perhaps did not fully succeed but was noble in its ends.

Thrown into Johnson's lap was the consuming issue of what to do with the rebellious South. By instinct, Johnson wanted to punish the South. Born literally in a log cabin, he had grown up distrusting and disliking the slave-owning plantation class, whom he regarded as effete aristocrats. But when the weight of decision making fell on him, he realized that restoration of the Union required a gentler hand. In May 1865 he issued a set of proclamations that ushered in what is called the period of Presidential Reconstruction (as opposed to the period of Congressional Reconstruction from 1867 to 1877). Among these proclamations was a pardon to former Confederates with the exception of the rebellion's leaders and the wealthy planters, who, he believed, had led otherwise innocent people into rebellion. Further, he appointed provisional governors in the states and developed plans for the creation of new state governments. He imposed only three requirements: that states outlaw slavery, repudiate any further secession efforts, and cancel the Confederate debt. Otherwise, he gave the states wide scope in conducting their own affairs.

Many northerners opposed the president's policies. They wanted revenge for Lincoln's assassination and for the war in general. They were dismayed to see the southern states elect former leaders of the Confederacy to their legislatures. They were particularly incensed by the slow pace of racial integration and the harsh "Black Codes"—legislation passed first in South Carolina and Mississippi and later in other southern states. These codes allowed freed slaves to rent land only in rural areas, effectively keeping them on plantations. They required freed slaves to sign yearlong labor contracts; any person who failed to fulfill the terms of the contract could be arrested for vagrancy. Blacks could apprentice their children only with the consent of their former owners. Penalties for violations of these codes were harsh. In this context, the Radical Republicans in Congress and even many moderate Republicans came to oppose Johnson's Reconstruction policies.

Johnson's annual message, then, was in large measure a justification of his policies based on the concept of states' rights. In the first paragraph of this excerpt, he looks back to the framers of the Constitution and to the tension that existed even then between the "General Government"—that is, the federal government—and those who feared that the federal government would dominate the states; alternatively, there were fears that if the states retained too much independence, they could spin off from the Union. He notes, though, that the federal government's legitimate concerns are many and that if it meddled in the affairs of the states, it would collapse under the weight of too much to do. In the second paragraph, Johnson balances his support of states' rights with his desire to see the Union survive, arguing that a state does not have the right to "renounce its own place in the Union or to nullify the laws of the Union." He goes on to say that the Confederacy's doctrine of the "sovereignty of the States" was a false one and points out that the Constitution makes federal doctrine "the supreme law of the land."

Johnson then appeals to the language of the Declaration of Independence in arguing that the power of all governments, both state and federal, should be limited. The alternative is the tyranny that was historically exercised over individuals in such matters as religious beliefs. He then returns to a discussion of states and their role in the polity. He notes that the Declaration of Independence was adopted by the individual states, that the Constitution was ratified by the states, and that the Constitution can be amended only with the consent of the states. He summarizes the reciprocal relations between the Union and the states by saying, "The whole can not exist without the parts, nor the parts without the whole. So long as the Constitution of the United States endures, the States will endure. The destruction of the one is the destruction of the other; the preservation of the one is the preservation of the other."

On the basis of this balancing of state and federal interests, Johnson explains and justifies his Reconstruction policies. The first question he faced as president was whether to install a military government in the South. Johnson rejected this alternative, arguing that such a military government was susceptible to corruption and, by hindering the free movement of people between North and South, would delay the achievement of harmony. He also argues that a military government would imply that somehow the states of the South had ceased to exist by rebellion. Johnson rejects this view by saying that secession was a "pretended" act that was "null and void" because a state cannot be guilty of treason any more than it can usurp the functions of the federal government, such as to make treaties. Rather, what the states did was abandon their proper functions. Johnson then argues that his policies—provisional governors; election of governors, state legislatures, and representatives to Congress; restoration of the postal service; the removal of federal blockades; and the reopening of courts—are designed to reenergize the states and their governments, hastening their restoration to the Union.

Johnson turns to the issue of presidential pardons. He knew that many people in the North objected to the pardoning of rebels and traitors. In his address, however, Johnson appeals to a spirit of reconciliation and argues that the rebels could reaffirm their allegiance to the United States only if they were pardoned. He notes, though, that pardon was contingent on "binding force of the laws of the United States and an unqualified acknowledgment of the great social change of condition in regard to slavery which has grown out of the war." Accordingly, he says, he has invited the southern states to take part in the process of amending the Constitution to eliminate slavery. Johnson maintains that only by constitutionally ending slavery can the nation heal its wounds and put the bloody rebellion behind it. By participating in the task of amending the Constitution, the South can affirm its loyalty to the United States and thus help reunite the country.

◆ Veto of the Freedmen's Bureau Bill

In March 1865 Congress established the Bureau of Refugees, Freedmen, and Abandoned Lands, commonly known as the Freedmen's Bureau. The purpose of the bureau, a federal agency administered by the Department of War, was to look to the material and social welfare of freed slaves and those made destitute by the Civil War by providing food, shelter, medical aid, and education; helping former slaves find paying work on former plantations or accept sharecropping and tenancy arrangements; reuniting families; and ensuring that freedmen received fair treatment in legal proceedings. The bureau had mixed results, principally because of inadequate funding and the lack of agents in the field. Further, the bureau attempted to relocate freed slaves on some 850,000 acres of abandoned southern land the North had seized during the Civil War. When Andrew Johnson pardoned many former Confederates, their land was restored to them, frustrating the bureau's efforts.

In 1866 Congress passed a bill to extend the life of the bureau—and to increase its powers. On February 19, 1866, Johnson sent the bill back to Congress with his veto. Congress overrode his veto, and the bureau survived until 1868, although some of its work, principally education and veterans' relief, continued until 1872. Often working in tandem with aid societies and missionaries, the bureau established some 4,300 schools and a hundred hospitals; Howard University, a historically black college, was named after Major General Oliver O. Howard, the bureau's commissioner.

It is fair to say that large numbers of white southerners detested the Freedmen's Bureau, and even in the North the bureau's mandate met with resistance. During the 1866 gubernatorial race in Pennsylvania, for example, racist posters attacking the bureau were circulated in support of a white supremacist candidate. The caption on the posters read "The Freedman's Bureau! An agency to keep the Negro in idleness at the expense of the white man." The poster characterized the freedman's "estimate of freedom" as consisting of "Candy," "Rum, Gin, Whiskey," "Sugar Plums," "Indolence," "White Women," "Apathy," "White Sugar," "Idleness," "Fish Balls," "Clams," "Stews," and "Pies." In the South, bureau agents met with wide resistance. White southerners objected to the establishment of special courts that handled cases involving blacks, arguing that such courts were unconstitutional. In particular, they resented the military tribunals the bureau used to try whites accused of violating the rights of freedmen. White planters, restored to their land, generally harassed freedmen and exploited their labor. Numerous freedmen were lynched, but rarely was anyone prosecuted for the crimes. Indeed, during the months following the war, guerrilla actions continued. as some desperate southerners believed that the South could rise again and defeat the hated North. In many cases, however, objections to the Freedmen's Bureau were based on the more moderate belief that the states should look after the welfare of freedmen so that they did not become permanent wards of the federal government, a view held by General Howard himself.

It was in this context that Johnson vetoed the bill to extend the life of the Freedmen's Bureau. In his lengthy

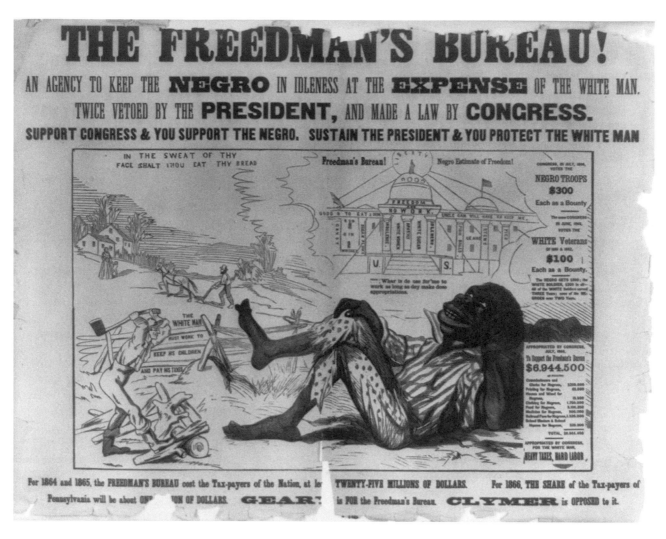

One in a series of racist posters attacking Radical Republicans on the issue of black suffrage, issued during the Pennsylvania gubernatorial election of 1866 (Library of Congress)

veto, he enumerates his objections to particular provisions of the bill as it was presented to him, but in this excerpt he emphasizes the constitutional issues. First, Johnson objects to the formation of military jurisdiction over the parts of the country served by the bureau. Although Johnson does not use the term, his objections to the imposition of a military government in the South prefigured the Posse Comitatus Act of 1878, passed in the wake of Reconstruction to limit the ability of the federal government to use federal troops on American soil. The Latin phrase *posse comitatus* (the source of the word *posse*) means "power of the county" and refers to a county sheriff's authority under the act to assemble men to keep order, pursue criminals, and the like.

Johnson also objects to the bill because it "subjects any white person who may be charged with depriving a freedman of any civil rights or immunities belonging to white persons to imprisonment or fine, or both, without, however, defining the civil rights and immunities which are thus to be secured to the freedmen by military law." The bill would expand the number of bureau agents, who then would be given unsupervised power to enforce the provisions of the bill in courts. Johnson sees this as a violation of the Fifth Amendment of the Constitution. The procedures under which such courts would operate would be arbitrary. The usual rules of evidence would not apply. Punishments meted out would be capricious. There would be no right of appeal to higher courts. The actions that could be considered punishable are overly extensive. In addition, trials by military tribunal would violate the fundamental constitutional right of a trial by an impartial jury in the state or district where the alleged crime took place. In response to the president's veto, Congress modified and passed a new bill, which Johnson once again promptly vetoed. The new bill was passed over his veto on July 16, 1866.

◆ **Veto of the Civil Rights Act**

Johnson's struggle with the Radical Republicans continued when the Senate passed a civil rights bill designed to protect the rights of African Americans. The key provision of the Civil Rights Act of 1866—more formally, "An Act to pro-

> "The whole can not exist without the parts, nor the parts without the whole. So long as the Constitution of the United States endures, the States will endure. The destruction of the one is the destruction of the other; the preservation of the one is the preservation of the other."
>
> (First Annual Message to Congress)

> "The adoption of the amendment [to abolish slavery] reunites us beyond all power of disruption; it heals the wound that is still imperfectly closed: it removes slavery, the element which has so long perplexed and divided the country; it makes of us once more a united people, renewed and strengthened, bound more than ever to mutual affection and support."
>
> (First Annual Message to Congress)

> "I have, with Congress, the strongest desire to secure to the freedmen the full enjoyment of their freedom and their property and their entire independence and equality in making contracts for their labor. But the bill before me contains provisions which, in my opinion, are not warranted by the Constitution and are not well suited to accomplish the end in view."
>
> (Veto of the Freedmen's Bureau Bill)

> "In all our history, in all our experience as people living under Federal and State law, no such system as that contemplated by the details of this bill has ever before been proposed or adopted. They establish for the security of the colored race safeguards which go infinitely beyond any that the General Government has ever provided for the white race. In fact, the distinction of race and color is by the bill made to operate in favor of the colored and against the white race."
>
> (Veto of the Civil Rights Act)

tect all Persons in the United States in their Civil Rights, and furnish the Means of their vindication"—was to state that "All persons within the jurisdiction of the United States shall have the same right in every State and Territory to make and enforce contracts, to sue, be parties, give evidence, and to the full and equal benefit of all laws and proceedings for the security of persons and property as is enjoyed by white citizens, and shall be subject to like punishment, pain, penal-ties, taxes, licenses, and exactions of every kind, and to no other." The effect of the bill was to grant full citizenship to newly freed slaves; it was written with a view to countering the Black Codes taking effect through the post–Civil War southern states in response to the passage of the Thirteenth Amendment freeing slaves. In most instances the legisla-tures of the southern states that passed these codes had been installed as a result of Johnson's policies in 1865.

Johnson's veto of the bill on March 27, in the wake of his veto of the Freedmen's Bureau Bill, marked a decisive break with the Republican Party. Johnson was now seen as allied more with southern Democrats, who opposed the expansion of civil rights for former slaves, than with his own party. The Republican-controlled Congress overrode the veto by votes of 182 to 41 in the House and 33 to 15 in the Senate. It must be remembered that although Johnson had tried to readmit the southern states to Congress, Congress opposed him and refused to seat the representatives and senators from the eleven states of the Confederacy. These states were overwhelmingly Democratic, in contrast to the North, which had strong Republican majorities. A coalition of Radical and moderate Republicans had the votes to overturn any presidential veto.

After announcing that he is vetoing the bill, Johnson explains his reasons. His first objection is that the bill would grant U.S. citizenship to classes of people. But consistent with his unwavering support for states' rights, he objects that doing so imposes on the states the obligation of granting state citizenship. Further, Johnson argues, the Constitution already makes all native-born persons citizens of the United States; if African Americans (even those born in the United States) are not citizens, as the language of the bill implies, then Johnson believes that legislation making them citizens should not be enacted when eleven of the states that will be affected by the legislation are unrepresented in Congress. Johnson goes on to argue that the Constitution already grants rights, even to noncitizens, so he objects to "special legislation" granting rights to classes of people. A further argument is that to grant citizenship to freed slaves at the stroke of a pen is unfair to other noncitizens, who are required to pass through "a certain probation" before becoming citizens. In this respect, Johnson reflected the widely held view that newly freed slaves were not capable of exercising the responsibilities of citizenship.

Johnson then justifies his position on racial grounds. By extending such rights to "every State and Territory in the United States," an effort is being made to fix "by Federal law" "a perfect equality of the white and colored races" without allowing the states to make distinctions between the races. What troubles Johnson is that, historically, the rights enumerated in the bill have been protected under

Questions for Further Study

1. Discuss the opposing viewpoints on Reconstruction policy presented by Johnson and other "moderates" on the one hand, and the Radical Republicans and their supporters on the other. What were the most and least valid arguments for each position? Be sure to cite particular statements, especially those of Johnson, to illustrate your points.

2. How did Johnson's Reconstruction policies change over the course of his presidency? Discuss the differences between his positions in the 1865 message to Congress, wherein he takes a relatively positive view of Reconstruction efforts in the South, and the far more oppositional perspective reflected in the two later documents. What factors brought about this change? In addition to those external factors, what aspects of Johnson's personality and experiences might have influenced his break with a large portion of the Republican Party?

3. Critique the logic Johnson applies to justify his vetoes of the Freedmen's Bureau Bill and the Civil Rights Act. Based on his statements in these two documents, what are his views on the nature of the Union and the place within it of the states and individual persons—particularly freed slaves?

4. Consider Johnson's analysis of the meaning of citizenship in the second and third paragraphs of the Civil Rights Act veto. Do you agree or disagree with his claim that the Constitution already grants African Americans full rights as citizens? What is "state citizenship," as opposed to citizenship under the federal government, and how did its legal status change as a result of the Civil War and Reconstruction?

5. Compare and contrast the circumstances surrounding the impeachment proceedings against Andrew Johnson and those against Bill Clinton, as well as the threatened impeachment that ultimately brought an end to the administration of Richard Nixon. In each case, what were the specific offenses and the arguments for and against the president? Give the outcome of the proceedings in each case.

the auspices of the states; it is the state, for example, that enforces contracts, conducts trials, and the like. If the federal government has the power to pass a law that requires states to give special consideration to protected classes of people, it would then by implication have the power to pass any law that would intrude on the prerogatives of the states. Johnson contends that Congress does have the power to "make rules and regulations" in the territories, but it does not have such power with regard to the states.

Impact and Legacy

History has not been kind to Andrew Johnson. He is often ranked as one of the nation's "worst" presidents, and until Bill Clinton was impeached in 1998, he was the only president to face an impeachment trial in the Senate. Further, it is difficult to acquit Johnson of the charge of racism. Although he cited constitutional and other grounds for many of his decisions, it is also clear that he regarded the United States as a nation of whites that should be ruled by whites. His stubbornness and refusal to compromise with Congress, and particularly with members of his own party, created a climate of contention that soured the Reconstruction debate. Opposition to him and his policies ran so deep that the Radical Republicans were able to determine the course of Reconstruction until 1877. And while those Republicans were actuated by principles of equality and racial reconciliation, their own policies came to be regarded as heavy-handed in the South, further impeding the process of integration.

In any event, the chief impact of Johnson's views as expressed in his annual message to Congress and his two vetoes was to strengthen the Radical Republicans. In the 1866 elections, Johnson campaigned for senators and representatives, but many Americans had come to see him as a buffoon, and his campaigning actually harmed the election and reelection bids of members of his party. When the southern states voted against ratification of the Fourteenth Amendment granting due process and equal protection under the law, the Radicals took matters into their own hands, inaugurating the period known as Congressional Reconstruction, sometimes called Radical Reconstruction. In 1867 they passed a series of Reconstruction acts that divided the South into military districts and subdistricts. These acts also outlined the ways in which new state governments would be established, and they mandated universal suffrage (for men). In effect, by stubbornly opposing the Radical Republicans, Johnson strengthened their hand, allowing them to impose Republican governments on the South. The resentment felt in the South gave rise to a countermovement that resulted in the end of Republican government in 1877, the ascendancy of the Democrats, the passage of Jim Crow laws, and the racial injustices and atrocities that followed.

Key Sources

Andrew Johnson's speeches are printed in *Speeches of Andrew Johnson, President of the United States* (1970), edited by Frank Moore. This volume was reprinted in 2005 as part of the Michigan Historical Reprint Series by the University of Michigan Library. The chief source for Johnson's papers, letters, and speeches is the sixteen-volume *The Papers of Andrew Johnson* (1967–2000), edited by Ralph W. Haskins et al.

Further Reading

■ Books

Beale, Howard K. *The Critical Year. A Study of Andrew Johnson and Reconstruction*. New York: Harcourt Brace, 1930.

Benedict, Michael Les. *The Impeachment and Trial of Andrew Johnson*, 2nd ed. New York: W. W. Norton, 1999.

Castel, Albert E. *The Presidency of Andrew Johnson*. Lawrence: Regents Press of Kansas, 1979.

Foster, G. Allen. *Impeached: The President Who Almost Lost His Job*. New York: Criterion Books, 1964.

McKitrick, Eric L. *Andrew Johnson and Reconstruction*. Chicago: University of Chicago Press, 1960.

Mantell, Martin E. *Johnson, Grant, and the Politics of Reconstruction*. New York: Columbia University Press, 1973.

Means, Howard. *The Avenger Takes His Place: Andrew Johnson and the 45 Days That Changed the Nation*. Orlando, Fla.: Harcourt, 2006.

Trefousse, Hans L. *Andrew Johnson: A Biography*. New York: W. W. Norton, 1989.

■ Web Sites

"Andrew Johnson (1808–1875)." Miller Center of Public Affairs, American President Web site.
http://millercenter.org/academic/americanpresident/johnson.

—Michael J. O'Neal

FIRST ANNUAL MESSAGE TO CONGRESS

Fellow-Citizens of the Senate and House of Representatives:...

It is not strange that the framers of the Constitution, which had no model in the past, should not have fully comprehended the excellence of their own work. Fresh from a struggle against arbitrary power, many patriots suffered from harassing fears of an absorption of the State governments by the General Government, and many from a dread that the States would break away from their orbits. But the very greatness of our country should allay the apprehension of encroachments by the General Government. The subjects that come unquestionably within its jurisdiction are so numerous that it must ever naturally refuse to be embarrassed by questions that lie beyond it. Were it otherwise the Executive would sink beneath the burden, the channels of justice would be choked, legislation would be obstructed by excess, so that there is a greater temptation to exercise some of the functions of the General Government through the States than to trespass on their rightful sphere. The "absolute acquiescence in the decisions of the majority" was at the beginning of the century enforced by Jefferson as "the vital principle of republics;" and the events of the last four years have established, we will hope forever, that there lies no appeal to force.

The maintenance of the Union brings with it "the support of the State governments in all their rights," but it is not one of the rights of any State government to renounce its own place in the Union or to nullify the laws of the Union. The largest liberty is to be maintained in the discussion of the acts of the Federal Government, but there is no appeal from its laws except to the various branches of that Government itself, or to the people, who grant to the members of the legislative and of the executive departments no tenure but a limited one, and in that manner always retain the powers of redress.

"The sovereignty of the States" is the language of the Confederacy, and not the language of the Constitution. The latter contains the emphatic words—

This Constitution and the laws of the United States which shall be made in pursuance thereof, and all treaties made or which shall be made under the authority of the United States, shall be the supreme law of the land, and the judges in every State shall be bound thereby, anything in the constitution or laws of any State to the contrary notwithstanding.

Certainly the Government of the United States is a limited government, and so is every State government a limited government. With us this idea of limitation spreads through every form of administration—general, State, and municipal—and rests on the great distinguishing principle of the recognition of the rights of man. The ancient republics absorbed the individual in the state—prescribed his religion and controlled his activity. The American system rests on the assertion of the equal right of every man to life, liberty, and the pursuit of happiness, to freedom of conscience, to the culture and exercise of all his faculties. As a consequence the State government is limited—as to the General Government in the interest of union, as to the individual citizen in the interest of freedom.

States, with proper limitations of power, are essential to the existence of the Constitution of the United States. At the very commencement, when we assumed a place among the powers of the earth, the Declaration of Independence was adopted by States; so also were the Articles of Confederation: and when "the people of the United States" ordained and established the Constitution it was the assent of the States, one by one, which gave it vitality. In the event, too, of any amendment to the Constitution, the proposition of Congress needs the confirmation of States. Without States one great branch of the legislative government would be wanting. And if we look beyond the letter of the Constitution to the character of our country, its capacity for comprehending within its jurisdiction a vast continental empire is due to the system of States. The best security for the perpetual existence of the States is the "supreme authority" of the Constitution of the United States. The perpetuity of the Constitution brings with it the perpetuity of the States; their mutual relation makes us what we are, and in our political system their connection is indissoluble. The whole can not exist without the parts, nor the parts without the whole. So long as the Constitution of the United States endures, the States will endure. The destruction of the one is the destruction of the other; the preservation of the one is the preservation of the other.

I have thus explained my views of the mutual relations of the Constitution and the States, because they unfold the principles on which I have sought to solve the momentous questions and overcome the appalling difficulties that met me at the very commencement of my Administration. It has been my steadfast object to escape from the sway of momentary passions and to derive a healing policy from the fundamental and unchanging principles of the Constitution.

I found the States suffering from the effects of a civil war. Resistance to the General Government appeared to have exhausted itself. The United States had recovered possession of their forts and arsenals, and their armies were in the occupation of every State which had attempted to secede. Whether the territory within the limits of those States should be held as conquered territory, under military authority emanating from the President as the head of the Army, was the first question that presented itself for decision.

Now military governments, established for an indefinite period, would have offered no security for the early suppression of discontent, would have divided the people into the vanquishers and the vanquished, and would have envenomed hatred rather than have restored affection. Once established, no precise limit to their continuance was conceivable. They would have occasioned an incalculable and exhausting expense. Peaceful emigration to and from that portion of the country is one of the best means that can be thought of for the restoration of harmony, and that emigration would have been prevented; for what emigrant from abroad, what industrious citizen at home, would place himself willingly under military rule? The chief persons who would have followed in the train of the Army would have been dependents on the General Government or men who expected profit from the miseries of their erring fellow-citizens. The powers of patronage and rule which would have been exercised under the President, over a vast and populous and naturally wealthy region are greater than, unless under extreme necessity, I should be willing to intrust to any one man. They are such as, for myself, I could never, unless on occasions of great emergency, consent to exercise. The willful use of such powers, if continued through a period of years, would have endangered the purity of the general administration and the liberties of the States which remained loyal.

Besides, the policy of military rule over a conquered territory would have implied that the States whose inhabitants may have taken part in the rebellion had by the act of those inhabitants ceased to exist. But the true theory is that all pretended acts of secession were from the beginning null and void. The States can not commit treason nor screen the individ-

ual citizens who may have committed treason any more than they can make valid treaties or engage in lawful commerce with any foreign power. The States attempting to secede placed themselves in a condition where their vitality was impaired, but not extinguished; their functions suspended, but not destroyed.

But if any State neglects or refuses to perform its offices there is the more need that the General Government should maintain all its authority and as soon as practicable resume the exercise of all its functions. On this principle I have acted, and have gradually and quietly, and by almost imperceptible steps, sought to restore the rightful energy of the General Government and of the States. To that end provisional governors have been appointed for the States, conventions called, governors elected, legislatures assembled, and Senators and Representatives chosen to the Congress of the United States. At the same time the courts of the United States, as far as could be done, have been reopened, so that the laws of the United States may be enforced through their agency. The blockade has been removed and the custom-houses reestablished in ports of entry, so that the revenue of the United States may be collected. The Post-Office Department renews its ceaseless activity, and the General Government is thereby enabled to communicate promptly with its officers and agents. The courts bring security to persons and property; the opening of the ports invites the restoration of industry and commerce; the post-office renews the facilities of social intercourse and of business. And is it not happy for us all that the restoration of each one of these functions of the General Government brings with it a blessing to the States over which they are extended? Is it not a sure promise of harmony and renewed attachment to the Union that after all that has happened the return of the General Government is known only as a beneficence?

I know very well that this policy is attended with some risk; that for its success it requires at least the acquiescence of the States which it concerns; that it implies an invitation to those States, by renewing their allegiance to the United States, to resume their functions as States of the Union. But it is a risk that must be taken. In the choice of difficulties it is the smallest risk; and to diminish and if possible to remove all danger, I have felt it incumbent on me to assert one other power of the General Government— the power of pardon. As no State can throw a defense over the crime of treason, the power of pardon is exclusively vested in the executive government of the United States. In exercising that power I have taken every precaution to connect it with the clearest recognition of the binding force of the laws of the

United States and an unqualified acknowledgment of the great social change of condition in regard to slavery which has grown out of the war.

The next step which I have taken to restore the constitutional relations of the States has been an invitation to them to participate in the high office of amending the Constitution. Every patriot must wish for a general amnesty at the earliest epoch consistent with public safety. For this great end there is need of a concurrence of all opinions and the spirit of mutual conciliation. All parties in the late terrible conflict must work together in harmony. It is not too much to ask, in the name of the whole people, that on the one side the plan of restoration shall proceed in conformity with a willingness to cast the disorders of the past into oblivion, and that on the other the evidence of sincerity in the future maintenance of the Union shall be put beyond any doubt by the ratification of the proposed amendment to the Constitution, which provides for the abolition of slavery forever within the limits of our country. So long as the adoption of this amendment is delayed, so long will doubt and jealousy and uncertainty prevail. This is the measure which will efface the sad memory of the past; this is the measure which will most certainly call population and capital and security to those parts of the Union that need them most. Indeed, it is not too much to ask of the States which are now resuming their places in the family of the Union to give this pledge of perpetual loyalty and peace. Until it is done the past, however much we may desire it, will not be forgotten. The adoption of the amendment reunites us beyond all power of disruption; it heals the wound that is still imperfectly closed: it removes slavery, the element which has so long perplexed and divided the country; it makes of us once more a united people, renewed and strengthened, bound more than ever to mutual affection and support.

Glossary

agency	action
Articles of Confederation	the constitution for the thirteen original U.S. states from 1777 until 1787, when it was replaced by the U.S. Constitution
General Government	federal government
patronage	political corruption characterized by exchanges of favors between more and less influential persons
republic	political system in which citizens elect their leaders—as opposed to a monarchy, dictatorship, or other government not popularly elected

VETO OF THE FREEDMEN'S BUREAU BILL

To THE SENATE OF THE UNITED STATES: I have examined with care the bill which originated in the Senate, and has been passed by the two Houses of Congress, to amend an act entitled "an act to establish a bureau for the relief of freedmen and refugees, and for other purposes." Having, with much regret, come to the conclusion that it would not be consistent with the public welfare to give my approval to the measure, I return the bill to the Senate with my objections to its becoming a law....

I have, with Congress, the strongest desire to secure to the freedmen the full enjoyment of their freedom and their property and their entire independence and equality in making contracts for their labor. But the bill before me contains provisions which, in my opinion, are not warranted by the Constitution and are not well suited to accomplish the end in view. The bill proposes to establish by authority of Congress military jurisdiction over all parts of the United States containing refugees and freedmen. It would, by its very nature, apply with most force to those parts of the United States in which the freedmen most abound; and it expressly extends the existing temporary jurisdiction of the Freedmen's Bureau, with greatly enlarged powers, over those States in which the ordinary course of judicial proceedings has been interrupted by the rebellion. The source from which this military jurisdiction is to emanate is none other than the President of the United States, acting through the War Department and the Commissioner of the Freedmen's Bureau. The agents to carry out this military jurisdiction are to be selected either from the army or from civil life. The country is to be divided into districts and sub-districts, and the number of salaried agents to be employed may be equal to the number of counties or parishes in all the United States where freedmen and refugees are to be found. The subjects over which this military jurisdiction is to extend in every part of the United States, include protection to all employees, agents, and officers of this bureau in the exercise of the duties imposed upon them by the bill. In eleven States it is farther to extend over all cases affecting freedmen and refugees discriminated against by local law, custom, or prejudice. In those eleven States the bill subjects any white person who may be charged with depriving a freedman of any civil rights or immunities belonging to white persons to imprisonment or fine, or both, without, however, defining the civil rights and immunities which are thus to be secured to the freedmen by military law. This military jurisdiction also extends to all questions that may arise respecting contracts. The

Glossary

a capital or otherwise infamous crime	a crime punishable by death, or any other serious crime
court-martial	a legal proceeding in a military court whereby a member of the armed services is tried and, if found guilty, punished by loss of rank and other penalties
militia	a military force composed of citizens rather than professional military personnel
parishes	in Louisiana, the equivalent of counties
presentment	a formal legal statement
veto	Latin for "I forbid," the exercise of executive power, usually by a president, to overrule proposed legislation
War Department	pre-1947 name for what is now known as the Department of Defense
writ of error	a legal document ordering a court to review, and possibly correct, rulings by another court

agent, who is thus to exercise the office of a military judge, may be a stranger, entirely ignorant of the laws of the place, and exposed to the errors of judgment to which all men are liable. The exercise of power over which there is no legal supervision, by so vast a number of agents as is contemplated by the bill, must, by the very nature of man, be attended by acts of caprice, injustice, and passion. The trials having their origin under this bill are to take place without the intervention of a jury and without any fixed rules of law or evidence. The rules on which offences are to be heard and determined by the numerous agents, are such rules and regulations as the President, through the War Department, shall prescribe. No previous presentment is required, nor any indictment charging the commission of a crime against the laws; but the trial must proceed on charges and specifications. The punishment will be not what the law declares, but such as a court-martial may think proper; and from these arbitrary tribunals there lies no appeal, no writ of error to any of the courts in which the Constitution of the United States vests exclusively the judicial power of the country; while the territory and the class of actions and offences that are made subject to this measure are so extensive, that the bill itself, should it become a law, will have no limitation in point of time, but will form a part of the permanent legislation of the country. I cannot reconcile a system of military jurisdiction of this kind with the words of the Constitution, which declare that "no person shall be held to answer for a capital or otherwise infamous crime unless on a presentment or indictment of a grand jury, except in cases arising in the land or naval forces or in the militia when in actual service in time of war or public danger"; and that in all criminal prosecutions the accused shall enjoy the right to a speedy and public trial by an impartial jury of the State or district wherein the crime shall have been committed.

VETO OF THE CIVIL RIGHTS ACT

WASHINGTON, D.C.,
March 27, 1866.

To the Senate of the United States:

I regret that the bill, which has passed both Houses of Congress, entitled "An act to protect all persons in the United States in their civil rights and furnish the means of their vindication," contains provisions which I can not approve consistently with my sense of duty to the whole people and my obligations to the Constitution of the United States. I am therefore constrained to return it to the Senate, the House in which it originated, with my objections to its becoming a law.

By the first section of the bill all persons born in the United States and not subject to any foreign power, excluding Indians not taxed, are declared to be citizens of the United States.... It does not purport to give these classes of persons any status as citizens of States, except that which may result from their status as citizens of the United States. The power to confer the right of State citizenship is just as exclusively with the several States as the power to confer the right of Federal citizenship is with Congress. The right of Federal citizenship thus to be conferred on the several excepted races before mentioned is now for the first time proposed to be given by law. If, as is claimed by many, all persons who are native born already are, by virtue of the Constitution, citizens of the United States, the passage of the pending bill can not be necessary to make them such. If, on the other hand, such persons are not citizens, as may be assumed from the proposed legislation to make them such, the grave question presents itself whether, when eleven of the thirty-six States are unrepresented in Congress at the present time, it is sound policy to make our entire colored population and all other excepted classes citizens of the United States. Four millions of them have just emerged from slavery into freedom....

It may also be asked whether it is necessary that they should be declared citizens in order that they may be secured in the enjoyment of the civil rights proposed to be conferred by the bill. Those rights are, by Federal as well as State laws, secured to all domiciled aliens and foreigners, even before the completion of the process of naturalization; and it may safely be assumed that the same enactments are sufficient to give like protection and benefits to those for whom this bill provides special legislation.

Besides, the policy of the Government from its origin to the present time seems to have been that persons who are strangers to and unfamiliar with our institutions and our laws should pass through a certain probation, at the end of which, before attaining the coveted prize, they must give evidence of their fitness to receive and to exercise the rights of citizens as contemplated by the Constitution of the United States. The bill in effect proposes a discrimination against large numbers of intelligent, worthy, and patriotic foreigners, and in favor of the negro, to whom, after long years of bondage, the avenues to freedom and intelligence have just now been suddenly opened....

The first section of the bill also contains an enumeration of the rights to be enjoyed by these classes so made citizens "in every State and Territory in the United States." These rights are "to make and enforce contracts; to sue, be parties, and give evidence; to inherit, purchase, lease, sell, hold, and convey real and personal property," and to have "full and equal benefit of all laws and proceedings for the security of person and property as is enjoyed by white citizens." So, too, they are made subject to the same punishment, pains, and penalties in common with white citizens, and to none other. Thus a perfect equality of the white and colored races is attempted to be fixed by Federal law in every State of the Union over the vast field of State jurisdiction covered by these enumerated rights. In no one of these can any State ever exercise any power of discrimination between the different races....

Hitherto every subject embraced in the enumeration of rights contained in this bill has been considered as exclusively belonging to the States. They all relate to the internal police and economy of the respective States. They are matters which in each State concern the domestic condition of its people, varying in each according to its own peculiar circumstances and the safety and well-being of its own citizens. I do not mean to say that upon all these subjects there are not Federal restraints—as, for instance, in the State power of legislation over contracts there is a Federal limitation that no State shall pass a law impairing the obligations of contracts; and, as to crimes, that no State shall pass an *ex post facto* law; and, as to money, that no State shall make anything but gold and silver a legal tender; but where can we find a Federal prohibition against the power of any

State to discriminate, as do most of them, between aliens and citizens, between artificial persons, called corporations, and natural persons, in the right to hold real estate? If it be granted that Congress can repeal all State laws discriminating between whites and blacks in the subjects covered by this bill, why, it may be asked, may not Congress repeal in the same way all State laws discriminating between the two races on the subjects of suffrage and office? If Congress can declare by law who shall hold lands, who shall testify, who shall have capacity to make a contract in a State, then Congress can by law also declare who, without regard to color or race, shall have the right to sit as a juror or as a judge, to hold any office, and, finally, to vote "in every State and Territory of the United States." As respects the Territories, they come within the power of Congress, for as to them the lawmaking power is the Federal power; but as to the States no similar provision exists vesting in Congress the power "to make rules and regulations" for them....

In all our history, in all our experience as people living under Federal and State law, no such system as that contemplated by the details of this bill has ever before been proposed or adopted. They establish for the security of the colored race safeguards which go infinitely beyond any that the General Government has ever provided for the white race. In fact, the distinction of race and color is by the bill made to operate in favor of the colored and against the white race. They interfere with the municipal legislation of the States, with the relations existing exclusively between a State and its citizens, or between inhabitants of the same State—an absorption and assumption of power by the General Government which, if acquiesced in, must sap and destroy our federative system of limited powers and break down the barriers which preserve the rights of the States. It is another step, or rather stride, toward centralization and the concentration of all legislative powers in the National Government. The tendency of the bill must be to resuscitate the spirit of rebellion and to arrest the progress of those influences which are more closely drawing around the States the bonds of union and peace.

Glossary

artificial persons, called corporations	in U.S. law, groups or other nonindividual entities, as opposed to individuals ("natural persons")
convey	transfer legal ownership to
the coveted prize	citizenship
ex post facto	Latin for "after the fact," a term describing a retroactive law, or a law that criminalizes acts that occurred prior to the time the law was adopted
federative	organized along federal lines, with both a national government and semi-sovereign or self-ruling state governments
legal tender	a unit or units of value that, by law, must be accepted as payment for a debt
suffrage and office	the right to vote and to be elected to public office

Lyndon Baines Johnson (Library of Congress)

LYNDON BAINES JOHNSON   1908–1973

Thirty-sixth President of the United States

Featured Documents
- ◆ Speech to a Joint Session of Congress on Assuming the Presidency (1963)
- ◆ Commencement Address at the University of Michigan (1964)
- ◆ Remarks on the Gulf of Tonkin Incident (1964)
- ◆ Speech to a Joint Session of Congress on Civil Rights (1965)

Overview

Lyndon Baines Johnson was born in 1908 in rural southwestern Texas and grew up in a household saturated with politics. He went to Washington in 1931 as a secretary to Representative Richard Kleberg. He returned to Texas in 1935 as the state director of the National Youth Administration. Johnson defeated nine other candidates in 1937 to win a special election to the U.S. House of Representatives. In the 1948 Democratic primary for senator, his eighty-seven-vote margin of victory brought charges of fraud and earned Johnson the mocking nickname "Landslide Lyndon." Despite the charges and mockery, Johnson became a master of the legislative process. He worked two years as Senate majority whip, two as Senate minority leader, and six as Senate majority leader.

In 1960 Johnson campaigned for the Democratic presidential nomination but was defeated in the primary by John F. Kennedy. Kennedy surprised observers by naming Johnson as his vice presidential choice. In November the Kennedy-Johnson ticket defeated the Republican candidate, Richard Nixon. Kennedy's 1963 assassination thrust Johnson into the presidency. As president, Johnson pledged to continue his predecessor's policies, beginning with a speech delivered to Congress five days after Kennedy's assassination. After a bitter battle in Congress, he secured passage of the landmark 1964 Civil Rights Act. Soundly defeating Barry Goldwater in the 1964 election, Johnson embarked on a far-ranging legislative program. He introduced bills creating Medicare and Medicaid, guaranteeing voting rights for minority groups, and providing financial aid for elementary and secondary schools and grants for college students. Urban renewal, consumer protection, environmental quality, and the War on Poverty were other Johnson' initiatives. The set of domestic programs that Johnson created, which he outlined in his commencement address at the University of Michigan in 1964, were collectively termed the Great Society. Johnson also began his push for additional civil rights in the form of voting rights legislation, which he supported in a speech to a joint session of Congress and before a television audience in March 1965. The Voting Rights Act was passed in August of that year.

During Johnson's presidency the country became mired in the Vietnam War, a war fought from the mid-1950s to 1976 between Communist North Vietnam and its allies and the government of South Vietnam. In August 1964, the USS *Maddox* was on a secret support mission in the waters of the Gulf of Tonkin when it engaged with North Vietnamese torpedo boats. The incident led to the large-scale involvement of U.S. troops in the conflict in Southeast Asia, a plan that Johnson announced to the American people on August 4. Despite Johnson's sending more than half a million troops into battle, the United States and South Vietnam were unable to defeat the Vietcong. Opponents of the war challenged Johnson for the 1968 Democratic presidential nomination. After a close New Hampshire Democratic primary, Johnson announced he would not seek reelection. In 1969 Johnson retired to his Texas ranch; his health declined, and he died of a heart attack in 1973.

Explanation and Analysis of Documents

During the five years of Lyndon Johnson's presidency the United States was buffeted by conflict both overseas and on the home front. Johnson responded to the demands of civil rights protesters by proposing two major pieces of legislation—the Civil Rights Act of 1964 and the Voting Rights Act of 1965. He grappled with the underlying problem of economic deprivation by creating ambitious antipoverty programs collectively termed the Great Society. At the same time, he tried to deal with the worsening military situation in Southeast Asia. His success in enacting his domestic agenda was offset by his failure in Vietnam. Johnson's most important documents were his speeches to Congress and to the American people advancing his domestic agenda and defending his Vietnam policy.

◆ Speech to a Joint Session of Congress on Assuming the Presidency

Lyndon Johnson had not been a popular choice when John F. Kennedy named the Texan as his vice presidential running mate. The northern liberals who advised Kennedy were deeply suspicious of Johnson's strong ties to powerful southern conservatives such as Georgia's Senator Richard Russell, Jr. Robert Kennedy, John F. Kennedy's brother and campaign manager, was especially hostile. But John Kennedy knew that Johnson's name on the ticket would provide the geographic balance needed to win the election

Time Line

1908
- **August 27**
  Lyndon Baines Johnson is born in Stonewall, Texas.

1937
- **April 10**
  Johnson is elected to the U.S. House of Representatives.

1948
- **August 28**
  Johnson wins the Democratic nomination to the U.S. Senate by an eighty-seven-vote margin.
- **November 2**
  Johnson is elected to the U.S. Senate.

1955
- **January**
  Johnson is named Senate majority leader.

1960
- **July 14**
  Johnson is nominated as the Democratic candidate for vice president.
- **November 8**
  Johnson is elected vice president of the United States.

1963
- **November 22**
  John F. Kennedy is assassinated in Dallas, and Johnson is sworn in as the thirty-sixth president.
- **November 27**
  Johnson delivers his speech to a joint session of Congress on assuming the presidency.

1964
- **May 22**
  Johnson delivers the commencement address at the University of Michigan, in which he calls for "the Great Society."
- **July 2**
  Johnson signs the Civil Rights Act.
- **August 4**
  Johnson orders attacks on North Vietnam following the Gulf of Tonkin incident.

in November, and Texas's electoral votes did, in fact, help tip the election in Kennedy's favor.

As vice president, Johnson languished in obscurity. He was mostly relegated to performing ceremonial duties and was excluded from Kennedy's inner circle of advisers. Johnson had difficulty adjusting to this minor role; he missed the power he had wielded as Senate majority leader. All of that changed in an instant on November 22, 1963, when John Kennedy was struck down in Dallas by an assassin's bullet. Standing next to Jacqueline Kennedy, Johnson took the oath of office aboard Air Force One as the plane prepared to return John Kennedy's body to Washington, D.C., for a state funeral.

The most urgent challenge facing Johnson as he took office was convincing Kennedy's supporters and the American public that he was capable of carrying out the awesome duties of the presidency. In fact, few men were better prepared to assume the office. Johnson's service in the House and Senate had given him intimate knowledge of the legislative process. His friendship with congressional leaders was a resource he would use to considerable advantage in gaining support for his policies. Although his sometimes crude and overbearing personal style differed markedly from that of the witty and sophisticated Kennedy, Johnson displayed great sensitivity to the needs of the Kennedy family as he assured a worried nation that his administration would continue the policies of the martyred president.

Five days after the assassination, Johnson stood before a joint session of Congress. A national television audience joined the legislators waiting to hear the new president's first major address. It was the most important speech of Johnson's political career. He needed to outline his agenda in terms that would rally support for his administration and convince the nation's grieving citizens that he could restore their shattered dreams. On both counts he did not disappoint. Johnson begins by expressing his deep regret over the circumstances that make his remarks necessary. He links his sorrow at Kennedy's death to the heartache experienced by the nation. Then he quickly sounds his main theme—his determination to advance the policies of the Kennedy administration. He lists some of Kennedy's major initiatives—the space program, the Peace Corps, aid to education, health care for the elderly, civil rights—and pledges to make these his own priorities. He tells Americans that he will push Congress to make sure they are enacted.

Turning his attention to foreign affairs, Johnson praises Kennedy's courage and leadership. In a thinly veiled reference to the Cuban missile crisis (when the United States confronted the Soviets about their buildup of missile bases in Cuba), Johnson applauds his predecessor's willingness to risk war while standing up to America's enemies. Just as Kennedy had done, he promises to stand strong against those enemies who oppose peace and seek to impose the "yoke of tyranny" on innocent people. More specifically, he renews America's commitment to defend South Vietnam and Berlin. He pledges to balance U.S. military strength with restraint and not to seek special privileges in other lands.

Shifting the focus to his new administration, Johnson vows to rise above sectional loyalties and govern on behalf of the entire nation. He will use his thirty-two years of Washington experience to develop wise, just, and enlightened programs. Despite the national trauma of the assassination, he will lead the country forward. Echoing John F. Kennedy's inaugural address, in which he had said, "Let us begin," Johnson forcefully implores, "Let us continue." Johnson announces that his most urgent priority will be passage of the civil rights bill that Kennedy had sent to Congress six months earlier. The time for talk has passed, Johnson observes; now is the time for action. He urges Congress to enact the bill as a fitting memorial to the slain leader. Reminding his audience that he had led the fight to pass two civil rights bills as Senate majority leader, he expresses his determination to continue the fight against discrimination and racial oppression.

Returning to his original theme, he beseeches his listeners to move from grief to action and to honor Kennedy's memory by becoming a nation dedicated to tolerance and mutual respect, free of hatred and bigotry. With a renewed sense of unity, he urges Americans to resolve that "John Fitzgerald Kennedy did not live—or die—in vain." In a closing benediction, he quotes the great patriotic hymn "America the Beautiful," asking God to "shed His grace" on the shattered nation.

◆ **Commencement Address at the University of Michigan**

Democratic presidents of the twentieth century coined catchy slogans to label their political agendas. Woodrow Wilson proclaimed a New Freedom; Franklin Roosevelt championed the New Deal; for Harry Truman it was the Fair Deal; John F. Kennedy spoke of the New Frontier. When Lyndon Johnson described his vision for America, he talked about the Great Society. Because he had not campaigned for the presidency, Johnson lacked a slogan for his programs when he assumed office, but he soon felt the need for one in order to distinguish his agenda from Kennedy's. When the presidential speechwriter Richard Goodwin suggested "the Great Society," Johnson decided to build a major address around it. The occasion was the commencement ceremony at the University of Michigan on May 22, 1964. Johnson, who had been president for six months, used this speech to set forth a conceptual framework for his domestic agenda. Goodwin prepared a speech that outlined in broad terms the kind of programs Johnson hoped to implement and spelled out his vision for the American nation. Johnson wanted to demonstrate that he was a politician with a grand blueprint for change, and he needed to build popular support for the measures he would soon introduce to Congress. In addition, the president hoped that this speech would convince those liberal intellectuals who remained loyal to Kennedy's memory that he was a leader with bold ideas for reshaping American society.

In many respects, Johnson's agenda for the Great Society was an updated version of Roosevelt's New Deal. Johnson had come of age during the Roosevelt years. When he

Time Line

1964
- **November 3**
  Johnson is elected president with 61 percent of the popular vote.

1965
- **March 15**
  Johnson delivers his speech to a joint session of Congress on civil rights.
- **August 6**
  Johnson signs the Voting Rights Act.

1968
- **March 31**
  Johnson announces that he will not seek a second term.

1973
- **January 22**
  Johnson dies of a heart attack at his Texas ranch.

was just twenty-six years old, Roosevelt had appointed him to be the Texas head of the National Youth Administration. In Johnson's first run for Congress in 1937, his platform had given 100 percent support to Roosevelt's New Deal policies. He shared Roosevelt's optimism about the ability of the federal government to solve pressing social problems. As president, he made sure that many of his domestic proposals addressed issues for which his Democratic predecessors had not been able to implement solutions.

Speaking before more than eighty thousand people jammed into the university's football stadium, Johnson states that the fundamental challenge facing America is the way it deals with its unprecedented abundance. Americans first conquered the frontier; then they constructed a mighty industrial system; now they have the opportunity to create the Great Society. Johnson refers to his major initiatives to expand civil rights and combat poverty, but these would not be enough. In his vision of the future, all children would be challenged to develop their minds and enlarge their talents; their parents would make productive use of their leisure time; cities would become places of beauty and community spirit; people would be "more concerned with the quality of their goals than the quantity of their goods." There was much to be accomplished. "The Great Society," Johnson says, "is not a safe harbor, a resting place, a final objective, a finished work. It is a challenge constantly renewed, beckoning us toward a destiny where the meaning of our lives matches the marvelous products of our labor."

Rebuilding American cities to accommodate a growing population was an essential component of the Great Society. Erecting new housing, enlarging transportation facilities, and preserving open space were all areas that needed

The U.S. Navy destroyer USS Maddox (AP/Wide World Photos)

to be addressed. Preserving the natural environment was another priority. Air and water would have to be freed from pollution, green spaces had to be preserved, and more parks and recreational facilities would have to be created. Improving education was the third piece of his grand plan. This would require building more classrooms. It would also mean recruiting and training new teachers and increasing their pay as well as developing new teaching techniques. Johnson does not advance specific proposals to reach these goals. Instead, he promises to bring together the country's best minds in a series of White House conferences to work on solutions. Johnson concludes with an exhortation to the graduates, their families, and the university faculty to work together with him to shape the future of America in the image of his Great Society.

◆ Remarks on the Gulf of Tonkin Incident

The most fateful action of Lyndon Johnson's presidency was his decision to expand American military involvement in South Vietnam. Previous presidents had sent aid to the region, but Johnson presided over a massive buildup that dwarfed earlier efforts. President Dwight Eisenhower had provided material support for the French in their war against the Viet Minh, a Vietnamese national liberation movement initially formed to seek independence from France. In 1954 the French negotiated peace accords, which divided the land into North Vietnam (with a Communist government) and South Vietnam until unifying elections could take place. The United States backed the newly formed government of South Vietnam. Unifying elections never took place. By the late 1950s a South Vietnamese Communist insurgency, the Vietcong, had actively begun to fight a guerrilla war. President John F. Kennedy dispatched U.S. military advisers to prop up the weak South Vietnamese army, but only sixteen thousand American troops were on the ground in South Vietnam at the time of his assassination. The growing strength of the Vietcong and the North Vietnamese army and the continued poor performance of the South Vietnamese army added pressure on Johnson to send more U.S. forces.

On August 2, 1964, the U.S. destroyer *Maddox*, patrolling sixteen miles off the coast of North Vietnam, was attacked by three North Vietnamese torpedo boats. The American vessel suffered only minor damage and no injuries to its personnel. In the early morning hours of August 4, the *Maddox* and a sister ship, the *Turner Joy*, reported a second attack. American forces fired at what they believed to be North Vietnamese torpedo boats, although none were actually sighted. Later that day the commander of the *Maddox* sent word that the indications of an attack might have been triggered by freak weather effects or misreadings by overeager sonar men.

The president and his advisers conferred over the best course of action. In addition to military and foreign policy considerations, Johnson weighed the consequences of inaction on his upcoming presidential election campaign. Barry Goldwater, the Republican nominee, was calling for a more aggressive response to the Communist threat in South Vietnam; Johnson did not want to be seen as a weak leader. He ordered no retaliation for the initial attack, but the second incident, despite its dubious credibility, was treated as a deliberate provocation. Johnson dispatched air strikes against North Vietnamese targets and met with congressional leaders to seek their support for a resolution he would soon submit to them.

At 11:36 PM on August 4, a grave Johnson went before a national television audience to announce his response to the incident. He begins by briefly describing "hostile actions against United States ships on the high seas in the Gulf of Tonkin." Making no mention of the uncertain military intelligence, he depicts the second incident as involving "a number of hostile vessels attacking two U.S. destroyers with torpedoes." After outlining the immediate military response, Johnson characterizes the U.S. role in Southeast Asia as protecting the "peaceful villagers of South Viet Nam" against a campaign of "aggression by terror" being waged by the Vietcong and their North Vietnamese allies. He says nothing about the provocative actions of the American ships prior to the incident. Despite the belligerent actions of the North Vietnamese, Johnson assures his listeners that the American response will be "limited and fitting." Using a phrase he will repeat many times in coming months, the commander in chief tells the nation, "We still seek no wider war."

But authority to wage a wider war is exactly what Johnson was requesting. He announces that he will send a resolution to Congress expressing American "determination to take all necessary measures" to defend the government of South Vietnam. Johnson was convinced that there would be little opposition to this move, and he was correct. On August 7, after perfunctory hearings and minimal debate, the House passed the Gulf of Tonkin Resolution unanimously. In the Senate, there were only two dissenting votes. With this vote congressional leaders gave Johnson a blank check to use in pursuing his goals in Vietnam. A few months after his November landslide election victory, Johnson sent the first U.S. combat troops to Vietnam. When 3,500 Marines waded ashore at Da Nang in March 1965 the wider war that Johnson had pledged to avoid became a reality. By 1969 more than half a million American military personnel were fighting in Vietnam. Critics of the war pointed to Johnson's Gulf of Tonkin speech as a key example of the presidential deception that led the United States into this costly and divisive Southeast Asian quagmire.

◆ Speech to a Joint Session of Congress on Civil Rights

Johnson was an unlikely champion of civil rights. For most of his congressional career he voted with the southern bloc to oppose legislation offering protection to African Americans. As Senate majority leader, however, Johnson's outlook changed. He realized that he would never win the national office he desired unless he shed the segregationist label. In 1957 the Texas senator engineered passage of the first civil rights legislation since Reconstruction. By breaking with his southern colleagues, Johnson began refashioning his image.

On assuming the presidency, Johnson made passage of Kennedy's civil rights bill a top priority. In his first speech as president, Johnson urged Congress to pass the stalled civil rights bill as a memorial to the slain president. Then Johnson went to work, exercising his legendary political skills to persuade reluctant Republican senators to join with northern Democrats supporting the bill. After an unsuccessful southern filibuster, the bill passed and was signed into law on July 2, 1964. Johnson understood that the Civil Rights Act alone would not solve all the problems facing African Americans. He believed that voting was the key to black advancement. Johnson's aides prepared additional legislation, but he held off advancing it because he felt Congress would not pass another civil rights bill so soon after the 1964 act. Then Selma happened.

Martin Luther King, Jr., had targeted the central Alabama town to draw attention to the widespread discrimination against would-be black voters. He did so not only because less than 1 percent of Selma's African American citizens had been able to register to vote but also because Sheriff Jim Clark of Dallas County was a stereotypical southern bigot. During January and February 1965, civil rights workers organized demonstrations to highlight the denial of voting rights and the heavy-handed methods of law officers. These protests climaxed on March 7 when a band of six hundred marchers attempted to walk to the state capital of Montgomery. State troopers and Sheriff Clark's mounted posse attacked the nonviolent marchers with tear gas and billy clubs. Television news coverage of the brutal assault triggered outrage across the country. Thousands of civil rights supporters joined King's forces in Selma. Tension increased when a Unitarian minister from Boston died after a vicious beating administered by a gang of local whites.

In the wake of this incident Lyndon Johnson decided that it was time to introduce voting rights legislation. Rather than sending the bill to Congress by messenger, Johnson dramatized his request by speaking to a rare joint session of Congress and a television audience of 70 million people. One week after the events of "Bloody Sunday," the

president made the case for his sweeping proposal. He begins by reminding his audience of the events in Selma, describing them as "a turning point in man's unending search for freedom" equivalent to the battles of the American Revolution and Civil War. In the face of the "cries of pain" from the "long-suffering men and women" who were peacefully protesting, Johnson appeals to the representatives and senators to take action. The problem of racial inequality is a challenge to the basic values of American democracy, he asserts. At issue is the most fundamental right of free citizens—the right to vote. "There is no reason which can excuse the denial of that right," he thunders.

Johnson then recites some of the devices used to disqualify potential black voters: limited opportunities to register, trivial errors on the application forms, discriminatory literacy tests. He concludes that "the only way to pass these barriers is to show a white skin." The president outlines key provisions of his bill—eliminating "illegal barriers to the right to vote," establishing "a simple, uniform standard" for voter registration, and prohibiting interference with the right to vote. Johnson endorses the civil rights movement as a valiant effort by "American Negroes to secure for themselves the full blessings of American life." But support for the movement should not come only from African Americans, he says, because all U.S. citizens stand to benefit from its success. All Americans need to "overcome the crippling legacy of bigotry and injustice." Here Johnson pauses for emphasis and then slowly and deliberately declares, "And we shall overcome." Listeners around the nation were shocked and amazed to hear the southern-born president repeat the refrain of the civil rights movement's best-known anthem.

Johnson links his proposal to Abraham Lincoln's Emancipation Proclamation. It has been more than one hundred years since Lincoln freed the slaves, but African Americans are not yet free, says Johnson. It was time for Congress to act to ensure justice for the courageous people who risked their lives while seeking their constitutionally guaranteed rights. In an abrupt change of pace, Johnson reminisces about his first job as a schoolteacher in the tiny town of Cotulla, Texas. His students there were poor Mexican American children. He describes the hardships they endured and the prejudice they faced. Johnson tells how the memories of those days stayed with him and how they motivated him to enter politics so that he could help the "sons and daughters of those students." Rarely has the nation been treated to such a powerful and deeply felt oration by an American president.

Impact and Legacy

No American president left a more conflicted legacy than Lyndon Johnson. None can match his record of legislative accomplishment, but few left office more widely disliked. Taking advantage of large Democratic majorities in the House and Senate, Johnson guided a staggering number of bills through the Eighty-ninth Congress, creating many programs that became a permanent part of the U.S. government.

When it came to advancing the rights of African Americans, Johnson can rightfully be compared to Abraham Lincoln. He deserves credit for passing the 1964 Civil Rights Act. His 1965 Voting Rights Act effectively dismantled Jim Crow barriers that prevented blacks from voting in much of the South. In addition, Johnson appointed the first black Supreme Court justice, Thurgood Marshall, and the first black cabinet secretary, Robert C. Weaver. Despite these achievements, many young African Americans were not satisfied. Only days after Johnson signed the Voting Rights Act, the Watts neighborhood of Los Angeles erupted in a five-day outbreak of rioting and looting. Over the next three summers, nearly every American city experienced similar urban rebellions. Black Power advocates showed no gratitude to the man who had protected their constitutional rights.

Johnson understood that enhanced economic opportunities were just as essential to black progress as expanded political rights. In 1964 he declared his War on Poverty and, while poverty was not eliminated during his administration, it was significantly reduced. Among the many antipoverty programs created by Johnson were Head Start, food stamps, the Job Corps, Volunteers in Service to America, and increased Social Security benefits. As a former teacher, Johnson had a strong commitment to educational improvement. He was responsible for the first direct federal financial aid to local school districts and introduced legislation to provide federal grants and loans to low-income college students. The most costly pieces of Johnson's antipoverty initiative were two health insurance programs—Medicare for the elderly and Medicaid for low-income families. Johnson greatly enlarged the federal government's role in environmental protection by authoring the Clean Air Act and the Clean Water Act. He advanced culture by creating the National Endowment for the Arts and the National Endowment for the Humanities.

Notwithstanding this impressive list of accomplishments, it can be argued that Johnson's optimistic rhetoric contained the seeds of his own downfall. By promising more than he could deliver, such as an end to poverty, he created unrealistic expectations that, when not speedily realized, resulted in disillusionment and frustration. His vigorous support of black civil rights alienated white southern voters, who soon shifted their allegiance to the Republican Party. His misleading statements on Vietnam undermined the credibility of the White House. By creating numerous large government programs, some of which were poorly conceived and hastily put together, he fueled right-wing criticism of big government. The conservative resurgence that culminated in the 1980 election of Ronald Reagan can be seen, in part, as a reaction to what some saw as the excesses of the Johnson years.

Johnson's Vietnam policy remains a matter of bitter debate decades after the war's end. Vietnam hawks argue that Johnson did not pursue a sufficiently aggressive strategy, forcing American commanders to fight a limited war. Doves fault him for misleading the American people and needlessly squandering the lives of American soldiers in a country of little strategic importance. There can be no doubt that the Vietnam War casts a shadow over all of Johnson's domestic programs and remains the most controversial part of his legacy. Johnson possessed great energy and enormous political skills. Like his hero, Franklin D. Roosevelt, Johnson believed that government's proper role was to protect those in need and to improve the lives of average citizens. Even with his considerable legislative accomplishments, his presidency was haunted by the divisive and futile Vietnam War.

Key Sources

The Lyndon Baines Johnson Library is the official repository for documents from Johnson's presidential administration and his early career. The library's Web site (http://www.lbjlib.utexas.edu/) includes a full directory of resources including oral history transcripts, presidential speeches, photographs, and audiovisual materials. Full texts of Johnson's official statements can be found in *Public Papers of the Presidents of the United States: Lyndon B. Johnson* (1965–1970). In retirement, with the uncredited assistance of the historian Doris Kearns Goodwin, Johnson wrote a memoir of his presidency, *The Vantage Point; Perspectives of the Presidency, 1963–1969* (1971). The excellent four-hour documentary *LBJ* (1997), written by David G. McCullough and David Grubin, was originally shown on the PBS American Experience series. *The LBJ Tapes* (1997) features reenactments of Johnson's tape-recorded telephone conversations while president.

Further Reading

■ Books

Califano, Joseph A. *The Triumph and Tragedy of Lyndon Johnson: The White House Years*. New York: Simon and Schuster, 1991.

Caro, Robert. *The Years of Lyndon Johnson: The Path to Power*. New York: Alfred A. Knopf, 1982.

_____. *The Years of Lyndon Johnson: Means of Ascent*. New York: Alfred A. Knopf, 1990.

_____. *The Years of Lyndon Johnson: Master of the Senate*. New York: Alfred A. Knopf, 2002.

Dallek, Robert. *Lone Star Rising: Lyndon Johnson and His Times, 1908–1960*. New York: Oxford University Press, 1991.

_____. *Flawed Giant: Lyndon Johnson and His Times, 1961–1973*. New York: Oxford University Press, 1998.

Mackenzie, G. Calvin, and Robert A. Weisbrot. *The Liberal Hour: Washington and the Politics of Change in the 1960s*. New York: Penguin, 2008.

—Paul T. Murray

"John F. Kennedy told his countrymen that our national work would not be finished 'in the first thousand days, nor in the life of this administration, nor even perhaps in our lifetime on this planet. But,' he said, 'let us begin.' Today, in this moment of new resolve, I would say to all my fellow Americans, let us continue."

(Speech to a Joint Session of Congress on Assuming the Presidency)

"No memorial oration or eulogy could more eloquently honor President Kennedy's memory than the earliest possible passage of the civil rights bill for which he fought so long. We have talked long enough in this country about equal rights. We have talked for one hundred years or more. It is time now to write the next chapter, and to write it in the books of law."

(Speech to a Joint Session of Congress on Assuming the Presidency)

"The Great Society is not a safe harbor, a resting place, a final objective, a finished work. It is a challenge constantly renewed, beckoning us toward a destiny where the meaning of our lives matches the marvelous products of our labor."

(Commencement Address at the University of Michigan)

"The determination of all Americans to carry out our full commitment to the people and to the government of South Viet-Nam will be redoubled by this outrage. Yet our response, for the present, will be limited and fitting. We Americans know, although others appear to forget, the risks of spreading conflict. We still seek no wider war."

(Remarks on the Gulf of Tonkin Incident)

"What happened in Selma is part of a far larger movement which reaches into every section and State of America. It is the effort of American Negroes to secure for themselves the full blessings of American life. Their cause must be our cause too. Because it is not just Negroes, but really it is all of us, who must overcome the crippling legacy of bigotry and injustice. And we shall overcome."

(Speech to a Joint Session of Congress on Civil Rights)

1. Three U.S. presidents are known familiarly by their initials. First there was Franklin D. Roosevelt, nicknamed FDR; then John F. Kennedy, who encouraged the use of JFK in reference to himself precisely because it harkened back to one of his heroes; and, finally, Johnson, who, in a conscious effort to identify his name with those of his two great predecessors, became known as LBJ. Discuss the influence on Johnson exerted by Roosevelt, under whose administration LBJ cut his teeth politically, and Kennedy, in whose shadow Johnson served as a vice president with very little share of real power and influence. To what extent did these two men provide a guide and model to Johnson, and to what extent did he feel a need to transcend that influence and become his own man? Pay special attention to his use of phrases or ideas associated with Roosevelt or Kennedy and the ways his policies coincided or contrasted with those of the other two men.

2. Friends and foes alike conceded at least one thing about Lyndon B. Johnson: that he had a salty, sometimes off-color sense of humor that fit well with his image as a strong, take-charge leader. Discuss Johnson's use of humor, particularly in the University of Michigan address, which contains several jokes and what appear to be jokes about coeducational learning, the self-sacrificing attitude of youth "trying so hard live at the level of the people" in the richest nation on earth, and so on. How effective and appropriate is his use of humor here and in other instances? What do his jokes and his sometimes outlandish acts (for instance, pulling a dog's ears in front of a group of reporters) say about Johnson's background and his view of his role as chief executive?

3. One of the most controversial aspects of Johnson's legacy was the set of social programs collectively titled the Great Society. Critics maintain that the Great Society resulted in massive spending increases with results that were at best questionable and at worst counterproductive, while others judged it an overwhelming success. Discuss the specifics of the Great Society and evaluate its outcome, citing both factual information and opinions such as those of critics and supporters. Compare the results of Johnson's programs with his promises and predictions, particularly in his 1963 message to Congress and his University of Michigan commencement address the following year.

4. Evaluate Johnson's remarks on the Gulf of Tonkin incident in light of what is now known about the event itself and the war whose escalation it helped bring about. In what specific ways does Johnson deviate from the truth and for what purposes? On the other hand, what are his most valid points? Why do you think he chose to make Vietnam one of the focal issues of his administration?

5. Whereas his Great Society programs have received mixed reviews and his escalation of the Vietnam conflict is now generally regarded as a great mistake that marred his legacy and prevented him from seeking reelection in 1968, Johnson's record with regard to civil rights is clearly a great achievement of his administration. What role did his background as a southerner play in his emergence as a champion of racial equality? To what degree did his southern background actually give him an advantage in this arena? It could be said that just as Richard Nixon's staunch reputation made him an ideal proponent of normalized relations with China because no one would accuse him of being soft on Communism, so Johnson made a credible defender of equal opportunity precisely because he was not a northern liberal. To what degree did he have to evolve and adjust his thinking to accommodate to changes in the racial and political landscape? Was he sincere in his support for the civil rights movement, or was his backing of civil rights legislation merely a calculated political move?

SPEECH TO A JOINT SESSION OF CONGRESS ON ASSUMING THE PRESIDENCY (1963)

Mr. Speaker, Mr. President, Members of the House, Members of the Senate, my fellow Americans:

All I have I would have given gladly not to be standing here today.

The greatest leader of our time has been struck down by the foulest deed of our time. Today, John Fitzgerald Kennedy lives on in the immortal words and works that he left behind. He lives on in the mind and memories of mankind. He lives on in the hearts of his countrymen. No words are sad enough to express our sense of loss. No words are strong enough to express our determination to continue the forward thrust of America that he began.

The dream of conquering the vastness of space, the dream of partnership across the Atlantic—and across the Pacific as well—the dream of a Peace Corps in less developed nations, the dream of education for all of our children, the dream of jobs for all who seek them and need them, the dream of care for our elderly, the dream of an all-out attack on mental illness, and above all, the dream of equal rights for all Americans, whatever their race or color. These and other American dreams have been vitalized by his drive and by his dedication. And now the ideas and the ideals which he so nobly represented must and will be translated into effective action.

Under John Kennedy's leadership, this nation has demonstrated that it has the courage to seek peace, and it has the fortitude to risk war. We have proved that we are a good and reliable friend to those who seek peace and freedom. We have shown that we can also be a formidable foe to those who reject the path of peace and those who seek to impose upon us or our allies the yoke of tyranny. This nation will keep its commitments from South Vietnam to West Berlin. We will be unceasing in the search for peace, resourceful in our pursuit of areas of agreement—even with those with whom we differ—and generous and loyal to those who join with us in common cause.

In this age when there can be no losers in peace and no victors in war, we must recognize the obligation to match national strength with national restraint. We must be prepared at one and the same time for both the confrontation of power and the limitation of power. We must be ready to defend the national interest and to negotiate the common interest. This is the path that we shall continue to pursue.

Those who test our courage will find it strong, and those who seek our friendship will find it honorable. We will demonstrate anew that the strong can be just in the use of strength and the just can be strong in the defense of justice.

And let all know we will extend no special privilege and impose no persecution. We will carry on the fight against poverty, and misery, and disease, and ignorance, in other lands and in our own. We will serve all the nation, not one section or one sector or one group, but all Americans.

These are the United States: A united people with a united purpose.

Our American unity does not depend upon unanimity. We have differences; but now, as in the past, we can derive from those differences strength, not weakness; wisdom, not despair. Both as a people and a government, we can unite upon a program, a program which is wise and just, enlightened and constructive.

For 32 years Capitol Hill has been my home. I have shared many moments of pride with you, pride in the ability of the Congress of the United States to act, to meet any crisis, to distill from our differences strong programs of national action. An assassin's bullet has thrust upon me the awesome burden of the Presidency. I am here today to say I need your help. I cannot bear this burden alone. I need the help of all Americans, and all America.

This nation has experienced a profound shock, and in this critical moment, it is our duty, yours and mine, as the Government of the United States, to do away with uncertainty and doubt and delay, and to show that we are capable of decisive action; that from the brutal loss of our leader we will derive not weakness, but strength; that we can and will act and act now.

From this chamber of representative government, let all the world know and none misunderstand that I rededicate this Government to the unswerving support of the United Nations, to the honorable and determined execution of our commitments to our allies, to the maintenance of military strength second to none, to the defense of the strength and the stability of the dollar, to the expansion of our foreign trade, to the reinforcement of our programs of mutual assistance and cooperation in Asia and Africa, and to our Alliance for Progress in this hemisphere.

On the 20th day of January, in 19 and 61, John F. Kennedy told his countrymen that our national work would not be finished "in the first thousand days, nor in the life of this administration, nor even perhaps in our lifetime on this planet." "But," he said, "let us begin."

Today in this moment of new resolve, I would say to all my fellow Americans, *let us continue*.

This is our challenge—not to hesitate, not to pause, not to turn about and linger over this evil moment, but to continue on our course so that we may fulfill the destiny that history has set for us.

Our most immediate tasks are here on this Hill. First, no memorial oration or eulogy could more eloquently honor President Kennedy's memory than the earliest possible passage of the Civil Rights Bill for which he fought so long. We have talked long enough in this country about equal rights. We have talked for a hundred years or more. It *is* time now to write the next chapter, and to write it in the books of law. I urge you again, as I did in 19 and 57 and again in 19 and 60, to enact a civil rights law so that we can move forward to eliminate from this nation every trace of discrimination and oppression that is based upon race or color. There could be no greater source of strength to this nation both at home and abroad.

And second, no act of ours could more fittingly continue the work of President Kennedy than the early passage of the tax bill for which he fought all this long year. This is a bill designed to increase our national income and Federal revenues, and to provide insurance against recession. That bill, if passed without delay, means more security for those now working, more jobs for those now without them, and more incentive for our economy.

In short, this is no time for delay. It is a time for action—strong, forward-looking action on the pending education bills to help bring the light of learning to every home and hamlet in America; strong, forward-looking action on youth employment opportunities; strong, forward-looking action on the pending foreign aid bill, making clear that we are not forfeiting our responsibilities to this hemisphere or to the world, nor erasing Executive flexibility in the conduct of our foreign affairs; and strong, prompt, and forward-looking action on the remaining appropriation bills.

In this new spirit of action, the Congress can expect the full cooperation and support of the executive branch. And, in particular, I pledge that the expenditures of your Government will be administered with the utmost thrift and frugality. I will insist that the Government get a dollar's value for a dollar spent. The Government will set an example of prudence and economy.

This does not mean that we will not meet our unfilled needs or that we will not honor our commitments. We will do both.

As one who has long served in both Houses of the Congress, I firmly believe in the independence and the integrity of the legislative branch. And I promise you that I shall always respect this. It is deep in the marrow of my bones. With equal firmness, I believe in the capacity and I believe in the ability of the Congress, despite the divisions of opinions which characterize our nation, to act—to act wisely, to act vigorously, to act speedily when the need arises.

The need is here. The need is now. I ask your help.

Glossary

19 and 61	a slightly old-fashioned and formal way of identifying years, used here and elsewhere—"nineteen and sixty-one," meaning 1961
Alliance for Progress	an organization of North and South American nations established by President John F. Kennedy in 1961 to counteract the influence of Communism in the Western Hemisphere
appropriation bills	legislation for the purpose of funding particular undertakings
Peace Corps	an independent federal agency, founded by President Kennedy in 1961 with the mission of promoting world peace and understanding by sending American volunteers to serve in needy communities throughout the third world
the tax bill	legislation proposed by President Kennedy in December 1962 to lower income taxes in order to increase tax revenues, an initiative that Johnson helped bring to fruition with the passage of the Revenue Act of 1964

We meet in grief, but let us also meet in renewed dedication and renewed vigor. Let us meet in action, in tolerance, and in mutual understanding.

John Kennedy's death commands what his life conveyed—that America must move forward.

The time has come for Americans of all races and creeds and political beliefs to understand and to respect one another. So let us put an end to the teaching and the preaching of hate and evil and violence. Let us turn away from the fanatics of the far left and the far right, from the apostles of bitterness and bigotry, from those defiant of law, and those who pour venom into our nation's bloodstream.

I profoundly hope that the tragedy and the torment of these terrible days will bind us together in new fellowship, making us one people in our hour of sorrow.

So let us here highly resolve that John Fitzgerald Kennedy did not live or die in vain.

And on this Thanksgiving eve, as we gather together to ask the Lord's blessing, and give Him our thanks, let us unite in those familiar and cherished words:

America, America,
God shed His grace on thee,
And crown thy good
With brotherhood
From sea to shining sea.

COMMENCEMENT ADDRESS AT THE UNIVERSITY OF MICHIGAN (1964)

President Hatcher, Governor Romney, Senators McNamara and Hart, Congressmen Meader and Staebler, and other members of the fine Michigan delegation, members of the graduating class, my fellow Americans:

It is a great pleasure to be here today. This university has been coeducational since 1870, but I do not believe it was on the basis of your accomplishments that a Detroit high school girl said, "In choosing a college, you first have to decide whether you want a coeducational school or an educational school."

Well, we can find both here at Michigan, although perhaps at different hours.

I came out here today very anxious to meet the Michigan student whose father told a friend of mine that his son's education had been a real value. It stopped his mother from bragging about him.

I have come today from the turmoil of your Capital to the tranquility of your campus to speak about the future of your country.

The purpose of protecting the life of our Nation and preserving the liberty of our citizens is to pursue the happiness of our people. Our success in that pursuit is the test of our success as a Nation.

For a century we labored to settle and to subdue a continent. For half a century we called upon unbounded invention and untiring industry to create an order of plenty for all of our people.

The challenge of the next half century is whether we have the wisdom to use that wealth to enrich and elevate our national life, and to advance the quality of our American civilization.

Your imagination, your initiative, and your indignation will determine whether we build a society where progress is the servant of our needs, or a society where old values and new visions are buried under unbridled growth. For in your time we have the opportunity to move not only toward the rich society and the powerful society, but upward to the Great Society.

The Great Society rests on abundance and liberty for all. It demands an end to poverty and racial injustice, to which we are totally committed in our time. But that is just the beginning.

The Great Society is a place where every child can find knowledge to enrich his mind and to enlarge his talents. It is a place where leisure is a welcome chance to build and reflect, not a feared cause of boredom and restlessness. It is a place where the city of man serves not only the needs of the body and the demands of commerce but the desire for beauty and the hunger for community.

It is a place where man can renew contact with nature. It is a place which honors creation for its own sake and for what it adds to the understanding of the race. It is a place where men are more concerned with the quality of their goals than the quantity of their goods.

But most of all, the Great Society is not a safe harbor, a resting place, a final objective, a finished work. It is a challenge constantly renewed, beckoning us toward a destiny where the meaning of our lives matches the marvelous products of our labor.

So I want to talk to you today about three places where we begin to build the Great Society—in our cities, in our countryside, and in our classrooms.

Many of you will live to see the day, perhaps 50 years from now, when there will be 400 million Americans—four-fifths of them in urban areas. In the remainder of this century urban population will double, city land will double, and we will have to build homes, highways, and facilities equal to all those built since this country was first settled. So in the next 40 years we must rebuild the entire urban United States.

Aristotle said: "Men come together in cities in order to live, but they remain together in order to live the good life." It is harder and harder to live the good life in American cities today.

The catalog of ills is long: there is the decay of the centers and the despoiling of the suburbs. There is not enough housing for our people or transportation for our traffic. Open land is vanishing and old landmarks are violated.

Worst of all, expansion is eroding the precious and time honored values of community with neighbors and communion with nature. The loss of these values breeds loneliness and boredom and indifference.

Our society will never be great until our cities are great. Today the frontier of imagination and innovation is inside those cities and not beyond their borders.

New experiments are already going on. It will be the task of your generation to make the American city a place where future generations will come, not only to live but to live the good life.

I understand that if I stayed here tonight I would see that Michigan students are really doing their best to live the good life.

This is the place where the Peace Corps was started. It is inspiring to see how all of you, while you are in this country, are trying so hard to live at the level of the people.

A second place where we begin to build the Great Society is in our countryside. We have always prided ourselves on being not only America the strong and America the free, but America the beautiful. Today that beauty is in danger. The water we drink, the food we eat, the very air that we breathe, are threatened with pollution. Our parks are overcrowded, our seashores overburdened. Green fields and dense forests are disappearing.

A few years ago we were greatly concerned about the "Ugly American." Today we must act to prevent an ugly America.

For once the battle is lost, once our natural splendor is destroyed, it can never be recaptured. And once man can no longer walk with beauty or wonder at nature his spirit will wither and his sustenance be wasted.

A third place to build the Great Society is in the classrooms of America. There your children's lives will be shaped. Our society will not be great until every young mind is set free to scan the farthest reaches of thought and imagination. We are still far from that goal.

Today, 8 million adult Americans, more than the entire population of Michigan, have not finished 5 years of school. Nearly 20 million have not finished 8 years of school. Nearly 54 million—more than one-quarter of all America—have not even finished high school.

Each year more than 100,000 high school graduates, with proved ability, do not enter college because they cannot afford it. And if we cannot educate today's youth, what will we do in 1970 when elementary school enrollment will be 5 million greater than 1960? And high school enrollment will rise by 5 million. College enrollment will increase by more than 3 million.

In many places, classrooms are overcrowded and curricula are outdated. Most of our qualified teachers are underpaid, and many of our paid teachers are unqualified. So we must give every child a place to sit and a teacher to learn from. Poverty must not be a bar to learning, and learning must offer an escape from poverty.

But more classrooms and more teachers are not enough. We must seek an educational system which grows in excellence as it grows in size. This means better training for our teachers. It means preparing youth to enjoy their hours of leisure as well as their hours of labor. It means exploring new techniques of teaching, to find new ways to stimulate the love of learning and the capacity for creation.

These are three of the central issues of the Great Society. While our Government has many programs directed at those issues, I do not pretend that we have the full answer to those problems.

But I do promise this: We are going to assemble the best thought and the broadest knowledge from all over the world to find those answers for America. I intend to establish working groups to prepare a series of White House conferences and meetings—on the cities, on natural beauty, on the quality of education, and on other emerging challenges. And from these meetings and from this inspiration and from these studies we will begin to set our course toward the Great Society.

The solution to these problems does not rest on a massive program in Washington, nor can it rely solely on the strained resources of local authority. They require us to create new concepts of cooperation, a creative federalism, between the National Capital and the leaders of local communities.

Woodrow Wilson once wrote: "Every man sent out from his university should be a man of his Nation as well as a man of his time."

Within your lifetime powerful forces, already loosed, will take us toward a way of life beyond the realm of our experience, almost beyond the bounds of our imagination.

For better or for worse, your generation has been appointed by history to deal with those problems and to lead America toward a new age. You have the chance never before afforded to any people in any age. You can help build a society where the demands of morality, and the needs of the spirit, can be realized in the life of the Nation.

So, will you join in the battle to give every citizen the full equality which God enjoins and the law requires, whatever his belief, or race, or the color of his skin?

Will you join in the battle to give every citizen an escape from the crushing weight of poverty?

Will you join in the battle to make it possible for all nations to live in enduring peace—as neighbors and not as mortal enemies?

Will you join in the battle to build the Great Society, to prove that our material progress is only the foundation on which we will build a richer life of mind and spirit?

There are those timid souls who say this battle cannot be won; that we are condemned to a soulless wealth. I do not agree. We have the power to shape the civilization that we want. But we need your will, your labor, your hearts, if we are to build that kind of society.

Those who came to this land sought to build more than just a new country. They sought a new world. So I have come here today to your campus to say that you can make their vision our reality. So let us from this moment begin our work so that in the future men will look back and say: It was then, after a long and weary way, that man turned the exploits of his genius to the full enrichment of his life.

Glossary

Aristotle	highly influential Greek philosopher of the fourth century BCE who was noted for his writings on politics, among other subjects
the city of man	a reference to a concept in *The City of God*, in which the fifth-century church father Augustine contrasts heavenly with earthly authority
federalism	a political system in which states hold considerable authority within their jurisdictions while remaining subordinate to a national government
Peace Corps	an independent federal agency, founded by President Kennedy in 1961 with the mission of promoting world peace and understanding by sending American volunteers to serve in needy communities throughout the third world
President Hatcher, Governor Romney, Senators McNamara and Hart, Congressmen Meader and Staebler	University of Michigan president Harlan Hatcher, U.S. senators Patrick V. McNamara and Philip A. Hart, and U.S. representatives George Meader and Ned Staebler
the "Ugly American"	a critical term describing what many perceived to be the arrogant and inconsiderate behavior of Americans in other countries

REMARKS ON THE GULF OF TONKIN INCIDENT (1964)

My fellow Americans:

As President and Commander in Chief, it is my duty to the American people to report that renewed hostile actions against United States ships on the high seas in the Gulf of Tonkin have today required me to order the military forces of the United States to take action in reply.

The initial attack on the destroyer Maddox, on August 2, was repeated today by a number of hostile vessels attacking two U.S. destroyers with torpedoes. The destroyers and supporting aircraft acted at once on the orders I gave after the initial act of aggression. We believe at least two of the attacking boats were sunk. There were no U.S. losses.

The performance of commanders and crews in this engagement is in the highest tradition of the United States Navy. But repeated acts of violence against the Armed Forces of the United States must be met not only with alert defense, but with positive reply. That reply is being given as I speak to you tonight. Air action is now in execution against gunboats and certain supporting facilities in North Viet-Nam which have been used in these hostile operations.

In the larger sense this new act of aggression, aimed directly at our own forces, again brings home to all of us in the United States the importance of the struggle for peace and security in Southeast Asia. Aggression by terror against the peaceful villagers of South Viet-Nam has now been joined by open aggression on the high seas against the United States of America.

The determination of all Americans to carry out our full commitment to the people and to the government of South Viet-Nam will be redoubled by this outrage. Yet our response, for the present, will be limited and fitting. We Americans know, although others appear to forget, the risks of spreading conflict. We still seek no wider war.

I have instructed the Secretary of State to make this position totally clear to friends and to adversaries and, indeed, to all. I have instructed Ambassador Stevenson to raise this matter immediately and urgently before the Security Council of the United Nations. Finally, I have today met with the leaders of both parties in the Congress of the United States and I have informed them that I shall immediately request the Congress to pass a resolution making it clear that our Government is united in its determination to take all necessary measures in support of freedom and in defense of peace in southeast Asia.

I have been given encouraging assurance by these leaders of both parties that such a resolution

Glossary

Ambassador Stevenson	former Illinois governor and two-time Democratic presidential candidate Adlai Stevenson, U.S. ambassador to the United Nations from 1961 to 1965
destroyer	a fast, maneuverable warship designed to protect larger vessels in a convoy
Gulf of Tonkin	an arm of the South China Sea bordered by northern Vietnam (whose capital, Hanoi, was once known as Tonkin) and China
Maddox	third U.S. naval destroyer named after William A. T. Maddox, a marine captain in the nineteenth century, the *Maddox* (DD-731) was launched after a Nazi dive-bomber sank its predecessor in the Mediterranean in 1943
Security Council of the United Nations	a body within the United Nations consisting of five permanent members (the United States, Russia, China, Great Britain, and France) and ten elected members; preserving peace is its goal
Senator Goldwater	Barry Goldwater, Republican senator from Arizona and Johnson's opponent in the 1964 presidential election

will be promptly introduced, freely and expeditiously debated, and passed with overwhelming support. And just a few minutes ago I was able to reach Senator Goldwater and I am glad to say that he has expressed his support of the statement that I am making to you tonight.

It is a solemn responsibility to have to order even limited military action by forces whose overall strength is as vast and as awesome as those of the United States of America, but it is my considered conviction, shared throughout your Government, that firmness in the right is indispensable today for peace; that firmness will always be measured. Its mission is peace.

SPEECH TO A JOINT SESSION OF CONGRESS ON CIVIL RIGHTS (1965)

Mr. Speaker, Mr. President, Members of the Congress:

I speak tonight for the dignity of man and the destiny of democracy.

I urge every member of both parties, Americans of all religions and of all colors, from every section of this country, to join me in that cause.

At times history and fate meet at a single time in a single place to shape a turning point in man's unending search for freedom. So it was at Lexington and Concord. So it was a century ago at Appomattox. So it was last week in Selma, Alabama.

There, long-suffering men and women peacefully protested the denial of their rights as Americans. Many were brutally assaulted. One good man, a man of God, was killed.

There is no cause for pride in what has happened in Selma. There is no cause for self-satisfaction in the long denial of equal rights of millions of Americans. But there is cause for hope and for faith in our democracy in what is happening here tonight.

For the cries of pain and the hymns and protests of oppressed people have summoned into convocation all the majesty of this great Government—the Government of the greatest Nation on earth.

Our mission is at once the oldest and the most basic of this country: to right wrong, to do justice, to serve man....

There is no Negro problem. There is no Southern problem. There is no Northern problem. There is only an American problem. And we are met here tonight as Americans—not as Democrats or Republicans—we are met here as Americans to solve that problem....

Many of the issues of civil rights are very complex and most difficult. But about this there can and should be no argument. Every American citizen must have an equal right to vote. There is no reason which can excuse the denial of that right. There is no duty which weighs more heavily on us than the duty we have to ensure that right.

Yet the harsh fact is that in many places in this country men and women are kept from voting simply because they are Negroes.

Every device of which human ingenuity is capable has been used to deny this right. The Negro citizen may go to register only to be told that the day is wrong, or the hour is late, or the official in charge is absent. And if he persists, and if he manages to present himself to the registrar, he may be disqualified because he did not spell out his middle name or because he abbreviated a word on the application.

And if he manages to fill out an application he is given a test. The registrar is the sole judge of whether he passes this test. He may be asked to recite the entire Constitution, or explain the most complex provisions of State law. And even a college degree cannot be used to prove that he can read and write.

For the fact is that the only way to pass these barriers is to show a white skin.

Experience has clearly shown that the existing process of law cannot overcome systematic and ingenious discrimination. No law that we now have on the books—and I have helped to put three of them there—can ensure the right to vote when local officials are determined to deny it.

In such a case our duty must be clear to all of us. The Constitution says that no person shall be kept from voting because of his race or his color. We have all sworn an oath before God to support and to defend that Constitution. We must now act in obedience to that oath.

Wednesday I will send to Congress a law designed to eliminate illegal barriers to the right to vote....

This bill will strike down restrictions to voting in all elections—federal, state, and local—which have been used to deny Negroes the right to vote.

This bill will establish a simple, uniform standard which cannot be used, however ingenious the effort, to flout our Constitution.

It will provide for citizens to be registered by officials of the United States Government if the State officials refuse to register them.

It will eliminate tedious, unnecessary lawsuits which delay the right to vote.

Finally, this legislation will ensure that properly registered individuals are not prohibited from voting....

What happened in Selma is part of a far larger movement which reaches into every section and State of America. It is the effort of American Negroes to secure for themselves the full blessings of American life.

Their cause must be our cause too. Because it is not just Negroes, but really it is all of us, who must overcome the crippling legacy of bigotry and injustice. And we shall overcome.

As a man whose roots go deeply into Southern soil, I know how agonizing racial feelings are. I know how difficult it is to reshape the attitudes and the structure of our society.

But a century has passed, more than a hundred years, since the Negro was freed. And he is not fully free tonight.

It was more than a hundred years ago that Abraham Lincoln, a great President of another party, signed the Emancipation Proclamation, but emancipation is a proclamation and not a fact.

A century has passed, more than a hundred years, since equality was promised. And yet the Negro is not equal.

A century has passed since the day of promise. And the promise is unkept.

The time of justice has now come. I tell you that I believe sincerely that no force can hold it back. It is right in the eyes of man and God that it should come. And when it does, I think that day will brighten the lives of every American....

My first job after college was as a teacher in Cotulla, Texas, in a small Mexican-American school. Few of them could speak English, and I couldn't speak much Spanish. My students were poor and they often came to class without breakfast, hungry. They knew even in their youth the pain of prejudice. They never seemed to know why people disliked them. But they knew it was so, because I saw it in their eyes. I often walked home late in the afternoon, after the classes were finished, wishing there was more that I could do. But all I knew was to teach them the little that I knew, hoping that it might help them against the hardships that lay ahead.

Somehow you never forget what poverty and hatred can do when you see its scars on the hopeful face of a young child.

I never thought then, in 1928, that I would be standing here in 1965. It never even occurred to me in my fondest dreams that I might have the chance to help the sons and daughters of those students and to help people like them all over this country.

But now I do have that chance—and I'll let you in on a secret—I mean to use it. And I hope that you will use it with me.

Glossary

Appomattox	Virginia site of the final battle of the Civil War, on April 9, 1965
Lexington and Concord	Massachusetts sites of important battles in the Revolutionary War
Mr. Speaker, Mr. President	a reference to the Speaker of the House, John McCormack, and Hubert Humphrey, who in his capacity as vice president served as president of the Senate

Barbara Jordan (AP/Wide World Photos)

BARBARA JORDAN

1936–1996

U.S. Congresswoman

Featured Documents
- "The Constitutional Basis for Impeachment" (1974)
- "Who Then Will Speak for the Common Good?" (1976)
- "Change: From What to What?" (1992)

Overview

Barbara Jordan was born in Houston, Texas, in 1936 and grew up during a time of racial segregation throughout the South. As an African American, she became increasingly aware of the limitations imposed by segregation when she traveled outside the South as a member of the Texas Southern University debate team in the early 1950s. In 1959 she earned a law degree at racially integrated Boston University and then returned to Houston, where she began her law practice and soon became involved in politics.

In 1966, after two unsuccessful campaigns as a Democrat for a seat in the Texas House of Representatives, Jordan successfully ran for a seat in the Texas Senate. The Voting Rights Act of 1965 had eliminated state-imposed prerequisites for voting, including the Texas poll tax, which had impaired the voting rights of many African Americans. In 1972, by Supreme Court–mandated reapportionment, Houston gained a new congressional district. Jordan ran for that seat and won an overwhelming victory to represent the new Eighteenth Congressional District of Texas in the U.S. Congress.

Jordan was the first African American woman elected to the Texas Senate and the first African American elected to that body since Reconstruction. When she joined the U.S. House of Representatives, she became the first African American to represent Texas in Congress and one of the first two African Americans elected to Congress since Reconstruction. Jordan quickly became a political insider. Pragmatic, she learned the rules, analyzed the power structures, cultivated connections, and became skilled at negotiating compromises and trading votes to gain support for legislation that was important to her constituents. Her willingness to compromise and work with conservatives drew criticism, however, from Houston's liberals as well as from the Congressional Black Caucus.

Jordan came to the nation's attention in 1974 when, as a member of the House Judiciary Committee, she made an introductory statement in the nationally televised committee hearings on the impeachment of President Richard Nixon. The year 1974 was the first time presidential impeachment had been seriously considered since 1868, when Andrew Johnson was impeached by the House. Jordan's remarks were well received, and in 1976 her fellow Texan Robert Strauss asked her to be one of two keynote speakers at the Democratic National Convention. This was the first time that either a woman or an African American had been a keynote speaker at any major party's national convention. After the 1976 keynote address, there were calls for Jordan's nomination as Jimmy Carter's running mate.

In 1977, for reasons of ill health, Jordan announced she would not seek another term. Before her third term in Congress ended, Jordan accepted a position teaching at the Lyndon B. Johnson School of Public Affairs at the University of Texas at Austin, where for almost twenty years she taught graduate courses in policy and ethics. She continued to speak about ethics, accountability, and citizen participation before business and civic organizations and at graduation ceremonies. She also accepted positions on corporate boards of directors, often as the first African American on the board. After Ann Richards was elected governor of Texas, Jordan served as her ethics adviser. In 1992, when Richards was the chair of the Democratic National Convention, Bill Clinton, the party's presumptive nominee, asked Jordan to deliver a keynote address at the convention. Jordan died in Austin in 1996.

Explanation and Analysis of Documents

Jordan's speeches are best experienced through audio recordings. Her words and ideas by themselves are important, but her delivery gave them the strength that propelled her to national notice. She used her distinctive voice as an instrument, and her timing, emphasis, and repetition of key words combined with her voice to produce a powerful effect. Jordan studied the effect of emphasizing specific words. In her opinion, "the people" rather than "of" should be emphasized when quoting "of the people, by the people, and for the people" from Abraham Lincoln's Gettysburg Address. Jordan herself frequently referred to "the people" in her speeches and commonly used inclusive language. She spoke in terms of "we" rather than "you" or "I." Accordingly, with respect to ideas, she emphasized accountability and ethics and promoted the belief that, for all its diversity, the United States is one undivided nation, made up of many but united as one—"E pluribus unum."

Jordan originally honed her speaking skills in high school and college; in law school, she discovered that speaking well was not enough, as one also had to present convincing support for what was said. Her awareness of

Time Line

1936
- **February 21**
  Barbara Jordan is born in Houston, Texas.

1956
- Jordan graduates magna cum laude from Texas Southern University.

1959
- Jordan receives a law degree from Boston University Law School.

1966
- **May 8**
  Jordan wins her district's Democratic primary and, with no opposing-party candidate, is thereby elected to the Texas Senate.

1972
- **November 7**
  Jordan is elected to the U.S. House of Representatives, becoming the first African American elected to represent Texas in Congress.

1974
- **July 25**
  As part of the House Judiciary Committee hearings on the impeachment of Richard Nixon, Jordan presents "The Constitutional Basis for Impeachment" to a national television audience.

1976
- **July 12**
  At the Democratic National Convention, Jordan gives a televised keynote speech, "Who Then Will Speak for the Common Good?"

1979
- Jordan joins the faculty of the Lyndon B. Johnson School of Public Affairs at the University of Texas at Austin.

- Jordan joins the board of directors of Texas Commerce Bank, becoming the first African American to serve on a major bank's board.

---

this is most apparent in her examination of President Richard Nixon's involvement in the Watergate scandal and the constitutional reasons for his impeachment. After Watergate, the country was in need of healing, and the Democratic Party needed unity. Jordan's speech at the 1976 Democratic National Convention, "Who Then Will Speak for the Common Good?" provided each. Jordan refrained from attacking Republicans and instead brought the Democratic Party together through her use of inclusive language, her emphasis on the shared beliefs of party members, and her vision of a national community. She continued the theme of national unity and repeated the importance of individual involvement to benefit the national community when she later delivered another keynote speech at the 1992 Democratic National Convention: "Change: From What to What?" The three speeches examined here are the best known of the more than three hundred delivered by Jordan over the course of her career.

◆ "The Constitutional Basis for Impeachment"

The involvement of President Nixon and some of his key aides in the planning and subsequent cover-up of the break-in at the Democratic National Committee's headquarters in the Watergate office building in Washington, D.C., on June 17, 1972, dominated much of Jordan's first term in the House of Representatives. In early 1974 the House Judiciary Committee began considering the impeachment of the president. The committee met in closed sessions for a number of months, examining documents. Finally, in late July, the committee began televised public hearings. Each committee member was allowed to present a fifteen-minute introductory statement.

Jordan approached the impeachment process very seriously and personally researched the subject. As she addressed the committee and the nation, her sober tone made it clear that she recognized the historic importance of the decision that the committee had to make. She begins by pointing out that when the Constitution was written, she—that is, in various respects, as a representative of both her race and her gender—was not included in its mention of "We, the people." She then notes that she has by the present been included through court cases and amendments. Jordan proceeds to state that she has complete faith in the Constitution, assuring listeners that she believes in the nation's founding document and will remain true to it. She does not intend to allow the Constitution to be undermined by anyone—not even a president.

After describing the process of impeachment and the role of the House as prosecutor but not judge, Jordan carefully examines impeachment from the standpoint of the federal Constitutional Convention of 1787, the Federalist Papers, and the ratification conventions in several states. She explains that impeachment of the president is a narrow exception to the general separation-of-powers doctrine. It is a grave remedy reserved for serious offenses. She assures the public that Congress has too much to do for the committee to engage in pettiness; to counter assertions that some evidence is thin, she lists what the president knew

---

with regard to the Watergate break-in. Explaining why the hearings should not be postponed to allow the president more time to provide information, she states, "The fact is that on yesterday, the American people waited with great anxiety for eight hours, not knowing whether their president would obey an order of the Supreme Court of the United States."

At this point Jordan expresses her intention "to juxtapose a few of the impeachment criteria with some of the actions the president has engaged in." She provides criteria from several primary sources, in each case quoting the source and explaining which of the president's actions fit that source's standards for impeachment. Before moving to the next example, she again quotes from the primary source, reinforcing its applicability to the circumstances presented. Jordan concludes by suggesting that the Constitution is worthless paper if its impeachment provisions do not apply to the offenses attributed to the president. However, she counsels reason rather than passion in the ensuing deliberations. Her own remarks provided an example of a reasoned approach to impeachment. Although Nixon was a Republican and Jordan a Democrat, her remarks were notably nonpartisan. Public response to Jordan's speech was mixed. Although many were impressed by her forcefulness and logic, others considered her arrogant. Some, including Republicans, expressed their admiration and their willingness to vote for her if she ever ran for president.

In its televised hearings of July 24–30, 1974, the House Judiciary Committee agreed on three articles of impeachment against President Nixon. Each of the three articles of impeachment charged him with actions Jordan had referred to in her remarks.

On August 9, 1974, before the articles of impeachment were formally reported to the full House, Nixon resigned, becoming the first U.S. president to do so. Gerald Ford, Nixon's successor, later granted him a full pardon for all acts that he had or might have committed against the United States while president.

◆ **"Who Then Will Speak for the Common Good?"**

When the Democratic National Convention was held in July 1976, the identity of the Republican Party's candidate for president was still uncertain. Ronald Reagan was challenging President Gerald Ford for the nomination. Ford became the Republican candidate only after a close vote at the party's convention in August. Although Jordan never directly names Ford in her speech, she alludes to his liberal use of the veto power—he had vetoed twenty bills in 1976—toward the end when she says, "This we must do as individuals, and if we do it as individuals, there is no president of the United States who can veto that decision." The comment received enthusiastic applause.

After beginning her speech with a short history of the Democratic Party and its conventions, Jordan quickly focused her audience's attention on the present—and elicited a standing ovation—by proclaiming that there was something different and special about this particular evening: "I, Barbara Jordan, am a keynote speaker." As in her Judicial

Time Line

1981
- **June 18**
  Supporting the extension of the Voting Rights Act, Jordan testifies before the House Judiciary Committee.

1985
- Jordan is the only American to serve on a U.N. panel examining corporate influence on apartheid in South Africa and Namibia.

1992
- **July 13**
  Jordan gives a keynote speech, "Change: From What to What?" at the Democratic National Convention, her last nationally televised appearance.

1994
- Jordan receives the Presidential Medal of Freedom.
- **September 30**
  Jordan delivers her first report to Congress as chair of the U.S. Commission on Immigration Reform.

1996
- **January 17**
  Jordan dies in Austin, Texas.

Committee remarks, she does not explicitly state the intended meaning behind her words, leaving it to the listener to put emphasis on her race, her gender, or both. Jordan was both the first African American and the first woman to deliver a keynote speech at any major party's convention.

With congenial self-deprecation, she then asks, "Now that I have this grand distinction, what in the world am I supposed to say?" She states what she chooses not to do: She will not simply attack the Republicans and praise the Democrats, and she will not list America's problems without offering solutions. Instead, she chooses to advance the idea of a national community. Jordan had been interested in the need for a national community since the days of the Nixon impeachment hearings. In her 1976 keynote speech she rarely uses the pronoun "I"; rather, to establish and to speak from commonality, she uses "we" and "our." Repeatedly saying "We are a people," she echoes the beginning words of the preamble to the Constitution: "We the people."

Jordan asserts that the United States is still one nation, despite mistakes, fears, distrust, and private concerns.

The hearing room of the House Judiciary Committee in Washington on July 25, 1974, during the debate on the impeachment of Richard Nixon (AP/Wide World Photos)

However, there was a danger that America could become a collection of interest groups—a divided nation. The country had to master the future, and it could do so through a national community. Jordan explains that forming this community would require individual effort by citizens. Elected public officials, however, must set examples for the country's citizens. Officials had to deliver on their promises. They had to be accountable and willing to sacrifice if they asked the people to sacrifice.

Toward the close of her address, Jordan expresses her faith in the governmental system established by the Constitution but asserts that new ways could be found to use the system and realize America's destiny. Earlier in the speech, she refers to "the promise of America" and "our national purpose"—the establishment of a society in which all are equal. This is the destiny to be realized through a national community, she states. Jordan ends her speech by quoting Lincoln, a Republican president, asking her audience to relate his words to the concept of a participatory national community.

Jordan's keynote speech inspired a sense of unity and enthusiasm that had been missing in the Democratic Party. The speech was enthusiastically received by the delegates; she was interrupted by applause some twenty times and received at least two standing ovations. The next morning, "Barbara Jordan for Vice President" buttons appeared. Recognizing that the time was not yet right for her to be a serious candidate for the vice presidency, Jordan issued a press statement indicating her lack of interest in being a token. While conducting her own successful campaign for a third term in Congress, she also campaigned for Jimmy Carter (and his ultimate selection for a running mate, Walter Mondale), who won the election. Midway through her term, Jordan announced that she would not again run for reelection to the House. In 1980 she declined to campaign for Carter, who lost the election to the Republican candidate, Ronald Reagan.

◆ **"Change: From What to What?"**

"Change" was the theme of the Democratic National Convention in 1992. The White House had been occupied by a Republican since January 1981: Ronald Reagan had served two terms as president; his vice president, George H. W. Bush, won the presidential election in 1988 and was running for reelection in 1992. Jordan's speech was the last of three keynote speeches on the first night of the 1992 Democratic National Convention, where Arkansas governor Bill Clinton received the party's nomination for president. The *Wall Street Journal* described Jordan's speech as remarkable. Once again, the power of the speech lay in her delivery as well as in her words.

Jordan reminds the audience that she was a keynote speaker in 1976, when the Democratic candidate won. She asks, "Why not repeat that performance in 1992?" She then discusses change—as the watchword in the year's campaigns, as a means of economic expansion, as a return to the American dream, and as a path to national unity. She identifies the Democratic Party and its presidential nominee as the catalysts that would bring about change. In her first keynote address, Jordan conceded that the Democratic Party had made mistakes but described them as mistakes of the heart. This time, she insists, "We must frankly acknowledge our complicity in the creation of the unconscionable budget deficits." Addressing the national deficit would require equitable sacrifice by all: retirees, laborers, corporate executives, professors, and politicians alike.

Returning to a favored theme, Jordan emphasizes the unity of all Americans. This time, however, she does not use the phrase "national community"; instead, she recalls the American motto "E Pluribus Unum"—from many, one—and asserts, "That still identifies us." She describes the Democratic Party as a party that has no place for xenophobia and "will not tolerate bigotry under any guise," rejecting "both white racism and black racism." She also emphasizes the need to include women in politics, acknowledging that this change had already begun.

Jordan points out that the political affiliation of the president makes an important difference in who is appointed to the Supreme Court and in the principles, policies, and programs that are promoted. She acknowledges that character had become an issue in the campaign and that it could be a proper concern, but she contends that the current slant on the topic was more emotional than factual. Echoing words she used in "The Constitutional Basis for Impeachment," she declares, "It is reason and not passion which should guide our decisions." She asserts that the important question is "Who can best lead this country at this moment in our history?"

As in her 1976 keynote speech, in closing Jordan quotes an earlier president—this time a Democrat. By quoting Franklin Roosevelt, who was elected during the Great Depression, Jordan alludes to the economic losses many people were feeling in 1992 after twelve years of "trickle down economics," emphasizes the importance of the people's involvement, and suggests the positive change that might come with the election of a Democratic president.

Jordan's 1992 keynote garnered praise as well as criticism, but response to it was lukewarm compared with the responses to her 1976 keynote. Although the *Wall Street Journal* devoted an entire article to reporting on Jordan's 1992 speech, most newspapers included only brief mentions of it in reports on the convention and referred to each of the three keynote speakers. An article in the *Washington Post*, written before the speech was delivered, praised Jordan and anticipated the effect her speech might have at the convention. The same paper, the day after the speech, dismissively referred to it as "an academic essay." A number of the articles noted Jordan's use of the term *black racism*. Her usage was rejected by some people who viewed "racism" as necessarily involving systemic power rather than individual biases against another race.

Bill Clinton was elected in 1992 and during his eight years as president, the federal budget went from deficit to surplus. As Jordan had predicted, sacrifice was necessary; taxes were raised, and welfare was reformed. Although Jordan had asserted that the character issues of the 1992 campaign were more emotional than factual, it was one of those character issues that came to dominate Clinton's second term in office. The president's less than forthright response to allegations of marital infidelity led to his impeachment by the House of Representatives on December 19, 1998, on two charges: lying under oath to a grand jury and obstruction of justice. Although he was impeached by the House, Clinton was not convicted by the Senate. Jordan did not live to see or comment on the impeachment proceedings.

Impact and Legacy

Jordan spent seventeen years teaching and considered that the most important role of her life. Her most lasting impact, then, may be felt through her graduate students from the Lyndon B. Johnson School of Public Affairs. Her students' comments reveal the effect she had on them: "Her ideas of social commitment and social consciousness have framed my life," one wrote. Said another, "She is convincing us that we have to, in a sense, pay rent for the space that we occupy." A third commented, "Above all else, she has taught me that greatness, more than power or fame, is something you do every day" (Sherman, p. 2). The degree to which her impact on her students will extend to the nation remains to be seen.

The societal benefits of Jordan's twelve years in legislative assemblies, on the other hand, are more readily apparent. She was responsible for various laws with enduring effects, such as the first minimum wage law in Texas. In the U.S. Congress, she introduced the Consumer Goods Pricing Act of 1975, which eliminated manufacturers' ability to set fixed retail prices for their products. Consumers continue to save money by shopping around for lower prices on brand-name products. Jordan's work in Congress may be most remembered for her efforts to extend and expand the 1965 Voting Rights Act, which was set to expire in 1975. The "pre-clearance" provision, which previously applied only to seven states in the Deep South, was extended by the 1975 act to require Texas to seek prior approval from the Justice Department before implementing any changes in election law or procedures that might limit minority voters' rights. Additionally, the 1975 act required all states to provide voting materials in languages other than English in areas where numerous citizens spoke another language. Earlier, in the Texas senate, Jordan helped block legislation that would have limited voting rights for minorities.

It seems likely that through her speeches at Nixon's impeachment proceedings and at the 1976 and 1992 Democratic National Conventions, Jordan bore some influence on the determination of who would be president of the United States, although the extent of her influence is impossible to quantify. Jordan's 1974 Judiciary Committee statement may not have directly led to Nixon's resignation, but her rational approach to the proceedings raised the impeachment consideration above partisan politics, perhaps contributing to the Judiciary Committee's ultimate approval of the three articles of impeachment. Jordan's two convention addresses, in turn, may have helped Carter and Clinton win their first presidential elections—and they may also have contributed to the election of a third Democratic president, Barack Obama, whose speeches tend to echo the national community theme of Jordan's keynote addresses in language and in tone. Responses to Jordan's speeches in 1974, 1976, and 1992 indicate that in those years, some Americans were willing to consider the possibility of an African American woman as president. Jordan recognized that she would have been a token candidate in 1976; changes in attitude take time before they affect the majority of the population. However, the changes evident in the public's responses to Jordan's speeches may have helped pave the way for the historic 2008 presidential election.

"My faith in the Constitution is whole; it is complete; it is total, and I am not going to sit here and be an idle spectator to the diminution, the subversion, the destruction of the Constitution."

("The Constitutional Basis for Impeachment")

"If the impeachment provision in the Constitution of the United States will not reach the offenses charged here, then perhaps that eighteenth-century Constitution should be abandoned to a twentieth-century paper shredder."

("The Constitutional Basis for Impeachment")

"We are a people in a quandary about the present. We are a people in search of our future. We are a people in search of a national community. We are a people trying not only to solve the problems of the present: unemployment, inflation—but we are attempting on a larger scale to fulfill the promise of America."

("Who Then Will Speak for the Common Good?")

"This is the great danger America faces—that we will cease to be one nation and become instead a collection of interest groups: city against suburb, region against region, individual against individual. Each seeking to satisfy private wants. If that happens, who then will speak for America? Who then will speak for the common good?"

("Who Then Will Speak for the Common Good?")

"More is required of public officials than slogans and handshakes and press releases. More is required. We must hold ourselves strictly accountable. We must provide the people with a vision of the future."

("Who Then Will Speak for the Common Good?")

"The American dream is not dead. It is not dead! It is gasping for breath, but it is not dead.... There is no time to waste because the American Dream is slipping away from too many people."

("Change: From What to What?")

In her career, Barbara Jordan amassed a number of "firsts" as an African American, a woman, or both. Some would be remembered only for that trailblazing role, but Jordan is remembered for more. She was an interesting mix of pragmatic politician and ethicist, and she demonstrated that it was possible to be both ethical and politically effective. She had a strong sense of the importance of justice in a democratic society, a keen ear to hear the concerns of the people, and a voice to convey the concerns of the people and the need for justice to any audience.

Key Sources

The Barbara Jordan Archives are located at Texas Southern University in Houston, Texas. The first of Jordan's papers were deposited there on August 16, 1978, and Jordan continued to donate material throughout her lifetime. In 1979 Jordan published the autobiography *Barbara Jordan: A Self-Portrait*, coauthored by Shelby Hearon. Max Sherman, ed., *Barbara Jordan: Speaking the Truth with Eloquent Thunder* (2007), includes a DVD with videos of Jordan giving her Judiciary Committee remarks from Nixon's impeachment hearings and the 1976 and 1992 keynote addresses; eight of Jordan's speeches appear in the book. Sandra Parnham, ed., *Barbara C. Jordan: Selected Speeches* (1999), includes twenty of Jordan's speeches. Addresses by Jordan can also be found in the Barbara Jordan commemorative issue of the *Texas Journal of Women and the Law*, vol. 5 (1996). The transcript of a 1984 interview with Jordan by Roland C. Hayes is stored in the Lyndon Baines Johnson Library and is available online (http://www.lbjlib.utexas.edu/johnson/archives.hom/oral-history.hom/JordanB/Jordan-b.PDF).

Further Reading

■ Articles

German, Kathleen M. "Hitting the Key Note: A Rhetorical Trio." *National Forensic Journal* 10, no. 2 (Fall 1992): 89–100.

Hamilton, Dagmar S. "Barbara Jordan: Constitutional Lawyer." *Texas Journal of Women and the Law* 5 (1996): 153–160.

Questions for Further Study

1. Jordan's impeachment speech mentions a number of events associated with the Watergate break-in and the subsequent cover-up. Research and discuss these events, as well as the individuals involved in them, using Jordan's account as a framework for your discussion. How clearly does her narrative correspond to events? Further, how did her speech play into the larger drama that was Watergate?

2. In her 1976 speech before the Democratic Party Convention, Jordan noted the historic nature of the event—that she, an African American woman elected to federal office, should address the gathered delegates of a major political party. To what extent do you think she perceived her status as a disadvantage and to what degree an advantage? More specifically, what were the barriers to her success, and in what ways did her unique role improve her visibility in a nation awakening to the idea of racial equality as a fact of political life? Be sure to use Jordan's own words on these subjects as support for your analysis.

3. A number of themes become apparent in Jordan's most significant speeches: for instance, a discussion of the past, present, and future or a question of what the American dream has come to mean for her listeners. Look for these themes and others—for example, her recurring emphasis on historic American leaders from James Madison to Abraham Lincoln to Franklin Roosevelt. How did she employ and develop these motifs, and what does her use of them say about her views on American history and politics?

4. Jordan's speeches allude to a number of affiliations that she felt strongly, though these were not necessarily what some might have expected: Rather than focusing on her identity as an African American or a woman, she seems to have been far more concerned about what defined her and others as members of the Democratic Party and ultimately as Americans. Discuss these different frameworks for identification and loyalty as contained in her speeches and talk about her perspective on each. Which was most important to her? How did she portray her political party, and what principles did she consider foundational to being an American?

■ **Books**

Bryant, Ira B. *Barbara Charline Jordan: From the Ghetto to the Capitol*. Houston: D. Armstrong, 1977.

Fenno, Richard F. *Going Home: Black Representatives and Their Constituents*. Chicago: University of Chicago Press, 2003.

Holmes, Barbara A. *A Private Woman in Public Spaces: Barbara Jordan's Speeches on Ethics, Public Religion, and Law*. Harrisburg, Penn.: Trinity Press International, 2000.

Mendelsohn, James. *Barbara Jordan: Getting Things Done*. Brookfield, Conn.: Twenty-First Century Books, 2000.

Rogers, Mary Beth. *Barbara Jordan: American Hero*. New York: Bantam Books, 1998.

■ **Web Sites**

Scarborough, Megan. "A Voice That Could Not Be Stilled: Barbara Jordan's Legacy of Equality and Justice." University of Texas at Austin Web site.
   http://www.utexas.edu/features/archive/2003/jordan.html.

—Carol A. Pettit

"THE CONSTITUTIONAL BASIS FOR IMPEACHMENT"

Earlier today we heard the beginning of the Preamble to the Constitution of the United States: "We, the people." It's a very eloquent beginning. But when that document was completed, on the seventeenth of September in 1787, I was not included in that "We, the people." I felt, somehow, for many years, that George Washington and Alexander Hamilton just left me out by mistake. But through the process of amendment, interpretation, and court decision, I have finally been included in "We, the people."

Today, I am an inquisitor. An hyperbole would not be fictional and would not overstate the solemnness that I feel right now. My faith in the Constitution is whole; it is complete; it is total, and I am not going to sit here and be an idle spectator to the diminution, the subversion, the destruction of the Constitution.

"Who can so properly be the inquisitors for the nation as the representatives of the nation themselves?" "The subjects of its jurisdiction are those offenses which proceed from the misconduct of public men." And that's what we are talking about. In other words, [the jurisdiction comes] from the abuse of violation of some public trust.

It is wrong, I suggest, it is a misreading of the Constitution for any member here to assert that for a member to vote for an article of impeachment means that that member must be convinced that the president should be removed from office. The Constitution doesn't say that. The powers relating to impeachment are an essential check in the hands of the body, the legislature, against and upon the encroachments of the executive. [In establishing] the division between the two branches of the legislature, the House and the Senate—assigning to the one the right to accuse and to the other the right to judge— the framers of this Constitution were very astute. They did not make the accusers and the judges the same person.

We know the nature of impeachment.... It is chiefly designed for the president and his high ministers to somehow be called into account. It is designed to "bridle" the executive if he engages in excesses. "It is designed as a method of national inquest into the conduct of public men." The framers confide in the Congress the power, if need be, to remove the president in order to strike a delicate balance between a president swollen with power and grown tyrannical, and preservation of the independence of the executive.

The nature of impeachment—a narrowly channeled exception to the separation-of-powers maxim; the federal convention of 1787 said that. It limited impeachment to high crimes and misdemeanors and discounted and opposed the term "maladministration."...

Of the impeachment process, it was Woodrow Wilson who said that "nothing short of the grossest offenses against the plain law of the land will suffice to give them speed and effectiveness. Indignation so great as to overgrow party interest may secure a conviction; but nothing else can."

Common sense would be revolted if we engaged upon this process for petty reasons. Congress has a lot to do: appropriations, tax reform, health insurance, campaign finance reform, housing, environmental protection, energy sufficiency, mass transportation. Pettiness cannot be allowed to stand in the face of such overwhelming problems. So today we're not being petty. We're trying to be big because the task we have before us is a big one.

This morning, in a discussion of the evidence, we are told that the evidence which purports to support the allegations of misuse of the CIA by the president is thin. We're told that that evidence is insufficient. What that recital of the evidence this morning did not include is what the president did know on June the twenty-third, 1972.

The president did know that it was Republican money, that it was money from the Committee for the Re-Election of the President, which was found in the possession of one of the burglars arrested on June the seventeenth. What the president did know on the twenty-third of June was the prior activities of E. Howard Hunt, which included his participation in the break-in of Daniel Ellsberg's psychiatrist, which included Howard Hunt's participation in the Dita Beard ITT affair, which included Howard Hunt's fabrication of cables designed to discredit the Kennedy administration.

We were further cautioned today that perhaps these proceedings ought to be delayed because certainly there would be new evidence forthcoming from the president of the United States. There has not even been an obfuscated indication that this committee would receive any additional materials from the president. The committee subpoena is outstanding, and if the president wants to supply that material, the committee sits here. The fact is that on yesterday, the American people waited with great anxiety for eight hours, not knowing whether their president would obey an order of the Supreme Court of the United States.

At this point, I would like to juxtapose a few of the impeachment criteria with some of the actions the president has engaged in.

Impeachment criteria: James Madison, from the Virginia ratification convention: "If the president be connected in any suspicious manner with any person

and there be grounds to believe that he will shelter him, he may be impeached."

We have heard time and time again that the evidence reflects the payment to defendants—money. The president had knowledge that these funds were being paid and these were funds collected for the 1972 presidential campaign. We know that the president met with Mr. Henry Petersen twenty-seven times to discuss matters related to Watergate and immediately thereafter met with the very persons who were implicated in the information Mr. Petersen was receiving.

The words are: "If the president is connected in any suspicious manner with any person and there be

Glossary

"It is designed as a method of national inquest…"	quotation from Alexander Hamilton, Federalist 65
"nothing short of the grossest offenses…"	quotation from Woodrow Wilson's *Congressional Government* (1901)
"The subjects of its jurisdiction…"	quotation from John Jay, Federalist 64
"Who can so properly be the inquisitors…"	quotation from Alexander Hamilton, Federalist 65
Daniel Ellsberg	author of the *Pentagon Papers*, a study critical of the conduct of the war in Vietnam
Dita Beard ITT affair	reference to Dita Beard, a lobbyist for International Telephone and Telegraph Corporation, and allegations that the government dismissed an antitrust suit against the company in exchange for a large cash contribution to the Republican Party in 1972
Dr. Fielding	Lewis Fielding, Daniel Ellsberg's psychiatrist, whose office was broken into by the White House "plumbers"
E. Howard Hunt	former Central Intelligence Agency agent who worked for President Richard Nixon
Ehrlichman	John Ehrlichman, a key adviser to President Richard Nixon before and during the Watergate scandal
Henry Petersen	member of the Justice Department who was the initial investigator of the Watergate break-in
Huston plan	a report outlining proposed security plans written by White House aide Timothy Huston in 1970
Justice Story	Joseph Story, associate justice of the U.S. Supreme Court (1812–1845)
Woodrow Wilson	twenty-eighth president of the United States
Young	David R. Young, an assistant to Secretary of State Henry Kissinger in the Nixon administration

grounds to believe that he will shelter that person, he may be impeached."

Justice Story: "Impeachment is intended for occasional and extraordinary cases where a superior power acting for the whole people is put into operation to protect their rights and rescue their liberties from violations."

We know about the Huston plan. We know about the break-in of the psychiatrist's office. We know that there was absolute complete direction on September third when the president indicated that a surreptitious entry had been made in Dr. Fielding's office after having met with Mr. Ehrlichman and Mr. Young.

"Protect their rights." "Rescue their liberties from violation."…

Beginning shortly after the Watergate break-in and continuing to the present time, the president has engaged in a series of public statements and actions designed to thwart the lawful investigation by government prosecutors. Moreover, the president has made public announcements and assertions bearing on the Watergate case which the evidence will show he knew to be false.

These assertions: false assertions. Impeachable: those who misbehave. Those who "behave amiss or betray the public trust."

James Madison again at the Constitutional Convention: "A president is impeachable if he attempts to subvert the Constitution."

The Constitution charges the president with the task of taking care that the laws be faithfully executed, and yet the president has counseled his aides to commit perjury, willfully disregard the secrecy of grand jury proceedings, conceal surreptitious entry, attempt to compromise a federal judge while publicly displaying his cooperation with the processes of criminal justice.…

If the impeachment provision in the Constitution of the United States will not reach the offenses charged here, then perhaps that eighteenth-century Constitution should be abandoned to a twentieth-century paper shredder. Has the president committed offenses and planned and directed and acquiesced in a course of conduct which the Constitution will not tolerate? That's the question.…We know the question. We should now forthwith proceed to answer the question. It is reason, and not passion, which must guide our deliberations, guide our debate, and guide our decision.

"WHO THEN WILL SPEAK FOR THE COMMON GOOD?" (1976)

It was one hundred and forty-four years ago that members of the Democratic Party first met in convention to select a presidential candidate. Since that time, Democrats have continued to convene once every four years and draft a party platform and nominate a presidential candidate. And our meeting this week is a continuation of that tradition.

But there is something different about tonight. There is something special about tonight. What is different? What is special? I, Barbara Jordan, am a keynote speaker.

A lot of years passed since 1832, and during that time, it would have been most unusual for any national political party to ask a Barbara Jordan to deliver a keynote address, but tonight, here I am. And I feel … that notwithstanding the past that my presence here is one additional bit of evidence that the American Dream need not forever be deferred.

Now that I have this grand distinction what in the world am I supposed to say? I could easily spend this time praising the accomplishments of this party and attacking the Republicans, but I don't choose to do that. I could list the many problems which Americans have. I could list the problems which cause people to feel cynical, angry, frustrated: problems which include lack of integrity in government; the feeling that the individual no longer counts; the reality of material and spiritual poverty; the feeling that the grand American Experiment is failing or has failed. I could recite these problems, and then, I could sit down and offer no solutions. But I don't choose to do that either. The citizens of America expect more. They deserve and they want more than a recital of problems.

We are a people in a quandary about the present. We are a people in search of our future. We are a people in search of a national community. We are a people trying not only to solve the problems of the present: unemployment, inflation—but we are attempting on a larger scale to fulfill the promise of America. We are attempting to fulfill our national purpose: to create and sustain a society in which all of us are equal.

Throughout our history, when people have looked for new ways to solve their problems and to uphold the principles of this nation, many times they have turned to political parties. They have often turned to the Democratic Party.…

What is it about the Democratic Party that makes it the instrument the people use when they search for ways to shape their future?…I believe the answer to that question lies in our concept of governing. Our concept of governing is derived from our view of people. It is a concept deeply rooted in a set of beliefs firmly etched in the national conscience of all of us.

Now what are these beliefs?

First, we believe in equality for all and privileges for none. This is a belief that each American, regardless of background, has equal standing in the public forum—all of us. Because we believe this idea so firmly, we are an inclusive rather than an exclusive party.…

I think it no accident that most of those immigrating to America in the nineteenth century identified with the Democratic Party. We are a heterogeneous party made up of Americans of diverse backgrounds. We believe that the people are the source of all governmental power; that the authority of the people is to be extended, not restricted. This can be accomplished only by providing each citizen with every opportunity to participate in the management of the government. They must have that.…

We believe that the government which represents the authority of all the people, not just one interest group, but all the people, has an obligation to actively—underscore "actively"—seek to remove those obstacles which would block individual achievement—obstacles emanating from race, sex, economic condition. The government must remove them—seek to remove them.

We are a party … of innovation. We do not reject our traditions, but we are willing to adapt to changing circumstances when change we must. We are willing to suffer the discomfort of change in order to achieve a better future. We have a positive vision of the future founded on the belief that the gap between the promise and reality of America can one day be finally closed.…

This, my friends, is the bedrock of our concept of governing. This is a part of the reason why Americans have turned to the Democratic Party. These are the foundations upon which a national community can be built.

Let all understand that these guiding principles cannot be discarded for short-term political gains.

They represent what this country is all about. They are indigenous to the American idea. And these are principles which are not negotiable.

In other times, I could stand here and give this kind of exposition on the beliefs of the Democratic Party and that would be enough. But today that is not enough. People want more. That is not sufficient reason for the majority of the people of this country to decide to vote Democratic. We have made mistakes. We realize that. We admit our mistakes. In our haste to do all things for all people, we did not foresee the full consequences of our actions. And when the people raised their voices, we didn't hear. But our deafness was only a temporary condition, and not an irreversible condition.

Even as I stand here and admit that we have made mistakes, I still believe that as the people of America sit in judgment on each party, they will recognize that our mistakes were mistakes of the heart....

Now we must look to the future. Let us heed the voice of the people and recognize their common sense. If we do not, we not only blaspheme our political heritage, we ignore the common ties that bind all Americans.

Many fear the future; many are distrustful of their leaders and believe that their voices are never heard. Many seek only to satisfy their private work wants, to satisfy their private interests. But this is the great danger America faces—that we will cease to be one nation and become instead a collection of interest groups: city against suburb, region against region, individual against individual. Each seeking to satisfy private wants. If that happens, who then will speak for America? Who then will speak for the common good? This is the question which must be answered in 1976: Are we to be one people bound together by common spirit, sharing in a common endeavor, or will we become a divided nation?

For all of its uncertainty, we cannot flee the future. We must not become the new puritans and reject our society. We must address and master the future together. It can be done if we restore the belief that we share a sense of national community, that we share a common national endeavor....

There is no executive order; there is no law that can require the American people to form a national community. This we must do as individuals, and if we do it as individuals, there is no president of the United States who can veto that decision.

As a first step, we must restore our belief in ourselves. We are a generous people so why can't we be generous with each other? We need to take to heart the words spoken by Thomas Jefferson: "Let us restore to social intercourse that harmony and that affection without which liberty and even life are but dreary things."

A nation is formed by the willingness of each of us to share in the responsibility for upholding the common good. A government is invigorated when each one of us is willing to participate in shaping the future of this nation.

In this election year, we must define "the common good" and begin again to shape a common future. Let each person do his or her part. If one citizen is unwilling to participate, all of us are going to suffer. For the American idea, though it is shared by all of us, is realized in each one of us....

What are those of us who are elected public officials supposed to do? We call ourselves public servants, but I'll tell you this: we as public servants must set an example for the rest of the nation. It is hypocritical for the public official to admonish and exhort the people to uphold the common good if we are derelict in upholding the common good.... More is required of public officials than slogans and handshakes and press releases. More is required. We must hold ourselves strictly accountable. We must provide the people with a vision of the future.

If we promise as public officials, we must deliver. If we as public officials propose, we must produce. If we say to the American people: "It is time for you to be sacrificial"; sacrifice. If the public official says

Glossary

"As I would not be a slave ..."	quotation from Abraham Lincoln
"Let us restore ..."	quotation from Thomas Jefferson's first inaugural address
blaspheme	exhibit disrespect to
puritans	reference to New England's earliest settlers, known for moral rigidity

that, we must be the first to give. We must be. And again, if we make mistakes, we must be willing to admit them....What we have to do is strike a balance between the idea that government should do everything, and the idea—the belief—that government ought to do nothing....

Let there be no illusions about the difficulty of forming this kind of a national community. It's tough, difficult, not easy. But a spirit of harmony will survive in America only if each of us remembers that we share a common destiny. If each of us remembers, when self-interest and bitterness seem to prevail, that we share a common destiny, I have confidence that we can form this kind of national community. I have confidence that the Democratic Party can lead the way. I have that confidence.

We cannot improve on the system of government handed down to us by the founders of the Republic, there is no way to improve upon that, but what we can do is to find new ways to implement that system and realize our destiny.

Now, I began this speech by commenting to you on the uniqueness of a Barbara Jordan making a keynote address. Well, I am going to close my speech by quoting a Republican president, and I ask you that as you listen to these words of Abraham Lincoln, relate them to the concept of a national community in which every last one of us participates:

"As I would not be a slave, so I would not be a master. This expresses my idea of democracy. Whatever differs from this, to the extent of the difference is no democracy."

"Change: From What to What?" (1992)

It was at this time; it was at this place; it was at this event sixteen years ago, I presented a keynote address to the Democratic National Convention. I remind you, with modesty, I remind you, that that year—1976—we won the presidency. We won it.... Why not repeat that performance in 1992? We can do it. We can do it....

What we need to do, Democrats, is believe that it is possible to win.... We can do it. Now, you have heard a lot about change tonight. Every speaker here has said something about change. And I want you to talk with me for a few minutes about change, but I want you to listen to way I have entitled my remarks—"Change: From What to What?" From what to what? This change, which is very rhetorically oriented, this change acquires substance when each of us contemplates the public mind. What about the public mind?

There appears to be a general apprehension in the country about the future. That apprehension undermines our faith in each other and our faith in ourselves.... The idea that America today will be better tomorrow has become destabilized...because of the recession and the sluggishness of the economy. Jobs lost have become permanent unemployment rather than cyclical unemployment.... Public policy makers are held in low regard. Mistrust abounds. In this kind of environment, it is understandable that change would become the watchword of this time.

What is the catalyst which will bring about the change we are all talking about? I say that catalyst is the Democratic Party and our nominee for president.

We are not strangers to change. Twenty years ago, we changed the whole tone of the nation after Watergate abuses.... We know how to change. We have been the instrument of change in the past. We know what needs to be done. We know how to do it. We know that we can impact policies which affect education, human rights, civil rights, economic and social opportunity, and the environment.

These are policies...which are imbedded in the soul of the Democratic Party, and imbedded in our soul they will not disappear easily. We as a party will do nothing to erode our essence. We will not.

But there are some things which ought to change. We need to change them, but the fact that we are going to change things should not cause any apprehension in our minds because the Democratic Party is alive and well....We will change in order to satisfy the present, in order to satisfy the future, but we will not die. We will change, but we will not die.

From what to what? Why not change from a party with a reputation of "tax and spend" to one with a reputation of "investment and growth"? Change. Change. A growth economy is a must. We can grow the economy and sustain an improved environment at the same time. When the economy is growing and we are taking care of our air and soil and water, we all prosper....

When I say something like that, I certainly do not mean the thinly disguised racism and elitism which is some kind of "trickle down economics."...I will tell you the kind of economy I'm talking about. I'm talking about an economy where a young black woman or a young black man, born in the Fifth Ward of Houston—my town—or South-Central Los Angeles, or a young person in the *colonias* of the lower Rio Grande valley—I'm talking about an economy where those persons can go to a public school, learn the skills that will enable her or him to prosper. We must have an economy that does not force that migrant worker's child to miss school for a full day so that she can work at less than the minimum wage—and, doing that, the family can still only afford one meal a day. That...is the moral bankruptcy of trickle down economics. Change. Change. Change.

We can change the direction...of America's economic engine and become competitive again. We can make that change and become proud of the country that we are.

Friends in the Democratic Party, the American Dream is not dead. It is not dead! It is gasping for breath, but it is not dead. We can applaud that statement and know that there is no time to waste because the American Dream is slipping away from too many people. It is slipping away from too many black and brown mothers and their children. The American Dream is slipping away from the homeless—of every color, of every sex. It's slipping away from those immigrants living in communities without water and sewer systems. The American Dream is slipping away from those persons who have jobs, jobs which no longer will pay the benefits which will enable them to live and thrive because America seems to be better at building war equipment to sit in warehouses and rot than in building decent housing. It's slipping away.…The American Dream is slipping away from those workers who are on indefinite layoffs while their chief executive officers are taking home bonuses which equal more than the worker will ever make in ten, twenty, or thirty years.

We need to change the decaying inner cities from decay to places where hope lives. As we undergo that change, we must be prepared to answer Rodney King's haunting question: "Can we all get along?" "Can we all get along?" I say…we answer that question with a resounding "Yes!" Yes. Yes.

We must change that deleterious environment of the eighties, that environment which was characterized by greed and hatred and selfishness and megamergers and debt overhang. Change it to what? Change that environment of the eighties to an environment which is characterized by a devotion to the public interest, public service, tolerance, and love. Love. Love. Love.

We are one, we Americans. We're one and we reject any intruder who seeks to divide us on the basis of race and color. We honor, we honor cultural identity. We always have; we always will.… Separatism is not allowed. Separatism is not the American way. We must not allow ideas like political correctness to divide us and cause us to reverse hard-won achievements in human rights and civil rights. Xenophobia has no place in the Democratic Party. We seek to unite people not divide them. As we seek to unite people, we reject both white racism and black racism. This party will not tolerate bigotry under any guise.

Our strength in this country is rooted in our diversity. Our history bears witness to that fact. E Pluribus Unum—from many, one. It was a good idea when the country was founded and it's a good idea today. From many…one. That still identifies us.

We must frankly acknowledge our complicity in the creation of the unconscionable budget deficits—acknowledge our complicity and recognize, painful though it may be, that in order to seriously address the budget deficits, we must address the question of entitlements also. That's not easy.…But we have to do it; we have to do it because [of] the idea of justice between generations—that idea mandates that the baby-boomers … and their progeny are entitled to a secure future.… However, if we are going to ask those who receive benefits to sacrifice, there must be equity in sacrifice.…That idea says that we will sacrifice for growth, but that everybody must join in the sacrifice, not just a few. Equity in sacrifice means that all will sacrifice equally.… That is the person who is retired on a fixed income, the day laborer, the corporate executive, the college professor, the member of Congress. All must sacrifice for equity.

One … overdue change, which you have already heard a lot about, is already under way. And…that is reflected in the number of women now challenging the councils of political power. These women are challenging those councils of political power because they have been dominated by white, male policy makers, and that's wrong. That horizon…of gender equity is limitless for us. And what we see today is simply a dress rehearsal for the day and time we meet in convention to nominate Madame President. This country can ill afford to continue to function using less than half its human resources, less than half its kinetic energy, less than half its brain power.

We had a nineteenth-century visitor from France named de Tocqueville. De Tocqueville came to America.… "If I were asked," he said, "to what singular substance do I mainly attribute the prosperity and growing strength of the American people, I should reply…to the superiority of their women." I can only say the twentieth century will not close without the presence of women being keenly felt.

We must leave this convention tonight with a determination to convince the American people to trust us. The American electorate must be persuaded to trust us, the Democrats, to govern again. That is not easy, but we can do it.…

Public apprehension and fears about the future have provided very fertile ground for a chorus of cynics, and these cynics go around saying that it makes no difference who is elected president of the United States. You must say to those cynics, "You are perpetuating a fraud." It does…make a difference who is president. It makes a difference.…A Democrat—a Democratic president—a Democratic president would appoint a Supreme Court Justice who protects liberty, rather than burden[s] liberty. A Democratic president … would promote principles, programs, policies which help us help ourselves.…

Character has become an item on the political agenda of 1992. The question of character is a proper one, but if you were to exercise a well-reasoned examination…of the question of character, what you [would] discover is that the whole question falls into emotionalism rather than fact. You know how dangerous it is for us to make decisions based on emotion rather than reason. James Madison, the founder of the Constitution—the father of the Constitution, warned us of the perils of relying on passion rather than reason.

There is an editor, a late editor, of the Emporia, Kansas, Gazette…—William White—who had this to say about reason, and it's very, very pertinent …: "Reason has never failed man. Only fear and oppression have made the wrecks of the world." It is reason…. It is reason and not passion which should guide our decisions….

The question persists: Who can best lead this country at this moment in our history?

I close my remarks by quoting from Franklin Roosevelt—Franklin Roosevelt's [first] inaugural address, which he made in 1933. Franklin Roosevelt made that address to a people longing for change from the darkness and despair of the Great Depression. And this is what Roosevelt said: "In every dark hour of our national life, a leadership of frankness and vigor has met with that understanding and support of the people themselves which is essential to victory."

Given … the ingredients of today's national environment, maybe, maybe, just maybe, we Americans are poised for a second "Rendezvous with Destiny."

Glossary

colonias	subdivisions in the American Southwest where people of limited income can buy inexpensive land that would otherwise go unused
cyclical unemployment	unemployment resulting from the natural fluctuations in the nation's economy
de Tocqueville	Alexis de Tocqueville, a nineteenth-century French political thinker and author of *Democracy in America*.
entitlements	government aid to which a person is entitled by virtue of belonging to a class of people, such as old-age retirement benefits
mega-mergers	mergers involving large corporations, common in the 1980s
Rendezvous with Destiny	phrase used by President Franklin D. Roosevelt in his acceptance speech at the 1936 Democratic National Convention
Rodney King	an African American whose beating by a group of Los Angeles police officers was caught on tape in 1991, leading to a highly publicized legal case and civil unrest

George F. Kennan (AP/Wide World Photos)

GEORGE F. KENNAN   1904–2005

Diplomat and Presidential Adviser

Featured Documents
- The "Long Telegram" (1946)
- "The Sources of Soviet Conduct" (1947)
- "PPS/23: Review of Current Trends in U.S. Foreign Policy" (1948)
- "Introducing Eugene McCarthy" (1968)
- "A Modest Proposal" (1981)

Overview

George Frost Kennan, acclaimed as the chief architect of U.S. cold war strategy and policy, was born on February 16, 1904, in Milwaukee, Wisconsin. He attended St. John's Northwestern Military Academy in Delafield, Wisconsin, and studied at Princeton University, where he earned his B.A. in 1925. After graduating, Kennan joined the Foreign Service, which he later described as the first and last sensible decision he ever made regarding his career. Kennan, who had a natural aptitude for languages, learned that his service entitled him to undertake graduate work without leaving the Foreign Service, so he arranged to study in Berlin, where he focused on Russian and Russian history. The polyglot Kennan also mastered German, French, Polish, Czech, Portuguese, and Norwegian.

Kennan spent several years at the end of World War II trying to convince U.S. policy makers that it was naive to expect the friendly relations between the United States and the USSR to continue, to no effect. Only when the USSR spurned the International Monetary Fund and the World Bank, two international organizations established at the end of World War II to expedite the economic recovery of Europe and the international stability of currency markets, did Kennan's writings find a receptive audience. His famous "Long Telegram" and "The Sources of Soviet Conduct" made Kennan's career and reputation and became foundational documents of postwar U.S. foreign policy. Still, to the end of his life, Kennan lamented that what he had intended as political containment was turned into military containment, spawning the nuclear arms race, which he decried as foolish and dangerous. Kennan's later writings bemoan this overemphasis on the military aspects of containment, particularly in his opposition to the Vietnam War and his abiding opposition to the nuclear arms race.

The "Long Telegram" and "The Sources of Soviet Conduct" helped form the basis for the Truman Doctrine, President Harry Truman's declaration that the United States would provide economic and military support to free peoples facing either external military threats or internal insurrections by armed—and presumably Communist —minorities. Kennan was also the principal intellectual architect of the European Recovery Program, better known as the Marshall Plan, the economic assistance plan designed to rebuild the war-torn European economies, which built on ideas articulated in these two documents. An outspoken critic of what he called hysterical anti-Communism, Kennan spoke out publicly against the red scare, the anti-Communist hysteria of the late 1940s and 1950s, led by Wisconsin senator Joseph McCarthy, that resulted in witch hunts, blacklisting, and other social and professional persecution of suspected Communists.

As a policy planner, Kennan held to his belief that a coherent foreign policy could not be formed by focusing solely on specific threats but had to consider events from a worldwide perspective. Only on the basis of such a perspective, Kennan argued, could specific policies be formed and evaluated in terms of their projected benefits and expected costs, and he dedicated considerable energies toward efforts in this direction. At the Institute for Advanced Study at Princeton, Kennan continued to work on policy matters, ultimately writing more than twenty books, two of which won Pulitzer Prizes, and dozens of major articles and essays. He died in Princeton, New Jersey, in 2005.

Explanation and Analysis of Documents

Kennan's reputation as the chief intellectual architect of the cold war policy of containment rests primarily on two documents. "The Long Telegram," which Kennan sent from Moscow in 1946, lays out what he saw as the chief features of the Soviet state and its approach to world affairs. In it he suggested that trying to contain the USSR would be more effective in the long run than would direct confrontation. He elaborated on these ideas in 1947 in "The Sources of Soviet Conduct," which continued and broadened his analysis of the conflict between the United States and the USSR and made recommendations regarding how the United States should approach its foreign policy in the context of that conflict.

Although he was an expert on Russian history and affairs, Kennan did not focus solely on the Soviet Union. As the director of the State Department's Policy Planning Staff, he worked toward coordinating American foreign policy around the world. "PPS/23: Review of Current Trends in U.S. Foreign Policy" is one of his attempts to identify the major global problems facing American policy makers and

Time Line

suggest strategies for coordinating policy decisions based on cost/benefit analyses. Although Kennan's influence on foreign policy was strong, he was unable to prevent containment from being implemented almost exclusively as a military policy rather than the economic and political strategy that he had envisioned. In devising the policy of containment, Kennan envisaged policy makers choosing their conflicts in such a way as to maximize potential gains while minimizing potential losses, in terms of life, political capital, and economic resources. He believed that the Vietnam War was a major mistake of policy and strategy, as he makes clear in his 1968 speech "Introducing Eugene McCarthy." Another element of American cold war strategy that Kennan rejected was the nuclear arms race, which he saw as a contest that could not end with victory for any side, as he explains in his 1981 essay, "A Modest Proposal."

◆ The "Long Telegram"

As World War II ground its way to a close, Kennan was among the many watching the wartime Soviet-American alliance begin to falter and then break apart. In early 1945 a majority of Americans viewed the USSR as their country's strongest ally; by 1947 the majority of Americans saw the Soviet Union as the country's greatest threat. Kennan had been writing analytical essays and position papers from Moscow, but no one seemed to be reading or reacting to them, and he grew increasingly frustrated with what he saw as a confused policy toward the Soviet Union developing in Washington.

When the Soviet Union declined to support the World Bank and the International Monetary Fund, the Treasury Department asked the State Department to explain the USSR's behavior. Kennan seized on a minor request for information to give what he described as the whole truth. Acknowledging in his memoirs that his answer was disproportionate to the question but nevertheless was a truth that needed to be told, Kennan grasped the opportunity to lay out in detail his understanding of the Soviet state and its leader. The eight-thousand-word telegram was well received and, together with "The Sources of Soviet Conduct," became the basis for what became known as the policy of "containment."

The telegram consists of an outline of the basic features of the USSR's postwar outlook; the background of this view; a description of how it informed Soviet policy, both officially and unofficially; and what the United States could learn from this outlook and then adapt to its own policy. Kennan carefully and explicitly lays out the USSR's understanding of its position in the world, characterizing the Soviet state as believing itself encircled and besieged by capitalist states naturally combative and inclined toward hostility against the USSR. The USSR was convinced that its standing on the world stage must be increased at all costs, preferably at the expense of the United States. Kennan makes clear that this is the position of the inner circle of the Communist Party and does not reflect on the Russian people, who are ruled by a tyrant. Kennan further points out that the party's viewpoint that there can be no peaceful coexistence between Communist and capitalist countries is simply false, subtly suggesting to his superiors that they could consider a foreign policy that emphasized coexistence, rather than combativeness, once conditions improved.

The first step toward an intelligent policy with regard to the Soviets, Kennan says, is to take the time and effort necessary to understand the nation and the Communist movement. Only then, he argues, could policy be profitably formed. Kennan notes that the Soviet state and Stalin, in particular, were impervious to logic or argument. The dictator Stalin was far too insecure and suspicious to be persuaded; he would assume that he was being lied to and act accordingly. Kennan points out that however resistant Stalin was to argumentation, he was highly sensitive to judicious application of force. Rather than relying on goodwill gestures or efforts to engage the Soviet leadership in negotiations, Kennan proposes engagement with the Soviet Union where it tried to expand and threaten vital American interests—with sufficient force to compel the USSR to withdraw. Kennan argues that subtlety would not work, and it would be better to react too strongly than too weakly.

Kennan also makes the point that the public needed to be educated about the Soviets, thereby lessening irrational fears of the unknown. Moreover, America should look to its own society and try to solve its internal problems, lest Stalin's regime profit by comparison. Kennan urges the development and promulgation of a constructive vision of the future world. It is not enough, he says, to encourage people to emulate American ways; rather, the United States should articulate a vision that could be achieved by cooperation, under U.S. guidance. Last, Kennan warns against adopting Soviet tactics in confronting the Soviet Union. The show trials and employment purges of the Red Scare represent the kind of mirroring of Soviet actions in the name of confronting the USSR that Kennan warns against in the telegram.

◆ "The Sources of Soviet Conduct"

One of the officials who took a profound interest in Kennan's "Long Telegram" was Secretary of the Navy James Forrestal, who asked Kennan in late 1946 to prepare a paper dealing with Marxism in relation to Soviet power. On January 31, 1947, Kennan submitted the paper, which discussed the nature of Soviet power in terms of the policy problems it presented. Forrestal wrote Kennan that he was impressed and was forwarding the paper to Secretary of State George Marshall. Kennan subsequently sought and obtained permission to publish a modified version of it in *Foreign Affairs*, which he did in the summer of 1947 under the byline "X," in a vain attempt to hide the fact that he was the author.

The article lays out Kennan's understanding of the Soviet Union. In it he uses, for the first time, the word *containment*. He recapitulates several themes from the "Long Telegram," including the need to understand the Soviets and their outlook. He reiterates that the Soviet leadership must be understood in terms of their ideology, which per-

Time Line

1948

■ **February 24**
Kennan submits "PPS/23: Review of Current Trends in U.S. Foreign Policy," a Policy Planning Staff paper detailing the problems facing the development of a coordinated, coherent U.S. foreign policy.

1950

■ **September**
Kennan joins the faculty of the Institute for Advanced Study at Princeton University while on leave from the State Department.

1951

■ **December 27**
Kennan is appointed ambassador to the Soviet Union, effective May 1952.

1952

■ **September**
Kennan's ambassadorship ends owing to a dispute with the Soviet government.

1956

■ Kennan returns to the Institute for Advanced Study, where he remains for most of the remainder of his career.

1961–1963

■ Kennan serves as ambassador to Yugoslavia.

1968

■ **April 11**
"Introducing Eugene McCarthy" is published in the *New York Review of Books*, describing McCarthy as the presidential candidate who presented the best chance of ending the Vietnam War.

1981

■ **July 16**
"A Modest Proposal" is published in the *New York Review of Books*, laying out Kennan's thoughts on cold war challenges and the folly of the nuclear arms race.

2005

■ **March 17**
Kennan dies in Princeton, N.J.

mitted no cooperation between capitalism and Communism and which served as the basis for their dictatorial rule. Kennan stresses the outward-focused nature of this ideology; given the party's success in stamping out capitalism within the USSR's borders, the perceived threat had to be shifted to an external capitalist foe. Everything that the USSR did on the international stage, he notes, would be premised and justified by this perception. Kennan is careful to depict the nature of the foe that he believes the United States faces in the USSR. The Soviets were going to be difficult to deal with, he says, but the United States should not act as though the USSR intended to destroy them at the first available opportunity. The leaders of the USSR believed that they would ultimately triumph and were willing to be as patient as necessary to see the conflict through, necessitating an equally patient approach on the part of the United States.

Kennan suggests that the United States needed to "contain" the Soviet Union, to prevent it from expanding beyond its current borders. By applying appropriate counterforce to any aggressive Soviet maneuvers, the United States would be able to keep the USSR in check long enough for the internal flaws within the Soviet system to ensure its collapse. The Soviets, he says, were wholly uninterested in cooperation and would seek to apply constant pressure against the capitalist states to try to cause their destruction; the American response should be a commensurately constant application of counter-pressure.

Kennan articulates two cogent and prescient insights. First, he observes that the United States did not possess the power by itself to bring about the destruction of the Soviet Union. Rather, the United States could make it continually and progressively more difficult for Moscow to operate as it wished. Second, he warns that while the Soviets would be inclined toward patience and withdrawing from confrontation, they would not do so at the expense of their prestige. He echoes a warning from the "Long Telegram," where he cautioned that the USSR considered its standing of paramount importance. Putting the Soviets in a position in which they could not back down without losing face would provoke armed conflict between the two powers, even if the Soviets knew that it was in their interest to avoid war. The key, he says, would be to behave coolly and rationally and always make sure to give the Soviets a way to both back down and save face.

Despite the article's impact on U.S. policy—and indeed *because* of that impact—Kennan always regretted what he saw as the article's failings, particularly its lack of clarity regarding the type of counterforce that should be applied. Kennan viewed the cold war principally in economic and political, rather than military, terms and meant "containment" in this light—the application of the appropriate economic and political pressure at the right times. While Kennan's idea of containment drove U.S. cold war policy for decades, it resulted in military containment. Kennan also regretted not having been more specific about the geographic limitations of containment. He did not envision a constant and global response to any move that the Soviets

might make, but instead the application of counterforce where it was most appropriate and necessary and also the most likely to have the desired effect—USSR withdrawal.

◆ **"PPS/23: Review of Current Trends in U.S. Foreign Policy"**

In 1947 Secretary of State George C. Marshall ordered Kennan to form a Policy Planning Staff, which Kennan was to head. In February 1948, after several months of preparation, Kennan delivered "PPS/23: Review of Current Trends in U.S. Foreign Policy" to Marshall and Undersecretary of State Robert A. Lovett. The paper detailed the development of U.S. foreign policy, beginning with past actions and continuing through present circumstances, with the idea that seeing where they had been would show something about where they were going. Kennan deals particularly and explicitly with two arenas of conflict that presented pressing questions for U.S. policy makers: Germany and the Far East.

In "PPS/23," Kennan repeatedly advocates a Western European union, one that Great Britain also would be able to support, as a counterweight to a Soviet-dominated Eastern Europe. A disorganized West would never stand up to an organized East, Kennan says, and thus the West needed to be brought together into a federation. This federation would serve a second critical objective, he argues: containing Germany within the West. Here Kennan speaks in terms of what some historians refer to as "double containment," the need to contain the Soviet Union and also to keep Germany within the Western configuration, thereby preventing Germany from either aligning with the USSR or returning to its imperialistic ambitions. Kennan deeply distrusted Germany and gives reasons for this distrust in the paper; but he also recognized the need to have a functioning European federation that would incorporate the western portions of Germany and permit its reindustrialization, while limiting the risk that a rebuilt German state would reembark on conquest.

More controversially, Kennan also deals bluntly here with the question of the Far East. He describes the area as too different ideologically from the United States to be effectively "led" from Washington. Further, he notes, there is a drastic material divide between the United States, with roughly 6 percent of the world's population controlling nearly 50 percent of the world's wealth, and the desperately poor regions of East Asia. This material divide meant two things to Kennan. First, the imbalance would result in a great deal of envy and resentment, and the task for U.S. policy makers was to devise ways to maintain this disparity without causing harm to national security arrangements. Second, the United States needed to recognize that this very material disparity further limited its possibilities for effective action in this region of the world. Because these areas were so poor, they would more naturally incline toward Moscow than Washington.

Kennan advises patience and discretion in dealing with East Asia. Patience was necessary because Moscow's ideology would be more attractive in the short term, while discretion was necessary because the United States could not extend itself into the whole region but must instead be extremely selective about where it would become engaged in the region in pursuit of its interests. Kennan perceived Japan and the Philippines as being of greater significance to U.S. interests than the Asian mainland. Last, he observes that the time was coming when the United States would have to deal with the region with strength, rather than slogans.

◆ "Introducing Eugene McCarthy"

In 1968 Kennan's was among the voices calling out for change in U.S. foreign policy, particularly with regard to Vietnam. Minnesota senator Eugene McCarthy, an outspoken opponent of the Vietnam War, challenged incumbent President Lyndon B. Johnson, and while Johnson beat McCarthy 49 percent to 42 percent in the New Hampshire primary, the result underscored the fact that Johnson was vulnerable and that the war was the primary reason for this vulnerability.

Kennan introduced McCarthy at a fund-raising dinner on February 29, 1968, shortly before the primary, and took advantage of the opportunity to explain his opposition to the Vietnam War, which he articulated in language he had previously used to define containment. The war, which he believed was a catastrophic mistake that had damaged American society, needed to be ended, and Kennan here introduces McCarthy as the candidate who presented the best chance of ending the war.

In supporting McCarthy and condemning current policy regarding Vietnam, Kennan revisits language he used in the "Long Telegram" and his article on "The Sources of Soviet Conduct," expanding upon and clarifying the ideas contained in those two pieces. Kennan begins by stating that the Vietnam War was poorly conceived because it had no discernible goal, but he quickly moves to the crux of his complaint—that Vietnam was not important enough to merit the kind of resources that the United States had committed to the war and that the conflict had distracted the United States from working toward rectifying its own social problems. This first idea is in some respects a contextual clarification of one of the failings Kennan saw in his "Sources" article. If before he failed to distinguish between vital and less vital geographic regions within which to push back against Communist expansion, Kennan leaves no doubt here: He did not consider Vietnam important in that regard. Second, Kennan repeats a caution that he had made both in the "Long Telegram" and the "Sources" article: that in the struggle against Communist expansion, the United States should take care never to overlook or relegate to second-class importance its own social problems.

Kennan also berates the arrogance of the Johnson administration, blaming it for spurning erstwhile allies, for acting as though the United States had no need of informed advice from other nations. The war had seriously divided public opinion at home, he notes, referencing the antiwar student movements of the late 1960s, and had helped turn world opinion against the United States. If

The Minuteman 2 is fired from an underground silo at Cape Kennedy on September 24, 1964. The weapon was being developed to deliver a nuclear payload nearly eight thousand miles away. (AP/Wide World Photos)

Kennan saw anything fortunate about this situation, it was the fact that 1968 was an election year and the people thus had the opportunity to bring a new president into office with a clear electoral mandate to end the war. In order for this to happen, though, there had to be a candidate that genuinely stood for ending the war, not a candidate who would equivocate and try to please both sides simultaneously; otherwise, the people who believed that ending the war should be the new president's top priority would have no one for whom they could vote.

◆ "A Modest Proposal"

Cold war tensions, which had relaxed somewhat during the 1970s, suddenly heightened again in the early 1980s. With these new tensions, a new arms race was begun, threatening the stability of the Strategic Arms Limitations Treaties. It seemed to Kennan and others that the USSR and United States were once again heading down a political and diplomatic path that could and perhaps had to lead to war. It was to this problem that Kennan addressed his proposal. He begins by stating that the current arms race was the result of actions undertaken by both sides. The

USSR had indeed rejected the Baruch Plan, which would have placed atomic energy and weapons under international control; but the United States had instigated each development in the race in its pursuit of more powerful weapons. It did no good to cast blame in this situation, because there was enough to go around and because the weapons were powerful enough to make the discussion pointless. Rather, he says, the United States had to focus on how to resolve the problem.

Kennan saw no real chance of success in the Strategic Arms Limitation Treaties negotiations, which he describes as part of the problem, because the two powers approached the talks trying to preserve a "relative advantage" in weaponry, an idea that Kennan considered meaningless in a discussion nuclear weapons. What he advocated instead was an across-the-board reduction of all weaponry on both sides by 50 percent. He further supported pursuing this goal as an end in itself. The minute one side started wondering whether the other side had a relative advantage in remaining weapons, the arms race would continue. If 50 percent could be cut from each side's arsenal, then Kennan would advocate a second round of talks, with the aim of reducing by two-thirds the remaining nuclear arsenal of each.

Kennan acknowledges that this would be only a first step. Making this proposal in support of President Ronald Reagan's professed desire to negotiate with the USSR for as long as necessary (to bring the number of nuclear weapons down to the point that neither side could obliterate the other) would challenge people to think of a major arms reduction as the beginning of a process, rather than an end in itself. In the early 1980s such a view was gaining traction, and Kennan here gives voice to the idea and its attendant problems eloquently and thoughtfully.

Impact and Legacy

Kennan's impact on U.S. foreign policy can hardly be overstated. He was, in many ways, the right person at the right time, given his capacity to empathize with the USSR and to articulate his understanding of the Soviets clearly. Kennan was vital to the implementation of the European Recovery Program and to efforts to persuade the United States to support European unity efforts and programs. He was also a public critic both of the nuclear arms race, which he considered a disastrous mistake on both sides, and of "red baiting" and the Red Scare of the late 1940s and early 1950s. Most important, it was Kennan's vision that gave rise to the policy of containment, which for all of its failures and successes was the guiding principle of the United States toward the USSR for the remainder of the cold war.

Kennan would not have assessed his career and impact only in terms of the positives, however. Despite his literary talent, his writings did not always present his opinions forcefully or clearly enough to be understood. This shortcoming was particularly the case with his early writings on containment, which failed to distinguish sufficiently between military and political/economic containment. At

the same time, however, it is clear from Kennan's writings that he had several critical insights that some of his contemporaries failed to recognize. First, he saw that Stalin did not want and could not afford war with the United States. This insight helped him put forward a policy of economic and political engagement and confrontation, which, he believed, would hasten the end of the cold war without running the risk of a major military conflict. Throughout his life Kennan retained his sense of the importance of being willing to tell the truth to those in power, including the president, even when they disagreed. He also repeatedly stressed the need to understand the adversary, to try to think as he did. He criticized simplistic depictions of the USSR as unreasonable, irrational, or nonhuman because he felt that these depictions fed irrational fears that undermined foreign and domestic needs. Studying Kennan's writings provides profound insight into both the successes and the failings of U.S. foreign policy during the cold war.

Key Sources

The George F. Kennan Papers at the Mudd Manuscript Library at Princeton University is the largest collection of Kennan's writings, spanning the period from 1925 to 1969. Kennan two-volume autobiography—*Memoirs: 1925–1950* (1967), which won the Pulitzer Prize, and *Memoirs: 1950–1963* (1972)—are the classic starting point. *Sketches from a Life* (1989) and *At a Century's Ending: Reflections 1982–1995* (1996) combine autobiography with a critical evaluation of cold war history. *From Prague after Munich: Diplomatic Papers, 1938–1940* (1968) shows Kennan's developing understanding of foreign affairs in the early years of World War II. Kennan wrote extensively on Russia; among his writings are *Russia, the Atom, and the West* (1958), *Soviet Foreign Policy 1917–1941* (1960), and *Russia and the West under Lenin and Stalin* (1961). He also wrote numerous books analyzing U.S. foreign policy during the cold war, including *The Cloud of Danger: Current Realities of American Foreign Policy* (1977), *The Nuclear Delusion: Soviet-American Relations in the Atomic Age* (1982), and *Around the Cragged Hill: A Personal and Political Philosophy* (1993). Kennan's *Russia Leaves the War* (1956) also won the Pulitzer Prize.

Further Reading

■ Books

Gellman, Barton D. *Contending with Kennan: Towards a Philosophy of American Power*. New York: Praeger Press, 1984.

Hixson, Walter L. *George F. Kennan: Cold War Iconoclast*. New York: Columbia University Press, 1989.

Kennan, George F., and John Lukacs. *George F. Kennan and the Origins of Containment, 1944–1946: The Kennan-Lukacs Correspondence*. Columbia: University of Missouri Press, 1997.

"Soviet power… is neither schematic nor adventuristic. It does not work by fixed plans. It does not take unnecessary risks. Impervious to logic of reason, and it is highly sensitive to logic of force. For this reason it can easily withdraw—and usually does when strong resistance is encountered at any point. Thus, if the adversary has sufficient force and makes clear his readiness to use it, he rarely has to do so. If situations are properly handled there need be no prestige-engaging showdowns."

(The "Long Telegram")

"Soviet pressure against the free institutions of the Western world is something that can be contained by the adroit and vigilant application of counterforce at a series of constantly shifting geographical and political points, corresponding to the shifts and maneuvers of Soviet policy, but which cannot be charmed or talked out of existence."

("The Sources of Soviet Conduct")

"The day is not far off when we are going to have to deal in straight power concepts. The less we are then hampered by idealistic slogans, the better."

("PPS/23: Review of Current Trends in U.S. Foreign Policy")

"[The Vietnam War] has riveted an undue amount of our attention and resources to a single secondary theatre of world events. It has left us poorly prepared, if not helpless, to meet other crises that might occur simultaneously elsewhere in the world. And finally, it has proceeded at the cost of the successful development of our life here in this country."

("Introducing Eugene McCarthy")

"I see [the arms race] taking possession of men's imagination and behavior, becoming a force in its own right, detaching itself from the political differences that initially inspired it, and then leading both parties, invariably and inexorably, to the war they no longer know how to avoid."

("A Modest Proposal")

Kennan, George F.

Lukacs, John. *George Kennan: A Study of Character*. New Haven, Yale University Press, 2007.

Mayers, David Allan. *George Kennan and the Dilemmas of U.S. Foreign Policy*. New York: Oxford University Press, 1988.

Miscamble, Wilson D. *George F. Kennan and the Making of American Foreign Policy, 1947–1950*. Princeton, N.J.: Princeton University Press, 1992.

—Anthony Santoro

Questions for Further Study

1. Study the record of Russian and Soviet history and compare it with the account Kennan gives in his famous "Long Telegram." Do you agree or disagree with his analysis of the factors that shaped the Russian and later Soviet views of the world—for instance, his assertion that the Russians began as "a peaceful agricultural people" or his distinction between "Russian rulers" and "the Russian people"? How does he regard the Soviets and particularly their leaders? (Consider, for instance, his implied comparison of the Soviet leadership to mental patients.) Based on his interpretation of the Soviet mind-set, do you think his conclusions in the latter half of the document are correct? In other words, if the Soviets were as devious and potentially dangerous as he suggests, was he correct in recommending a cautious, generally nonmilitary approach in dealing with them?

2. Examine the principles of Marxism-Leninism, which Kennan discusses in the three documents from the late 1940s included here. What is the Marxist-Leninist view of history, and how did this perspective influence the actions of Communist leaders? Compare and contrast Marxism-Leninism as a doctrine with the liberal ideas of individual freedom that form the basis of the U.S. Constitution—ideas that are likewise based in part on the writings of philosophers, most notably John Locke. What are the common points in the origins of American and Soviet political philosophy, and what are the differences?

3. How might Kennan have regarded events of the late twentieth and early twenty-first century—specifically, the downfall of Communism in Europe, the unification of much of that continent under the European Union (EU), and the emergence of Islamic fundamentalist terrorism as a new threat to American freedom and security? Would he have regarded the EU as a fulfillment of the unified Continental framework he envisioned in his 1948 report included here? How would he have explained the downfall of Soviet Communism? How would he regard the U.S. response to Islamic fundamentalist terror, particularly the war in Iraq? Would he have seen American behavior in that situation as yet another instance of the reliance on military rather than other solutions to the problem, or would he have taken some other position?

4. In his early career, Kennan established himself as a staunch anti-Communist, but that did not mean he supported every possible measure against Communist aggression. Thus he strongly opposed the Vietnam War, which, though it was ostensibly fought to halt the spread of Communism in Southeast Asia, seemed to him a tremendous waste of lives and resources. Examine his speech on Eugene McCarthy and discuss why Kennan—whose positions on Communism seemed to identify him as a conservative—would have supported the most liberal, antiwar candidate in the 1968 primaries. Given his reasons for supporting McCarthy and opposing the war, how might he have analyzed the Iraq war of the early twenty-first century? Would he have seen it as another Vietnam? Use Kennan's own words to support your position.

The "Long Telegram" (1946)

At bottom of Kremlin's neurotic view of world affairs is traditional and instinctive Russian sense of insecurity. Originally, this was insecurity of a peaceful agricultural people trying to live on vast exposed plain in neighborhood of fierce nomadic peoples. To this was added, as Russia came into contact with economically advanced West, fear of more competent, more powerful, more highly organized societies in that area. But this latter type of insecurity was one which afflicted rather Russian rulers than Russian people; for Russian rulers have invariably sensed that their rule was relatively archaic in form, fragile and artificial in its psychological foundation, unable to stand comparison or contact with political systems of Western countries. For this reason they have always feared foreign penetration, feared direct contact between Western world and their own, feared what would happen if Russians learned truth about world without or if foreigners learned truth about world within. And they have learned to seek security only in patient but deadly struggle for total destruction of rival power, never in compacts and compromises with it.

It was no coincidence that Marxism, which had smoldered ineffectively for half a century in Western Europe, caught hold and blazed for first time in Russia. Only in this land which had never known a friendly neighbor or indeed any tolerant equilibrium of separate powers, either internal or international, could a doctrine thrive which viewed economic conflicts of society as insoluble by peaceful means. After establishment of Bolshevist regime, Marxist dogma, rendered even more truculent and intolerant by Lenin's interpretation, became a perfect vehicle for sense of insecurity with which Bolsheviks, even more than previous Russian rulers, were afflicted. In this dogma, with its basic altruism of purpose, they found justification for their instinctive fear of outside world, for the dictatorship without which they did not know how to rule, for cruelties they did not dare not to inflict, for sacrifice they felt bound to demand. In the name of Marxism they sacrificed every single ethical value in their methods and tactics. Today they cannot dispense with it. It is fig leaf of their moral and intellectual respectability. Without it they would stand before history, at best, as only the last of that long succession of cruel and wasteful Russian rulers who have relentlessly forced country on to ever new

heights of military power in order to guarantee external security of their internally weak regimes. This is why Soviet purposes must always be solemnly clothed in trappings of Marxism, and why no one should underrate importance of dogma in Soviet affairs. Thus Soviet leaders are driven [by?] necessities of their own past and present position to put forward which [apparent omission] outside world as evil, hostile and menacing, but as bearing within itself germs of creeping disease and destined to be wracked with growing internal convulsions until it is given final Coup de grace by rising power of socialism and yields to new and better world. This thesis provides justification for that increase of military and police power of Russian state, for that isolation of Russian population from outside world, and for that fluid and constant pressure to extend limits of Russian police power which are together the natural and instinctive urges of Russian rulers. Basically this is only the steady advance of uneasy Russian nationalism, a centuries old movement in which conceptions of offense and defense are inextricably confused. But in new guise of international Marxism, with its honeyed promises to a desperate and war torn outside world, it is more dangerous and insidious than ever before....

We have now seen nature and background of Soviet program. What may we expect by way of its practical implementation?...

Toward colonial areas and backward or dependent peoples, Soviet policy, even on official plane, will be directed toward weakening of power and influence and contacts of advanced Western nations, on theory that in so far as this policy is successful, there will be created a vacuum which will favor Communist-Soviet penetration....

The Soviet regime is a police regime par excellence, reared in the dim half world of Tsarist police intrigue, accustomed to think primarily in terms of police power. This should never be lost sight of in [gauging] Soviet motives.

Part 5: [Practical Deductions from Standpoint of US Policy]

In summary, we have here a political force committed fanatically to the belief that with US there can be no permanent modus vivendi [;] that it is desirable and necessary that the internal harmony of our society be disrupted, our traditional way of life be destroyed, the international authority of our state be broken, if Soviet power is to be secure....

(1) Soviet power, unlike that of Hitlerite Germany, is neither schematic nor adventuristic. It does not work by fixed plans. It does not take unnecessary risks. Impervious to logic of reason, and it is highly sensitive to logic of force. For this reason it can easily withdraw—and usually does when strong resistance is encountered at any point. Thus, if the adversary has sufficient force and makes clear his readiness to use it, he rarely has to do so. If situations are properly handled there need be no prestige-engaging showdowns....

(4) All Soviet propaganda beyond Soviet security sphere is basically negative and destructive. It should therefore be relatively easy to combat it by any intelligent and really constructive program.

For those reasons I think we may approach calmly and with good heart problem of how to deal with Russia. As to how this approach should be made, I only wish to advance, by way of conclusion, following comments:

1. Our first step must be to apprehend, and recognize for what it is, the nature of the movement with which we are dealing. We must study it with same courage, detachment, objectivity, and same determination not to be emotionally provoked or unseated by it, with which doctor studies unruly and unreasonable individual.

2. We must see that our public is educated to realities of Russian situation. I cannot over-emphasize importance of this.... I am convinced that there would be far less hysterical anti-Sovietism in our country today if realities of this situation were better understood by our people. There is nothing as dangerous or as terrifying as the unknown. It may also be argued that to reveal more information on our difficulties with Russia would reflect unfavorably on Russian-American relations....

4. We must formulate and put forward for other nations a much more positive and constructive picture of sort of world we would like to see than we have put forward in past. It is not enough to urge people to develop political processes similar to our own....

5. Finally we must have courage and self-confidence to cling to our own methods and conceptions of human society. After all, the greatest danger that can befall us in coping with this problem of Soviet communism is that we shall allow ourselves to become like those with whom we are coping.

Glossary

Bolshevist	reference to the native political party that led the Russian Revolution of 1917, the forerunner of the nation's Communist Party
Coup de grace	death blow, blow that kills
fig leaf	a covering that conceals or obscures something only partly
Kremlin	a fortified complex of buildings in the heart of Moscow, Russia; as a figure of speech, the government of the Soviet Union
Lenin	Vladimir Lenin, the founder of the Bolshevist Party and first leader of the Soviet Union
Marxism	the economic and social philosophy advocated by Karl Marx, often used synonymously with "Communism"
modus vivendi	an agreement or accommodation between adversaries
Tsarist	reference to the Russian monarchs, or tsars (czars), prior to the advent of Communism

"The Sources of Soviet Conduct" (1947)

Now it lies in the nature of the mental world of the Soviet leaders, as well as in the character of their ideology, that no opposition to them can be officially recognized as having any merit or justification whatsoever. Such opposition can flow, in theory, only from the hostile and incorrigible forces of dying capitalism. As long as remnants of capitalism were officially recognized as existing in Russia, it was possible to place on them, as an internal element, part of the blame for the maintenance of a dictatorial form of society. But as these remnants were liquidated, little by little, this justification fell away; and when it was indicated officially that they had been finally destroyed, it disappeared altogether. And this fact created one of the most basic of the compulsions which came to act upon the Soviet regime: since capitalism no longer existed in Russia and since it could not be admitted that there could be serious or widespread opposition to the Kremlin springing spontaneously from the liberated masses under its authority, it became necessary to justify the retention of the dictatorship by stressing the menace of capitalism abroad....

But least of all can the rulers dispense with the fiction by which the maintenance of dictatorial power has been defended. For this fiction has been canonized in Soviet philosophy by the excesses already committed in its name; and it is now anchored in the Soviet structure of thought by bonds far greater than those of mere ideology....

It must invariably be assumed in Moscow that the aims of the capitalist world are antagonistic to the Soviet regime, and therefore to the interests of the peoples it controls.... Basically, the antagonism [between capitalism and communism] remains. It is postulated. And from it flow many of the phenomena which we find disturbing in the Kremlin's conduct of foreign policy: the secretiveness, the lack of frankness, the duplicity, the wary suspiciousness and the basic unfriendliness of purpose. These phenomena are there to stay, for the foreseeable future.

This means that we are going to continue for a long time to find the Russians difficult to deal with. It does not mean that they should be considered as embarked upon a do-or-die program to overthrow our society by a given date....

In these circumstances it is clear that the main element of any United States policy toward the Soviet Union must be that of a long-term, patient but firm and vigilant containment of Russian expansive tendencies. It is important to note, however, that such a policy has nothing to do with outward histrionics: with threats or blustering or superfluous gestures of outward "toughness." While the Kremlin is basically flexible in its reaction to political realities, it is by no means unamenable to considerations of prestige. Like almost any other government, it can be placed by tactless and threatening gestures in a position where it cannot afford to yield even though this might be dictated by its sense of realism. The Russian leaders are keen judges of human psychology, and as such they are highly conscious that loss of temper and of self-control is never a source of strength in political affairs. They are quick to exploit such evidences of weakness. For these reasons, it is a sine qua non of successful dealing with Russia that the foreign government in question should remain at all times cool and collected and that its demands on Russian policy should be put forward in such a manner as to leave the way open for a compliance not too detrimental to Russian prestige.

In the light of the above, it will be clearly seen that the Soviet pressure against the free institutions of the Western world is something that can be contained by the adroit and vigilant application of counterforce at a series of constantly shifting geographical and political points, corresponding to the shifts and maneuvers of Soviet policy, but which cannot be charmed or talked out of existence....

Thus the future of Soviet power may not be by any means as secure as Russian capacity for self-delusion would make it appear to the men in the Kremlin.... The possibility remains (and in the opinion of this writer it is a strong one) that Soviet power, like the capitalist world of its conception, bears within it the seeds of its own decay, and that the sprouting of these seeds is well advanced.

It is clear that the United States cannot expect in the foreseeable future to enjoy political intimacy with the Soviet regime. It must continue to regard the Soviet Union as a rival, not a partner, in the political arena. It must continue to expect that Soviet policies will reflect no abstract love of peace and stability, no real faith in the possibility of a permanent happy coexistence of the Socialist and capitalist worlds, but rather a cautious, persistent pressure toward the disruption and weakening of all rival influence and rival power.

Balanced against this are the facts that Russia, as opposed to the western world in general, is still by far the weaker party, that Soviet policy is highly flexible, and that Soviet society may well contain deficiencies which will eventually weaken its own total potential. This would of itself warrant the United States entering with reasonable confidence upon a policy of firm containment, designed to confront the Russians with unalterable counterforce at every point where they show signs of encroaching upon the interest of a peaceful and stable world....

It would be an exaggeration to say that American behavior unassisted and alone could exercise a power of life and death over the Communist movement and bring about the early fall of Soviet power in Russia. But the United States has it in its power to increase enormously the strains under which Soviet policy must operate, to force upon the Kremlin a far greater degree of moderation and circumspection than it has had to observe in recent years, and in this way to promote tendencies which must eventually find their outlet in either the breakup or the gradual mellowing of Soviet power. For no mystical, messianic movement—and particularly not that of the Kremlin — can face frustration indefinitely without eventually adjusting itself in one way or another to the logic of that state of affairs.

Thus the decision will really fall in large measure on this country itself. The issue of Soviet-American relations is in essence a test of the overall worth of the United States as a nation among nations. To avoid destruction the United States need only measure up to its own best traditions and prove itself worthy of preservation as a great nation.

Glossary

incorrigible	incapable of being reformed, improved, or corrected
Kremlin	a fortified complex of buildings in the heart of Moscow, Russia; as a figure of speech, the government of the Soviet Union
messianic	relating to a a leader who promises deliverance or salvation
sine qua non	essential condition, requirement
unamenable	not disposed or willing to comply

"PPS/23: Review of Current Trends in U.S. Foreign Policy" (1948)

In the long run there can be only three possibilities for the future of western and central Europe. One is German domination. Another is Russian domination. The third is a federated Europe, into which the parts of Germany are absorbed but in which the influence of the other countries is sufficient to hold Germany in her place.

If there is no real European federation and if Germany is restored as a strong and independent country, we must expect another attempt at German domination. If there is no real European federation and if Germany is not restored as a strong and independent country, we invite Russian domination, for an unorganized Western Europe cannot indefinitely oppose an organized Eastern Europe. The only reasonably hopeful possibility for avoiding one of these two evils is some form of federation in western and central Europe....

We cannot rely on any such Germany to fit constructively into a pattern of European union of its own volition. Yet without the Germans, no real European federation is thinkable. And without federation, the other countries of Europe ran have no protection against a new attempt at foreign domination.

If we did not have the Russians and the German communists prepared to take advantage politically of any movement on our part toward partition we could proceed to partition Germany regardless of the will of the inhabitants, and to force the respective segments to take their place in a federated Europe. But in the circumstances prevailing today, we cannot do this without throwing the German people politically into the arms of the communists. And if that happens, the fruits of our victory in Europe will have been substantially destroyed.

Our possibilities are therefore reduced, by the process of exclusion, to a policy which, without pressing the question of partition in Germany, would attempt to bring Germany, or western Germany, into a European federation, but do it in such a way as not to permit her to dominate that federation or jeopardize the security interests of the other western European countries. And this would have to be accomplished in the face of the fact that we cannot rely on the German people to exercise any self-restraint of their own volition, to feel any adequate sense of responsibility vis-à-vis the other western nations, or to concern themselves for the preservation of western values in their own country and elsewhere in Europe....

Furthermore, we have about 50% of the world's wealth but only 6.3% of its population. This disparity is particularly great as between ourselves and the peoples of Asia. In this situation, we cannot fail to be the object of envy and resentment. Our real task in the coming period is to devise a pattern of relationships which will permit us to maintain this position of disparity without positive detriment to our national security. To do so, we will have to dispense with all sentimentality and day-dreaming; and our attention will have to be concentrated everywhere on our immediate national objectives. We need not deceive ourselves that we can afford today the luxury of altruism and world-benefaction.

For these reasons, we must observe great restraint in our attitude toward the Far Eastern areas.... This process of adaptation will also be long and violent. It is not only possible, but probable, that in the course of this process many peoples will fall, for varying periods, under the influence of Moscow, whose ideology has a greater lure for such peoples, and probably greater reality, than anything we could oppose to it. All this, too, is probably unavoidable....

In the face of this situation we would be better off to dispense now with a number of the concepts which have underlined our thinking with regard to the Far East. We should dispense with the aspiration to "be liked" or to be regarded as the repository of a high-minded international altruism. We should stop putting ourselves in the position of being our brothers' keeper and refrain from offering moral and ideological advice. We should cease to talk about vague and—for the Far East—unreal objectives such as human

Glossary

Moscow	in 1848, the capital of the USSR; here representing the Soviet government

rights, the raising of the living standards, and democratization. The day is not far off when we are going to have to deal in straight power concepts. The less we are then hampered by idealistic slogans, the better.

"Introducing Eugene McCarthy" (1968)

It is now several years that our country has been heavily involved in the war in Vietnam. During most of this time, it has been inescapably evident that the entire venture was in several ways grievously unsound. It was unsound in the first place because it was devoid of a plausible, coherent, and realistic object. The regime in South Vietnam has been throughout too weak, too timid, too selfish, too uninspiring, to form a suitable or promising object of our support. And even if this regime had been a most vigorous and effective one, we would still be faced with the fact that the methods to which we have found ourselves driven, in the effort to crush by purely military means an elusive and disguised adversary, have been so destructive of civilian life, even in South Vietnam itself, that no conceivable political outcome could justify the attendant suffering and destruction.

And that's not the only way this effort has been unsound. It has also been unsound in its relation to our own world responsibilities and to our responsibilities here at home.... It has riveted an undue amount of our attention and resources to a single secondary theatre of world events. It has left us poorly prepared, if not helpless, to meet other crises that might occur simultaneously elsewhere in the world. And finally, it has proceeded at the cost of the successful development of our life here in this country. It has distracted us and hampered us in our effort to come to grips with domestic problems of such gravity as to cry out...for the concentrated, first-priority attention of both our government and our public....

Nevertheless, in the face of all these elements of unsoundness, the Administration...has pushed stubbornly ahead with the prosecution of this military effort, steadily increasing the degree of our commitment, rendering any peaceful liquidation of the conflict steadily more difficult, burning one bridge after another behind itself and ourselves, cutting off one after the other of the possible paths of retreat. It has done this in the face of a long series of pleas and warnings from wise and experienced people.... It has done it despite the clearly expressed misgivings of a great many of our friends and allies throughout the world. It has done it in disregard of the friendly suggestions and recommendations of the greatest political and spiritual leaders of the world community. It has acted as though it had never heard the suggestion that a country such as ours owed "a decent respect to the opinions of mankind."

It has persisted, furthermore, in the face of the fact that the war was obviously splitting American opinion in the sharpest and most unfortunate way, that it was having, in particular, a seriously disturbing effect on large sections of our student youth. It was, and is, filling many of our young people with bitterness and bewilderment, poisoning their relationship to the very society of which they and we are a part—the very society to the successful development of which their faith and enthusiasm are essential. In the face of all these warning voices, and all these warning signals, our governmental leaders, I reiterate, have pushed stubbornly and heedlessly ahead, like men in a dream, seemingly insensitive to outside opinion, seemingly unable to arrive at any realistic assessment of the effects of their own acts.

Now it is fortunate for us...that the crisis in Vietnam is occurring in the year of a presidential election ...because if any serious attempt is ever to be made to resolve this conflict by peaceful means, the chances for success will be far greater if our part in it is carried forward by fresh faces—and particularly by people who have sought and obtained a clear elec-

Glossary

"a decent respect to the opinions of mankind"	phrase from the Declaration of Independence
chimera	a monster, based on the fire-breathing creature of Greek mythology; more generally, an illusion

toral mandate to bring the conflict to an early end, to an end short of national humiliation but short, also, of the fateful chimera of total victory....

But in order that this possibility may have reality there must be at least one presidential candidate who is prepared to make himself the spokesman of the feelings of such people. If the only candidates at this stage are ones who either are already committed by their previous conduct to the indefinite and uncompromising prosecution of this struggle or ones who equivocate in the hope that they can straddle the issue and attract votes from both wings of opinion, then the anguish experienced by a large part of our public over the present policy will find no political expression at all, and many of us will have no choice but to be swept helplessly into disasters against which we have never had the opportunity to register an electoral protest.

"A Modest Proposal" (1981)

How have we got ourselves into this dangerous mess?

Let us not confuse the question by blaming it all on our Soviet adversaries. They have, of course, their share of the blame, and not least in their cavalier dismissal of the Baruch Plan so many years ago. They too have made their mistakes; and I should be the last to deny it. But we must remember that it has been we Americans who, at almost every step of the road, have taken the lead in the development of this sort of weaponry. It was we who first produced and tested such a device; we who were the first to raise its destructiveness to a new level with the hydrogen bomb; we who introduced the multiple warhead; we who have declined every proposal for the renunciation of the principle of "first use"; and we alone, so help us God, who have used the weapon in anger against others, and against tens of thousands of helpless noncombatants at that....

What is it, then, if not our own will, and not the supposed wickedness of our opponents, that has brought us to this pass?

The answer, I think, is clear. It is primarily the inner momentum, the independent momentum, of the weapons race itself—the compulsions that arise and take charge of great powers when they enter upon a competition with each other in the building up of major armaments of any sort.

This is nothing new. I am a diplomatic historian. I see this same phenomenon playing its fateful part in the relations among the great European powers as much as a century ago. I see this competitive build-up of armaments, conceived initially as a means to an end, becoming the end in itself. I see it taking possession of men's imagination and behavior, becoming a force in its own right, detaching itself from the political differences that initially inspired it, and then leading both parties, invariably and inexorably, to the war they no longer know how to avoid....

Is it possible to break out of this charmed and vicious circle? It is sobering to recognize that no country, at least to my knowledge, has yet done so. But no country, for that matter, has ever been faced with such great catastrophe, such plain and inalterable catastrophe, at the end of the line. Others, in earlier decades, could befuddle themselves with dreams of something called "victory." We, perhaps fortunately, are denied this seductive prospect. We have to break out of the circle. We have no other choice.

How are we to do it?

I must confess that I see no possibility of doing this by means of...the...SALT...negotiations, that is, in which each side is obsessed with the chimera of relative advantage and strives only to retain a maximum of the weaponry for itself while putting its opponent to the maximum disadvantage—I have no illusion that such negotiations could ever be adequate to get us out of this hole, They are not a way of escape from the weapons race; they are an integral part of it....

Whoever does not understand that when it comes to nuclear weapons the whole concept of relative advantage is illusory—whoever does not understand that when you are talking about preposterous quantities of overkill the relative sizes of arsenals have no serious meaning—whoever does not understand that the danger lies not in the possibility that someone else might have more missiles and warheads than you do, but in the very existence of those unconscionable quantities of highly poisonous explosives, and their existence, above all, in hands as weak and shaky and undependable as those of ourselves or our adversaries or any other mere human beings: whoever does not understand these things is never going to guide us out of this increasingly dark and menacing forest of bewilderments into which we have all wandered.

I can see no way out of this dilemma other than by a bold and sweeping departure...that would cut surgically through all the exaggerated anxieties, the self-engendered nightmares, and the sophisticated mathematics of destruction in which we have all been entangled over these recent years, and would permit us to move smartly, with courage and decision, to the heart of the problem.

President Reagan recently said, and I think very wisely, that he would "negotiate as long as necessary to reduce the numbers of nuclear weapons to a point where neither side threatens the survival of the other." Now that is, of course, precisely the thought to which these present observations of mine are addressed. And I wonder whether the negotiations would really have to be at such great length. What I would like to see the President do, after proper consultation with the Congress, would be to propose to the Soviet government an immediate across-the-boards reduction by 50 percent of the nuclear arsenals now being maintained by the two superpowers—a reduction affecting in equal measure all forms of the weapon, strategic, medium-range, and tactical, as well as all means of their delivery—all this to be implemented at once and without further wrangling among the experts, and to be subject to such national means of verification as now lie at the disposal of the two powers.

Whether the balance of reduction would be precisely even—whether it could be construed to favor statistically one side or the other—would not be the question. Once we start thinking that way, we would be back on the same old fateful track that has brought us where we are today. Whatever the precise results of such a reduction, there would still be plenty of overkill left—so much so that if this first operation were successful, I would then like to see a second one put in hand to rid us of at least two thirds of what would be left....

What I have suggested is, of course, only a beginning. But a beginning has to be made somewhere; and if it has to be made, is it not best that it should be made where the dangers are the greatest, and their necessity the least? If a step of this nature could be successfully taken, people might find heart to tackle with greater confidence and determination the many problems that would still remain.

Glossary

Baruch Plan	a plan written by the financier and presidential adviser Bernard Baruch, submitted to the United Nations in 1946, for the peaceful use of atomic energy
chimera	a monster, based on the fire-breathing creature of Greek mythology; more generally, an illusion
President Reagan	Ronald Reagan, fortieth president of the United States
SALT	Strategic Arms Limitation Talks

John F. Kennedy (AP/Wide World Photos)

JOHN F. KENNEDY   1917–1963

Thirty-fifth President of the United States

Featured Documents
- Inaugural Address (1961)
- Report to the American People on the Soviet Arms Buildup in Cuba (1962)
- Report to the American People on Civil Rights (1963)

Overview

During his thousand days in the White House, John F. Kennedy made a profound and enduring impression on millions of Americans. Kennedy's record of achievement, especially in domestic affairs, was hardly exceptional; his eloquence and style accounted for much of his appeal. Kennedy was only forty-three years old when he took the oath of office, making him the youngest chief executive to be elected in American history. He was handsome, cool, and articulate, qualities that made him particularly effective on television when that electronic medium first became a powerful force in national politics. Kennedy inspired, moved, and motivated so many people because he was remarkably effective at giving expression to the nation's hopes and dreams.

John Fitzgerald Kennedy was born on May 29, 1917, in Brookline, Massachusetts, into a wealthy and politically prominent family. He graduated from Harvard University in 1940 and enlisted in the U.S. Navy the following year. He earned public acclaim for his heroism in August 1943, when a Japanese destroyer rammed the ship he commanded, *PT-109*, and he led the survivors in the weeklong ordeal in the South Pacific before being rescued. He entered politics as a Democrat in 1946 and won election to the U.S. House of Representatives in a Boston-area district. In 1952 Massachusetts voters elected him to the U.S. Senate. Kennedy secured the Democratic nomination for president in 1960, declaring during the campaign that it was time to get the country "moving again" (Giglio, p. 16). He complained that President Dwight D. Eisenhower had let the Soviet Union make dangerous advances in the cold war by launching *Sputnik I*, the world's first artificial satellite, in October 1957 and by gaining an advantage in long-range nuclear missiles. (Kennedy found the latter charge to be inaccurate after he became president.) In November 1960, Kennedy won a narrow victory over Vice President Richard M. Nixon, the Republican nominee.

As president, Kennedy compiled a modest record in domestic affairs. Congress failed to approve most of the measures that were part of the New Frontier, the name he gave to his domestic program. After campaign assurances that he would advance civil rights at a time when racial segregation was common in American life, Kennedy at first was cautious and hesitant but eventually took stronger action. When riots followed civil rights protests in Birmingham, Alabama, Kennedy told the American people on June 11, 1963, that racial justice was "a moral issue" and sent legislation to Congress to bar discrimination in employment and in public accommodations.

Kennedy was most concerned about the cold war and insisted that the United States needed to make more vigorous efforts to contain Soviet expansion and protect U.S. security. After a stormy meeting with the Soviet premier Nikita Khrushchev in Vienna, Austria, in June 1961, he faced a crisis over Berlin. The Soviets built a wall between East and West Berlin to prevent East Germans from fleeing Communist rule. Kennedy faced his most dangerous crisis over Cuba (which was ruled by the Marxist dictator Fidel Castro) when the Soviets sent nuclear missiles to the Caribbean nation. Kennedy imposed a blockade of Cuba in October 1962, and the Cuban missile crisis ended when the Soviets complied with Kennedy's demand to remove the missiles and nuclear warheads. During what would be his final year in office, Kennedy proclaimed that the United States needed to continue to take strong action to meet Communist advances in trouble spots around the world, such as South Vietnam. But he also hoped for an easing of cold war tensions, and he signed a treaty in October 1963 banning the testing of nuclear weapons in the atmosphere, the oceans, and outer space. After serving less than three years in office, Kennedy died of gunshot wounds inflicted during a political trip to Dallas, Texas, on November 22, 1963.

Explanation and Analysis of Documents

Kennedy's presidency was a time of great dreams and grave crises. He was a superb public speaker who inspired the American people during the exhilarating and perilous events of the early 1960s. He expressed soaring hopes for the future most eloquently in the first speech of his presidency, delivered in January 1961. Despite his lofty idealism, Kennedy spent much of his time in office confronting the perils of the cold war and the hard realities of a segregated society undergoing upheaval. He dealt with those difficult issues in reports to the American people on Soviet nuclear missiles in Cuba in October 1962 and on civil rights in June 1963.

Inaugural Address

Kennedy wanted his inaugural address to establish the tone for his presidency. Instead of proposing new initiatives

Time Line

1917 ■ **May 29**
John F. Kennedy is born in Brookline, Massachusetts.

1940 ■ **June 20**
Kennedy graduates from Harvard University.

1943 ■ **August 2**
PT-109, under Kennedy's command, is rammed by a Japanese destroyer in the South Pacific; Kennedy is rescued a week later.

1947 ■ **January 3**
Kennedy takes his elected seat in the U.S. House of Representatives.

1953 ■ **January 3**
Having defeated Henry Cabot Lodge, Jr., to win election, Kennedy takes his seat as U.S. senator from Massachusetts.

1960 ■ **November 8**
Kennedy defeats Richard M. Nixon in the presidential election.

1961 ■ **January 20**
Kennedy is sworn in as president and delivers his inaugural address.

1962 ■ **October 22**
Kennedy informs the American people in a radio and television address that the Soviet Union has put nuclear missiles in Cuba.

■ **October 28**
The Cuban missile crisis ends when the Soviets agree to remove nuclear missiles and warheads from Cuba.

1963 ■ **April–May**
Civil rights demonstrations in Birmingham, Alabama, produce brutal responses from local police and lead to violence and riots.

or outlining specific policies, he decided to concentrate on broad themes that would inspire the American people and express the national hope of extending freedom both abroad and at home. Kennedy's principal speechwriter, Theodore Sorensen, studied previous inaugural addresses and concluded that the most eloquent were usually the briefest. The speech Kennedy delivered proved to be one of the shortest in history, barely half the average length of previous inaugural addresses. He drew on suggestions from advisers, friends, and journalists, and Sorensen incorporated the various words and ideas into drafts that he kept revising until the day before Kennedy took the oath of office. Kennedy also realized that the speech would be only as good as his delivery. He practiced time and again in the days before the inauguration, even reading passages in the bathtub on the morning before the ceremony. Although Sorensen was responsible for much of the exact wording, the address that Kennedy delivered in the winter sunshine on January 20, 1961, was thoroughly his own.

Beginning with the theme of change amid continuity, Kennedy asserts that his new leadership would seek to preserve enduring American principles. He refers to the presidential oath that the framers of the Constitution had prescribed and to the beliefs that he and his fellow citizens had inherited from the nation's Founders. He then makes a bold declaration that "the torch has been passed to a new generation of Americans" who are proud of their "ancient heritage" and are determined to preserve the "human rights to which this nation has always been committed…at home and around the world." Kennedy believed that a fundamental shift had occurred, as the oldest president to that point in U.S. history was leaving the nation's highest office to the youngest president ever elected. The new generation that Kennedy represented would make a supreme national effort to protect the nation's security and advance American values around the world. Kennedy expresses this idea in one of the most memorable passages of his address, proclaiming that "we shall pay any price, bear any burden, meet any hardship, support any friend, oppose any foe to assure the survival and the success of liberty."

Next concentrating on international affairs, Kennedy gives high priority to developing nations, many of which had not chosen sides in the cold war. In the year that Kennedy was elected president, some seventeen African nations gained independence from European colonial rule. Many of those nations, as well as others in the developing world, endured grinding poverty, widespread hunger, and political turmoil. Kennedy promises to help these nations "break the bonds of mass misery" because it is the right thing to do. Cold war realism as well as altruism shaped his outlook. Kennedy was keenly aware that the third world—developing nations not aligned with either side in the cold war—had become an area of intense competition between the United States and the Soviet Union during the 1950s, and he contended that the Dwight Eisenhower administration had not done enough to counter the growth of Communist influence. In his address, he pledges that his administration would not allow colonial rule to be succeeded by "a far more iron tyranny," by which he means Communist domination. He also promises a new "alliance for progress" with the nations of Latin America. Behind his high-minded rhetoric was a realization that "the chains of poverty" created discontent and hopelessness that allowed Communist revolutionaries to win popular support.

Kennedy combines his determination to prosecute the cold war more vigorously with an appeal to America's cold war adversaries to make new efforts to achieve peace. He calls for agreements to control the growth of existing nuclear arsenals and the spread of "the deadly atom" to more nations. To those who worry that arms accords with the Soviets might weaken U.S. security, Kennedy declares, "Let us never negotiate out of fear. But let us never fear to negotiate." Kennedy looks forward to Soviet-American cooperation in using science not to develop more sophisticated weapons but to eradicate disease and explore space. He hopes that eventually a "world of law" will replace the "balance of power," such that all nations, strong and weak, might live in peace and security. He acknowledges that these great goals will take enormous efforts and considerable time—longer than "one thousand days" or "the life of this Administration" or even "our lifetime on this planet. But let us begin."

At the close of his address, Kennedy challenges the American people to serve and sacrifice in the "long twilight struggle … against the common enemies of man: tyranny, poverty, disease and war itself." He asserts that Americans in the 1960s faced the extraordinary task of "defending freedom in its hour of maximum danger." He hopes that his fellow citizens will welcome this obligation as he does, and he calls on them to meet their civic responsibility in what became the most famous line of his address: "And so, my fellow Americans: ask not what your country can do for you—ask what you can do for your country."

Kennedy earned high praise for an eloquent address that encouraged Americans to think about national challenges rather than individual success and to put the good of their country ahead of personal benefit. His appeal for service to a higher cause inspired many Americans to join the Peace Corps, a new organization created in 1961 to help people in developing nations, or to work at home for social justice by enlisting in the civil rights movement. The speech achieved its main purpose: Kennedy proclaimed his administration's challenge to the American people to make a new commitment to improving their society, bettering the world, and prevailing in the cold war.

◆ Report to the American People on the Soviet Arms Buildup in Cuba

When Kennedy delivered a televised address from the Oval Office on October 22, 1962, to reveal that U.S. intelligence had proof that the Soviets were building nuclear missile bases in Cuba, people around the world experienced one of the most frightening moments of the cold war. Cuba had been an inflammatory cold war concern since Fidel Castro had seized power in early 1959. Castro denounced the United States for supporting the dictator-

Time Line

1963

■ **June 11**
The University of Alabama's first African American students enroll despite the opposition of Governor George Wallace.

■ **June 11**
Kennedy addresses the American people on civil rights.

■ **June 19**
Kennedy sends civil rights legislation to Congress.

■ **October 7**
Kennedy signs the Limited Test Ban Treaty.

■ **November 22**
Kennedy is murdered in Dallas, Texas.

1964

■ **July 2**
President Lyndon B. Johnson signs the Civil Rights Act of 1964.

ship he had overthrown and for exploiting the Cuban economy, and he turned to the Soviet Union for economic and military aid. During his campaign for the presidency, Kennedy criticized the Eisenhower administration for allowing the Soviets to establish a Communist satellite less than a hundred miles from Florida.

What Kennedy did not know was that Eisenhower had authorized the Central Intelligence Agency to train an invasion force of anti-Castro Cubans. The invaders were not ready to take action when Eisenhower left the White House in January 1961, but the agency informed Kennedy that they were prepared in April 1961. The ensuing Bay of Pigs invasion proved a disastrous failure. Republicans began criticizing Kennedy for his inability to keep Soviet influence from increasing in Cuba, and Kennedy then authorized secret new initiatives, including assassination attempts, to get rid of Castro. In May 1962, Khrushchev made a stunning and reckless decision to install nuclear missiles in Cuba to protect Castro from a U.S. invasion and to gain a dramatic advantage in the nuclear arms race. American reconnaissance planes found evidence of the Soviet nuclear arms in October, before the bases were complete. After days of meetings with his advisers, Kennedy decided to make a televised speech to demand that the Soviets withdraw their missiles. More than 100 million Americans—the largest audience for a presidential address to that point in U.S. history—heard Kennedy reveal the news of a grave nuclear crisis.

In the first part of his speech Kennedy explains the kinds of weapons that the Soviets were installing in Cuba

*Photograph taken on October 23, 1962, of a medium-range ballistic missile site
under construction in the San Cristobal area of Cuba* (AP/Wide World Photos)

and the dangers they posed to the United States and other American nations. He uses clear, factual language, avoiding technicalities or complications so that every citizen would understand how these new weapons could inflict "sudden mass destruction" on cities from Canada to Peru. In the nuclear age, nations that waited to ensure their security until they faced actual attack could suffer catastrophic losses from which they might never recover. Kennedy states that he is taking action now, before the Soviets were able to launch their weapons, because "nuclear weapons are so destructive and ballistic missiles are so swift, that any substantially increased possibility of their use or any sudden change in their deployment may well be regarded as a definite threat to peace."

Kennedy frames the crisis as the result of provocative, deceptive, and unjustified Soviet action in violation of the Charter of the United Nations and at odds with the securi-

ty of the United States and other members of the world community. He does not mention the Bay of Pigs invasion, and he dismisses any notion that the missiles serve defensive purposes. He asserts that the crisis at hand is not a conflict with "the captive people of Cuba" or even expressly with the "puppets and agents of an international conspiracy" who rule them. It is rather a Soviet-American confrontation, one in which U.S. policy would be "to regard any nuclear missile launched from Cuba against any nation in the Western Hemisphere as an attack by the Soviet Union on the United States, requiring a full retaliatory response." Even as Kennedy announces a blockade of Cuba—which he calls a "quarantine," since a blockade is an act of war under international law—he declares that American diplomats were prepared to discuss proposals to reduce cold war tensions. Such conversations, however, could not occur "in an atmosphere of intimidation," and so he demands that Khrushchev "move the world back from the abyss of destruction" by withdrawing the nuclear weapons from Cuba.

For the next six days the two nations were "eyeball to eyeball," in the words of Secretary of State Dean Rusk, until the Soviets announced on October 28 that they were dismantling the missile sites (Dallek, p. 562). Kennedy won praise for resolute leadership that produced compliance with U.S. terms without either side's resorting to war. Yet neither the Soviet nor the U.S. government disclosed to the public all the provisions of the agreement that ended the Cuban missile crisis. The president's aides assured Soviet diplomats that the United States would remove nuclear missiles that it had based in Turkey, but it would wait several months to do so and would never acknowledge any secret deal. Kennedy seemed to have won a clear victory, but both sides made concessions to avoid what might have been an unimaginable catastrophe.

◆ **Report to the American People on Civil Rights**

No issue was more important, troubling, or divisive for Americans during the early 1960s than civil rights, the subject of a White House address by Kennedy on June 11, 1963. When Kennedy spoke, racial tensions had been high for months, especially in Alabama. In April and May, Martin Luther King, Jr., had organized peaceful demonstrations in Birmingham to desegregate lunch counters and open job opportunities to African Americans. Local authorities, however, used fire hoses and police dogs against the demonstrators, and the news photographs and film reports shocked many viewers. Kennedy sent Justice Department officials to help negotiate a compromise settlement, but a series of violent incidents threatened the fragile accord. The Alabama governor, George Wallace, inflamed the situation when he announced that he would personally block the admission of two African American students to the University of Alabama, the country's last all-white state institution of higher education. On June 11, as promised, Wallace stood in the "school house" door, before yielding to federal authority and allowing the students to register (Giglio, p. 180).

Aides warned Kennedy that conflicts over civil rights might yet erupt in dozens more cities during the summer, and so the president decided to speak to the American people later that same day about the nation's racial crisis. His intent was to address a problem that was affecting every part of the country and that raised fundamental questions of law, justice, and morality. He read from a text, one that Sorensen had finished only five minutes before the president faced the television camera. Kennedy, however, had spent much of the afternoon discussing what he would say with aides. At times during his address, he spoke extemporaneously, his words reflecting the urgency and conviction he felt. And, indeed, the speech revealed that the president's thinking about civil rights had changed. During his first year in office, Kennedy had made only tepid efforts to eliminate racial barriers, since he feared losing vital support from white southern Democrats. By mid-1963 Kennedy realized that inaction or delay was no longer possible.

Kennedy begins by placing the civil rights movement in the long sweep of American history and explaining that the movement's urgency arises from the discrimination and deprivation that afflicts African Americans in their daily lives. He indicates that he had come to believe that civil rights involved fidelity to basic American principles of decency, fairness, and equality: "One hundred years of delay have passed since President Lincoln freed the slaves, yet their heirs, their grandsons, are not fully free....And this Nation, for all its hopes and all its boasts, will not be fully free until all its citizens are free." Kennedy also connects civil rights to the cold war. He asserts that the United States could not "preach freedom" to other nations if it did not follow its own advice: "Are we to say to the world, and much more importantly, to each other that this is a land of the free except for the Negroes?" He goes on to declare, "The fires of frustration and discord are burning in every city, North and South, where legal remedies are not at hand." Americans faced "a moral crisis" that they could not resolve through "repressive police action" or "token moves or talk."

Kennedy proposes a combination of government and citizen action to ensure that "race has no place in American life or law." He announces that he will send Congress the most ambitious civil rights legislation since the end of Reconstruction in the 1870s, a bill that would end racial segregation "in facilities which are open to the public— hotels, restaurants, theaters, retail stores, and similar establishments," as well as outlaw discrimination in employment. New laws, necessary though they were, would not be enough; Kennedy also calls on his fellow citizens to examine their consciences—as he had his—and to work to make life better for all people in their communities "out of a sense of human decency."

Kennedy's speech was a landmark in the civil rights movement. Never before had a president declared that racial justice was a moral issue. Kennedy did not live, however, to see the passage of the legislation he submitted to Congress. Instead, President Lyndon B. Johnson used his extraordinary political skills to maneuver the legislation through Congress, calling on the public to rally behind it as a memorial to his slain predecessor. On July 2, 1964, Johnson signed the Civil Rights Act of 1964, one of the most important laws enacted in U.S. history.

Impact and Legacy

Americans have remembered Kennedy's presidency as a special time of optimism, achievement, and grand possibilities. Kennedy's untimely death encouraged many people to idealize his memory—to imagine what he might have done if only he had lived longer. Even his limited accomplishments, however, seemed to exceed those of his immediate successors. In the years after Kennedy's death, Americans experienced the nightmares of Vietnam, Watergate, economic turmoil, and violent explosions in inner cities. Their trust in government plummeted; their alienation and disil-

"Let the word go forth from this time and place, to friend and foe alike, that the torch has been passed to a new generation of Americans—born in this century, tempered by war, disciplined by a hard and bitter peace, proud of our ancient heritage—and unwilling to witness or permit the slow undoing of those human rights to which this nation has always been committed, and to which we are committed today at home and around the world."

(Inaugural Address)

"Let every nation know, whether it wishes us well or ill, that we shall pay any price, bear any burden, meet any hardship, support any friend, oppose any foe to assure the survival and the success of liberty."

(Inaugural Address)

"And so, my fellow Americans: ask not what your country can do for you— ask what you can do for your country."

(Inaugural Address)

"Neither the United States of America nor the world community of nations can tolerate deliberate deception and offensive threats on the part of any nation, large or small. We no longer live in a world where only the actual firing of weapons represents a sufficient challenge to a nation's security to constitute maximum peril. Nuclear weapons are so destructive and ballistic missiles are so swift, that any substantially increased possibility of their use or any sudden change in their deployment may well be regarded as a definite threat to peace."

(Report to the American People on the Soviet Arms Buildup in Cuba)

"It shall be the policy of this Nation to regard any nuclear missile launched from Cuba against any nation in the Western Hemisphere as an attack by the Soviet Union on the United States, requiring a full retaliatory response upon the Soviet Union."

(Report to the American People on the Soviet Arms Buildup in Cuba)

"We are confronted primarily with a moral issue. It is as old as the scriptures and is as clear as the American Constitution."

(Report to the American People on Civil Rights)

lusionment soared. The Kennedy years, whatever their problems, seemed by comparison to be "one brief, shining moment"—in the words from a song in the popular musical *Camelot*, which Kennedy admired—when government worked, leaders were trustworthy, and people were full of hope. Nostalgia and mythmaking do not by themselves explain Kennedy's continuing appeal. Kennedy understood the power of words and images to shape popular thinking. The hope and purpose he expressed so eloquently became his most enduring achievement.

Historians have divided views about Kennedy's presidency. They praise the brilliance of his inaugural address and recognize the power of his rhetoric to shape popular thinking about both domestic and international affairs. Yet they differ over the relationship between his words and deeds. Some see Kennedy as an eloquent but impassioned cold warrior whose zeal contributed to the frightening crises over Cuba and Berlin. Others emphasize his quest to lessen cold war tensions and slow the arms race. Some scholars fault Kennedy for showing more profile than

Questions for Further Study

1. Admirers of Kennedy regard him as a heroic figure who deeply and significantly influenced American history, whereas detractors tend to present him as an unsuccessful leader whose other shortcomings were overcome by his charisma and the image he projected. What do you think? To what extent was he a genuinely great president and to what extent was he merely a handsome, charming man who played well to the new medium of television? Support your position with quotations from the documents included here, paying special attention to Kennedy's use of language.

2. Kennedy's is one of the most famous inaugural addresses in American history. Discuss the background and development of the speech, most notably the emphasis on economy of words encouraged by the speechwriter Theodore Sorensen. Consider the document as it relates to larger currents of American expression—public and personal, verbal and literary, practical and artistic—as well as its impact on subsequent political oratory. (It has been noted, for example, that none other than Richard Nixon, one of his bitterest foes, used words echoing Kennedy's inaugural in his own first inaugural address.) Another fruitful line of inquiry might be to compare and contrast Kennedy's speech and the opening of *A Farewell to Arms* by Ernest Hemingway: Although the two texts might initially seem to bear no relation to each other, both have been cited as models of concision in the use of language.

3. Discuss the events of the Cuban missile crisis. Was Kennedy's handling of it a success or not? On the one hand, he has been credited with averting a third world war in October 1962, which clearly sounds like a success on the face of it. Critics of Kennedy, however, point out the concessions he ended up making to the Soviets and maintain that in so far as the two superpowers really were on the brink of nuclear war, Kennedy's mismanagement had made that situation possible. What do you think? Use quotes from Kennedy to support your position.

4. Examine the development of Kennedy's views on extending full civil rights to African Americans. Whereas he began his career taking a more cautious approach to that issue, by the time of his 1963 report on the subject, he had clearly experienced a significant shift in his views. What factors influenced this change? How did his later positions contrast (or not contrast) with those of his predecessor, Dwight Eisenhower—who likewise used National Guard troops to enforce school desegregation? How significant is Kennedy's use of a moral argument for the extension of full civil rights? How does it signify a radical shift from the statements of earlier presidents on the issue?

5. How would Kennedy have dealt with the greatest crises of later eras, particularly 9/11? In what ways would he have brought his rhetorical abilities to bear in reassuring the nation and calling for action in response to the terrorist attacks? Write the speech he might have given on September 11, 2001, being sure to emulate the style of his inaugural address, his speech on Cuba, and the other documents included here.

courage in dealing with civil rights during most of his presidency. Others credit him for altering his views and declaring that Americans had a fundamental obligation to end racial discrimination. Even if historians disagree about Kennedy's goals and achievements, it is widely recognized that he was remarkably effective at mobilizing popular support for his policies and inspiring Americans to imagine a better future.

Key Sources

Kennedy's personal, congressional, and presidential papers are in the John F. Kennedy Presidential Library and Museum in Boston. His public statements, proclamations, speeches, and news conferences are in *Public Papers of the Presidents of the United States: John F. Kennedy*, 3 vols. (1962–1964); an online version of this collection is accessible on the American Presidency Project Web page of the University of California, Santa Barbara (http://www.presidency.ucsb.edu/ws/). As president, Kennedy secretly recorded meetings with his advisers during 1962–1963, including those that occurred during the Cuban missile crisis. A selection of those tapes, including transcripts, can be found in Philip Zelikow and Ernest May, eds., *John F. Kennedy: The Great Crises*, 3 vols. (2001), part of the Presidential Recordings series.

Further Reading

■ Books

Dallek, Robert. *An Unfinished Life: John F. Kennedy, 1917–1963.* Boston: Little, Brown, 2003.

Fursenko, Aleksandr, and Timothy Naftali. *"One Hell of a Gamble": Khrushchev, Castro, and Kennedy, 1958–1964.* New York: W. W. Norton, 1997.

Giglio, James N. *The Presidency of John F. Kennedy.* 2nd ed. Lawrence: University Press of Kansas, 2006.

———, and Stephen G. Rabe. *Debating the Kennedy Presidency.* Lanham, Md.: Rowman & Littlefield, 2003.

Parmet, Herbert S. *JFK: The Presidency of John F. Kennedy.* New York: Penguin Books, 1984.

Sorensen, Theodore C. *Kennedy.* New York: Harper & Row, 1965.

■ Web Sites

"John Fitzgerald Kennedy (1917–1963)." Miller Center of Public Affairs "American President" Web site.
http://millercenter.org/academic/americanpresident/kennedy.

—Chester Pach

Inaugural Address (1961)

We observe today not a victory of party but a celebration of freedom—symbolizing an end as well as a beginning—signifying renewal as well as change. For I have sworn before you and Almighty God the same solemn oath our forebears prescribed nearly a century and three quarters ago.

The world is very different now. For man holds in his mortal hands the power to abolish all forms of human poverty and all forms of human life. And yet the same revolutionary beliefs for which our forebears fought are still at issue around the globe—the belief that the rights of man come not from the generosity of the state but from the hand of God.

We dare not forget today that we are the heirs of that first revolution. Let the word go forth from this time and place, to friend and foe alike, that the torch has been passed to a new generation of Americans—born in this century, tempered by war, disciplined by a hard and bitter peace, proud of our ancient heritage—and unwilling to witness or permit the slow undoing of those human rights to which this nation has always been committed, and to which we are committed today at home and around the world.

Let every nation know, whether it wishes us well or ill, that we shall pay any price, bear any burden, meet any hardship, support any friend, oppose any foe to assure the survival and the success of liberty.

This much we pledge—and more.

To those old allies whose cultural and spiritual origins we share, we pledge the loyalty of faithful friends. United, there is little we cannot do in a host of cooperative ventures. Divided, there is little we can do—for we dare not meet a powerful challenge at odds and split asunder.

To those new states whom we welcome to the ranks of the free, we pledge our word that one form of colonial control shall not have passed away merely to be replaced by a far more iron tyranny. We shall not always expect to find them supporting our view. But we shall always hope to find them strongly supporting their own freedom—and to remember that, in the past, those who foolishly sought power by riding the back of the tiger ended up inside.

To those peoples in the huts and villages of half the globe struggling to break the bonds of mass misery, we pledge our best efforts to help them help themselves, for whatever period is required—not because the communists may be doing it, not because we seek their votes, but because it is right. If a free society cannot help the many who are poor, it cannot save the few who are rich.

To our sister republics south of our border, we offer a special pledge—to convert our good words into good deeds—in a new alliance for progress—to assist free men and free governments in casting off the chains of poverty. But this peaceful revolution of hope cannot become the prey of hostile powers. Let all our neighbors know that we shall join with them to oppose aggression or subversion anywhere in the Americas. And let every other power know that this Hemisphere intends to remain the master of its own house.

To that world assembly of sovereign states, the United Nations, our last best hope in an age where the instruments of war have far outpaced the instruments of peace, we renew our pledge of support—to prevent it from becoming merely a forum for invective—to strengthen its shield of the new and the weak—and to enlarge the area in which its writ may run.

Finally, to those nations who would make themselves our adversary, we offer not a pledge but a request: that both sides begin anew the quest for peace, before the dark powers of destruction unleashed by science engulf all humanity in planned or accidental self-destruction.

We dare not tempt them with weakness. For only when our arms are sufficient beyond doubt can we be certain beyond doubt that they will never be employed.

But neither can two great and powerful groups of nations take comfort from our present course—both sides overburdened by the cost of modern weapons, both rightly alarmed by the steady spread of the deadly atom, yet both racing to alter that uncertain balance of terror that stays the hand of mankind's final war.

So let us begin anew—remembering on both sides that civility is not a sign of weakness, and sincerity is always subject to proof. Let us never negotiate out of fear. But let us never fear to negotiate.

Let both sides explore what problems unite us instead of belaboring those problems which divide us.

Let both sides, for the first time, formulate serious and precise proposals for the inspection and control of arms—and bring the absolute power to destroy other nations under the absolute control of all nations.

Let both sides seek to invoke the wonders of science instead of its terrors. Together let us explore the stars, conquer the deserts, eradicate disease, tap the ocean depths and encourage the arts and commerce.

Let both sides unite to heed in all corners of the earth the command of Isaiah—to "undo the heavy burdens...(and) let the oppressed go free."

And if a beach-head of cooperation may push back the jungle of suspicion, let both sides join in creating a new endeavor, not a new balance of power, but a new world of law, where the strong are just and the weak secure and the peace preserved.

All this will not be finished in the first one hundred days. Nor will it be finished in the first one thousand days, nor in the life of this Administration, nor even perhaps in our lifetime on this planet. But let us begin.

In your hands, my fellow citizens, more than mine, will rest the final success or failure of our course. Since this country was founded, each generation of Americans has been summoned to give testimony to its national loyalty. The graves of young Americans who answered the call to service surround the globe.

Now the trumpet summons us again—not as a call to bear arms, though arms we need—not as a call to battle, though embattled we are—but a call to bear the burden of a long twilight struggle, year in and year out, "rejoicing in hope, patient in tribulation"—a struggle against the common enemies of man: tyranny, poverty, disease and war itself.

Can we forge against these enemies a grand and global alliance, North and South, East and West, that can assure a more fruitful life for all mankind? Will you join in that historic effort?

In the long history of the world, only a few generations have been granted the role of defending freedom in its hour of maximum danger. I do not shrink from this responsibility—I welcome it. I do not believe that any of us would exchange places with any other people or any other generation. The energy, the faith, the devotion which we bring to this endeavor will light our country and all who serve it—and the glow from that fire can truly light the world.

And so, my fellow Americans: ask not what your country can do for you—ask what you can do for your country.

My fellow citizens of the world: ask not what America will do for you, but what together we can do for the freedom of man.

Finally, whether you are citizens of America or citizens of the world, ask of us here the same high standards of strength and sacrifice which we ask of you. With a good conscience our only sure reward, with history the final judge of our deeds, let us go forth to lead the land we love, asking His blessing and His help, but knowing that here on earth God's work must truly be our own.

Glossary

Isaiah	biblical prophet, author of parts of the book of Isaiah
"rejoicing in hope,..."	famous quotation from Paul's Epistle to the Romans (Romans 12:12)
writ	power, authority, or influence

REPORT TO THE AMERICAN PEOPLE ON THE SOVIET ARMS BUILDUP IN CUBA (1962)

Good evening, my fellow citizens:

This Government, as promised, has maintained the closest surveillance of the Soviet military buildup on the island of Cuba. Within the past week, unmistakable evidence has established the fact that a series of offensive missile sites is now in preparation on that imprisoned island. The purpose of these bases can be none other than to provide a nuclear strike capability against the Western Hemisphere....

The characteristics of these new missile sites indicate two distinct types of installations. Several of them include medium range ballistic missiles, capable of carrying a nuclear warhead for a distance of more than 1,000 nautical miles. Each of these missiles, in short, is capable of striking Washington, D.C., the Panama Canal, Cape Canaveral, Mexico City, or any other city in the southeastern part of the United States, in Central America, or in the Caribbean area.

Additional sites not yet completed appear to be designed for intermediate range ballistic missiles—capable of traveling more than twice as far—and thus capable of striking most of the major cities in the Western Hemisphere, ranging as far north as Hudson Bay, Canada, and as far south as Lima, Peru. In addition, jet bombers, capable of carrying nuclear weapons, are now being uncrated and assembled in Cuba, while the necessary air bases are being prepared.

This urgent transformation of Cuba into an important strategic base—by the presence of these large, long-range, and clearly offensive weapons of sudden mass destruction—constitutes an explicit threat to the peace and security of all the Americas, in flagrant and deliberate defiance of the Rio Pact of 1947, the traditions of this Nation and hemisphere, the joint resolution of the 87th Congress, the Charter of the United Nations, and my own public warnings to the Soviets on September 4 and 13. This action also contradicts the repeated assurances of Soviet spokesmen, both publicly and privately delivered, that the arms buildup in Cuba would retain its original defensive character, and that the Soviet Union had no need or desire to station strategic missiles on the territory of any other nation....

Neither the United States of America nor the world community of nations can tolerate deliberate deception and offensive threats on the part of any nation, large or small. We no longer live in a world where only the actual firing of weapons represents a sufficient challenge to a nation's security to constitute maximum peril. Nuclear weapons are so destructive and ballistic missiles are so swift, that any substantially increased possibility of their use or any sudden change in their deployment may well be regarded as a definite threat to peace....

But this secret, swift, and extraordinary buildup of Communist missiles—in an area well known to have a special and historical relationship to the United States and the nations of the Western Hemisphere, in violation of Soviet assurances, and in defiance of American and hemispheric policy—this sudden, clandestine decision to station strategic weapons for the first time outside of Soviet soil—is a deliberately provocative and unjustified change in the status quo which cannot be accepted by this country, if our courage and our commitments are ever to be trusted again by either friend or foe.

The 1930's taught us a clear lesson: aggressive conduct, if allowed to go unchecked and unchallenged, ultimately leads to war. This nation is opposed to war. We are also true to our word. Our unswerving objective, therefore, must be to prevent the use of these missiles against this or any other country, and to secure their withdrawal or elimination from the Western Hemisphere.

Our policy has been one of patience and restraint, as befits a peaceful and powerful nation, which leads a worldwide alliance. We have been determined not to be diverted from our central concerns by mere irritants and fanatics. But now further action is required—and it is under way; and these actions may only be the beginning. We will not prematurely or unnecessarily risk the costs of worldwide nuclear war in which even the fruits of victory would be ashes in our mouth—but neither will we shrink from that risk at any time it must be faced.

Acting, therefore, in the defense of our own security and of the entire Western Hemisphere, and under the authority entrusted to me by the Constitution as endorsed by the resolution of the Congress, I have directed that the following initial steps be taken immediately:

First: To halt this offensive buildup, a strict quarantine on all offensive military equipment under shipment to Cuba is being initiated. All ships of any kind bound for Cuba from whatever nation or port will, if found to contain cargoes of offensive weapons, be turned back. This quarantine will be extended, if needed, to other types of cargo and carriers. We are not at this time, however, denying the necessities of life as the Soviets attempted to do in their Berlin blockade of 1948.

Second: I have directed the continued and increased close surveillance of Cuba and its military buildup. The foreign ministers of the OAS, in their communiqué of October 6, rejected secrecy on such matters in this hemisphere. Should these offensive military preparations continue, thus increasing the threat to the hemisphere, further action will be justified. I have directed the Armed Forces to prepare for any eventualities; and I trust that in the interest of both the Cuban people and the Soviet technicians at the sites, the hazards to all concerned of continuing this threat will be recognized.

Third: It shall be the policy of this Nation to regard any nuclear missile launched from Cuba against any nation in the Western Hemisphere as an attack by the Soviet Union on the United States, requiring a full retaliatory response upon the Soviet Union....

Sixth: Under the Charter of the United Nations, we are asking tonight that an emergency meeting of the Security Council be convoked without delay to take action against this latest Soviet threat to world peace. Our resolution will call for the prompt dismantling and withdrawal of all offensive weapons in Cuba, under the supervision of U.N. observers, before the quarantine can be lifted.

Seventh and finally: I call upon Chairman Khrushchev to halt and eliminate this clandestine, reckless, and provocative threat to world peace and

to stable relations between our two nations. I call upon him further to abandon this course of world domination, and to join in an historic effort to end the perilous arms race and to transform the history of man. He has an opportunity now to move the world back from the abyss of destruction—by returning to his government's own words that it had no need to station missiles outside its own territory, and withdrawing these weapons from Cuba by refraining from any action which will widen or deepen the present crisis—and then by participating in a search for peaceful and permanent solutions....

But it is difficult to settle or even discuss these problems in an atmosphere of intimidation. That is why this latest Soviet threat—or any other threat which is made either independently or in response to our actions this week—must and will be met with determination. Any hostile move anywhere in the world against the safety and freedom of peoples to whom we are committed—including in particular the brave people of West Berlin—will be met by whatever action is needed.

Finally, I want to say a few words to the captive people of Cuba, to whom this speech is being directly carried by special radio facilities. I speak to you as a friend, as one who knows of your deep attachment to your fatherland, as one who shares your aspirations for liberty and justice for all. And I have watched and the American people have watched with deep sorrow how your nationalist revolution was betrayed—and how your fatherland fell under foreign domination. Now your leaders are no longer Cuban leaders inspired by Cuban ideals. They are puppets and agents of an international conspiracy which has turned Cuba against your friends and

Glossary

ballistic missile	any missile that follows a suborbital flight path and is designed to deliver a warhead
Berlin blockade of 1948	efforts by the Soviet Union and Communist East Germany to cut off and isolate West Berlin, which was surrounded by East Germany
Chairman Khrushchev	Nikita Khrushchev, premier of the Soviet Union from 1958 to 1964
clandestine	secret, hidden
nautical miles	a unit of measurement used at sea; one nautical mile equals 1.1508 miles
OAS	Organization of American States, an agency that promotes cooperation among the nations of North, Central, and South America
Rio Pact of 1947	a defense pact signed by most of the nations of the Western Hemisphere

neighbors in the Americas and turned it into the first Latin American country to become a target for nuclear war—the first Latin American country to have these weapons on its soil.

These new weapons are not in your interest. They contribute nothing to your peace and well-being. They can only undermine it. But this country has no wish to cause you to suffer or to impose any system upon you. We know that your lives and land are being used as pawns by those who deny your freedom....

My fellow citizens: let no one doubt that this is a difficult and dangerous effort on which we have set out. No one can foresee precisely what course it will take or what costs or casualties will be incurred. Many months of sacrifice and self-discipline lie ahead—months in which both our patience and our will will be tested—months in which many threats and denunciations will keep us aware of our dangers. But the greatest danger of all would be to do nothing.

The path we have chosen for the present is full of hazards, as all paths are—but it is the one most consistent with our character and courage as a nation and our commitments around the world. The cost of freedom is always high—but Americans have always paid it. And one path we shall never choose, and that is the path of surrender or submission.

Our goal is not the victory of might, but the vindication of right—not peace at the expense of freedom, but both peace and freedom, here in this hemisphere, and, we hope, around the world.

REPORT TO THE AMERICAN PEOPLE ON CIVIL RIGHTS (1963)

This afternoon, following a series of threats and defiant statements, the presence of Alabama National Guardsmen was required on the University of Alabama to carry out the final and unequivocal order of the United States District Court of the Northern District of Alabama. That order called for the admission of two clearly qualified young Alabama residents who happened to have been born Negro.

That they were admitted peacefully on the campus is due in good measure to the conduct of the students of the University of Alabama, who met their responsibilities in a constructive way.

I hope that every American, regardless of where he lives, will stop and examine his conscience about this and other related incidents. This Nation was founded by men of many nations and backgrounds. It was rounded on the principle that all men are created equal, and that the rights of every man are diminished when the rights of one man are threatened.

Today we are committed to a worldwide struggle to promote and protect the rights of all who wish to be free. And when Americans are sent to Viet-Nam or West Berlin, we do not ask for whites only. It ought to be possible, therefore, for American students of any color to attend any public institution they select without having to be backed up by troops.

It ought to be possible for American consumers of any color to receive equal service in places of public accommodation, such as hotels and restaurants and theaters and retail stores, without being forced to resort to demonstrations in the street, and it ought to be possible for American citizens of any color to register and to vote in a free election without interference or fear of reprisal.

It ought to be possible, in short, for every American to enjoy the privileges of being American without regard to his race or his color. In short, every American ought to have the right to be treated as he would wish to be treated, as one would wish his children to be treated. But this is not the case.

The Negro baby born in America today, regardless of the section of the Nation in which he is born, has about one-half as much chance of completing a high school as a white baby born in the same place on the same day, one-third as much chance of completing college, one-third as much chance of becoming a professional man, twice as much chance of becoming unem-ployed, about one-seventh as much chance of earning $10,000 a year, a life expectancy which is 7 years shorter, and the prospects of earning only half as much.

This is not a sectional issue. Difficulties over segregation and discrimination exist in every city, in every State of the Union, producing in many cities a rising tide of discontent that threatens the public safety. Nor is this a partisan issue. In a time of domestic crisis men of good will and generosity should be able to unite regardless of party or politics. This is not even a legal or legislative issue alone. It is better to settle these matters in the courts than on the streets, and new laws are needed at every level, but law alone cannot make men see right.

We are confronted primarily with a moral issue. It is as old as the scriptures and is as clear as the American Constitution.

The heart of the question is whether all Americans are to be afforded equal rights and equal opportunities, whether we are going to treat our fellow Americans as we want to be treated. If an American, because his skin is dark, cannot eat lunch in a restaurant open to the public, if he cannot send his children to the best public school available, if he cannot vote for the public officials who represent him, if, in short, he cannot enjoy the full and free life which all of us want, then who among us would be content to have the color of his skin changed and stand in his place? Who among us would then be content with the counsels of patience and delay?

One hundred years of delay have passed since President Lincoln freed the slaves, yet their heirs, their grandsons, are not fully free. They are not yet freed from the bonds of injustice. They are not yet freed from social and economic oppression. And this Nation, for all its hopes and all its boasts, will not be fully free until all its citizens are free.

We preach freedom around the world, and we mean it, and we cherish our freedom here at home, but are we to say to the world, and much more importantly, to each other that this is a land of the free except for the Negroes; that we have no second-class citizens except Negroes; that we have no class or caste system, no ghettoes, no master race except with respect to Negroes?

Now the time has come for this Nation to fulfill its promise. The events in Birmingham and elsewhere have so increased the cries for equality that no city or State or legislative body can prudently choose to ignore them.

The fires of frustration and discord are burning in every city, North and South, where legal remedies are not at hand. Redress is sought in the streets, in demonstrations, parades, and protests which create tensions and threaten violence and threaten lives.

We face, therefore, a moral crisis as a country and as a people. It cannot be met by repressive police action. It cannot be left to increased demonstrations in the streets. It cannot be quieted by token moves or talk. It is a time to act in the Congress, in your State and local legislative body and, above all, in all of our daily lives....

Those who do nothing are inviting shame as well as violence. Those who act boldly are recognizing right as well as reality.

Next week I shall ask the Congress of the United States to act, to make a commitment it has not fully made in this century to the proposition that race has no place in American life or law. The Federal judiciary has upheld that proposition in a series of forthright cases. The executive branch has adopted that proposition in the conduct of its affairs, including the employment of Federal personnel, the use of Federal facilities, and the sale of federally financed housing.

But there are other necessary measures which only the Congress can provide, and they must be provided at this session. The old code of equity law under which we live commands for every wrong a remedy, but in too many communities, in too many parts of the country, wrongs are inflicted on Negro citizens and there are no remedies at law. Unless the Congress acts, their only remedy is in the street.

I am, therefore, asking the Congress to enact legislation giving all Americans the right to be served in facilities which are open to the public—hotels, restaurants, theaters, retail stores, and similar establishments.

This seems to me to be an elementary right. Its denial is an arbitrary indignity that no American in 1963 should have to endure, but many do....

I am also asking Congress to authorize the Federal Government to participate more fully in lawsuits designed to end segregation in public education. We have succeeded in persuading many districts to desegregate voluntarily. Dozens have admitted Negroes without violence. Today a Negro is attending a State-supported institution in every one of our 50 States, but the pace is very slow....

Other features will be also requested, including greater protection for the right to vote. But legislation, I repeat, cannot solve this problem alone. It must be solved in the homes of every American in every community across our country.

In this respect, I want to pay tribute to those citizens North and South who have been working in their communities to make life better for all. They are acting not out of a sense of legal duty but out of a sense of human decency.

Like our soldiers and sailors in all parts of the world they are meeting freedom's challenge on the firing line, and I salute them for their honor and their courage.

My fellow Americans, this is a problem which faces us all—in every city of the North as well as the South. Today there are Negroes unemployed, two or three times as many compared to whites, inadequate in education, moving into the large cities, unable to find work, young people particularly out of work without hope, denied equal rights, denied the opportunity to eat at a restaurant or lunch counter or go to a movie theater, denied the right to a decent education, denied almost today the right to attend a State university even though qualified. It seems to me that these are matters which concern us all, not merely Presidents or Congressmen or Governors, but every citizen of the United States.

This is one country. It has become one country because all of us and all the people who came here had an equal chance to develop their talents.

We cannot say to 10 percent of the population that you can't have that right; that your children can't have the chance to develop whatever talents they have; that the only way that they are going to get their rights is to go into the streets and demonstrate. I think we owe them and we owe ourselves a better country than that.

Therefore, I am asking for your help in making it easier for us to move ahead and to provide the kind of equality of treatment which we would want our-

Glossary

Justice Harlan	John Marshall Harlan, associate justice of the U.S. Supreme Court (1877–1911) and a vigorous supporter of racial equality

selves; to give a chance for every child to be educated to the limit of his talents....

We have a right to expect that the Negro community will be responsible, will uphold the law, but they have a right to expect that the law will be fair, that the Constitution will be color blind, as Justice Harlan said at the turn of the century.

This is what we are talking about and this is a matter which concerns this country and what it stands for, and in meeting it I ask the support of all our citizens.

Robert F. Kennedy (Library of Congress)

ROBERT F. KENNEDY 1925–1968

U.S. Attorney General, Senator, and Presidential Candidate

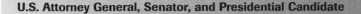

Featured Documents
◆ Tribute to John F. Kennedy at the Democratic National Convention (1964)
◆ Day of Affirmation Address at the University of Cape Town (1966)
◆ Address at the University of California, Berkeley (1966)
◆ Remarks on the Death of Martin Luther King (1968)

Overview

Born in 1925 in Brookline, Massachusetts, Robert F. Kennedy was the seventh of nine children of a close-knit political family. After serving in the military and then graduating from college and law school, Kennedy became campaign manager for his brother John F. Kennedy's successful bid to reach the U.S. Senate in 1952. Throughout the 1950s Robert Kennedy served on a number of Senate committees as legal counsel and made a name for himself in hearings that investigated labor racketeering. In 1960 he managed John's successful presidential campaign, and he served in his brother's administration as attorney general and one of his closest advisers. Robert Kennedy spearheaded the administration's participation in the civil rights movement, especially the drive to integrate universities and protect the rights of blacks in public accommodations. At the same time he continued his pursuit of labor union corruption, targeting the International Brotherhood of Teamsters president James Hoffa.

In the aftermath of President Kennedy's assassination in November 1963, Robert Kennedy resigned from the cabinet and sought election to the U.S. Senate from New York, winning a seat in 1964. Many people expected him to carry on in his brother's footsteps, anticipating that he might one day thereby reclaim the White House. At the same time, they noticed that he had become more philosophical and reflective, prone to engage in battles for the underprivileged in contests his older brother would have shunned. Visits to South American nations and to South Africa reinforced Kennedy's impression that the United States needed to play a leading role in the politics of developing countries and in battling against racism, oppression, and poverty. Somewhat more slowly, he came to question the involvement of the United States in the Vietnam War, believing the American military action to be counterproductive.

After much hesitation, Kennedy decided to challenge Lyndon B. Johnson for the Democratic nomination for president in 1968. When Johnson unexpectedly withdrew, Kennedy found himself competing against the Minnesota senator Eugene McCarthy in a series of primaries, while Vice President Hubert Humphrey prepared to battle Kennedy and McCarthy for the nomination at the party's convention in Chicago that August. Although Kennedy won several primaries, McCarthy bested him elsewhere, and the

two men faced off in California in June. Kennedy claimed victory, but moments after he addressed a crowd celebrating his triumph at the Ambassador Hotel in Los Angeles, he was felled by an assassin's bullet. Kennedy died on June 6. After an emotional funeral ceremony, he was buried at Arlington National Cemetery, near where his brother had been laid to rest nearly five years earlier.

Kennedy's death left many people wondering what might have been. Skeptics continued to portray him as a ruthlessly ambitious politician; supporters believed that they had seen Kennedy evolve into a far more compassionate and thoughtful leader who was committed to fundamental changes in accordance with his principled political beliefs. It is a sign of how he could arouse such deep emotions that it has taken some time for subsequent generations to arrive at a more balanced assessment of the person of Robert Kennedy, his political career, and to the degree to which he might have changed the United States had he lived.

Explanation and Analysis of Documents

Robert Kennedy's speeches indicate how his thought evolved in the years between the death of his brother and his own death in 1968. After celebrating his brother's accomplishments at the Democratic National Convention in August 1964, he then took it upon himself to lead the way in implementing the vision he had so vaguely outlined in that address. Not for another year or so would he be able to explicate his vision of political leadership. A visit to South Africa provided an opportunity for him to give what may remain his most substantial explanation of the interrelationship of generational shift, social progress, and political leadership that was contributing to the growing desire for foundational change in the United States. In that national effort to achieve change, he saw it as the obligation of young Americans, particularly those from privileged backgrounds, to heed the call to public service and take the lead in shaping the American future; he conveyed that message to California college students in 1966. He saw the divisions within the United States as tremendous obstacles to American progress toward the ideals of freedom, liberty, and equality. So it was with a heavy heart born of personal experience as well as political awareness that he addressed a predominantly African American crowd in Indianapolis,

Time Line

1925
- **November 20**
  Robert F. Kennedy is born in Brookline, Massachusetts.

1946
- **February 1**
  Kennedy begins a four-month stint of service in the U.S. navy.

1948
- **June 10**
  Kennedy graduates from Harvard College.

1951
- **June 11**
  Kennedy graduates from the University of Virginia Law School.

1952
- **December**
  Kennedy is appointed to serve on Senator Joseph McCarthy's Permanent Subcommittee on Investigations.

1954
- **March–June**
  During the Army-McCarthy hearings, Kennedy serves as Democratic counsel.

1957
- **February**
  Kennedy begins serving as counsel for the special Senate committee investigating labor racketeering.

1960
- **November 8**
  With Kennedy as his campaign manager, John F. Kennedy wins the presidential election.

1961
- **January 20**
  Kennedy assumes his appointment as attorney general.

1964
- **August 27**
  Kennedy addresses the Democratic National Convention in Atlantic City, New Jersey.

Indiana, on the night of the death of Martin Luther King, Jr., who had provided incomparable leadership during the civil rights movement.

◆ **Tribute to John F. Kennedy at the Democratic National Convention**

Robert Kennedy long labored in the shadow of his brother John. He assisted his brother during various Senate hearings in the 1950s, sometimes taking center stage with his earnest questioning of committee witnesses; he served first as his brother's campaign manager and then as attorney general in his cabinet. With President Kennedy's assassination on November 22, 1963, Robert Kennedy found himself burdened with the prospect of carrying on his slain brother's legacy. Still a crusader on behalf of principle (at least as he understood it), Kennedy now balanced his inclination for confrontation with a determination to mobilize others in favor of change. Having developed a deeper appreciation of civil rights during his tenure as attorney general, he began to expand his concern with helping the impoverished, downtrodden, and disadvantaged. Meanwhile, his stern cold war approach to foreign policy showed signs of giving way to a different appreciation of the place of the United States in the world as a flawed purveyor of democratic change in the name of human freedom and equality. That reorientation led him to reassess several aspects of American foreign policy, most notably the nation's involvement in the Vietnam War.

One milestone in Kennedy's ideological transition was his appearance before the 1964 Democratic National Convention. There had been talk of Kennedy running as vice president on a ticket led by Lyndon B. Johnson, but neither Johnson nor Kennedy desired that arrangement; the two men disliked each other and were wary of each other's politics. Moreover, Kennedy knew that it would be political suicide for him to challenge Johnson for the 1964 presidential nomination. Thus, he ran for the U.S. Senate from New York (where he had spent some of his childhood, although that did not shield him from charges of being a carpetbagger). In speaking before the convention, he was foremost a representative of his deceased brother but also a senatorial candidate in his own right.

Starting slowly and hesitantly, Kennedy thanks the delegates for supporting President Kennedy as a candidate and in office. He struggles with his facts: Thomas Jefferson and James Madison took their trip sometime before 1800, for the Democratic Party was already formed by that time. In retracing the party's history, he does little more than recycle the usual convention verbiage about great Democratic presidents; his effort to ground President Kennedy's legacy in his accomplishments and efforts in office actually fell flat with the delegates. But Robert Kennedy starts hitting his stride when he speaks of "the next generation" making the world "a better place." His quoting of William Shakespeare's *Romeo and Juliet* brought redoubled applause, though some listeners would later link "the garish sun" with Lyndon Johnson, who had a reputation for coarseness.

As Kennedy builds to the climax of what was, after all, a short speech introducing a film about the late president, he reminds everyone that much remains to be done. In quoting Robert Frost's "but I have promises to keep and miles to go before I sleep," Kennedy may well have been implicitly identifying himself as the person who would carry the martyred president's legacy forward.

Here, as in many of his speeches, Kennedy expressly quotes great writers and poets, not necessarily political leaders, to advance his theme. It was only natural on this occasion for Kennedy to quote his brother's remarks as president, but for years to come the younger brother would recite the words of the older brother on many occasions, always taking care to refer to him as President Kennedy. In the fall contest, Robert Kennedy won New York's Senate race, while Lyndon Johnson won election to the presidency in his own right. Both men continued to eye each other as rivals, and it would not take long for Senator Kennedy to question administration policies.

◆ **Day of Affirmation Address at the University of Cape Town**

Robert Kennedy traveled widely across the world. He easily made comparisons between the United States and other countries, not to offer contrasts that would presumably demonstrate the superiority of the United States but to detect and highlight common ground and common concerns. He was one of the first major American politicians to recognize the challenges of the developing world, and he was not always comfortable with the way the United States flexed its muscle in developing countries. In 1965 Kennedy protested President Johnson's decision to intervene with military force in the Dominican Republic; he drew a parallel with the escalation of the American presence in Vietnam, suggesting that he was perhaps now questioning cold war assumptions about the spread of Communism.

In keeping with his concerns with the developing world, Kennedy was among the first American political leaders to take a serious interest in Africa. In June 1966 he paid a visit to South Africa, in large part because he saw parallels between the experiences of the United States and that country regarding race relations. Indeed, South African college students had been inspired by the achievements of the American civil rights movement to take steps against apartheid in their homeland. South Africa's government looked dimly upon Kennedy's visit, blocking members of the media from accompanying him and his wife, declining to meet with him, and finally "banning" the head of the student organization from attending the event at which he spoke. None of that mattered to Kennedy, who met instead with opposition leaders (including the president of the student organization). On June 6 he gave the keynote address during the "Day of Affirmation" ceremonies at the University of Cape Town.

Kennedy notes in his address that the United States and South Africa have much in common, with those commonalities including a troubled history with respect to race relations. As much as Americans could take pride in recent changes, Kennedy reminds the audience that his own

Time Line

1964

■ **November 3**
Kennedy wins a U.S. Senate seat from New York.

1966

■ **June 6**
At the University of Cape Town, in South Africa, Kennedy gives his "Day of Affirmation" speech.

■ **October 22**
Kennedy gives a campaign speech at the University of California, Berkeley.

1968

■ **April 4**
Kennedy addresses a crowd in Indianapolis, Indiana, on the evening of the death of Martin Luther King, Jr.

■ **June 5**
In the course of seeking the Democratic presidential nomination, Kennedy is shot in Los Angeles, California.

■ **June 6**
Kennedy dies from his wounds.

country had a long way to go to meet the promise of its rhetoric of equality. He enumerates several tenets of fundamental importance, including freedom of speech, the accountability of government, and limits on the degree to which government could interfere with basic human rights and freedoms. Such populist notions distinguish democracies from Communist nations, and yet the absence of Communism does not ensure democracy, for regimes of other natures seek to control their populations in ways contrary to democratic principles.

Kennedy asks, then, how freedom can be achieved for those burdened by oppression of any kind. Above all, he argues, people must be willing to honor the principle of human equality and value everyone. Progress toward ideals might well be slow, he admits, and the example provided by the United States might not be suitable to political situations elsewhere in the world. So long as various nations sought to establish the ideals of human freedom, liberty, and equality, they might choose paths suitable to their circumstances and heritage. For the achievement of change, Kennedy looks to the young and to an attitude of youthfulness—"not a time of life but a state of mind." In urging change, Kennedy warns against the beliefs that nothing can be done by any single person, that it may be better to deal with things as they are than to seek to alter them to

James Hoffa, president of the Teamsters Union, points to a paper held by Robert Kennedy, counsel of the Senate committee investigating racketeering. (AP/Wide World Photos)

what we want them to be, that fear might justly deter one from acting, and that the desire for comfort and ease might legitimize the following of a more mundane path.

This speech, which Senator Edward Kennedy quoted in his moving eulogy of his brother, reveals several of Robert Kennedy's traits in public address. He liked to offer arguments in a fairly straightforward, logical fashion, listing his main points. Again, he loved to quote from the classics and other renowned works, not in efforts to talk down to his audience but in attempts to draw them up and interact with them on an intellectual as well as an emotional basis. Finally, he was prone after November 22, 1963, to inject passages from his older brother's speeches, as if to offer assurance that he was still keeping the faith and following in his brother's footsteps.

Kennedy's visit to South Africa drew much attention there as well as in the United States. He gave several more speeches, incorporating remarks about the shooting of James Meredith in Mississippi to remind people that in critical ways the United States and South Africa shared common problems with respect to race. Over the course of his sojourn, when he spoke about race, it was now with a greater appreciation for the injuries racism could inflict and a greater passion about what needed to be done to overcome it.

◆ **Address at the University of California, Berkeley**

By the fall of 1966 Kennedy's political prominence had risen in the popular estimation; he surpassed President Lyndon Johnson in one poll as the preferred choice of Democrats and independents for the 1968 Democratic presidential nomination. The New York senator took to the campaign trail during the 1966 election season on behalf

of Democratic congressional candidates, making one appearance at the University of California, Berkeley, long known for its tradition of student protest and radicalism.

In this speech Kennedy embraces the Berkeley tradition of dissent, asking students to use it to confront the problems of America and the world. Aware that protesters had recently shouted down a speech by the Johnson loyalist and UN ambassador Arthur J. Goldberg, Kennedy tells the students that they must turn the energies unleashed by the spirit of critical dissent to reforming the world around them, communicating that the Goldberg protest was "merely self-indulgence" that "will not have brightened or enriched the life of a single portion of humanity in a single part of the globe." Although the bulk of the speech concerns the status of African Americans in the United States, Kennedy's remarks serve as a model of his call for service in constructive engagement with social and political challenges. He would return to this theme in speech after speech, building upon the call for youth to serve that he had sounded in South Africa.

Kennedy's point is a simple one: With opportunity and privilege comes an obligation to serve others. He highlights that theme to college students who are beneficiaries of much of the best that life has to offer young Americans. Moreover, he believes that young people are well positioned to meet the challenge of being among "those who can blend passion, reason, and courage in a personal commitment to the ideals and great enterprises of American society." Criticism and dissent were necessary but by no means sufficient: "Those who are serious about the future have the obligation to direct those energies and talents toward concrete objectives consistent with the ideas they profess." Young people would bring to that endeavor fresh ideas and new energy.

◆ **Remarks on the Death of Martin Luther King**

Kennedy announced that he was running for president on March 16, 1968. That decision had been a long time in coming. He had weighed the advantages and disadvantages of running against an incumbent president from within his own party as well as the changing political circumstances of 1967 and 1968. The Minnesota senator Eugene McCarthy showed no such hesitation, and his surprisingly strong performance in the New Hampshire primary suggested that Lyndon Johnson was politically vulnerable. That circumstance was due in large part to public perception of the situation in Vietnam following the Tet Offensive, in which the North Vietnamese and Vietcong launched a series of attacks that convinced many Americans that victory was as far off as ever, if obtainable at all.

Only two weeks after Kennedy's announcement, on March 31, 1968, Johnson withdrew from the presidential race. Four days later, fresh from a meeting with the president, Kennedy was campaigning in Indiana. As he left Muncie on a short flight to Indianapolis, he learned that the civil rights leader Martin Luther King, Jr., had been shot in Memphis, Tennessee; when the plane landed, he learned that King was dead. Setting aside warnings that he might be putting his life at risk, Kennedy decided to keep his commitment to appear at a rally at an African American community center. When he arrived, he saw at once that few people in the crowd of thousands were aware of King's assassination. Ignoring the rain drizzling down as darkness approached, Kennedy mounted the platform, asked the crowd to put down their signs, and then relayed the "sad news" of King's death. From the crowd there were anguished cries.

Reminding the crowd that King had "dedicated his life to love and to justice" for all, Kennedy tells those gathered before him that "it's perhaps well to ask what kind of a nation we are and what direction we want to move in." He understood that blacks might well be angry at what had happened and might even want revenge—but those sentiments would lead the nation toward "greater polarization," with whites and blacks battling, "filled with hatred toward one another." Americans could also, to the contrary, choose to learn from what had happened "and replace that violence...with an effort to understand, compassion and love." As the brother of a victim of an assassin's bullet, he reminds his listeners that he knows how some people feel; at this point in time, however, it is more important for American to move beyond division and hatred toward "love and wisdom, and compassion toward one another, and a feeling of justice toward those who still suffer within our country, whether they be white or whether they be black." Over the next several days, riots broke out in many American cities, as people responded with anger to King's death. But all remained quiet in Indianapolis.

Impact and Legacy

Although one can debate exactly how much the assassination of John F. Kennedy affected the life of Robert F. Kennedy, many observers at the time and later argued that his brother's death initiated a period of introspection and reflection from which Robert Kennedy emerged with a deeper and more profound sense of mission in public life. Even as he dealt somewhat uneasily with having to serve as the inheritor of his slain brother's legacy, he knew that he could use President Kennedy's image to advance causes in which he deeply believed.

The Robert Kennedy of the 1950s believed in rooting out, confronting, and defeating evil. Sometime during his tenure as attorney general he began to rethink the way he approached this task. His later speeches demonstrate that he wrestled with the need to persuade other people to help him in a crusade to change the world as it moved forward. That process proved ever changing and sometimes problematic, for Kennedy's actions did not always match his words. In several cases it took him some time to assume the positions with which he would later be associated in the popular mind, including his support for civil rights, his attack on poverty, and his reassessment of the place of the United States in the world, especially regarding its Vietnam policy.

Kennedy inspired people during the final years of his political career, but a dispassionate assessment remains a difficult task, precisely because in the wake of his untimely death one can only speculate about what might have been. Thus, a key component of Robert Kennedy's legacy is that Americans continue to reshape their memory of him as they reflect on what he did accomplish as well as on what he ultimately wished to accomplish. Many look toward the future with what they believe would have been Kennedy's own values, beliefs, and spirit, while others question whether this remains an exercise in fanciful historical projection.

Key Sources

Robert F. Kennedy's papers are housed at the John F. Kennedy Presidential Library in Boston, Massachusetts. This extensive collection, covering his entire life, is partially open to researchers. There is substantial material covering his career as legal counsel for Senate committees in the 1950s, his work managing his brother John's campaigns, his tenure as attorney general, his service in the U.S. Senate, and his own presidential candidacy as well as a sizable collection of condolence mail and tributes which remains closed. The library provides a number of Kennedy's speeches online (http://www.jfklibrary.org/Historical+Resources/Archives/Reference+Desk/Speeches/Speeches+of+Robert+F.+Kennedy.htm). *Robert Kennedy, in His Own Words: The Unpublished Recollections of the Kennedy Years* (1988), edited by Edwin O. Guthman and Jeffrey Shulman, contains a selection of interviews with Kennedy. George Plimpton edited interviews conducted by Jean Stein for *American Journey: The Times of Robert Kennedy* (1970), a chatty and admiring oral history offered by Kennedy's associates. Edwin O. Guthman and C. Richard Allen edited *RFK: Collected Speeches* (1993). Kennedy's own writings include *The Enemy Within* (1960), the story of his battle, during his years as legal counsel in the Senate, against James "Jimmy" Hoffa; *The Pursuit of Justice* (1964), which offers an early vision of the interplay between politics and society; *To Seek a Newer World* (1967), which brings together his speeches as U.S. senator; and, most famously, *Thirteen Days: A Memoir of the Cuban Missile Crisis* (1969).

Further Reading

■ Books

Hilty, James W. *Robert Kennedy: Brother Protector*. Philadelphia: Temple University Press, 1997.

Palermo, Joseph A. *In His Own Right: The Political Odyssey of Senator Robert F. Kennedy*. New York: Columbia University Press, 2001.

———. *Robert F. Kennedy and the Death of American Idealism*. New York: Pearson Longman, 2008.

Schlesinger, Arthur M., Jr. *Robert Kennedy and His Times*. New York: Ballantine, 1978.

"When I think of President Kennedy, I think of what Shakespeare said in Romeo and Juliet: 'When he shall die take him and cut him out into stars and he shall make the face of heaven so fine that all the world will be in love with night and pay no worship to the garish sun.'"

(Tribute to John F. Kennedy at the Democratic National Convention)

"We must recognize the full human equality of all of our people before God, before the law, and in the councils of government."

(Day of Affirmation Address at the University of Cape Town)

"It is from numberless diverse acts of courage and belief that human history is shaped. Each time a man stands up for an ideal, or acts to improve the lot of others, or strikes out against injustice, he sends forth a tiny ripple of hope, and crossing each other from a million different centers of energy and daring those ripples build a current which can sweep down the mightiest walls of oppression and resistance."

(Day of Affirmation Address at the University of Cape Town)

"The future does not belong to those who are content with today, apathetic toward common problems and their fellow man alike, timid and fearful in the face of new ideas and bold projects. Rather it will belong to those who can blend passion, reason, and courage in a personal commitment to the ideals and great enterprises of American society. It will belong to those who see that wisdom can only emerge from the clash of contending views, the passionate expression of deep and hostile beliefs."

(Address at the University of California, Berkeley)

"What we need in the United States is not division; what we need in the United States is not hatred; what we need in the United States is not violence and lawlessness, but is love and wisdom, and compassion toward one another, and a feeling of justice toward those who still suffer within our country, whether they be white or whether they be black."

(Remarks on the Death of Martin Luther King)

Steel, Ronald. *In Love with Night: The American Romance with Robert Kennedy*. New York: Simon & Schuster, 2000.

Thomas, Evan. *Robert Kennedy: His Life*. New York: Simon & Schuster, 2000.

—Brooks D. Simpson

Questions for Further Study

1. What differences do you see between the 1964 tribute to John F. Kennedy and the 1966 speeches included here? How eloquent and forceful does Kennedy seem at the Democratic National Convention compared with his tone in the addresses in Cape Town and Berkeley? Which do you regard as the weakest of these speeches and which the strongest? Why? Is the difference only a matter of wording and use of language, or is it tied to other changes in Kennedy that took place during those years?

2. Although the life and political career of Robert F. Kennedy was even shorter than that of his brother John, he went through a number of phases as a political thinker and leader. Whereas he worked for the extreme right-wing senator Joseph McCarthy in the mid-1950s, the mid-1960s found him shifting to the farther reaches of the Democratic Party's liberal wing. What events brought about these changes? What were the pivotal moments in his career as they related to his overall view of the American political framework? To what degree did he really change and to what degree were his later views consistent with his earlier ones? How sincere was Kennedy about his ideals, and to what degree was he presenting an image? How might his views have evolved if he had lived long enough to gain some historical perspective on the events of the 1960s?

3. Examine Kennedy's University of Cape Town address for what it says about the speaker and the world he envisioned. From his comments on the role of individuals in the opening paragraph to his vision of the world's future presented near the middle to his warnings at the end, trace the outline of Bobby Kennedy's universe as displayed in this speech. Discuss the people and events he mentions in the second half of the speech, which bristles with historical references, and consider what they meant to Kennedy and why he included them in his speech.

4. In hindsight, Kennedy is often viewed as working hand in hand with the student activists of the 1960s, but this simplistic portrayal does not bear up to scrutiny. With his clean-cut looks, his traditional family life, and his role as a political figure working within the political system, Kennedy must have seemed like a "square" to the student radicals of the time. What does Kennedy's Berkeley speech say about the differences between him and the emerging movements of hippies, free-speech activists, and other opponents of the "establishment"? What, in his view, are the strongest and weakest aspects of the emerging student movements?

5. Write a "behind the scenes" report on Kennedy's speech in Indianapolis following the assassination of the Reverend Martin Luther King, Jr., on April 4, 1968. As noted in the overview, it was a drizzly night with darkness falling as Kennedy began to speak, relaying terrible news of which few people in the audience were aware. What are some of the most emotionally compelling aspects of this scene, in your opinion? What sorts of thoughts were going through Kennedy's mind as he spoke, and what do you think were the reactions of his listeners? Go beyond obvious points, such as the fact that people were sad King had been shot, and genuinely try to see the moment through the eyes of people who were there.

TRIBUTE TO JOHN F. KENNEDY AT THE DEMOCRATIC NATIONAL CONVENTION (1964)

I first want to thank all of you delegates to the Democratic National Convention and the supporters of the Democratic Party for all that you did for President John F. Kennedy.

I want to express my appreciation to you for the efforts that you made on his behalf at the convention four years ago, the efforts that you made on his behalf for his election in November of 1960, and perhaps most importantly, the encouragement and the strength that you gave him after he was elected President of the United States.

I know that it was a source of the greatest strength to him to know that there were thousands of people all over the United States who were together with him, dedicated to certain principles and to certain ideals.

No matter what talent an individual possesses, what energy he might have, no matter how much integrity and how much honesty…, if he is by himself, and particularly a political figure, he can accomplish very little. But if he is sustained, as President Kennedy was, by the Democratic Party all over the United States, dedicated to the same things that he was attempting to accomplish, he can accomplish a great deal.

No one knew that more than President John F. Kennedy. He used to take great pride in telling of the trip that Thomas Jefferson and James Madison made up the Hudson River in 1800 on a botanical expedition searching for butterflies; that they ended up down in New York City and that they formed the Democratic Party.

He took great pride in the fact that the Democratic Party was the oldest political Party in the world, and he knew that this linkage of Madison and Jefferson with the leaders in New York combined the North and South, and combined the industrial areas of the country with the rural farms and that this combination was always dedicated to progress and all of our Presidents have been dedicated to progress.

He thought of Thomas Jefferson in the Louisiana Purchase, and also when Jefferson realized that the United States could not remain on the Eastern Seaboard and sent Lewis and Clark to the West Coast; of Andrew Jackson; of Woodrow Wilson; of Franklin Roosevelt who saved our citizens who were in great despair because of the financial crisis; of Harry Truman who not only spoke but acted for freedom.

So, when he became President he not only had his own principles and his own ideals but he had the strength of the Democratic Party. As President he wanted to do something for the mentally ill and the mentally retarded; for those who were not covered by Social Security; for those who were not receiving an adequate minimum wage; for those who did not have adequate housing; for our elderly people who had difficulty paying their medical bills; for our fellow citizens who are not white and who had difficulty living in this society. To all this he dedicated himself.

But he realized also that in order for us to make progress here at home, that we had to be strong overseas, that our military strength had to be strong. He said one time, "Only when our arms are sufficient, without doubt, can we be certain, without doubt, that they will never have to be employed." So when we had the crisis with the Soviet Union and the Communist Bloc in October of 1962, the Soviet Union withdrew their missiles and bombers from Cuba.

Even beyond that, his idea really was that this country, that this world, should be a better place when we turned it over to the next generation than when we inherited it from the last generation. That is why—with all of the other efforts that he made—the Test Ban Treaty, which was done with Averell Harriman, was so important to him.

And that's why he made such an effort and was committed to the young people not only of the United States but to the young people of the world. And in all of these efforts you were there all of you.

When there were difficulties, you sustained him.

When there were periods of crisis, you stood beside him. When there were periods of happiness, you laughed with him. And when there were periods of sorrow, you comforted him. I realize that as individuals we can't just look back, that we must look forward. When I think of President Kennedy, I think of what Shakespeare said in Romeo and Juliet:

When he shall die take him and cut him out into stars and he shall make the face of heaven so fine that all the world will be in love with night and pay no worship to the garish sun.

I realize that as individuals, and even more important, as a political party and as a country, we can't just look to the past, we must look to the future.

So I join with you in realizing that what started four years ago—what everyone here started four years ago—that is to be sustained; that is to be continued.

The same effort and the same energy and the same dedication that was given to President John F. Kennedy must be given to President Lyndon Johnson and Hubert Humphrey.

If we make that evident, it will not only be for the benefit of the Democratic Party, but, far more important, it will be for the benefit of this whole country.

When we look at this film we must think that President Kennedy once said:

We have the capacity to make this the best generation in the history of mankind, or make it the last.

If we do our duty, if we meet our responsibilities and our obligations, not just as Democrats, but as American citizens in our local cities and towns and farms and our states and in the country as a whole, then this generation of Americans is going to be the best generation in the history of mankind.

He often quoted from Robert Frost—and said it applied to himself—but we could apply it to the Democratic Party and to all of us as individuals:

The woods are lovely, dark and deep, but I have promises to keep and miles to go before I sleep, and miles to go before I sleep.

Glossary

Averell Harriman	W. Averell Harriman, twentieth-century U.S. statesman
Hubert Humphrey	U.S. senator, later vice president under President Lyndon Johnson
Lewis and Clark	Meriwether Lewis and William Clark, who explored the American West (1803–1806) under President Thomas Jefferson's direction
Louisiana Purchase	purchase of some 829,000 square miles of land from France in 1803, doubling the size of the United States
"Only when our arms are sufficient…"	quotation from John F. Kennedy's inaugural address
Robert Frost	American poet, author of the poem "Stopping by Woods on a Snowy Evening," from which the quotation is taken
"We have the capacity…"	quotation from speech to the United Nations in 1963

DAY OF AFFIRMATION ADDRESS AT THE UNIVERSITY OF CAPE TOWN (1966)

This is a Day of Affirmation, a celebration of liberty. We stand here in the name of freedom. At the heart of that Western freedom and democracy is the belief that the individual man, the child of God, is the touchstone of value, and all society, groups, the state, exist for his benefit. Therefore the enlargement of liberty for individual human beings must be the supreme goal and the abiding practice of any Western society....

Many nations have set forth their own definitions and declarations of these principles. And there have often been wide and tragic gaps between promise and performance, ideal and reality. Yet the great ideals have constantly recalled us to our duties. And—with painful slowness—we have extended and enlarged the meaning and the practice of freedom for all our people.

For two centuries, my own country has struggled to overcome the self-imposed handicap of prejudice and discrimination based on nationality, social class, or race-discrimination profoundly repugnant to the theory and command of our Constitution. Even as my father grew up in Boston, signs told him that No Irish Need Apply. Two generations later President Kennedy became the first Catholic to head the nation; but how many men of ability had, before 1961, been denied the opportunity to contribute to the nation's progress because they were Catholic, or of Irish extraction? How many sons of Italian or Jewish or Polish parents slumbered in slums—untaught, unlearned, their potential lost forever to the nation and human race? Even today, what price will we pay before we have assured full opportunity to millions of Negro Americans?...

So the road toward equality of freedom is not easy, and great cost and danger march alongside us. We are committed to peaceful and nonviolent change, and that is important for all to understand though all change is unsettling. Still, even in the turbulence of protest and struggle is greater hope for the future, as men learn to claim and achieve for themselves the rights formerly petitioned from others.

And most important of all, all the panoply of government power has been committed to the goal of equality before the law, as we are now committing ourselves to the achievement of equal opportunity in fact.

We must recognize the full human equality of all of our people before God, before the law, and in the councils of government. We must do this, not because it is economically advantageous, although it is; not because the laws of God command it, although they do; not because people in other lands wish it so. We must do it for the single and fundamental reason that it is the right thing to do.

We recognize that there are problems and obstacles before the fulfillment of these ideals in the United States, as we recognize that other nations, in Latin America and Asia and Africa, have their own political, economic, and social problems, their unique barriers to the elimination of injustices.

In sum, there is concern that change will submerge the rights of a minority, particularly where the minority is of a different race from the majority. We in the United States believe in the protection of minorities; we recognize the contributions they can make and the leadership they can provide; and we do not believe that any people—whether minority, majority, or individual human beings—are "expendable" in the cause of theory or policy. We recognize also that justice between men and nations is imperfect, and that humanity sometimes progresses slowly.

All do not develop in the same manner, or at the same pace. Nations, like men, often march to the beat of different drummers, and the precise solutions of the United States can neither be dictated nor transplanted to others. What is important is that all nations must march toward increasing freedom; toward justice for all; toward a society strong and flexible enough to meet the demands of all its own people, and a world of immense and dizzying change....

It is these qualities which make of youth today the only true international community. More than this I think that we could agree on what kind of a world we would all want to build. It would be a world of independent nations, moving toward international community, each of which protected and respected the basic human freedoms. It would be a world which demanded of each government that it accept its responsibility to insure social justice. It would be a world of constantly accelerating economic progress—not material welfare as an end in itself, but as a means to liberate the capacity of every human being to pursue his talents and to pursue his hopes. It would, in short, be a world that we would be proud to have built....

Our answer is the world's hope; it is to rely on youth. The cruelties and obstacles of this swiftly changing planet will not yield to obsolete dogmas and outworn slogans. It cannot be moved by those who cling to a present which is already dying, who prefer the illusion of security to the excitement and danger which comes with even the most peaceful progress.

This world demands the qualities of youth; not a time of life but a state of mind, a temper of the will, a quality of the imagination, a predominance of courage over timidity, of the appetite for adventure over the love of ease. It is a revolutionary world we live in, and thus, as I have said in Latin America and Asia, in Europe and in the United States, it is young people who must take the lead. Thus you, and your young compatriots everywhere, have had thrust upon you a greater burden of responsibility than any generation that has ever lived.

"There is," said an Italian philosopher, "nothing more difficult to take in hand, more perilous to conduct, or more uncertain in its success than to take the lead in the introduction of a new order of things." Yet this is the measure of the task of your generation, and the road is strewn with many dangers.

First, is the danger of futility: the belief there is nothing one man or one woman can do against the enormous array of the world's ills—against misery and ignorance, injustice and violence. Yet many of the world's greatest movements, of thought and action, have flowed from the work of a single man. A young monk began the Protestant Reformation, a young general extended an empire from Macedonia to the borders of the earth, and a young woman reclaimed the territory of France. It was a young Italian explorer who discovered the New World, and the thirty-two-year-old Thomas Jefferson who proclaimed that all men are created equal.

"Give me a place to stand," said Archimedes, "and I will move the world." These men moved the world, and so can we all. Few will have the greatness to bend history itself, but each of us can work to change a small portion of events, and in the total of all those acts will be written the history of this generation. Thousands of Peace Corps volunteers are making a difference in isolated villages and city slums in dozens of countries. Thousands of unknown men and women in Europe resisted the occupation of the Nazis and many died, but all added to the ultimate strength and freedom of their countries. It is from numberless diverse acts of courage and belief that human history is shaped. Each time a man stands up for an ideal, or acts to improve the lot of others, or strikes out against injustice, he sends forth a tiny rip-ple of hope, and crossing each other from a million different centers of energy and daring those ripples build a current which can sweep down the mightiest walls of oppression and resistance.

"If Athens shall appear great to you," said Pericles, "consider then that her glories were purchased by valiant men, and by men who learned their duty." That is the source of all greatness in all societies, and it is the key to progress in our time.

The second danger is that of expediency; of those who say that hopes and beliefs must bend before immediate necessities. Of course, if we would act effectively we must deal with the world as it is. We must get things done. But if there was one thing President Kennedy stood for that touched the most profound feelings of young people around the world, it was the belief that idealism, high aspirations, and deep convictions are not incompatible with the most practical and efficient of programs—that there is no basic inconsistency between ideals and realistic possibilities, no separation between the deepest desires of heart and of mind and the rational application of human effort to human problems. It is not realistic or hardheaded to solve problems and take action unguided by ultimate moral aims and values, although we all know some who claim that it is so. In my judgment, it is thoughtless folly. For it ignores the realities of human faith and of passion and of belief—forces ultimately more powerful than all of the calculations of our economists or of our generals. Of course to adhere to standards, to idealism, to vision in the face of immediate dangers takes great courage and takes self-confidence. But we also know that only those who dare to fail greatly can ever achieve greatly.

It is this new idealism which is also, I believe, the common heritage of a generation which has learned that while efficiency can lead to the camps at Auschwitz, or the streets of Budapest, only the ideals of humanity and love can climb the hills of the Acropolis.

A third danger is timidity. Few men are willing to brave the disapproval of their fellows, the censure of their colleagues, the wrath of their society. Moral courage is a rarer commodity than bravery in battle or great intelligence. Yet it is the one essential, vital quality of those who seek to change a world which yields most painfully to change. Aristotle tells us that "At the Olympic games it is not the finest and the strongest men who are crowned, but they who enter the lists.... So too in the life of the honorable and the good it is they who act rightly who win the prize." I believe that in this generation those with the courage to enter the moral conflict will find themselves with companions in every corner of the world.

For the fortunate among us, the fourth danger is comfort, the temptation to follow the easy and familiar paths of personal ambition and financial success so grandly spread before those who have the privilege of education. But that is not the road history has marked out for us. There is a Chinese curse which says, "May he live in interesting times." Like it or not we live in interesting times. They are times of danger and uncertainty; but they are also more open to the creative energy of men than any other time in history. And everyone here will ultimately be judged—will ultimately judge himself—on the effort he has contributed to building a new world society and the extent to which his ideals and goals have shaped that effort.

Glossary

Acropolis	a citadel in ancient Athens, Greece
Archimedes	Greek philosopher of the third century BCE
Aristotle	Greek philosopher of the fourth century BCE
Budapest	Hungarian city, scene in 1956 of a rebellion, supressed by Soviet troops, against the country's Communist government
camps at Auschwitz	Nazi concentration camp in Poland during World War II
Italian philosopher	Niccolò Machiavelli (1469–1527), author of *The Prince and Other Discourses*, the source of the quotation
march to the beat of different drummers	an allusion to *Walden* by the nineteenth-century American author Henry David Thoreau: "If a man does not keep pace with his companions, perhaps it is because he hears a different drummer. Let him step to the music which he hears, however measured or far away."
No Irish Need Apply	a sign commonly placed in the window of a business looking to hire employees in the nineteenth and early twentieth centuries
Pericles	Greek statesman and general of the fifth century BCE
touchstone	standard, basis for comparison
young general	Alexander the Great (356–323 BCE)
young Italian explorer	Christopher Columbus (1451–1506)
young monk	Martin Luther (1483–1546)
young woman	Joan of Arc (1412–1431)

ADDRESS AT THE UNIVERSITY OF CALIFORNIA, BERKELEY (1966)

The future does not belong to those who are content with today, apathetic toward common problems and their fellow man alike, timid and fearful in the face of new ideas and bold projects. Rather it will belong to those who can blend passion, reason, and courage in a personal commitment to the ideals and great enterprises of American society. It will belong to those who see that wisdom can only emerge from the clash of contending views, the passionate expression of deep and hostile beliefs. Plato said: "A life without criticism is not worth living."

This is the seminal spirit of American democracy. It is this spirit which can be found among many of you. It is this which is the hope of our nation.

For it is not enough to allow dissent. We must demand it. For there is much to dissent from.

We dissent from the fact that millions are trapped in poverty while the nation grows rich.

We dissent from the conditions and hatreds which deny a full life to our fellow citizens because of the color of their skin.

We dissent from the monstrous absurdity of a world where nations stand poised to destroy one another, and men must kill their fellow men.

We dissent from the sight of most of mankind living in poverty, stricken by disease, threatened by hunger, and doomed to an early death after a life of unremitting labor.

We dissent from cities which blunt our senses and turn the ordinary acts of daily life into a painful struggle.

We dissent from the willful, heedless destruction of natural pleasure and beauty.

We dissent from all those structures—of technology and of society itself—which strip from the individual the dignity and warmth of sharing in the common tasks of his community and his country.

These are among the objects of our dissent. Yet we must, as thinking men, distinguish between the right of dissent and the way we choose to exercise that right. It is not enough to justify or explain our actions by the fact that they are legal or constitutionally protected. The Constitution protects wisdom and ignorance, compassion and selfishness alike. But that dissent which consists simply of sporadic and dramatic acts sustained by neither continuing labor or research—that dissent which seeks to demolish while lacking both the desire and direction for rebuilding, that dissent which contemptuously or out of laziness, casts aside the practical weapons and instruments of change and progress—that kind of dissent is merely self-indulgence. It is satisfying, perhaps to those who make it.

But it will not solve the problems of our society. It will not assist those seriously engaged in the difficult and frustrating work of the nation. And, when it is all over, it will not have brightened or enriched the life of a single portion of humanity in a single part of the globe.

All of us have the right to dissipate our energies and talent as we desire. But those who are serious about the future have the obligation to direct those energies and talents toward concrete objectives consistent with the ideals they profess. From those of you who take that course will come the fresh ideas and leadership, which are the compelling needs of America....

This is one of the many crossroads at which American life now stands. In the world and at home, you have the opportunity and the responsibility to help make the choices which will determine the greatness of this nation. You are a generation which is coming of age at one of the rarest moments in history—a time when all around us the old order of things is crumbling and a new world society is painfully struggling to take shape. If you shrink from this struggle, and these many difficulties, you will betray the trust which your own position forces upon you.

You live in the most privileged nation on earth. You are the most privileged citizens of that privileged nation; for you have been given the opportunity to study and learn, to take your place among the tiny

Glossary

Plato	Greek philosopher of the fifth to fourth centuries BCE

minority of the world's educated men. By coming to this school you have been lifted onto a tiny, sunlit island while all around you lies an ocean of human misery, injustice, violence, and fear. You can use your enormous privilege and opportunity to seek purely private pleasure and gain. But history will judge you, and, as the years pass, you will ultimately judge yourself, on the extent to which you have used your gifts to lighten and enrich the lives of your fellow man. In your hands, not with presidents or leaders, is the future of your world and the fulfillment to the best qualities of your own spirit.

REMARKS ON THE DEATH OF MARTIN LUTHER KING (1968)

I have some very sad news for all of you, and I think sad news for all of our fellow citizens, and people who love peace all over the world, and that is that Martin Luther King was shot and was killed tonight in Memphis, Tennessee.

Martin Luther King dedicated his life to love and to justice between fellow human beings. He died in the cause of that effort. In this difficult day, in this difficult time for the United States, it's perhaps well to ask what kind of a nation we are and what direction we want to move in.

For those of you who are black—considering the evidence evidently is that there were white people who were responsible—you can be filled with bitterness, and with hatred, and a desire for revenge.

We can move in that direction as a country, in greater polarization—black people amongst blacks, and white amongst whites, filled with hatred toward one another. Or we can make an effort, as Martin Luther King did, to understand and to comprehend, and replace that violence, that stain of bloodshed that has spread across our land, with an effort to understand, compassion and love.

For those of you who are black and are tempted to be filled with hatred and mistrust of the injustice of such an act, against all white people, I would only say that I can also feel in my own heart the same kind of feeling. I had a member of my family killed, but he was killed by a white man.

But we have to make an effort in the United States, we have to make an effort to understand, to get beyond these rather difficult times.

My favorite poet was Aeschylus. He once wrote: "Even in our sleep, pain which cannot forget falls drop by drop upon the heart, until, in our own despair, against our will, comes wisdom through the awful grace of God."

What we need in the United States is not division; what we need in the United States is not hatred; what we need in the United States is not violence and lawlessness, but is love and wisdom, and compassion toward one another, and a feeling of justice toward those who still suffer within our country, whether they be white or whether they be black.

So I ask you tonight to return home, to say a prayer for the family of Martin Luther King, … but more importantly to say a prayer for our own country, which all of us love—a prayer for understanding and that compassion of which I spoke. We can do well in this country. We will have difficult times. We've had difficult times in the past. And we will have difficult times in the future. It is not the end of violence; it is not the end of lawlessness; and it's not the end of disorder.

But the vast majority of white people and the vast majority of black people in this country want to live together, want to improve the quality of our life, and want justice for all human beings that abide in our land.

Let us dedicate ourselves to what the Greeks wrote so many years ago: to tame the savageness of man and make gentle the life of this world.

Let us dedicate ourselves to that, and say a prayer for our country and for our people.

Glossary

Aeschylus	Greek poet and playwright (ca. 525–456 BCE), author of the play *Agamemnon*, from which the quotation is taken

Martin Luther King, Jr. (AP/Wide World Photos)

Civil Rights Leader

Featured Documents
- "Letter from a Birmingham Jail" (1963)
- "I Have a Dream" Speech (1963)
- Speech in Opposition to the Vietnam War (1967)

Overview

Martin Luther King, Jr., was the eloquent voice of the modern civil rights movement. More than any other individual, he articulated the aspirations and grievances of African Americans who sought the rights promised by the U.S. Constitution. King pioneered the use of civil disobedience against racial segregation and discrimination. His powerful oratory invoked religious and patriotic imagery in support of full civil rights for all Americans. He inspired thousands of sympathizers to join his nonviolent crusade and persuaded untold millions of the justice of his cause.

King was born and raised in Atlanta, Georgia, the son, grandson, and great-grandson of Baptist preachers. A precocious student, he entered Morehouse College at age fifteen. He prepared for a career in the ministry by studying at Crozer Theological Seminary in Chester, Pennsylvania, and then pursued doctoral studies at Boston University, receiving the degree in 1955. In 1954 he accepted the pastorate of Dexter Avenue Baptist Church in Montgomery, Alabama. On December 1, 1955, Rosa Parks, a Montgomery seamstress, was arrested for refusing to surrender her seat on a city bus to a white passenger. Four days later, King was elected president of the Montgomery Improvement Association, an organization formed to protest the city's segregated transportation system. King and the association conducted a year-long boycott of city buses. His advocacy of nonviolent resistance against segregation adapted techniques used by India's famous leader Mohandas K. Gandhi to the American situation. When the buses finally were integrated in December 1956, King was hailed as a dynamic young leader of the emerging civil rights movement.

Over the next decade King remained the foremost champion of African American equality. His success in Montgomery inspired other activists to develop direct-action tactics for use in the civil rights movement. In 1960 King supported African American college students who staged sit-in demonstrations at segregated lunch counters. When the Freedom Riders encountered mob violence in 1961, King urged them to continue their battle to integrate interstate transportation. In Albany, Georgia, the following year King led mass marches against segregation, resulting in hundreds of arrests, but he was unable to wrest any concessions from an unyielding city administration. The lessons King learned from his Albany setback were applied in Birmingham, Alabama, where he spearheaded weeks of demonstrations against segregation in 1963. While confined in the Birmingham jail, King penned a passionate letter defending his confrontational methods. National opinion turned in favor of civil rights when Police Commissioner Eugene "Bull" Connor turned police dogs and fire hoses on youthful protesters. The Birmingham crisis persuaded President John F. Kennedy to sponsor legislation requiring integration of public accommodations. On August 28, 1963, King delivered his memorable, "I have a dream" speech at a Washington, D.C., rally of 250,000 people supporting Kennedy's civil rights bill.

King's leadership of the civil rights movement was recognized in 1964 when he was awarded the Nobel Peace Prize. His prominence brought increased scrutiny from the Federal Bureau of Investigation, whose director, J. Edgar Hoover, increased his surveillance of King's activities and orchestrated efforts to discredit his leadership. After the Civil Rights Act was passed in 1964, King turned his attention to voting rights. When Alabama state troopers attacked demonstrators attempting to march from Selma to Montgomery on March 7, 1965, public outrage again forced the federal government to act. Five months later, President Lyndon B. Johnson signed the Voting Rights Act, which protected African American citizens attempting to vote.

King responded to growing unrest in urban ghettoes by leading a 1966 crusade against slum housing in Chicago. He also raised his voice to condemn the Vietnam War. His 1967 speech at Riverside Church in New York City, in which he spoke out against the war, placed him in the front rank of antiwar activists. In the final year of his life, King concentrated on issues of economic justice. He began organizing a campaign to bring delegations of poor people to Washington, D.C., to lobby for increased antipoverty funding. A request to support striking sanitation workers drew King to Memphis, Tennessee, where, on April 4, 1968, he was killed by a shot from a high-powered rifle. James Earl Ray, a white man with a prison record, was convicted of King's murder. In 1986 the nation honored King's memory when his birthday was declared a national holiday.

Explanation and Analysis of Documents

Martin Luther King, Jr., was first and foremost a black Baptist preacher, raised in the traditions of African American spirituality. Although he wrote four books to help

Time Line

1929

- **January 15**
  Martin Luther King, Jr., is born in Atlanta, Georgia.

1954

- **October 31**
  King is called to be pastor of Dexter Avenue Baptist Church in Montgomery, Alabama.

1955

- **December 1**
  Rosa Parks is arrested for failing to give her seat to a white passenger in Montgomery.

- **December 5**
  King is elected president of the Montgomery Improvement Association and assumes leadership of the Montgomery bus boycott.

1956

- **December 20**
  King's boycott leads to buses in Montgomery being integrated.

1957

- **February 14**
  King founds the Southern Christian Leadership Conference.

1961

- **December 15**
  King arrives in Albany, Georgia, to lead protests against segregated facilities.

1963

- **April 12**
  King is arrested in Birmingham, Alabama, and begins writing his letter from a Birmingham jail.

- **August 28**
  King delivers his "I have a dream" speech at the March on Washington.

1964

- **December 10**
  King is awarded the Nobel Peace Prize in Oslo, Norway.

---

advance the cause of civil rights, it was through his oratory that he reached his widest audience. In speeches that combined biblical quotations with references to leading intellectuals, King embraced the role of biblical prophet, speaking against the evils of his society and articulating a vision of a more just and democratic nation. His words live on as a monument to the power of his message.

◆ "Letter from a Birmingham Jail"

Birmingham, Alabama, was reputed to be the most segregated city in the United States. During the 1950s a series of unsolved bombings directed at African Americans earned it the dubious nickname "Bombingham." The police department was directed by Commissioner Eugene "Bull" Connor, an outspoken segregationist. His failure to act against white thugs who attacked Freedom Riders arriving in Birmingham in May 1961 confirmed suspicions that Connor was in league with the Ku Klux Klan.

In January 1963 the Southern Christian Leadership Conference targeted Birmingham for its next desegregation campaign. During 1962 King had led a series of protests against segregation in Albany, Georgia, but had been unable to win any concessions from a stubborn city administration. He badly needed a victory to revive the movement's sagging morale. The Reverend Fred Shuttlesworth, a fiery local civil rights leader, argued that despite its dangerous reputation, Birmingham was ripe for change; the short-tempered Connor could be provoked to retaliate against civil rights demonstrators, and that, in turn, would generate sympathy for the movement.

Moderate business leaders realized that Connor's heavy-handed tactics hurt their city's prospects for economic development and backed a drive to oust Connor from power. King delayed the start of demonstrations until Connor was defeated in a runoff election for mayor. Connor, however, refused to give up his office. Birmingham's divided white leadership was embroiled in controversy when the Southern Christian Leadership Conference launched its protest against segregated facilities in downtown stores. With the Easter shopping season in full swing, civil rights forces hoped to pressure business owners by hitting them in the pocketbook. Connor promptly arrested scores of sit-in demonstrators. King announced his intention to fill the jails with adherents to his nonviolent philosophy, just as Gandhi had done in India. When a city judge issued an injunction against further demonstrations, King marched in defiance of the order. Arrested on Good Friday, King refused bail and was locked in solitary confinement.

The same day King was jailed, a group of eight prominent clergymen published an appeal to Birmingham's African Americans urging them to abandon public protests. The white religious leaders argued that these demonstrations were unnecessarily disruptive and provocative. The city was making progress, they claimed, and protesters should allow the new government time to address their concerns. They suggested that local blacks should reject outside guidance and send King back to Atlanta. After reading their plea, King began writing an impassioned rebuttal.

His letter was smuggled out of jail and published in pamphlet form a few weeks later. King's powerful defense of his confrontational tactics was soon recognized as one of the most influential documents of the civil rights movement.

King begins his epistle in a tone of Christian brotherhood. While confined in the city jail, he had read the clergymen's statement describing his campaign as "'unwise and untimely.'" Although he rarely answered critics, he says that he has decided to respond to their statement because he considers them "men of genuine goodwill." He first speaks to their objection to his outsider status. He maintains that he is present in Birmingham because injustice is there. King likens himself to early Christian evangelists, such as the apostle Paul, who faced persecution as they roamed the ancient world proclaiming the Gospel message. His mission, he says, requires him to answer a cry for assistance, no matter what its source. The "Macedonian call" refers to a biblical passage (Acts 16:9–10) in which Paul responds to the vision of a Macedonian man calling for his aid. In the modern world, communities are linked in what King calls an "inescapable network of mutuality." The presence of injustice is sufficient reason to bring him to Birmingham. King rejects the offensive label of "'outside agitator.'" According to King, a person from another state should not be considered an outsider because all Americans are citizens of the same nation.

Next, King addresses the criticism of the demonstrations he led. He faults the statement's authors for "superficial" analysis because they failed to consider the underlying conditions giving rise to the protests. He concedes that protests are "unfortunate" but not for the same reasons set forth by his critics. He considers the inaction of Birmingham's white leaders deplorable because it leaves African Americans no option other than public dissent.

King poses the question, why are demonstrations necessary? Is negotiation not a better alternative? He agrees that negotiation would be preferable, but meaningful dialogue is not possible unless both parties are willing to face the issues. He readily admits that his direct action campaign aims to create a crisis. Rather than avoiding confrontation, he embraces it. Only by forcefully calling attention to their grievances can powerless people force community leaders to sit down and bargain. King asserts that tension is not something to be avoided; if it contributes to healing and progress, it can be constructive. Just as Socrates insisted that tension between opposing ideas was necessary for intellectual growth, King claims conflict is needed to move from prejudice to brotherhood. He frankly acknowledges that the goal of his campaign is to create crisis conditions that will "open the door to negotiation."

Borrowing a line from the great abolitionist Frederick Douglass, King states that "freedom is never voluntarily given by the oppressor; it must be demanded by the oppressed." For this reason, those in power will never consider a protest to be "'well timed.'" At a moment when many white leaders were advising civil rights forces to not press so hard for change, King angrily rejects their appeal for patience. "'Wait'" is a word hated by African Americans

Time Line	
1965	■ **March 21–25** King leads the Selma to Montgomery march for voting rights.
1967	■ **April 4** King speaks against the Vietnam War at New York's Riverside Church. ■ **November 27** King announces plans for a "poor people's campaign" in 1968.
1968	■ **April 4** King is assassinated in Memphis, Tennessee.

because it almost always means "'Never.'" King refuses to go slowly in his quest for civil rights. Black people, he believes, have waited for more than three centuries to attain basic human rights and cannot delay any longer.

In the most remarkable passage of his letter, King recites a stinging litany of abuses contributing to African American dissatisfaction with the glacial rate of change. He cites the history of lynching, vicious police brutality, and pervasive poverty among the reasons for their impatience. In an instance that may be based on personal experience, he describes the plight of a black parent who must explain to his young daughter why she cannot go to the segregated amusement park she has seen advertised on television. In the same vein, he voices the complaint of a boy who asks why white people are so mean to black people. He recounts the humiliation of African American travelers who cannot find a motel that will accept them; the degrading names directed at black adults; the multitude of daily fears and slights experienced by African Americans. If his critics can appreciate the cumulative effect of these insults, then they may be able to understand the "legitimate and unavoidable impatience" felt by civil rights protesters.

King then raises an issue fundamental to his philosophy of civil disobedience—his willingness to break the law. He rhetorically asks how civil rights leaders can condemn southern whites for failing to obey the Supreme Court's 1954 *Brown v. Board of Education* school desegregation decision and, at the same time, advocate disobeying laws requiring segregation in public facilities in the South. There are two types of law, he answers, just and unjust. Here King introduces the concept of natural law articulated by Thomas Aquinas. A just law is one rooted in natural law; it affirms the dignity of human beings. An unjust law is not in harmony with natural law; it degrades and damages the human personality. By this logic, all segregation laws are unjust; therefore, they can be broken without moral blame.

Police haul away a black demonstrator following a protest march in Birmingham, Alabama, in April 1963. (AP/Wide World Photos)

The shortcomings of southern white moderates are a major disappointment for King. By blindly insisting on law and order without considering segregation's basic injustice, they have become an obstacle to progress. When moderates fault civil rights leaders for generating tension with their demonstrations, they fail to acknowledge the positive contributions of these protests. Direct action against segregation brings hidden conflicts to the surface where they can be addressed and resolved. King asserts that exposing injustice is healthy and a necessary precondition for creating a just social order. Too many moderates advocate gradualism, he says, believing that progress is inevitable; according to them, there is no need to push for change because it will come with the passage of time. King effectively refutes that notion. "Time is neutral," he asserts; it can be used for good or evil. Too many white moderates had failed to speak against the racist policies of white politicians during the past decade. He condemns "the appalling silence of the good people." Progress will come only through "the tireless efforts and persistent work" of dedicated people. He urges his readers to use time creatively and work to "make real the promise of democracy."

The tepid response of white churches to the civil rights movement is another source of dismay to King. As a believer whose activism had been nurtured by his religious faith, he expected better. He cites his experience in Montgomery, where some white clergy actively opposed the bus boycott, while others feared to give open support. The same experience was being repeated in Birmingham. He admonishes white church leaders for not viewing the denial of African American civil rights as a burning moral issue. Some religious leaders urged compliance with court-ordered school desegregation because it was the law; King would prefer to hear them tell their congregations to support integration because it is morally right. He decries their "pious irrelevancies and sanctimonious trivialities."

Despite lack of backing from white churches, King expresses confidence that his movement ultimately will prevail because the quest for freedom is a fundamental American value. The experience of African Americans is inextricably linked with the history of the United States. Black people endured two centuries of slavery and another century of second-class citizenship and still press for equality. King believes that they will not be denied because the nation's heritage and the will of God are on their side. He concludes his letter by expressing the hope that he will be able to meet the authors of the statement on some future day when love and brotherhood will replace the prejudice and misunderstanding that currently separate them.

◆ "I Have a Dream" Speech

In January 1963 the veteran African American labor leader A. Philip Randolph announced plans for a mass march on Washington, D.C., to urge government action on problems of poverty and unemployment in black communities. His idea generated only modest enthusiasm until King lent his backing. Following his successful desegregation campaign in Birmingham, Alabama, King realized that such a march was an ideal vehicle to keep public attention focused on civil rights. With his endorsement, the objective of the march shifted from jobs to support for President John F. Kennedy's recently announced civil rights bill. Kennedy initially tried to discourage the march organizers, fearing that possible disorder would spark a backlash against this legislation. When civil rights leaders refused to cancel their plans, however, the president offered the assistance of government agencies to ensure a well-managed gathering.

On the morning of August 28, 1963, nearly a quarter million black and white marchers arrived in the nation's capital. Assembled around the reflecting pool of the Lincoln Memorial, the peaceful crowd listened to songs by the African American gospel singer Mahalia Jackson and the folk-singing trio Peter, Paul, and Mary and a series of short speeches by religious and civil rights leaders. The day's final speaker was Martin Luther King, Jr. He had toiled late into the previous night crafting an address that would capture the spirit of the momentous occasion. Cameras of three television networks would broadcast his words into millions of homes across the nation.

King begins by acknowledging the legacy of Abraham Lincoln, whose memorial forms the symbolic backdrop for the day's events. Using the archaic "five score" instead of "one hundred," he echoes the Gettysburg Address. He reminds his listeners that a century earlier Lincoln had signed the Emancipation Proclamation, freeing those held in slavery. However, the work begun by the Great Emancipator remains unfinished. African Americans, he maintains, still do not enjoy the freedom they were promised. Segregation, racial discrimination, and poverty exclude black citizens from the mainstream of American society. The March on Washington continues their quest for freedom.

King uses the familiar image of a checking account to represent the promise made by the Founding Fathers that all men are created equal and endowed with "unalienable rights of life, liberty, and the pursuit of happiness." This promissory note applies to all citizens, but for African Americans the check has not been honored; it has been returned for "insufficient funds." Continuing the banking metaphor, King states his belief that the treasury of justice is not bankrupt. The assembled marchers have come to Washington to cash that check, to demand that the government fulfill its promise of freedom. He rejects the advice voiced by white politicians that the civil rights movement slow its protests and begin a "cooling off" period. King insists that this is not a time for gradualism. Rather, it is an opportune moment to realize the promise of American democracy, to abandon segregation and discrimination in favor of brotherhood and equality.

Speaking directly to white Americans, he promises that African Americans will continue to march and demonstrate until they achieve the dual goals of freedom and equal rights. The day's events should not be dismissed as an occasion for blacks to "blow off steam." Protests will continue until freedom is won. King says that America will not enjoy peace and tranquility until African Americans gain their constitutionally guaranteed rights.

Next, King speaks to his fellow black citizens. They must act with dignity and respect; they cannot indulge in bitterness and hatred. The struggle for civil rights must be conducted on a high moral plane. King rejects the Black Nationalist assertion that whites should be viewed as enemies. Rather, he insists that white people also carry the burden of past injustices. When blacks gain their freedom, whites also will be freed. When will African Americans be satisfied? King asks. He presents a list of long-standing grievances, including police brutality, segregated hotels and motels, confinement in urban ghettos, humiliating segregated restrooms and water fountains, denial of voting rights, and lack of meaningful political participation. Quoting the biblical prophet Amos, he declares that African Americans will not be satisfied until "justice rolls down like waters and righteousness like a mighty stream." Speaking to veterans of the civil rights movement in his audience who have endured beatings and served sentences in southern jails, King urges them not to abandon the nonviolent fight. Their suffering is redemptive, he contends. They should return to southern towns and northern slums to continue working for the cause of freedom.

At this point, King departs from his prepared text to reprise a theme he sounded in several earlier speeches—his dream for a renewed America. In that society the promise that "all men are created equal" finally will be realized. It will be a place where blacks and whites overcome the legacy of slavery and treat each other as brothers. "I have a dream today," King thunders. With each new recitation, the vocal crowd joins in a chorus of affirmation, urging him to continue elaborating his vision. Even Mississippi, the most racist state in the nation, will become "an oasis of freedom." In this future time King's four small children will be judged not "by the color of their skin but by the content of their character." Alabama, where Governor George Wallace defied federal authorities seeking to integrate its schools, will become a place where black children can walk hand in hand with white children. Falling back once again on biblical imagery, he invokes the prophet Isaiah to proclaim that on that day "every valley shall be exalted; every hill and mountain shall be made low."

Next King gives a testament of his faith. His credo includes the belief that the present sounds of conflict will become a "beautiful symphony of brotherhood." He believes that by working, praying, struggling, and standing up together for civil rights, his movement will achieve its goal of freedom. The patriotic hymn "America" furnishes the refrain for King's closing recitation. If America is to become a truly great nation, then freedom shall ring throughout the land, he says. It will ring from mountain-

Martin Luther King, Jr. (Library of Congress)

tops in the East and the West; it will ring even in the segregated states of Georgia, Tennessee, and Mississippi. Summoning his full oratorical powers, King proclaims that on that day when Americans let freedom ring from "every village and every hamlet," people of all colors and creeds will be able to sing, "Free at Last! Free at last! Thank God Almighty, we are free at last!"

◆ Speech in Opposition to the Vietnam War

As a religious leader and advocate of nonviolence, King was troubled by the growing American military involvement in the Vietnam War. Although he was not a pacifist, he questioned the morality of indiscriminate bombing and attacks on civilian populations. As the foremost African American spokesman of his era, he was deeply concerned about the disproportionate casualties suffered by black soldiers and government policies that placed more African Americans in dangerous combat assignments. As an advocate for the poor, he was disheartened by the enormous sums spent to support the war—funds that could be better spent on antipoverty programs.

King had made earlier statements critical of the American war effort. These remarks were condemned by other civil rights leaders, largely for political reasons. They argued

that King should limit his energies to fighting for civil rights. By embracing other causes, he weakened the movement. More important, they feared that his criticism of the Vietnam War would antagonize the commander in chief. President Lyndon Johnson had surprised black leaders by becoming the most effective champion of African American freedom since Abraham Lincoln, but Johnson was known for his vindictiveness toward those who opposed his policies. King's public dissent from Johnson's Vietnam policies threatened to dampen presidential enthusiasm for civil rights legislation. As the peace movement gained momentum, King became increasingly outspoken in his opposition to the Vietnam War. His most notable criticism came in an address delivered one year before his death to a meeting of the antiwar organization, Clergy and Laymen Concerned about Vietnam, in New York's Riverside Church.

King opens by announcing his agreement with the organization's antiwar objectives and endorsing its statement: "'A time comes when silence is betrayal.'" This statement became the keynote for his remarks. He acknowledges the problem of opposing one's government in wartime and the difficult task of sorting out complex issues, but this cannot be an excuse for inaction. He speaks of the personal conflicts he has encountered as he moved to oppose American policies in Vietnam. Many people said that he was "hurting the cause" of his people by speaking out against the war. This criticism, he insists, is based on a fundamental misunderstanding of his mission. King states that his activist career that began with the Montgomery bus boycott leads directly to his present antiwar stance.

King outlines several reasons for his opposition to the Vietnam War. He argues that war is the enemy of the poor. The huge cost of fighting in Vietnam, he claims, takes money away from the domestic war against poverty. He points out that among African American soldiers, there have been a disproportionate number of combat casualties. It is a "cruel irony" that black and white GIs can fight and die side by side in Vietnam when they cannot live together in the United States. King reminds his listeners that he has urged young black rioters in northern ghettoes to refrain from violence. They, in turn, ask, "What about Vietnam?" He must be consistent and demand that the government abandon violence overseas. King rejects the notion that he should limit himself to civil rights advocacy. He cites the motto of the Southern Christian Leadership Conference— "'To save the soul of America.'" This mission includes the quest for peace as well as the struggle for civil rights. King contends that America's soul is being poisoned by the Vietnam War and that those who care about the nation's health must protest the war.

As a recipient of the Nobel Peace Prize, King felt a special responsibility to strive for peace. His duty to work for "'the brotherhood of man'" is universal, he says; it requires him to disregard national boundaries. Ultimately, however, King's dedication to the cause of peace was rooted in his Christian faith. He believes that all men are sons of the same God who cares for His children regardless of "race or nation or creed." King boldly declares, "Somehow this madness must cease." He speaks on behalf of Vietnamese victims of the war and poor Americans who bear the burden of the fighting. He speaks both as a citizen of the world and as a patriotic American. He calls upon leaders of the United States to stop the conflict. What America needs, King maintains, is a "radical revolution of values." The country must move away from racism, materialism, and militarism to become a more "person-oriented society." If this revolution occurs, Americans will question the wisdom of many national policies; they will realize that true compassion requires basic changes in the structure of society. King calls on American capitalists to stop extracting profits from overseas investments with no concern for the welfare of third world people. He urges world leaders to end the awful human cost of modern warfare. He calls on American leaders to embrace this revolution of values so that the pursuit of peace becomes the highest national priority. In conclusion, King asks his audience to dedicate themselves to the struggle for a new world order. Despite many difficulties, the choice is clear. As sons of God, they must embrace the cause of peace.

Impact and Legacy

Few twentieth-century leaders could match Martin Luther King's far-reaching influence. As the most visible and articulate spokesperson of the modern civil rights movement, King led a crusade that fundamentally altered the legal and social status of African Americans. In little more than a decade, the country's system of legally sanctioned racial segregation was discredited and dismantled. Signed by President Lyndon B. Johnson on July 2, 1964, the Civil Rights Act removed segregation barriers in restaurants, theaters, and hotels. After the Voting Rights Act became law the next year, black political participation increased dramatically, especially in the South, where hundreds of black candidates were elected to local, state, and national offices. African American students enrolled in schools and colleges that had previously been closed to them. Newly opened employment opportunities enabled many black families to enjoy greater economic security and enter the middle class. The success of the civil rights movement encouraged other minorities to press for equal rights. The women's liberation movement, the American Indian movement, the gay rights movement, the disability rights movement, and others all drew inspiration from King's leadership. Overseas, participants in popular struggles against repressive regimes in South Africa, Poland, and China sang the civil rights anthem "We Shall Overcome" as they adopted King's techniques of nonviolent resistance.

King's leadership was not limited to racial issues. He realized that African Americans' low standing in American society would not be elevated by the passage of civil rights laws alone. That is why he increasingly advocated programs to fight poverty among people of all races. He joined the antiwar movement for moral reasons but also because he saw military spending draining funds away from badly needed domestic spending. King's preeminent stature was equally the result of his powerful oratory and his philosophy of nonviolent resistance. His ability to deliver a ringing, inspirational message was honed by his immersion in the rich tradition of the black Baptist church. Unlike many of his clerical contemporaries, however, King was well versed in the leading intellectual currents of his day. His speeches combined familiar biblical references with concepts borrowed from prominent philosophers and theologians. King also buttressed his argument for equal rights with quotations from patriotic documents, including the Declaration of Independence and the Constitution.

His philosophy of civil disobedience and nonviolent resistance to government oppression was borrowed from Gandhi's Indian independence movement and based on the writings of the nineteenth-century American writer Henry David Thoreau. King's original contribution was the addition of a uniquely Christian perspective. He used Jesus' admonitions to "turn the other cheek" and to "do good to those who hate you" to persuade his followers to remain nonviolent, even in the face of violent repression. King's use of religious justifications helped his followers claim the moral high ground in the contest for public support. He shrewdly realized that the main resource at the disposal of African American people was their ability to appeal to the conscience of the nation with disciplined, nonviolent protests.

King's final years were marked by his criticism of the pervasive poverty and economic inequality that characterized American society and his opposition to U.S. military operations in Vietnam. At the same time, his vision of racial integration and his emphasis on nonviolence were rejected by militant Black Power advocates. Only after his assassination was King recognized as the leading spokesman for the American ideals of justice and equality.

Key Sources

Martin Luther King, Jr., was the author of four books: *Stride toward Freedom: The Montgomery Story* (1958), *The Strength to Love* (1963), *Why We Can't Wait* (1964), and *Where Do We Go From Here: Chaos or Community?* (1967). *The Autobiography of Martin Luther King, Jr.* (2001) is a posthumous work edited by Clayborne Carson from King's writings, speeches, and personal documents. King's papers are held at the King Center in Atlanta. His important correspondence, sermons, speeches, published writings, and unpublished manuscripts are being published in a projected fourteen-volume series by the University of California Press. Volume 6, published in 2007, is the latest book of this series. An online inventory of 1,750 documents can be accessed at http://www.stanford.edu/group/King/mlkpapers/. The PBS video series *Eyes on the Prize: America's Civil Rights Years* (1986) covers King's public career in the context of the emerging civil rights movement. *The Speeches of Martin Luther King* (1990) is a film collection of King's major addresses.

We know through painful experience that freedom is never voluntarily given by the oppressor; it must be demanded by the oppressed…. For years now I have heard the words 'Wait!' It rings in the ear of every Negro with a piercing familiarity. This 'Wait' has almost always meant 'Never.'"

("Letter from a Birmingham Jail")

"When you have seen vicious mobs lynch your mothers and fathers at will and drown your sisters and brothers at whim; when you have seen hate filled policemen curse, kick, brutalize and even kill your black brothers and sisters with impunity; when you see the vast majority of your twenty million Negro brothers smothering in an airtight cage of poverty in the midst of an affluent society;…then you will understand why we find it difficult to wait."

("Letter from a Birmingham Jail")

"I have a dream that one day on the red hills of Georgia the sons of former slaves and the sons of former slave owners will be able to sit down together at the table of brotherhood…. I have a dream that my four little children will one day live in a nation where they will not be judged by the color of their skin but by the content of their character…. I have a dream that one day, down in Alabama… little black boys and black girls will be able to join hands with little white boys and white girls as sisters and brothers."

("I Have a Dream" Speech)

"Let freedom ring from Stone Mountain of Georgia. Let freedom ring from Lookout Mountain of Tennessee. Let freedom ring from every hill and molehill of Mississippi. From every mountainside, let freedom ring."

("I Have a Dream" Speech)

"We have been repeatedly faced with the cruel irony of watching Negro and white boys on TV screens as they kill and die together for a nation that has been unable to seat them together in the same schools. And so we watch them in brutal solidarity burning the huts of a poor village, but we realize that they would hardly live on the same block in Chicago."

(Speech in Opposition to the Vietnam War)

Further Reading

■ Books

Branch, Taylor. *Parting the Waters: America in the King Years 1954–63.* New York: Simon & Schuster, 1988.

———. *Pillar of Fire: America in the King Years 1963–65.* New York: Simon & Schuster, 1998.

———. *At Canaan's Edge: America in the King Years 1965–68.* New York: Simon & Schuster, 2006.

Carson, Clayborne, and Kris Shepard, eds. *A Call to Conscience: The Landmark Speeches of Martin Luther King, Jr.* New York: Intellectual Properties Management/Warner Books, 2001.

———, and Peter Holloran, eds. *Knock at Midnight: Inspiration from the Great Sermons of Reverend Martin Luther King,*

Questions for Further Study

1. Discuss the logical formation of the arguments King employs in his famous "Letter from a Birmingham Jail." Outline his points step by step and give his justification for them. How does he use examples from history, literature, philosophy, and American history? Of the painful experiences to which he alludes in the lengthy seventh paragraph, which do you think were King's own? Use evidence from this speech or other information about King to back up your position.

2. Compare and contrast King's "I have a dream" speech with the two addresses by Malcolm X included in this volume. Use each man's actual words to set forth their relative positions and examine the many ways in which they disagreed about the proper approach to questions of racial justice in America as well those ways in which they agreed. For what qualities might each man have praised the other?

3. In his "Letter from a Birmingham Jail," King makes disparaging comparisons between the speed of racial progress in America compared with that of Africa and Asia, and in his speech against the Vietnam War four years later he lambastes the United States as the "greatest purveyor of violence" in the world. Were such criticisms fair? What did subsequent events show about the progress of racial and social reform in America relative to that in the then newly emergent third world nations King lauded in 1963? How did America's record of violence overseas and at home in the 1960s compare with that of the Soviet Union, China, and other Communist countries? What was the "world revolution" King references in his Vietnam speech, and were the aims of its leaders and supporters truly aligned with those of King and other civil rights leaders in the United States? In what ways might King have taken issue with third world nationalism and Socialism?

4. As remarkable a figure as King was, his views did not all originate with him but bore the strong imprint of other influences. Much has been made of the degree to which he reflected the nonviolent philosophies of Mohandos K. Gandhi and the social activism of the African American church, but this was far from the extent of his education. Discuss the influence on King of other thinkers such as his namesake, Martin Luther; the German philosopher G. W. F. Hegel, whose work King studied as a postgraduate student; and others, including twentieth-century philosophers and theologians. What might King have said about these influences, and for what particular aspects of his thought might he have credited each of them?

5. King, himself a Baptist minister who gained his greatest prominence as a political leader, did not live to see the battles over "separation of church and state" that began to take an increasingly prominent place in the U.S. political landscape from the 1970s onward. How would he have approached this controversy, given the fact that he was committed to a broad social movement encompassing numerous groups and faiths? What would he have seen as the limits for appropriate religious involvement in politics? Would he have viewed religious movements among people of color as having no greater or lesser right to a political role than white or multiracial churches?

Jr. New York: Intellectual Properties Management /Warner Books, 1998.

———, Tenisha Armstrong, Susan Carson, Erin Cook, and Susan Englander, eds. *The Martin Luther King, Jr., Encyclopedia* Westport, Conn: Greenwood Press, 2008.

Dyson, Michael Eric. *I May Not Get There with You: The True Martin Luther King, Jr.* New York: Free Press, 2000.

Garrow, David J. *The FBI and Martin Luther King: From "Solo" to Memphis.* New York: W. W. Norton, 1981.

———. *Bearing the Cross: Martin Luther King, Jr., and the Southern Christian Leadership Conference.* New York: Vintage Books, 1986.

Hansen, Drew D. *The Dream: Martin Luther King, Jr., and the Speech That Inspired a Nation.* New York: HarperCollins, 2003.

Lischer, Richard. *The Preacher King: Martin Luther King, Jr., and the Word That Moved America.* New York: Oxford University Press, 1995.

—Paul Murray

"Letter from a Birmingham Jail" (1963)

My Dear Fellow Clergymen:

While confined here in the Birmingham City Jail, I came across your recent statement calling our present activities "unwise and untimely." Seldom, if ever, do I pause to answer criticism of my work and ideas. If I sought to answer all the criticisms that cross my desk, my secretaries would be engaged in little else in the course of the day, and I would have no time for constructive work. But since I feel that you are men of genuine goodwill and your criticisms are sincerely set forth, I would like to answer your statement in what I hope will be patient and reasonable terms....

I am in Birmingham because injustice is here. Just as the eighth century prophets left their little villages and carried their "thus saith the Lord" far beyond the boundaries of their home towns; and just as the Apostle Paul left his little village of Tarsus and carried the gospel of Jesus Christ to practically every hamlet and city of the Greco-Roman world, I too am compelled to carry the gospel of freedom beyond my particular home town. Like Paul, I must constantly respond to the Macedonian call for aid.

Moreover, I am cognizant of the interrelatedness of all communities and states. I cannot sit idly by in Atlanta and not be concerned about what happens in Birmingham. Injustice anywhere is a threat to justice everywhere. We are caught in an inescapable network of mutuality, tied in a single garment of destiny. Whatever affects one directly affects all indirectly. Never again can we afford to live with the narrow, provincial "outside agitator" idea. Anyone who lives inside the United States can never be considered an outsider anywhere in this country.

You deplore the demonstrations that are presently taking place in Birmingham. But I am sorry that your statement did not express a similar concern for the conditions that brought the demonstrations into being. I am sure that each of you would want to go beyond the superficial social analyst who looks merely at effects, and does not grapple with underlying causes. I would not hesitate to say that it is unfortunate that so-called demonstrations are taking place in Birmingham at this time, but I would say in more emphatic terms that it is even more unfortunate that the white power structure of this city left the Negro community with no other alternative....

You may well ask: "Why direct action? Why sit-ins, marches, etc.? Isn't negotiation a better path?" You are exactly right in your call for negotiation. Indeed, this is the purpose of direct action. Nonviolent direct action seeks to create such a crisis and establish such creative tension that a community that has constantly refused to negotiate is forced to confront the issue. It seeks so to dramatize the issue that it can no longer be ignored. I just referred to the creation of tension as a part of the work of the nonviolent resister. This may sound rather shocking. But I must confess that I am not afraid of the word tension. I have earnestly worked and preached against violent tension, but there is a type of constructive nonviolent tension that is necessary for growth. Just as Socrates felt that it was necessary to create a tension in the mind so that individuals could rise from the bondage of myths and half-truths to the unfettered realm of creative analysis and objective appraisal, we must see the need of having nonviolent gadflies to create the kind of tension in society that will help men to rise from the dark depths of prejudice and racism to the majestic heights of understanding and brotherhood. So the purpose of the direct action is to create a situation so crisis-packed that it will inevitably open the door to negotiation. We, therefore, concur with you in your call for negotiation. Too long has our beloved Southland been bogged down in the tragic attempt to live in monologue rather than dialogue....

We know through painful experience that freedom is never voluntarily given by the oppressor; it must be demanded by the oppressed. Frankly, I have never yet engaged in a direct action movement that was "well timed," according to the timetable of those who have not suffered unduly from the disease of segregation. For years now I have heard the word "Wait!" It rings in the ear of every Negro with a piercing familiarity. This "Wait" has almost always meant "Never." We must come to see with the distinguished jurist of yesterday that "justice too long delayed is justice denied."

We have waited for more than three hundred and forty years for our constitutional and God-given rights. The nations of Asia and Africa are moving with jet-like speed toward the goal of political independence, and we still creep at horse and buggy pace toward the gaining of a cup of coffee at a lunch counter. I guess it is easy for those who have never felt the stinging darts of segregation to say, "Wait." But when you have seen vicious mobs lynch your mothers and fathers at will and drown your sisters and brothers at whim; when you have seen hate filled policemen curse, kick, brutalize and even kill your black brothers and sisters with impunity; when you see the vast majority of your twenty million Negro brothers smothering in an airtight cage of poverty in the midst of an affluent society; when you suddenly find your tongue twisted and your speech stammering as you seek to explain to your six-year-old daughter why she can't go to the public amusement park that has just been advertised on television, and see tears welling up in her eyes when she is told that Funtown is closed to colored children, and see the depressing clouds of inferiority begin to form in her little mental sky, and see her begin to distort her little personality by unconsciously developing a bitterness toward white people; when you have to concoct an answer for a five-year-old son asking in agonizing pathos: "Daddy, why do white people treat colored people so mean?"; when you take a cross-country drive and find it necessary to sleep night after night in the uncomfortable corners of your automobile because no motel will accept you; when you are humiliated day in and day out by nagging signs reading "white" and "colored"; when your first name becomes "nigger," your middle name becomes "boy" (however old you are) and your last name becomes "John," and your wife and mother are never given the respected title "Mrs."; when you are harried by day and haunted by night by the fact that you are a Negro, living constantly at tip-toe stance never quite knowing what to expect next, and plagued with inner fears and outer resentments; when you are forever fighting a degenerating sense of "nobodiness"; then you will understand why we find it difficult to wait. There comes a time when the cup of endurance runs over, and men are no longer willing to be plunged into an abyss of despair. I hope, sirs, you can understand our legitimate and unavoidable impatience.

You express a great deal of anxiety over our willingness to break laws. This is certainly a legitimate concern. Since we so diligently urge people to obey the Supreme Court's decision of 1954 outlawing segregation in the public schools, it is rather strange and paradoxical to find us consciously breaking laws. One may well ask: "How can you advocate breaking some laws and obeying others?" The answer is found in the fact that there are two types of laws: There are just and there are unjust laws. I would agree with Saint Augustine that "An unjust law is no law at all."

Now, what is the difference between the two? How does one determine when a law is just or unjust? A just law is a man-made code that squares with the moral law or the law of God. An unjust law is a code that is out of harmony with the moral law. To put it in the terms of Saint Thomas Aquinas, an unjust law is a human law that is not rooted in eternal and natural law. Any law that uplifts human personality is just. Any law that degrades human personality is unjust. All segregation statutes are unjust because segregation distorts the soul and damages the personality. It gives the segregator a false sense of superiority, and the segregated a false sense of inferiority.... So I can urge men to disobey segregation ordinances because they are morally wrong....

I had hoped that the white moderate would understand that law and order exist for the purpose of establishing justice, and that when they fail to do this they become dangerously structured dams that block the flow of social progress. I had hoped that the white moderate would understand that the present tension in the South is merely a necessary phase of the transition from an obnoxious negative peace, where the Negro passively accepted his unjust plight, to a substance-filled positive peace, where all men will respect the dignity and worth of human personality. Actually, we who engage in nonviolent direct action are not the creators of tension. We merely bring to the surface the hidden tension that is already alive. We bring it out in the open where it can be seen and dealt with. Like a boil that can never be cured as long as it is covered up but must be opened with all its pus-flowing ugliness to the natural medicines of air and light, injustice must likewise be exposed, with all of the tension its exposing creates, to the light of human conscience and the air of national opinion before it can be cured....

I had also hoped that the white moderate would reject the myth of time....It is the strangely irrational notion that there is something in the very flow of time that will inevitably cure all ills. Actually time is neutral. It can be used either destructively or constructively. I am coming to feel that the people of ill-will have used time much more effectively than the people of good will. We will have to repent in this generation not merely for the vitriolic words and actions of the bad people, but for the appalling silence of the good people. We must come to see that human progress never rolls in on wheels of inevitability. It comes through the tireless efforts and persistent work of men willing to be co-workers with God, and without this hard work time itself becomes an ally of the forces of social stagnation. We must use time creatively, and forever realize that the time is always ripe to do right. Now is the time to make real the promise of democracy, and transform our pending national elegy into a creative psalm of brotherhood. Now is the time to lift our national policy from the quicksand of racial injustice to the solid rock of human dignity....

I must honestly reiterate that I have been disappointed with the church. I do not say that as one of those negative critics who can always find something wrong with the church. I say it as a minister of the gospel, who loves the church; who was nurtured in its bosom; who has been sustained by its spiritual blessings and who will remain true to it as long as the cord of life shall lengthen.

I had the strange feeling when I was suddenly catapulted into the leadership of the bus protest in Montgomery several years ago, that we would have the support of the white church. I felt that the white ministers, priests and rabbis of the South would be some of our strongest allies. Instead, some have been outright opponents, refusing to understand the freedom movement and misrepresenting its leaders; all too many others have been more cautious than courageous and have remained silent behind the anesthetizing security of the stained-glass windows.

In spite of my shattered dreams of the past, I came to Birmingham with the hope that the white religious leadership of this community would see the justice of our cause, and with deep moral concern, serve as the channel through which our just grievances would get to the power structure. I had hoped that each of you would understand. But again I have been disappointed. I have heard numerous religious leaders of the South call upon their worshippers to comply with a desegregation decision because it is the law, but I have longed to hear white ministers say, "Follow this decree because integration is morally right and the Negro is your brother." In the midst of blatant injustices inflicted upon the Negro, I have watched white churches stand on the sideline and merely mouth pious irrelevancies and sanctimonious trivialities. In the midst of a mighty struggle to rid our nation of racial and economic injustice, I have heard so many ministers say, "Those are social issues with which the gospel has no real concern." And I have watched so many churches commit themselves to a completely other-worldly religion which made a strange distinction between body and soul, the sacred and the secular....

I hope the church as a whole will meet the challenge of this decisive hour. But even if the church does not come to the aid of justice, I have no despair about the future. I have no fear about the outcome of our struggle in Birmingham, even if our motives are presently misunderstood. We will reach the goal of freedom in Birmingham and all over the nation, because the goal of America is freedom. Abused and scorned though we may be, our destiny is tied up with the destiny of America. Before the pilgrims

Glossary

bus protest in Montgomery	the Montgomery bus boycott (1955–1956) initiated by the refusal of Rosa Parks, an African American, to relinquish her seat on a bus to a white passenger
distinguished jurist	possibly British statesman William Gladstone (1809–1898), though the source of the phrase, commonly used in legal circles, is disputed
eighth century prophets	the biblical prophets Isaiah, Amos, Micah, and Judah
gadflies	pests, persistently annoying people
Macedonian	describing a region and its people on the Balkan Peninsula, on the border of ancient Greece and the center of an empire in the fourth century BCE
Saint Augustine	Bishop of Hippo, in North Africa; influential fourth-century theologian
Saint Thomas Aquinas	(c. 1225–1274) an Italian philosopher and theologian of the Catholic Church
Socrates	ancient Greek philosopher (c. 469–399 BCE)
Supreme Court's decision of 1954	the landmark decision in *Brown v. Board of Education*, which ordered the integration of public schools

landed at Plymouth we were here. Before the pen of Jefferson etched across the pages of history the majestic words of the Declaration of Independence, we were here. For more than two centuries our fore-parents labored in this country without wages; they made cotton king; and they built the homes of their masters in the midst of brutal injustice and shameful humiliation—and yet out of a bottomless vitality they continued to thrive and develop. If the inexpressible cruelties of slavery could not stop us, the opposition we now face will surely fail. We will win our freedom because the sacred heritage of our nation and the eternal will of God are embodied in our echoing demands....

I hope this letter finds you strong in the faith. I also hope that circumstances will soon make it possible for me to meet each of you, not as an integrationist or a civil rights leader, but as a fellow clergyman and a Christian brother. Let us all hope that the dark clouds of racial prejudice will soon pass away and the deep fog of misunderstanding will be lifted from our fear-drenched communities and in some not too distant tomorrow the radiant stars of love and brotherhood will shine over our great nation with all their scintillating beauty.

Yours for the cause of Peace and Brotherhood,
Martin Luther King, Jr.

"I Have a Dream" Speech (1963)

Five score years ago, a great American, in whose symbolic shadow we stand today, signed the Emancipation Proclamation. This momentous decree came as a great beacon light of hope to millions of Negro slaves who had been seared in the flames of withering injustice. It came as a joyous daybreak to end the long night of their captivity.

But one hundred years later, the Negro still is not free. One hundred years later, the life of the Negro is still sadly crippled by the manacles of segregation and the chains of discrimination. One hundred years later, the Negro lives on a lonely island of poverty in the midst of a vast ocean of material prosperity. One hundred years later, the Negro is still languishing in the corners of American society and finds himself an exile in his own land. So we have come here today to dramatize a shameful condition.

In a sense we have come to our nation's capital to cash a check. When the architects of our republic wrote the magnificent words of the Constitution and the Declaration of Independence, they were signing a promissory note to which every American was to fall heir. This note was a promise that all men, yes, black men as well as white men, would be guaranteed the unalienable rights of life, liberty, and the pursuit of happiness.

It is obvious today that America has defaulted on this promissory note insofar as her citizens of color are concerned. Instead of honoring this sacred obligation, America has given the Negro people a bad check, a check which has come back marked "insufficient funds." But we refuse to believe that the bank of justice is bankrupt. We refuse to believe that there are insufficient funds in the great vaults of opportunity of this nation. So we have come to cash this check—a check that will give us upon demand the riches of freedom and the security of justice. We have also come to this hallowed spot to remind America of the fierce urgency of now. This is no time to engage in the luxury of cooling off or to take the tranquilizing drug of gradualism. Now is the time to make real the promises of democracy. Now is the time to rise from the dark and desolate valley of segregation to the sunlit path of racial justice. Now is the time to lift our nation from the quicksands of racial injustice to the solid rock of brotherhood. Now is the time to make justice a reality for all of God's children.

It would be fatal for the nation to overlook the urgency of the moment. This sweltering summer of the Negro's legitimate discontent will not pass until there is an invigorating autumn of freedom and equality. Nineteen sixty-three is not an end, but a beginning. Those who hope that the Negro needed to blow off steam and will now be content will have a rude awakening if the nation returns to business as usual. There will be neither rest nor tranquility in America until the Negro is granted his citizenship rights. The whirlwinds of revolt will continue to shake the foundations of our nation until the bright day of justice emerges.

But there is something that I must say to my people who stand on the warm threshold which leads into the palace of justice. In the process of gaining our rightful place we must not be guilty of wrongful deeds. Let us not seek to satisfy our thirst for freedom by drinking from the cup of bitterness and hatred.

We must forever conduct our struggle on the high plane of dignity and discipline. We must not allow our creative protest to degenerate into physical violence. Again and again we must rise to the majestic heights of meeting physical force with soul force. The marvelous new militancy which has engulfed the Negro community must not lead us to a distrust of all white people, for many of our white brothers, as evidenced by their presence here today, have come to realize that their destiny is tied up with our destiny. They have come to realize that their freedom is inextricably bound to our freedom. We cannot walk alone.

As we walk, we must make the pledge that we shall always march ahead. We cannot turn back. There are those who are asking the devotees of civil rights, "When will you be satisfied?" We can never be satisfied as long as the Negro is the victim of the unspeakable horrors of police brutality. We can never be satisfied, as long as our bodies, heavy with the fatigue of travel, cannot gain lodging in the motels of the highways and the hotels of the cities. We cannot be satisfied as long as the Negro's basic mobility is from a smaller ghetto to a larger one. We can never be satisfied as long as our children are stripped of their selfhood and robbed of their dignity by signs stating "For Whites Only." We cannot be satisfied as long as a Negro in Mississippi cannot vote and a Negro in New York believes he has nothing for which

King, Martin Luther Jr.

to vote. No, no, we are not satisfied, and we will not be satisfied until justice rolls down like waters and righteousness like a mighty stream.

I am not unmindful that some of you have come here out of great trials and tribulations. Some of you have come fresh from narrow jail cells. Some of you have come from areas where your quest for freedom left you battered by the storms of persecution and staggered by the winds of police brutality. You have been the veterans of creative suffering. Continue to work with the faith that unearned suffering is redemptive.

Go back to Mississippi, go back to Alabama, go back to South Carolina, go back to Georgia, go back to Louisiana, go back to the slums and ghettos of our northern cities, knowing that somehow this situation can and will be changed. Let us not wallow in the valley of despair.

I say to you today, my friends, so even though we face the difficulties of today and tomorrow, I still have a dream. It is a dream deeply rooted in the American dream.

I have a dream that one day this nation will rise up and live out the true meaning of its creed: "We hold these truths to be self-evident: that all men are created equal."

I have a dream that one day on the red hills of Georgia the sons of former slaves and the sons of former slave owners will be able to sit down together at the table of brotherhood.

I have a dream that one day even the state of Mississippi, a state sweltering with the heat of injustice, sweltering with the heat of oppression, will be transformed into an oasis of freedom and justice.

I have a dream that my four little children will one day live in a nation where they will not be judged by the color of their skin but by the content of their character.

I have a dream today.

I have a dream that one day, down in Alabama, with its vicious racists, with its governor having his lips dripping with the words of interposition and nullification; one day right there in Alabama, little black boys and black girls will be able to join hands with little white boys and white girls as sisters and brothers.

I have a dream today.

I have a dream that one day every valley shall be exalted, every hill and mountain shall be made low, the rough places will be made plain, and the crooked places will be made straight, and the glory of the Lord shall be revealed, and all flesh shall see it together.

This is our hope. This is the faith that I go back to the South with. With this faith we will be able to hew out of the mountain of despair a stone of hope. With this faith we will be able to transform the jangling discords of our nation into a beautiful symphony of brotherhood. With this faith we will be able to work together, to pray together, to struggle together, to go to jail together, to stand up for freedom together, knowing that we will be free one day.

This will be the day when all of God's children will be able to sing with a new meaning, "My country, 'tis of thee, sweet land of liberty, of thee I sing. Land where my fathers died, land of the pilgrim's pride, from every mountainside, let freedom ring."

And if America is to be a great nation this must become true. So let freedom ring from the prodigious hilltops of New Hampshire. Let freedom ring from the mighty mountains of New York. Let freedom ring from the heightening Alleghenies of Pennsylvania!

Let freedom ring from the snowcapped Rockies of Colorado!

Let freedom ring from the curvaceous slopes of California!

But not only that; let freedom ring from Stone Mountain of Georgia!

Let freedom ring from Lookout Mountain of Tennessee!

Let freedom ring from every hill and molehill of Mississippi. From every mountainside, let freedom ring.

Glossary

five score	one hundred, with one score equal to twenty
governor	George C. Wallace, elected governor of Alabama in 1962
great American	President Abraham Lincoln, who issued the Emancipation Proclamation
nullification	the doctrine that a state has the right to refuse to implement or enforce a law passed by the U.S. Congress
promissory note	a document that represents a promise to pay a debt at some future date

And when this happens, when we allow freedom to ring, when we let it ring from every village and every hamlet, from every state and every city, we will be able to speed up that day when all of God's children, black men and white men, Jews and Gentiles, Protestants and Catholics, will be able to join hands and sing in the words of the old Negro spiritual, "Free at last! Free at last! Thank God Almighty, we are free at last!"

SPEECH IN OPPOSITION TO THE VIETNAM WAR (1967)

I come to this magnificent house of worship tonight because my conscience leaves me no other choice. I join you in this meeting because I am in deepest agreement with the aims and work of the organization which has brought us together: Clergy and Laymen Concerned about Vietnam. The recent statements of your executive committee are the sentiments of my own heart, and I found myself in full accord when I read its opening lines: "A time comes when silence is betrayal." And that time has come for us in relation to Vietnam.

The truth of these words is beyond doubt, but the mission to which they call us is a most difficult one. Even when pressed by the demands of inner truth, men do not easily assume the task of opposing their government's policy, especially in time of war. Nor does the human spirit move without great difficulty against all the apathy of conformist thought within one's own bosom and in the surrounding world. Moreover, when the issues at hand seem as perplexed as they often do in the case of this dreadful conflict, we are always on the verge of being mesmerized by uncertainty; but we must move on.

And some of us who have already begun to break the silence of the night have found that the calling to speak is often a vocation of agony, but we must speak. We must speak with all the humility that is appropriate to our limited vision, but we must speak. And we must rejoice as well, for surely this is the first time in our nation's history that a significant number of its religious leaders have chosen to move beyond the prophesying of smooth patriotism to the high grounds of a firm dissent based upon the mandates of conscience and the reading of history. Perhaps a new spirit is rising among us. If it is, let us trace its movements and pray that our own inner being may be sensitive to its guidance, for we are deeply in need of a new way beyond the darkness that seems so close around us.

Over the past two years, as I have moved to break the betrayal of my own silences and to speak from the burnings of my own heart, as I have called for radical departures from the destruction of Vietnam, many persons have questioned me about the wisdom of my path. At the heart of their concerns this query has often loomed large and loud: "Why are you speaking about the war, Dr. King?" "Why are you joining the voices of dissent?" "Peace and civil rights don't mix," they say. "Aren't you hurting the cause of your people?" they ask. And when I hear them, though I often understand the source of their concern, I am nevertheless greatly saddened, for such questions mean that the inquirers have not really known me, my commitment or my calling. Indeed, their questions suggest that they do not know the world in which they live.

In the light of such tragic misunderstanding, I deem it of signal importance to try to state clearly, and I trust concisely, why I believe that the path from Dexter Avenue Baptist Church—the church in Montgomery, Alabama, where I began my pastorate—leads clearly to this sanctuary tonight.

Since I am a preacher by trade, I suppose it is not surprising that I have seven major reasons for bringing Vietnam into the field of my moral vision. There is at the outset a very obvious and almost facile connection between the war in Vietnam and the struggle I, and others, have been waging in America. A few years ago there was a shining moment in that struggle. It seemed as if there was a real promise of hope for the poor—both black and white—through the poverty program. There were experiments, hopes, new beginnings. Then came the buildup in Vietnam, and I watched this program broken and eviscerated, as if it were some idle political plaything of a society gone mad on war, and I knew that America would never invest the necessary funds or energies in rehabilitation of its poor so long as adventures like Vietnam continued to draw men and skills and money like some demonic destructive suction tube. So, I was increasingly compelled to see the war as an enemy of the poor and to attack it as such.

Perhaps the more tragic recognition of reality took place when it became clear to me that the war was doing far more than devastating the hopes of the poor at home. It was sending their sons and their brothers and their husbands to fight and to die in extraordinarily high proportions relative to the rest of the population. We were taking the black young men who had been crippled by our society and sending them eight thousand miles away to guarantee liberties in Southeast Asia which they had not found in southwest Georgia and East Harlem. And so we have been repeatedly faced with the cruel irony of watching

Negro and white boys on TV screens as they kill and die together for a nation that has been unable to seat them together in the same schools. And so we watch them in brutal solidarity burning the huts of a poor village, but we realize that they would hardly live on the same block in Chicago. I could not be silent in the face of such cruel manipulation of the poor.

My third reason moves to an even deeper level of awareness, for it grows out of my experience in the ghettos of the North over the last three years—especially the last three summers. As I have walked among the desperate, rejected, and angry young men, I have told them that Molotov cocktails and rifles would not solve their problems. I have tried to offer them my deepest compassion while maintaining my conviction that social change comes most meaningfully through nonviolent action. But they ask—and rightly so—what about Vietnam? They ask if our own nation wasn't using massive doses of violence to solve its problems, to bring about the changes it wanted. Their questions hit home, and I knew that I could never again raise my voice against the violence of the oppressed in the ghettos without having first spoken clearly to the greatest purveyor of violence in the world today—my own government. For the sake of those boys, for the sake of this government, for the sake of the hundreds of thousands trembling under our violence, I cannot be silent.

For those who ask the question, "Aren't you a civil rights leader?" and thereby mean to exclude me from the movement for peace, I have this further answer. In 1957 when a group of us formed the Southern Christian Leadership Conference, we chose as our motto: "To save the soul of America." We were convinced that we could not limit our vision to certain rights for black people, but instead affirmed the conviction that America would never be free or saved from itself until the descendants of its slaves were loosed completely from the shackles they still wear....

Now, it should be incandescently clear that no one who has any concern for the integrity and life of America today can ignore the present war. If America's soul becomes totally poisoned, part of the autopsy must read: Vietnam. It can never be saved so long as it destroys the deepest hopes of men the world over. So it is that those of us who are yet determined that America will be are led down the path of protest and dissent, working for the health of our land.

As if the weight of such a commitment to the life and health of America were not enough, another burden of responsibility was placed upon me in 1964; and I cannot forget that the Nobel Prize for Peace was also a commission—a commission to work hard-er than I had ever worked before for "the brotherhood of man." This is a calling that takes me beyond national allegiances, but even if it were not present I would yet have to live with the meaning of my commitment to the ministry of Jesus Christ....

And finally, as I try to explain for you and for myself the road that leads from Montgomery to this place I would have offered all that was most valid if I simply said that I must be true to my conviction that I share with all men the calling to be a son of the living God. Beyond the calling of race or nation or creed is this vocation of sonship and brotherhood, and because I believe that the Father is deeply concerned especially for his suffering and helpless and outcast children, I come tonight to speak for them....

Somehow this madness must cease. We must stop now. I speak as a child of God and brother to the suffering poor of Vietnam. I speak for those whose land is being laid waste, whose homes are being destroyed, whose culture is being subverted. I speak for the poor of America who are paying the double price of smashed hopes at home, and death and corruption in Vietnam. I speak as a citizen of the world, for the world as it stands aghast at the path we have taken. I speak as one who loves America, to the leaders of our own nation: The great initiative in this war is ours; the initiative to stop it must be ours....

I am convinced that if we are to get on the right side of the world revolution, we as a nation must undergo a radical revolution of values. We must rapidly begin...the shift from a thing-oriented society to a person-oriented society. When machines and computers, profit motives and property rights, are considered more important than people, the giant triplets of racism, extreme materialism, and militarism are incapable of being conquered.

A true revolution of values will soon cause us to question the fairness and justice of many of our past and present policies. On the one hand, we are called to play the Good Samaritan on life's roadside, but that will be only an initial act. One day we must come to see that the whole Jericho Road must be transformed so that men and women will not be constantly beaten and robbed as they make their journey on life's highway. True compassion is more than flinging a coin to a beggar. It comes to see that an edifice which produces beggars needs restructuring.

A true revolution of values will soon look uneasily on the glaring contrast of poverty and wealth. With righteous indignation, it will look across the seas and see individual capitalists of the West investing huge sums of money in Asia, Africa, and South America, only to take the profits out with no concern for the social betterment of the countries, and say, "This is not just." It will look at our alliance with the landed gentry of South America and say, "This is not just." The Western arrogance of feeling that it has everything to teach others and nothing to learn from them is not just.

A true revolution of values will lay hand on the world order and say of war, "This way of settling differences is not just." This business of burning human beings with napalm, of filling our nation's homes with orphans and widows, of injecting poisonous drugs of hate into the veins of peoples normally humane, of sending men home from dark and bloody battlefields physically handicapped and psychologically deranged, cannot be reconciled with wisdom, justice, and love. A nation that continues year after year to spend more money on military defense than on programs of social uplift is approaching spiritual death.

America, the richest and most powerful nation in the world, can well lead the way in this revolution of values. There is nothing except a tragic death wish to prevent us from reordering our priorities so that the pursuit of peace will take precedence over the pursuit of war. There is nothing to keep us from molding a recalcitrant status quo with bruised hands until we have fashioned it into a brotherhood....

Now let us begin. Now let us rededicate ourselves to the long and bitter, but beautiful, struggle for a new world. This is the calling of the sons of God, and our brothers wait eagerly for our response. Shall we say the odds are too great? Shall we tell them the struggle is too hard? Will our message be that the forces of American life militate against their arrival as full men, and we send our deepest regrets? Or will there be another message—of longing, of hope, of solidarity with their yearnings, of commitment to their cause, whatever the cost? The choice is ours, and though we might prefer it otherwise, we must choose in this crucial moment of human history.

Glossary

Good Samaritan	reference to the central character is a parable told by Jesus (Luke 10:29–37) about a man from Samaria who gave aid to a stranger who had been beaten and robbed
Jericho Road	the road that connects Jericho and Jerusalem, the setting for the parable of the Good Samaritan
landed gentry	the landowning class, usually the owners of tenanted estates
militate against	to influence or have force against
Molotov cocktails	improvised firebombs, named after Vyacheslav Molotov, a foreign minister of the Soviet Union
napalm	a highly flammable liquid used to create incendiary bombs
recalcitrant	resistant

Robert La Follette (Library of Congress)

ROBERT LA FOLLETTE   1855–1925

Governor, U.S. Congressman, and Senator

Featured Documents
- Speech on the Amendment of National Banking Laws (1908)
- Speech Opposing War with Germany (1917)
- Platform of the Conference for Progressive Political Action (1924)

Overview

Robert Marion La Follette, a son of farmers, was born on June 14, 1855, in Primrose, Wisconsin. At age twenty he entered the University of Wisconsin, graduating in 1879. In 1880, after briefly attending law school, he was elected district attorney of Dane County, where Madison, the capital of Wisconsin, is located. In 1884 he was elected as the youngest member of U.S. House of Representatives, where he was so orthodox in his Republicanism that he ardently supported the high rates of the McKinley Tariff. The victim of a Democratic landslide in 1890, he resumed his law practice in Madison. An attempted bribe by the Wisconsin senator Philetus Sawyer, who asked La Follette to intervene in a case in which his brother-in-law was judge, radicalized the young attorney, who henceforth became a strong foe of entrenched interests.

After two abortive bids for Wisconsin's governorship, La Follette won the race in 1900 and was reelected in both 1902 and 1904. He pushed through a battery of reform measures, including conservation acts, antilobbying laws, regulation of telephone and telegraph companies, educational expansion, public utility controls, consumer protection, tax and civil service legislation, a direct primary, and railroad and industrial commissions. He also pioneered what was called the "Wisconsin idea," by which university experts aided in drafting significant legislation. While still governor, he was chosen in January 1905 by the state legislature to represent Wisconsin in the U.S. Senate, where he would serve until his death in 1925.

In the Senate, La Follette was one of the more vocal members, focusing in particular on giant business, which he saw as an evil in itself. In 1906, breaking the unwritten rule that freshman senators should not speak, he delivered an address on strengthening the pending Hepburn Act, a railroad regulation bill that was so detailed that it filled 148 pages of the *Congressional Record*. He produced similar documentation in advocating the direct election of senators, more powerful antitrust legislation, income redistribution, lower tariffs, and protection for American workers. He led the attack against the Aldrich-Vreeland bill in 1908, a measure to allow banks to issue emergency currency against securities and bonds. In his presentation, he claimed that fewer than a hundred men dominated and controlled business and industry in America. Although he was nominally a Republican, he broke with the presidency of William Howard Taft over the high Payne-Aldrich Tariff and over alleged corruption in the Department of the Interior. He sought to gain the Republican presidential nomination of 1912, but his major supporters abandoned him once former President Theodore Roosevelt entered the race.

When Woodrow Wilson became president in 1913, La Follette backed such "New Freedom" proposals as the Underwood Tariff and the Federal Reserve System. La Follette authored only one major bill, the Seamen's Act, legislation that abrogated one-year contracts and mandated safety measures for passengers and crew. Always a foe of military intervention, he spoke forcefully against armed involvement in Mexico and the Caribbean. In March 1917 he led a filibuster against Wilson's proposal to arm American merchant ships in the aftermath of Germany's declaration of unrestricted submarine warfare, at which point the president snapped, "A little group of willful men, representing no opinion but their own, have rendered the great Government of the United States helpless and contemptible" (Link, p. 362). La Follette was equally outspoken in his opposition to American entrance into World War I, conscription, the curbing of the freedoms of speech and the press, the Treaty of Versailles, and entry into the League of Nations. In 1924 he ran for president on an independent Progressive Party ticket, gaining 4.8 million votes. His platform included collective bargaining, public ownership of water power and railroads, aid to farmers, a ban on child labor, and the recall of federal judges. On June 18, 1925, he died of heart failure in Washington, D.C.

Explanation and Analysis of Documents

Throughout much of his adult life, Robert M. La Follette was known as "Fighting Bob," and the appellation was most apt. He was admittedly by nature combative and suspicious. At the same time, he was an indefatigable researcher who could often intimidate opponents with mounds of supporting data. He always characterized himself as a spokesman for a public trampled by predatory capitalists and Wall Street speculators. In 1908, while attacking a major banking bill, he indicted the entire financial system, which he saw grinding down the true producers of the nation. In April 1917 he sought to parry President Wilson's call for war with Germany by denying that the United States had ever been neutral. When he heeded the call

1855
- **June 14**
Robert Marion La Follette is born in Primrose, Wisconsin.

1879
- **June 18**
La Follette graduates from the University of Wisconsin.

1880
- La Follette is elected district attorney of Dane County, Wisconsin.

1884
- **November 4**
La Follette is elected to the U.S. House of Representatives, where he would serve for six years.

1901
- **January 7**
La Follette is inaugurated governor of Wisconsin.

1906
- **January 4**
La Follette takes the oath of office as a U.S. senator, for the first time

1908
- **March 17**
La Follette attacks corporate oligarchy on the Senate floor in a speech on the amendment of national banking laws.

1917
- **April 4**
La Follette opposes President Woodrow Wilson's call for a declaration of war on Germany.

1924
- **July 6**
The text of La Follette's Progressive Party platform is released.

1925
- **June 18**
La Follette dies of heart failure in Washington, D.C.

---

to lead the Progressive Party in 1924, he advanced a platform that embodied many of the major reforms sought by Theodore Roosevelt and Wilson.

◆ **Speech on the Amendment of National Banking Laws**

By the beginning of the twentieth century, the corporation became the linchpin of the American economy. Moreover, thanks to such devices as the trust and the holding company, many of these enterprises became increasingly concentrated in fewer hands. By 1904 two-fifths of all manufacturing was controlled by 305 industrial combinations possessing an aggregate capital of $7 billion. The epitome of such consolidation of power was John D. Rockefeller's Standard Oil Company, a firm that by 1900 dominated the petroleum industry. The imbalanced situation was fostered by Wall Street investment banks, particularly J. P. Morgan & Company. These banks would raise needed capital for new corporations by selling their stocks and bonds and would, at the same time, police these new ventures by placing their own representatives on the boards of directors and by controlling sources of credit. Critics of this new centralization, such as La Follette, referred to the phenomenon as the "money trust."

On March 17, 1908, La Follette began a series of speeches attacking the money trust. This first speech was triggered by the Aldrich currency bill, proposed in the aftermath of the Panic of 1907. Nelson Aldrich, the powerful chairman of the Senate Finance Committee, proposed the issue of $500 million in emergency currency that would be backed by state, municipal, and private railroad bonds. Edward B. Vreeland of New York offered a similar bill in the House. Aldrich soon renounced the clause involving railroad bonds, acting out of the fear that the proposal would injure the Finance Committee members William B. Allison of Iowa and Chester I. Long of Kansas in their forthcoming races for reelection. La Follette had intended to blast Aldrich's original proposal, but he hastily rewrote his speech, with the result containing some of the most sensationalist charges ever made on the floor of Congress.

In his Senate speech of March 17, 1908, La Follette begins with the accusation that about a hundred men "hold in their hands the business of the country." He lists the enterprises they controlled, ranging from railroads to mining, from cotton to food. He then points to the domination of American banking by Wall Street, which he found to be involved in destructive speculation. The Wisconsin senator refers to a special committee, established in 1905 by the New York State Legislature and headed by the state senator William M. Armstrong, which investigated the corrupt use of life insurance funds. Wall Street banks either established connections with trust companies or organized such firms themselves so as to sell securities, underwrite bonds, and float loans that ordinary banks could not openly sponsor. La Follette then produces a massive "List of Men Who Control Industrial, Franchise, Transportation, and Financial Business of the United States, with Their Directorships and Offices in Various Corporations." This document covered ten pages of fine print in the *Congressional Record*. Here, La Follette argues, was firm evidence showing the control exercised by Morgan and Standard Oil at the expense of ordinary Americans.

In the last part of his speech, La Follette accuses the Morgan and Standard Oil banks of creating the Panic of 1907 so as to line their own pockets. During the October panic, the great New York financial institutions were unable to supply funds to needy banks in the interior of the country. Therefore, bankruptcies took place among several large industrial corporations and many small western and southern banks as well. Only intervention by J. P. Morgan himself, who switched funds from one bank to another as well as to securities markets, could save the day. La Follette, however, does not see Morgan as a redeemer but as one who profited unjustly from the crisis. He quotes predictions of impending disaster made that summer by James J. Hill, chairman of the Great Northern Railway Company, and Edward Payson Ripley, president of the Atchison, Topeka and Santa Fe Railway. He also notes warnings of banking concentration made by Thomas F. Woodlock, former editor of the *Wall Street Journal*; Charles J. Bullock, an economist at Williams College; and the commercial expert Edward E. Pratt.

It was Morgan's effort to squeeze out a conglomeration centering on the Heinze United Copper Company that created the panic. Only after it became obvious that "every countinghouse, factory, and shop in America" might be affected did J. P. Morgan and James Stillman, board chairman of the Rockefeller-controlled National City Bank of New York, meet on October 24 to end the crisis. La Follette concludes by denouncing the Morgan and Rockefeller interests for sacrificing "the distressed merchant and manufacturer" to the interests of "the speculating banker." His final remark, "By their fruits ye shall know them!" was taken from Jesus' Sermon on the Mount (Matthew 7:20).

La Follette's claims were widely publicized. Not surprisingly, he was immediately challenged. The president of the First National Bank of Chicago, one of the men on the senator's list, called the speech "worse than rot" and said that it was "a deliberate stirring up of passion and rage among people who have no facility for acquiring knowledge at first hand and are dependent upon men whom they trust" (*New York Times*, March 19, 1908). Such attacks did not faze La Follette, who concluded his series of addresses on March 24. On this occasion he denied that he was attacking such figures as Rockefeller, Morgan, and E. H. Harriman, of the Union Pacific Railroad, as individuals, remarking that they were merely types, the embodiment of an evil. It was what drove them that had to be destroyed in order to safeguard America's free institutions.

Some business interests backed La Follette, among them the New York Board of Trade, which distributed copies of the speech among its most active members. Indeed, in contrast to earlier requests, this time it was companies in the Northeast, not the Midwest, that sought many reprints. Aldrich accepted a La Follette amendment prohibiting banks from investing in the securities of other firms in which they had interlocking directorates. However, defeated by a vote of thirty-seven to thirteen was a La Follette proposal to forbid banks from making loans to people who were officers of the same banks. On May 29, La Follette proved furious enough to start a filibuster of the Aldrich-Vreeland bill. Battling a cold and addressing his Senate colleagues in ninety-degree heat, La Follette spoke for a record nineteen hours, but parliamentary blundering by allies led to the bill's adoption, by a vote of forty-three to twenty-two. Only with the adoption of the Federal Reserve System in 1913 were genuine reforms made to the nation's banking and credit system.

◆ Speech Opposing War with Germany

On April 2, 1917, President Woodrow Wilson asked Congress for a declaration of war against Germany. On January 31, the imperial German government had announced that on the following day its submarines would sink without warning all ships, including those belonging to neutral nations, in a broad war zone that covered the seas around Britain, France, Italy, and the eastern Mediterranean. Then, in late February, it became known that Arthur Zimmermann, the German foreign minister, had proposed an alliance with Mexico in the event that Kaiser Wilhelm's government went to war against the United States. In return, Mexico would receive vast territories lost in the Mexican-American War of 1846–1848. Wilson sought to keep U.S. involvement limited to "armed neutrality" but found his hand forced on March 18 by the German sinking of three American ships.

On April 4, the Senate met to vote upon Wilson's call for a war declaration. Debate began at ten in the morning and lasted until late that night. Only five senators spoke against the declaration—the first four being James K. Vardaman (D-Miss.), William J. Stone (D-Mo.), George Norris (R-Nebr.), and Asle Gronna (R-N.D.). Then, in the afternoon, La Follette addressed his colleagues. La Follette's daughter, Fola, later captured the excitement of this event, writing, "Senators who had been in the smoking room hurried to their seats; men and women in the crowded galleries leaned forward expectantly. The stir of interest was followed by unusual quiet in the galleries and on the floor" (La Follette and La Follette, vol. 1, p. 657).

In the record of the speech, La Follette begins by claiming that senators have the duty to vote their convictions, irrespective of whether they are backing the president. He then defends his opposition to the armed-ship bill, claiming that polls revealed strong opposition to entrance into the European war and portraying himself as representing "the poor," that is, those powerless Americans who would be making the major sacrifices. Once such people experienced 300 percent price increases in life's necessities and a quadrupling of taxes to enrich J. P. Morgan, they would be heard—though, of course, in a peaceful manner.

Citing Wilson's call for "practicable cooperation" with Germany's foes, La Follette warns that the United States would thereby be embracing Britain's "shameful methods of warfare," against which he had continually protested.

CLASS OF SERVICE DESIRED

| Fast Day Message |
| Day Letter |
| Night Message |
| Night Letter |

Patrons should mark an X opposite the class of service desired; OTHERWISE THE TELEGRAM WILL BE TRANSMITTED AS A FAST DAY MESSAGE.

WESTERN UNION TELEGRAM

NEWCOMB CARLTON, PRESIDENT

Send the following telegram, subject to the terms on back hereof, which are hereby agreed to

Time Filed

via Galveston

JAN 19 1917

GERMAN LEGATION

MEXICO CITY

```
  130    13042   13401    8501     115    3528    416    17214    6491    11310
18147    18222   21560   10247   11518   23677  13605    3494    14936
98092     5905   11311   10392   10371    0302  21290    5161    39695
23571    17504   11269   18276   18101    0317   0228    17694    4473
23284    22200   19452   21589   67893    5569  13918    8958    12137
 1333     4725    4458    5905   17166   13851   4458   17149   14471    6706
13850    12224    6929   14991    7382   15857  67893   14218   36477
 5870    17553   67893    5870    5454   16102  15217   22801   17138
21001    17388    7446   23638   18222    6719  14331   15021   23845
 3156    23552   22096   21604    4797    9497  22464   20855    4377
23610    18140   22260    5905   13347   20420  39689   13732   20667
 6929     5275   18507   52262    1340   22049  13339   11265   22295
10439    14814    4178    6992    8784    7632   7357    6926   52262   11267
21100    21272    9346    9559   22464   15874  18502   18500   15857
 2188     5376    7381   98092   16127   13486   9350    9220   76036   14219
 5144     2831   17920   11347   17142   11264   7667    7762   15099    9110
10482    97556    3569    3870
```

BERNSTORFF.

Charge German Embassy.

The Zimmermann telegram of 1917: a coded message from the German foreign minister Arthur Zimmermann to a Mexican official, offering to help Mexico regain territory lost to the United States (AP/Wide World Photos)

Such "practicable cooperation" would, in fact, mean the starving of children, the aged, and the infirm in Germany. Furthermore, the United States would be binding itself to British war aims, "of which we know nothing." He was certain, however, of one thing: Britain was a hereditary monarchy based on restricted suffrage and the grinding exploitation of its laborers. Indeed, with the exception of France and Russia (where, he states, democracy had just been established), America's new allies all represented the old order, one that had not even kept pace with the municipal and social reforms of the new German enemy. Furthermore, the United States had not even made its support of Britain conditional upon home rule for the rebellious nations of Ireland, Egypt, and India. La Follette notes that Wilson had called the war one for democracy, which the president defined as a condition wherein "those who submit to authority" possess "a voice in their own government." Yet if such were really the case, why was the very issue of entering the war not being presented directly to the American people? The senator then answers his own question, claiming that the public would vote ten to one against entering any such conflict. Instead of permitting a popular referendum, the government was considering forced conscription and "espionage" bills, both of which, he asserts, would violate traditional American liberties.

La Follette points to centuries of American tension with Britain, which he contrasts to long-standing friendly relations with Germany. He blames the outbreak of the current conflict on a small minority of greedy and ambitious men who sought profit and power while being indifferent to any suffering inflicted on the masses. He finds much credence in the German claim that France, Britain, and Russia had long been secret allies. The senator goes on at length, quoting various documents to support his claim that the United States acquiesced in Britain's continued violation of neutral rights, in particular, British efforts to prevent American goods from reaching Germany. Making an even more serious accusation, La Follette calls the United States itself highly non-neutral, for applying one standard to Britain and a far more rigorous one to Germany. Rather than go to war, he asserts, the United States should demand that both belligerents respect American commercial rights and should furthermore enforce these rights against the two major powers. If the nation did not choose this option, it could withdraw food supplies to both sides, which would force them to honor American commerce.

The senator finished his address after nearly three hours. The Democratic senator John Sharp Williams of Mississippi immediately reported that La Follette's speech "would have better become Herr Bethmann-Hollweg," a reference to Germany's chancellor. Williams continued, "I heard from him a speech which was pro-German, pretty nearly pro-Goth, and pro-Vandal, which was anti-American President and anti-American Congress, and anti-American people" (La Follette and La Follette, vol. 1, pp. 665–666). After six other speeches, all backing entrance into war, the Senate voted, just after eleven. The clerk announced the final tally at 82 to 6. On the next day House members sup-ported their Senate colleagues 373 to 50. On April 6 Wilson signed the declaration, and the United States was at war. Only after the conflict was over and a postwar disillusionment set in did many Americans see La Follette as having uttered prophetic words.

◆ **Platform of the Conference for Progressive Political Action**

"The two old parties have betrayed the people," said La Follette in the early summer of 1924 (La Follette and La Follette, vol. 2, p. 1110). His words found firm support at the 1924 convention of the Conference for Progressive Political Action, which met early in July. This organization was composed of a coalition of old-time progressives, dissident agrarians, college students, trade union leaders, and socialists of all shades. A majority of the delegates were under forty, though the seventy-year-old Jacob Coxey, leader of a famed march of the unemployed in 1894, was present. So, too, was the poet Edwin Markham, author of the proletarian verse "The Man with the Hoe," and the New York congressman Fiorello La Guardia. The group met on Independence Day in the same Cleveland auditorium where the Republican Party had nominated President Calvin Coolidge for reelection less than a month earlier. On the following day the Conference for Progressive Political Action nominated La Follette for president by acclamation. As the Wisconsin senator had remained in Washington, D.C., his son Robert M. La Follette, Jr., read a platform drafted by his father to the assembly.

One of the briefer political programs on record, it begins with the general claim that since the inception of the Republic the American people have been engaged in a struggle of freedom against tyranny. La Follette juxtaposes ruthless competition with "the progressive principle of cooperation," whereby government "offers" the greatest possible amount of well-being to its people. In lieu of a society wherein one class gains at the expense of another, he envisions a society based on mutual support and interdependence.

The platform then moves on to specific points. Foremost is an assault on "private monopoly." Unlike such Progressives as Theodore Roosevelt, who sought the regulation—not necessarily the breakup—of oligopolistic and monopolistic concerns, La Follette believed that concentration in itself was inefficient; only competition could lead to lower prices and higher wages. The platform then affirms the freedoms of speech, press, and assembly, all of which had been flagrantly violated by the Wilson administration once the United States entered World War I. It calls for the public ownership of water and hydroelectric power; the latter was swiftly becoming a major enterprise, for electricity was fostering changes in the nation's life as radical as those caused by the automobile. In a separate, more detailed statement, La Follette pointed to the massive nitrate complex at Muscle Shoals, Alabama, later the linchpin of the Tennessee Valley Authority, as a model for such development. His desire for public ownership of the railroads was rooted in his opposition to the Esch-Cummins

Act (1920), which legislated greater control by the Interstate Commerce Commission but fell short of total nationalization. The call for the conservation of coal, iron, oil, and timber lands echoed his abortive opposition in 1920 to the Mineral Leasing Act and the Federal Water Power Act, legislation that granted corporations fifty-year leases to develop minerals and water power on public lands. His plea for public works to relieve unemployment can be traced to the demands of "Coxey's Army."

Much of the Progressive platform centers on finance. La Follette was seeking increased taxes on incomes, dividends, estates, and inheritances, all of which ran counter to the economic philosophy of Treasury Secretary Andrew W. Mellon, who believed that low taxes and laissez-faire would create greater prosperity for all citizens. In attacking high tariffs, the platform was responding to the recent Fordney-McCumber Tariff, enacted in 1922, which embodied a massive increase over previous rates. All such proposals were rooted in La Follette's efforts to force those businesses that most benefited from profits gained during the recent world war to bear most of the subsequent cost of the conflict; compensation to veterans would certainly be included among these.

The platform calls for the federal and state protection of cooperatives, government loans to farmers, and a government marketing corporation. These measures were a response to the agricultural depression created at the end of World War I, when overextended cotton and wheat growers found prices on the world market sharply declining. In 1921 Congress had expanded the Federal Farm Loan System and had legislated the Packers and Stockyards Act, which sought to preserve competition among packers. It had passed the Agricultural Credits Act (1923) as well. To La Follette, however, international finance still controlled America.

La Follette was seeking various labor reforms, such as a federal child labor amendment, the legalized right to collective bargaining, and an end to injunctions, or court orders that prohibited efforts to organize workers. Particularly controversial was La Follette's challenge to elected federal judges and congressional powers to validate federal laws declared unconstitutional by the Supreme Court. In 1922 the high court had declared invalid a tax on firms employing children. With an eye to his Wisconsin base, the senator was also seeking the construction of a seaway along the St. Lawrence River.

Foreign policy planks include a war referendum, radical disarmament, the condemnation of State Department protection for overseas Wall Street investments, and the revision of the Treaty of Versailles, which deprived the nations defeated in World War I of much territory and imposed severe financial indemnities. In light of the strong influence of the newly formed Communist Party among the American Left, the platform concludes by opposing dictatorship either by plutocracy or by the proletariat.

La Follette, together with his vice presidential candidate Senator Burton K. Wheeler (D-Mont.), ran against the incumbent Calvin Coolidge and the Democratic candidate John W. Davis, a Wall Street banker. Although his ticket was endorsed by both the Socialist Party and the American Federation of Labor, it fared badly at the polls. Electoral votes came only from La Follette's home state of Wisconsin. Throughout the campaign, La Follette was facing an uphill battle, for most of the nation was experiencing economic boom. To his countrymen, the large corporation was a creator of material bounty, not a source of crushing poverty. Moreover, the Progressive platform was silent on such controversial matters as the newly resurgent Ku Klux Klan, civil rights for African Americans, and the prohibition of alcoholic beverages.

Impact and Legacy

In 1957 the Senate voted La Follette one of its five most significant members in history, along with Daniel Webster, Henry Clay, John C. Calhoun, and Robert A. Taft. Yet, aside from the Seamen's Act, La Follette's name has never been attached to any national legislation. Very often, he was speaking for those elements of American society—in particular, the small town and the farm—that were losing traditional prominence in giving way to the impersonal forces of industrialization and urbanization. Despite La Follette's attacks on "the system," the massive corporation remained. Similarly, major innovations in transportation and communication came to make his isolationism obsolete. In many ways, time was not on his side.

There was also the matter of personality. In his home state, he had been a most effective governor, controlling his own party machine with an iron discipline. Still, in a wider arena, he was too much of a "loner" to spearhead significant bills. He was always seen as "Battling Bob," the perpetual insurgent who engaged in one crusade after another, fighting in turn the "money trust," "financial imperialism," the munitions makers. Although he mobilized his arguments in a most thorough way, offering barrages of charts and statistics, he would often convey obsession with conspiracy, so much so that one biographer, Nancy C. Unger, offers the following traits as terms in her index: paranoia, sense of moral superiority, self-righteousness, exaggerations and fabrications, sanctimoniousness, self-absorption, black-and-white worldview, inability to work as member of team, self-destructive behavior. Although such negative qualities undoubtedly weakened La Follette's effectiveness, he remains a prophetic figure. Admittedly, La Follette too often fell prey to inflammatory rhetoric and overly simplistic logic. Yet his pursuit of a more democratic society, one focusing on the common good rather than on the welfare of the privileged, should give him a leading place in any civic pantheon.

Key Sources

The La Follette family papers are located in the Library of Congress. Robert La Follette's gubernatorial papers are at the Wisconsin Historical Society, in Madison. *La Follette's*

"I have placed before you the record evidence that less than one hundred men own and control railroads, traction, shipping, cable, telegraph, telephone, express, mining, coal, oil, gas, electric light, copper, cotton, sugar, tobacco, agricultural implements, and the food products, as well as banking and insurance."

(Speech on the Amendment of National Banking Laws)

"Sir, can any sane man doubt the power of a little group of men in whose hands are lodged the control of the railroads and the industries, outside of agriculture, as well as the great banks, insurance, and trust companies of the principal money center of the country, to give commercial banking and general business a shock at will?"

(Speech on the Amendment of National Banking Laws)

"The poor, sir, who are the ones called upon to rot in the trenches, have no organized power, have no press to voice their will upon this question of peace or war; but, oh, Mr. President, at some time they will be heard."

(Speech Opposing War with Germany)

"For my own part, I believe that this war, like nearly all others, originated in the selfish ambition and cruel greed of a comparatively few men in each government who saw in war an opportunity for profit and power for themselves, and who were wholly indifferent to the awful suffering they knew that war would bring to the masses."

(Speech Opposing War with Germany)

"It is our faith that we all go up or down together—that class gains are temporary delusions and that eternal laws of compensation make every man his brother's keeper."

(Platform of the Conference for Progressive Political Action)

"The nation may grow rich in the vision of greed. The nation will grow great in the vision of service."

(Platform of the Conference for Progressive Political Action)

Autobiography: A Personal Narrative of Political Experiences (1911) was timed for the author's intended 1912 presidential bid. *The Political Philosophy of Robert M. La Follette as Revealed in His Speeches and Writings* (1920), edited by Ellen Torelle, gives excepts of his speeches and articles, as does Robert S. Maxwell, ed., *La Follette* (1969), which also includes excerpts from works by historians.

Further Reading

■ Articles

Cooper, John Milton. "Robert M. La Follette: Political Prophet." *Wisconsin Magazine of History* 69 (Winter 1985–1986): 91–105.

"Forgan Attacks LaFollette." *New York Times* March 19, 1908, p. 5.

■ Books

Burgchardt, Carl R. *Robert M. La Follette, Sr.: The Voice of Conscience.* New York: Greenwood Press, 1992.

La Follette, Belle Case, and La Follette, Fola. *Robert M. La Follette, June 14, 1855–June 18, 1925.* 2 vols. New York: Macmillan, 1953.

Link, Arthur S. *Wilson: Campaigns for Progressivism and Peace, 1916–1917.* Princeton, N.J.: Princeton University Press, 1965.

MacKay, Kenneth C. *The Progressive Movement of 1924.* New York: Columbia University Press, 1947.

Maxwell, Robert S. *La Follette and the Rise of the Progressives in Wisconsin.* Madison: State Historical Society of Wisconsin, 1956.

Thelen, David P. *Robert M. La Follette and the Insurgent Spirit.* Boston: Little, Brown, 1976.

Unger, Nancy C. *Fighting Bob La Follette: The Righteous Reformer.* Chapel Hill: University of North Carolina Press, 2000.

—Justus Doenecke

Questions for Further Study

1. Much has changed since the early twentieth century, when many of the positions held by the two leading political parties in America were opposite to what they are today. The Republican Party of La Follette's time attracted social progressives such as Jane Addams, whereas the Democrats tended to be more conservative. La Follette (particularly in his platform for the Progressive Party) anticipated many ideas that would become part of American government, largely through the influence of Democrats, such as public ownership of utilities and an emphasis on environmentalism. In what ways was La Follette very much a man of his era and in what ways was he ahead of his time?

2. Study La Follette's 1908 speech on the national banking laws with an eye toward evaluating his statements. Investigate his claims regarding the degree to which a very small number of individuals controlled most of the wealth in the United States, identify the figures he discusses, and explain technical terms such as "floating stocks" or "buying in short." How accurate was his critique at the time, and how does his portrayal contrast with America today? On the other hand, how relevant is his criticism of "fictitious wealth" to the economic landscape of twenty-first century America?

3. How justified was La Follette in his opposition to American military intervention against Germany, as exemplified in his 1917 speech? A number of factors must be considered in answering this question. The Germans made enormous use of slave labor near the war's end; their employment of poison gas exceeded that of the British and French; and by helping the Bolsheviks win power in Russia, they perpetuated horrors that would cloud subsequent decades. Yet there is some historical evidence to support La Follette's assertion that Germany was not a hereditary monarchy like Britain or that Germany was more advanced politically than the United States. Also, consider his position in light of the massive anti-German sentiment that prevailed in America during World War I as well as the fact that he came from the northern Midwest, which at the time had a sizable population of recent immigrants from Germany.

SPEECH ON THE AMENDMENT OF NATIONAL BANKING LAWS (1908)

Eighteen hundred and ninety-eight was the beginning of great industrial reorganization. Men directly engaged in production brought about in the first instance an association of the independent concerns which they had built up. These reorganizations were at the outset limited to those turning out finished products similar in kind. Within a period of three years following, 149 such reorganizations were effected with a total stock and bond capitalization of $3,784,000,000. In making these reorganizations, the opportunity for a large paper capitalization offered too great a temptation to be resisted. This was but the first stage in the creation of fictitious wealth. The success of these organizations led quickly on to a consolidation of combined industries, until a mere handful of men controlled the industrial production of the country.

The opportunity to associate the reorganization of the industrial institutions of the country with banking capital presented itself. Such connections were a powerful aid to reorganization, and reorganization offered an unlimited field for speculation....

I have compiled a list of about one hundred men with their directorships in the great corporate business enterprises of the United States. It furnishes indisputable proof of the community of interest that controls the industrial life of the country....

It discloses their connections with the transportation, the industrial, and the commercial life of the American people. This exhibit will make it clear to anyone that a small group of men hold in their hands the business of this country.

No student of the economic changes in recent years can escape the conclusion that the railroads, telegraph, shipping, cable, telephone, traction, express, mining, iron, steel, coal, oil, gas, electric light, cotton, copper, sugar, tobacco, agricultural implements, and the food products are completely controlled and mainly owned by these hundred men; that they have through reorganization multiplied their wealth almost beyond their own ability to know its amount with accuracy....

But the country seems not to understand how completely great banking institutions in the principal money centers have become bound up with the control of industrial institutions, nor the logical connection of this relationship to the financial depression which we have so recently suffered, nor the dangers which threaten us from this source in the future....

The closeness of business association between Wall Street and the centralized banking power of New York can, unfortunately, be but imperfectly traced through the official reports. It would seem that the radical changes taking place in the banking business of the country, suggesting to the conservative, economic, and financial authorities the gravest possible dangers to our industrial and commercial integrity, might well have caused the Treasury Department to recognize the necessity of so directing its investigations of the national banks in the greater cities which are centers of speculation and to so classify their returns as to inform itself and the country definitely respecting such changes. This has not been done....

It is, however, possible to find evidence which establishes the diversion of a large volume of the bank resources to securities which are the subject of speculative operation in the stock exchange....

Official figures do not show the real condition. The reports from banks upon which statistics are based fail to make clear the actual investment in speculative securities.... These banks have either established connections with trust companies or have organized inside trust companies as a protection and convenience.... These companies afford a convenient cover for the banks.... Their securities can be borrowed and shuffled back and forth to make a good showing. The trust companies can handle securities which the banks can not touch. They can underwrite bonds and float loans for which the banks could not openly stand sponsor. They can deal with themselves in innumerable ways to their own benefit and the detriment of the public....

The effect of the proposed legislation becomes more apparent as we investigate the grouping together of the great financial institutions holding these railroad bonds and other special securities and then trace their connection with the companies issuing these bonds....

The twenty-three directors of the National City Bank, the head of the Standard Oil group, and the directors of the National Bank of Commerce, thirty-nine in number, hold 1,007 directorships on the great transportation, industrial, and commercial institutions of this country....

Fourteen of the directors of the National City Bank are at the head of fourteen great combinations representing 38 per cent of the capitalization of all the industrial trusts of the country.

The railroad lines represented on the board of this one bank cover the country like a network.... These same twenty-three directors, through their various connections, represent more than 350 other banks, trust companies, railroads, and industrial corporations, with an aggregate capitalization of more than twelve thousand million dollars....

It was inevitable that this massing of banking power should attract to itself the resources of other banks throughout the country. Capital attracts capital. It inspires confidence. It appeals to the imagination....

The law providing that 15 per cent of the deposits of a country bank should be held for the protection of its depositors conveniently permits three-fifths of the amount to be deposited in reserve city banks, and of the 25 per cent of reserve for the protection of depositors in reserve city banks one-half may be deposited with central reserve city banks. As there are but three central reserve cities, one of which, of course, is New York City, the alluring interest rates which these all-powerful groups could offer inevitably tended to draw the great proportion of lawful reserves subject to transfer from the country and reserve banks....

The power which the New York banks derive through these vast accumulations of the resources of other national banks strengthen their position so that they could draw in the surplus money of all the other financial institutions of the country, State, private, and savings banks and trust companies....

The ability of these group banks of New York through their connected interests to engage in underwriting, to finance promotion schemes, where the profits resulting from overcapitalization represent hundreds of millions of dollars, places them beyond let or hindrance from competitors elsewhere in the country. Their ability to take advantage of conditions in Wall Street...would enable them to command, almost at will, the capital of the country for these speculative purposes.

But one result could follow. Floating the stocks and bonds in overcapitalized transportation, traction, mining, and industrial organizations does not create wealth, but it does absorb capital. Through the agency of these great groups hundreds of millions of dollars of the wealth of the country have been tied up....

The plain truth is that legitimate commercial banking is being eaten up by financial banking. The greatest banks of the financial center of the country have ceased to be agents of commerce and have become primarily agencies of promotion and speculation.... Trained men, who a dozen years ago stood first among the bankers of the world as heads of the greatest banks of New York City, are, in the main, either displaced or do the bidding of men who are not bankers, but masters of organization....

Sir, can any sane man doubt the power of a little group of men in whose hands are lodged the control of the railroads and the industries, outside of agriculture, as well as the great banks, insurance, and trust companies of the principal money center of the country, to give commercial banking and general business a shock at will?...

Taking the general conditions of the country, it is difficult to find any sufficient reason outside of manipulation for the extraordinary panic of October, 1907....

The panic came. It had been scheduled to arrive. The way had been prepared. Those who were directing it were not the men to miss anything in their way as it advanced....

The panic was working well. The stock market had gone to smash. Harriman was buying back Union Pacific shorts, but still smashing the market. Morgan was buying in short steel stocks and bonds, but still smashing the market.... The country banks were begging for their balances. Business was being held up.... On the street and in the brokers' offices the strain of apprehension was intense. In the midst of a Wall Street fight, when fear supersedes reason, it is difficult for those who are in it, but not directing it, to determine how much is real, how much is sham. Some of the guns are loaded only with blank cartridges to alarm; some are loaded with powder and ball to kill....

The floor of the stock exchange was chosen as the scene for the closing act, October 24 the time.

The men who had created the money stringency, who had absorbed the surplus capital of the country with promotions and reorganization schemes, who had deliberately forced a panic and frightened many innocent depositors to aid them by hoarding, who had held up the country banks by lawlessly refusing to return their deposits, never lost sight of one of the chief objects to be attained. The cause of currency revision was not neglected for one moment. It was printed day by day in their press; it passed from mouth to mouth.... High interest rates should be made to plead for emergency money through the telegraph dispatches of October 24 in every countinghouse, factory, and shop in America. The banks refused credit to old customers—all business to new customers. Call loans for money were at last denied at any price....It spelled ruin....

How perfect the stage setting! How real it all seemed! But back of the scenes Morgan and Stillman were in conference. They had made their representations at Washington. They knew when the next installment of aid would reach New York.... They awaited its arrival and deposit. Thereupon they pooled an equal amount. But they held it....Interest rates soared. Wall street was driven to a frenzy....The smashing of the market became terrific. Still they waited....Men looked into each other's ghastly faces. Then, at precisely 2.15, the curtain went up with Morgan and Standard Oil in the center of the stage with money—real money, twenty-five millions of money—giving it away at 10 per cent....

And so ended the panic.

How beautifully it all worked out. They had the whole country terrorized. They had the money of the deposits of the banks of every State in the Union to the amount of five hundred million, nearly all of which was in the vaults of the big group banks. This served two purposes—it made the country banks join in the cry for currency revision and it supplied the big operators with money to squeeze out investors and speculators at the very bottom of the decline, taking in the stock at an enormous profit.... The operations of Morgan and the Standard Oil furnish additional evidence of the character of this panic. We have record proof of their utter contempt for commercial interests.... Did they give aid and support to the distressed merchant and manufacturer?...Alas, no. They pursued the course of the speculating banker.... They let great commercial houses, great manufacturing concerns,... down to ruin and dishonor, while they protected their speculative patrons. No better evidence could be asked to establish the character of this panic or the character of the men who were in command. By their fruits ye shall know them!

Glossary

capitalization	the total value of a company, based usually on the total value of the company's shares of stock
Harriman	E. H. Harriman, father of W. Averell Harriman and director of the Union Pacific Railroad
Morgan	James Pierpont Morgan, American financier in the steel industry
shorts	also called "short sales," an investment technique that involves first selling a stock one does not own with the expectation of later buying the stock back at a lower price when its value falls, thus realizing a profit in a falling market
speculative securities	investments that are highly risky but hold the potential for large profits
Stillman	James Stillman, American financier and banker
trust companies	combinations of companies, usually formed with the purpose of driving out competition
underwrite	to guarantee financial support; to finance stocks or bonds and sell them to the public
Wall Street	the street in Lower Manhattan where the New York Stock Exchange is located; as a figure of speech, the financial sector of the economy

SPEECH OPPOSING WAR WITH GERMANY (1917)

Mr. President, I had supposed until recently that it was the duty of senators and representatives in congress to vote and act according to their convictions on all public matters that came before them for consideration and decision....

For myself I shall support the president in the measures he proposes when I believe them to be right. I shall oppose measures proposed by the president when I believe them to be wrong....

If, unhappily, on such momentous questions the most patient research and conscientious consideration we could give to them leave us in disagreement with this president, I know of no course to take except to oppose, regretfully but not the less firmly, the demands of the executive....

The poor, sir, who are the ones called upon to get in the trenches, have no organized power, have no press to voice their will upon this question of peace or war but, oh, Mr. President, at some time they will be heard.

I hope and I believe they will be heard in an orderly and a peaceful way. I think they may be heard from before long. I think, sir, if we take this step, when the people today who are staggering under the burden of supporting families at the present prices of the necessaries of life find those prices multiplied, when they are raised a hundred percent, or 300 per cent, as they will be quickly, aye, sir, when beyond that those who pay taxes come to have their taxes doubled and again doubled to pay the interest on the nontaxable bonds held by Morgan and his combinations, which have been issued to meet this war, there will come an awakening: they will have their day and they will be heard.

It will be as certain and as inevitable as the return of the tides, and as resistless, too....

In his message of April 2, the president said:

We have no quarrel with the German people—it was not upon their impulse that their government acted in entering this war; it was not with their previous knowledge or approval....

At least, the German people, then, are not outlaws. What is the thing the president asks us to do to these German people of whom he speaks so highly and whose sincere friend he declares us to be?

Here is what he declares we shall do in this war. We shall undertake, he says—

The utmost practicable cooperation in counsel and action with the governments now at war with Germany, and as an incident to that, the extension to these governments of the most liberal financial credits in order that our resources may, so far as possible, be added to theirs.

"Practical cooperation!" Practicable cooperation with England and her allies in starving to death the old men and women, the children, the sick and maimed of Germany. The thing we are asked to do is the thing I have stated.

It is idle to talk of a war upon a government only. We are leagued in this war, or it is the president's proposition that we shall be so leagued, with the hereditary enemies of Germany. Any war with Germany, or any other country for that matter, would be bad enough, but there are not words strong enough to voice my protest against the proposed combination with the entente allies.

When we cooperate with those governments we endorse their methods, we endorse the violations of international law, we endorse the shameful methods of warfare against which we have again and again protested in this war....

Finally when the end comes, whatever it may be, we find ourselves in cooperation with our ally, Great Britain, and if we cannot resist now the pressure she is exerting to carry us into the war, how can we hope to resist, then, the thousandfold greater pressure she will exert to bend us to her purposes and compel compliance with her demands?...

Once enlisted, once in the co-partnership, we will be carried through with the purposes, whatever they may be, of which we know nothing.

Sir, if we are to enter upon this war in the manner the president demands, let us throw pretense to the winds, let us be honest, let us admit that this is a ruthless war against not only Germany's army and navy but against her civilian population as well, and frankly state that the purpose of Germany's hereditary European enemies has become our purpose....

Just a word of comment more upon one of the points in the president's address. He says that this is a war "for the things we have always carried nearest to our hearts—for democracy, for the right of those who submit to authority to have a voice in their own government."...

It is a sentiment peculiarly calculated to appeal to American hearts and, when accompanied by acts consistent with it, is certain to receive our support; but in this same connection, and strangely enough, the president says that we have become convinced that the German government as it now exists— "Prussian autocracy" he calls it—can never again maintain friendly relations with us....

Who has registered the knowledge or approval of the American people of the course this congress is called upon to take in declaring war upon Germany? Submit the question to the people, you who support it. You who support it dare not do it, for you know that by a vote of more than 10 to one the American people as a body would register their declaration against it....

The espionage bills, the conscription bills, and other forcible military measures which we understand are being ground out of the war machine in this country is the complete proof that those responsible for this war fear that it has no popular support and that armies sufficient to satisfy the demand of the entente allies cannot be recruited by voluntary enlistments....

I have said that with the causes of the present war we have nothing to do. That is true. We certainly are not responsible for it. It originated from causes beyond the sphere of our influence and outside the realm of our responsibility. It is not inadmissible, however, to say that no responsible narrator of the events which have led up to this greatest of all wars has failed to hold that the government of each country engaged in it is at fault for it.

For my own part, I believe that this war, like nearly all others, originated in the selfish ambition and cruel greed of a comparatively few men in each government who saw in war an opportunity for profit and power for themselves, and who were wholly indifferent to the awful suffering they knew that war would bring to the masses....

The offenses of Great Britain and Germany against us can not be treated as they might be treated if those nations were not at war with each other. Undoubtedly, if those nations were not at war with each other we could suffer one to violate international law to our injury and make no protest and take no action against the nations so offending and hold the other to strict accountability and compel her to respect to the limit our rights under international law, and if she refused we would be justified in going to war about it.

But when we are dealing with Germany and Great Britain, warring against each other, so evenly balanced in strength that a little help to one or a little hindrance to the other turns the scale and spells victory for one and defeat for the other, in that situation I say the principle of international law steps in which declares that any failure on our part to enforce our rights equally against both is a gross act of un-neutrality....

There can be no greater violation of our neutrality than the requirement that one of two belligerents shall adhere to the settled principles of law and that the other shall have the advantage of not doing so. The respect that German naval authorities were required to pay to the rights of our people upon the high seas would depend upon the question whether we had exacted the same rights from Germany's enemies.

If we had not done so we lost our character as a neutral nation, and our people unfortunately had lost the protection that belongs to neutrals. Our responsibility was joint in the sense that we must exact the same conduct from both belligerents....

Had the plain principle of international law announced by Jefferson been followed by us, we

Glossary

autocracy	a political system in which power is concentrated in the hands of a single person
belligerents	warring parties
entente allies	the Triple Entente allies—Great Britain, France, and Russia—opposed to the Central Powers, led by Germany and Austria-Hungary, in World War I
Morgan	James Pierpont Morgan, American financier in the steel industry
Prussian	referring to the leading state in the nineteenth- and early-twentieth-century German empire

would not be called on today to declare war upon any of the belligerents. The failure to treat the belligerent nations of Europe alike, the failure to reject the unlawful "war zones" of both Germany and Great Britain, is wholly accountable for our present dilemma.

We should not seek to hide our blunder behind the smoke of battle, to inflame the mind of our people by half truths into the frenzy of war, in order that they may never appreciate the real cause of it until it is too late. I do not believe that our national honor is served by such a course. The right way is the honorable way.

One alternative is to admit our initial blunder to enforce our rights against Great Britain as we have enforced our rights against Germany; demand that both those nations shall respect our neutral rights upon the high seas to the letters and give notice that we will enforce those rights from that time forth against both belligerents and then live up to that notice.

The other alternative is to withdraw our commerce from both. The mere suggestion that food supplies would be withheld from both sides impartially would compel belligerents to observe the principle of freedom of the seas for neutral commerce.

PLATFORM OF THE CONFERENCE FOR PROGRESSIVE POLITICAL ACTION (1924)

For 148 years the American people have been seeking to establish a government for the service of all and to prevent the establishment of a government for the mastery of the few. Free men of every generation must combat renewed efforts of organized force and greed to destroy liberty. Every generation must wage a new war for freedom against new forces that seek through new devices to enslave mankind.

Under our representative democracy the people protect their liberties through their public agents.

The test of public officials and public policies alike must be: Will they serve, or will they exploit, the common need?

The reactionary continues to put his faith in mastery for the solution of all problems. He seeks to have what he calls the "strong men and best minds" rule and impose their decision upon the masses of their weaker brethren.

The progressive, on the contrary, contends for less autocracy and more democracy in government, and for less power of privilege and greater obligation of service.

Under the principle of ruthless individualism and competition, that government is deemed best which offers to the few the greatest chance of individual gain.

Under the progressive principle of cooperation, that government is deemed best which offers to the many the highest level of average happiness and well-being.

It is our faith that we all go up or down together …that eternal laws of compensation make every man his brother's keeper.

In that faith we present our program of public services.

(1) The use of power of the Federal Government to crush private monopoly, not to foster it.

(2) Unqualified enforcement of the constitutional guarantees of freedom of speech, press and assemblage.

(3) Public ownership of the nation's waterpower and creation of a public superpower system. Strict public control and permanent conservation of all national resources, including coal, iron and other ores, oil and timber lands, in the interest of the people. Promotion of public works in times of business depression.

(4) Retention of surtaxes on swollen incomes: restoration of the tax on excess profits, on stock dividends, profits undistributed to evade taxes, rapidly progressive taxes on large estates and inheritances and repeal of excessive tariff duties, especially on trust-controlled necessities of life, and of nuisance taxes on consumption, to relieve the people of the present unjust burden of taxation and compel those who profited by the war to pay their share of the war's costs and to provide the funds for adjusted compensation solemnly pledged to the veterans of the World War.

(5) Reconstruction of the Federal Reserve and Federal farm loan systems to provide for direct public control of the nation's money and credit, to make it available on fair terms to all, and national and State Legislatures to permit and promote cooperative banking

(6) Adequate laws to guarantee to farmers and industrial workers the right to organize and bargain collectively, through representatives of their own choosing, for the maintenance or improvement of their standards of life.

(7) Creation of Government marketing corporation to provide a direct route between farm producer and city consumer, and to assure farmers fair prices for their products and protect consumers from the profiteers in food stuffs and other necessaries of life. Legislation to conduct the meat packing industry.

(8) Protection and aid of cooperative enterprises by national and State legislation.

(9) Common international action to effect the economic recovery of the world from the effects of the World War.

(10) Repeal of the Cummins-Esch law. Public ownership of railroads, with the democratic

La Follette, Robert

operation, with definite safeguards against bureaucratic control.

(11) Abolition of the tyranny and usurpation of the courts, including the practice of nullifying legislation in conflict with the political, social or economic theories in labor disputes and of the power to punish for contempt without trial by jury. Election of all Federal Judges without party designation for limited terms.

(12) Prompt satisfaction of the child labor amendment, and subsequent enactment of a Federal law to protect children in industry. Removal of legal discriminations against women by measures not prejudicial to legislation necessary for the protection of women and for the advancement of social welfare.

(13) A deep waterway from the Great Lakes to the sea.

(14) We denounce the mercenary system of foreign policy under recent administrations in the interests of financial imperialists, oil monopolists and International bankers, which has at times degraded our State Department from its high service as a strong and kindly intermediary of defenseless Governments to a trading outpost for those interests and concession seekers engaged in the exploitation of weaker nations, as contrary to the will of the American people, destructive of domestic development and provocative of war. We favor an active foreign policy to bring about a revision of the Versailles Treaty in accordance with the terms of the armistice, and to promote firm treaty agreements with all nations to outlaw wars, abolish conscription, dramatically reduce land, air and naval armaments and guarantee public referendums on peace and war.

In supporting this program we are applying to the needs of today the fundamental principles of American democracy opposing equally the dictatorship of plutocracy and the dictatorship of the proletariat.

We appeal to all Americans without regard to partisan affiliation, and we raise the standards of our faith so that all of like purpose may rally and march in this campaign under the banners of progressive union.

The nation may grow rich in the vision of greed. The nation will grow great in the vision of service.

Glossary

autocracy	a political system in which power is concentrated in the hands of a single person
Cummins-Esch law	more formally, the Transportation Act of 1920, which created the U.S. Railroad Labor Board and returned ownership of the railroads to private hands
plutocracy	a political system in which power is concentrated in the hands of wealthy people
progressive taxes	a tax system in which the rate of taxation increases at higher income or profit levels
proletariat	the working class
reactionary	an extreme conservative, opposed to progress
surtaxes	extra taxes, usually on luxury items or on high incomes or profits

Robert E. Lee (Library of Congress)

Robert E. Lee

1807–1870

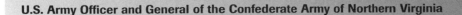

U.S. Army Officer and General of the Confederate Army of Northern Virginia

Featured Documents
- Letter to Mary Lee (1856)
- Letter to Custis Lee (1861)
- Letter to Jefferson Davis (1862)
- Letter to Jefferson Davis (1863)
- Letter to Jefferson Davis (1864)
- Letter to Andrew Hunter (1865)
- General Order No. 9 (1865)

Overview

Robert E. Lee was born on January 19, 1807, on the plantation of Stratford Hall, Virginia, just south of the Potomac River. Lee's father died in disgrace and disrepute when his son was eleven years old, a victim of bad business decisions and poor health, leaving Lee to be brought up by his mother in Alexandria, Virginia. In 1825 he secured an appointment to the U.S. Military Academy at West Point, where he achieved exceptional marks, graduating second in the class of 1829. Assigned to the Army Corps of Engineers, Lee spent much of the next sixteen years shifting from post to post, performing noteworthy work on the Missouri and Mississippi rivers as well as the harbor facilities at St. Louis between 1837 and 1840.

In 1846 Lee jumped at the chance to see action in the Mexican-American War; early the following year he was assigned to the staff of Winfield Scott, and he distinguished himself during Scott's campaign from Vera Cruz to Mexico City. After the war, he won appointment as superintendent at West Point, a post he held from 1852 to 1855, and then became a lieutenant colonel assigned to the newly established Second U.S. Cavalry. Upon the death of his father-in-law in 1857, Lee returned home to Virginia and established a residence at Arlington, just across the Potomac from Washington, D.C. He found managing the slaves at Arlington an onerous business and gained notoriety in 1859 when the *New York Tribune* reported that Lee had whipped some of the very slaves that he was supposed to free under the terms of his father-in-law's will. Later that year, he hurried west to Harpers Ferry to take command of a detachment of U.S. Marines to subdue the abolitionist John Brown, who had seized a federal arsenal as the first step in his plan to incite a slave insurrection.

Lee anxiously watched as several southern states declared that they were seceding from the United States in the aftermath of the election of Abraham Lincoln. As of early 1861 Lee was determined not to take part in any conflict so long as Virginia remained in the Union. On the heels of Virginia's decision to secede, made in the wake of Lincoln's call for troops after the Union surrender of Fort Sumter, Lee turned down a general's commission in the U.S. Army, resigned his colonelcy, and joined first the Virginia militia and then the Confederate forces, winning elevation to general in a matter of months. From June 1862 until April 1865 he led the Army of Northern Virginia, winning plaudits for his generalship, but he found himself forced to surrender to Ulysses S. Grant on April 9, 1865, at Appomattox Court House, Virginia. After the war, Lee accepted the presidency of Washington College (which was renamed Washington and Lee University after his death), in Lexington, Virginia. Although he advised his fellow former Confederates to accept the outcome of the war, he remained uneasy about emancipation and contemplated writing a history of his army's operations to suggest that the South had been overwhelmed and not outfought. After a short illness, he died on October 12, 1870.

Explanation and Analysis of Documents

Although Lee was engaged in a successful military career in the U.S. Army, he tended to identify himself as a Virginian and sympathized with the interests of the slaveholding South. Regarding slavery itself, his views reflected a mixture of misgivings about the impact of slavery on whites and a belief that the institution was the best that could be done for blacks so long as they lived in the United States. He never doubted white supremacy; he blamed abolitionists for the controversy over slavery. Once he identified his interests with those of the Confederacy, Lee looked to wage aggressive war in order to beat back Union battalions and weaken northern public support for the war effort. He was always aware of the wider dimensions of his military operations; by 1865 he was prepared to accept the enlistment of African Americans in the Confederate army as a means of reviving his military manpower. Never questioning the correctness of the Confederate cause, even in defeat, Lee steadfastly maintained that the Union victory was the result of overwhelming resources, not superior military skill.

The documents produced by Lee—primarily personal correspondence—focus upon two themes. First, Lee dealt throughout his adult life, in various ways, with questions of slavery, freedom, and race. He was a slaveholder, and for a

Time Line

1807
- **January 19**
  Lee is born at Stratford Hall, Westmoreland County, Virginia.

1829
- **June**
  Lee graduates from the U.S. Military Academy at West Point, New York.

1837– 1840
- Lee supervises the refashioning of channels of the Missouri and Mississippi rivers and improves the harbor at St. Louis, Missouri.

1846
- Lee begins serving in the Mexican-American War, which ends in 1848.

1852
- Lee accepts the post of superintendent at West Point.

1855
- Lee is appointed lieutenant colonel in the Second U.S. Cavalry.

1856
- **December 27**
  Lee writes a letter to his wife, Mary Lee, sharing his thoughts on President Franklin Pierce's annual message to Congress.

1859
- **October**
  Lee leads a contingent of U.S. Marines to suppress John Brown's raid on the federal arsenal at Harpers Ferry, Virginia.

1861
- **January 23**
  Lee writes a letter to Custis Lee sharing his thoughts on secession and the Confederacy.

1861
- **April**
  Lee resigns his commission as colonel in the U.S. Army to become a major general in charge of Virginia's forces; he is soon confirmed as a full general by the Confederate Congress.

brief period he managed a plantation. Never did he question white supremacy or black inferiority, and if he questioned slavery at all, it was because it presented a burden to southern whites and not because of its impact upon the lives of southern blacks. He faulted abolitionists for their agitation of the slavery question. However, as a pragmatic matter, he came to accept that in order for the Confederacy to survive, it might have to enlist blacks into military service and offer them the reward of freedom. Lee's second realm of concern was that of military strategy. As a military commander, Lee demonstrated an appreciation of the broader concerns of national policy and an understanding that the manner in which war is waged should be shaped by the ends sought in waging it. He was acutely aware of the importance of public support for any war effort, and at several opportune moments he suggested to the Confederate president Jefferson Davis that northern morale and public opinion were viable targets of Confederate war making.

◆ **Letter to Mary Lee (1856)**

In 1831 Robert E. Lee married Mary Anna Randolph Custis at Arlington House, Virginia. Mary was a granddaughter of Martha Washington (the wife of George Washington); by wedding her, Lee married into the Washington legacy and benefited from the estate of the Custis family, including Arlington and its slaves. For the next twenty-five years Lee was often away from his wife while serving in the military, including during the Mexican-American War of 1846–1848. In 1856 he was on duty in Texas when he read President Franklin Pierce's annual message to Congress, and he hurried to share his impressions with his wife.

The year 1856 had proved a critical one in American politics, with the discussion over slavery and its expansion looming large. In his last annual message to Congress, Pierce blamed northern agitators for the violence of the past year, whether it took place on the plains of Kansas, as proslavery and antislavery forces vied to determine the fate of that territory, or on Capitol Hill; the Massachusetts senator Charles Sumner was beaten by the South Carolina representative Preston Brooks in the Senate chamber in retaliation for a speech by Sumner attacking slavery and its advocates, particularly Brooks's kinsman Senator Andrew Butler.

In the letter to his wife, Lee expresses his relief that the Republican Party failed to prevail in the presidential contest that had concluded the previous month. Agreeing with Pierce, Lee charges that the North bore responsibility for the sectional crisis because of northerners' continual agitation against slavery. Although Lee considers slavery "a moral & political evil," he argues that its primary victims were whites. Black slaves, he asserts, "are immeasurably better off here than in Africa, morally, socially & physically." Lee expresses the belief that if it is to be successful, emancipation must come gradually, and he measures that process in centuries and millennia, not months or years. He defers to God's will over the question of when slavery should end, meanwhile deploring any agitation of the issue as needless and counterproductive. In short, Lee was a supporter of the "peculiar institution" of slavery and shared in its white supremacist assumptions. Never did he hold southern whites accountable for their role in the sectional crisis that exploded in violence in the 1860s.

◆ Letter to Custis Lee (1861)

The debate over slavery and its future escalated during the late 1850s. In November 1860 the antislavery Republican Party at last triumphed in the presidential contest with the election of Abraham Lincoln. Several southern states then hastened to declare that they would leave the Union and set up their own slaveholding republic in order to protect slavery from the encroachment of a Republican-controlled White House. Texas was among the first states to secede; as it prepared to do so, Colonel Lee contemplated his own next move. He shared his thoughts in a letter that was most probably addressed to his son Custis.

In this letter of 1861 Lee again blames the crisis on northern agitators, although he displays impatience with convoluted theories of secession. It would be better, he thought, to label the departure of the southern states for what it was—a revolution, with the goal of independence. Regardless, he admits to having no interest in serving on the side of the United States in any war that might result. If fighting were to break out, he would assess his fortunes according to what the state of Virginia decided to do. If it stayed within the Union, he would set aside his commission and watch from the sidelines; if Virginia cast its fate with the Confederacy, he would side with his state and offer his military services. He professes to deplore the idea of a country held together by force rather than sentiment, explicitly noting that he would not take up arms against the Confederacy. Not until Virginia chose to secede and join the Confederacy in the wake of the Union surrender of Fort Sumter and Lincoln's call for volunteers did Lee's course become clear. Any notion that he might have led U.S. forces against the Confederacy is belied by his own correspondence from when he was considering his options.

◆ Letter to Jefferson Davis (1862)

Lee took command of the Army of Northern Virginia on June 1, 1862. At that time, the men of the Union general George B. McClellan's Army of the Potomac could see the church spires in the Confederate capital at Richmond, Virginia. Within a month, however, Lee succeeded in driving McClellan away from Richmond and toward the James River. Once he learned that the Union high command had decided to order McClellan to evacuate his position and take his army north via water to join John Pope's Army of Virginia in central Virginia, Lee moved quickly to strike at Pope before McClellan arrived in full force. After smashing Pope at the Second Battle of Bull Run (also called Second Manassas) at the end of August, Lee decided to advance into Maryland. The decision reflected his belief that the Confederacy's best chance to achieve independence lay in undermining support for the Union war effort through a series of Confederate victories. Invading Maryland, he believed, might well bolster the cause of secession in that state; it might also persuade European powers that the

Time Line

1862

- **June 1**
  After serving as the Confederate president Jefferson Davis's military adviser, Lee accepts command of the Army of Northern Virginia, which he leads for the next thirty-four months.

- **September 8**
  Lee writes a letter to Davis in which he advocates negotiations for peace and Confederate independence.

1863

- **June 10**
  Lee writes to Davis further discussing strategy for achieving both peace and victory .

1864

- **March 25**
  Lee writes to Davis about General Ulysses S. Grant's expected advances on Virginia.

1865

- **January 11**
  Lee writes a letter to the Virginia legislator Andrew Hunter explaining his opinions on the idea of enlisting blacks in the Confederate army.

- **April 9**
  Lee surrenders to Grant at Appomattox Court House, Virginia.

- **April 10**
  Lee issues General Order No. 9, dismissing Confederate soldiers.

- **October 2**
  Lee becomes president of Washington College, in Lexington, Virginia.

1870

- **October 12**
  Lee dies in Lexington, where he is buried.

time had come to intervene. For the moment, it appeared that Lee had indeed caught the Union off balance, with its armies still recovering from defeat.

In September 1862 Lee decided to take the war north of the Potomac River into Maryland and Union territory. Even as he pressed forward, Lee thought it time to alert Jefferson Davis to the possible political advantages to be gained by coupling an invasion north of the Potomac with a call for peace negotiations, to result in the recognition of Confederate independence. As he puts it, it "would show conclusively to the world that our sole object is the establishment of our independence and the attainment of an honorable peace." Nothing came of this proposal; in less than two weeks Lee had returned to Virginia after having held off McClellan at the Battle of Antietam in the bloodiest day of combat in the American Civil War.

◆ Letter to Jefferson Davis (1863)

Although he scored several key victories in his first year as commander of the Army of Northern Virginia, Lee bemoaned the fact that he could not transform any of those battlefield triumphs into an event of far larger strategic significance. After he beat back a series of Union attacks at Fredericksburg on December 13, 1862, despite the damage he inflicted upon the enemy, he regretted that the outcome was not beneficial enough. Nor was he completely satisfied with the results of his most spectacular battlefield triumph, at Chancellorsville (April 30–May 6, 1863), where he defeated an enemy force twice the size of his own, though at heavy cost. Once more he chose to cross the Potomac north; once more he sought to impress his president with the political advantages that might accrue from such an offensive.

In this letter to Davis, Lee argues that it is important for Confederate politicians to say nothing that might dampen talk of a peaceful resolution of the conflict by northerners. By 1863 some northern Democrats were charging that the war was a failure, that reunion by coercion was doomed, and that the time had come to negotiate a settlement. Whether Confederate independence would be part of such a settlement remained open to discussion. Lee argues, then, that it would be best not to preclude any efforts at negotiation; if such negotiations were to take place, northerners might well come to accept Confederate independence as talks dragged on without evidence of Union progress on the battlefield. Implicit in Lee's letter is the notion that Confederate resources were not inexhaustible: "Our resources in men are constantly diminishing." Lee believes it critical for the Confederacy to use whatever means are available, including deception, to weaken northern resolve. Thus, he concludes, it would be important to welcome any talk of negotiations without mentioning any preconditions, including the recognition of Confederate independence. Lee remarks that should his invasion of Pennsylvania prove a success, that result would add to the northern cry for peace and an acceptance of an independent Confederacy.

Davis might well have replied that to enter into such negotiations without any assurance regarding independence could demoralize support for the Confederacy in the South. Other observers might have noted that Lee was perhaps overestimating the number of northerners willing to talk peace, especially at a time when the Union general Ulysses S. Grant's Army of Tennessee was laying siege to Vicksburg, Mississippi. The Confederate defeat at Gettysburg, Pennsylvania, which proved costly in terms of both manpower and leadership losses, rendered the discussion moot. Lee may have at first secured the upper hand on the battlefield, but by the end of 1863 it was evident that his victories had come at such a cost that he was unable to exploit them to much advantage.

◆ Letter to Jefferson Davis (1864)

If Lee understood that his defeat at Gettysburg represented a setback for Confederate fortunes in 1863, he did not assume that it represented the turning point of the war. As spring came to Virginia in 1864, he prepared once more to check Union offensive operations in that state. He looked forward to meeting Grant in battle. In a March 1864 letter to Davis, Lee shared his speculations about Grant's plans based upon close observation of northern newspaper reports about the Union general's activities. Lee professes to believe it obvious that Grant will plan to make Richmond the objective of a spring campaign and, as the new Union commander, will come to Virginia to supervise that offensive. Lee remarks, "Energy and activity on our part, with a constant readiness to seize any opportunity to strike a blow, will embarrass, if not entirely thwart the enemy in concentrating his different armies, and compel him to conform his movements to our own." In short, Lee holds that Confederate commanders must be ready to repel Union advances and take the initiative when necessary, even undertaking offensive operations of their own.

Lee's stance remained aggressive, as he was looking to land a blow to keep his foe off balance and perhaps seize the initiative; he repeatedly sought reinforcements to enable him to take advantage of whatever opportunities presented themselves. He was also mindful that 1864 was an election year, such that Union military reverses might well lead to the repudiation of Lincoln and the Republicans at the polls. However, in May and June 1864, he discovered that in Grant he had met a general who matched up well against him. Grant refused to surrender the initiative and seemed undeterred from achieving his objectives. By June, Lee found himself clinging to Richmond and Petersburg, fending off Grant's efforts to cut his supply lines. Lee's efforts to regain the offensive failed; if Grant could not defeat Lee outright, he at least pinned the Confederacy's most able military leader in place while Union armies elsewhere scored the military triumphs that reassured the reelection of Abraham Lincoln.

◆ Letter to Andrew Hunter (1865)

During the course of the Civil War, Lee did not question the cause of the preservation of slavery. His army swept through the countryside of Maryland and Pennsylvania looking to gather up blacks suspected of being fugitive slaves; in 1864 he put black Union prisoners of war to work on fortifications within range of Union weaponry, relenting only when Grant responded in kind by deploying Confederate prisoners in the same way. Lee dragged his feet when it came to emancipating his family's slaves in accordance with his father-in-law's will. Desperation for manpower, however, drove him to consider the idea of enlisting black

Bodies of fallen troops lie on the field after the Battle of Antietam,
the bloodiest one-day battle of the American Civil War. (AP/Wide World Photos)

slaves in the Confederate army, especially when it became a topic of political debate in the winter of 1864–1865.

Although Lee prided himself on being apolitical, he often gave advice and shared his sentiments privately, and nowhere was his willingness to do so more evident than in this letter to Andrew Hunter, a member of the Virginia state legislature who had solicited Lee's views on the subject of black enlistment for the Confederacy. Lee's response, written in January 1865, is richly suggestive of the way in which he sought to balance the preferred ideal from a white southern perspective with the reality of the Confederacy's situation. Although he still praises slavery as the best way to define the relationship between black and white Americans, he recognizes that with the Union now tapping into black manpower to bolster its military effort, if the Confederacy did not do the same, it would be overwhelmed and crushed. He professes to be, unlike some others, willing to offer emancipation to black soldiers and their families as a reward for faithful military service. Noteworthy in light of modern-day controversies about the extent and nature of black service in the Confederate armies is Lee's failure to mention any such service as a way to combat objections to the plan for enlisting blacks. In later years Lee would claim that he had always been in favor of gradual emancipation, but this letter sets that claim in a more limited context, suggesting that he would have preferred emancipation only if

accompanied by the colonization of the former slaves and other blacks outside the United States.

◆ General Order No. 9 (1865)

Lee looked to continue the Civil War through 1865. His first mission early in the year was to evade Grant and evacuate Richmond and Petersburg in such a fashion as to render a pursuit difficult. However, his initial effort to achieve this proved a disaster when his attack on Fort Stedman of March 25 was soundly repulsed; a week later, after Grant took the offensive, Lee abandoned Richmond and Petersburg and headed west. Grant then launched a vigorous pursuit, cutting off Lee's efforts to venture into North Carolina and smashing his rear guard. Hungry and ill supplied, Lee's command began to disintegrate, until at last he accepted the inevitable and surrendered to Grant on April 9, 1865, at Appomattox Court House.

By the next day, the staff officer Charles Marshall had drafted a farewell order, which Lee edited before issuing it to the twenty-five thousand or so men who remained in the ranks. The order states nothing about the cause for which the Confederates had been fighting; Lee suggests that the ultimate outcome was due to their being overwhelmed by superior Union numbers, and he commends the men on their bravery and sacrifice. These themes would help form the basis of what is sometimes called the mythology of the Lost

> *"Secession is nothing but revolution."*
>
> (Letter to Custis Lee, 1861)

> *"Still, a Union that can only be maintained by swords and bayonets, and in which strife and civil war are to take the place of brotherly love and kindness, has no charm for me. I shall mourn for my country and for the welfare and progress of mankind. If the Union is dissolved, and the Government disrupted, I shall return to my native State and share the miseries of my people, and save in defence will draw my sword on none."*
>
> (Letter to Custis Lee, 1861)

> *"We should neglect no honorable means of dividing and weakening our enemies that they may feel some of the difficulties experienced by ourselves. It seems to me that the most effectual mode of accomplishing this object, now within our reach, is to give all the encouragement we can, consistently with truth, to the rising peace party of the North."*
>
> (Letter to Jefferson Davis, 1863)

> *"Considering the relation of master and slave, controlled by humane laws and influenced by Christianity and an enlightened public sentiment, as the best that can exist between the white and black races while intermingled as at present in this country, I would deprecate any sudden disturbance of that relation unless it be necessary to avert a greater calamity to both."*
>
> (Letter to Andrew Hunter, 1865)

> *"After four years of arduous service, marked by unsurpassed courage and fortitude, the Army of Northern Virginia has been compelled to yield to overwhelming numbers and resources."*
>
> (General Order No. 9, 1865)

Cause, including the notion that the Confederacy was over-whelmed by sheer weight of numbers despite their soldiers' superior fighting ability. Lee concludes, "With an increasing admiration of your constancy and devotion to your country, and a grateful remembrance of your kind and generous con-siderations for myself, I bid you all an affectionate farewell."

Impact and Legacy

Had there been no American Civil War, Robert E. Lee would have been remembered, if at all, as an extremely competent army officer. His brilliant military leadership brought the Confederacy as close as it ever came to battlefield victory, but at heavy costs that would be felt during the latter years of the war, as Lee found he could no longer replace his losses. Moreover, as tremendous as some of his military triumphs might have been, he proved unable to exploit them, and both of his invasions north across the Potomac River resulted in defeats that might have turned into disasters were it not for the inability of Union forces to capitalize on their own opportunities. Nevertheless, the Confederacy may have survived as long as it did because of Lee's leadership, and not until he encountered Grant did he find himself unable to reverse Union offensives.

After the war, Lee came to be portrayed as a simple soldier who went along with his state because he embraced a simple conception of duty. In truth, not all Virginians shared his particular notions of duty and loyalty, including George H. Thomas, who rose to become one of the Union's greatest generals. Nor was he nearly as opposed to slavery as some eulogists would have it: His writings suggest that he was comfortable with white supremacy and that his commitment to abolition was strictly practical and qualified by conditions. He understood the advantages of abolition primarily in relation to the potential impact on military operations. While identifying himself as a Virginian, Lee took the southern view when it came to slavery, emphasizing that it was a burden upon white people but the best status that blacks could enjoy in first the United and then the Confederate States of America.

For most of the years since the end of the Civil War, Lee has been accorded iconic status by many Americans, although he has always had his critics. Several biographical efforts sought to celebrate his greatness as a general and his goodness of character while distancing his persona from issues of slavery and the nature of the Confederate cause. Indeed, for some, Lee became the model of southern honor and gentility; his image was used to refashion the essence of Confederate identity as being detached from slavery and white supremacy. In more recent years, some scholars have raised questions about Lee both as a general and as a white southerner, especially regarding his views on slavery and race, and have rendered him as a somewhat more complex character. However, old images die hard, and as the bicentennial of Lee's birth passed, it was clear that many white Americans still held him in high regard.

Key Sources

Major collections of Robert E. Lee's papers can be found at the Virginia Historical Society and the Library of Congress; smaller collections are at the University of Virginia, the Library of Virginia, the Museum of the Confederacy, the Huntington Library (in San Marino, California), and Duke University, as well as at Lee's birthplace in Stratford Hall and at Washington and Lee University. Many of Lee's formal dispatches appear in *The War of the Rebellion: A Compilation of the Official Records of the Union and Confederate Armies*, 128 vols. (1880–1901). A published

Questions for Further Study

1. In the popular imagination of the United States as a whole and the South in particular, Robert E. Lee is typically regarded as a heroic figure. Although most Americans, even in the former Confederate states, would say that the Confederate causes of slavery and secession were wrong, Lee himself is often viewed as a victim of circumstances—a man of principle who, while he did not personally support these causes, nevertheless remained loyal to his state of Virginia. Judging from Lee's writings, how justified is this portrayal? What were his positions on slavery and secession?

2. In the 1863 letter to Confederate president Jefferson Davis, Lee critiques what in modern times would be called "the media," maintaining that the southern press was actually hurting the Confederate cause by giving northerners little reason to believe that the issues underlying the Civil War might even then be settled by peaceful means. Likewise, the 1864 letter to Davis opens with an analysis of northern newspaper reports on the movements of troops under his counterpart, General Ulysses Grant. How did Lee regard the media, in terms of both its impact on popular opinion and its reliability as a guide to what was really happening in wartime situations? How might he have viewed the role of journalists in later conflicts, such as World War II, Vietnam, and the two conflicts involving Iraq?

3. Discuss the specifics mentioned by Lee in his 1864 letter to Jefferson Davis. Give a day-by-day account of events leading up to the moment when he composed that letter and consider how we would have viewed Confederate chances of victory at that point in the war.

collection is Clifford Dowdey, ed., *The Wartime Papers of Robert E. Lee* (1961).

Further Reading

■ Books

Carmichael, Peter S., ed. *Audacity Personified: The Generalship of Robert E. Lee*. Baton Rouge: Louisiana State University Press, 2004.

Fellman, Michael. *The Making of Robert E. Lee*. New York: Random House, 2000.

Freeman, Douglas S. *R. E. Lee: A Biography*. 4 vols. New York: Charles Scribner's Sons, 1934–1935.

———. *Lee's Lieutenants: A Study in Command*. 3 vols. New York: Charles Scribner's Sons, 1942–1944.

Gallagher, Gary W., ed. *Lee the Soldier*. Lincoln: University of Nebraska Press, 1996.

Nolan, Alan T. *Lee Considered: General Robert E. Lee and Civil War History*. Chapel Hill: University of North Carolina Press, 1991.

Thomas, Emory M. *Robert E. Lee: A Biography*. New York: W. W. Norton, 1995.

—Brooks D. Simpson

Letter to Mary Lee (1856)

The steamer also brought the President's message to Cong; & the reports of the various heads of Depts; the proceedings of Cong: &c &c. So that we are now assured, that the Govt: is in operation, & the Union in existence, not that we had any fears to the Contrary, but it is Satisfactory always to have facts to go on. They restrain Supposition & Conjecture, Confirm faith, & bring Contentment: I was much pleased with the President's message & the report of the Secy of War, the only two documents that have reached us entire. Of the others synopsis have only arrived. The views of the Pres: of the Systematic & progressive efforts of certain people of the North, to interfere with & change the domestic institutions of the South, are truthfully & faithfully expressed. The Consequences of their plans & purposes are also clearly set forth, & they must also be aware, that their object is both unlawful & entirely foreign to them & their duty; for which they are irresponsible & unaccountable; & Can only be accomplished by them through the agency of a Civil & Servile war. In this enlightened age, there are few I believe, but what will acknowledge, that slavery as an institution, is a moral & political evil in any Country. It is useless to expatiate on its disadvantages. I think it however a greater evil to the white man than to the black race, & while my feelings are strongly enlisted in behalf of the latter, my sympathies are more strong for the former. The blacks are immeasurably better off here than in Africa, morally, socially & physically. The painful discipline they are undergoing, is necessary for their instruction as a race, & I hope will prepare & lead them to better things. How long their subjugation may be necessary is known & ordered by a wise Merciful Providence. Their emancipation will sooner result from the mild & melting influence of Christianity, than the storms & tempests of fiery Controversy. This influence though slow, is sure. The doctrines & miracles of our Saviour have required nearly two thousand years, to Convert but a small part of the human race, & even among Christian nations, what gross errors still exist! While we see the Course of the final abolition of human Slavery is onward, & we give it the aid of our prayers & all justifiable means in our power, we must leave the progress as well as the result in his hands who sees the end; who Chooses to work by slow influences; & with whom two thousand years are but as a Single day. Although the Abolitionist must know this, & must See that he has neither the right or power of operating except by moral means & suasion, & if he means well to the slave, he must not Create angry feelings in the Master; that although he may not approve the mode which it pleases Providence to accomplish its purposes, the result will nevertheless be the same; that the reasons he gives for interference in what he has no Concern, holds good for every kind of interference with our neighbors when we disapprove their Conduct; Still I fear he will persevere in his evil Course. Is it not strange that the descendants of those pilgrim fathers who Crossed the Atlantic to preserve their own freedom of opinion, have always proved themselves intolerant of the Spiritual liberty of others?

Glossary

expatiate	elaborate, write or speak in detail

LETTER TO CUSTIS LEE (1861)

The South, in my opinion, has been aggrieved by the acts of the North, as you say. I feel the aggression, and am willing to take every proper step for redress. It is the principle I contend for, not individual or private gain. As an American citizen, I take great pride in my country, her prosperity and institutions, and would defend any State if her rights were invaded. But I can anticipate no greater calamity for the country than a dissolution of the Union. It would be an accumulation of all the evils we complain of, and I am willing to sacrifice everything but honor for its preservation. I hope therefore, that all constitutional means will be exhausted before there is a recourse to force. Secession is nothing but revolution. The framers of our Constitution never exhausted so much labor, wisdom and forbearance in its formation, and surrounded it with so many guards and securities, if it was intended to be broken by every member of the Confederacy at will. It was intended for "perpetual union" so expressed in the preamble, and for the establishment of a government, not a compact, which can only be dissolved by revolution, or the consent of all the people in convention assembled. It is idle to talk of secession. Anarchy would have been established, and not a government by Washington, Hamilton, Jefferson, Madison, and the other patriots of the Revolution.... Still, a Union that can only be maintained by swords and bayonets, and in which strife and civil war are to take the place of brotherly love and kindness, has no charm for me. I shall mourn for my country and for the welfare and progress of mankind. If the Union is dissolved, and the Government disrupted, I shall return to my native State and share the miseries of my people, and save in defence will draw my sword on none.

LETTER TO JEFFERSON DAVIS (1862)

HEADQUARTERS.
Near Fredericktown, Md., September 8, 1862.
His Excellency JEFFERSON DAVIS,
President of the Confederate States, Richmond,
　　Va.:

MR. PRESIDENT: The present position of affairs, in my opinion, places it in the power of the Government of the Confederate States to propose with propriety to that of the United States the recognition of our independence. For more than a year both sections of the country have been devastated by hostilities which have brought sorrow and suffering upon thousands of homes, without advancing the objects which our enemies proposed to themselves in beginning the contest. Such a proposition, coming from us at this time, could in no way be regarded as suing for peace; but, being made when it is in our power to inflict injury upon our adversary, would show conclusively to the world that our sole object is the establishment of our independence and the attainment of an honorable peace. The rejection of this offer would prove to the country that the responsibility of the continuance of the war does not rest upon us, but that the party in power in the United States elect to prosecute it for purpose of their own. The proposal of peace would enable the people of the United States to determine at their coming elections whether they will support those who favor a prolongation of the war, or those who wish to bring it to a termination, which can but be productive of good to both parties without affecting the honor of either.

I have the honor to be, with high respect, your obedient servant,
　　R. E. LEE,
　　General.

LETTER TO JEFFERSON DAVIS (1863)

To JEFFERSON DAVIS
Richmond, Virginia
Headquarters, Army of Northern Virginia
June 10, 1863

Mr. President:

I beg leave to bring to your attention a subject with reference to which I have thought that the course pursued by writers and speakers among us has had a tendency to interfere with our success. I refer to the manner in which the demonstration of a desire for peace at the North has been received in our country.

I think there can be no doubt that journalists and others at the South, to whom the Northern people naturally look for a reflection of our opinions, have met these indications in such wise as to weaken the hands of the advocates of a pacific policy on the part of the Federal Government, and give much encouragement to those who urge a continuance of the war.

Recent political movements in the United States, and the comments of influential newspapers upon them, have attracted my attention particularly to this subject, which I deem not unworthy of the consideration of Your Excellency, nor inappropriate to be adverted to by me in view of its connection with the situation of military affairs.

Conceding to our enemies the superiority claimed by them in numbers, resources, and all the means and appliances for carrying on the war, we have no right to look for exemptions from the military consequences of a vigorous use of these advantages, excepting by such deliverance as the mercy of Heaven may accord to the courage of our soldiers, the justice of our cause, and the constancy and prayers of our people. While making the most we can of the means of resistance we possess, and gratefully accepting the measure of success with which God has blessed our efforts as an earnest of His approval and

favor, it is nevertheless the part of wisdom to carefully measure and husband our strength, and not to expect from it more than in the ordinary course of affairs it is capable of accomplishing. We should not therefore conceal from ourselves that our resources in men are constantly diminishing, and the disproportion in this respect between us and our enemies, if they continue united in their efforts to subjugate us, is steadily augmenting. The decrease of the aggregate of this army as disclosed by the returns affords an illustration of this fact. Its effective strength varies from time to time, but the falling off in its aggregate shows that its ranks are growing weaker and that its losses are not supplied by recruits.

Under these circumstances we should neglect no honorable means of dividing and weakening our enemies that they may feel some of the difficulties experienced by ourselves. It seems to me that the most effectual mode of accomplishing this object, now within our reach, is to give all the encouragement we can, consistently with truth, to the rising peace party of the North.

Nor do I think we should in this connection make nice distinctions between those who declare for peace unconditionally and those who advocate it as a means of restoring the Union however much we may prefer the former.

We should bear in mind that the friends of peace at the North must make concessions to the earnest desire that exists in the minds of their countrymen for a restoration of the Union, and that to hold out such a result as an inducement is essential to the success of their party.

Should the belief that peace will bring back the Union become general, the war would no longer be supported, and that after all is what we are interested in bringing about. When peace is proposed to us it will be time enough to discuss its terms, and it is not the part of prudence to spurn the proposition in advance, merely because those who wish to make it

Glossary

adverted to	referred to
subjugate	subdue, defeat

believe, or affect to believe, that it will result in bringing us back to the Union. We entertain no such apprehensions, nor doubt that the desire of our people for a distinct and independent national existence will prove as steadfast under the influence of peaceful measures as it has shown itself in the midst of war.

If the views I have indicated meet the approval of Your Excellency you will best know how to give effect to them. Should you deem them inexpedient or impracticable, I think you will nevertheless agree with me that we should at least carefully abstain from measures or expressions that tend to discourage any party whose purpose is peace.

With the statement of my own opinion on the subject, the length of which you will excuse, I leave to your better judgment to determine the proper course to be pursued.

I am with great respect, your obt servt

R. E. LEE

Genl

LETTER TO JEFFERSON DAVIS (1864)

To JEFFERSON DAVIS
Richmond, Virginia
Headquarters, Army of Northern Virginia
March 25, 1864

Mr. President:

I have the honor to acknowledge the receipt of the letter forwarded to me by your directions, containing the views of the writer as to the intentions of the enemy in the approaching campaign.

I have read the speculations of the Northern papers on the subject, and the order of Genl Grant published in our papers yesterday, but I am not disposed to believe from what I now know, that the first important effort will be directed against Richmond.

The Northern papers, particularly if they derive their information from official sources, as they profess, do not in all probability represent the real purpose of the Federal Government, but are used to create false impressions. The order of Genl Grant, closely considered, is not inconsistent with this idea. There was no apparent occasion for the publication at such a time and place of his intention to take up his headquarters with the Army of the Potomac, and the announcement appears to me to be made with some hidden purpose. It will be remembered that Northern papers of the 14th instant represented Genl Grant as en route for Tennessee to arrange affairs there preparatory to assuming immediate command of the Army of the Potomac. What those arrangements were, we do not know, but if of sufficient moment to require Genl Grant's personal presence in the West just on the eve of his entering upon active duties with another army, it can not be probable that he had completed them by the time his order bears date, March 17th, especially as several of the few days intervening between his departure from Washington and the publication of the order, must have been consumed in travelling. The establishment of an office in Washington to which communications from other armies than that which Genl Grant accompanies shall be addressed, evidently leaves everything to go on under the direction of the former authorities as before, and allows no room for inferences as to whether any army will be active or not, merely from the fact of the presence of Genl Grant. There is to my mind an appearance of design

about the order which makes it of a piece with the publications in the papers, intended to mislead us as to the enemy's intention, and if possible, induce corresponding preparation on our part. You will remember that a like ruse was practised at Vicksburg. Just before the Federal Army went down the river, the indications given out were such, that it was thought the attempt on Vicksburg would be abandoned, and that it was proper to reinforce Genl Bragg, whose army it was supposed would next be attacked. It is natural that the enemy should try to conceal the point which he intends to assail first, as he may suppose that our armies, being connected by shorter lines than his, can concentrate more rapidly. In confirmation of these views, I cannot learn that the army of Genl Meade has been reinforced by any organized troops, nor can I learn of any coming east over the Baltimore & Ohio Railroad which I have ordered to be closely watched. A dispatch from Genl Imboden dated March 23rd states that it is reported that the enemy was moving troops westwards over that road all last week. The report is vague but if true, the troops referred to may be recruits, convalescents & furloughed men going to the corps from the east now serving in the west, or they may be reinforcements for the Army of Tennessee. I have reiterated my order about watching the road, and directed the rumor above mentioned to be carefully investigated. From present indications, I am inclined to believe that the first efforts of the enemy will be directed against Genl Johnston or Genl Longstreet, most probably the former. If it succeeds, Richmond will no doubt be attacked. The condition of the weather and the roads will probably be more favorable for active operations at an early day in the South than in Virginia where it will be uncertain for more than a month. Although we cannot do more than weigh probabilities, they are useful in stimulating and directing a vigilant observation of the enemy, and suggesting such a policy on our part as may determine his. His object can be ascertained with the greatest certainty by observing the movements of his armies closely. I would advise that we make the best preparations in our power to meet an advance in any quarter, but be careful not to suffer ourselves to be misled by feigned movements into strengthening one point at the expense of others, equally exposed and equally important. We should hold ourselves in constant readiness to concentrate as rapidly as possible wherever it may be necessary, but do nothing without reasonably certain information except prepare. This information I have already said, can be best obtained by unremitting vigilance in observing those armies that will most probably be active in the campaign, and I trust that Your Excellency will impress this fact, and the importance of energy, accuracy, and intelligence in collecting information upon all officers in a position to do so. Should a movement be made against Richmond in large force, its preparation will no doubt be indicated by the withdrawal of troops from other quarters, particularly the Atlantic coast and the West. The officers commanding in these regions should endeavor to get early and accurate information of such withdrawal. Should Genl Johnston or Genl Longstreet find the forces opposed to them reduced sufficiently to justify attacking them, they might entirely frustrate the enemy's plans by defeating him. Energy and activity on our part, with a constant readiness to seize any opportunity to strike a blow, will embarrass, if not entirely thwart the enemy in concentrating his different armies, and compel him to conform his movements to our own. If Genl Johnston could be put in a condition to operate successfully against the army opposed to him, he would effectually prevent a combination against Richmond. In the meantime, to guard against any contingency, everything not immediately required should be sent away from Richmond, and stores of food and other supplies collected in suitable and safe places for the use of the troops that it may become necessary to assemble for its defence. I beg to repeat that the utmost vigilance and circumspection, coupled with active and energetic preparation are of the first moment to us.

With high respect, your obt servt
R. E. LEE
Genl

Glossary

Army of the Potomac	the chief Union army in the eastern theater during the Civil War
Genl Bragg	General Braxton Bragg, commander of the Confederacy's army in the western theater
Genl Grant	General Ulysses S. Grant, general of the army who became head of the Union forces in 1863; later eighteenth president of the United States
Genl Imboden	General John Imboden, a Confederate cavalry commander
Genl Johnston	General Joseph Johnston, a senior general in the Confederate army
Genl Longstreet	General James Longstreet, General Robert E. Lee's chief subordinate officer
Genl Meade	General George Meade, Union general who distinguished himself at the Battle of Gettysburg
instant	of this month
Richmond	capital city of Virginia and capital of the Confederacy during the Civil War
Vicksburg	a city in Mississippi, the site of a major campaign (1862–1863) during the Civil War

LETTER TO ANDREW HUNTER (1865)

Headquarters Army of Northern Virginia,
January 11, 1865.
Hon. Andrew Hunter,
Richmond, Va.:
Dear Sir:

I have received your letter of the 7th instant, and without confining myself to the order of your interrogatories, will endeavor to answer them by a statement of my views on the subject. I shall be most happy if I can contribute to the solution of a question in which I feel an interest commensurate with my desire for the welfare and happiness of our people.

Considering the relation of master and slave, controlled by humane laws and influenced by Christianity and an enlightened public sentiment, as the best that can exist between the white and black races while intermingled as at present in this country, I would deprecate any sudden disturbance of that relation unless it be necessary to avert a greater calamity to both. I should therefore prefer to rely upon our white population to preserve the ratio between our forces and those of the enemy, which experience has shown to be safe. But in view of the preparations of our enemies, it is our duty to provide for continued war and not for a battle or a campaign, and I fear that we cannot accomplish this without overtaxing the capacity of our white population.

Should the war continue under existing circumstances, the enemy may in course of time penetrate our country and get access to a large part of our negro population. It is his avowed policy to convert the able-bodied men among them into soldiers, and to emancipate all. The success of the Federal arms in the South was followed by a proclamation of President Lincoln for 280,000 men, the effect of which will be to stimulate the Northern States to procure as substitutes for their own people the negroes thus brought within their reach. Many have already been obtained in Virginia, and should the fortune of war expose more of her territory, the enemy would gain a large accession to his strength. His progress will thus add to his numbers, and at the same time destroy slavery in a manner most pernicious to the welfare of our people. Their negroes will be used to hold them in subjection, leaving the remaining force of the enemy free to extend his conquest. Whatever may be the effect of our employing negro troops, it cannot be as mischievous as this. If it end in subverting slavery it will be accomplished by ourselves, and we can devise the means of alleviating the evil consequences to both races. I think, therefore, we must decide whether slavery shall be extinguished by our enemies and the slaves be used against us, or use them ourselves at the risk of the effects which may be produced upon our social institutions. My own opinion is that we should employ them without delay. I believe that with proper regulations they can be made efficient soldiers. They possess the physical qualifications in an eminent degree. Long habits of obedience and subordination, coupled with the moral influence which in our country the white man possesses over the black, furnish an excellent foundation for that discipline which is the best guaranty of military efficiency. Our chief aim should be to secure their fidelity.

There have been formidable armies composed of men having no interest in the cause for which they fought beyond their pay or the hope of plunder. But it is certain that the surest foundation upon which the fidelity of an army can rest, especially in a service which imposes peculiar hardships and privations, is the personal interest of the soldier in the issue of the contest. Such an interest we can give our negroes by giving immediate freedom to all who enlist, and freedom at the end of the war to the families of those who discharge their duties faithfully (whether they survive or not), together with the privilege of residing at the South. To this might be added a bounty for faithful service.

We should not expect slaves to fight for prospective freedom when they can secure it at once by going to the enemy, in whose service they will incur no greater risk than in ours. The reasons that induce me to recommend the employment of negro troops at all render the effect of the measures I have suggested upon slavery immaterial, and in my opinion the best means of securing the efficiency and fidelity of this auxiliary force would be to accompany the measure with a well-digested plan of gradual and general emancipation. As that will be the result of the continuance of the war, and will certainly occur if the enemy succeed, it seems to me most advisable to adopt it at once, and thereby obtain all the benefits that will accrue to our cause.

The employment of negro troops under regulations similar in principle to those above indicated would, in my opinion, greatly increase our military strength and enable us to relieve our white population to some extent. I think we could dispense with the reserve forces except in cases of necessity.

It would disappoint the hopes which our enemies base upon our exhaustion, deprive them in a great measure of the aid they now derive from black troops, and thus throw the burden of the war upon their own people. In addition to the great political advantages that would result to our cause from the adoption of a system of emancipation, it would exercise a salutary influence upon our whole negro population, by rendering more secure the fidelity of those who become soldiers, and diminishing the inducements to the rest to abscond.

I can only say in conclusion that whatever measures are to be adopted should be adopted at once. Every day's delay increases the difficulty. Much time will be required to organize and discipline the men, and action may be deferred until it is too late.

Very respectfully, your obedient servant,

R. E. LEE,

General.

Glossary

accession	increase
deprecate	disapprove of
instant	of this month
interrogatories	questions

GENERAL ORDER NO. 9 (1865)

Headquarters, Army of Northern Virginia
April 10, 1865

After four years of arduous service, marked by unsurpassed courage and fortitude, the Army of Northern Virginia has been compelled to yield to overwhelming numbers and resources.

I need not tell the brave survivors of so many hard fought battles, who have remained steadfast to the last, that I have consented to the result from no distrust of them.

But feeling that valor and devotion could accomplish nothing that would compensate for the loss that must have attended the continuance of the contest, I determined to avoid the useless sacrifice of those whose past services have endeared them to their countrymen.

By the terms of the agreement officers and men can return to their homes and remain until exchanged. You will take with you the satisfaction that proceeds from the consciousness of duty faithfully performed, and I earnestly pray that a Merciful God will extend to you His blessing and protection.

With an increasing admiration of your constancy and devotion to your country, and a grateful remembrance of your kind and generous considerations for myself, I bid you all an affectionate farewell.

R. E. LEE
Genl

Abraham Lincoln (Library of Congress)

ABRAHAM LINCOLN   1809–1865

Sixteenth President of the United States

Featured Documents
◆ "House Divided" Speech (1858)
◆ First Inaugural Address (1861)
◆ Gettysburg Address (1863)
◆ Second Inaugural Address (1865)

Overview

By almost every standard, Abraham Lincoln is rated as America's greatest president. This recognition stems from five factors. First, Lincoln presided, with ultimate success, over the direst crisis in American history. Had he been less skilled or less determined, the Civil War might very well have ended in the permanent division of the nation. Second, Lincoln accomplished the abolition of slavery in the United States and led the nation in taking its first steps toward racial justice. Third, Lincoln was one of the most impeccable craftsmen of the English language to ever hold political office in the United States. Indeed, with the possible exception of Thomas Jefferson, no other national politician ever demonstrated such a stunning ability to express himself and inspire others through language and text. Fourth, Lincoln came from the humblest background of any person elected to the presidency. Born in a log cabin on the Kentucky frontier, lacking any formal education, scrupulously honest, and enormously hardworking, Lincoln embodied values that almost all Americans admire while symbolizing the idea that any American can escape poverty to achieve greatness. His two nicknames—"Honest Abe" and "the Rail Splitter"—convey his honesty, his humble roots, and his willingness to work hard to improve himself and his nation. Finally, Lincoln's death at the hands of an assassin mere days after the U.S. army's triumph in the Civil War made him into a hero and a national martyr of almost mythic proportions. The national outpouring of grief at his death, even in parts of the defeated South, was unprecedented.

Lincoln was born on February 12, 1809, in a log cabin near Hodgenville, Hardin County, Kentucky. His parents, Thomas and Nancy Hanks Lincoln, were illiterate farmers. The family later moved to Knob Creek, where Lincoln learned the alphabet but little more while attending school for a few weeks. When he was seven, the family moved to Indiana, which had just been admitted to the Union. Uncertain land titles in Kentucky helped prompt the move, but Thomas Lincoln also belonged to a church that opposed slavery, and thus the free state of Indiana was doubly attractive. When Lincoln was nine, his mother died; a year later his father married Sarah Bush Johnston. Sarah was literate and encouraged her young stepson to read, which he did, despite his father's belief that his love of

learning was a sign of weakness and laziness. This led to tension between father and son that was never resolved. Thomas hired Abraham out to neighbors, collecting all his wages, and the teenager grew to resent this form of "slavery" imposed by his overbearing father. In 1828 the young Lincoln took a flatboat down the Mississippi, widening his horizons in part by encountering the horrors of true slavery for the first time. He would later claim that he was "naturally antislavery" and could "not remember when" he "did not so think, and feel" (Basler, 1953–1955, vol. 7, p. 281).

In 1830 the Lincolns moved to Illinois, and in the summer of 1831 Lincoln left his father's house, settling in New Salem. For the next six years he worked as a mill hand, store clerk, and postmaster. He was the part owner of a general store that went bankrupt; while his partner left town, Lincoln remained and gradually paid off all their creditors, leading to his nickname "Honest Abe." Lincoln also expanded his education, developing his oratorical skills by participating in a debate society. In 1832, during the Black Hawk War, he was elected captain of his militia company, reflecting his comrades' recognition of his natural leadership abilities. In 1834 he easily won a seat as county representative, running as a Whig. While in the legislature, where he would remain through 1841, he studied law under John Todd Stuart, the Whigs' leader. In 1836 Lincoln was admitted to the bar, and in 1837 he moved to Springfield, the new state capital, where he became Stuart's law partner. As one of a handful of state legislators to oppose a resolution condemning abolitionists, Lincoln instead offered a resolution condemning slavery, which was overwhelmingly defeated.

In 1846 Lincoln was elected to the U.S. House of Representatives, having promised to serve only one term. In Congress he opposed the Mexican-American War, as did most of his fellow Whigs. After his term ended, Lincoln returned to Illinois and left politics, focusing on his law practice. The 1854 passage of the Kansas-Nebraska Act, which repealed most of the Missouri Compromise and allowed slavery in most of the western territories, brought Lincoln back into politics. In fact, opposition to this law led to a political revolution. Lincoln successfully ran for the state legislature by opposing the spread of slavery to the western territories. He hoped that the new legislature, now dominated by a rickety coalition of Whigs and Democrats who opposed the Kansas-Nebraska Act, would send him to

1809
- **February 12**
  Abraham Lincoln is born near Hodgenville, Kentucky.

1816
- **December**
  The Lincoln family moves to Pigeon Creek, Indiana, where Lincoln grows up in an atmosphere that is both hostile to slavery and hostile to free blacks.

1828
- In the first of two trips to New Orleans, Lincoln encounters slavery for the first time; he is ever after opposed to the institution.

1832
- **April 21–June 11**
  Lincoln serves in the Illinois militia during the Black Hawk War.
- **August**
  Lincoln is defeated in running for the state legislature.

1834
- **August 4**
  Lincoln is elected to the Illinois General Assembly from Sangamon County, to gain reelection three times and serve throughout 1841.

1836
- **September 9**
  Lincoln is admitted to the practice of law in Illinois.

1837
- **April 15**
  Lincoln moves to Springfield and joins the law practice of his mentor, John Todd Stuart.

1846
- **August 3**
  Lincoln is elected to the U.S. House of Representatives.

1849
- Lincoln's term in Congress ends; after failing to secure a position in the new Zachary Taylor administration, he returns to Illinois to practice law.

the U.S. Senate. Although he led for six ballots, he could not gain enough votes to win. Lincoln continued to make speeches against the spread of slavery, crisscrossing the state and the Midwest. By 1855 the movement against the Kansas-Nebraska Act had coalesced in the creation of the Republican Party.

In 1856 Lincoln made an unsuccessful bid to gain the new party's vice presidential nomination. After the election, he concentrated his efforts on unseating the state's incumbent Democratic senator—the author of the Kansas-Nebraska Act—Stephen A. Douglas. In March 1857, the Supreme Court held in *Dred Scott v. Sandford* that Congress could never ban slavery from the territories. In his brilliant critiques of that opinion Lincoln alleged that the decision was part of a conspiracy to nationalize slavery that included Chief Justice Roger B. Taney, President James Buchanan, and Senator Douglas. Lincoln's challenge to Douglas began with his "house divided" speech and continued through the 1858 campaign, as he debated Douglas seven times in cities and towns across Illinois. Although he lost the election, Lincoln emerged as one of the new party's most prominent speakers. At a dramatic convention in 1860 he secured the presidential nomination of the Republican Party. His campaign centered on ending the spread of slavery into the territories but not harming the institution where it existed. He was not on the ballot in most of the slave states, but he carried every northern state, won a plurality of the popular votes, and won a commanding majority of the electoral votes. By the time he was inaugurated, seven states had seceded from the Union, asserting that a Lincoln presidency threatened slavery.

No president before or since Lincoln ever faced a comparable crisis. The nation was coming apart; with seven states having created a new government as the Confederate States of America, war seemed inevitable. Lincoln's first inaugural address was a masterpiece of conciliation. Lincoln believed that by taking the oath or "preserve, protect and defend the Constitution of the United States," he was under a moral obligation to prevent the destruction of the Union. While Lincoln asserted from the beginning of the Civil War that its purpose was to preserve the Union, everyone in the nation knew, as he would later admit in his second inaugural, that slavery was the war's cause. By early 1862 Lincoln had decided to move against the institution. He spent much of the summer working on the Emancipation Proclamation but waited to present it, telling his critics that it would be foolish to try to end slavery without the military standing to do so. Following the Union's strategic victory at the Battle of Antietam on September 17, Lincoln issued the proclamation, which would take effect on January 1, 1863. Detailing how and where slaves would be freed, the decree was a dry legal document designed not to inspire the nation but to impress lawyers and, more important, the Supreme Court. It was in the Gettysburg address, given in November 1863, that Lincoln provided America with an eloquent and stirring argument for freedom and for the fulfillment of the Declaration of Independence. Finally, in his second inaugural address, with the war almost won and slavery virtually ended, Lincoln spoke to the future, when peace would be restored and freedom would finally be a national policy. A month and a half later, Lincoln lay dead, murdered by John Wilkes Booth, a pro-Confederate fanatic.

Explanation and Analysis of Documents

Lincoln was a master of the English language. He was largely self-educated but was widely read and had a fine ear for language. He clearly stated the complicated and difficult issues facing his audience and the nation. Lincoln was also brilliant at creating phrases that would resonate with his audience. His appeal to the "better angels of our nature" in his first inaugural was a remarkable plea to the people of the nation to act on their highest principles. Similarly, his phrasing in the last sentence of the Gettysburg address brilliantly conveyed two remarkable ideas. First, he asserted that the Civil War was justified to create "a new birth of freedom," which included an end to slavery. Second he tied the war to the preservation of democracy, saying that if the war was won, "government of the people, by the people, for the people" would not "perish from the earth." These ideas were easily captured by those who heard him speak or who read the speech. Likewise, in his second inaugural, he memorably asked Americans—"with malice toward none, with charity for all"—to avoid vengeance and retaliation in the wake of such a bloody war.

◆ "House Divided" Speech

In the nineteenth century, before the adoption of the Seventeenth Amendment (1913), state legislatures chose the U.S. senators, often with deals and compromises made by members of the majority party. Thus, candidates rarely directly ran for the Senate; the 1858 race in Illinois was different. In June the new Republican Party held a state convention and formally nominated Abraham Lincoln as its candidate. He later challenged the incumbent senator, Stephen A. Douglas, to a series of seven debates, to be forever known as the Lincoln-Douglas debates. Lincoln's campaign began at the state Republican convention, where he gave his famous "house divided" speech. His goal was to inspire his fellow Republicans to vigorously campaign for the party's candidates for the state legislature so that enough might win to send him to the U.S. Senate.

Although he was not particularly pious and not much of a churchgoer, Lincoln knew the Bible well, as did most educated men of his age. In the opening paragraph of this speech, he offers a biblical quotation: "A house divided against itself cannot stand." Everyone in the audience would have recognized this line from Matthew 12:25, and many would have recalled the full verse: "And Jesus knew their thoughts, and said unto them, Every kingdom divided against itself is brought to desolation; and every city or house divided against itself shall not stand." Lincoln's message was clear: The United States was facing a crisis over slavery. The house was the nation, and if the nation did not address the problem of slavery, "desolation" would follow.

Time Line

1854

■ **November 7**
Lincoln is elected to the Illinois legislature but resigns twenty days later to pursue a seat in the U.S. Senate, which he fails to obtain.

1857

■ **March 6**
Chief Justice Roger B. Taney announces the decision in *Dred Scott v. Sandford*, a decision that dramatically affects northern politics and sets the stage for Lincoln's rise as a national figure.

1858

■ **June 16**
The Republican convention in Illinois nominates Lincoln to run for the U.S. Senate, and he gives his "house divided" speech.

■ **August–October**
Lincoln gains renown by debating Stephen A. Douglas seven times; he loses the election.

1860

■ **May 18**
The Republican National Convention nominates Lincoln for president.

■ **November 6**
Lincoln is elected president.

■ **December 20**
South Carolina becomes the first state to secede from the Union.

1861

■ **March 4**
Lincoln is inaugurated as president of the United States and delivers his first inaugural address.

■ **April 12**
The American Civil War begins when Confederate troops in Charleston, South Carolina, fire on Fort Sumter.

■ **April 15**
Lincoln calls for seventy-five thousand volunteers to defend the nation; shortly thereafter, Virginia, Arkansas, North Carolina, and Tennessee secede from the Union.

1862

■ **September 16–18**
The Battle of Antietam provides Lincoln with the needed military victory to announce the Emancipation Proclamation.

■ **September 22**
Lincoln issues the preliminary version of the Emancipation Proclamation, giving Confederate states one hundred days to return to the Union.

1863

■ **January 1**
Lincoln issues the final Emancipation Proclamation, declaring that most of the slaves in the Confederacy are free.

■ **January 1–4**
Major U.S. victories at Gettysburg and Vicksburg end any chance of Confederate victory.

■ **November 19**
Lincoln gives an address at Gettysburg to dedicate the national cemetery there.

1864

■ **November 8**
Lincoln is reelected president.

1865

■ **March 4**
Lincoln is again inaugurated and gives his second inaugural address.

■ **April 9**
General Robert E. Lee surrenders his army to General Ulysses S. Grant, effectively ending the Civil War.

■ **April 14**
Lincoln is assassinated at Ford's Theatre by the pro-Confederate actor John Wilkes Booth; the president dies the next day.

Overall, the speech was an extended attack on Lincoln's opponent, Douglas, as well as on President Buchanan and Chief Justice Taney. It was also a warning that if the nation continued on its present path, the conspiracy of those men would be fulfilled, and slavery would become legal throughout the nation. Lincoln warns his fellow citizens, "We shall lie down pleasantly dreaming that the people of Missouri are on the verge of making their State free, and we shall awake to the reality instead, that the Supreme Court has made Illinois a slave State." While the statement is seen as an exaggeration today, many Republicans truly feared that the supporters of slavery would never stop until it was protected everywhere in the nation. The election of Lincoln would help prevent this.

As a campaign document, the "house divided" speech was enormously successful in defining Lincoln and his issues as well as his opponent. Throughout the campaign, Douglas was forced to both defend and disassociate himself from the *Dred Scott* decision. Lincoln ended up losing the election among the state legislators in part because that body had not been reapportioned in many years. By 1858 a majority of the Illinois population lived in the northern part and were underrepresented; had there been a popular election, Lincoln probably would have won. In the 1860 presidential election, Lincoln would win more than half the popular vote in Illinois, while Douglas would carry only 47 percent. The "house divided" speech catapulted Lincoln into a leadership position in the new Republican Party by virtue of his strong rhetorical arguments and his ability not only to delineate why the *Dred Scott* decision was wrong but also to tie the result to the leading Democrats of the decade, the former president, Franklin Pierce, President Buchanan, and Senator Douglas.

◆ **First Inaugural Address**

Lincoln's first address as president may have been the most important inaugural address in history. As he stood to take the oath of office, the nation was collapsing. Seven states had declared that they were no longer in the United States but were part of a new nation, the Confederate States of America. Lincoln's ambitious goal in his inaugural was to bring these states back into the Union. He begins by confronting the fears of the South—that his administration would seek to disestablish slavery in the South. He bluntly declares, "I have no purpose, directly or indirectly, to interfere with the institution of slavery in the States where it exists. I believe I have no lawful right to do so, and I have no inclination to do so."

Hoping the Deep South might return to the Union, Lincoln reminds all Americans—in the North and the South—of their shared heritage. He invokes the Founders, making specific references to the Declaration of Independence and the inauguration of George Washington. He notes that the Constitution was designed to create a "more perfect Union" and that he had taken an oath under God to protect the Constitution and the nation.

Lincoln reminds the South of its ties to the rest of the country, of its historical and physical connections to the

---

Abraham Lincoln's handwritten draft of the Gettysburg Address (AP/Wide World Photos)

North. He promises not to send troops to the South and not to unnecessarily antagonize the region. But he also promises to keep the Union together and, where necessary, to enforce federal laws. He closes with a plea for peace and unity crafted with an eloquence rarely seen in inaugural addresses:

> We are not enemies, but friends. We must not be enemies. Though passion may have strained it must not break our bonds of affection. The mystic chords of memory, stretching from every battlefield and patriot grave to every living heart and hearthstone all over this broad land, will yet swell the chorus of the Union, when again touched, as surely they will be, by the better angels of our nature.

In the end Lincoln's plea for unity failed, and, as he would say in his second inaugural address, "the war came." But with his entreaty on behalf of the Union and his promise not to harm slavery in the South, Lincoln placed his administration on the side of peace and compromise. Thus, when the Civil War began, most northerners saw the South as a relentless aggressor against an administration that offered peace. This helped rally northerners to defend the nation after the Confederate firing on Fort Sumter.

◆ **Gettysburg Address**

Only 266 words long, the Gettysburg address is perhaps the most famous short speech in the English language;

whole books have been written analyzing it. The address was part of a ceremony to dedicate the military cemetery located at the site of the Battle of Gettysburg. Lincoln was not the featured speaker, and his speech was so short that much of the day's audience probably missed it. However, when published, the address immediately captivated the nation for its simplicity, directness, and somber yet uplifting message.

The context of the speech is crucial to understanding its relevance. From July 1 to July 3, 1863, the Union army fought a pitched battle against the Confederate army at Gettysburg. The United States registered its casualties at 23,049, with 3,155 killed in action, 14,529 wounded, and 5,365 missing or captured. Confederate losses were less certain because the Confederate army fled the battle in disarray; whole units were decimated, and so many officers were killed, wounded, or captured that no one was left in command to even tally the losses. The best scholarship has estimated Confederate casualties at 24,000, with at least 3,500 killed, 15,250 wounded (6,800 of whom were also captured), and 5,425 captured unwounded. By any standard, the three-day Battle of Gettysburg was the bloodiest in American history. The battle was also an overwhelming and decisive victory for the United States and an equally catastrophic defeat for the Confederate army and its commander, General Robert E. Lee.

The battle was the clear turning point of the Civil War; never again would Lee's army be in a position to launch an offensive against the United States. With the fall of Vicksburg on the Mississippi River on July 4, President Lincoln could be confident that victory would eventually be achieved. Six months before Gettysburg, Lincoln had issued the Emancipation Proclamation, making the war a struggle for liberty as well as a conflict necessary to save the nation. Lincoln was thus able to use the dedication of the Gettysburg military cemetery, four and a half months after the battle, to underscore the high moral purposes of the war, for which so many U.S. soldiers died on this battlefield and all the others.

The address itself is rhetorically powerful, in part because of its simplicity. In an age of lengthy and complex speeches, Lincoln delivered an amazingly short one on November 19, 1863. The speech is almost religious in nature, creating images of what scholars call civil religion. It begins in a biblical fashion, using the term "score" (meaning twenty) to count the years instead of simply stating the exact number. Lincoln ties this scripture-like dating system to "our fathers"—not religious fathers but the fathers of the nation. What happened eighty-seven years ago, in 1776, was the writing and signing of the Declaration of Independence. The text then paraphrases that document, noting that the nation was "conceived in liberty and dedicated to the proposition that all men are created equal." In the rest of the speech, Lincoln describes the struggle of the United States as a "testing" of the theory of liberty and equality set out in the Declaration of Independence. The message is clear: The "unfinished work" of those who died at Gettysburg is not merely victory but nationwide freedom and equality as well. Lincoln's final sentence is especially powerful and stirring. He asks his countrymen to finish the task before them, that of saving the Union and expanding liberty:

> It is rather for us to be here dedicated to the great task remaining before us—that from these honored dead we take increased devotion to that cause for which they gave the last full measure of devotion— that we here highly resolve that these dead shall not have died in vain, that this nation under God shall have a new birth of freedom, and that government of the people, by the people, for the people shall not perish from the earth.

The final message—that the American experiment in democracy was on the verge of a "new birth of freedom"— reminds the audience that the Civil War was a struggle to destroy not only Confederate treason but also the institution of slavery.

◆ Second Inaugural Address

The circumstances of Lincoln's second inaugural address were far different from those of the first. For almost four years the nation had been at war. Nearly one million Americans, in Union blue and Confederate gray, had already been killed or wounded in battle. Huge amounts of property had been destroyed. Most of the Confederacy had been conquered, but still the rebel armies fought on, in an inevitably losing cause. Union victory was in sight and, with it, a total end to slavery. At the beginning of the war, blacks were not even considered citizens of the United States and had almost no legal rights. By the time Lincoln gave his second inaugural, nearly two hundred thousand African Americans had served in the army and navy, many with great distinction. Laws discriminating against blacks had been repealed in a number of states, and federal laws were beginning to establish equality. Two acts creating streetcar lines in the District of Columbia, for instance, prohibited segregated seating—a small but important step toward equality in the nation's capital. The most prominent African American in the nation, Frederick Douglass, had met with Lincoln, drank tea with him in public, and would be invited to attend the inaugural party that night.

Lincoln's second inaugural address reflected these massive changes. He notes that when the war began, "neither party expected ... the magnitude or the duration which it has already attained." Indeed, both sides had expected a short war with few casualties. But the conflict had lasted for four years, with staggering numbers of soldiers dead and wounded. Lincoln points out that when it began "one-eighth of the whole population were colored slaves, not distributed generally over the Union, but localized in the southern part of it," and that "these slaves constituted a peculiar and powerful interest. All knew that this interest was somehow the cause of the war." Even though Lincoln had initially fought the war in order to preserve the Union, he admits here that he knew, as all had known, that slavery was the root cause—and he could now declare that the conflict had ended slavery.

He ends this speech with an appeal for peace, even as he understood that there would be more violence before the war was over. But, once it was over, he would seek some measure of reconciliation, not vengeance. Thus, with true grace he concludes,

> With malice toward none, with charity for all, with firmness in the right as God gives us to see the right, let us strive on to finish the work we are in, to bind up the nation's wounds, to care for him who shall have borne the battle and for his widow and his orphan, to do all which may achieve and cherish a just and lasting peace among ourselves and with all nations.

Exactly what Lincoln intended for the future was unclear. He was committed to black freedom and to justice for those who had fought in the war, including the two hundred thousand or so black soldiers and sailors. His goal of a "just and lasting peace" would have precluded punishments of former Confederates but would have necessarily included the protection of former slaves. Yet, whatever he had hoped for, Lincoln would not be able to carry it out. A month and a half after this speech, he would be murdered by a Confederate sympathizer whose motive was malice and who could not stand the idea that peace had come at the expense of the Confederacy.

Impact and Legacy

It is hard to underestimate Lincoln's impact on history. By standing up to the secessionists, Lincoln preserved the nation. His predecessor, James Buchanan, did nothing to stop secession and, in fact, stated that neither the president nor Congress could prevent the southern slave states from tearing apart the nation. Lincoln disagreed and firmly opposed secession. The cost of this nationalism was high; more than 350,000 Union soldiers and nearly as many Confederate soldiers died in the Civil War, and the destruction of buildings, land, railroads, and infrastructure was enormous. Equally important to Unionism was Lincoln's making the end of slavery a goal of the war, such that he became the first American president to take a stand against the institution. At the beginning of the war, most blacks in America were slaves, none were able to serve in the army, and no president had ever met a black on equal terms. By the war's end, almost all slaves were free, and the few remaining slaves would gain their freedom at the end of 1865 with the ratification of the Thirteenth Amendment. More than two hundred thousand African Americans had served with honor and bravery in the U.S. Army and Navy, most as enlisted men but some as officers. More than twenty were presented with the congressional Medal of Honor for disproving racist notions that blacks would not or could not be admirable soldiers. Had Lincoln not authorized the enlistment of black troops, the outcome of the war might have been altered, and the conflict would have had a different meaning. Finally, Lincoln publicly met with blacks, ate with them, shook their hands, and sought their advice. These acts violated contemporary social taboos and so helped break down racism. At a party after his second inauguration, Lincoln walked arm in arm with Frederick Douglass, introducing him as his friend.

Lincoln's legacy is somewhat more complex and contested. For nearly a century he was sacrosanctly seen as "Father Abraham," the "Great Emancipator." More recently, some scholars have focused on his slow movement toward emancipation and black enlistment in the military. Others have suggested that by running away, many slaves effectively liberated themselves. Both points have some validity; but most historians understand that successful emancipation required deft, if delayed, political maneuvering and strong presidential leadership. Near the end of the war, some Confederate leaders were willing to end the conflict and bring their states back into the Union if Lincoln would revoke the Emancipation Proclamation. The president refused to consider such a plan. Providing another perspective, some scholars have argued that Lincoln abused civil liberties during the war, by suspending habeas corpus in some places and allowing the military to arrest civilians. Others point out, however, that this was indeed civil war and that the Constitution specifically allows the suspension of habeas corpus during a rebellion. Scholars also note that the Confederacy, under Jefferson Davis, was far more abusive of civil liberties than was the United States under Lincoln.

In the end, Lincoln's impression on the course of American history was enormous. He was central to preserving the Union, abolishing slavery, and moving the United States toward greater recognition of civil rights. Early in his career, Lincoln opposed black suffrage, as did almost all other politicians of the era. By the end of his days, he had come to support black suffrage just as he had come to support the ending of slavery everywhere in the nation and the enlisting of black troops. Arguably, the most important aspect of Lincoln's character was his ability to grow, change, and adapt, which led him to always seek progress on such issues as liberty and freedom. And with his moral strength, Lincoln proved able to give Americans a new direction, such that the nation at last rejected its support for slavery and embraced the notions "that this nation under God shall have a new birth of freedom, and that government of the people, by the people, for the people shall not perish from the earth."

Key Sources

The records of Lincoln's presidency and life are scattered across the nation. Most of his letters and speeches can be found in Roy P. Basler, ed., *The Collected Works of Abraham Lincoln*, 9 vols. (1953–1955), and its continuations, Roy P. Basler, ed., *Supplement, 1832–1865* (1974), and Roy P. Basler and Christian O. Basler, eds., *Second Supplement, 1848–1865* (1990). The original collection by Basler is available online through the Abraham Lincoln Association and the University of Michigan (http://quod.lib.umich.edu/l/lincoln). Documents from Lincoln's legal work are in Daniel W. Stowell, ed., *The Papers of Abraham Lincoln: Legal Documents and Cases*, 4 vols. (2008), and Martha L. Benner and Cullom Davis, eds., *The Law Practice of Abraham Lincoln: Complete Documentary Edition* (2000), an electronic resource on three discs. Online collections of Lincoln's papers include the Abraham Lincoln Papers at the Library of Congress (http://lcweb2.loc.gov/ammem/alhtml/malhome.html) and the Papers of Abraham Lincoln as presented by the Illinois Historic Preservation Agency and the Abraham Lincoln Presidential Library and Museum (http://www.papersofabrahamlincoln.org).

Further Reading

■ Books

Donald, David Herbert. *Lincoln*. New York: Simon & Schuster, 1996.

Holzer, Harold. *Lincoln President-Elect: Abraham Lincoln and the Great Secession Winter, 1860–1861*. New York: Simon & Schuster, 2008.

Lehrman, Lewis E. *Lincoln at Peoria: The Turning Point; Getting Right with the Declaration of Independence*. Mechanicsburg, Pa: Stackpole Books, 2008.

"*I do not expect the Union to be dissolved—I do not expect the house to fall—but I do expect it will cease to be divided.*"

("House Divided" Speech)

"*I have no purpose, directly or indirectly, to interfere with the institution of slavery in the States where it exists. I believe I have no lawful right to do so, and I have no inclination to do so.*"

(First Inaugural Address)

"*We are not enemies, but friends. We must not be enemies. Though passion may have strained it must not break our bonds of affection. The mystic chords of memory, stretching from every battlefield and patriot grave to every living heart and hearthstone all over this broad land, will yet swell the chorus of the Union, when again touched, as surely they will be, by the better angels of our nature.*"

(First Inaugural Address)

"*That we here highly resolve that these dead shall not have died in vain, that this nation under God shall have a new birth of freedom, and that government of the people, by the people, for the people shall not perish from the earth.*"

(Gettysburg Address)

"*Neither party expected for the war the magnitude or the duration which it has already attained. Neither anticipated that the cause of the conflict might cease with or even before the conflict itself should cease. Each looked for an easier triumph, and a result less fundamental and astounding.*"

(Second Inaugural Address)

"*With malice toward none, with charity for all, with firmness in the right as God gives us to see the right, let us strive on to finish the work we are in, to bind up the nation's wounds.*"

(Second Inaugural Address)

McPherson, James M. *Tried by War: Abraham Lincoln as Commander in Chief*. New York: Penguin Press, 2008.

Oates, Stephen. *With Malice toward None: A Life of Abraham Lincoln*. New York: Harper and Row, 1977.

Paludan, Phillip Shaw. *The Presidency of Abraham Lincoln*. Lawrence: University Press of Kansas, 1994.

Peterson, Merrill D. *Lincoln in American Memory*. New York: Oxford University Press, 1994.

Striner, Richard. *Father Abraham: Lincoln's Relentless Struggle to End Slavery*. New York: Oxford University Press, 2006.

—Paul Finkelman

Questions for Further Study

1. Carefully outline and discuss the arguments Lincoln makes in his "house divided" speech. What links does he identify between slavery and secession, and how were these views reflected seven years later, in his second inaugural address? Trace the process he outlines, whereby proponents of slavery sought to impose their will on the nation first through the Kansas-Nebraska Act and later through the decision in the *Dred Scott* case. How valid are Lincoln's arguments, such as his claim that secessionists deliberately confused the identity of states with that of territories?

2. Compare and contrast Lincoln with his opponents. An obvious figure among the latter was Stephen Douglas, one of whose speeches from the celebrated debates between the two men is included elsewhere in this series. Yet Douglas, as a northern Democrat, was a moderate compared with southern Democrats, who viewed Lincoln as a threat to their states' rights of sovereignty. How justified was this fear, and how did Lincoln, particularly in his first inaugural address, attempt to allay the fears of potential secessionists and persuade them to remain in the Union?

3. Lincoln's first inaugural address is indeed among the most important of its kind in world history, coming at a time when the nation stood on the brink of civil war. Discuss the method by which Lincoln attempts to extend an olive branch to those who called for secession, even as he remained true to his own principles. What does he offer to the southern states if they will simply remain in the Union? In what ways is his tone toward secessionists and advocates of slavery almost apologetic and in what other ways is it sarcastic or otherwise firmly oppositional?

4. Examine the Gettysburg Address both as a moment in American history and as a lasting part of world literature. Discuss the circumstances surrounding its delivery, including the battle that had taken place at the site just four months earlier, the fact that the much-anticipated keynote speaker at the dedication ceremony was not Lincoln himself but the former secretary of state Edward Everett, and the immediate reception of Everett's and Lincoln's speeches compared with the ultimate verdict of history. Try rewriting the speech as it might have been delivered by a less effective communicator—conveying the same ideas but with more words, and less compelling ones at that. (An interesting and humorous example can be found in *Writing Well*, by Donald Hall.) Then discuss the importance of Lincoln's economy of words and careful use of vocabulary.

5. Compare and contrast Lincoln's first and second inaugural addresses. Note that Lincoln himself did part of the job, offering in his 1865 speech a number of ways in which the situation of his second inaugural (and the attendant speech) differs from that of four years earlier. In particular, how did his portrayal of the causes behind the national conflict differ between his first and second inaugurals? How aware does he seem that victory lay, as subsequent events would show, just a few weeks in the future? And how might he have handled the postwar reconstruction of the United States if he had lived to see it?

"HOUSE DIVIDED" SPEECH (1858)

If we could first know where we are, and whither we are tending, we could better judge what to do, and how to do it. We are now far into the fifth year since a policy was initiated with the avowed object, and confident promise, of putting an end to slavery agitation. Under the operation of that policy, that agitation has not only has not ceased but has constantly augmented. In my opinion it will not cease until a crisis shall have been reached and passed. "A house divided against itself cannot stand." I believe this government cannot endure permanently half slave and half free. I do not expect the Union to be dissolved—I do not expect the house to fall—but I do expect it will cease to be divided. It will become all one thing, or all the other. Either the opponents of slavery will arrest the further spread of it, and place it where the public mind shall rest in the belief that it is in the course of ultimate extinction; or its advocates will push it forward, till it shall become alike lawful in all the States, old as well as new—North as well as South.

Have we no tendency to the latter condition?

Let any one who doubts, carefully contemplate that now almost complete legal combination—piece of machinery, so to speak—compounded of the Nebraska doctrine, and the *Dred Scott* decision. Let him consider not only what work the machinery is adapted to do, and how well adapted; but also, let him study the history of its construction, and trace, if he can, or rather fail, if he can, to trace the evidences of design, and concert of action, among its chief architects, from the beginning.

The new year of 1854 found slavery excluded from more than half the States by State Constitutions, and from most of the national territory by Congressional prohibition. Four days later, commenced the struggle which ended in repealing that Congressional prohibition. This opened all the national territory to slavery, and was the first point gained.

But, so far, Congress only had acted; and an indorsement by the people, real or apparent, was indispensable, to save the point already gained, and give chance for more.

This necessity had not been overlooked; but had been provided for, as well as might be, in the notable argument of "squatter sovereignty," otherwise called "sacred right of self-government," which latter phrase, though expressive of the only rightful basis of any government, was so perverted in this attempted use of it as to amount to just this: That if any one man choose to enslave another, no third man shall be allowed to object. That argument was incorporated into the Nebraska bill itself, in the language which follows: "It being the true intent and meaning of this act not to legislate slavery into any Territory or State, nor to exclude it therefrom; but to leave the people thereof perfectly free to form and regulate their domestic institutions in their own way, subject only to the Constitution of the United States." Then opened the roar of loose declamation in favor of "Squatter Sovereignty," and "sacred right of self-government." "But," said opposition members, "let us amend the bill so as to expressly declare that the people of the Territory may exclude slavery." "Not we," said the friends of the measure; and down they voted the amendment.

While the Nebraska bill was passing through Congress, a law case involving the question of a negro's freedom, by reason of his owner having voluntarily taken him first into a free State and then into a Territory covered by the Congressional prohibition, and held him as a slave for a long time in each, was passing through the U. S. Circuit Court for the District of Missouri; and both Nebraska bill and law suit were brought to a decision in the same month of May, 1854. The negro's name was "Dred Scott," which name now designates the decision finally made in the case. Before the then next Presidential election, the law case came to, and was argued in, the Supreme Court of the United States; but the decision of it was deferred until after the election. Still, before the election, Senator Trumbull, on the floor of the Senate, requested the leading advocate of the Nebraska bill to state his opinion whether the people of a Territory can constitutionally exclude slavery from their limits; and the latter answers: "That is a question for the Supreme Court."

The election came. Mr. Buchanan was elected, and the indorsement, such as it was, secured. That was the second point gained. The indorsement, however, fell short of a clear popular majority by nearly four hundred thousand votes, and so, perhaps, was not overwhelmingly reliable and satisfactory. The outgoing President, in his last annual message, as impressively as possible echoed back upon the people the weight and authority of the indorsement. The Supreme Court met again; did not announce their decision, but ordered a reargument. The Presidential inauguration came, and still no decision of the court; but the incoming President in his inaugural address, fervently exhorted the people to abide by the forthcoming decision, whatever it might be. Then, in a few days, came the decision.

The reputed author of the Nebraska bill finds an early occasion to make a speech at this capital indorsing the *Dred Scott* decision, and vehemently denouncing all opposition to it. The new President, too, seizes the early occasion of the Silliman letter to indorse and strongly construe that decision, and to express his astonishment that any different view had ever been entertained!

At length a squabble springs up between the President and the author of the Nebraska bill, on the mere question of fact, whether the Lecompton Constitution was or was not, in any just sense, made by the people of Kansas; and in that quarrel the latter declares that all he wants is a fair vote for the people, and that he cares not whether slavery be voted down or voted up. I do not understand his declaration that he cares not whether slavery be voted down or voted up, to be intended by him other than as an apt definition of the policy he would impress upon the public mind—the principle for which he declares he has suffered so much, and is ready to suffer to the end. And well may he cling to that principle. If he has any parental feeling, well may he cling to it. That principle is the only shred left of his original Nebraska doctrine. Under the *Dred Scott* decision "squatter sovereignty" squatted out of existence, tumbled down like temporary scaffolding—like the mould at the foundry served through one blast and fell back into loose sand—helped to carry an election, and then was kicked to the winds. His late joint struggle with the Republicans, against the Lecompton Constitution, involves nothing of the original Nebraska doctrine. That struggle was made on a point—the right of a people to make their own constitution—upon which he and the Republicans have never differed.

The several points of the *Dred Scott* decision, in connection, with Senator Douglas's "care not" policy, constitute the piece of machinery, in its present state of advancement. This was the third point gained. The working points of that machinery are:

First, That no negro slave, imported as such from Africa, and no descendant of such slave, can ever be a citizen of any State, in the sense of that term as used in the Constitution of the United States. This point is made in order to deprive the negro, in every possible event, of the benefit of that provision of the United States Constitution, which declares that "The citizens of each State, shall be entitled to all privileges and immunities of citizens in the several States."

Secondly, That "subject to the Constitution of the United States," neither Congress nor a Territorial Legislature can exclude slavery from any United States territory. This point is made in order that individual men may fill up the Territories with slaves, without danger of losing them as property, and thus to enhance the chances of permanency to the institution through all the future.

Thirdly, That whether the holding a negro in actual slavery in a free State, makes him free, as against the holder, the United States courts will not decide, but will leave to be decided by the courts of any slave State the negro may be forced into by the master. This point is made, not to be pressed immediately; but, if acquiesced in for awhile, and apparently indorsed by the people at an election, then to sustain the logical conclusion that what Dred Scott's master might lawfully do with Dred Scott, in the free State of Illinois, every other master may lawfully do with any other one, or one thousand slaves, in Illinois, or in any other free State.

Auxiliary to all this, and working hand in hand with it, the Nebraska doctrine, or what is left of it, is to educate and mould public opinion, at least Northern public opinion, not to care whether slavery is voted down or voted up. This shows exactly where we now are; and partially, also, whither we are tending.

It will throw additional light on the latter, to go back, and run the mind over the string of historical facts already stated. Several things will now appear less dark and mysterious than they did when they were transpiring. The people were to be left "perfectly free," "subject only to the Constitution." What the Constitution had to do with it, outsiders could not then see. Plainly enough now, it was an exactly fitted niche, for the *Dred Scott* decision to afterward come in, and declare the perfect freedom of the people to be just no freedom at all. Why was the amendment, expressly declaring the right of the people, voted down? Plainly enough now: the adoption of it would have spoiled the niche for the *Dred Scott* decision. Why was the court decision held up? Why even a Senator's individual opinion withheld, till after the Presidential election? Plainly enough now: the speaking out then would have damaged the perfectly free argument upon which the election was to be carried. Why the outgoing President's felicitation on the indorsement? Why the delay of a reargument? Why the incoming President's advance exhortation in favor of the decision? These things look like the cautious patting and petting of a spirited horse preparatory to mounting him, when it is dreaded that he may give the rider a fall. And why the hasty after-indorsement of the decision by the President and others?

We cannot absolutely know that all these exact adaptations are the result of preconcert. But when we see a lot of framed timbers, different portions of which we know have been gotten out at different times and places and by different workmen—Stephen, Franklin, Roger and James, for instance—and when we see these timbers joined together, and see they exactly make the frame of a house or a mill, all the tenons and mortices exactly fitting, and all the lengths and proportions of the different pieces exactly adapted to their respective places, and not a piece too many or too few—not omitting even scaffolding—or, if a single piece be lacking, we see the place in the frame exactly fitted and prepared yet to bring such a piece in—in such a case, we find it impossible not to believe that Stephen and Franklin and Roger and James all understood one another from the beginning, and all worked upon a common plan or draft drawn up before the first blow was struck.

It should not be overlooked that, by the Nebraska bill, the people of a State as well as Territory, were to be left "perfectly free," "subject only to the Constitution." Why mention a State? They were legislating for Territories, and not for or about States. Certainly the people of a State are and ought to be subject to the Constitution of the United States; but why is mention of this lugged into this merely Territorial law? Why are the people of a Territory and the people of a State therein lumped together, and their relation to the Constitution therein treated as being precisely the same? While the opinion of the court, by Chief Justice Taney, in the *Dred Scott* case, and the separate opinions of all the concurring Judges, expressly declare that the Constitution of the United States neither permits Congress nor a Territorial Legislature to exclude slavery from any United States Territory, they all omit to declare whether or not the same Constitution permits a State, or the people of a State, to exclude it. Possibly, this is a mere omission; but who can be quite sure, if McLean or Curtis had sought to get into the opinion a declaration of unlimited power in the people of a State to exclude slavery from their limits, just as Chase and Mace sought to get such declaration, in behalf of the people of a Territory, into the Nebraska bill;—I ask, who can be quite sure that it would not have been voted down in the one case as it had been in the other? The nearest

approach to the point of declaring the power of a State over slavery, is made by Judge Nelson. He approaches it more than once, using the precise idea, and almost the language, too, of the Nebraska act. On one occasion, his exact language is, "except in cases where the power is restrained by the Constitution of the United States, the law of the State is supreme over the subject of slavery within its jurisdiction." In what cases the power of the States is so restrained by the United States Constitution, is left an open question, precisely as the same question, as to the restraint on the power of the Territories, was left open in the Nebraska act. Put this and that together, and we have another nice little niche, which we may, ere long, see filled with another Supreme Court decision, declaring that the Constitution of the United States does not permit a State to exclude slavery from its limits. And this may especially be expected if the doctrine of "care not whether slavery be voted down or voted up," shall gain upon the public mind sufficiently to give promise that such a decision can be maintained when made.

Such a decision is all that slavery now lacks of being alike lawful in all the States. Welcome, or unwelcome, such decision is probably coming, and will soon be upon us, unless the power of the present political dynasty shall be met and overthrown. We shall lie down pleasantly dreaming that the people of Missouri are on the verge of making their State free, and we shall awake to the reality instead, that the Supreme Court has made Illinois a slave State. To meet and overthrow the power of that dynasty, is the work now before all those who would prevent that consummation. That is what we have to do. How can we best do it?

There are those who denounce us openly to their own friends, and yet whisper us softly, that Senator Douglas is the aptest instrument there is with which to effect that object. They wish us to infer all, from the fact that he now has a little quarrel with the present head of the dynasty; and that he has regularly voted with us on a single point, upon which he and we have never differed. They remind us that he is a great man, and that the largest of us are very small ones. Let this be granted. But "a living dog is better than a dead lion." Judge Douglas, if not a dead lion, for this work, is at least a caged and toothless one. How can he oppose the advances of slavery? He don't care anything about it. His avowed mission is impressing the "public heart" to care nothing about it. A leading Douglas democratic newspaper thinks Douglas's superior talent will be needed to resist the revival of the African slave trade. Does Douglas believe an effort to revive that trade is approaching? He has not said so. Does he really think so? But if it is, how can he resist it? For years he has labored to prove it a sacred right of white men to take negro slaves into the new Territories. Can he possibly show that it is less a sacred right to buy them where they can be bought cheapest? And unquestionably they can be bought cheaper in Africa than in Virginia. He has done all in his power to reduce the whole question of slavery to one of a mere right of property; and as such, how can he oppose the foreign slave trade— how can he refuse that trade in that "property" shall be "perfectly free"—unless he does it as a protection to the home production? And as the home producers will probably not ask the protection, he will be wholly without a ground of opposition.

Senator Douglas holds, we know, that a man may rightfully be wiser to-day than he was yesterday—that he may rightfully change when he finds himself wrong. But can we, for that reason, run ahead, and infer that he will make any particular change, of which he, himself, has given no intimation? Can we safely base our action upon any such vague inference? Now, as ever, I wish not to misrepresent Judge Douglas's position, question his motives, or do aught that can be personally offensive to him. Whenever, if ever, he and we can come together on principle so that our cause may have assistance from his great ability, I hope to have interposed no adventitious obstacle. But clearly, he is not now with us—he does not pretend to be—he does not promise ever to be.

Our cause, then, must be intrusted to, and conducted by, its own undoubted friends—those whose hands are free, whose hearts are in the work—who do care for the result. Two years ago the Republicans of the nation mustered over thirteen hundred thou-

Glossary

Buchanan	James Buchanan, fifteenth president of the United States
Chase and Mace	Ohio senator Salmon P. Chase, later chief justice of the Supreme Court, and Daniel Mace, U.S. representative from Indiana
Chief Justice Taney	Roger Taney, chief justice of the United States and author of the Supreme Court's decision in the *Dred Scott* case
Dred Scott decision	reference to the U.S. Supreme Court's decision in *Dred Scott v. Sandford* (1854), which declared that slaves were not citizens
Judge Nelson	Samuel Nelson, associate justice of the U.S. Supreme Court
Lecompton Constitution	one of four proposed constitutions for the state of Kansas
McLean or Curtis	Supreme Court justices James McLean and Benjamin Curtis, who dissented from the majority opinion in the *Dred Scott* case
Nebraska doctrine	reference to the Kansas-Nebraska Act of 1854, which repealed the Missouri Compromise of 1820
Senator Douglas	Stephen A. Douglas, Illinois senator who had been Lincoln's opponent in the 1860 presidential election
Senator Trumbull	Lyman Trumball, U.S. senator from Illinois
Silliman letter	letter of August 15, 1857, written to Benjamin Silliman and made public by President James Buchanan, who had protested the use of federal troops in Kansas
Squatter Sovereignty	belief that the people of any state or territory had the right to conduct their domestic institutions as they saw fit, particularly the institution of slavery
tenons and mortices	types of woodworking joints
whither	to where

sand strong. We did this under the single impulse of resistance to a common danger, with every external circumstance against us. Of strange, discordant, and even hostile elements, we gathered from the four winds, and formed and fought the battle through, under the constant hot fire of a disciplined, proud and pampered enemy. Did we brave all then, to falter now?—now, when that same enemy is wavering, dissevered and belligerent? The result is not doubtful. We shall not fail—if we stand firm, we shall not fail. Wise counsels may accelerate, or mistakes delay it, but, sooner or later, the victory is sure to come.

First Inaugural Address (1861)

In compliance with a custom as old as the Government itself, I appear before you to address you briefly and to take in your presence the oath prescribed by the Constitution of the United States to be taken by the President before he enters on the execution of this office.

I do not consider it necessary at present for me to discuss those matters of administration about which there is no special anxiety or excitement.

Apprehension seems to exist among the people of the Southern States that by the accession of a Republican Administration their property and their peace and personal security are to be endangered. There has never been any reasonable cause for such apprehension. Indeed, the most ample evidence to the contrary has all the while existed and been open to their inspection. It is found in nearly all the published speeches of him who now addresses you. I do but quote from one of those speeches when I declare that "I have no purpose, directly or indirectly, to interfere with the institution of slavery in the States where it exists. I believe I have no lawful right to do so, and I have no inclination to do so."

Those who nominated and elected me did so with full knowledge that I had made this and many similar declarations and had never recanted them; and more than this, they placed in the platform for my acceptance, and as a law to themselves and to me, the clear and emphatic resolution which I now read:

"Resolved, That the maintenance inviolate of the rights of the States, and especially the right of each State to order and control its own domestic institutions according to its own judgment exclusively, is essential to that balance of power on which the perfection and endurance of our political fabric depend; and we denounce the lawless invasion by armed force of the soil of any State or Territory, no matter what pretext, as among the gravest of crimes."

I now reiterate these sentiments, and in doing so I only press upon the public attention the most conclusive evidence of which the case is susceptible that the property, peace, and security of no section are to be in any wise endangered by the now incoming Administration. I add, too, that all the protection which, consistently with the Constitution and the laws, can be given will be cheerfully given to all the States when lawfully demanded, for whatever cause—as cheerfully to one section as to another.

There is much controversy about the delivering up of fugitives from service or labor. The clause I now read is as plainly written in the Constitution as any other of its provisions:

"No person held to service or labor in one State, under the laws thereof, escaping into another, shall in consequence of any law or regulation therein be discharged from such service or labor, but shall be delivered up on claim of the party to whom such service or labor may be due."

It is scarcely questioned that this provision was intended by those who made it for the reclaiming of what we call fugitive slaves; and the intention of the lawgiver is the law. All members of Congress swear their support to the whole Constitution—to this provision as much as to any other. To the proposition, then, that slaves whose cases come within the terms of this clause "shall be delivered up" their oaths are unanimous. Now, if they would make the effort in good temper, could they not with nearly equal unanimity frame and pass a law by means of which to keep good that unanimous oath?

There is some difference of opinion whether this clause should be enforced by national or by State authority, but surely that difference is not a very material one. If the slave is to be surrendered, it can be of but little consequence to him or to others by which authority it is done. And should anyone in any case be content that his oath shall go unkept on a merely unsubstantial controversy as to how it shall be kept?

Again: In any law upon this subject ought not all the safeguards of liberty known in civilized and humane jurisprudence to be introduced, so that a free man be not in any case surrendered as a slave? And might it not be well at the same time to provide by law for the enforcement of that clause in the Constitution which guarantees that "the citizens of each State shall be entitled to all privileges and immunities of citizens in the several States"?

I take the official oath to-day with no mental reservations and with no purpose to construe the Constitution or laws by any hypercritical rules; and while I do not choose now to specify particular acts of Congress as proper to be enforced, I do suggest that it will be much safer for all, both in official and private stations, to conform to and abide by all those acts which stand unrepealed than to violate any of them trusting to find impunity in having them held to be unconstitutional.

It is seventy-two years since the first inauguration of a President under our National Constitution. During that period fifteen different and greatly distinguished citizens have in succession administered the executive branch of the Government. They have conducted it through many perils, and generally with great success. Yet, with all this scope of precedent, I now enter upon the same task for the brief constitutional term of four years under great and peculiar difficulty. A disruption of the Federal Union, heretofore only menaced, is now formidably attempted.

I hold that in contemplation of universal law and of the Constitution the Union of these States is perpetual. Perpetuity is implied, if not expressed, in the fundamental law of all national governments. It is safe to assert that no government proper ever had a provision in its organic law for its own termination. Continue to execute all the express provisions of our National Constitution, and the Union will endure forever, it being impossible to destroy it except by some action not provided for in the instrument itself.

Again: If the United States be not a government proper, but an association of States in the nature of contract merely, can it, as a contract, be peaceably unmade by less than all the parties who made it? One party to a contract may violate it—break it, so to speak—but does it not require all to lawfully rescind it?

Descending from these general principles, we find the proposition that in legal contemplation the Union is perpetual confirmed by the history of the Union itself. The Union is much older than the Constitution. It was formed, in fact, by the Articles of Association in 1774. It was matured and continued by the Declaration of Independence in 1776. It was further matured, and the faith of all the then thirteen States expressly plighted and engaged that it should be perpetual, by the Articles of Confederation in 1778. And finally, in 1787, one of the declared objects for ordaining and establishing the Constitution was "to form a more perfect Union."

But if destruction of the Union by one or by a part only of the States be lawfully possible, the Union is less perfect than before the Constitution, having lost the vital element of perpetuity.

It follows from these views that no State upon its own mere motion can lawfully get out of the Union; that resolves and ordinances to that effect are legally void, and that acts of violence within any State or States against the authority of the United States are insurrectionary or revolutionary, according to circumstances.

I therefore consider that in view of the Constitution and the laws the Union is unbroken, and to the extent of my ability, I shall take care, as the Constitution itself expressly enjoins upon me, that the laws of the Union be faithfully executed in all the States. Doing this I deem to be only a simple duty on my part, and I shall perform it so far as practicable unless my rightful masters, the American people, shall withhold the requisite means or in some authoritative manner direct the contrary. I trust this will not be regarded as a menace, but only as the declared purpose of the Union that it will constitutionally defend and maintain itself.

In doing this there needs to be no bloodshed or violence, and there shall be none unless it be forced upon the national authority. The power confided to me will be used to hold, occupy, and possess the property and places belonging to the Government and to collect the duties and imposts; but beyond what may be necessary for these objects, there will be no invasion, no using of force against or among the people anywhere. Where hostility to the United States in any interior locality shall be so great and universal as to prevent competent resident citizens from holding the Federal offices, there will be no attempt to force obnoxious strangers among the people for that object. While the strict legal right may exist in the Government to enforce the exercise of these offices, the attempt to do so would be so irritating and so nearly impracticable withal that I deem it better to forego for the time the uses of such offices.

The mails, unless repelled, will continue to be furnished in all parts of the Union. So far as possible the people everywhere shall have that sense of perfect security which is most favorable to calm thought and reflection. The course here indicated will be followed unless current events and experience shall show a modification or change to be proper, and in every case and exigency my best discretion will be exercised, according to circumstances actually existing and with a view and a hope of a peaceful solution of the national troubles and the restoration of fraternal sympathies and affections.

That there are persons in one section or another who seek to destroy the Union at all events and are glad of any pretext to do it I will neither affirm nor deny; but if there be such, I need address no word to them. To those, however, who really love the Union may I not speak?

Before entering upon so grave a matter as the destruction of our national fabric, with all its benefits, its memories, and its hopes, would it not be wise to ascertain precisely why we do it? Will you hazard so desperate a step while there is any possibility that any portion of the ills you fly from have no real existence? Will you, while the certain ills you fly to are greater than all the real ones you fly from, will you risk the commission of so fearful a mistake?

All profess to be content in the Union if all constitutional rights can be maintained. Is it true, then, that any right plainly written in the Constitution has been denied? I think not. Happily, the human mind is so constituted that no party can reach to the audacity of doing this. Think, if you can, of a single instance in which a plainly written provision of the Constitution has ever been denied. If by the mere force of numbers a majority should deprive a minority of any clearly written constitutional right, it might in a moral point of view justify revolution; certainly would if such right were a vital one. But such is not our case. All the vital rights of minorities and of individuals are so plainly assured to them by affirmations and negations, guaranties and prohibitions, in the Constitution that controversies never arise concerning them. But no organic law can ever be framed with a provision specifically applicable to every question which may occur in practical administration. No foresight can anticipate nor any document of reasonable length contain express provisions for all possible questions. Shall fugitives from labor be surrendered by national or by State authority? The Constitution does not expressly say. May Congress prohibit slavery in the Territories? The Constitution does not expressly say. Must Congress protect slavery in the Territories? The Constitution does not expressly say.

From questions of this class spring all our constitutional controversies, and we divide upon them into majorities and minorities. If the minority will not acquiesce, the majority must, or the Government must cease. There is no other alternative, for continuing the Government is acquiescence on one side or the other. If a minority in such case will secede rather than acquiesce, they make a precedent which in turn will divide and ruin them, for a minority of their own will secede from them whenever a majority refuses to be controlled by such minority. For instance, why may not any portion of a new confederacy a year or two hence arbitrarily secede again, precisely as portions of the present Union now claim to secede from it? All who cherish disunion sentiments are now being educated to the exact temper of doing this.

Is there such perfect identity of interests among the States to compose a new union as to produce harmony only and prevent renewed secession?

Plainly the central idea of secession is the essence of anarchy. A majority held in restraint by constitutional checks and limitations, and always changing easily with deliberate changes of popular opinions and sentiments, is the only true sovereign of a free people. Whoever rejects it does of necessity fly to anarchy or to despotism. Unanimity is impossible. The rule of a minority, as a permanent arrangement, is wholly inadmissible; so that, rejecting the majority principle, anarchy or despotism in some form is all that is left.

I do not forget the position assumed by some that constitutional questions are to be decided by the Supreme Court, nor do I deny that such decisions must be binding in any case upon the parties to a suit as to the object of that suit, while they are also entitled to very high respect and consideration in all parallel cases by all other departments of the Government. And while it is obviously possible that such decision may be erroneous in any given case, still the evil effect following it, being limited to that particular case, with the chance that it may be overruled and never become a precedent for other cases, can better be borne than could the evils of a different practice. At the same time, the candid citizen must confess that if the policy of the Government upon vital questions affecting the whole people is to be irrevocably fixed by decisions of the Supreme Court, the instant they are made in ordinary litigation between parties in personal actions the people will have ceased to be their own rulers, having to that extent practically resigned their Government into the hands of that eminent tribunal. Nor is there in this view any assault upon the court or the judges. It is a duty from which they may not shrink to decide cases properly brought before them, and it is no fault of theirs if others seek to turn their decisions to political purposes.

One section of our country believes slavery is right and ought to be extended, while the other believes it is wrong and ought not to be extended. This is the only substantial dispute. The fugitive-slave clause of the Constitution and the law for the suppression of the foreign slave trade are each as well enforced, perhaps, as any law can ever be in a community where the moral sense of the people imperfectly supports the law itself. The great body of the people abide by the dry legal obligation in both cases, and a few break over in each. This, I think, can not be perfectly cured, and it would be worse in both cases after the separation of the sections than before. The foreign slave trade, now imperfectly suppressed, would be ultimately revived without restriction in one section, while fugitive slaves, now only partially surrendered, would not be surrendered at all by the other.

Physically speaking, we can not separate. We can not remove our respective sections from each other nor build an impassable wall between them. A husband and wife may be divorced and go out of the presence and beyond the reach of each other, but the different parts of our country can not do this. They can not but remain face to face, and intercourse, either amicable or hostile, must continue between them. Is it possible, then, to make that intercourse more advantageous or more satisfactory after separation than before? Can aliens make treaties easier than friends can make laws? Can treaties be more faithfully enforced between aliens than laws can among friends? Suppose you go to war, you can not fight always; and when, after much loss on both sides and no gain on either, you cease fighting, the identical old questions, as to terms of intercourse, are again upon you.

This country, with its institutions, belongs to the people who inhabit it. Whenever they shall grow weary of the existing Government, they can exercise their constitutional right of amending it or their revolutionary right to dismember or overthrow it. I can not be ignorant of the fact that many worthy and patriotic citizens are desirous of having the National Constitution amended. While I make no recommendation of amendments, I fully recognize the rightful authority of the people over the whole subject, to be exercised in either of the modes prescribed in the instrument itself; and I should, under existing circumstances, favor rather than oppose a fair opportunity being afforded the people to act upon it. I will venture to add that to me the convention mode seems preferable, in that it allows amendments to originate with the people themselves, instead of only permitting them to take or reject propositions originated by others, not especially chosen for the purpose, and which might not be precisely such as they would wish to either accept or refuse. I understand a proposed amendment to the Constitution—which amendment, however, I have not seen—has passed Congress, to the effect that the Federal Government shall never interfere with the domestic institutions of the States, including that of persons held to service. To avoid misconstruction of what I have said, I depart from my purpose not to speak of particular amendments so far as to say that, holding such a pro-

vision to now be implied constitutional law, I have no objection to its being made express and irrevocable.

The Chief Magistrate derives all his authority from the people, and they have referred none upon him to fix terms for the separation of the States. The people themselves can do this if also they choose, but the Executive as such has nothing to do with it. His duty is to administer the present Government as it came to his hands and to transmit it unimpaired by him to his successor.

Why should there not be a patient confidence in the ultimate justice of the people? Is there any better or equal hope in the world? In our present differences, is either party without faith of being in the right? If the Almighty Ruler of Nations, with His eternal truth and justice, be on your side of the North, or on yours of the South, that truth and that justice will surely prevail by the judgment of this great tribunal of the American people.

By the frame of the Government under which we live this same people have wisely given their public servants but little power for mischief, and have with equal wisdom provided for the return of that little to their own hands at very short intervals. While the people retain their virtue and vigilance no Administration by any extreme of wickedness or folly can very seriously injure the Government in the short space of four years.

My countrymen, one and all, think calmly and well upon this whole subject. Nothing valuable can be lost by taking time. If there be an object to hurry any of you in hot haste to a step which you would never take deliberately, that object will be frustrated by taking time; but no good object can be frustrated by it. Such of you as are now dissatisfied still have the old Constitution unimpaired, and, on the sensitive point, the laws of your own framing under it; while the new Administration will have no immediate power, if it would, to change either. If it were admitted that you who are dissatisfied hold the right side in the dispute, there still is no single good reason for precipitate action. Intelligence, patriotism, Christianity, and a firm reliance on Him who has never yet forsaken this favored land are still competent to adjust in the best way all our present difficulty.

In your hands, my dissatisfied fellow-countrymen, and not in mine, is the momentous issue of civil war. The Government will not assail you. You can have no conflict without being yourselves the aggressors. You have no oath registered in heaven to destroy the Government, while I shall have the most solemn one to preserve, protect, and defend it.

I am loath to close. We are not enemies, but friends. We must not be enemies. Though passion may have strained it must not break our bonds of affection. The mystic chords of memory, stretching from every battlefield and patriot grave to every living heart and hearthstone all over this broad land, will yet swell the chorus of the Union, when again touched, as surely they will be, by the better angels of our nature.

Glossary

Articles of Association	signed on October 20, 1774, and written in response to Great Britain's Coercive Acts (sometimes called the Intolerable Acts), passed in Parliament to punish the colonies, especially Massachusetts, for defying Parliament through such actions as the Boston Tea Party
Chief Magistrate	the chief executive, the president
clause in the Constitution	Article IV, Section 2, Clause 1, the so-called privileges and immunities clause
imposts	tariffs
organic law	law that determines the fundamental principles of a government

Gettysburg Address (1863)

Fourscore and seven years ago our fathers brought forth on this continent a new nation, conceived in liberty and dedicated to the proposition that all men are created equal. Now we are engaged in a great civil war, testing whether that nation or any nation so conceived and so dedicated can long endure. We are met on a great battlefield of that war. We have come to dedicate a portion of that field as a final resting-place for those who here gave their lives that that nation might live. It is altogether fitting and proper that we should do this. But in a larger sense, we cannot dedicate, we cannot consecrate, we cannot hallow this ground. The brave men, living and dead who struggled here have consecrated it far above our poor power to add or detract. The world will little note nor long remember what we say here, but it can never forget what they did here. It is for us the living rather to be dedicated here to the unfinished work which they who fought here have thus far so nobly advanced. It is rather for us to be here dedicated to the great task remaining before us—that from these honored dead we take increased devotion to that cause for which they gave the last full measure of devotion—that we here highly resolve that these dead shall not have died in vain, that this nation under God shall have a new birth of freedom, and that government of the people, by the people, for the people shall not perish from the earth.

Glossary

fourscore	eighty, with a score equal to twenty
hallow	to make holy or sacred

SECOND INAUGURAL ADDRESS (1865)

At this second appearing to take the oath of the Presidential office there is less occasion for an extended address than there was at the first. Then a statement somewhat in detail of a course to be pursued seemed fitting and proper. Now, at the expiration of four years, during which public declarations have been constantly called forth on every point and phase of the great contest which still absorbs the attention and engrosses the energies of the nation, little that is new could be presented. The progress of our arms, upon which all else chiefly depends, is as well known to the public as to myself, and it is, I trust, reasonably satisfactory and encouraging to all. With high hope for the future, no prediction in regard to it is ventured.

On the occasion corresponding to this four years ago all thoughts were anxiously directed to an impending civil war. All dreaded it, all sought to avert it. While the inaugural address was being delivered from this place, devoted altogether to saving the Union without war, insurgent agents were in the city seeking to destroy it without war—seeking to dissolve the Union and divide effects by negotiation. Both parties deprecated war, but one of them would make war rather than let the nation survive, and the other would accept war rather than let it perish, and the war came.

One-eighth of the whole population were colored slaves, not distributed generally over the Union, but localized in the southern part of it. These slaves constituted a peculiar and powerful interest. All knew that this interest was somehow the cause of the war. To strengthen, perpetuate, and extend this interest was the object for which the insurgents would rend the Union even by war, while the Government claimed no right to do more than to restrict the territorial enlargement of it. Neither party expected for the war the magnitude or the duration which it has already attained. Neither anticipated that the cause of the conflict might cease with or even before the conflict itself should cease. Each looked for an easier triumph, and a result less fundamental and astounding. Both read the same Bible and pray to the same God, and each invokes His aid against the other. It may seem strange that any men should dare to ask a just God's assistance in wringing their bread from the sweat of other men's faces, but let us judge not, that we be not judged. The prayers of both could not be answered. That of neither has been answered fully. The Almighty has His own purposes. "Woe unto the world because of offenses; for it must needs be that offenses come, but woe to that man by whom the offense cometh." If we shall suppose that American slavery is one of those offenses which, in the providence of God, must needs come, but which, having continued through His appointed time, He now wills to remove, and that He gives to both North and South this terrible war as the woe due to those by whom the offense came, shall we discern therein any departure from those divine attributes which the believers in a living God always ascribe to Him? Fondly do we hope, fervently do we pray, that this mighty scourge of war may speedily pass away. Yet, if God wills that it continue until all the wealth piled by the bondsman's two hundred and fifty years of unrequited toil shall be sunk, and until every drop of blood drawn with the lash shall be paid by another drawn with the sword, as was said three thousand years ago, so still it must be said "the judgments of the Lord are true and righteous altogether."

With malice toward none, with charity for all, with firmness in the right as God gives us to see the right, let us strive on to finish the work we are in, to bind up the nation's wounds, to care for him who shall have borne the battle and for his widow and his orphan, to do all which may achieve and cherish a just and lasting peace among ourselves and with all nations.

Glossary

"the judgments of the Lord ..."	quotation from the Bible (Psalms 19:9)
"Woe unto the world because of offenses ..."	quotation from the Bible (Matthew 18:7)

Henry Cabot Lodge (Library of Congress)

HENRY CABOT LODGE — 1850–1924

U.S. Congressman and Senator

Featured Documents
- ◆ Speech on the Retention of the Philippine Islands (1900)
- ◆ Speech on Mexico (1915)
- ◆ Speech on President Woodrow Wilson's Plan for a World Peace (1917)
- ◆ Speech Opposing the League of Nations (1919)

Overview

Henry Cabot Lodge was born in Boston on May 12, 1850, the son of a wealthy Brahman merchant and shipowner. After receiving his BA from Harvard in 1871, he enrolled at Harvard Law School, earning an LLB degree in 1874. At the same time, he took up graduate work in medieval history at Harvard under the direction of the historian and writer Henry Adams. In 1876 he received one of the first history PhDs in the United States and published his dissertation under the title *Anglo-Saxon Law*. From 1873 to 1876 he served as assistant editor of the *North American Review*, the foremost intellectual monthly in the United States, after which he became coeditor of the *International Review*. During the academic year 1878–1879 he taught American history at Harvard.

Feeling uneasy concerning a life of pure scholarship, Lodge entered the world of politics. He began his career as a liberal independent, but finding such a reformist stance futile, he quickly became a Republican regular, a position from which he never deviated. In 1879 he was elected to the Massachusetts legislature, where he served two terms. All this time Lodge was writing history—a life of his great-grandfather, the merchant and senator George Cabot (1877); a college textbook on American colonial history (1881); and lives of Alexander Hamilton (1882), Daniel Webster (1883), and George Washington (1889). He also edited the papers of Hamilton in nine volumes (1885–1886).

In 1886 Lodge was elected to Congress, where he served for six years. In addition to promoting civil service, effective copyright legislation, and a high tariff, he took the lead in fighting to protect the voting rights of African Americans in the South. His federal elections bill, commonly known as the Lodge force bill, introduced in 1890, called for federal supervision of elections there. It easily passed the House but was filibustered in the Senate by southern Democrats. In 1893 the Massachusetts legislature elected Lodge to the Senate, where he backed such causes as immigration restriction, hard money, and economic protectionism. Yet when his close friend Theodore Roosevelt became president in 1901, Lodge went along with most of Roosevelt's more liberal domestic policies. Moderate change, he believed, was preferable to such radical measures as government ownership of public utilities. A believer in noblesse oblige, Lodge had only scorn for the newer breed of millionaires, who ignored law and custom in their ruthless search for wealth. Even so, Lodge fought progressive efforts at instituting a more direct democracy—initiative, referendum, recall, and the popular election of senators. When Roosevelt ran for president in 1912 on a platform that included recall of state judicial decisions, Lodge remained with his party's old guard and its candidate, William Howard Taft. In 1899 Lodge was reelected to the Senate, as he was every six years until his death in 1924.

Lodge was closer to Roosevelt on matters of foreign policy, which was always Lodge's primary focus. A staunch defender of what was called the "large policy" (control of the Caribbean and parts of the Pacific and seizure of strategic islands like Cuba, Hawaii, and the Philippines), Lodge supported the U.S. navy flag officer Alfred Thayer Mahan in his desire to maximize naval strength. Mahan sought coaling stations (crucial to sustain shipping) in order to expedite major commercial expansion. Lodge also backed the Spanish-American War. He opposed President Woodrow Wilson's handling of relations with Mexico and believed that the favored Mexican leaders Venustiano Carranza and Francisco "Pancho" Villa were no better than the much-scorned Mexican president Victoriano Huerta. When World War I broke out, Lodge strongly supported the allies (Britain, France, Italy, Russia, Serbia, Romania, and Belgium), so much so that in May 1915, when the *Lusitania* was sunk, he called for severing diplomatic relations with Germany.

Although Lodge backed Wilson's war measures when the United States entered the conflict, he bitterly fought the president once the war ended. As chairman of the Senate Foreign Relations Committee, he strongly objected to Article 10 of the League of Nations covenant, which called for members to respect and preserve the independence and territorial integrity of all members. He feared that this would tie America's hands to such a degree that vital decisions would be out of the control of Congress. Lodge insisted on Senate ratification of a series of reservations before the United States could join the League. By the end of 1919 both Wilson's unadulterated league and Lodge's reservations had gone down to defeat. The senator participated in the Washington Disarmament Conference of 1921–1922, which sought to establish a new order in the Pacific similar to the one established by the Versailles Treaty concerning Europe. Lodge died on November 9, 1924, in Cambridge, Massachusetts.

Time Line

1850
- **May 12**
  Henry Cabot Lodge is born in Boston.

1871
- Lodge graduates from Harvard.

1873–1876
- Lodge serves as an assistant editor of the *North American Review.*

1874
- Lodge earns an LLB from Harvard Law School.

1876
- Lodge receives a PhD from Harvard.

1878–1879
- Lodge teaches American history at Harvard.

1879
- Lodge is elected to the Massachusetts legislature.

1880–1881
- Lodge is coeditor of the *International Review.*

1886
- **November 2**
  Lodge is elected to Congress for the first of four terms.

1893
- **November 7**
  Lodge is elected to the Senate for the first of six terms.

1900
- **March 7**
  Lodge gives a Senate speech favoring the acquisition of the Philippines.

1915
- **January 6**
  Lodge gives a Senate speech on Mexican policy.

1917
- **February 1**
  Lodge gives a Senate speech on Wilson's "peace without victory" address.

Explanation and Analysis of Documents

Lodge advocated a militant foreign policy, one based on the premise that the United States was a great power and should always act as such. In his 1900 speech favoring the acquisition of the Philippines, he portrayed an American destiny that would soon encompass mastery of the entire Pacific. At the same time he could also urge caution, as when he attacked President Wilson in 1915 for engaging in a blundering and destructive intervention in Mexico. The president again met with Lodge's scorn in February 1917 when Lodge condemned Wilson's call for "peace without victory" and for seeking to create a binding league to enforce this peace; both policies, he claimed, were utterly unrealistic. In his critique of the League of Nations covenant that Wilson brought back from the Paris Peace Conference, Lodge stressed the dangers inherent in any indissoluble alliance.

◆ Speech on the Retention of the Philippine Islands

On December 10, 1898, the Treaty of Paris was signed, formally ending the Spanish-American War. During the negotiations, President William McKinley had demanded cession of the Philippines, which were transferred to the United States for $20 million. Eleven days after the peace was signed, McKinley issued a presidential proclamation, in which he pledged the "benevolent assimilation" of the Filipinos. By February 1899, however, a national rebellion was taking place, led by the guerrilla leader Emilio Aguinaldo. As American occupation forces were becoming increasingly enmeshed in ruthless suppression of the Filipino insurgents, Senator John C. Spooner sought to give the president personal authority to govern the islands until the Congress should decide otherwise—in reality, until the insurrection had been suppressed. Conversely the Democrats sought to make their opposition to imperialism and, in particular, to the Philippine conflict a major issue in the coming presidential campaign.

On March 7, 1900, Lodge defended the Spooner bill, and with it McKinley's Philippine policy, for three hours. Serving both as chairman of the Standing Committee on the Philippines and the Senate's Committee on Foreign Relations, Lodge discusses all aspects of island policy, ranging from the character of Aguinaldo to the commercial potential of the islands. His address ably articulates the imperialism proclaimed by defenders of the "large policy" that found the nation's welfare integrally tied to overseas expansion.

Lodge attacks the Democratic Party for betraying its own heritage of expansionism, which could be traced to Thomas Jefferson's Louisiana Purchase and to later demands for annexing Hawaii and Cuba. By engaging in partisan opposition for its own sake, Democrats were spurning a prosperous trade with all of Asia. Conscious that much of the Democratic Party's strength was rooted in the American South, Lodge finds that southern "tenderness for the rights of men with dark skins" living in the Pacific stands in sharp contrast with southerners' treatment of African Americans at home.

In contrast to arguments made by anti-imperialists, the Massachusetts senator denies that the Filipinos are ready for self-government. Within the past two months, he notes, the Democratic Party leader William Jennings Bryan had acknowledged their limitations. Indeed, Lodge claims, Bryan really wanted to abandon this people, whereas he—Lodge—would "lead them along the path of freedom." Using Haiti and Santo Domingo as negative examples, Lodge warns that continued anarchy and native dictatorship on the islands would lead to European intervention. Sounding a bit like Rudyard Kipling's poem "The White Man's Burden," which itself was originally subtitled "The United States and the Philippine Islands," the senator denies that Americans are grasping new powers; rather, they are assuming fresh and essential responsibilities.

While not oblivious to the new market that the Philippines might provide, Lodge stresses their role as a stepping-stone to far more significant trade with China. It was Admiral George Dewey's capture of Manila in May 1898, he maintains, that made the United States an Eastern power, one that could now gain the commerce needed to assure prosperity to American farmers and laborers. In the last part of his speech, Lodge offers an updated version of "Manifest Destiny," the slogan of the 1840s. He points as well to the "hands off" warnings to Europe embodied in the Monroe Doctrine. Instead of limiting himself to the matter of continental expansion, however, he invokes "the true laws of our being," which—he asserts—involve mastery of the Pacific. To violate such laws would only lead to national ruin and disgrace. Reflecting his learning, he concludes his address with a selection from William Ernest Henley's poem "Invictus" and offers a Latin quotation invoking divine protection.

Lodge's Philippine committee reported the bill, but the Republican majority decided to delay any vote until after the 1900 election. In that election, Bryan, who spoke for Filipino rights, was defeated in his second bid for the presidency. Only on February 28, 1901, did Spooner's proposal pass Congress, in the form of an amendment to an army appropriation bill. Lodge's hopes for a thriving China market remained unfulfilled for close to a century. In the short term, however, his immediate imperialist aims were gratified. By mid-1902 the Filipino resistance had ended. That year Congress declared the islands an unorganized territory in which an American commission, headed by William Howard Taft, then a federal circuit judge, would establish a civil government.

◆ **Speech on Mexico**

If there was one issue that caused Lodge to lose respect for Woodrow Wilson, it was the president's policy toward Mexico. In May 1911 the dictator Porfirio Díaz was overthrown by the idealistic but naive Francisco Madero. In February 1913 Madero, in turn, was murdered by the strongman Victoriano Huerta, who was ruling Mexico when Wilson took office. Infuriated by Huerta's conduct, Wilson refused to recognize his regime. In an effort to force the new dictator's abdication, the president sent an unoffi-

Time Line

1919

■ **February 28**
Lodge gives a Senate speech opposing League of Nations.

1924

■ **November 9**
Lodge dies of a cerebral hemorrhage in Cambridge, Massachusetts.

cial representative, the former Minnesota governor John Lind, to press for the election of a constitutional government. President Wilson backed the "Constitutionalist" case of Huerta's leading opponent, Venustiano Carranza, governor of the northern province of Coahuila. In April 1914 Wilson occupied the port of Veracruz in order to aid Carranza's forces.

Lodge's speech of January 6, 1915, offers a step-by-step critique of Wilson's policy. The senator concedes that Huerta possessed a villainous character but finds that most Mexican rulers had gained power through violent means. Had the United States intervened in Mexico to restore order and protect the lives and property of American citizens, rather than to depose a ruler personally abhorrent to President Wilson, it would have been engaged in "a worthy national policy."

Lodge offers a detailed, if partisan, description of the Tampico incident of April 9, 1914, in which an unarmed paymaster and the crew of the USS *Dolphin* were inadvertently arrested in the Mexican city of Tampico by Huerta's troops; they were promptly released, and an apology was made. Admiral Henry T. Mayo, who commanded the American squadron off Veracruz, demanded—without authorization—that the Mexican government give a twenty-one-gun salute. Huerta caustically agreed, provided an American warship returned a simultaneous volley. Had Wilson conceded, he would in effect have been recognizing the Huerta government. On April 20, Congress granted Wilson's request to use armed force to enforce his demands. On the following day the United States occupied Veracruz. Although the president had stressed the need to uphold American rights and honor, he was in reality seeking to humiliate the Mexican ruler. In Lodge's view, the chief executive was indeed duplicitous.

Lodge is even more critical of Wilson's occupation of Veracruz. On April 21, Wilson had been informed that the German ship *Ypiranga*, loaded with munitions for Huerta, was approaching the city. He ordered Rear Admiral Charles J. Badger immediately to seize Veracruz with five battleships and three thousand men. Because President Wilson did not foresee the sharp resistance that the students at the Mexican naval academy mounted, he was—in Lodge's eyes—responsible for the death of nineteen Americans and several hundred Mexicans. On May 20, Wilson accepted the offer of Argentina, Brazil, and Chile (called the "ABC

Powers") to meet at Niagara Falls to mediate the conflict. The conference failed in its efforts, but within two months the Constitutionalists whom Wilson favored captured Mexico City. On July 15, Huerta was forced to leave office. In October 1915, Wilson extended recognition to the Carranza regime, which had assumed power two months earlier. At the time Lodge was speaking, however, Emiliano Zapata and Francisco "Pancho" Villa were leading a full-scale insurgency against Carranza's forces. Mexico was again engulfed in civil war.

In concluding his speech, Lodge takes slaps at the Mexican people, claiming their mixed blood made them ill disposed toward democracy. Mexico's current condition, he maintains, was one of anarchy. The United States should have used all its powers to enforce its rights under international law or should have occupied the entire nation. As the United States did neither, it had possibly lost a billion dollars in investment and had sacrificed up to two hundred American lives. Although people today would find Lodge's anti-Mexican racism abhorrent, the senator was correct in showing the naive blundering embodied in Wilson's policies. Carranza was far from being the Wilsonian model of a democratic ruler, as evidenced by his crackdown on trade unions and his subsequent murder of the agrarian reformer Zapata.

◆ Speech on President Woodrow Wilson's Plan for a World Peace

On January 22, 1917, in an address before the Congress, President Wilson endorsed a "peace without victory" in the European war, one that would involve no indemnities or annexations. By this time, however, Germany had abandoned any hope of negotiating peace with the Allies. Just a little over a week after Wilson spoke, Germany announced that on February 1 its submarines would sink without warning all ships bound for enemy waters, whether they belonged to belligerent or neutral powers. American ships could sail through only at their peril.

Lodge begins his speech of February 1 with a call to back the president in the immediate crisis with Germany and then moves on to attack Wilson's "peace without victory" concept as being naive. None of the belligerents, he says, were making "such awful sacrifices" in order simply to return to the conditions of 1914. The senator then criticizes the president's insistence that any lasting peace must be based upon the principle, in Wilson's own words (which he quotes), "that governments derive all their just powers from the consent of the governed" and that no right exists to hand people "from sovereignty to sovereignty as if they were property." Although he found the tenet admirable in the abstract, Lodge asks how it can possibly be enforced in such diverse areas as Korea, Hindustan, Alsace-Lorraine, and Armenia. Certainly the very history of America's own expansion belied such a principle, for the United States had annexed such major areas as California and the Louisiana Territory without consulting any indigenous population. The senator also questions the president's call for "the freedom of the seas," which the chief executive saw as

part of the free intercourse of nations. Such a proposal, says Lodge, could violate international law, especially because long-honored rules of contraband and blockade would be scrapped. He also sees impracticalities in Wilson's notion that all "great peoples" have access to major bodies of water. By mentioning such landlocked nations as Bolivia, Paraguay, and Afghanistan, Lodge sought to indicate the absurdity of such a proposal.

Wilson's proposal for a league of nations met with Lodge's strong suspicion. Lodge invokes the tenets of George Washington, Thomas Jefferson, and James Monroe to bolster his claim that American and European interests are poles apart. To enter into a postwar league for peace would necessitate placing American military and naval forces at the service of other nations. The United States, he claims, is by no means ready for such a commitment. The senator ends his address by calling for a peace based on "righteousness." Given the fact that he had been sympathetic to Britain and France from the outset of the war, Lodge is claiming that only an Allied victory can create a genuine international order.

◆ Speech Opposing the League of Nations

In December 1918, Wilson sailed to Europe to participate in the Paris Peace Conference that would draft treaties with the Central Powers (Germany, Austria-Hungary, the Ottoman Empire, and Bulgaria). On February 14 a special commission, over which the president presided, submitted a draft covenant for a proposed League of Nations to the conference's plenary session. Ten days later Wilson briefly returned to the United States, in part to defuse anticipated Senate criticism. Arriving in Boston, he gave a speech in Mechanics Hall in which he claimed that peace could not last a single generation unless it was guaranteed by all the civilized world.

As a result of the 1918 congressional elections, the Republicans had gained control of both houses of Congress. Lodge, who had become chairman of the Senate Foreign Relations Committee, was quick to challenge the president. Addressing his senatorial colleagues on February 28, 1919, Lodge first concedes the universal desire for a lasting peace and then starts critiquing the draft covenant. He points to its loose phrasing and equivocal language, which he finds inappropriate to what of necessity was a legal document.

Far more important, Lodge notes that the covenant reverses the policy of George Washington by committing the United States to a binding alliance. Similarly, the Monroe Doctrine, with its stress upon the settling of American questions by Americans alone, was being violated. Of particular concern was Article 10 of the proposed league, which required members to preserve the integrity and independence of other member nations against acts of aggression. Article 10 frightened Lodge, since it committed the United States to involve itself in questions invoking Europe, Asia, and Africa. At issue for Lodge were matters involving Asia Minor, where there was soon talk of an American mandate for Constantinople and Armenia, and the Balkans, a region so full of ethnic and tribal rivalries that World War I itself

*Cartoon depicting result of the proposed League of Nations: Uncle Sam watching
wounded and dead soldiers come off a ship, while John Bull (the personification of Great Britain)
says, "Hi Sam! Send me over a new army!"* (Library of Congress)

had originated there. Similarly, European and Asian nations would be given the right to exercise police powers on the American continent, which authority even extended to the highly strategic Panama Canal. As Lodge saw it, the nation's very sovereignty was at stake.

After he delivered this speech, Lodge fought a rearguard action against Wilson's league. He drafted fourteen "reservations" to the covenant, the most important being one that Article 10 was inapplicable unless Congress were to uphold it by act or resolution Yet Lodge was not irreconcilable on the matter. He favored a society of nations; unlike the one envisioned by Wilson, however, Lodge's lacked coercive powers. Because Wilson refused to accept Lodge's reservations, the entire peace treaty went down to defeat, first in November 1919 and then again in March 1920.

Impact and Legacy

Because of his bitter dispute with Wilson over the League of Nations, Lodge has often been demonized. In part, this negative image was the senator's own fault. He and Wilson detested each other, and, despite disclaimers,

his contempt was all too visible. An aloof man, Lodge possessed a haughtiness bordering on arrogance. Far too often, he acted out of bitterness, cynicism, and extreme partisanship when the welfare of his nation demanded compromise and sacrifice. Lodge also had positive qualities, however. He was learned enough to deserve the title "scholar in politics," one that he could share with his enemy Wilson. He was conservative, as evidenced by his support of the gold standard and immigration restriction; but he was no reactionary, for he backed suffrage rights for blacks and curbs on corporate power. He was a skilled legislator, avoiding conflicts of interest and being particularly effective in committees.

It is wrong to think of Lodge as a quintessential isolationist. He was fundamentally a nationalist and possessed more than a touch of imperialism. His foreign policy was akin to that of Theodore Roosevelt, who linked the preservation of peace to the appropriate application of force. In 1919, for example, Lodge favored a binding alliance between Britain, France, and the United States as the best way to ensure world tranquility. Despite the intense animosity between Lodge and Wilson, there was far more at stake in the League fight than personal pique. To Wilson the United States had a moral obligation to engage in the type of collective securi-

"I do not believe that this nation was raised up for nothing. I do not believe that it is the creation of blind chance. I have faith that it has a great mission in the world—a mission of good, a mission of freedom.... I wish to see it master of the Pacific."

(Speech on the Retention of the Philippine Islands)

"I should be sorry to shed the blood of a single American soldier or sailor for the sake of restoring order in Mexico, but nothing, it seems to me, can possibly justify shedding the blood of a single American soldier or sailor for the sake of putting one blood-stained Mexican in the place occupied by another."

(Speech on Mexico)

"As a practical question for us, dealing with a condition on which we are to build a future league for peace to which we are to be a party, how are we going to provide that it shall be a peace without victory? How are we to arrange that there shall be no victories?"

(Speech on President Woodrow Wilson's Plan for a World Peace)

"It seems to me that this plan for securing free access to the sea to all the great nations of Europe, and still more to the nations, both great and small, would involve us in some very difficult questions wholly outside our proper sphere of influence; and yet the President states this as one of the essentials for the lasting peace which we are to covenant to bring about and to enforce."

(Speech on President Woodrow Wilson's Plan for a World Peace)

"The wisdom of Washington's policy, supplemented by that of Monroe, has been demonstrated by the experience of more than a century, and this at least must be said, that we should not depart from it without most powerful reasons and without knowing exactly where that departure would lead."

(Speech on President Woodrow Wilson's Plan for a World Peace)

"No question has ever confronted the United States which equals in importance that which is involved in the league of nations intended to secure the future peace of the world."

(Speech Opposing the League of Nations)

ty embodied in Article X; to Lodge any such obligation—moral or legal—could lead only to disaster. As decades of subsequent international involvement has shown, the questions raised by Lodge do not permit easy answers.

Key Sources

The Henry Cabot Lodge papers are at the Massachusetts Historical Society, Boston, and are also on microfilm. The Theodore Roosevelt papers at the Library of Congress contain much correspondence between Lodge and the twenty-sixth president. Lodge also edited *Selections from the Correspondence of Theodore Roosevelt and Henry Cabot Lodge, 1884–1918* (1925), which, because of Lodge's later excisions, should be used with care. Lodge wrote a revealing autobiography, *Early Memories* (1913). Collections of his speeches can be found in *Speeches and Addresses, 1884–1909* (1909) and *War Addresses, 1915–1917* (1917). Lodge's *Senate and the League of Nations* (1925) not only contains a narrative account of his fight with Wilson but also offers an appendix that includes the entire text of speeches dated January 22, 1917; February 28, 1919; and August 12, 1919 as well as a record of a major meeting of the entire Senate Foreign Relations Committee with Wilson on August 19, 1919.

Further Reading

■ Articles
Mervin, David. "Henry Cabot Lodge and the League of Nations." *Journal of American Studies* 4 (February 1971): 201–214.

■ Books
Garraty, John A. *Henry Cabot Lodge: A Biography*. New York: Alfred A. Knopf, 1953.

Widenor, William C. *Henry Cabot Lodge and the Search for an American Foreign Policy*. Berkeley: University of California Press, 1980.

Questions for Further Study

1. Consider Lodge's speech on the Philippines from various perspectives. To what degree do his views align with those of William McKinley, as expressed in the "benevolent assimilation" speech? How valid are the points he brings to bear against Democrats—that they had a history of expansionism and, by supporting slavery in the past, had no moral ground to stand on in condemning U.S. colonization of the Philippines? What about his claim that the Monroe Doctrine, which applied primarily to the Western Hemisphere, could be used to justify expansion in the Pacific? Regarding his allusions to poems by Rudyard Kipling and William Ernest Henley, how did those works—and the viewpoints they represented—seem to support his own position? Finally, how might the history of World War II (in which the United States took on the majority of the fighting against the Japanese) have been different if the nation had not taken a strong interest in Asian and Pacific affairs, as Lodge recommended?

2. Evaluate Lodge's 1915 speech on Mexico. Discuss his apparently racist views toward Mexicans compared with those expressed by Andrew Jackson toward Native Americans in his address on Indian removal and John C. Calhoun toward African Americans in a number of speeches. On the other hand, to what extent was he correct in his assertion that the United States had simply switched its support from one dictator to another in Mexico? How justified is he in his criticism of President Woodrow Wilson's Mexican policy?

3. How valid are the arguments Lodge employs in his 1917 critique of President Wilson's plan for world peace or his 1919 speech opposing the League of Nations? How justified was he in supporting a position of American exceptionalism—the view that the United States was very different from other nations and therefore did not have to abide by perceived international standards? How relevant for today is his skepticism regarding the position of Wilson and others on self-determination, with its implication that every nationality deserves to possess its own nation? Was his opposition to the league simply a matter of isolationism, or was he motivated by a concern, dating back at least to George Washington's Farewell Address, for keeping the United States free of formal entanglements? How did his views on the League appear in light of events during the 1930s, when the organization failed to stop expansion by nations that would ultimately form the Axis powers in World War II?

Zimmermann, Warren. *First Great Triumph: How Five Americans Made Their Country a World Power*. New York: Farrar, Straus and Giroux, 2002.

—Justus Doenecke

Speech on the Retention of the Philippine Islands (1900)

One of the great political parties of the country has seen fit to make what is called "an issue" of the Philippines. They have no alternative policy to propose which does not fall to pieces as soon as it is stated. A large and important part of their membership, North and South, is heartily in favor of expansion, because they are Americans, and have not only patriotism but an intelligent perception of their own interests. They are the traditional party of expansion, the party which first went beyond seas and tried to annex Hawaii, which plotted for years to annex Cuba, which have in our past acquisitions of territory their one great and enduring monument. In their new wanderings they have developed a highly commendable, if somewhat hysterical, tenderness for the rights of men with dark skins dwelling in the islands of the Pacific, in pleasing contrast to the harsh indifference which they have always manifested toward those American citizens who "wear the shadowed livery of the burnished sun" within the boundaries of the United States. The Democratic party has for years been the advocate of free trade and increased exports, but now they shudder at our gaining control of the Pacific and developing our commerce with the East....

Once more our opponents insist that we shall be the only political party devoted to American policies. As the standard of expansion once so strongly held by their great predecessors drops from their nerveless hands we take it up and invite the American people to march with it. We offer our policy to the American people, to Democrats and to Republicans, as an American policy, alike in duty and honor, in morals and in interest, as one not of skepticism and doubt, but of hope and faith in ourselves and in the future, as becomes a great young nation which has not yet learned to use the art of retreat or to speak with the accents of despair....

The next argument of the opponents of the Republican policy is that we are denying self-government to the Filipinos. Our reply is that to give independent self-government at once, as we understand it, to a people who have no just conception of it and no fitness for it, is to dower them with a curse instead of a blessing. To do this would be to entirely arrest their progress instead of advancing them on the road to the liberty and free government which we wish them to achieve and enjoy. This contention rests, of course, on the proposition that the Filipinos are not to-day in the least fitted for self-government, as we understand it....

They think that we should abandon the Philippines because they are not fit for self-government. I believe that for that very reason we should retain them and lead them along the path of freedom until they are able to be self-governing, so far, at least, as all their own affairs are concerned....

We are also told that the possession of these islands brings a great responsibility upon us. This, Mr. President, I freely admit. A great nation must have great responsibilities. It is one of the penalties of greatness. But the benefit of responsibilities goes hand in hand with the burdens they bring....

Men who have done great things are those who have never shrunk from trial or adventure. If a man has the right qualities in him, responsibility sobers, strengthens, and develops him. The same is true of nations. The nation which fearlessly meets its responsibilities rises to the task when the pressure is upon it. I believe that these new possessions and these new questions, this necessity for watching over the welfare of another people, will improve our civil service, raise the tone of public life, and make broader and better all our politics and the subjects of political discussion. My faith in the American people is such that I have no misgiving as to their power to meet these responsibilities and to come out stronger and better for the test, doing full justice to others as well as to themselves....

Thus, Mr. President, I have shown that duty and interest alike, duty of the highest kind and interest of the highest and best kind, impose upon us the retention of the Philippines, the development of the islands, and the expansion of our Eastern commerce. All these things, in my belief, will come to pass, whatever the divisions of the present moment, for no people who have come under our flag have ever sought to leave it, and there is no territory which we have acquired that any one would dream of giving up....

Even now we can abandon the Monroe doctrine, we can reject the Pacific....

Or we may follow the true laws of our being, the laws in obedience to which we have come to be what we are, and then we shall stretch out into the Pacific; we shall stand in the front rank of the world powers....

I do not believe that this nation was raised up for nothing. I do not believe that it is the creation of blind chance. I have faith that it has a great mission in the world—a mission of good, a mission of freedom. I believe that it can live up to that mission; therefore I want to see it step forward boldly and take its place at the head of the nations. I wish to see it master of the Pacific. I would have it fulfill what I think is its manifest destiny if it is not false to the laws which govern it. I am not dreaming of a primrose path....

Onward and forward it will still be, despite stumblings and mistakes as before, while we are true to ourselves and obedient to the laws which have ruled our past and will still govern our future.

Glossary

dower	to endow with
"wear the shadowed livery of the burnished sun"	quotation adapted from William Shakespeare's *Merchant of Venice*, act 2, scene 1

Speech on Mexico (1915)

This amendment, which is purely formal, proposes to strike out the clause supplying the deficiency in the appropriations for the War Department caused by the leasing of transports to take troops to Vera Cruz. It is an honest debt, honestly incurred, and must of course be paid; but I think, Mr. President, it is not amiss at this time and in this connection to review briefly the circumstances which have led to the necessity for this appropriation, and which will lead to the necessity for other appropriations to cover other deficiencies arising from the same source. I wish, in as compact a manner as possible, to call attention to the events in Mexico which have led to these appropriations and to the condition of affairs in Mexico at the present moment....

Mr. President, I was not one of those who was disposed to find fault with the refusal to recognize General Huerta, although there was much to be said in favor of recognition. There were broad international grounds and sound international grounds upon which that refusal could have been based....

The ground on which recognition of Huerta was refused was what was called a moral ground; that he was a man of bad character, who had reached the highest position in Mexico by treacherous and murderous methods....

But when we put our refusal of recognition on the personal ground that the character of the head of the Mexican Government at that time was unsatisfactory to us, to that extent we intervened. We had an absolute right on international grounds to refuse recognition, but when we say to another nation, We object to the man who is at the head of your government or at the head of the only government you have got because he is a person of obnoxious character, we intervene in the affairs of that nation. The refusal, however, to recognize General Huerta was based upon this ground, and while it undoubtedly embarrassed the Huerta Government, it did not overthrow it....

The policy of the United States in regard to Mexico, speaking from the international point of view, was to secure as soon as possible the pacification of the country, the reëstablishment of order, the removal of all our many causes of complaint, the security of the lives and property of our own citizens and also of the citizens or subjects of other nations....

This would have been a worthy national policy, but the business of driving Huerta from power and putting somebody else in his place was not a policy at all....

Mr. President, I fear that it is now too late to adopt any policy which would be effective there except a complete military occupation of the country at great cost, which all of us wish to avoid, but it is certain that when the Mexican question was first presented to us there were but two possible policies. I am speaking now of policies and not of personal animosities. One policy was to begin by exerting all the power and influence we had under international law and under treaties and in accordance with the comity of nations to stop outrages, to prevent wrongs, and to try to bring about pacification. This was never effectively attempted, but that is the way we should have begun, and then, in line with the policy of avoiding war at all hazards, we should have refrained from any intervention beyond the efforts warranted by international law.

The other course was to enter Mexico in sufficient force to take possession of and pacify the country and try to establish a government there which would have the capacity of fulfilling its international obligations and at least maintain order. To that course the United States was opposed, and quite naturally and rightly; but the course we did pursue was neither one nor the other. It combined with singular dexterity the evils of both and the advantages of neither. We did not stay out and we did not go in effectively. I should be sorry to shed the blood of a single American soldier or sailor for the sake of restoring order in Mexico, but nothing, it seems to me, can possibly justify shedding the blood of a single American soldier or sailor for the sake of putting one blood-stained Mexican in the place occupied by another. We have our reward for what we have done in the condition of Mexico to-day....

I have no intention of doing otherwise than vote for this deficiency bill and for the others which are to follow. The Secretary of War has done his duty; but I cannot let the matter go by, Mr. President, without thus calling attention to what has happened in Mexico; without saying that, in my opinion, even in the midst of the dreadful disasters to humanity and civilization which are now filling

Europe and the world, we should not forget what has taken place and is now going on in Mexico—a situation so bad that when the President of the United States delivered his annual message to Congress the best way in which he could deal with it was by complete silence.

General Huerta	Victoriano Huerta, president of Mexico
Secretary of War	Lindley M. Garrison, secretary of war under President Woodrow Wilson

Speech on President Woodrow Wilson's Plan for a World Peace (1917)

As I understand it, the President is aiming at two objects....—to bring to an end the war now raging in Europe, and to make provision for the future and permanent peace of the world....

In the first place, it must be a peace without victory....

Peace without victory can only mean ... that neither side is to gain anything by the terms of peace through victory in the field.... In other words, all the lives have been given in this war and all the money spent in vain and Europe is to emerge from the conflict in exactly the same situation as when she entered it. It seems to me incredible that people who have made such awful sacrifices as have been made by the belligerents should be content to forgo the prospect of victory, in the hope of bringing the war to an end, with everything left just as it was. In such a result they might well think that all their efforts and losses, all their miseries and sorrows and sacrifices were a criminal and hideous futility.... There is no doubt of the reality of the desire among many of the great nations of Europe to close this war with a victory which will give them a peace worth having, and not a mere breathing-space filled with the up-building of crushing armaments and then another and a worse war. Such, I think, is their point of view; but as a practical question for us, dealing with a condition on which we are to build a future league for peace to which we are to be a party, how are we going to provide that it shall be a peace without victory? How are we to arrange that there shall be no victories?...

The next condition precedent stated by the President, without which we can have no peace that "can last or ought to last," is the universal acceptance of the idea that governments derive all their just powers from the consent of the governed and that any peace which does not recognize and accept this principle will inevitably be upset....

As a preliminary of the peace which we are to help enforce must we insist that it cannot exist if there are any people under any government who have been handed from sovereignty to sovereignty as if they were property? I am not contesting the justice of the principle,—far from it,—but we may well ask how we are going to compel the adoption of that principle by other governments, and this is no idle question....

The next condition ... is that to obtain a firm and lasting peace we must have "freedom of the seas."... To attain this end we should have to begin by sweeping away all existing doctrines as to the rights of belligerents at sea in time of war.... These doctrines were established by us in the face of very general opposition and have been since accepted and acted upon by belligerents in other wars as the sound construction of international rights. We should therefore have to begin at once by tearing down the fabric of law on this point which we ourselves created and built up....

It will also be necessary, for the firm and lasting peace which the league proposed by the President is to bring about, that every great people now struggling toward a full development of its resources and its powers be assured a direct outlet to the sea. The President confines this important right to the "great peoples."... If the right of access to the sea is to be confined, as the President says, to "every great people," small nations are excluded. We have ample access to two great oceans, so that this proposed reform of the President has the enormous advantage of being wholly altruistic. It is entirely for the benefit of others....

Every one must feel, as I do, the enormous importance of securing in some way the peace of the world and relieving the future of humanity from such awful struggles as that which is now going on in Europe, but if the only advance is to be made through the creation of an international force, we are brought face to face with the difficulties of that system....

The policy of the United States hitherto has been the policy laid down by Washington, and its corollary expressed in the message of President Monroe....

The wisdom of Washington's policy, supplemented by that of Monroe, has been demonstrated by the experience of more than a century, and this at least must be said, that we should not depart from it without most powerful reasons and without knowing exactly where that departure would lead. We are now invited to depart from it by giving our adherence to a league for peace when the present war closes, without knowing how far it is proposed to go or what is to be demanded of us....

The first service which the United States can render to the cause of peace is to preserve its own. I do not mean within its own borders, but to preserve its peace with the other nations of the earth….A league for peace has a most encouraging sound, but this is altogether too grave a question to be satisfied with words. We must realize that a league for peace means putting force behind peace and making war on any nation which does not obey the decisions of the league. It may be that the world's peace can be secured in this manner, but we should not attempt it without a full appreciation of just what it involves. Effective leagues for peace cannot be sustained by language alone nor by moral suasion as their only weapons….

We cannot secure our own safety or build up the lasting peace of the world upon peace at any price. The peace of the world, to be enduring, must be based on righteousness at any cost.

Glossary

belligerents	warring parties
condition precedent	an event that must occur before something else can occur

Speech Opposing the League of Nations (1919)

Mr. President, all people, men and women alike, who are capable of connected thought abhor war and desire nothing so much as to make secure the future peace of the world....We ought to lay aside once and for all the unfounded and really evil suggestion that because men differ as to the best method of securing the world's peace in the future, anyone is against permanent peace, if it can be obtained, among all the nations of mankind.... We all earnestly desire to advance toward the preservation of the world's peace, and difference in method makes no distinction in purpose....No question has ever confronted the United States Senate which equals in importance that which is involved in the league of nations intended to secure the future peace of the world. There should be no undue haste in considering it. My one desire is that not only the Senate, which is charged with responsibility, but that the press and the people of the country should investigate every proposal with the utmost thoroughness and weigh them all carefully before they make up their minds....

In the first place, the terms of the league...must be so plain and so explicit that no man can misunderstand them.... The Senate can take no action upon it, but it lies open before us for criticism and discussion. What is said in the Senate ought to be placed before the peace conference and published in Paris, so that the foreign Governments may be informed as to the various views expressed here.

In this draft prepared for a constitution of a league of nations,...there is hardly a clause about the interpretation of which men do not already differ. As it stands there is serious danger that the very nations which sign the constitution of the league will quarrel about the meaning of the various articles before a twelvemonth has passed. It seems to have been very hastily drafted, and the result is crudeness and looseness of expression, unintentional, I hope. There are certainly many doubtful passages and open questions obvious in the articles which can not be settled by individual inference, but which must be made so clear and so distinct that we may all understand the exact meaning of the instrument to which we are asked to set our hands. The language of these articles does not appear to me to have the precision and unmistakable character which a constitution, a treaty, or a law ought to present....Arguments and historical facts have no place in a statute or a treaty. Statutory and legal language must assert and command, not argue and describe. I press this point because there is nothing so vital to the peace of the world as the sanctity of treaties. The suggestion that we can safely sign because we can always violate or abrogate is fatal not only to any league but to peace itself. You can not found world peace upon the cynical "scrap of paper" doctrine so dear to Germany. To whatever instrument the United States sets its hand it must carry out the provisions of that instrument to the last jot and tittle, and observe it absolutely both in letter and in spirit. If this is not done the instrument will become a source of controversy instead of agreement, of dissension instead of harmony. This is all the more essential because it is evident, although not expressly stated, that this league is intended to be indissoluble, for there is no provision for its termination or for the withdrawal of any signatory. We are left to infer that any nation withdrawing from the league exposes itself to penalties and probably to war. Therefore, before we ratify, the terms and language in which the terms are stated must be exact and precise, as free from any possibility of conflicting interpretations, as it is possible to make them.

The explanation or interpretation of any of these doubtful passages is not sufficient if made by one man, whether that man be the President of the United States, or a Senator, or anyone else. These questions and doubts must be answered and removed by the instrument itself.

It is to be remembered that if there is any dispute about the terms of this constitution there is no court provided that I can find to pass upon differences of opinion as to the terms of the constitution itself. There is no court to fulfill the function which our Supreme Court fulfills. There is provision for tribunals to decide questions submitted for arbitration, but there is no authority to decide differing interpretations as to the terms of the instrument itself....

I now come to questions of substance, which seem to me to demand the most careful thought of the entire American people, and particularly of those charged with the responsibility of ratification. We abandon entirely by the proposed constitution the policy laid down by Washington in his Farewell Address and the Monroe doctrine.... I know that some of the ardent advocates of the plan submitted to us regard any suggestion of the importance of the Washington policy as foolish and irrelevant.... Perhaps the time has come when the policies of Washington should be abandoned; but if we are to cast them aside I think that at least it should be done respectfully and with a sense of gratitude to the great man who formulated them. For nearly a century and a quarter the policies laid down in the Farewell Address have been followed and adhered to by the Government of the United States and by the American people. I doubt if any purely political declaration has ever been observed by any people for so long a time. The principles of the Farewell Address in regard to our foreign relations have been sustained and acted upon by the American people down to the present moment. Washington declared against permanent alliances.... He did not close the door on temporary alliances for particular purposes. Our entry in the great war just closed was entirely in accord with and violated in no respect the policy laid down by Washington. When we went to war with Germany we made no treaties with the nations engaged in the war against the German Government. The President was so careful in this direction that he did not permit himself ever to refer to the nations by whose side we fought as "allies," but always as "nations associated with us in the war."...Now, in the twinkling of an eye, while passion and emotion reign, the Washington policy is to be entirely laid aside and we are to enter upon a permanent and indissoluble alliance. That which we refuse to do in war we are to do in peace, deliberately, coolly, and with no war exigency. Let us not overlook the profound gravity of this step.

Washington was not only a very great man but he was also a very wise man. He looked far into the future and he never omitted human nature from his calculations.... He was so great a man that the fact that this country had produced him was enough of itself to justify the Revolution and our existence as a Nation. Do not think that I overstate this in the fondness of patriotism and with the partiality of one of his countrymen. The opinion I have expressed is the opinion of the world....

But if we put aside forever the Washington policy in regard to our foreign relations we must always remember that it carries with it the corollary known as the Monroe doctrine. Under the terms of this league draft reported by the committee to the peace conference the Monroe doctrine disappears. It has been our cherished guide and guard for nearly a century. The Monroe doctrine is based on the principle of self-preservation. To say that it is a question of protecting the boundaries, the political integrity, or the American States, is not to state the Monroe doctrine.... The real essence of that doctrine is that American questions shall be settled by Americans alone; that the Americas shall be separated from Europe in purely American questions. That is the vital principle of the doctrine.

I have seen it said that the Monroe doctrine is preserved under article 10 [calling for a collective security agreement among League members]; that we do not abandon the Monroe doctrine, we merely extend it to all the world. How anyone can say this passes my comprehension. The Monroe doctrine exists solely for the protection of the American Hemisphere, and to that hemisphere it was limited. If you extend it to all the world, it ceases to exist,...Under this draft of the constitution of the league of nations, American questions and European questions and Asian and African questions are all alike put within the control and jurisdiction of the league. Europe will have the right to take part in the settlement of all American questions, and we, of course, shall have the right to share in the settlement of all questions in Europe and Asia and Africa....Perhaps the time has come when it is necessary to do this, but it is a very grave step, and I wish now merely to point out that the American people ought never to abandon the Washington policy and the Monroe doctrine without being perfectly certain that they earnestly wish to do so. Standing always firmly by these great policies, we have thriven and prospered and have done more to preserve the world's peace than any nation, league, or alliance which ever existed. For this reason I ask the press and the public and, of course, the Senate to consider well the gravity of this proposition before it takes the heavy responsibility of finally casting aside these policies which we have adhered to for a century and more and under which we have greatly served the cause of peace both at home and abroad.

Glossary

abrogate	renounce, go back on

Huey Long (AP/Wide World Photos)

HUEY LONG

Governor and U.S. Senator

1893–1935

Featured Documents
- ◆ "Every Man a King" Address (1934)
- ◆ "Share Our Wealth" Address (1935)
- ◆ "Our Growing Calamity" Address (1935)

Overview

Born on August 30, 1893, Huey Pierce Long, Jr., was the seventh of nine children. Although he often spoke of his childhood as one of extreme poverty, in fact he grew up in comfortable, if not affluent, surroundings. A precocious and articulate child, he was also undisciplined and prone to rebel against the requirements of formal education. After desultory work as a traveling salesman, Long entered Tulane University Law School. Although he managed to finish less than a year of coursework, he persuaded state officials to give him a bar exam, which he passed, becoming a lawyer at the age of twenty-one.

Long admitted that for him the law was merely a means to a political career, which he began in 1918 with his election as a state railroad commissioner. A lifelong member of the Democratic Party, he established himself from the beginning as a populist—more specifically, as a crusading underdog who attacked corporations like Standard Oil and establishment politicians who did the bidding of big business. After serving on the Louisiana Public Service Commission and running unsuccessfully for governor in 1924, he won the governorship in 1928 on a platform promising free textbooks for schoolchildren and a massive highway-building program. Long consolidated his power quickly by putting his cronies in state offices and by establishing his own newspaper. His abuse of power led to impeachment proceedings, which he was able to quash by bribing and intimidating state legislators.

Called a dictator, Long retained and enhanced his power by winning a seat in the U.S. Senate in 1930 but holding his position as governor until 1932; in that election year, his close associate and chosen successor, O. K. Allen, won the governorship. Initially supporting Franklin Roosevelt in the 1932 election for president, Long became increasingly disenchanted with Roosevelt's unwillingness to implement the radical share-the-wealth program that Long advocated in national radio addresses and on the Senate floor. In 1933 he published his autobiography, *Every Man a King*. With a serious mass following throughout the country, Long might have mounted a vigorous challenge to Roosevelt's reelection campaign in 1936, but he was assassinated; Long was shot on September 8, 1935, and died two days later. His visionary work *My First Days in the White House* was published after his death.

Explanation and Analysis of Documents

By all accounts Huey Long was a spellbinding speaker. No matter the platform—the radio, the Senate floor, or small towns and large cities alike during campaigns—Long was a consummate performer who could adjust the level of his talk to his audience. In rural Louisiana he was a common man, using plain and simple language. On the Senate floor he could be eloquent in tearing apart legislation by his colleagues that either ignored or did not do enough to relieve the economic plight of Americans. Over the radio, he appealed directly to Depression-era audiences of millions, addressing poverty, joblessness, and the growing influence of corporations and wealthy individuals who, in Long's view, prevented the "everyman" from becoming a king—that is, master of his own fate, on equal terms with every other man. Long approached populism with religious fervor, claiming no special insight of his own but rather simply maintaining a dogged insistence on following the teachings of the Bible, the U.S. Constitution, and the Declaration of Independence. The latter document was his key authority for attacking the Roosevelt administration and politicians who did not support the radical egalitarian programs that Long believed should follow from the crucial statement that "all men are created equal." While Long played on people's emotions in portraying himself as a simple, plainspoken man, he also could cite facts and figures to buttress his arguments, demonstrating the legal training that enabled him to be a shrewd and relentless opponent of the status quo.

◆ "Every Man a King" Address

Why is it that the wealth of the country is concentrated in the hands of a few? This is the main question that Long puts forth in his signature speech, in a way that is direct and forceful, since he contrasts the power of twelve men with that of 120 million people (some 5 million less than the nation's population at the time), also emphasizing that his concern is with the future of America's children. Often called a populist—a politician who speaks for the people and works for their desires—Long states that the country is not facing a difficult problem. That is only the view in Washington, he insists, as he lays out a program in his limited time of thirty minutes, which, in fact, lends both urgency and cogency to his remarks. Long often imbued his audiences with the feeling that he was a man in a hurry while other politicians wasted the public's time, especially

1893
- **August 30**
  Huey Pierce Long is born in Winnfield, Louisiana.

1915
- Long passes the Louisiana state bar exam.

1916
- Long opens a law practice specializing in attacking corporate interests and defending the rights of the people.

1918
- Long wins election to the Louisiana Railroad Commission.

1924
- Long runs for governor and is defeated.

1928
- Long is elected governor of Louisiana.

1929
- While overcoming impeachment efforts, Long passes legislation initiating free textbooks for schoolchildren and a major highway-building program.

1930
- Long wins election to the U.S. Senate but does not take his seat in Washington, holding his position as governor until 1932, when his term expires.

1932
- **January 25**
  Long assumes his seat in the U.S. Senate.

1934
- **February 23**
  Long delivers a radio address to be known by the motto he heralds for his "Share Our Wealth Society"— "Every Man a King"; that year he establishes the Share Our Wealth clubs.

---

when they suggested that problems were difficult to solve. Long begins by suggesting that the problem is not the issue itself but rather the lack of political will to do something about it, which must involve confronting the superrich who are not willing to share their wealth.

Continuing in the same vein, Long praises Americans' love of their country but also points out that in a land in which the wealth is not shared, the first paragraph of the Declaration of Independence cannot be implemented. That paragraph stipulates that all men are created equal. The laws and form of government are predicated on this principle, yet—as Long points out—a child can inherit $10 million or nothing. Equality cannot have the meaning intended in the Declaration of Independence as long as so many children begin life in such unequal conditions.

Next Long elaborates on the notion that life, liberty, and the pursuit of happiness are not possible in a country where certain children can live on inherited wealth while others starve. Returning to his opening statement about the twelve and the 120 million, Long engages in the kind of simple refrain that made many of his speeches memorable and quotable. Rather than citing many statistics, he embeds this one key numerical comparison in a series of questions tending to expose the outrageous unfairness of depriving millions of children of what a very small number of wealthy ones receive.

The answer to the imbalance of wealth, Long states, is to return the government of the United States to its core principles as expressed in the Declaration of Independence—and as first delineated in the ultimate authority, the scriptures. Long made ample use of the Bible in his speeches, often quoting long passages from memory, because he believed—as he states in this radio address—that he was doing no more than returning his country to the teachings of Moses, Jesus, and the Lord, from whom all power and rights derived. The Bible argues against the concentration of wealth and for the relief of debt, Long notes; a powerful point in his career of attacks against banks that foreclosed on property and provided no escape from the cycle of poverty. In effect, Long then implies, the superrich have become anti-Christian and are living in defiance of the Bible, which teaches concern for the community's welfare, not just for the well-being of certain individuals.

Long then makes his interpretation of the Bible explicit: "I believe that was the judgment and the view and the law of the Lord, that we would have to distribute wealth every so often, in order that there could not be people starving to death in a land of plenty, as there is in America today." He notes that many people cannot afford to buy homes or feed their families, even though farmers produce more than the country can consume.

Having invoked the Bible as his standard, Long is able to cast his criticism of the superrich in moral and religious terms, using vivid imagery:

> We have trouble, my friends, in the country ... because the greed of a few men is such that they

think it is necessary that they own everything, and their pleasure consists in the starvation of the masses, and in their possessing things they cannot use, and their children cannot use, but who bask in the splendor of sunlight and wealth, casting darkness and despair and impressing it on everyone else.

Using such loaded words as *greed*, Long depicts the wealthy as positively enjoying the misery of the poor, depriving them not merely of happiness but also of knowledge, leaving them in darkness. His language becomes apocalyptic as his words draw on a biblical sense of evil overcoming the good.

Long pursues his pointby specifing how the accumulation of debt and of massive fortunes has stifled the lives of millions of Americans. Not only the Bible but also the greatest philosophers of the classical age denounce accumulation of great wealth that deprives the average man of a living. Even Presidents Herbert Hoover and Roosevelt have argued for the decentralization of wealth, Long points out, but they have done nothing about it.

Erly on Long states that love of country is a kind of religion, a theme he develops by suggesting that the people must reclaim their rights as a kind of religious principle. Long's own contribution to this movement comes in the form of his "Share Our Wealth" societies, first mentioned in this speech. Long proposes to limit fortunes, provide old-age pensions, limit hours of work, and provide opportunities for adults to return to school. According to his plans, every man will be a king in the sense that no man will starve and every man will have a livable wage and income, based on calculations of national wealth to be redistributed as soon as the huge fortunes of the few have been reduced.

Long insists that only a comprehensive program such as the one he proposes will solve the country's fundamental problems, and this is why he rejects Roosevelt's piecemeal programs, which he refers to by their "alphabetical codes," such as NRA (National Recovery Act) and PWA (Public Works Administration). These programs only serve to hide or mask the underlying economic problems. Only through concerted community action can the designs of a central government be thwarted, Long argues, touting his Share Our Wealth societies. In effect, Long was appealing directly to the American people, suggesting that only through their efforts could the country change. His speech features this direct appeal: "Get together in your community tonight or tomorrow and organize your Share Our Wealth Societies. A senator himself, Long cast himself as an outsider relying on the people to change the institutions of government and thereby create their own prosperity.

At the very end of his speech, Long asks the public to write to him and share their ideas. He ends on a personal note by sending his regards to his family and friends in Louisiana, thus burnishing his reputation as a straight-talking, down-to-earth man who is calling upon his government to abide by the country's democratic principles and by Christian beliefs. In his last sentence he effectively merges his own efforts with those of his clubs in the minds of the

Time Line

1935

■ **January 14**
Long delivers his "Share Our Wealth" radio address, which is entered in the *Congressional Record* that day; that year he declares open opposition to Franklin Delano Roosevelt and most New Deal Programs and announces his intention to run for president in 1936.

■ **January 19**
Long delivers his "Our Growing Calamity" radio address, which is entered in the *Congressional Record* on January 23.

■ **September 8**
Long is shot in Baton Rouge, Louisiana; he dies two days later.

people listening to his speech: "I thank you, my friends, for your kind attention, and I hope you will enroll with us, take care of your own work in the work of this Government, and share or help in our Share Our Wealth society."

◆ "Share Our Wealth" Address

Addressing a nationwide radio audience on January 14, 1935, Long wasted no time in attacking President Roosevelt. In the third year of the Roosevelt administration conditions had grown worse, Long argued. The president could no longer be regarded as the country's savior, or as Long put it pithily, "It is not Roosevelt or ruin; it is Roosevelt's ruin." The nation's leader had not acted on his promises to redistribute wealth and shorten the working hours of Americans who labored in a land of abundance.

Long personalizes the attack on Roosevelt by suggesting that the president prefers the companionship of rich men like John D. Rockefeller, Jr. Long even criticizes himself here, admitting that perhaps he should have known better than to trust Roosevelt to redistribute wealth, given the figures he befriended. As usual, Long presents himself as a simple man who has grown distrustful of the government's promises. Roosevelt, by implication, becomes the symbol of the politician who talks a good line but fails to deliver what he proposes. It is time, Long says, to begin an immediate program to share the country's wealth. And the vehicle for this program, he suggests, will be his Share Our Wealth societies. His expressed goal is to establish one hundred thousand societies that will meet and talk and work to ensure that the land produces everything that the nation's people need.

Long then sets out his seven-point program. The first aim would be to reduce individual fortunes to no more than a few million dollars. After the first million earned, a person would be taxed an increasing percentage of his income; after more than $8 million has been earned, the person's income would be taxed at 100 percent. Second, no person could inherit more than $1 million a year. Third, the taxes on the rich would be redistributed to every family so that all have "common conveniences," such as automobiles, radios, and freedom from debt. Fourth, a full-employment economy and a thirty-hour workweek would be instituted. Fifth, the Louisiana education program would be expanded to provide free education to all Americans, a plan that would also entail the employment of one hundred thousand new teachers. Sixth, pension plans would be put in place for those over sixty years of age. The final aspect of Long's program would be a moratorium on all unpayable debts.

Long believed that such a program could be instituted within two months. He provides few details about how such a massive redistribution of wealth would actually be administered, instead relying on basic language about his intentions, which are to "straighten things out." The phrase implies, of course, that the country is not governed fairly and that it is in the grip of crooked men. He reinforces this notion by suggesting that the wealth of the country has been "locked in a vise" by a few powerful and wealthy men.

Long emphasizes that he is not against wealth per se—that, in fact, his plan would increase the number of millionaires by redistributing the enormous wealth of the few. No one would really be injured, and millions would benefit from his plan. "The only difference," he contends in a memorable phrase, "would be that maybe 10,000 people would own a concern instead of 10 people owning it." As usual, Long uses elementary facts and figures to make his dramatic point that wealth should be held in common. And, as usual, Long invokes the Bible, suggesting that his plan is part of the divine economy: "But, my friends, unless we do share our wealth, unless we limit the size of the big man so as to give something to the little man, we can never have a happy or free people. God said so! He ordered it."

Near the very end of his address, Long resorts to one of his favorite ploys: presenting his plans as a kind of parable. In this case he presents an image of the country's wealth as a barbecue that could provide enough for everyone to eat, and yet 90 percent of the food is taken by one man, even though he cannot eat all of it and will have to abandon much of it to rot. This is Long's analogy for the functioning of a capitalist economy that produces goods in abundance and yet leaves people to starve. In his customary way, he presents the national depression in melodramatic terms, suggesting a sharp dichotomy between those who have all the wealth and those who are starving—the haves and the have-nots.

Finally, Long portrays America as God's paradise, a land of plenty—indeed, the site of a feast. It is the Rockefellers and their ilk who are despoiling this paradise, and it is now time, Long concludes, to demand that these thieves "put some of it back." Even more than in his "Every Man a King" address—a phrase Long also uses in this speech—he expresses outrage not only at the wealthy but also at President Roosevelt personally, who is treated as a man who has reneged on his assurances to help the American people. Consequently, Long's

only hope is the people themselves. They must govern themselves when their leaders seem unwilling to do God's work, which should also be America's work.

◆ "Our Growing Calamity" Address
In this radio speech delivered on January 19, 1935, and read into the *Congressional Record* on January 23, 1935, Long continues his attack on Roosevelt. He soon concludes that Roosevelt has so complicated the issue of providing old-age pensions on a national basis that his real aim must be to "scuttle [the pension plan] inside and out." The reason Roosevelt's program will not work, Long explains, is the president's reluctance to tax multimillionaires and billionaires. Instead, Roosevelt would tax working people, placing an additional burden on them and on the states in which they reside.

Long presents his own argument with customary plainness. There is no way that Roosevelt can pay for his programs to help the American people "unless that money is scraped off the big piles at the top and spread among the people at the bottom, who have nothing." One of Long's political gifts was his ability to present his economic arguments in clear, picturesque language. Next he portrays the president as fearful of Wall Street's reaction to his economic programs: Indeed, Roosevelt has been unwilling to propose a comprehensive relief agenda, which would, in Wall Street's view, hamper economic recovery. As a result, Long asserts, the depression has actually worsened: "The Roosevelt depression is just a double dose of the Hoover depression."

After providing statistics to show how the economy has worsened under Roosevelt, Long draws the following conclusions: The worker's standard of living has been lowered, the average worker cannot support his family in "health and decency," and the gap between rich and poor is growing greater. Here Long attacks Roosevelt's credibility, suggesting that the president is intentionally vague about what he proposes to do: "You could tell what Mr. Hoover meant to do, or rather meant not to do, whereas understanding what Mr. Roosevelt means to do compared to what he does do is difficult."

Again invoking the Bible, Long uses some verses from the book of Nehemiah to frame the plight of Depression-bathed Americans and to spell out the debt-relief measures he believes should now be adoped. Additional scriptural quotations describe the ancient Hebrew concept of the Jubilee year, which the senator would like to see honored. This presents himself as a kind of prophet and moral guide. Even nonbelievers, Long insists, should heed the words of great American figures from Thomas Jefferson to Theodore Roosevelt who believed that society would prosper only if all of its citizens shared its wealth.

Long implies that like Rome, America may fall because its common people cannot prosper. Acknowledging that he is a Baptist, Long quotes an attack on greed, by the sitting pope, Pius XI, which seems to anticipate Long's own excoriations of the superrich. The antidote to the concentration of resources is for the American people to establish Share Our Wealth clubs in their communities. Long sees himself as fighting for humanity. Only through a mass movement, he suggests, can

Shacks of unemployed and destitute men dot the waterfront of Seattle, Washington (March 20, 1933), once one of the busiest industrial sites on the Pacific Coast. (AP/Wide World Photos)

Roosevelt and the Washington politicians be forced to act to help impoverished people. The problem, in Long's view, is not overwhelming. Indeed, he affirms the potential of his solution to the crisis in one sentence: "All this can be done with ease only if we will say to the rich, 'None shall be too rich!'"

Impact and Legacy

Huey Long has often been described as the dictator of Louisiana. To be sure, he consolidated power in his own person in a way that was unprecedented in American politics. This is why Harnett T. Kane subtitled his book on Long "American Rehearsal for Dictatorship." In Louisiana, Long interfered with the legislative process, drafting laws himself and paying off and intimidating legislators to vote his way. In the U.S. Senate, Long tried to bully his colleagues and would filibuster any piece of legislation he chose so that it could not be voted upon.

Even Long's achievements for his state—such as paving roads and providing free schoolbooks—were the result of underhanded and roughshod methods that abused the democratic system. As with his attacks on Roosevelt, Long tended to personalize politics, making every problem a matter of personality and not of policy or administration. He preyed on people's emotions rather than challenging them to deal thoughtfully with complex problems. Still, Long's populism was not an entirely malign legacy. He was the first politician in Louisiana to appeal directly to the people, to challenge the political machines in the cities. Although he, in turn, established his own political machine, his notion that the people can empower themselves and organize to mount a tide of public opinion that can change government is one that has historically been an enormous tool for good. Long remains for many in Louisiana and elsewhere a kind of folk hero, one who stood up for the common man and rightfully questioned the way wealth and political power are distributed in a democratic society.

Key Sources

The place to start in research on Huey Long is Hill Memorial Library at Louisiana State University, which holds nearly all of Long's papers (including personal letters, his law practice records, documents about his personal finances, and political campaign literature). The library also includes related materials in the collections of Earl Long,

John Fournet, Seymour Weiss, and other Long associates and family members. The New Orleans Public Library contains the papers of Long's local political contemporaries, such as Mayor Semmes Walmsley. Northwestern University also houses papers of Long's associates. Richard D. White, Jr., notes that in his research for his biography of Long, he contacted all sixty-four parish libraries in Louisiana, and several responded with unique material on Long's life.

Further Reading

■ Books

Brinkley, Alan. *Voices of Protest: Huey Long, Father Coughlin, and the Great Depression.* New York: Knopf, 1982.

Hair, William Ivy. *The Kingfish and His Realm: The Life and Times of Huey P. Long.* Baton Rouge: Louisiana State University Press, 1991.

Essential Quotes

> "Now was it the meaning of the Declaration of Independence when it said that they held that there were certain rights that were inalienable—the right of life, liberty, and the pursuit of happiness. Is that right of life, my friends, when the young children of this country are being reared into a sphere which is more owned by 12 men than it is by 120,000,000 people?"
>
> ("Every Man a King" Address)

> "I believe that was the judgment and the view and the law of the Lord, that we would have to distribute wealth every so often, in order that there could not be people starving to death in a land of plenty, as there is in America today."
>
> ("Every Man a King" Address)

> "It is not Roosevelt or ruin; it is Roosevelt's ruin."
>
> ("Share Our Wealth" Address)

> "But, my friends, unless we do share our wealth, unless we limit the size of the big man so as to give something to the little man, we can never have a happy or free people. God said so! He ordered it."
>
> ("Share Our Wealth" Address)

> "The Roosevelt depression is just a double dose of the Hoover depression."
>
> ("Our Growing Calamity" Address)

> "All this can be done with ease only if we will say to the rich, 'None shall be too rich!'"
>
> ("Our Growing Calamity" Address)

Jeansonne, Glen. *Messiah of the Masses: Huey P. Long and the Great Depression*. New York: HarperCollins, 1993.

Kane, Harnett T. *Huey Long's Louisiana Hayride: The American Rehearsal for Dictatorship, 1928–1940*. New York: Morrow, 1941.

White, Richard D., Jr. *Kingfish: The Reign of Huey P. Long*. New York: Random House, 2006.

Williams, T. Harry. *Huey Long*. New York: Knopf, 1969.

■ Web Sites

"Huey Long." Social Security Online Web site. http://www.ssa.gov/history/hlong1.html.

—Carl Rollyson

Questions for Further Study

1. Critique Long's interpretation of equality, particularly as it is expressed in his "every man a king" address. According to Long, equality under the law is not enough; for true equality to exist, wealth should be shared. Do you agree or disagree and why?

2. In both his "every man a king" and "share our wealth" speeches, Long expresses what might be called a "zero sum" philosophy—the idea that when one person gains, another loses. According to this viewpoint, wealth is finite; for someone to become wealthy, other people must necessarily be in poverty. Contrasted to this is the free-market idea that wealth can be created and that, by reducing government intervention in the marketplace, it is possible for everyone in a society to benefit economically. Take one of these positions and analyze Long's speeches in light of that position.

3. How was Long's philosophy of government and the economy like that of Soviet Russia and the Fascist states of central Europe at that time? How was it different, for instance in its use of themes from Christianity? Particularly notable is the comparison to Italy under Benito Mussolini, to whom Long has often been compared.

4. Long appears, in fictional form at least, as the protagonist of Robert Penn Warren's 1946 novel *All the King's Men*. Compare and contrast Long, particularly in his speechmaking, with his literary counterpart, Willy Stark.

"EVERY MAN A KING" ADDRESS (1934)

I contend, my friends, that we have no difficult problem to solve in America, and that is the view of nearly everyone with whom I have discussed the matter here in Washington and elsewhere throughout the United States—that we have no very difficult problem to solve.

It is not the difficulty of the problem which we have; it is the fact that the rich people of this country—and by rich people I mean the super-rich—will not allow us to solve the problems, or rather the one little problem that is afflicting this country, because in order to cure all of our woes it is necessary to scale down the big fortunes, that we may scatter the wealth to be shared by all of the people.

We have a marvelous love for this Government of ours; in fact, it is almost a religion, and it is well that it should be, because we have a splendid form of government and we have a splendid set of laws. We have everything here that we need, except that we have neglected the fundamentals upon which the American Government was principally predicated.

How many of you remember the first thing that the Declaration of Independence said? It said, "We hold these truths to be self-evident, that there are certain inalienable rights of the people, and among them are life, liberty, and the pursuit of happiness"; and it said, further, "We hold the view that all men are created equal."

Now, what did they mean by that? Did they mean, my friends, to say that all men were created equal and that that meant that any one man was born to inherit $10 billion and that another child was to be born to inherit nothing?...

Is that right of life, my friends, when the young children of this country are being reared into a sphere which is more owned by twelve men than it is by 120 million people? Is that, my friends, giving them a fair shake of the dice...when we have today in America thousands and hundreds of thousands and millions of children on the verge of starvation in a land that is overflowing with too much to eat and too much to wear?...

I quote you the Scripture, rather refer you to the Scripture, because whatever you see there you may rely upon will never be disproved so long as you or your children or anyone may live; and you may further depend upon the fact that not one historical fact that the Bible has ever contained has ever yet been disproved by any scientific discovery or by reason of anything that has been disclosed to man through his own individual mind or through the wisdom of the Lord which the Lord has allowed him to have....

I believe that was the judgment and the view and the law of the Lord, that we would have to distribute wealth every so often, in order that there could not be people starving to death in a land of plenty, as there is in America today. We have in America today more wealth, more goods, more food, more clothing, more houses than we have ever had. We have everything in abundance here....

We have trouble, my friends, in the country, because...the greed of a few men is such that they think it is necessary that they own everything, and their pleasure consists in the starvation of the masses, and in their possessing things they cannot use, and their children cannot use, but who bask in the splendor of sunlight and wealth, casting darkness and despair and impressing it on everyone else....

Now, my friends, if you were off on an island where there were 100 lunches, you could not let one man eat up the hundred lunches, or take the hundred lunches and not let anybody else eat any of them. If you did, there would not be anything else for the balance of the people to consume....

Then we have heard of the great Greek philosopher, Socrates, and the greater Greek philosopher, Plato, and we have read the dialog between Plato and Socrates, in which one said that great riches brought on great poverty, and would be destructive of a country. Read what they said. Read what Plato said; that you must not let any one man be too poor, and you must not let any one man be too rich; that the same mill that grinds out the extra rich is the mill that will grind out the extra poor, because, in order that the extra rich can become so affluent, they must necessarily take more of what ordinarily would belong to the average man....

That was the view of the English statesmen. That was the view of American statesmen. That was the view of American statesmen like Daniel Webster, Thomas Jefferson, Abraham Lincoln, William Jennings Bryan, and Theodore Roosevelt, and even as late as Herbert Hoover and Franklin D. Roosevelt.

Both of these men, Mr. Hoover and Mr. Roosevelt, came out and said there had to be a decentralization of wealth, but neither one of them did anything about it....

It is necessary to save the Government of the country, but is much more necessary to save the people of America. We love this country. We love this Government. It is a religion, I say....

Now, we have organized a society, and we call it "Share Our Wealth Society," a society with the motto "every man a king." Every man a king, so there would be no such thing as a man or woman who did not have the necessities of life, who would not be dependent upon the whims and caprices and ipse dixit of the financial barons for a living. What do we propose by this society? We propose to limit the wealth of big men in the country. There is an average of $15,000 in wealth to every family in America. That is right here today....

We will not say we are going to try to guarantee any equality, or $15,000 to families. No; but we do say that one third of the average is low enough for any one family to hold, that there should be a guaranty of a family wealth of around $5,000; enough for a home, an automobile, a radio, and the ordinary conveniences, and the opportunity to educate their children; a fair share of the income of this land thereafter to that family so there will be no such thing as merely the select to have those things, and so there will be no such thing as a family living in poverty and distress.

We have to limit fortunes. Our present plan is that we will allow no one man to own more than $50,000,000. We think that with that limit we will be able to carry out the balance of the program. It may be necessary that we limit it to less than $50,000,000. It may be necessary, in working out of the plans, that no man's fortune would be more than $10,000,000 or $15,000,000....

Another thing we propose is old-age pension of $30 a month for everyone that is 60 years old. Now, we do not give this pension to a man making $1,000 a year, and we do not give it to him if he has $10,000 in property, but outside of that we do.

We will limit hours of work. There is not any necessity of having over-production. I think all you have got to do, ladies and gentlemen, is just limit the hours of work to such an extent as people will work only so long as is necessary to produce enough for all of the people to have what they need....

We will not have any trouble taking care of the agricultural situation. All you have to do is balance your production with your consumption. You simply have to abandon a particular crop that you have too much of, and all you have to do is store the surplus for the next year, and the Government will take it over. When you have good crops in the area in which the crops that have been planted are sufficient for another year, put in your public works in the particular year when you do not need to raise any more, and by that means you get everybody employed....

You cannot solve these things through these various and sundry alphabetical codes. You can have the N.R.A. and P.W.A. and C.W.A. and the U.U.G. and G.I.N. and any other kind of "dadgummed" lettered code. You can wait until doomsday and see 25 more alphabets, but that is not going to solve this proposition. Why hide? Why quibble? You know what the trouble is. The man that says he does not know what the trouble is just hiding his face to keep from seeing the sunlight....

We had these great incomes in this country; but the farmer, who plowed from sunup to sundown, who labored here from sunup to sundown for 6 days a week, wound up at the end...with practically nothing.

And we ought to take care of the veterans of the wars in this program. That is a small matter. Suppose it does cost a billion dollars a year—that means that the money will be scattered throughout this country. We ought to pay them a bonus. We can do it. We ought to take care of every single one of the sick and disabled veterans. I do not care whether a man got sick on the battlefield or did not; every man that wore the uniform of this country is entitled to be taken care of, and there is money enough to do it;

Glossary

impressing	forcing
ipse dixit	describing baseless claims; the Latin means "he himself spoke"
N.R.A. and P.W.A. and C.W.A. and the U.U.G. and G.I.N	in a play on the many acronyms for New Deal programs (nicknamed "alphabet soup" agencies by detractors), references to the National Recovery, Public Works, and Civil Works administrations along with two fictional agencies

and we need to spread the wealth of the country, which you did not do in what you call the N.R.A....

Get together in your community tonight or tomorrow and organize one of our Share Our Wealth societies. If you do not understand it, write me and let me send you the platform; let me give you the proof of it....

Now that I have but a minute left, I want to say that I suppose my family is listening in on the radio in New Orleans, and I will say to my wife and three children that I am entirely well and hope to be home before many more days, and I hope they have listened to my speech tonight, and I wish them and all their neighbors and friends everything good that may be had.

I thank you, my friends, for your kind attention, and I hope you will enroll with us, take care of your own work in the work of this Government, and share or help in our Share Our Wealth society.

"SHARE OUR WEALTH" ADDRESS (1935)

We are in our third year of the Roosevelt depression, with the conditions growing worse....

We must now become awakened! We must know the truth and speak the truth. There is no use to wait three more years. It is not Roosevelt or ruin; it is Roosevelt's ruin....

We ran Mr. Roosevelt for the presidency of the United States because he promised to us by word of mouth and in writing:

*That the size of the big man's fortune would be reduced so as to give the masses at the bottom enough to wipe out all poverty; and

*That the hours of labor would be so reduced that all would share in the work to be done and in consuming the abundance mankind produced.

Hundreds of words were used by Mr. Roosevelt to make these promises to the people, but they were made over and over again. He reiterated these pledges even after he took his oath as President. Summed up, what these promises meant was: "Share our wealth."

When I saw him spending all his time of ease and recreation with the business partners of Mr. John D. Rockefeller, Jr., with such men as the Astors, etc., maybe I ought to have had better sense than to have believed he would ever break down their big fortunes to give enough to the masses to end poverty—maybe some will think me weak for ever believing it all, but millions of other people were fooled the same as myself. I was like a drowning man grabbing at a straw, I guess. The face and eyes, the hungry forms of mothers and children, the aching hearts of students denied education were before our eyes, and when Roosevelt promised, we jumped for that ray of hope.

So therefore I call upon the men and women of America to immediately join in our work and movement to share our wealth.

There are thousands of share-our-wealth societies organized in the United States now. We want 100,000 such societies formed for every nook and corner of this country—societies that will meet, talk, and work, all for the purpose that the great wealth and abundance of this great land that belongs to us may be shared and enjoyed by all of us....

So in this land of God's abundance we propose laws, viz.:

1. The fortunes of the multimillionaires and billionaires shall be reduced so that no one person shall own more than a few million dollars to the person. We would do this by a capital levy tax. On the first million that a man was worth, we would not impose any tax. We would say, "All right for your first million dollars, but after you get that rich you will have to start helping the balance of us." So we would not levy any capital levy tax on the first million one owned. But on the second million a man owns, we would tax that 1 percent, so that every year the man owned the second million dollars he would be taxed $10,000. On the third million we would impose a tax of 2 percent. On the fourth million we would impose a tax of 4 percent. On the fifth million we would impose a tax of 8 percent. On the sixth million we would impose a tax of 16 percent. On the seventh million we would impose a tax of 32 percent. On the eighth million we would impose a tax of 64 percent; and on all over the eighth million we would impose a tax of 100 percent....

2. We propose to limit the amount any one man can earn in one year or inherit to $1 million to the person.

3. Now, by limiting the size of the fortunes and incomes of the big men, we will throw into the government Treasury the money and property from which we will care for the millions of people who have nothing; and with this money we will provide a home and the comforts of home, with such common conveniences as radio and automobile, for every family in America, free of debt.

4. We guarantee food and clothing and employment for everyone who should work by shortening the hours of labor to thirty hours per week, maybe less, and to eleven months per year, maybe less. We would have the hours shortened just so much as would give work to

everybody to produce enough for everybody; and if we were to get them down to where they were too short, then we would lengthen them again. As long as all the people working can produce enough of automobiles, radios, homes, schools, and theaters for everyone to have that kind of comfort and convenience, then let us all have work to do and have that much of heaven on earth.

5. We would provide education at the expense of the states and the United States for every child, not only through grammar school and high school but through to a college and vocational education. We would simply extend the Louisiana plan to apply to colleges and all people. Yes; we would have to build thousands of more colleges and employ 100,000 more teachers; but we have materials, men, and women who are ready and available for the work. Why have the right to a college education depend upon whether the father or mother is so well-to-do as to send a boy or girl to college? We would give every child the right to education and a living at birth.

6. We would give a pension to all persons above sixty years of age in an amount sufficient to support them in comfortable circumstances, excepting those who earn $1,000 per year or who are worth $10,000.

7. Until we could straighten things out—and we can straighten things out in two months under our program—we would grant a moratorium on all debts which people owe that they cannot pay.

And now you have our program, none too big, none too little, but every man a king....

Our plan would injure no one. It would not stop us from having millionaires—it would increase them tenfold, because so many more people could make $1 million if they had the chance our plan gives them. Our plan would not break up big concerns.

The only difference would be that maybe 10,000 people would own a concern instead of 10 people owning it.

But, my friends, unless we do share our wealth, unless we limit the size of the big man so as to give something to the little man, we can never have a happy or free people. God said so! He ordered it.

We have everything our people need. Too much of food, clothes, and houses—why not let all have their fill and lie down in the ease and comfort God has given us? Why not? Because a few own everything—the masses own nothing.

I wonder if any of you people who are listening to me were ever at a barbecue! We used to go there—sometimes 1,000 people or more. If there were 1,000 people, we would put enough meat and bread and everything else on the table for 1,000 people. Then everybody would be called and everyone would eat all they wanted. But suppose at one of these barbecues for 1,000 people that one man took 90 percent of the food and ran off with it and ate until he got sick and let the balance rot. Then 999 people would have only enough for 100 to eat and there would be many to starve because of the greed of just one person for something he couldn't eat himself.

Well, ladies and gentlemen, America, all the people of America, have been invited to a barbecue. God invited us all to come and eat and drink all we wanted. He smiled on our land and we grew crops of plenty to eat and wear. He showed us in the earth the iron and other things to make everything we wanted. He unfolded to us the secrets of science so that our work might be easy. God called: "Come to my feast."

Glossary

the Astors	one of the wealthiest families in America
capital levy tax	a tax on property
Morgan	a reference to John Pierpont Morgan Jr. (1867–1943), financier and one of the wealthiest men in America
to the person	per person
viz.	abbreviation for the Latin *videlicet*, meaning "namely"

Then what happened? Rockefeller, Morgan, and their crowd stepped up and took enough for 120 million people and left only enough for 5 million for all the other 125 million to eat. And so many millions must go hungry and without these good things God gave us unless we call on them to put some of it back.

"OUR GROWING CALAMITY" ADDRESS (1935)

Ladies and gentlemen, the only means by which any practical relief may be given to the people is in taking the money with which to give such relief from the big fortunes at the top....

Now, we have been clamoring for a number of relief measures. Among them was the old-age pension....

Now, along comes Mr. Roosevelt and says that he is for the old-age pension of $30 a month, but he says that it shall be paid by the States....

What the Roosevelt pronouncement for old-age pensions means is that he would scuttle it inside and out. In other words, he will proceed to show how unreasonable, how impossible an old-age pension system can be, and how much harm can be done by trying to bring it about....

The only way you can get $3 billion is by taxing the billionaires and multimillionaires, and nobody else, because if you tax the poor wage earner, who is barely making a living now, you will do more harm than good in trying to build up an old-age pension system....

He rode into the President's office on the platform of redistributing wealth. He has done no such thing and has made no effort to do any such thing since he has been there.... We can pass laws today providing for education, for old-age pensions, for unemployment insurance, for doles, public buildings,... and still none of them would be worth anything unless we provided the money for them. And the money cannot be provided for them without these things doing twice as much harm as they do good unless that money is scraped off the big piles at the top and spread among the people at the bottom, who have nothing....

The big interests realize Roosevelt's plan would not cost them anything, which is the same as saying it will be no relief to the poor....

The big men of Wall Street were a little bit apprehensive for fear Roosevelt would provide some relief or social legislation that would cost them something, but they are glad to see whatever he does will be self-sustaining. That is, the poor people who get relief will pay for it....

Now, our conditions today are much more deplorable than they were in [Herbert] Hoover's depression. The Roosevelt depression is just a double dose of the Hoover depression....

The average worker's income of nearly $1,099 in 1934 is below the minimum necessary to support a family of five in health and decency by $813, or 43 percent....

In other words, according to these accredited figures, those so fortunate as to be employed are living 43 percent below a reasonable standard of living at the end of the year 1934 under Roosevelt's depression....

We have the same promises from Mr. Roosevelt now that we had before he was elected, with the exception he says you must not pass any such law as will put them into effect in actual fact.

The only difference in Roosevelt before election and now is that Roosevelt now says he is still for them, but that you must not do anything about them. The only difference between Mr. Roosevelt and Mr. Hoover is that things are much worse in every degree under Mr. Roosevelt than ever under Mr. Hoover; and you could tell what Mr. Hoover meant to do, or rather meant not to do, whereas understanding what Mr. Roosevelt means to do compared to what he does do is difficult.

There is only one way to save our people; only one way to save America. How? Pull down wealth from the top and spread wealth at the bottom; free people of these debts they owe; God told just exactly how to do it all.

There was once a country in exactly the same shape as America is today. God's prophet was there and applied the laws as God had prescribed them. If you would just recognize that God is still alive, that His law still lives, America would not grope today. Here is the written record of that country that was in the same fix as America is today. Here is what they did under the command of God's prophet. Hear me, I read from the Bible, Nehemiah, chapter 5....

Some also there were that said, We have mortgaged our lands, vineyards, and houses, that we might buy corn, because of the dearth....

Then I consulted with myself, and I rebuked the nobles, and the rulers, and said unto them, Ye exact usury, every one of his brother....

Restore, I pray you, to them, even this day, their lands, their vineyards, their olive yards, and their houses, also the hundredth part of the money, and of the corn, the wine, and the oil, that ye exact of them.

Then said they, We will restore them, and will require nothing of them, so will we do as thou sayest....

Hear me, people of America, God's laws live today. Keep them and none suffer, disregard them and we go the way of the missing. His word said that. Here is what He said:...

"And ye shall hallow the fiftieth year, and proclaim liberty throughout all the land unto all the inhabitants thereof; it shall be a jubilee unto you; and ye shall return every man unto his possession, and ye shall return every man unto his family." Leviticus: chapter 25, verse 10.

"At the end of every 7 years thou shalt make a release...Every creditor that lendeth ought unto his neighbor shall release it; he shall not exact it of his ...brother; because it is called the Lord's release." Deuteronomy: Chapter 15, verses 1 and 2.

Maybe you do not believe the Bible; maybe you do not accept God as your Supreme Lawgiver....If you do not, then all I ask of you is to believe the simple problems of arithmetic....If you believe them, you will know that we cannot tolerate this condition of a handful of people owning nearly all and [nearly] all owning nearly nothing. In a land of plenty there is no need to starve unless we allow greed to starve us to please the vanity of someone else. I can read you what Theodore Roosevelt, Daniel Webster, Thomas Jefferson, Abraham Lincoln, Ralph Waldo Emerson, all other great Americans said. Their beliefs might be stated in the following lines of Emerson:...Give no bounties: make equal laws: secure life and prosperity and you need not give alms." Or maybe these words of Theodore Roosevelt would be proof: "We must pay equal attention to the distribution of prosperity. The only prosperity worth having is that which affects the mass of people."...

Here are the words of Pope Pius in his encyclical letter of May 18, 1932, which I, a Baptist, caused to be placed in the CONGRESSIONAL RECORD. Hear these words:

From greed arises mutual distrust that casts a blight on all human dealings; from greed arises hateful envy which makes a man consider the advantages of another as losses to himself; from greed arises narrow individualism which orders and subordinates everything to its own advantage without taking account of others, on the contrary, cruelly trampling under foot all rights of others. Hence the disorder and inequality from which arises the accumulation of the wealth of nations in the hands of a small group of individuals who manipulate the market of the world at their own caprice, to the immense harm of the masses.

I call and ask you now to organize a share-our-wealth society in your community now. Don't delay.... Help in our plan. What is it? I state it to you again:

We propose to limit the size of all big fortunes to not more than $3 to 4 million and to throw the balance in the United States Treasury; we will impose taxes every year to keep down these fortunes and to also limit the amount which any one may earn to $1 million per year, and to limit the amount any one can inherit to $1 million in a lifetime, throwing all surpluses into the United States Treasury.

Then from the immense money thus acquired we will guarantee to every family a home and the comforts of a home, including such conveniences as automobile and radio; we will guarantee education to every child and youth through college and vocational training, based upon the ability of the student and not upon the ability of the child's parents to pay the costs; we would pay flat and outright to all people over 60 years of age, a pension sufficient for their life and comfort; we would shorten the hours of work to

Glossary

encyclical	letter from a pope to, for example, the bishops of the church; a statement of papal policy
God's prophet	Nehemiah (fifth century BCE)
Horace	Roman poet of the first century BCE

30 hours per week, maybe less, and to eleven months per year, maybe less; and thus share our work at living wages and to those for whom we fail to find work we would pay insurance until we do find it; we would pay the soldiers' bonus and give a sufficient supply of money to carry on our work and business.

All this can be done with ease only if we will say to the rich, "None shall be too rich!"

Won't you help in this work? Is not humanity worth the effort?...

Good night, my friends. I thank you!

James Madison (Library of Congress)

Featured Documents
◆ "Memorial and Remonstrance against Religious Assessments" (1785)
◆ Speech on the New Jersey Plan to the Constitutional Convention (1787)
◆ Federalist 10 (1787)
◆ Speech to the House of Representatives Proposing a Bill of Rights (1789)
◆ Virginia Resolutions (1798)
◆ "Advice to My Country" (1834)

Overview

Although James Madison served two terms as president of the United States, he is historically better known for his role at the Constitutional Convention of 1787, for drafting the Bill of Rights, and for helping to form and lead the Democratic-Republican Party. Born in Port Conway, Virginia, in 1751, James Madison, Jr., was the eldest of twelve children, seven of whom survived into adulthood. His parents were James Madison, Sr., and Eleanor Rose Conway, prominent slaveholding landowners in Orange County, where Madison, Sr., was a justice of the peace.

In his early teens, Madison was tutored at a nearby plantation by Donald Robertson, from Scotland, and then by Thomas Martin, a local clergyman. He attended the College of New Jersey (now Princeton University) and studied under President John Witherspoon, also from Scotland, who distinguished himself as the only clergyman to sign the Declaration of Independence. Madison returned to Virginia after his college studies and was shocked to find that the nearby city of Culpeper had imprisoned Baptist ministers for their beliefs. He soon became caught up in the calls for revolution against Great Britain, and he was appointed to the committee that George Mason headed to draw up the Virginia Declaration of Rights. Madison insisted that a moderate proposal for toleration of religion be strengthened so as to provide for its "free exercise," language later reflected in the First Amendment to the U.S. Constitution.

Madison was elected to the Continental Congress and later to the Virginia legislature. His experiences in both bodies convinced him that the nation needed a stronger national government that would be able to resist inflationary and other schemes that states were promoting to gain popular favor. Madison was a key figure in the Annapolis convention of September 1786, which issued the call for a constitutional convention. In Philadelphia, at the Constitutional Convention, he exercised major influence in the development of the Virginia Plan, which opened the convention's proceedings. Rather than simple revision of the existing Articles of Confederation, the plan proposed an entirely new form of government, with a bicameral congress to replace the unicameral one and with three inde-pendent branches of the national government instead of one. Madison also proposed granting Congress a veto over state legislation. In addition to being one of the most prominent debaters during the Constitutional Convention, Madison served as a self-appointed secretary. Although his notes were not published until after his death, they remain the best single source for information about the convention's proceedings.

At the end of the Philadelphia convention, Madison actively worked for the adoption of the Constitution. Along with Alexander Hamilton and John Jay, he authored *The Federalist*, a series of eighty-five essays published originally in New York newspapers and subsequently in book form. He also led efforts for ratification in Virginia, where his reasoned arguments eventually overcame the more bombastic opposition of Patrick Henry. Initially tepid toward a bill of rights, Madison eventually agreed to work for such an addition after the U.S. Constitution was ratified. He led this fight as a member of the new House of Representatives in the nation's first Congress.

Although he had advocated a stronger national government at the Philadelphia convention, Madison became convinced that Secretary of Treasury Alexander Hamilton, of George Washington's administration, was seeking a central government that was too strong. Madison thus opposed Hamilton's proposals for establishing a national bank and for broad executive powers. In time, Madison joined his fellow Virginian Thomas Jefferson in forming the Democratic-Republican Party. When the Federalists adopted the Alien and Sedition Acts in 1798, Madison authored the Virginia Resolutions, opposing the laws both on the ground of states' rights and because they violated the First Amendment rights of freedom of speech and press. When Jefferson was elected president, he chose Madison as his secretary of state. During his service, the United States purchased the Louisiana Territory from France and imposed an embargo on shipping to Britain.

Madison was elected to succeed Jefferson, and he served two terms. During this time, the United States engaged in a war with Great Britain—the War of 1812—that resulted in a surge of nationalism. Madison prided himself on waging the war without imposing the restraints on speech that Adams had imposed during the nation's ear-

1751

■ **March 16**
James Madison is born in Port Conway, Virginia.

1771

■ Madison graduates from the College of New Jersey (now Princeton) after two years of study.

1776

■ Madison helps draft the Virginia Declaration of Rights.

1780

■ Madison is elected to the Continental Congress (which became the Confederation Congress in 1781), serving until 1783.

1784

■ Madison is elected to the Virginia House of Delegates, serving until 1786.

1785

■ **June 20**
Madison begins circulating his tract "Memorial and Remonstrance against Religious Assessments."

1786

■ **September**
Madison attends the Annapolis Convention.

1787

■ **May–September**
Madison attends the Constitutional Convention.

■ **June 19**
Madison gives his speech on the New Jersey Plan to the Constitutional Convention.

■ **November 22**
Madison publishes Federalist 10, "The Utility of the Union as a Safeguard against Domestic Faction and Insurrection."

1788

■ **June**
Madison attends the Virginia convention for ratification of the Constitution.

---

lier Quasi War with France. Overall, Madison was a far weaker president than Jefferson, even though Madison's wife, Dolley, helped to smooth personal conflicts that partisanship often stirred.

Madison retired to his estate, Montpelier, in Virginia after being succeeded by James Monroe, who had served as his secretary of state. He served on the University of Virginia's board of visitors; took part in the Virginia constitutional Convention of 1830; and warned, in posthumously circulated advice, of the increasing dangers of disunion.

Explanation and Analysis of Documents

Madison was a quiet speaker whom others often had to strain to hear, but his writings were known for their logical rigor and clarity, with Federalist 10 being perhaps the best example. He was a thorough researcher who was familiar with the weaknesses in the arguments of his opponents, whom he often sought to address; his speech on the New Jersey Plan is a particularly good example. His "Memorial and Remonstrance against Religious Assessments" used popular sentiment on behalf of principles of liberty, and his final "Advice to My Country" showed an ability to make use of figures of speech in forming an emotional appeal on behalf of national unity. Madison was rarely willing to compromise vital principles, and his advocacy of a Constitution that embodied some compromises that he had opposed, as well as his work on behalf of a bill of rights that he did not initially consider to be necessary, demonstrated that he could be flexible in pursuit of higher principles.

◆ **"Memorial and Remonstrance against Religious Assessments"**

Madison was firmly committed to religious liberty. His parents were members of the established Episcopal Church in Virginia, and he himself expressed some fairly warm religious sentiments during his college years. Yet because he did not freely share his personal religious beliefs in later life, scholars continue to debate the degree to which he remained orthodox or embraced the deism that was common among other notable American Founders. It is clear that Madison strongly opposed religious persecution while favoring fairly strict separation of church and state.

When Madison was serving as a state legislator in Virginia, Governor Patrick Henry gave his support to the Bill Establishing a Provision for Teachers of the Christian Religion. The bill was designed to use tax moneys to help support preachers who were teaching children at a time when public education was not available. On June 20, 1785, Madison began circulating a tract entitled "Memorial and Remonstrance against Religious Assessments" to secure signatures on petitions designed to defeat the bill. In this tract, Madison clearly grounds his analysis in natural rights theory. Government does not confer religious freedom; it recognizes that such freedom already exists by virtue of the prior duty that individuals owe to their Creator. On matters of religious exercise, Madison does not believe that "the will of the majority" should "trespass on the rights of the minority." Madison is less concerned about the amount of money involved in Henry's proposal than about the principles at issue. He thus cautions that citizens need "to take alarm at the first experiment on our liberties."

In addressing a population with significant numbers of religious people, Madison argues that governmental support for religion actually contradicts "the Christian Religion" itself. God preceded human government and laws, and divine religion does not need such secular support. Indeed, Madison observes that "ecclesiastical establishments" have historically been tied to "pride and indolence in the Clergy, ignorance and servility in the laity, in both, superstition, bigotry and persecution." Furthermore, Madison reasons that a government that can support Christian sects over non-Christian ones might also support one Christian group over another, and he fears that the state-sponsored establishment of religion in any form will provide a motive for those of minority religions to emigrate. He associates complete religious independence with "moderation and harmony" and with "equal and compleat liberty." He also observes that attempts to enforce obnoxious laws are likely "to enervate the laws in general, and to slacken the bands of Society." Madison notes that rights relative to religion are protected in the same Declaration of Rights (which he himself helped to formulate) that protects others. He thus fears that any diminution of the former rights might lead to similar destruction of those other rights.

Madison's "Memorial and Remonstrance" not only stirred sufficient concern to block Henry's proposed legislation but also provided support for Madison to push through the Virginia Statute for Religious Freedom, which Thomas Jefferson had first proposed in 1779 and would list as one of his three signature accomplishments on his tombstone. This law, in turn, was subsequently used to interpret the establishment clause of the First Amendment.

◆ **Speech on the New Jersey Plan to the Constitutional Convention**

Madison is often called the father of the U.S. Constitution. He attended the Annapolis convention, which issued the call for the Constitutional Convention, and helped persuade George Washington to attend the latter. In Philadelphia he participated actively in the debates and kept copious notes that continue to serve as a guide to the convention's proceedings. Prior to the convention, Madison read widely on the nature of government and composed two relevant essays. In "Of Ancient and Modern Confederacies," he examines the weaknesses of prior confederations, and in "Vices of the Political System of the United States," he examines problems of the state governments, many of which he observed firsthand in the Virginia legislature. As the first delegate to arrive from out of state before the Constitutional Convention, Madison spent his opening weeks in conjunction with other delegates from Virginia and Pennsylvania formulating a plan that the Virginia governor Edmund Randolph would introduce on May 29, 1787, the first day of convention deliberations. Although Congress had agreed

Time Line

1789
■ **June 8**
Madison gives a speech to the House of Representatives proposing a bill of rights.

1791
■ Madison helps found the Democratic-Republican Party.

1798
■ Madison authors the Virginia Resolutions, expressing opposition to the Alien and Sedition Acts.

1801
■ Madison is named secretary of state to Thomas Jefferson, serving until 1809.

1809
■ **March 4**
Madison is inaugurated as the fourth president of the United States, holding office for two terms.

1829–1830
■ Madison attends the Virginia Constitutional Convention in Richmond.

1834
■ **October**
Madison writes his political testament "Advice to My Country," which is not published until 1850.

1836
■ **June 28**
Madison dies at his home in Orange County, Virginia.

to call a convention to "revise and enlarge" the existing Articles of Confederation, the Virginia Plan called for a completely new form of government. Among the more innovative features proposed were a tripartite division of powers at the national level and a bicameral legislature wherein both houses would be apportioned according to population.

After about two weeks of debate, William Paterson introduced the rival New Jersey Plan. Although Paterson was willing to accede to the division of the national government into three branches, he questioned whether the convention was authorized to make other changes, such as rearranging the balance of powers between the national government and the states. As a representative of one of the less populous states, Paterson also expressed an unwillingness to part with the equal state representation provided for by the existing Articles of Confederation.

Madison delivered his speech on the New Jersey Plan on June 19, 1787. In responding to Paterson, Madison directs much of his address to demonstrating the need for a federal government with the power to operate directly upon individuals rather than through the states. One of the greatest difficulties that the Confederation Congress faced under the Articles of Confederation was that it could requisition the states for money or for troops, but it could not directly compel individuals to comply. Given weaknesses such as this one, Madison argues that there was nothing to prevent the Constitutional Convention from seeking a new system.

Madison proceeds to compare the system proposed by the Virginia Plan with that proposed by the New Jersey Plan, posing a series of six rhetorical questions to show the superiority of the former to the latter. He questions whether the New Jersey Plan would give sufficient power to Congress to prevent treaty violations on the part of the states, to "prevent encroachments on the federal authority," to "prevent trespasses of the States on each other," to "secure the internal tranquility of the States themselves," to "secure a good internal legislation & administration to the particular States," or to "secure the Union ag[ain]st the influence of foreign powers over its members." With a view to past experience, Madison argues that the Virginia Plan's provision for paying congressional delegates is better than the New Jersey Plan's leaving this pay dependent upon the states. He further warns that adherence to an impossible plan might result in the division of the continent into rival confederacies. Madison identifies the issue of representation as paramount and argues that any attempt to erase current boundaries and divide the states into equally populous entities would be impractical. He further suggests that the New Jersey Plan's provision for equal state representation would be an obstacle to the addition of new western states.

Not long after Madison's speech, the Constitutional Convention decided to proceed with the Virginia Plan. In time, however, delegates deleted Madison's proposal allowing for the congressional veto of state legislation, through which he had hoped to secure better internal state administration. Delegates further moderated the proposal for proportional representation in both houses of Congress through the Connecticut Compromise, which provided for equal state representation in the U.S. Senate. Once the compromise, which Madison strongly opposed, was adopted, constitutional deliberation went much more smoothly, and on September 17, 1787, thirty-nine of forty-two remaining delegates signed the new Constitution. The delegates then sent the document to the states for ratification by special conventions, a process they thought embodied the idea of popular sovereignty.

◆ **Federalist 10**

The Federalist was a work of advocacy designed to secure the ratification of the U.S. Constitution. The brainchild of Alexander Hamilton, who wrote the majority of the essays, the work was written under the pen name of a Roman statesman, Publius, and also featured essays by Madison and John Jay. Some of Madison's essays are among the most important: Federalist 39 remains a classic description of the system of federalism created by the new Constitution. Federalist 49 justifies the decision by members of the convention to exceed their commissions and propose an entirely new plan of government. Federalist 50 dissects and rejects a proposal by Thomas Jefferson for periodic revisions of the Constitution. Federalist 51 outlines a rationale for dividing the national government into three branches.

None of the essays has been the subject of greater analysis or praise than Federalist 10, "The Utility of the Union as a Safeguard against Domestic Faction and Insurrection," which focuses chiefly on the issue of factions, or interest groups. Antifederalist opponents of the Constitution, who cited Charles-Louis de Secondat, baron de Montesquieu (whom Federalists themselves relied upon for justification of the doctrine of separation of powers), were claiming that it was impossible to establish republican government over an area the size of the United States. By contrast, Madison had already developed a theory that the diversity of factions that he thought such a large land area would encompass could combat oppression by making it less likely that any single faction could dominate.

Madison presented this theory to the general public in New York's *Daily Advertiser* on November 22, 1787. In the essay, he acknowledges that the development of factions is inevitable in a nation based on liberty. He links factions to differences in opinion that stem from the "the reciprocal influence" of man's "opinions and his passions." Madison believes that "diversity in the faculties of men" contributes to property differences, which in turn create factions and classes: "A landed interest, a manufacturing interest, a mercantile interest, a moneyed interest, with many lesser interests, grow up of necessity in civilized nations, and divide them into different classes, actuated by different sentiments and views."

While some would look to "enlightened statesmen" to accommodate such varied interests, Madison seeks a more reliable institutional solution. In attempting to evade the force of Montesquieu's arguments about size, Madison distinguishes the "pure democracy" of ancient times from the modern republic. Whereas the former was necessarily limited to a city-state whose residents could gather together in one spot, the latter relied on a system of representation that permits its people to disperse over a larger land area. Madison proceeds to argue that the differences of the republic from the democracy would have positive effects. The republic's representatives would "refine and enlarge the public views, by passing them through the medium of a chosen body of citizens, whose wisdom may best discern the true interest of their country, and whose patriotism and love of justice will be least likely to sacrifice it to temporary or partial considerations." The greater land area covered by the republic, in turn, would increase the number of factions; and as the republican sphere expands, there would be less chance that a single faction

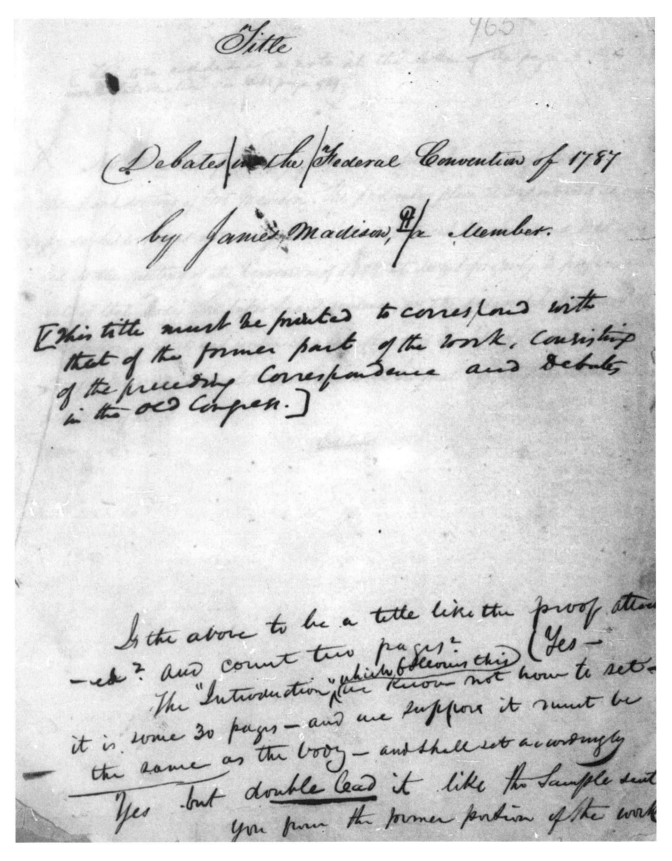

A page from James Madison's notes to the printer of his published version
of the debates in the Federal Convention of 1787 (AP/Wide World Photos)

would dominate. While individual states might be subject to contagions of opinion, any such "rage" would be less likely to sweep through the nation as a whole.

All citizens, then, could ratify the Constitution in the knowledge that it would be likely to provide greater security for liberty than would their own states.

Scholars continue to argue about whether Federalist 10 persuaded many Antifederalists to join the Federalist side as well as whether it embodies the philosophy of the Constitution as a whole. The essay certainly provided further justification for American expansionism, such as that later represented by the Louisiana Purchase. Modern scholars have cited the essay in economic interpretations of the Founders' intentions.

◆ Speech to the House of Representatives Proposing a Bill of Rights

During the state-by-state debates over ratification of the Constitution, Antifederalist opponents highlighted the absence of a bill of rights. Leading Federalist supporters, including Madison, initially argued that such a bill was unnecessary and might even be dangerous. In time, however, Madison recognized that support for such a bill was so strong that it could lead to a second constitutional convention that would potentially undo some of the hard work of the first. In seeking a seat in the first House of Representatives, Madison faced stiff opposition from James Monroe, who had distinguished himself in the Revolutionary War. Under pressure from Baptists and members of minority religious groups who feared religious persecution, Madison agreed that he would work for a bill of rights once the Constitution was ratified.

Madison subsequently compiled amending proposals made by the states and presented them to the First Congress, carefully focusing on amendments that would protect individual rights rather than on any rearranging of the structure of the proposed government. To his surprise, he found that some of the earlier advocates of a bill of rights had turned their attention to matters they considered more pressing with regard to getting the new government on its feet.

In his speech to the House of June 8, 1789, on behalf of a bill of rights, Madison cites "the duty which I owe to myself and my constituents" as well as the "prudence" of adopting such a bill in a timely fashion. Madison argues that the adoption of a bill of rights would be a way of convincing those who had opposed the adoption of the Constitution that the founding document's advocates "were as sincerely devoted to liberty and a republican government" as their opponents. He duly notes that the new Union will not be complete until Rhode Island and North Carolina ratify and join. At the time, the position of the new government remained precarious. Madison expresses the fear that should Congress fail to act, the door might be opened "for a re-consideration of the whole structure of the government—for a re-consideration of the principles and the substance of the powers given."

In contrast to Federalists who argued that the introduction of a bill of rights might be dangerous, Madison claims that adoption presented the opportunity for "something to gain" and "nothing to lose." He appeals to Federalist allies in observing that he is not proposing anything "which I do not wish to see take place, as intrinsically proper in itself, or proper because it is wished for by a respectable number of my fellow citizens." He further observes that the primary opposition to the Constitution had come from those who "disliked it because it did not contain effectual provision against encroachments on particular rights."

Madison next introduces his proposed amendments. His initial suggestion for a preamble declaring that the government was instituted for the people and that they had "an indubitable, unalienable, and indefeasible right to reform or change their government" was eventually deleted. Perhaps more notably, Madison proposed inserting individual amendments within the constitutional text rather than appending them to the end of the document, as Congress eventually voted to do (following the suggestion of Roger Sherman of Connecticut).

After outlining most of the provisions that would eventually make their way into the adopted Bill of Rights, Madison addresses specific arguments against them. Recognizing the implicit weakness of "paper barriers," he acknowledges that some thought a listing of rights was "unnecessary, because the powers [of Congress] are enumerated, and it follows that all that are not granted by the constitution are retained." Yet Madison thinks it is especially important to guard against legislative excesses. Effectively admitting the truth behind some Antifederalist criticisms, he acknowledges that some powers granted to Congress might be extended under the "necessary and proper" clause to embrace improper objects; he specifically notes that Congress might consider issuing "general warrants" for such purposes. It was just as logical, then, to restrict the national government on such matters as it was to restrict the states. As to relying on state bills of rights alone, they would be quite variable, and firmer security of rights would be needed.

As to the Federalist argument that a bill of rights could prove dangerous if its enumeration of particular rights was thought to "disparage those rights which were not placed in that enumeration," Madison points to the positive recognition of such unenumerated rights in the provision that would eventually become the Ninth Amendment. Relying in part on arguments that Thomas Jefferson had made to him in personal correspondence, Madison further answers the argument that provisions of the Bill of Rights would be ineffective paper barriers by asserting that, once enumerated, the rights would be enforced by the courts: "Independent tribunals of justice will consider themselves in a peculiar manner the guardians of those rights; they will be an impenetrable bulwark against every assumption of power in the legislative or executive." Moreover, state legislatures would also use such rights as rallying points against national oppression.

Madison's speech led to effective action. Congress proposed the Bill of Rights on September 25, 1789, and on December 15, 1791, the requisite number of states had ratified ten of twelve proposed amendments. Also by then,

Rhode Island and North Carolina had joined the Union. Time would test the effectiveness of these provisions.

◆ Virginia Resolutions

Despite the transparency of the First Amendment's declaration that Congress should make "no law...abridging freedom of speech or the press," Congress did exactly this during America's undeclared war at sea with France during the administration of John Adams. Well before the end of George Washington's first term, the initial hopes harbored by some for national unity were shattered by the division of the elected populace into two political parties. Although he professed to be above parties, Washington generally sided with the Federalist Party, which coalesced around Alexander Hamilton and his plans for the broad exercise of national powers, including the establishment of a national bank. Jefferson and Madison, in turn, rallied the Democratic-Republican opposition, which feared that the national government was already becoming too powerful and advocated strict constitutional construction as an antidote.

In 1798 the Federalist-dominated Congress enacted a series of controversial laws, the most important of which were the Alien and Sedition Acts. The first made it more difficult for immigrants, many of whom were joining the Democratic-Republican Party, to become citizens. The second made it a crime to criticize the government or president of the United States. As Federalists began arresting critics, Democratic-Republican leaders had to formulate a strategy.

When he had introduced the Bill of Rights before Congress, Madison not only had observed that courts might enforce its provisions but also had indicated that the amendments might serve as a rallying point for state governments. With the courts dominated by Federalist judges, Madison found himself secretly authoring resolutions that would be adopted by the Virginia legislature on December 24, 1798, to challenge what he considered to be unconstitutional legislation. Jefferson, then vice president and also acting secretly, was offering similar help to the Kentucky legislature, which was drawing up its own resolutions.

Indeed, Madison hoped to rally other state legislatures against clear violations of the Constitution. In phrases that others would later stretch into doctrines of state nullification of federal laws and even of state secession, Madison calls upon other state legislatures "to interpose for arresting the progress of the evil." He opposes the attempts of other congressional leaders to enlarge federal powers "by forced constructions of the constitutional charter," which he fears are transforming the nation's republican government "into an absolute, or at best a mixed monarchy." Madison further argues that the Alien and Sedition Acts violate constitutional principles: They represent an exercise of powers not simply denied to the national government but furthermore positively forbidden by the First Amendment. Virginia must accordingly declare such laws unconstitutional, with the hope that other states would join.

Madison's appeals for state intervention failed. Other states refused to join the appeals of Virginia and Kentucky, and some specifically repudiated the doctrine of state opposition advocated by Madison and Jefferson in favor of reliance on judicial review. While losing this battle, however, Madison and Jefferson won the larger and more important war: In the presidential contest of 1800, Jefferson, as the Democratic-Republican presidential candidate, defeated the incumbent Federalist John Adams and subsequently pardoned everyone who had been convicted under the Sedition Act. Not until the decision in *New York Times v. Sullivan* (1964) did the Supreme Court announce the obvious fact that the constitutionality of the Sedition Act had been judged deficient in the court of history.

Madison served as secretary of state throughout Jefferson's two terms as president. Despite rumblings over the embargo of New England ports, the favorable Democratic-Republican electoral tide continued, and Madison succeeded Jefferson as president. Although Madison's presidency witnessed the burning of the nation's capital during the War of 1812 with Great Britain, Madison did not seek to criminalize domestic opposition to the war. When America ended the war with victory over the British in New Orleans, national frustration with Democratic-Republican policies turned to pride in republican freedoms.

◆ "Advice to My Country"

Madison left the presidency in 1817 and retired to his home in Orange County, Virginia, where he and his wife continued the entertaining for which they had become famous in Washington, D.C. As he aged, however, Madison was troubled by others' using his name and reputation for political causes that he detested. He was particularly troubled by the South Carolina senator John C. Calhoun's attempts to draw parallels between Madison's reference in the Virginia Resolutions to "interposition," which he had used to defend civil liberties, and Calhoun's own doctrines of nullification (by which a single state could declare a federal law to be null and void) and secession (by which such a state, or group of states, could secede from the Union). Calhoun was using these doctrines in efforts to perpetuate slavery and state sovereignty.

Before Madison died at his Virginia home in 1836, he was the last surviving attendee of the Constitutional Convention of 1787. Madison's final political words, believed to have been penned in October 1834, did not reach the public until they were published in the *National Intelligencer* in 1850. Madison had, in effect, left a political statement as a kind of last will and testament.

In the essay, titled "Advice to My Country," Madison appeals to his own forty years of service to the nation and his commitment "to the cause of its liberty," sharing sentiments "nearest to my heart and deepest in my convictions." These sentiments, clearly meant to appeal both to the head and the heart, were for the perpetuation of the "Union of the States." Madison ends with a reference to classical thought and to the Bible. The enemies to union, most especially the unnamed Calhoun and other southern embodiments, were to be regarded "as a Pandora with her box opened" or "as the Serpent creeping with his deadly wiles into Paradise."

Madison's posthumous appeals were inadequate to stem the rising tide of secessionist sentiment. The issue of slavery ultimately overshadowed the significance of the diversity of factions that Madison had identified in Federalist 10. With pro-slavery and antislavery forces so sharply divided, each feared domination by the other, and there were no groups to mediate between them.

In time, the victory of northern forces in the Civil War led to the adoption of the Thirteenth through Fifteenth Amendments. The Fourteenth Amendment recognized the citizenship of all persons born or naturalized within the United States. Later, through a process of selective incorporation, the Supreme Court interpreted this amendment as mandating the application of most provisions of the Bill of Rights to the states as well as to the national government. As one who had initially advocated a congressional veto of state legislation and who later advocated an amendment to restrain state infringements on the rights to conscience, Madison was arguably vindicated.

Impact and Legacy

Standing about five feet, four inches tall, Madison did not have the physical presence of some of the more heralded founders. Intellectually, however, he was on par with his friend and colleague Thomas Jefferson and his sometime rival Alexander Hamilton. The title of "father" of the Constitution, which scholars have often bestowed upon Madison, is overly generous, but he certainly emerged as the first among equals at the Constitutional Convention, and he thus deserves the credit—or blame—for this document as much as anyone. Scholars often identify the whole system of checks and balances at the national level as a "Madisonian" system, and modern advocates of parliamentary democracy who would combine legislative and executive powers thus sometimes fault him for real or perceived inefficiencies in the current system.

The Constitution's greatest failure was, without doubt, its inability to avert the Civil War. Madison arguably shares the blame, then, for not using the convention to address the issue of slavery, although he should also receive credit for having opposed the extension of the slave trade. At the Constitutional Convention, Madison recognized that the division between the slave and free states was greater than the differences between large and small states.

Madison's work on the Bill of Rights earned him the moniker of "father" of that document as well. His initial lukewarm sentiments toward such a bill made his labors on its behalf even more impressive. Many scholars believe that the promise of a bill of rights helped secure constitutional ratification; its inclusion surely further bolstered faith in that document and, in time, helped protect civil liberties.

Madison also played a major role in the establishment of political parties. Scholars still debate the degree to which he anticipated such parties when he wrote Federalist 10, but he certainly provided vigorous leadership once it was apparent that they were around to stay. Although Madison could be unbending on matters of principle, he often moderated the passions of fellow party members. As president, Madison tended to ride popular tides rather than direct them. He carried over weak cabinet officers from Jefferson's administration and found it difficult to dismiss disloyal or incompetent subordinates, although he did wisely recognize and use the administrative strengths of James Monroe, who alternately served as both secretary of state and secretary of war. Madison's central strength stemmed from his ability to accept personal criticism without seeking to silence his critics.

In retirement, Madison fought a largely losing battle to prevent the appropriation of his own words on behalf of individual liberties for the causes of nullification and secession. He should not perhaps be overly blamed for his inability to solve a problem that the nation was eventually obliged to secure through force of arms. His posthumously published records of the Constitutional Convention continue to be a source of information about the birth of the U.S. Constitution.

Key Sources

Gaillard Hunt edited a nine-volume collection called *The Writings of James Madison* (1900–1910). The University of Chicago began editing *The Papers of James Madison* in 1962 and published ten volumes between then and 1977. The project was continued under the auspices of the University of Virginia. The papers are arranged in four series: the Congressional Series, consisting of seventeen volumes and covering the period 1751–1801; the Secretary of State Series, covering the years 1801–1809, of which eight of a projected sixteen volumes have been published; the Presidential Series, of which five of a projected twelve volumes covering the period 1809–1817 have been published; and the Retirement Series, covering the period 1817–1836, of which the first volume will soon be published. Many of Madison's writings are available online through the Library of Congress's American Memory project (http://memory.loc.gov/ammem/collections/madison_papers/). Madison's most accessible writings remain the essays he contributed to *The Federalist*, which have been collected and edited by Clinton Rossiter (1961). Two single-volume guides to Madison's major writings are Marvin Meyers, ed., *The Mind of the Founder: Sources of the Political Thought of James Madison* (1973), and Jack N. Rakove, ed., *Writings: James Madison* (1999). Adrienne Koch has published Madison's records of the Constitutional Convention of 1787 as *Notes of Debates in the Federal Convention of 1787: Reported by James Madison* (1987). Another source is Max Farrand, ed., *The Records of the Federal Convention of 1787*, 4 vols. (1966).

Madison, James

"*Ecclesiastical establishments, instead of maintaining the purity and efficacy of Religion, have had a contrary operation… [producing] pride and indolence in the Clergy, ignorance and servility in the laity, in both, superstition, bigotry and persecution.*"

("Memorial and Remonstrance against Religious Assessments")

"*The great difficulty lies in the affair of Representation; and if this could be adjusted, all others would be surmountable.*"

(Speech on the New Jersey Plan to the Constitutional Convention)

"*The latent causes of faction are thus sown in the nature of man; and we see them everywhere brought into different degrees of activity, according to the different circumstances of civil society.*"

(Federalist 10)

"*I should be unwilling to see a door opened for a re-consideration of the whole structure of the government—for a re-consideration of the principles and the substance of the powers given.*"

(Speech to the House of Representatives Proposing a Bill of Rights)

"*In case of a deliberate, palpable, and dangerous exercise of other powers, not granted [to the federal government] by the said compact, the states who are parties thereto, have the right, and are in duty bound, to interpose for arresting the progress of the evil, and for maintaining within their respective limits, the authorities, rights and liberties appertaining to them.*"

(Virginia Resolutions)

"*The advice nearest to my heart and deepest in my convictions is that the Union of the States be cherished and perpetuated.*"

("Advice to My Country")

Further Reading

■ Books

Banning, Lance. *The Sacred Fire of Liberty: James Madison and the Founding of the Federal Republic*. Ithaca, N.Y.: Cornell University Press, 1995.

Brant, Irving. *James Madison*. 6 vols. Indianapolis: Bobbs-Merrill, 1941–1961.

Goldwin, Robert. *From Parchment to Power: How James Madison Used the Bill of Rights to Save the Constitution*. Washington, D.C.: AEI Press, 1997.

Kaminski, John P. *James Madison: Champion of Liberty and Justice*. Madison, Wis.: Parallel, 2006.

Ketcham, Ralph. *James Madison: A Biography*. Charlottesville: University Press of Virginia, 1990.

Questions for Further Study

1. Given the views expressed in his 1785 commentary on efforts to support Christian teachers from state funds, how would Madison have viewed the contemporary debate over the separation of church and state? Would he favor those who oppose the use of any Judeo-Christian imagery in a state-supported setting, such as Christmas displays at government buildings, or would he be inclined to support their religious opponents? What words of caution might he have for Christian activists seeking to reinstate school prayer and other religious observances, as well as for secular humanists attempting to remove all trace of Christianity from American public life?

2. Examine Madison's 1787 speech against the New Jersey Plan at the Constitutional Convention, particularly the details of the Virginia Plan he offered. How was his system, involving a two-part legislature and a three-part separation of powers, different from any that had existed before? What merits were there in Paterson's New Jersey Plan, which emphasized the power of the states? (Thanks to the "Connecticut Compromise," certain aspects of both plans found their way into the Constitution, and there are many valid arguments, which resound to the present day, for Paterson's emphasis on equal representation for the states.)

3. In the tenth installment of the *The Federalist*, Madison discusses factionalism, or the division of the political arena into various groups competing for specific interests. According to his view, what is the relationship between factionalism and freedom? How would the presence of factional interests ensure the stability of the proposed constitutional government and facilitate geographic expansion from the thirteen states of 1787 to the transcontinental nation America became? How would he have viewed modern totalitarian states such as North Korea, in which differing viewpoints are treated as crimes and the people supposedly support their government without question?

4. Discuss the process by which Madison, who was initially opposed to the idea of a constitutional bill of rights, ultimately become its leading proponent. What were the arguments for and against such an enumeration of rights and how does he address them in his 1789 speech to the House of Representatives? What was his position on amending the Constitution, and how might he have viewed amendments of later years? (Consider, for instance, the differing appraisals he might have had for the Thirteenth through Fifteenth and the Nineteenth Amendments, which guaranteed equal rights for all Americans, as opposed to the Sixteenth Amendment, which imposed an income tax, and the Eighteenth, prohibiting the manufacture and sale of liquor.)

5. How did Madison regard the use of his words, in the 1798 Virginia Resolutions and other writings, to support calls for nullification of federal laws and secession from the United States? Examine his actual wording in the 1798 resolutions as well as the warnings and disclaimers in his 1834 political testament. Compare them to opposing views presented by Senator John C. Calhoun. What underlying factors in Madison's own belief system and education might have informed his opposition to separatism? Think about the influence of the philosophical ideas of the eighteenth century, which emphasized reason, individuality, and an international perspective, with those of the nineteenth century, which were characterized by an emphasis on emotion, ethnicity, and nationalism.

Labunski, Richard. *James Madison and the Struggle for the Bill of Rights*. New York: Oxford University Press, 2006.

McCoy, Drew R. *The Last of the Fathers: James Madison and the Republican Legacy*. New York: Cambridge University Press, 1989.

Rakove, Jack. *James Madison and the Creation of the American Republic*, 3rd. ed. New York: Pearson/Longman, 2007.

Rosen, Gary. *American Compact: James Madison and the Problem of Founding*. Lawrence: University Press of Kansas, 1999.

Vile, John R., William D. Pederson, and Frank Williams, eds. *James Madison: Philosopher, Founder, and Statesman*. Athens: Ohio University Press, 2008.

—John R. Vile

"MEMORIAL AND REMONSTRANCE AGAINST RELIGIOUS ASSESSMENTS" (1785)

We the subscribers, citizens of the said Commonwealth, having taken into serious consideration, a Bill ... entitled "A Bill establishing a provision for Teachers of the Christian Religion," and conceiving that the same if finally armed with the sanctions of a law, will be a dangerous abuse of power ... remonstrate against the said Bill,

1. Because we hold it for a fundamental and undeniable truth, "that religion or the duty which we owe to our Creator and the manner of discharging it, can be directed only by reason and conviction, not by force or violence." The Religion then of every man must be left to the conviction and conscience of every man, and it is the right of every man to exercise it as these may dictate. This right is in its nature an unalienable right. It is unalienable, because the opinions of men, depending only on the evidence contemplated by their own minds cannot follow the dictates of other men: It is unalienable also, because what is here a right towards men, is a duty towards the Creator.... This duty is precedent, both in order of time and in degree of obligation, to the claims of Civil Society. Before any man can be considered as a member of Civil Society, he must be considered as a subject of the Governour of the Universe: And if a member of Civil Society, do it with a saving of his allegiance to the Universal Sovereign. We maintain therefore that in matters of Religion, no man's right is abridged by the institution of Civil Society and that Religion is wholly exempt from its cognizance.... No other rule exists, by which any question which may divide a Society, can be ultimately determined, but the will of the majority; but it is also true that the majority may trespass on the rights of the minority.

2. Because Religion be exempt from the authority of the Society at large, still less can it be subject to that of the Legislative Body. The latter are but the creatures and vicegerents of the former.... The preservation of a free Government requires not merely, that the metes and bounds which separate each department of power be invariably maintained; but more especially that neither of them be suffered to overleap the great Barrier which defends the rights of the people. The Rulers who are guilty of such an encroachment ... are Tyrants. The People who submit to it are ... slaves.

3. Because it is proper to take alarm at the first experiment on our liberties. We hold this prudent jealousy to be the first duty of Citizens .... Who does not see that the same authority which can establish Christianity, in exclusion of all other Religions, may establish with the same ease any particular sect of Christians, in exclusion of all other Sects? ...

4. Because the Bill violates the equality which ought to be the basis of every law, and which is more indispensible, in proportion as the validity or expediency of any law is more liable to be impeached. If "all men are by nature equally free and independent," all men are to be considered as entering into Society on equal conditions.... Above all are they to be considered as retaining an "equal title to the free exercise of Religion according to the dictates of Conscience." Whilst we assert for ourselves a freedom to embrace, to profess and to observe the Religion which we believe to be of divine origin, we cannot deny an equal freedom to those whose minds have not yet yielded to the evidence which has convinced us. If this freedom be abused, it is an offence against God, not against man: To God, therefore, not to man, must an account of it be rendered....

5. Because the Bill implies either that the Civil Magistrate is a competent Judge of Religious Truth; or that he may employ Religion as an engine of Civil policy. The first is an arrogant pretension ...: the second an unhallowed perversion of the means of salvation.

6. Because the establishment proposed by the Bill is not requisite for the support of the Christian Religion. To say that it is, is a contradiction to the Christian Religion.... Nay, it is a

contradiction in terms; for a Religion not invented by human policy, must have pre-existed and been supported, before it was established by human policy. It is moreover to weaken in those who profess this Religion a pious confidence in its innate excellence and the patronage of its Author; and to foster in those who still reject it, a suspicion that its friends are too conscious of its fallacies to trust it to its own merits.

7. Because experience witnesseth that eccelsiastical establishments, instead of maintaining the purity and efficacy of Religion, have had a contrary operation.... What have been its fruits? More or less in all places, pride and indolence in the Clergy, ignorance and servility in the laity, in both, superstition, bigotry and persecution....

8. Because the establishment in question is not necessary for the support of Civil Government.... If Religion be not within the cognizance of Civil Government how can its legal establishment be necessary to Civil Government? What influence in fact have ecclesiastical establishments had on Civil Society? In some instances they have been seen to erect a spiritual tyranny on the ruins of the Civil authority; in many instances they have been seen upholding the thrones of political tyranny: in no instance have they been seen the guardians of the liberties of the people. Rulers who wished to subvert the public liberty, may have found an established Clergy convenient auxiliaries. A just Government instituted to secure & perpetuate it needs them not....

9. Because the proposed establishment is a departure from the generous policy, which, offering an Asylum to the persecuted and oppressed of every Nation and Religion, promised a lustre to our country. Instead of holding forth an Asylum to the persecuted, it is itself a signal of persecution. It degrades from the equal rank of Citizens all those whose opinions in Religion do not bend to those of the Legislative authority. Distant as it may be in its present form from the Inquisition, it differs from it only in degree. The one is the first step, the other the last in the career of intolerance....

10. Because it will have a like tendency to banish our Citizens.... To superadd a fresh motive to emigration by revoking the liberty which they now enjoy, would be the same species of folly which has dishonoured and depopulated flourishing kingdoms.

11. Because it will destroy that moderation and harmony which the forbearance of our laws to intermeddle with Religion has produced among its several sects....

12. Because the policy of the Bill is adverse to the diffusion of the light of Christianity.... It at once discourages those who are strangers to the light of revelation from coming into the Region of it; and countenances by example the nations who continue in darkness, in shutting out those who might convey it to them....

13. Because attempts to enforce by legal sanctions, acts obnoxious to so great a proportion of Citizens, tend to enervate the laws in general, and to slacken the bands of Society.... The American Theatre has exhibited proofs, that equal and compleat liberty... sufficiently destroys its ["narrow and rigorous" prescribed beliefs] malignant influence on the health and prosperity of the State.

14. Because a measure of such singular magnitude and delicacy ought not to be imposed, without the clearest evidence that it is called for by a majority of citizens Because the policy of the Bill is adverse to the diffusion of the light of Christianity....

Glossary

"all men are by nature equally free and independent"	quotation from the Virginia Declaration of Rights (1776)

15. Because finally, "the equal right of every citizen to the free exercise of his Religion according to the dictates of conscience" is held by the same tenure with all our other rights.... Either then, we must say, that the Will of the Legislature...may sweep away all our fundamental rights; or, that they are bound to leave this particular right untouched and sacred: Either we must say, that they may controul the freedom of the press, may abolish the Trial by Jury, may swallow up the Executive and Judiciary Powers of the State; nay that they may despoil us of our very right of suffrage, and erect themselves into an independent and hereditary Assembly or, we must say, that they have no authority to enact into the law the Bill under consideration.

SPEECH ON THE NEW JERSEY PLAN TO THE CONSTITUTIONAL CONVENTION (1787)

Proceeding to the consideration of Mr. Patterson's plan, he stated the object of a proper plan to be twofold. 1. to preserve the Union. 2. to provide a Governmt. that will remedy the evils felt by the States both in their united and individual capacities. Examine Mr. P.s plan, & say whether it promises satisfaction in these respects.

1. Will it prevent those violations of the law of nations & of Treaties which if not prevented must involve us in the calamities of foreign wars? The tendency of the States to these violations has been manifested in sundry instances.... The existing Confederacy does not sufficiently provide against this evil. The proposed amendment to it does not supply the omission. It leaves the will of the States as uncontrouled as ever.

2. Will it prevent encroachments on the federal authority? A tendency to such encroachments has been sufficiently exemplified, among ourselves, as well in every other confederated republic.... The plan... besides omitting a controul over the States as a general defence of the federal prerogatives was particularly defective in two of its provisions. 1. Its ratification was not to be by the people at large, but by the *legislatures*. It could not therefore render the Acts of Congs. in pursuance of their powers, even legally *paramount* to the Acts of the States. 2. It gave to the federal Tribunal an appellate jurisdiction only—even in the criminal cases enumerated. The necessity of any such provision supposed a danger of undue acquittals in the State tribunals....

3. Will it prevent trespasses of the States on each other?... He instanced Acts of Virga. & Maryland which give a preference to their own Citizens in cases where the Citizens of other States are entitled to equality of privileges by the Articles of Confederation. He considered the emissions of paper money & other kindred measures as also aggressions.... The plan of Mr. Patterson, not giving even a negative on the acts of the States, left them as much at liberty as ever to execute their unrighteous projects agst. each other.

4. Will it secure the internal tranquility of the States themselves? The insurrections in Massts. admonished all the States of the danger to which they were exposed. Yet the plan of Mr. P. contained no provisions for supplying the defect of the Confederation on this point....

5. Will it secure a good internal legislation & administration to the particular States?... Under this head he enumerated and animadverted on 1. the multiplicity of the laws passed by the several States. 2. the mutability of their laws. 3. the injustice of them. 4. the impotence of them: observing that Mr. Patterson's plan contained no remedy for this dreadful class of evils, and could not therefore be received as an adequate provision for the exigences of the Community.

6. Will it secure the Union agst. the influence of foreign powers over its members? He pretended not to say that any such influence had yet been tried: but it was naturally to be expected that occasions would produce it....

7. He begged the smaller States which were most attached to Mr. Patterson's plan to consider the situation in which it would leave them.... They would continue to bear the whole expence of maintaining their Delegates in Congress....As far as it led the small States to forbear keeping up a representation, by which the public business was delayed, it was evidently a matter of common concern....

8. He begged them to consider the situation in which they would remain in case their pertinacious adherence to an inadmissible plan, should prevent the adoption of any plan....Let the Union of the States be dissolved, and one of two consequences must happen. Either the States must remain individually independent & sovereign; or two or more Confederacies must be formed among them. In the first

event would the small States be more secure agst. the ambition & power of their larger neighbours, than they would be under a general Government pervading with equal energy every part of the Empire, and having an equal interest in protecting every part agst. every other part? In the second, can the smaller expect that their larger neighbours would confederate with them on the principle of the present confederacy, which gives to each member, an equal suffrage; or that they would exact less severe concessions from the smaller States, than are proposed in the scheme of Mr. Randolph?

The great difficulty lies in the affair of Representation; and if this could be adjusted, all others would be surmountable.

Glossary

animadverted on	remarked critically about
exigences	emergencies, urgent situations
Mr. Patterson	William Patterson, jurist and signer of the Constitution
Mr. Randolph	Edmund Randolph, lawyer, governor of Virginia, U.S. secretary of state, and U.S. attorney general
supplying the defect	overcoming or correcting the defect

FEDERALIST 10 (1787)

AMONG the numerous advantages promised by a well constructed Union, none deserves to be more accurately developed than its tendency to break and control the violence of faction.... The instability, injustice, and confusion introduced into the public councils, have, in truth, been the mortal diseases under which popular governments have everywhere perished....Complaints are everywhere heard..., that our governments are too unstable, that the public good is disregarded in the conflicts of rival parties, and that measures are too often decided, not according to the rules of justice and the rights of the minor party, but by the superior force of an interested and overbearing majority....

By a faction, I understand a number of citizens, whether amounting to a majority or a minority of the whole, who are united and actuated by some common impulse of passion, or of interest, adverse to the rights of other citizens, or to the permanent and aggregate interests of the community.

There are two methods of curing the mischiefs of faction: the one, by removing its causes; the other, by controlling its effects.

There are again two methods of removing the causes of faction: the one, by destroying the liberty which is essential to its existence; the other, by giving to every citizen the same opinions, the same passions, and the same interests....

The first remedy...[is] worse than the disease. Liberty is to faction what air is to fire, an aliment without which it instantly expires. But it could not be less folly to abolish liberty, which is essential to political life, because it nourishes faction, than it would be to wish the annihilation of air, which is essential to animal life, because it imparts to fire its destructive agency.

The second expedient is as impracticable as the first would be unwise. As long as the reason of man continues fallible, and he is at liberty to exercise it, different opinions will be formed. As long as the connection subsists between his reason and his self-love, his opinions and his passions will have a reciprocal influence on each other; and the former will be objects to which the latter will attach themselves. The diversity in the faculties of men, from which the rights of property originate, is not less an insuperable obstacle to a uniformity of interests. The protection of these faculties is the first object of government.

From the protection of different and unequal faculties of acquiring property, the possession of different degrees and kinds of property immediately results; and from the influence of these...ensues a division of the society into different interests and parties.

The latent causes of faction are thus sown in the nature of man; and we see them everywhere brought into different degrees of activity....A zeal for different opinions concerning religion, concerning government, and many other points...; an attachment to different leaders...or to persons of other descriptions ... have, in turn, divided mankind into parties, inflamed them with mutual animosity, and rendered them much more disposed to vex and oppress each other than to co-operate for their common good. So strong is this propensity of mankind to fall into mutual animosities, that ... the most frivolous and fanciful distinctions have been sufficient to kindle their unfriendly passions and excite their most violent conflicts. But the most common and durable source of factions has been the various and unequal distribution of property. Those who hold and those who are without property have ever formed distinct interests in society. Those who are creditors, and those who are debtors, fall under a like discrimination. A landed interest, a manufacturing interest, a mercantile interest, a moneyed interest, with many lesser interests, grow up of necessity in civilized nations, and divide them into different classes, actuated by different sentiments and views. The regulation of these various and interfering interests forms the principal task of modern legislation....

It is in vain to say that enlightened statesmen will be able to adjust these clashing interests, and render them all subservient to the public good. Enlightened statesmen will not always be at the helm....

The inference to which we are brought is, that the *causes* of faction cannot be removed, and that relief is only to be sought in the means of controlling its *effects*.

If a faction consists of less than a majority, relief is supplied by the republican principle, which enables the majority to defeat its sinister views by regular vote. It may clog the administration, it may convulse the society; but it will be unable to execute and mask its violence under the forms of the Constitution. When a majority is included in a faction, the form of popular government...enables it to sacrifice to its ruling passion or interest both the public good and the rights of other citizens. To secure the public good and private rights against the danger of such a faction, and at the same time to preserve the spirit and the form of popular government, is then the great object to which our inquiries are directed....

By what means is this object attainable?...Either the existence of the same passion or interest in a majority at the same time must be prevented, or the majority, having such coexistent passion or interest, must be rendered, by their number and local situation, unable to concert and carry into effect schemes of oppression. If the impulse and the opportunity be suffered to coincide, we well know that neither moral nor religious motives can be relied on as an adequate control....

It may be concluded that a pure democracy, by which I mean a society consisting of a small number of citizens, who assemble and administer the government in person, can admit of no cure for the mischiefs of faction. A common passion or interest will ...be felt by a majority of the whole; a communication and concert result from the form of government itself; and there is nothing to check the inducements to sacrifice the weaker party or an obnoxious individual.... Theoretic politicians ... have erroneously supposed that by reducing mankind to a perfect equality in their political rights, they would, at the same time, be perfectly equalized and assimilated in their possessions, their opinions, and their passions.

A republic, by which I mean a government in which the scheme of representation takes place, opens a different prospect, and promises the cure for which we are seeking.... The two great points of difference between a democracy and a republic are: first, the delegation of the government, in the latter, to a small number of citizens elected by the rest; secondly, the greater number of citizens, and greater sphere of country, over which the latter may be extended.

The effect of the first difference is...to refine and enlarge the public views, by passing them through the medium of a chosen body of citizens, whose wisdom may best discern the true interest of their country, and whose patriotism and love of justice will be least likely to sacrifice it to temporary or partial considerations. Under such a regulation, it may well happen that the public voice, pronounced by the representatives of the people, will be more consonant to the public good than if pronounced by the people themselves, convened for the purpose....

The other point of difference is, the greater number of citizens and extent of territory which may be brought within the compass of republican than of democratic government; and it is this circumstance principally which renders factious combinations less to be dreaded in the former than in the latter. The smaller the society, the fewer probably will be the distinct parties and interests composing it; the fewer the distinct parties and interests, the more frequently will a majority be found of the same party; and the smaller the number of individuals composing a majority, and the smaller the compass within which they are placed, the more easily will they concert and execute their plans of oppression. Extend the sphere, and you take in a greater variety of parties and interests; you make it less probable that a majority of the whole will have a common motive to invade the rights of other citizens; or if such a common motive exists, it will be more difficult for all who feel it to discover their own strength, and to act in unison....

The influence of factious leaders may kindle a flame within their particular States, but will be unable to spread a general conflagration through the other States....A rage for paper money, for an abolition of debts, for an equal division of property, or for any other improper or wicked project, will be less apt to pervade the whole body of the Union than a particular member of it; in the same proportion as such a malady is more likely to taint a particular county or district, than an entire State.

In the extent and proper structure of the Union, therefore, we behold a republican remedy for the diseases most incident to republican government.

SPEECH TO THE HOUSE OF REPRESENTATIVES PROPOSING A BILL OF RIGHTS (1789)

If I thought I could fulfill the duty which I owe to myself and my constituents, to let the subject pass over in silence, I most certainly should not trespass upon the indulgence of this House. But I cannot do this.... This house is bound by every motive of prudence, not to let the first session pass over without proposing to the state legislatures some things to be incorporated into the constitution, as will render it as acceptable to the whole people of the United States, as it has been found acceptable to a majority of them. I wish ... that those who have been friendly to the adoption of this constitution, may have the opportunity of proving to those who were opposed to it, that they were as sincerely devoted to liberty and a republican government, as those who charged them with wishing the adoption of this constitution in order to lay the foundation of an aristocracy or depotism....

Notwithstanding the ratification of this system of government by eleven of the thirteen United States...; yet still there is a great number of our constituents who are dissatisfied with it....We ought not to disregard their inclination, but, on principles of amity and moderation, conform to their wishes, and expressly declare the great rights of mankind secured under this constitution. The acquiescence which our fellow citizens shew under the government, calls upon us for a like return of moderation....A stronger motive ... for our going into a consideration of the subject ... is to provide those securities for liberty which are required by a part of the community. I allude in a particular manner to those two states who have not thought fit to throw themselves into the bosom of the confederacy:...A re-union should take place as soon as possible....

If all power is subject to abuse,...then it is possible the abuse of the powers of the general government may be guarded against in a more secure manner than is now done....We have in this way something to gain, and, if we proceed with caution, nothing to lose; and in this case it is necessary to proceed with caution.... I should be unwilling to see a door opened for a re-consideration of the whole structure of the government—for a re-consideration of the principles and substance of the powers given ... because I doubt ... if we should be very likely to stop at that point which would be safe to the government itself: But I do wish to see a door opened to consider, so far as to incorpo-

rate those provisions for the security of rights, against which I believe no serious objection has been made.... I will not propose a single alteration which I do not wish to see take place, as intrinsically proper in itself, or proper because it is wished for by a respectable number of my fellow citizens....

There have been objections of various kinds made against the constitution.... I believe that the great mass of the people who opposed it, disliked it because it did not contain effectual provision against encroachments on particular rights, and those safeguards which they have been long accustomed to have interposed between them and the magistrate who exercised the sovereign power....

The first of these amendments, relates to what may be called a bill of rights. I will own that I never considered this provision so essential to the federal constitution, as to make it improper to ratify it, until such an amendment was added; at the same time, I always conceived ... such a provision was neither improper nor altogether useless. I am aware, that a great number of the most respectable friends to the government and champions for republican liberty, have thought such a provision, not only unnecessary, but even improper...[or] dangerous....I acknowledge the ingenuity of those arguments which were drawn against the constitution, by a comparison with the policy of Great-Britain....

But altho' the case may be widely different, and it may not be thought necessary to provide limits for the legislative power in that country, yet a different opinion prevails in the United States. The people of many states, have thought it necessary to raise barriers against power in all forms and departments of government, and ... if once bills of rights are established in all the states as well as the federal constitution, we shall find that ... upon the whole, they will have a salutary tendency....

But whatever may be [the] form which the several states have adopted in making declarations in favor of particular rights, the great object in view is to limit and qualify the powers of government, by excepting out of the grant of power those cases in which the government ought not to act, or to act only in a particular mode....

In our government it is, perhaps, less necessary to guard against the abuse in the executive department than any other; because it is not the stronger branch of the system, but the weaker: It therefore must be levelled against the legislative, for it is the most powerful, and most likely to be abused, because it is under the least controul; hence, so far as a declaration of rights can tend to prevent the exercise of undue power, it cannot be doubted but such declaration is proper....In a government modified like this of the United States, the great danger lies rather in the abuse of the community than in the legislative body. The prescriptions in favor of liberty, ought to be levelled against that quarter where the greatest danger lies, namely, that which possesses the highest prerogative of power: But this [is]...found...in the body of the people, operating by the majority against the minority.

It may be thought all paper barriers against the power of the community are too weak to be worthy of attention.... They are not so strong as to satisfy gentlemen of every description...yet, as they have a tendency to impress some degree of respect for them, to establish the public opinion in their favor, and rouse the attention of the whole community, it may be one means to controul the majority from those acts to which they might be otherwise inclined.

It has been said [of]...a bill of rights...that they are unnecessary articles of a republican government, upon the presumption that the people have those rights in their own hands, and that is the proper place for them to rest. It would be a sufficient answer to say that this objection lies against such provisions under the state governments as well as under the general government; and...few gentlemen ...are inclined to push their theory so far as to say that a declaration of rights in those cases is either ineffectual or improper.

It has been said that in the federal government they are unnecessary, because the powers are enumerated, and it follows that all that are not granted by the constitution are retained: that the constitution is a bill of powers, the great residuum being the rights of the people; and therefore a bill of rights cannot be so necessary as if the residuum was thrown into the hands of the government.... These arguments are not...conclusive to the extent which

has been supposed. It is true the powers of the general government are...directed to particular objects; but even if government keeps within those limits, it has certain discretionary powers with respect to the means, which may admit of abuse to a certain extent ...; because in the constitution of the United States there is a clause granting to Congress the power to make all laws which shall be necessary and proper for carrying into execution all the powers vested in the government of the United States.... Now, may not laws be considered necessary and proper by Congress...to accomplish those special purposes which they may have in contemplation, which laws in themselves are neither necessary or proper?... The general government has a right to pass all laws which shall be necessary to collect its revenue; the means for enforcing the collection are within the direction of the legislature: may not general warrants be considered necessary for this purpose?... If there was reason for restraining the state governments from exercising this power, there is like reason for restraining the federal government....

It has been objected also against a bill of rights, that, by enumerating particular exceptions to the grant of power, it would disparage those rights which were not placed in that enumeration, and it might follow by implication, that those rights which were not singled out, were intended to be assigned into the hands of the general government, and were consequently insecure. This is one of the most plausible arguments I have ever heard urged against the admission of a bill of rights into this system; but, I conceive, that may be guarded against. I have attempted it....

It has been said, that it is necessary to load the constitution with this provision, because it was not found effectual in the constitution of the particular states.... There are a few particular states in which some of the most valuable articles have not, at one time or other, been violated; but does it not follow but they may have ... a salutary effect against the abuse of power. If they are incorporated into the constitution, independent tribunals of justice will consider themselves in a peculiar manner the guardians of those rights; they will be an impenetrable bulwark

Glossary

magistrate	executive, in this case, the president
shew	antique spelling of "show"
two states	Rhode Island and North Carolina

against every assumption of power in the legislative or executive; they will be naturally led to resist every encroachment upon rights expressly stipulated for in the constitution by the declaration of rights. Beside this security...the state legislatures will jealously and closely watch the operation of this government, and be able to resist with more effect every assumption of power than any other power on earth can do.

VIRGINIA RESOLUTIONS (1798)

RESOLVED, That the General Assembly of Virginia, doth unequivocally express a firm resolution to maintain and defend the Constitution of the United States, and the Constitution of this State, against every aggression either foreign or domestic, and that they will support the government of the United States in all measures warranted by the former.

That this assembly most solemnly declares a warm attachment to the Union of the States....

That this Assembly doth ... declare, that it views the powers of the federal government, as resulting from the compact, to which the states are parties; as limited by the plain sense and intention of the instrument constituting that compact; as no further valid than they are authorized by the grants enumerated in that compact; and that in case of a deliberate, palpable, and dangerous exercise of other powers, not granted by the said compact, the states who are parties thereto, have the right ... to interpose for arresting the progress of the evil, and for maintaining within their respective limits, the authorities, rights and liberties appertaining to them.

That the General Assembly doth also express its deep regret, that a spirit has in sundry instances, been manifested by the federal government, to enlarge its powers by forced constructions of the constitutional charter which defines them; and that implications have appeared of a design to expound certain general phrases ... so as to destroy the meaning and effect, of the particular enumeration which necessarily explains and limits the general phrases; and so as to consolidate the states by degrees, into one sovereignty, the obvious tendency and inevitable consequence of which would be, to transform the present republican system of the United States, into an absolute, or at best a mixed monarchy.

That the General Assembly doth particularly protest against the palpable and alarming infractions of the Constitution, in ... the "Alien and Sedition Acts"...; the first of which exercises a power no where delegated to the federal government ... and the other of which acts, exercises in like manner, a power not delegated by the constitution, but on the contrary, expressly and positively forbidden by one of the amendments ... which more than any other, ought to produce universal alarm, because it is levelled against that right of freely examining public characters and measures, and of free communication among the people thereon, which has ever been justly deemed, the only effectual guardian of every other right.

That this state having by its Convention, which ratified the federal Constitution, expressly declared, that among other essential rights, "the Liberty of Conscience and of the Press cannot be cancelled, abridged, restrained, or modified by any authority of the United States," and ... having with other states, recommended an amendment for that purpose, which amendment was, in due time, annexed to the Constitution it would mark a reproachful inconsistency ... if an indifference were now shown to the most palpable violation of one of the rights thus declared and secured....

That the good people of this commonwealth ... continuing to feel, the most sincere affection for their brethren of the other states; the truest anxiety for establishing and perpetuating the union of all; and the most scrupulous fidelity to that constitution ...; the General Assembly doth solemnly appeal to the like dispositions of the other states, in confidence that they will concur ... in declaring ... that the acts aforesaid, are unconstitutional; and that the necessary and proper measures will be taken by each, for co-operating ... in maintaining the Authorities, Rights, and Liberties, referred to the States respectively, or to the people.

Glossary

commonwealth	state; the official designation of Virginia, Massachusetts, Kentucky, and Pennsylvania

"ADVICE TO MY COUNTRY" (1834)

As this advice, if it ever see the light, will not do it till I am no more, it may be considered as issuing from the tomb, where truth alone can be respected, and the happiness of man alone consulted. It will be entitled therefore to whatever weight can be derived from good intentions, and from the experience of one who has served his country in various stations through a period of forty years, who espoused in his youth and adhered through his life to the cause of its liberty, and who has borne a part in most of the great transactions which will constitute epochs of its destiny.

The advice nearest to my heart and deepest in my convictions is that the Union of the States be cherished and perpetuated. Let the open enemy to it be regarded as a Pandora with her box opened; and the disguised one, as the Serpent creeping with his deadly wiles into Paradise.

Glossary

Pandora	in the mythology of ancient Greece, the first woman—famous for opening a jar, referred to later as Pandora's box, freeing all the evils of humankind

Malcolm X (AP/Wide World Photos)

MALCOLM X

1925–1965

Civil Rights Activist

Featured Documents
◆ **"Message to the Grass Roots" (1963)**
◆ **"The Ballot or the Bullet" Speech (1964)**

Overview

Malcolm X was born Malcolm Little on May 19, 1925, in Omaha, Nebraska. The family soon moved to Lansing, Michigan, where the six-year-old Malcolm's father was killed in 1931—possibly murdered by members of the Black Legion, a local Ku Klux Klan group. A good student, Malcolm nevertheless got into trouble early. He admired the energy and intelligence of criminals and soon became involved with the numbers racket and drugs. It did not help that his mother was committed to a mental institution and that having lost both parents he was placed in foster care. Living with his sister failed to provide enough stability for the unruly teenager, and at the age of twenty-one he was sent to prison for burglary, larceny, breaking and entering, and carrying a firearm.

Prison life provided Malcolm with the time to reflect on his criminal behavior and absorb the teachings of the Nation of Islam, a black nationalist and religious organization whose members are often called Black Muslims. During Malcolm X's life, the Nation of Islam proclaimed a belief in Allah as the supreme being and followed a theology that emphasized the freedom of the black man and the need to establish a self-governing and, if necessary, separate black nation. Malcolm came to see much of his law-breaking as a response to a repressive white society. At the same time, however, he did not absolve himself of responsibility for his actions. On the contrary, his fellow Black Muslim prisoners demanded that he take control of his own life rather than blame his plight on others. Only when Malcolm reformed himself, they counseled, could he set out to reform the world. Malcolm left prison with a new name, Malcolm X, jettisoning the last name he associated with his race's slave heritage. He became a preacher for the Nation of Islam, which called upon African Americans to develop their own independence and not base their sense of self-worth on the dictates of the white power structure.

A powerful public speaker, Malcolm X became the most well-known representative of the Nation of Islam. As his public speeches show, however, his appeal was not merely to audiences of Black Muslims or those who might wish to convert to the Nation of Islam but to African Americans of all creeds. Malcolm X presented himself as an alternative to the civil rights movement led by Martin Luther King, Jr., and other ministers steeped in the Christian tradition. While Malcolm X initially scorned the tactics of nonviolence and advocated self-defense in a revolutionary cause, at the same time—as is evident in his speech "The Ballot or the Bullet"—he was seeking ways to unite all African Americans in recognizing their oppression and urge them to create their own strong, self-governing communities.

As Malcolm X's understanding of the racial divide in America deepened, his last speeches—especially those in the last year of his life—exemplify a move away from sectarian beliefs. He sought new ways of binding the black community together and finding power at the grassroots level. His hope was that his views might triumph without the need for the bloody revolutions he had previously extolled as the only way to achieve freedom and dignity. Although his rhetoric against whites could seem quite harsh, he could be hard on the black community and its leaders as well. His speeches bristle with dynamism that make change seem not merely desirable but inevitable. Not afraid to dramatize the consequences of racial strife, Malcolm X also called for African Americans to scrutinize their own collaboration in second-class citizenship. By noting just how far America had fallen short of its democratic ideals, he also drew the support of many white critics of society. Indeed, his appeal enlarged the audience for black leaders even as he was redefining the conception of black leadership. This is why his speeches do not hesitate to attack those prominent black public figures who seem, in his view, to act in league with white leaders rather than develop an independent politics.

That Malcolm X eventually broke free from Elijah Muhammad, who had assumed leadership of the Nation of Islam in 1931, can be seen as an extension of his quest to develop a style of leadership entirely his own. His death on February 21, 1965, was viewed, in part, as the result of his unwillingness to submit to Elijah Muhammad's authority. (Two of his three assassins were Black Muslims.) But his death also confirmed his central position as a new kind of leader, seeking unity for his people in ways that conformed neither to the black separatist movement associated with the Nation of Islam nor to the integrationist movement led by King. Malcolm X's death cut short his effort to find a third way to freedom and equality, but his speeches give testimony to his relentless effort to speak truth to empower and galvanize people from the ground up.

Explanation and Analysis of Documents

Malcolm X gained great fame in his own lifetime largely as the result of his provocative—and some would say

Time Line

1925
- **May 19**
Malcolm Little is born in Omaha, Nebraska.

1931
- Malcolm's father dies, rumored to be a victim of a white supremacist group.

1946
- **February 27**
Malcolm begins serving an eight-year prison sentence.

1948
- In prison Malcolm learns about the teachings of Elijah Muhammad and the Black Muslims and changes his name to Malcolm X.

1952
- **August 7**
Malcolm X is released from prison early and begins attending Nation of Islam meetings in Detroit; he becomes a minister in 1953.

1959–1960
- Malcolm X travels to the Middle East as an ambassador for the Nation of Islam.

1963
- **November 10**
Malcolm X delivers "Message to the Grass Roots" to an audience in Detroit, Michigan.

1964
- Malcolm X begins collaborating with the American author Alex Haley on an autobiography.

- **March–April**
Malcolm X splits from the Nation of Islam and travels to Mecca, Saudi Arabia, Islam's holiest site.

- **April 12**
Malcolm X delivers "The Ballot or the Bullet" speech in Detroit, Michigan.

---

inflammatory—speeches. He created the persona of an angry black man, critical of mainstream civil rights leaders such as Martin Luther King, Jr. Malcolm X rejected the doctrine of nonviolence and the Christian tradition that inspired King and many of his followers. It seemed especially sinister to some that he advocated African American self-defense "by any means necessary" (a term he used in several speeches). It did not seem to be the case that he was preaching revolution, however, because as a minister of the Nation of Islam, he was committed to supporting a program of self-help within the African American community. Unlike radical groups such as the Black Panthers, Black Muslims did not engage in confrontations with the police; on the contrary, Black Muslims believed that African Americans should police themselves. But the Nation of Islam rejected the drive for integration and the gradual acceptance of African Americans into a white-dominated society.

Malcolm X, however, spoke with such eloquence and force that he aroused the sympathies of many outside the Black Muslim movement. Indeed, he became such a prominent figure in his own right that tensions developed between him and the Nation of Islam's leader, Elijah Muhammad, whom Malcolm came to know as a fallible man who engaged in adultery with his secretaries. For his part, Elijah Muhammad became increasingly disturbed with Malcolm X's controversial public statements and his links to other black nationalist groups. Gradually, in the last year of his life, Malcolm X not only became disillusioned with Elijah Muhammad but also began to modify the doctrine of black separatism, recognizing, for example, that Islam embraced peoples of varying colors and world outlooks. He seemed, in other words, to be moving toward some of King's positions even as King himself became more militant in opposing the U.S. power structure, especially in its involvement in the Vietnam War. It was out of this turbulent political atmosphere of dissension and protest that Malcolm X delivered his influential speeches.

◆ "Message to the Grass Roots"

Malcolm X's "Message to the Grass Roots" was delivered in Detroit in a Christian church and addressed to an audience of African Americans, many of whom came to hear him reflect on the results of the nonviolent movement dedicated to secure the freedom and equality of his people. He was famous for his direct, blunt statements: "America's problem is us," he tells his audience, emphasizing that African Americans cannot begin to act properly until they confront racism by recognizing that to be black is to be rejected in the United States. This uncompromising view is what led him to reject his last name, calling it a slave name because it was a name forced upon his family by whites, just as the word *Negro*, in his view, was a white invention. What hinders African Americans, he reiterates, is their blackness. Any other differences between blacks and blacks or blacks and whites hardly matter. Life for African Americans would not get better, he implies, until they came to realize that their blackness is their bond, which should cause them to unite.

Blacks did not like to acknowledge their history as slaves, he argues, and yet the crucial fact is that they were brought to this country in bondage by its very founders. (There were, in fact, no slaves on the *Mayflower* and only a handful of African American servants through the first decades of the 1600s. But he was perhaps making a broader point that slavery existed at the beginning of settlement in North America.) Slavery, in other words, was built into the origins of the nation. His uncompromising conclusion was that the white man is the enemy. Only time would tell whether he was wrong, he concedes. What he knew, however, was history, which suggested that only when people of color unite could they solve their problems—as they attempted to do at the Bandung Conference, a 1955 meeting of delegates from twenty-nine Asian and African states in Bandung, Indonesia, to discuss the effects of colonialism and cold war tensions on the East. But this unity was achieved only by excluding whites from participating. No matter their places of origin, all those at the Bandung Conference understood that white Europeans had colonized them and that whites had always been a factor in destroying the unity of people of color. Until the "dark man" realized that he belonged to a family of dark peoples oppressed by whites, the dark man would never be free.

What is more, Malcolm X points out in this speech that freedom would probably have to be obtained through revolution, which meant violence, as it did in the American, French, and Russian revolutions. Blacks would have to bleed for their freedom instead of bleeding for the white man's wars. Black churches, he concludes, were being bombed in the South, and yet blacks were afraid to shed blood in their own cause.

Like so many of Malcolm X's speeches, this one challenges his audience to take action by critically examining the black community's failings. African Americans have as much right to defend themselves as other nations have, including the new (at that time) African states. Countries such as Kenya and Algeria obtained their independence through violent revolution. Malcolm X argues that they are a model for black militancy. Rather than accept the terms and ideology of their colonial oppressors, these new African countries were determined to establish their own governments. African Americans should expect to do nothing less.

From this militant position, Malcolm goes on to reject the civil rights revolution. He implies that its goals are too modest, for it is not good enough to be able to coexist on the same level with whites in public spaces. Without land and control over their own lives in the form of their own government, blacks would never be self-determining. Thus he equates "Negro" with a white-dominated sense of "revolution," one that does not challenge the white power structure or result in fundamental freedoms for blacks. Whites knew that blacks would never be free if they did not follow the worldwide revolutions occurring in Asia and Latin America. Malcolm X contends that blacks wanted exactly what whites wanted when making revolutions: a sense of nationality and unity.

Time Line

1964

■ **June 28**
Malcolm X founds the Organization of Afro-American Unity, a civil rights group.

1965

■ **February 14**
Malcolm X's house is firebombed.

■ **February 21**
Malcolm X is assassinated while speaking at the Audubon Ballroom in Harlem.

But as much as Malcolm X attacked white supremacy, he also attacked traditional black civil rights leaders—those who counseled people not to become involved in black nationalism. These conventional leaders were afraid of revolution and were attempting to instill the same fears in Malcolm X's audience. In effect, in this speech he accuses the mainstream civil rights leadership of being house slaves, those members of the slave community who were closest to whites and imbibed white values. He refers to these black collaborators with the white power structure as "Uncle Toms," the character in Harriet Beecher Stowe's 1852 antislavery novel *Uncle Tom's Cabin* whose name became synonymous with black subservience to whites.

As a Black Muslim, Malcolm X preached that Christianity was a slave religion emphasizing suffering and the need to bleed rather than rebel. Christian black civil rights leaders, he says, have capitulated to whites, preaching that it is virtuous to turn the other cheek. Instead, Malcolm X argues for the superiority of the Muslim religion, which teaches self-defense and striking out for one's rights. Those black Christian preachers who taught nonviolence were traitors to the black cause. Indeed, they have been groomed by whites to stifle the strivings of the black community just as slave masters housed and indoctrinated their house slaves into the values of white supremacy. Malcolm X suggests that such leaders actually prided themselves on their influence with white people. In effect, they were the dupes of whites.

At this point, Malcolm engages in a full assault on the history of white oppression and the black collaboration in slavery as well as the role Christianity has played in subduing African Americans. By calling his audience "sheep," he also extends blame to blacks as a whole. They have not fought for their freedom and independence. Even Martin Luther King, Jr., is treated as a failure with a bankrupt organization, who did not succeed as a leader in areas of the South where he campaigned for desegregation. Other civil rights leaders are seen as fallen idols in Malcolm X's scornful analysis. Only when violence and the threat of more violence caught the attention of President John F. Kennedy did the white power structure begin to take the black revolution seriously. But as usual, that revolution was co-opted, infiltrated by several white leaders, so that in the end revolutionary action became impossible.

Malcolm X explains this adulterating of black revolution in a vivid simile:

> It's just like when you've got some coffee that's too black, which means it's too strong. What you do? You integrate it with cream; you make it weak. If you pour too much cream in, you won't even know you ever had coffee. It used to be hot, it becomes cool. It used to be strong, it becomes weak. It used to wake you up, now it'll put you to sleep. This is what they did with the march on Washington.

Malcolm X concludes by suggesting that the 1963 March on Washington that King led was nothing more than a spectacle, a show, a movie with black leaders ultimately playing the part the "white power structure" had organized for them. He questions the black leadership's level of commitment, and he challenges his audience to make history the only way it can be made: by exercising their power at the grass roots.

◆ "The Ballot or the Bullet" Speech

Much was made of Malcolm X's adherence to the theology of the Nation of Islam. Under the leadership of Elijah Muhammad, the Black Muslims developed a religion that cast the white race as an evil oppressor of the black man. Integration of the races was deemed impossible, and therefore collaboration with whites was rejected because it could only abet the white power structure. The Nation of Islam, a separatist organization, was spurned by many—even within the black community—as outside the mainstream of American life and inimical to the dreams and ambitions of African Americans. It was in this context that Malcolm X made his appeal to black congregations. He did not minimize the theological differences between Black Muslims and Christian black leaders, but as in this speech, given at the Cory Methodist Church in Cleveland, Ohio, and sponsored by the Congress on Racial Equality, he emphasized that as people of color African Americans could unite around a common experience of subjugation stemming from slavery. In other words, whatever might divide blacks in terms of religion and politics, the black nationalist movement held a set of principles that every African American could adopt.

Above all, black nationalism meant self-government—taking control of the black community's resources. Malcolm X believed that a new era in African American experience had emerged, so that the black community would no longer defer to white leadership or to "Negro" leaders working on behalf of the white power structure. The very term *Negro* was, in his view, a white invention, meant to segregate and dehumanize black people. In effect, he accuses the previous generation of black leaders of duplicity, seeming to act on behalf of African Americans while in fact serving only the interests of the dominant Caucasian culture.

Although Malcolm X often spoke in favor of bloody revolution, in this speech he clearly suggests that by banding together and understanding how the black community has heretofore served the interests of the white master class, African Americans could ultimately achieve independence and equality through peaceful means (the ballot). But this goal could be achieved only through reeducation and control over both the politics and the economy of black communities. He then describes a black community with businesses owned by others who did not live in the community. This paucity of black owners has led to powerlessness and poverty. Malcolm X insists that blacks have to own their means of production. This is what Black Muslims had done in their own communities, creating businesses that were black owned, that served the black community exclusively, and that invested the Nation of Islam's profits back into the community.

All African Americans were subject to the same fate: a government that had failed them. This failure was more than a political and economic catastrophe. When he speaks here of "social degradation," he is describing a people who have been debased and deprived of their self-respect. They could regain a sense of self-worth only by asserting authority over their own communities. To do anything less would be to ignore reality, to be "out of your mind." When he tells his audience "you do too much singing," he is suggesting that it is time for action, not just words. African Americans have been passive. The new black hero at the time was Cassius Clay, soon to take the name Muhammad Ali, a convert to the Nation of Islam. Like Clay, the African American community, Malcolm X says, should start "swinging," that is, behave aggressively. Malcolm's direct and even harsh words are a wake-up call, demanding that his listeners understand the failure of black leaders and the black community's collaboration in its own oppression. Until that complicity in evil is understood and acknowledged, the African American community could not progress toward liberty.

Malcolm X then takes direct aim at the philosophy and program of nonviolence led by Martin Luther King, Jr., a movement that urges blacks to "sit in" and sit down at restaurants and other public establishments that forbid blacks to enter or be served. These demonstrations in favor of integration, which often lead to arrests and police beatings of black demonstrators, are ineffective in Malcolm X's opinion. Black Muslims are a small minority within the black Christian community, but black nationalism, Malcolm X argues, is a self-help philosophy that all blacks can share. This is what he means by saying they all should be "thinking black." To think black means to hold a view of the common interests of African Americans in controlling the economy and culture of their own communities. So self-evident was the need for black nationalism that Malcolm X states that he feels sorry for those who cannot accept it. To him the absence of a black nationalist mentality meant that his people would continue to be oppressed. A nonviolent philosophy of passive resistance, of sitting down, was to him a form of emasculation, depriving black men of their manhood and the black nation of its energy and conviction.

Referring to black independence movements around the world, Malcolm X notes that none have been achieved through nonviolent resistance, by singing or sitting in.

African Americans were no different, in his view, from other colonial peoples. To be called a second-class citizen in America was the equivalent of being a colonial subject. The year 1964 was pivotal—a year in which blacks needed to make a choice: the ballot or the bullet. Even though he suggests in this speech and in earlier public talks that violence seemed to be the only way to attain independence, freedom, and equality, this speech marks a departure in indicating that blacks might yet achieve autonomy and self-respect by exercising the ballot (the vote). This sudden and seemingly bold departure from his previous argument in favor of revolution is, in fact, signaled near the beginning of the speech when he suggests that the consciousness of the African American community has been altered and that a process of reeducation is under way. Frustration in the black community was so profound and had built to such a peak that an explosion was ready to erupt with the force of an atomic bomb. This allusion to the cold war arms race—and to a period of history in which it seemed possible that America and the Soviet Union might blow each other up with their missiles and even destroy the world—was Malcolm X's bid to put black nationalism on a par with the major concern of his time.

At the same time, Malcolm X attacks King's historic March on Washington. It was not the ethic of nonviolence that would prevail but rather the aroused militancy of a new generation of blacks with a combustible energy that would ignite the nation if its force were not reflected in a new government obtainable through the ballot. To this new generation, it did not matter that whites outnumbered them or that they were part of the world's most powerful nation, which could crush them. This new generation of black militants could not be stopped any more than the white colonists who had attacked the British Empire could have been stopped. True revolutionaries, he says, are not daunted by the odds against them. Malcolm X concludes that this new generation understood that blacks have experienced not the American dream but the American "nightmare," and this is why the old generation of black leaders and their white liberal masters could no longer take the African American community for granted.

Malcolm X argues that if blacks united and used their political power to elect the next president and made him accountable to their support, then the ballot, not the bullet, might ultimately benefit black people. But they had to realize that they could not count on northern Democrats, who had collaborated with southern Democrats in oppressing African Americans. He cautions that these same politicians had to realize that their old tactics would not work: They could not simply placate blacks. Whites had to understand that worldwide they were outnumbered by people of color and that acknowledging and enforcing equal rights for black people was mandatory. If African Americans united around the black nationalist agenda, the white strategy to divide and conquer the black community would not succeed. For his part, Malcolm X pledges to collaborate with every organization regardless of its religious and political principles so long as it works to "eliminate the political, the economic, and the social evils that confront all of our people."

Malcolm X's New York City home is seen partially damaged after two molotov cocktails sparked a flash fire, on February 14, 1965. (AP/Wide World Photos)

Impact and Legacy

Part of Malcolm X's impact had to do with the way he stood apart from other African American leaders. Not only did he reject the nonviolent ways of Martin Luther King, Jr., and his followers—a civil rights movement that worked toward the gradual integration of African Americans into American society—but he also took issue with black churches and the role Christianity played in subduing the legitimate aspirations of African Americans. Still, Malcolm outgrew his role as Black Muslim dissenter, rejecting as well the black separatism of the Nation of Islam. This aspect of his evolution is reflected not so much in his public speeches as in his autobiography, in which he treats his life as a political and spiritual pilgrimage that ultimately led him to question his more radical views about revolution and the white power structure.

Malcolm X was no less strident in his determination to secure freedom and independence for African Americans. He became emblematic of the outspoken black leader who transcended the politics of black nationalism in order to become a symbol himself of individualism—that is, of the individual's role in interpreting and making history. Historically, however, Malcolm X also represents one extreme of black protest. During much of his life he was viewed as the diametrical opposite of King. But Malcolm X's growth as a thinker and public leader led him to adopt certain positions that, in part, converged with King's own critique of American culture. Above all, the spirit of self-criticism that Malcolm X brought to the discussion of African American lives makes him a figure who rises above the particular views he

"*America's problem is us…. The only reason she has a problem is she doesn't want us here.*"

("Message to the Grass Roots")

"*You haven't got a revolution that doesn't involve bloodshed. And you're afraid to bleed. I said, you're afraid to bleed.*"

("Message to the Grass Roots")

"*This is the way it is with the white man in America. He's a wolf and you're sheep.*"

("Message to the Grass Roots")

"*Today it's time to stop singing and start swinging. You can't sing up on freedom, but you can swing up on some freedom.*"

("The Ballot or the Bullet" Speech)

"*And 1964 looks like it might be the year of the ballot or the bullet.*"

("The Ballot or the Bullet" Speech)

"*We don't see any American dream; we've experienced only the American nightmare.*"

("The Ballot or the Bullet" Speech)

"*But when you go to a church and you see the pastor of that church with a philosophy and a program that's designed to bring black people together and elevate black people—join that church…. If you see where the NAACP is preaching and practicing that which is designed to make Black Nationalism materialize—join the NAACP. Join any kind of organization—civic, religious, fraternal, political, or otherwise that's based on lifting the black man up and making him master of his own community.*"

("The Ballot or the Bullet" Speech)

expressed in his speeches and makes him a symbol of the searching, independent mind.

Key Sources

The Schomberg Center for Research in Black Culture of the New York Public Library holds an extensive collection of Malcolm X's diaries, letters, and other materials. The collection also includes handwritten radio addresses, photographs, and other manuscripts. Malcolm X wrote his autobiography, *The Autobiography of Malcolm X*, with Alex Haley (1965). George Breitman edited *Malcolm X Speaks: Selected Speeches and Statements* (1965) and *Malcolm X: By Any Means Necessary* (2000), a collection of various statements, letters, and interviews. Speeches from the last two years of his life are in *Malcolm X: The Last Speeches*, edited by Bruce Perry (1989).

Questions for Further Study

1. In the eyes of supporters and detractors alike Malcolm X did not lack authenticity; in other words, he knew from experience about the issues of which he spoke. Having lost his father to murderers and his mother to mental health problems, Malcolm Little grew up in foster homes and might well have turned into a violent killer; instead, he became a great leader. How did the painful aspects of his background (some brought on him by others and some of his own doing) affect his development as a man?

2. In his "Message to the Grass Roots," Malcolm X discusses the phenomenon of "the house negro vs. the field negro," whereby white slave owners divided African Americans into two conflicting groups. Discuss Malcolm's portrayal of the situation and contrast it with the decidedly different portrayal provided by Margaret Mitchell in her 1936 novel *Gone with the Wind*. It would be easy to dismiss Mitchell's apparent sentimentalization of the relationship between the masters and the house slaves, but does Mitchell's narrative shed any light on Malcolm X's? Is his discussion too one-sided, too lacking in subtlety, nuance, or mitigating factors? Was he accurate in portraying nonviolent advocates of racial progress in the civil rights movement as "house negroes"?

3. "They even said they was going out to the airport and lay down on the runway and don't let no planes land." These words, from Malcolm X's "Message to the Grass Roots," were spoken by a highly educated man, who certainly recognized the many grammatical errors in the sentence but who also knew that the language of everyday people is sometimes more potent and engaging than the King's English. How did Malcolm use colloquialism, vivid metaphors, and expressions common in the African American community to communicate with his listeners? What are some of the best examples, in your opinion, from the speeches included here or from other writings?

4. Until his very last years, when he began to show changing views as expressed in "The Ballot or the Bullet," Malcolm X maintained that there was "no such thing as a nonviolent revolution"—a major point of contention between Malcolm X and Martin Luther King, Jr. Was he right? What would Malcolm X have had to say about successful nonviolent "revolutions"? What would he have had to say about the examples of the Philippines, South Africa, and many nations in Eastern Europe that overthrew dictatorships by largely peaceful means in the late 1980s and early 1990s? How might his views on nonviolence in the civil rights movement have changed?

5. As a Muslim, what view would Malcolm X have had regarding the early-twenty-first-century conflict between the United States and Muslim extremists? Although he infamously said that the assassination of John F. Kennedy in 1963 was a case of "chickens coming home to roost" (in other words, Kennedy's and America's use of violence had brought violence on the president and the nation), would he have said the same about the terrorist attacks of September 11, 2001? Keep in mind the changes in viewpoint taking place within him during his later years, his break with Elijah Muhammad and the mainstream of the Black Muslim movement, and his increasing willingness to work within the U.S. system.

Further Reading

■ Books

Breitman, George. *The Last Year of Malcolm X: The Evolution of a Revolutionary*. New York: Pathfinder Press, 1970.

Dyson, Michael Eric. *Making Malcolm: The Myth and Meaning of Malcolm X*. New York: Oxford University Press, 1995.

Jenkins, Robert L., and Mfanya Donald Tryman. *The Malcolm X Encyclopedia*. Westport, Conn.: Greenwood Press, 2002.

■ Web Sites

"The Detroit Speeches of Malcolm X." Malcolm Web site.
http://www.brothermalcolm.net/.

The Malcolm X Project at Columbia University Web site.
http://www.columbia.edu/cu/ccbh/mxp/.

Malcolm-X.org Web site.
http://www.malcolm-x.org/.

The Official Web Site of Malcolm X.
http://www.cmgww.com/historic/malcolm/home.php.

—Carl Rollyson

"MESSAGE TO THE GRASS ROOTS" (1963)

America's problem is us.... The only reason she has a problem is she doesn't want us here. And every time you look at yourself, be you black, brown, red, or yellow—a so-called Negro—you represent a person who poses such a serious problem for America because you're not wanted. Once you face this as a fact, then you can start plotting a course that will make you appear intelligent, instead of unintelligent.

What you and I need to do is learn to forget our differences. When we come together, we don't come together as Baptists or Methodists. You don't catch hell 'cause you're a Baptist, and you don't catch hell 'cause you're a Methodist. You don't catch hell 'cause you're a Methodist or Baptist. You don't catch hell because you're a Democrat or a Republican. You don't catch hell because you're a Mason or an Elk. And you sure don't catch hell 'cause you're an American; 'cause if you was an American, you wouldn't catch no hell. You catch hell 'cause you're a black man....All of us catch hell, for the same reason.

So we are all black people, so-called Negroes, second-class citizens, ex-slaves. You are nothing but an ex-slave. You don't like to be told that. But what else are you?...You didn't come here on the "Mayflower." You came here on a slave ship—in chains, like a horse, or a cow, or a chicken. And you were brought here by the people who came here on the "Mayflower." You were brought here by the so-called Pilgrims, or Founding Fathers. They were the ones who brought you here.

We have a common enemy. We have this in common: We have a common oppressor, a common exploiter, and a common discriminator. But once we all realize that we have this common enemy, then we unite on the basis of what we have in common. And what we have foremost in common is that enemy—the white man. He's an enemy to all of us. I know some of you all think that some of them aren't enemies. Time will tell.

In Bandung back in, I think, 1954, was the first unity meeting in centuries of black people. And once you study what happened at the Bandung conference, and the results of the Bandung conference, it actually serves as a model for the same procedure you and I can use to get our problems solved. At Bandung all the nations came together. There were dark nations from Africa and Asia. Some of them were Buddhists. Some of them were Muslim. Some of them were Christians. Some of them were Confucianists; some were atheists. Despite their religious differences, they came together. Some were communists; some were socialists; some were capitalists. Despite their economic and political differences, they came together. All of them were black, brown, red, or yellow.

The number-one thing that was not allowed to attend the Bandung conference was the white man. He couldn't come. Once they excluded the white man, they found that they could get together. Once they kept him out, everybody else fell...fell in line. This is the thing that you and I have to understand. And these people who came together didn't have nuclear weapons; they didn't have jet planes; they didn't have all of the heavy armaments that the white man has. But they had unity.

They were able to submerge their little petty differences and agree on one thing:...who their enemy was. The same man that was colonizing our people in Kenya was colonizing our people in the Congo. The same one in the Congo was colonizing our people in South Africa, and in Southern Rhodesia, and in Burma, and in India, and in Afghanistan, and in Pakistan. They realized all over the world where the dark man was being oppressed, he was being oppressed by the white man; where the dark man was being exploited, he was being exploited by the white man. So they got together under this basis—that they had a common enemy.... Instead of us airing our differences in public, we have to realize we're all the same family.... Put the white man out of our meetings ... and then sit down and talk shop with each other....

You haven't got a revolution that doesn't involve bloodshed. And you're afraid to bleed. I said, you're afraid to bleed....How are you going to be nonviolent in Mississippi, as violent as you were in Korea? How can you justify being nonviolent in Mississippi and Alabama, when your churches are being bombed, and your little girls are being murdered, and at the same time you're going to get violent with Hitler, and Tojo, and somebody else that you don't even know?

If violence is wrong in America, violence is wrong abroad. If it's wrong to be violent defending black women and black children and black babies and black men, then it's wrong for America to draft us and make us violent abroad in defense of her. And if it is right for America to draft us, and teach us how to be violent in defense of her, then it is right for you and me to do whatever is necessary to defend our own people right here in this country....

There's been a revolution, a black revolution, going on in Africa. In Kenya, the Mau Mau were revolutionaries; they were the ones who made the word "Uhuru." They were the ones who brought it to the fore.... They believed in scorched earth. They knocked everything aside that got in their way, and their revolution also was based on land, a desire for land. In Algeria, the northern part of Africa, a revolution took place. The Algerians were revolutionists; they wanted land. France offered to let them be integrated into France. They told France: to hell with France. They wanted some land, not some France. And they engaged in a bloody battle.

So I cite these various revolutions, brothers and sisters, to show you—you don't have a peaceful revolution. You don't have a turn-the-other-cheek revolution. There's no such thing as a nonviolent revolution. The only kind of revolution that's nonviolent is the Negro revolution. The only revolution based on loving your enemy is the Negro revolution. The only revolution in which the goal is a desegregated lunch counter, a desegregated theater, a desegregated park, and a desegregated public toilet.... That's no revolution. Revolution is based on land. Land is the basis of all independence. Land is the basis of freedom, justice, and equality.

The white man knows what a revolution is. He knows that the black revolution is world-wide in scope and in nature.... A revolution is bloody. Revolution is hostile. Revolution knows no compromise. Revolution overturns and destroys everything that gets in its way. And you, sitting around here like a knot on the wall, saying, "I'm going to love these folks no matter how much they hate me." No, you need a revolution. Whoever heard of a revolution where they lock arms, as Reverend Cleage was pointing out beautifully, singing "We Shall Overcome"? Just tell me. You don't do that in a revolution. You don't do any singing; you're too busy swinging....

When you want a nation, that's called nationalism....A revolutionary is a black nationalist. He wants a nation. I was reading some beautiful words by Reverend Cleage, pointing out why he couldn't get together with someone else here in the city because all of them were afraid of being identified with black nationalism. If you're afraid of black nationalism, you're afraid of revolution. And if you love revolution, you love black nationalism.

To understand this, you have to go back to what the young brother here referred to as the house Negro and the field Negro—back during slavery. There was two kinds of slaves. There was the house Negro and the field Negro. The house Negroes ... lived in the house with master. They dressed pretty good; they ate good 'cause they ate his food.... They lived in the attic or the basement, but still they lived near the master; and they loved their master more than the master loved himself. They would give their life to save the master's house quicker than the master would. The house Negro, if the master said, "We got a good house here," the house Negro would say, "Yeah, we got a good house here." Whenever the master said "we," he said "we." That's how you can tell a house Negro....

This modern house Negro loves his master. He wants to live near him. He'll pay three times as much as the house is worth just to live near his master, and then brag about "I'm the only Negro out here." "I'm the only one on my job." "I'm the only one in this school."... Just as the slavemaster of that day used Tom, the house Negro, to keep the field Negroes in check, the same old slavemaster today has Negroes who are nothing but modern Uncle Toms, 20th century Uncle Toms, to keep you and me in check, keep us under control, keep us passive and peaceful and nonviolent....

The white man do the same thing to you in the street,... put knots on your head and take advantage of you and don't have to be afraid of your fighting back. To keep you from fighting back, he gets these old religious Uncle Toms to teach you and me,...suffer peacefully. Don't stop suffering—just suffer peacefully. As Reverend Cleage pointed out, "Let your blood flow In the streets." This is a shame. And you know he's a Christian preacher. If it's a shame to him, you know what it is to me.

There's nothing in our book, the Quran ...that teaches us to suffer peacefully. Our religion teaches us to be intelligent. Be peaceful, be courteous, obey the law, respect everyone; but if someone puts his hand on you, send him to the cemetery. That's a good religion. In fact, that's that old-time religion. That's the one that Ma and Pa used to talk about: an eye for an eye, and a tooth for a tooth, and a head for a head, and a life for a life: That's a good religion. And doesn't nobody resent that kind of religion being taught but a wolf, who intends to make you his meal.

This is the way it is with the white man in America. He's a wolf and you're sheep. Any time a shepherd, a pastor, teach you and me not to run from the white man and, at the same time, teach us not to fight the white man, he's a traitor to you and me.

Don't lay down our life all by itself. No, preserve your life. It's the best thing you got. And if you got to give it up, let it be even-steven.

The slavemaster took Tom and dressed him well, and fed him well, and even gave him a little education…; gave him a long coat and a top hat and made all the other slaves look up to him. Then he used Tom to control them. The same strategy that was used in those days is used today, by the same white man. He takes a Negro…and make him prominent, build him up, publicize him, make him a celebrity. And then he becomes a spokesman for Negroes—and a Negro leader.

I would like to just mention just one other thing else quickly, and that is the method that the white man uses, how the white man uses these "big guns," or Negro leaders, against the black revolution. They are not a part of the black revolution. They're used against the black revolution.

When Martin Luther King failed to desegregate Albany, Georgia, the civil-rights struggle in America reached its low point. King became bankrupt almost, as a leader.… Even financially, the Southern Christian Leadership Conference was in financial trouble; plus it was in trouble, period, with the people when they failed to desegregate Albany, Georgia.…

As soon as King failed in Birmingham, Negroes took to the streets.…And as these Negroes of national stature began to attack each other, they began to lose their control of the Negro masses.

And Negroes was out there in the streets. They was talking about how we was going to march on Washington. By the way, right at that time Birmingham had exploded, and the Negroes in Birmingham—remember, they also exploded. They began to stab the crackers in the back and bust them upside their head—yes, they did. That's when Kennedy sent in the troops, down in Birmingham. So, and right after that, Kennedy got on the television and said "this is a moral issue." That's when he said he was going to put out a civil-rights bill. And when he mentioned civil-rights bill and the Southern crackers started talking about how they were going to boycott or filibuster it, then the Negroes started talking —about what? We're going to march on Washington, march on the Senate, march on the White House, march on the Congress, and tie it up, bring it to a halt; don't let the government proceed. They even said they was going out to the airport and lay down on the runway and don't let no airplanes land. I'm telling you what they said. That was revolution. That was revolution. That was the black revolution.

It was the grass roots out there in the street. It scared the white man to death, scared the white power structure in Washington, D.C. to death; I was there.…The same white element that put Kennedy in power—labor, the Catholics, the Jews, and liberal Protestants; the same clique that put Kennedy in power, joined the march on Washington.

Glossary

crackers	an insulting term for whites, especially southern whites
filibuster	the technique of obstructing a bill in a legislature by indefinitely prolonging debate
Mason or an Elk	reference to members of two fraternal and civic organizations
Mau Mau	secret terrorist organization that battled British colonial rule in Kenya from 1952 to 1960
Mayflower	the name of the ship that brought the Pilgrims, a group of religious separatists, to America in 1620
Quran	the sacred scripture of Islam
Reverend Cleage	Albert Cleage, an African American minister famous for arguing that Jesus was a black revolutionary leader
Tojo	Hideki Tojo, the Japanese prime minister during World War II
Uhuru	Swahili word for "freedom"
Uncle Tom	a central character in Harriet Beecher Stowe's 1852 novel *Uncle Tom's Cabin*; a character symbolic of black subservience to whites

It's just like when you've got some coffee that's too black, which means it's too strong. What you do? You integrate it with cream; you make it weak. If you pour too much cream in, you won't even know you ever had coffee. It used to be hot, it becomes cool. It used to be strong, it becomes weak. It used to wake you up, now it'll put you to sleep. This is what they did with the march on Washington. They joined it. They didn't integrate it; they infiltrated it. They joined it, became a part of it, took it over. And as they took it over, it lost its militancy. They ceased to be angry. They ceased to be hot. They ceased to be uncompromising. Why, it even ceased to be a march. It became a picnic, a circus. Nothing but a circus, with clowns and all.

No, it was a sellout. It was a takeover....And every one of those Toms was out of town by sundown. Now I know you don't like my saying this. But I can back it up. It was a circus, a performance that beat anything Hollywood could ever do, the performance of the year.

"THE BALLOT OR THE BULLET" SPEECH (1964)

So today, though Islam is my religious philosophy, my political, economic, and social philosophy is Black Nationalism.... If we bring up religion we'll have differences ... but when we come out here, we have a fight that's common to all of us against an enemy who is common to all of us.

The political philosophy of Black Nationalism only means that the black man should control the politics and the politicians in his own community.... The time when white people can come in our community and get us to vote for them so that they can be our political leaders and tell us what to do and what not to do is long gone. By the same token, the time when that same white man, knowing that your eyes are too far open, can send another negro into the community and get you and me to support him so he can use him to lead us astray—those days are long gone too.

The political philosophy of Black Nationalism only means that if you and I are going to live in a Black community—and that's where we're going to live, 'cause as soon as you move into one of their— soon as you move out of the Black community into their community, it's mixed for a period of time, but they're gone and you're right there all by yourself again.... So the political philosophy of Black Nationalism only means that we will have to carry on a program, a political program, of re-education to open our people's eyes, make us become more politically conscious, politically mature, and then we will— whenever we get ready to cast our ballot, that ballot will be—will be cast for a man of the community who has the good of the community of heart.

The economic philosophy of Black Nationalism only means that we should own and operate and control the economy of our community....You can't open up a black store in a white community. White men won't even patronize you. And he's not wrong. He's got sense enough to look out for himself. You the one who don't have sense enough to look out for yourself.... The white man is too intelligent to let someone else come and gain control of the economy of his community. But you will let anybody come in and take control of the economy of your community, control the housing, control the education, control the jobs, control the businesses, under the pretext that you want to integrate. No, you're out of your mind....

And you and I are in a double-track, because not only do we lose by taking our money someplace else and spending it, when we try and spend it in our own community we're trapped because we haven't had sense enough to set up stores and control the businesses of our community. The man who's controlling the stores in our community is a man who doesn't look like we do. He's a man who doesn't even live in the community. So you and I, even when we try and spend our money in the block where we live or the area where we live, we're spending it with a man who, when the sun goes down, takes that basket full of money in another part of the town....

So our people not only have to be reeducated to the importance of supporting black business, but the black man himself has to be made aware of the importance of going into business. And once you and I go into business, we own and operate at least the businesses in our community. What we will be doing is developing a situation wherein we will actually be able to create employment for the people in the community....

We're all in the same bag, in the same boat. We suffer political oppression, economic exploitation, and social degradation—all of them from the same enemy. The government has failed us; you can't deny that. Anytime you live in the twentieth century, 1964, and you walkin' around here singing "We Shall Overcome," the government has failed us.

This is part of what's wrong with you—you do too much singing. Today it's time to stop singing and start swinging. You can't sing up on freedom, but you can swing up on some freedom. Cassius Clay can sing, but singing didn't help him to become the heavyweight champion of the world; swinging helped him become the heavyweight champion....

And once we see that all these other sources to which we've turned have failed, we stop turning to them and turn to ourselves.... Before we can get a self-help program started we have to have a self-help philosophy.

Black Nationalism is a self-help philosophy. What's so good about it? You can stay right in the church where you are and still take Black Nationalism as your philosophy. You can stay in any kind of civic organization that you belong to and still take black nationalism as your philosophy. You can be an atheist and still take black nationalism as your philosophy. This is a philosophy that eliminates the necessity for division and argument. 'Cause if you're black you should be thinking black, and if you are black and you not thinking black at this late date, well I'm sorry for you....

As long as you gotta sit-down philosophy, you'll have a sit-down thought pattern, and as long as you think that old sit-down thought you'll be in some kind of sit-down action. They'll have you sitting in everywhere. It's not so good to refer to what you're going to do as a "sit-in." That right there castrates you. Right there it brings you down....Well you and I been sitting long enough, and it's time today for us to start doing some standing, and some fighting to back that up.

When we look...at other parts of this earth upon which we live, we find that black, brown, red, and yellow people in Africa and Asia are getting their independence. They're not getting it by singing "We Shall Overcome." No, they're getting it through nationalism....And it will take black nationalism...to bring about the freedom of 22 million Afro-Americans here in this country where we have suffered colonialism for the past 400 years.

America is just as much a colonial power as England ever was. America is just as much a colonial power as France ever was. In fact, America is more so a colonial power than they because she's a hypocritical colonial power behind it....

What do you call second class citizenship? Why, that's colonization.... They try and make you think they set you free by calling you a second class citizen. No, you're nothing but a 20th century slave.

Just as it took nationalism...to remove colonialism from Asia and Africa, it'll take black nationalism today to remove colonialism from the backs and the minds of 22 million Afro-Americans here in this country.

And 1964 looks like it might be the year of the ballot or the bullet....

Because Negroes have listened to the trickery, and the lies, and the false promises of the white man now for too long. And they're fed up. They've become disenchanted. They've become disillusioned. They've become dissatisfied, and all of this has built up frustrations in the black community that makes the black community throughout America today more explosive than all of the atomic bombs the Russians can ever invent....

And in 1964 this seems to be the year, because what can the white man use now to fool us after he put down that march on Washington? And you see all through that now. He tricked you, had you marching down to Washington. Yes, had you marching back and forth between the feet of a dead man named Lincoln and another dead man named George Washington singing "We Shall Overcome." He made a chump out of you....

And in 1964 you'll see this young black man, this new generation asking for the ballot or the bullet. That old Uncle Tom action is outdated. The young generation don't want to hear anything about the odds are against us. What do we care about odds?

When this country here was first being founded there were 13 colonies....The whites were colonized. They were fed up with this taxation without representation, so some of them stood up and said "liberty or death." Though I went to a white school over here in Mason, Michigan, the white man made the mistake of letting me read his history books. He made the mistake of teaching me that Patrick Henry was a patriot, and George Washington, wasn't nothing non-violent about old Pat or George Washington.

Liberty or death was what brought about the freedom of whites in this country from the English. They didn't care about the odds. Why they faced the wrath of the entire British Empire. And in those days they used to say that the British Empire was so vast and so powerful when the sun—the sun would never set on it. This is how big it was, yet these 13 little scrawny states, tired of taxation without representation, tired of being exploited and oppressed and degraded, told that big British Empire "liberty or death."

And here you have 22 million Afro-American black people today catching more hell than Patrick Henry ever saw....I'm here to tell you in case you don't know it—that you got a new...generation of black people in this country who don't care anything whatsoever about odds. They don't want to hear you old Uncle Tom handkerchief heads talking about the odds....

This is the year when all of the white politicians are going to come into the Negro community. You never see them until election time. You can't find them until election time. They're going to come in with false promises, and as they make these false promises they're gonna feed our frustrations and this will only serve to make matters worse....

I speak as a victim of America's so-called democracy....We don't see any American dream; we've experienced only the American nightmare. We haven't benefited from America's democracy; we've only suffered from America's hypocrisy. And the generation that's coming up now can see it and are not afraid to say it....

If you go to jail, so what? If you black, you were born in jail. If you black, you were born in jail, in the North as well as the South....

You're in a position to determine who will go to the White House and who will stay in the dog house. You're the one who has that power. You can keep Johnson in Washington D.C., or you can send him back to his Texas cotton patch. You're the one who sent Kennedy to Washington. You're the one who put the present Democratic Administration in Washington D.C. The whites were evenly divided. It was the fact that you threw 80 percent of your votes behind the Democrats that put the Democrats in the White House.

When you see this, you can see that the Negro vote is the key factor. And despite the fact that you are in a position…to be the determining factor, what do you get out of it? The Democrats have been in Washington D.C. only because of the Negro vote. They've been down there four years, and…all other legislation they wanted to bring up they brought it up and gotten it out of the way, and now they bring up you. And now, they bring up you. You put them first, and they put you last, 'cause you're a chump, a political chump….

I was in Washington a couple weeks ago while the Senators were filibustering, and I noticed in the back of the Senate a huge map, and on this map it showed the distribution of Negroes in America, and surprisingly the same Senators that were involved in the filibuster were from the states where there were the most Negroes. Why were they filibustering the civil rights legislation? Because the civil rights legislation is supposed to guarantee voting rights to Negroes in those states, and those senators from those states know that if the Negroes in those states can vote, those senators are down the drain….

These Northern Democrats are in cahoots with the Southern Democrats. They're playing a giant con game, a political con game. You know how it goes…. One of them comes to you and makes believe he's for you, and he's in cahoots with the other one that's not for you. Why? Because neither one of them is for you, but they got to make you go with one of them or the other….

Now you take your choice. You going to choose a Northern dog or a Southern dog? Because either dog you choose I guarantee you you'll still be in the dog house.

This is why I say it's the ballot or the bullet. It's liberty or it's death…. A revolution is bloody, but America is in a unique position. She's the only country in history in a position actually to become involved in a blood-less revolution….All she's got to do is give the black man in this country everything that's due him—everything.

I hope that the white man can see this, 'cause if he don't see it you're finished. If you don't see it you're going to be coming—you're going to become involved in some action in which you don't have a chance. And we don't care anything about your atomic bomb;…it's useless because other countries have atomic bombs. When two or three different countries have atomic bombs, nobody can use them, so it means that the white man today is without a weapon….If you want some action, you gotta come on down to Earth. And there's more black people on Earth than there are white people on Earth….

The strategy of the white man has always been divide and conquer. He keeps us divided in order to conquer us. He tells you I'm for separation and you're for integration to keep us fighting with each other.

Glossary

Cassius Clay	American boxer who later converted to Islam and adopted the name Muhammad Ali
filibustering	a way of obstructing a bill in a legislature by indefinitely prolonging debate
Johnson	President Lyndon B. Johnson
Kennedy	President John F. Kennedy
NAACP	the National Association for the Advancement of Colored People, a civil rights organization
Patrick Henry	American Revolutionary, most famous for his statement "Give my Liberty, or give me Death!"
Uncle Tom	a central character in Harriet Beecher Stowe's 1852 novel *Uncle Tom's Cabin*; a character symbolic of black subservience to whites

No, I'm not for separation and you're not for integration. What you and I is for is freedom. Only you think that integration will get you freedom, I think separation will get me freedom. We both got the same objective. We just got different ways of getting at it....

But when you go to a church and you see the pastor of that church with a philosophy and a program that's designed to bring black people together and elevate black people—join that church.... If you see where the NAACP is preaching and practicing that which is designed to make Black Nationalism materialize—join the NAACP. Join any kind of organization—civic, religious, fraternal, political, or otherwise that's based on lifting the black man up and making him master of his own community....

Anything that I can ever do, at any time, to work with anybody in any kind of program that is sincerely designed to eliminate the political, the economic, and the social evils that confront all of our people, in Detroit and elsewhere, all they got to do is give me a telephone call and I'll be on the next jet right on into the city.

George Marshall (Library of Congress)

MILESTONE DOCUMENTS OF AMERICAN LEADERS

GEORGE MARSHALL   1880–1959

U.S. Army Officer, Secretary of State, and Secretary of Defense

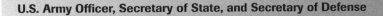

Featured Documents
- ◆ **Speech to the American Historical Association on the National Organization for War (1939)**
- ◆ **Speech to the Graduating Class of the U.S. Military Academy (1942)**
- ◆ **Washington's Birthday Remarks at Princeton University (1947)**
- ◆ **Marshall Plan Speech (1947)**
- ◆ **Nobel Peace Prize Acceptance Speech (1953)**

Overview

Born on December 31, 1880, in Uniontown, Pennsylvania, George Catlett Marshall spent his youth there until leaving in the fall of 1897 to attend the Virginia Military Academy, where he distinguished himself academically and as a leader. Commissioned a second lieutenant by the U.S. Army in 1902, Marshall commanded troops in the last months of heavy combat in the Philippine-American War (1899–1902). Afterward, Marshall rotated through a succession of peacetime postings. He helped revitalize officer education in the army and taught a variety of courses at Fort Leavenworth, Kansas. He served on General John J. Pershing's staff during World War I and helped plan the largest American offensives of that war. Widely regarded as one of the most capable officers in the army, Marshall continued to rise through the ranks after the war. President Franklin Roosevelt appointed him chief of staff of the army in 1939, and Marshall served in that position throughout World War II, helping lead the nation's mobilization and war effort.

As chief of staff, Marshall oversaw the massive expansion of the army as the nation prepared for war. Marshall's public speeches on military preparedness and his testimony before Congress paved the way for rearmament and proved critical in mobilizing the American people and preparing the nation for war. Under Marshall's direction the army grew from two hundred thousand soldiers in 1939 to 1,686,000 by the end of 1941 and to more than 8 million by the war's end. Marshall assembled an extraordinary group of generals to lead this army and took the lead in forming the Combined Chiefs of Staff, the joint American and British command organization that directed the war effort and is generally regarded as the closest and best functioning allied command organization in history. Marshall also closely monitored the appointments of many junior officers and took every opportunity to speak to them. Marshall retired as chief of staff on November 18, 1945.

Marshall had expected to retire from public life. Instead, he became an indispensable member of the administration of President Harry Truman, serving as special presidential emissary to China (1945–1947) and then secretary of state (1947–1949). Recalled again following the outbreak of the Korean War, he served one year as secretary of defense (1950–1951). In these years, Marshall helped craft Ameri-

can foreign policy and present it to the American public. In several important speeches, he argued for the linkage of military strategy to diplomacy and economics, civilian control of the military, preparation to fight limited as well as total wars, and an emphasis on Europe rather than Asia in American strategy. He spearheaded a number of diplomatic initiatives, most famously the European Recovery Program, better known as the Marshall Plan, an immense economic aid program to rehabilitate the industries and economies of Western Europe. Marshall played a key role in developing the alliance that would persevere through the cold war. He received the Nobel Peace Prize for the European Recovery Program in 1953, and his speech at the awards ceremony was his last major public address. Early in 1959 he suffered a stroke. He died on October 16 at Walter Reed Army Hospital in Washington, D.C.

Explanation and Analysis of Documents

Marshall directed the U.S. Army in the largest war in its history, building it from a tiny force to more than 8 million. Before Japan's attack on Pearl Harbor of December 7, 1941, Marshall led the effort to prepare the nation for war. Afterward, he helped direct the war effort and lead the United States and its allies to victory. Marshall became President Franklin Roosevelt's leading military adviser and helped draft many of his memos on strategy and military matters. He also helped craft American strategy to win World War II and secure peace in its aftermath. He played a leading role in fashioning American foreign policy, which centered on rebuilding Europe and containing the Soviet Union. The five speeches chosen to represent Marshall span the critical years of his career from 1939, shortly after he became army chief of staff, to 1953—at the height of the cold war. They highlight persistent themes in his thought, including the importance of a citizen army and civilian control of the military, the relevance of history and its vital role as an educational tool, the necessity of military preparedness, his hope that people would find a way to construct a lasting peace that made such preparedness unnecessary, and his belief that peace, prosperity, and democracy depended on one another. Marshall's carefully worded arguments often proved critical in swaying public, government, and military opinion.

Time Line

1880
- **December 31**
  George Marshall is born in Uniontown, Pennsylvania.

1902
- **February 3**
  Marshall is commissioned second lieutenant in the U.S. Army.

1939
- **July 1**
  Marshall assumes duties of acting chief of staff of the army.
- **September 1**
  Marshall is promoted to major general.
- **December 28**
  Marshall speaks to the American Historical Association on the national organization for war.

1942
- **May 29**
  Marshall addresses the graduating class of the U.S. Military Academy.

1944
- **December 16**
  Marshall is promoted to General of the Army.

1945
- **November 18**
  Marshall retires as chief of staff.
- **November 26**
  Marshall is awarded the Distinguished Service Medal.
- **November 27**
  Marshall is named special emissary to China.

1947
- **January 21**
  Marshall is appointed secretary of state.
- **February 27**
  Marshall delivers remarks at Princeton University to mark the birthday of George Washington.
- **June 5**
  Marshall delivers his Marshall Plan speech at the Harvard University commencement.

◆ **Speech to the American Historical Association on the National Organization for War**

Marshall assumed his position as army chief of staff a few hours after Germany invaded Poland on September 1, 1939, beginning World War II in Europe. Like President Roosevelt and other members of his administration, Marshall had served during the World War I and worried that the United States would be forced to enter this new world war as unprepared as it had been when it entered World War I. Over the next two years Marshall gave a series of speeches urging preparation for war. In this speech to the American Historical Association, the leading professional organization of historians in the United States, Marshall enunciates themes that recur in many of his speeches: the costs of military unpreparedness, the need to educate the public, the necessity for industrial as well as military preparedness, and the benefits of a citizen army, democratic government, and civilian direction of the military.

Marshall frequently sprinkled his speeches with historical references and urged people to study history to avoid mistakes of the past, particularly the United States' inadequate preparation for World War I. In this speech, he notes the problems the United States faced in mobilizing for war, particularly in modernizing and enlarging its small army. Marshall hoped to both shake Americans from their complacency and recruit historians to the cause of preparedness. In developing the latter point, he suggests that historians should expose past military failures to encourage the development of more effective military forces. While this study might not find a cure for the "deadly disease" of war, studying military history and preparing for war were essential to win wars at the least cost and for the United States to realize its potential to become the "strongest nation on earth." Time, he emphasizes, was of the essence, since the United States could not afford to wait until it was attacked. Germany's rapid conquest of Poland demonstrated that modern wars moved too quickly to allow the United States' traditionally slow pace of mobilization. This mobilization could proceed, however, only if widespread consensus favored it. For that reason, Marshall encourages the nation's historians to study war so that they would come to understand the urgent necessity of war preparation and then be able to help educate the American people on the subject.

As German victories mounted in 1940, Marshall elaborated on these points in a succession of speeches, particularly after France surrendered to Germany in June 1940. Shortly afterward, Marshall called for increased weapons production, activation of the National Guard, and conscription—calls that Congress answered with record military spending and the Selective Service Act, the first peacetime draft in U.S. history.

◆ **Speech to the Graduating Class of the U.S. Military Academy**

In the six months following Japan's attack on Pearl Harbor, American military forces suffered a series of demoralizing defeats. These defeats culminated with the surrender of the last American and Filipino defenders of the Philippines on May 8, 1942. In this speech Marshall addresses the cadets of the U.S. Military Academy at West Point, paying particular attention to the concerns of the graduating seniors who would soon leave their classrooms for the battlefield. Most of the other cadets would follow them in succeeding years as the academy accelerated its academic program to produce officers for the rapidly expanding American army. Marshall seeks to allay their fears, boost their morale, and give them some sense of the war they would be fighting and its importance. He reminds them that they would be leading the "finest personnel in the world," people who "are all that could be desired of soldiers." To defeat the enemy, they required only the necessary tools, support from the home front, and excellent leadership, like that Marshall expects these graduates to provide. The air force did not become an independent service until after World War II. During the war, it remained part of the U.S. Army, and Marshall praises the air force and its pilots and crews, the "flower of American manhood." He notes the recent success of the Doolittle raid in bombing Japan (named after its leader, Lieutenant Colonel James H. Doolittle) and assures his listeners that American airmen were eager to visit even more destruction on Japan and Germany. The war would present these future officers with great challenges and responsibilities, but Marshall expects them to rise to these challenges and responsibilities, to seize any opportunities presented to them, and to achieve great things.

Since Marshall became chief of staff, the army had grown from fewer than two hundred thousand officers and soldiers to more than 4 million. As the army continued to expand, West Point officers represented a decreasing percentage of the officer corps. Marshall warns the cadets that they would fight with, command, and even be commanded by men who lacked their West Point education but who were likely to be older and more experienced. Typical of Marshall's wartime speeches, he praised the American military tradition, its dedication to the ideal of citizen-soldiers, and Americans' ingenuity and fighting spirit. He assures the cadets that public attitudes have changed over the past year. The American people wholeheartedly supported the army and the war effort.

Twice, Marshall foreshadows what would become central parts of American policy and strategy in the war. He predicts that American forces would invade the continent of Europe to liberate France. Later, he argues that the United States and its allies must "utterly defeat" the German and Japanese war machines. The war had to end with a decisive conclusion. This statement anticipated by six months the official allied declaration of unconditional surrender as a war goal following the Casablanca Conference (January 14–24, 1943). In this speech Marshall also implies a new worldwide role for the United States, which would become a "symbol of freedom" and "overwhelming force" in the postwar world.

◆ Washington's Birthday Remarks at Princeton University

In his first speech as secretary of state, Marshall hoped to shock people out of complacency, much as he had in his

Marshall, George

Time Line

1949	**■ January 20** Marshall resigns as secretary of state. **■ October 1** Marshall is chosen as president of the American Red Cross.
1950	**■ September 21** Marshall is appointed secretary of defense.
1951	**■ September 12** Marshall resigns as secretary of defense.
1953	**■ December 11** Marshall delivers a speech accepting the Nobel Peace Prize.
1959	**■ October 16** Marshall dies at Walter Reed Army Hospital in Washington, D.C.

in prewar preparedness speeches. Returning to a theme that figured prominently in many of his wartime speeches, he argues that the world looked to the United States for leadership and that the United States needed to assume this role. As he had not in his earlier speeches, however, Marshall emphasizes that Americans needed to shape a new foreign policy for this new era. With the war over, "there is a natural tendency to relax, and to return to business as usual, politics as usual, pleasure as usual." Yet, the present situation was "even more critical." Marshall, who had studied the situation in Europe, warns Americans to avoid the mistakes of the Versailles Treaty and international settlement following World War I, particularly the United States' retreat to isolationism.

After World War I, the victorious allies, contrary to the hopes of President Woodrow Wilson, imposed a punitive peace on Germany in 1919. Required to pay reparations to the European Allies, Germany also lost territory and was forced to accept responsibility for starting the war and severe limits on the size of its military. Generally opposed to reparations and suspicious of the League of Nations, a new international organization designed to maintain international peace through collective action, the U.S. Senate rejected the Versailles Treaty and refused to join the League of Nations. The United States withdrew into isolation and remained aloof from international concerns when a new world war threatened in the 1930s. Without the United States, the world's largest economy and leading

A young girl holds a bouquet of hydrogen-filled balloons carrying a message of peace to Communist Eastern Europe at the spring fair in Vienna, Austria, on March 25, 1951. (AP/Wide World Photos)

naval power, the League of Nations proved unable to halt Japanese, Italian, or German aggression, which eventually brought about World War II.

Americans, Marshall argues, needed to study history to avoid the mistakes of the past and to inspire people, shape the world around them, and make it a better and more peaceful place. They needed to recognize the unique position of the United States "financially, militarily, and scientifically" in the postwar world and accept "responsibility for world order and security." Elsewhere, "fear and famine" prevailed. In the international arena, "order has yet to be brought out of confusion," and peace "has yet to be secured." With the world exhausted, only American leadership and assistance could restore shattered economies and democratic governments. The United States must not again sit idle while the international system devolves into chaos and opens the door to war. In this address Marshall offered no specific recommendations for American aid to Europe. He left those for his most important foreign policy address, delivered at Harvard University three and a half months later. Marshall here prepared the ground for the stunning proposals and reorientation of that forthcoming speech.

◆ Marshall Plan Speech

Marshall was not alone in calling for economic aid to reconstruct Europe. The journalist Walter Lippmann suggested it in a column two months later, and other govern-

ment officials also spoke in favor of the idea, including two key Marshall advisers, George Kennan and Charles Bohlen. These two helped Marshall draft his most famous speech, given at Harvard University in June. While they had yet to develop a formal economic aid proposal, they decided to seize the opportunity to publicize the idea when Harvard awarded Marshall an honorary degree. In this speech, Marshall expounds further on themes he developed for his Princeton speech. Only American support, he argues, could ensure the "rehabilitation of the economic structure of Europe" and hence stability and democratic government in Western Europe. Marshall had moved from warning against isolationism and providing aid to foreign nations to increasingly firm calls for action at Princeton and then Harvard.

Marshall never applied his name either to the idea of economic aid to Europe or to this particular speech. He consistently referred to plans for European economic aid by what became the official name: the European Recovery Program. Members of the press, though, overwhelmingly called it the Marshall Plan after President Truman used that term to describe proposals to aid Europe. The *New York Times* published the full text of this speech the following day, and it received nationwide attention.

Marshall describes the serious world situation, particularly Europe's situation, in more detail than in his Princeton speech and then firmly declares that the era of isolationism had ended. The United States had to involve itself positively in the wider world. Europe "must have substantial additional help or face economic, social, and political deterioration of a very grave character." Only the United States could break this "vicious circle" and restore European confidence. Referring to the Great Depression, Marshall argues that economic problems could precipitate political problems, destroy democratic governments, and create circumstances in which tyrants and dictators might come to power and threaten their neighbors, as happened in Italy and Germany in the 1920s and 1930s. Political stability, "free institutions," democracy, and international peace could come only from economic stability. While Marshall avoids supplying specific figures for aid, he hints that American aid to Europe must be substantial. It must be a cure, not a "mere palliative."

Reminiscent of his wartime speeches, Marshall argues for international cooperation and invites Europeans to take the lead in this effort. "The initiative," he notes, "must come from Europe." In fact, Marshall had consulted with European leaders before making this speech. Shortly after he delivered it, British foreign minister Ernest Bevin formally requested American aid. In a remark clearly directed at the Soviet Union, Marshall warns that any government that works against the plan or seeks to "perpetuate human misery in order to profit therefrom politically or otherwise will encounter the opposition of the United States."

Marshall's speech galvanized support for economic aid to Europe. Signed into law by Truman on April 3, 1948, the European Recovery Program funneled $17 billion in economic aid to more than a dozen nations in Western Europe over the next four years. From 1948 to 1952 the economies of many recipient nations grew at their fastest rates in history, and agricultural productivity soon exceeded that of the prewar years. The program proved remarkably successful.

◆ Nobel Peace Prize Acceptance Speech

Awarded the Nobel Peace Price in 1953 for the European Recovery Program, which expired that year, the ailing Marshall reflected on his long career in his acceptance speech, returning yet again to his favored themes: the importance of studying history, the dangers of complacency, the economic underpinnings of peace and democracy, and the need for military preparedness. Even more than in his other speeches, Marshall argues that education and prosperity lead to peace and democracy.

Delivered in the midst of the cold war, Marshall's speech focuses on the international situation, noting that "the rapid disintegration between 1945 and 1950" of American military power had led directly to "the brutal invasion of South Korea." Too often, efforts to preserve international peace succeeded only temporarily. While the cold war and the threat from the Soviet Union required a "very strong military posture," Marshall notes that military preparedness and deterrence was "too narrow a basis on which to build a dependable, long-enduring peace." National leaders "must find another solution," and it is on this that he focuses most of his speech. He firmly believes that prosperity and democracy would produce a peaceful world because tyranny must inevitably "retire before the tremendous moral strength of the gospel of freedom and self-respect for the individual."

Perhaps the most important ingredient to world peace, he suggests, "will be a spiritual regeneration to develop goodwill, faith, and understanding among nations," and the inspiration of "great principles." Marshall devotes most of his attention, however, to three specific and linked ideas: international cooperation, education, and aid to poorer nations by democratic nations. Schools should teach history "without national prejudices" to encourage international cooperation, and people should fight against intolerance. The wealthier nations had to address the needs of the poorer nations because "democratic principles do not flourish on empty stomachs." Growing prosperity would lead to democracy, which he sees as a "force holding within itself the seeds of unlimited progress by the human race." These must flow from the inspired leadership of democratic nations working together as they did in the great World War II alliance. Coercion, he warns, will not work to spread either prosperity or peace.

Impact and Legacy

George C. Marshall remains one of the most highly regarded American generals, a soldier and statesman routinely compared to George Washington. Lauded by both his contemporaries and more recent leaders, including former chairman of the Joint Chiefs of Staff Colin Powell, his self-less and dedicated service to his nation continues to inspire people. His legacy is immense and difficult to quantify. It includes not only Allied victory in World War II and the postwar reconstruction of Europe but also many of the hallmarks of today's international system. Marshall's calls for education and aid to poorer nations helped inspire the creation of government programs and private institutions ranging from educational exchange programs to the Peace Corps.

His belief in international cooperation helped produce the United Nations, the North Atlantic Treaty Organization, and a host of smaller international organizations aimed at improving international relations and preserving peace. His insistence on military preparedness and determined leadership prepared the United States for the challenges it would face in World War II and the cold war. Marshall firmly believed that only through economic and military strength and the determination to confront its enemies could the United States produce a peaceful world in which military force was no longer necessary. This was his legacy to those who succeeded him, and American foreign policy showed his influence throughout the twentieth century.

Key Sources

With the exception of *Memoirs of My Services in the World War, 1917–1918* (1976), Marshall refused to write his memoirs. He issued three biennial reports during World War II, published in *The War Reports of General of the Army George C. Marshall, Chief of Staff, General of the Army H. H. Arnold, Commanding General, Army Air Force, and Fleet Admiral Ernest J. King, Commander-in-Chief of the United States Fleet and Chief of Naval Operations* (1947). Documents detailing Marshall's participation in the major wartime conferences are contained in the conference volumes of the State Department's *Foreign Relations of the United States Diplomatic Papers: Washington, 1941–1942 and Casablanca, 1943; Washington and Quebec, 1943; Cairo and Tehran, 1943; Quebec, 1944; Malta and Yalta, 1945;* and *Berlin, 1945.* The 1946 volume of *Foreign Relations of the United States: Diplomatic Papers* contains documents from his mission to China. The 1947 and 1948 volumes cover his tenure as secretary of state. These volumes are all available online at http://digicoll. library.wisc.edu/FRUS. Marshall's papers are at the George C. Marshall Foundation Research Library and Museum, Virginia Military Institute, Lexington, Virginia. Larry Bland and Sharon Ritenour Stevens compiled and published five volumes of these papers titled *The Papers of George Catlett Marshall* (1981–2003). Two projected volumes will complete the set. Many of these documents, along with other materials about George Marshall, are available online from the library of the Marshall Foundation (http://www.marshallfoundation.org). Its extensive holdings include not only Marshall's papers and transcripts of the historian Forrest Pogue's interviews with Marshall but also interviews and papers of many of Marshall's friends and associates. Two documentary films are available on Marshall: *George*

"*I think it apparent that much of this misfortune in the life of our democracy could have been avoided by the influence of a better informed public on the decisions of the Congress.*"

(Speech to the American Historical Association on the National Organization for War)

"*We are determined that before the sun sets on this terrible struggle our flag will be recognized throughout the world as a symbol of freedom on the one hand and of overwhelming force on the other.*"

(Speech to the Graduating Class of the U.S. Military Academy)

"*The development of a sense of responsibility for world order and security, the development of a sense of overwhelming importance of this country's acts, and failures to act in relation to world order and security—these, in my opinion, are great 'musts' for your generation.*"

(Washington's Birthday Remarks at Princeton University)

"*Our policy is directed not against any country or doctrine but against hunger, poverty, desperation, and chaos. Its purpose should be the revival of a working economy in the world so as to permit the emergence of political and social conditions in which free institutions can exist.*"

(Marshall Plan Speech)

"*The cost of war in human lives is constantly spread before me, written neatly in many ledgers whose columns are gravestones. I am deeply moved to find some means or method of avoiding another calamity of war.*"

(Nobel Peace Prize Acceptance Speech)

"*We must present democracy as a force holding within itself the seeds of unlimited progress by the human race.*"

(Nobel Peace Prize Acceptance Speech)

Marshall and the American Century (1994), and *George C. Marshall: Soldier and Statesman* (1998).

Further Reading

■ Articles

Levine, Steven I. "A New Look at American Mediation in the Chinese Civil War: The Marshall Mission and Manchuria." *Diplomatic History* 3 (Fall 1979): 349–363.

May, Ernest R. "1947–48: When Marshall Kept the U.S. Out of War in China." *Journal of Military History* 66 (October 2002): 1001–1010.

Weigley, Russell F. "The George C. Marshall Lecture in Military History: The Soldier, the Statesman, and the Military Historian," *Journal of Military History* 63 (October 1999): 807–822.

■ Books

Cray, Ed. *General of the Army: George C. Marshall, Soldier and Statesman*. New York: W. W. Norton, 1990.

Ferrell, Robert H. *George C. Marshall as Secretary of State, 1947–1949*. New York: Cooper Square, 1966.

Hogan, Michael J. *The Marshall Plan: America, Britain and the Reconstruction of Western Europe, 1947–1952*. New York: Cambridge University Press, 1987.

Parrish, Thomas. *Roosevelt and Marshall: Partners in Politics and War*. New York: Morrow, 1989.

Pogue, Forrest C. *George C. Marshall*. Vol. 1: *Education of a General, 1880–1939*. New York: Viking, 1963. Vol. 2: *Ordeal and Hope, 1939–1942*. New York: Viking, 1966. Vol. 3: *Organizer of Victory, 1943–1945*. New York: Viking, 1973. Vol. 4: *Statesman, 1945–1959*. New York: Viking Press, 1989.

Stoler, Mark A. *George C. Marshall: Soldier-Statesman of the American Century*. Boston: Twayne, 1989.

Uldrich, Jack. *Soldier, Statesman, Peacemaker: Leadership Lessons from George C. Marshall*. New York: AMACOM, 2005.

—Stephen K. Stein

Questions for Further Study

1. George Marshall had not one but three careers, each of which was impressive. Yet the stages in Marshall's professional life—army officer, army chief of staff, and finally secretary of state and defense—marked successively greater achievements. Furthermore, he began his second career at the age of fifty-eight and his third at sixty-six years old. Discuss briefly Marshall's development over the course of those careers, from a junior office leading troops in battle to a general leading the greatest army in the worst war of all time, and from that to the architect of postwar peace and prosperity in the West. How did the Marshall of the second career, represented by two documents here, differ from the Marshall of the three later documents? On the other hand, what themes and issues remain over the span of the years represented by these five addresses?

2. What do Marshall's speeches teach us about the importance of education, particularly historical and political education, in his view? Examine the emphasis he places on the study of history in his 1939 address to history educators as well as the way that some of these same themes emerge in his remarks on Washington's birthday eight years later. What does he have to say specifically to high-schoolers in that first address, and what connections does he draw between the serious study of history on the one hand and national security on the other? How do these ideas reappear in his 1953 Nobel acceptance speech, when he discusses the consequences of failing to learn from history?

3. One of the most successful investment plans in history was the European Recovery Program, popularly known as the Marshall Plan. It helped prevent the economic panic and disorder that made possible the rise of totalitarian dictatorships in Europe after World War I and secured the future prosperity and stability of the West. Using Marshall's postwar speeches, particularly the 1947 Harvard address that introduced the European Recovery Program to the world, discuss his "principles of investment"—his ideas of how the United States could obtain the best possible return on the dollars it spent. Compare and contrast his ideas with those of George Kennan, who likewise urged U.S. leaders to maximize the value of the money they put into waging the cold war.

SPEECH TO THE AMERICAN HISTORICAL ASSOCIATION ON THE NATIONAL ORGANIZATION FOR WAR (1939)

Public appreciation of international affairs is of course important to a sound view regarding military policy, and the radio and press are doing a remarkable job of keeping the public informed. School children today are probably more fully informed on current international developments than were many high government officials of thirty years ago. But even more important are the lessons of history. Therefore, it is to the historian, to you gentlemen, that we must turn for the most essential service in determining the public policy relating to national defense.

Popular knowledge of history, I believe, is largely based on information derived from school textbooks, and unfortunately these sources often tell only a portion of the truth with regard to our war experiences. Historians have been inclined to record the victories and gloss over the mistakes and wasteful sacrifices. Cause and effect have been, to an important extent, ignored. Few Americans learn that we enrolled nearly 400,000 men in the Revolutionary War to defeat an enemy that numbered less than 45,000, or that we employed half a million in 1812 against an opponent whose strength never exceeded 16,000 at any one place, and fewer still have learned why these overwhelming numbers were so ineffective. The War between the States pointed numerous lessons for our future protection, yet seldom has a nation entered a war so completely unprepared, and yet so boastfully, as did the United States in 1898. Veterans of the World War often seem to overlook the fact that almost a year and a half elapsed after the declaration of war before we could bring a field army into being and even then its weapons, ammunition and other materiel were provided by our Allies. And many of them seem unaware of the fact that the partially trained state of our troops proved a costly and tragic business despite the eventual success.

What the casual student does learn is that we have won all our wars and he is, therefore, justified in assuming that since we have defeated the enemies of the past we shall continue to defeat the enemies of the future. This comfortable belief in our invincibility has been reflected legislatively in the inadequate military organization of past years, resulting in stupendous expenditures in each emergency, invariably followed by a parsimonious attitude, if not the complete neglect of ordinary military necessities. In

addition to the perils of war there is the issue of huge war debts with their aftermath of bitter years of heavy taxes. I think it apparent that much of this misfortune in the life of our democracy could have been avoided by the influence of a better informed public on the decisions of the Congress.

Personally I am convinced that the colossal wastefulness of our war organization in the past, and the near tragedies to which it has led us, have been due primarily to the character of our school textbooks and the ineffective manner in which history has been taught in the public schools of this country. In other words, I am saying that if we are to have a sound organization for war we must first have better school histories and a better technique for teaching history....

I might attempt a philosophical discussion this morning regarding the proper organization of this country for war, or, to put it more tactfully, for the national defense; but however convincing this might be, the effect would be negligible—or at least but momentary. The members of a Congress, wise on heels of a war, will legislate with serious purpose to avoid a repetition of the crises, the plights and frights of their recent experience; but what is done is usually undone, the military arrangements emasculated, the old story of unpreparedness continued on into the next chapter of repetitions, because of the pressure of public opinion.

To maintain a sound organization the public must understand the general requirements for the defense of this particular country—the requirements for the maintenance of peace as we soldiers believe, before Congress can be expected, year in and year out, to provide the necessary legislation with due regard both for the economics of the situation and for the essential requirements for an adequate Army and Navy, with the necessary industrial organization behind them. When the high-school student knows exactly what happened, and most important of all, why it happened, then our most serious military problem will be solved. Potentially the strongest nation on earth, we will become the strongest and at a much smaller cost than has been paid for our mistaken course in the past. The historian, the school history and its teacher are the important factors in the solution of the problem I am discussing so superficially this morning.

History as a science has many specialties. The military historian is a specialist. Normally he is not concerned in the preparation of school textbooks. Furthermore, military history, since it deals with wars, is unpopular, and probably more so today than at any other time. Yet I believe it is very important that the true facts, the causes and consequences that make our military history, should be matters of common knowledge. War is a deadly disease, which today afflicts hundreds of millions of people. It exists; therefore, there must be a reason for its existence. We should do everything in our power to isolate the disease, protect ourselves against it, and to discover the specific which will destroy it. A complete knowledge of the disease is essential before we can hope to find a cure. Daily we see attacks on war and tabulations regarding its cost, but rarely do we find a careful effort being made to analyze the various factors in order to determine the nature of war; to audit the accounts as it were, and to see to whom or to what each item of the staggering total is really chargeable.

As to the character of the organization for war suitable and acceptable to this country, I might say that certain definite policies have been developed through the years, and given a degree of permanence in the general amendments to the National Defense Act, of June 1920:

1st A small Regular Army as the keystone of our land defense program. It should provide the small force that might be immediately required for the security of the interests of this country, and supply the training standards and the training staff for the development of a citizen army.

2nd A territorial force, the National Guard, voluntarily maintained by the State governments in cooperation with the Federal Government, to supplement the small standing Army for the first phase of the defense of the country in the event of war.

3rd A democratic system for developing a Reserve of trained officer material—the ROTC and the CMTC, and a practical plan for the prompt procurement of man-power to fill up the ranks of the Regular Establishment and the National Guard, and later to provide the necessary replacements and the men for the new units which will be required.

4th A reserve of non-commercial munitions.

5th A practical set-up for the prompt mobilization of the industrial resources of the nation, to provide, with the least practicable delay, the munitions that are required.

And lastly, an adequate reserve of the raw materials essential for war purposes, which are not available in this country.

The foregoing policies have been generally accepted by the public and are a part of the organic law. Properly administered and developed, they provide a democratic basis for the national defense suitable to our form of government and to our particular international situation.

Glossary

"as did the United States in 1898"	reference to the Spanish-American War
CMTC	Citizens Military Training Camps, held in the summers from 1921 to 1940 and providing military training with no requirement that the trainee serve in the military
materiel	military equipment and supplies
Regular Establishment	the regular, full-time military, as opposed to reserve forces
ROTC	Reserve Officer Training Corps, a program located in colleges and universities to train military officers
War between the States	the American Civil War (1861–1865)

SPEECH TO THE GRADUATING CLASS OF THE U.S. MILITARY ACADEMY (1942)

I appreciate the honor of being here this morning, but I would like you young men to have a sympathetic realization of the fact that it is an obviously dangerous business for a soldier to make a speech these days. Nevertheless, I welcome the opportunity to talk for a few moments to you First Classmen on your day of graduation, and to the other members of the Corps who will carry the flag after you have gone.

Two weeks from now you join a great citizen-army. In physique, in natural ability, and in intelligence, the finest personnel in the world. In their eagerness to work, to endure, and to carry through any missions, they are all that could be desired of soldiers. They but require the modern tools of their profession, the support of the people back home and, most of all, understanding leadership. Preparation for that task of leadership has been the purpose of your course at the Military Academy....

In a few days you will find yourselves among thousands of officers who have recently won their commissions in a rigorous competition unique in the annals of our army. These officers are splendid types. They understand from personal experience the tasks, the duties and the daily problems of the private soldier. They have received intensive training in the technique of weapons and in minor tactics. They won their commissions because they proved conclusively in a grueling test that they were *leaders* and that they had the necessary intelligence and initiative. Already they are familiar with the concentrations and movements of large masses of men. Many of them have participated in maneuvers which extended over a period of months and involved hundreds of thousands of troops operating over tremendous areas, covering in one instance an entire state. In other words, you will be in fast company; you are to join virile, highly-developed forces. You will meet the citizen-soldiers of America at their best and, by the same token, you will have to work very hard to justify your heritage.

Within the past three years our military establishment has undergone a tremendous growth. When I became Chief of Staff, the active Army consisted of 175,000 men and 12,000 officers. Today it numbers almost as many officers as it formerly did soldiers. During the past four weeks alone it has been increased by 300,000 men, and this expansion will continue until by the end of the year there will be nearly four-and-a-half million in the ranks.

A large part of this expansion is taking place within the Air Forces. In spite of the high speed with which it must be accomplished, we know that our pilots represent the flower of American manhood, and our crews the perfection of American mechanical ingenuity. These men come from every section of the country, and pilots have been drawn from almost every college and university in the land. No finer body of men can be found. They are consumed with a determination to carry the fight into Germany and Japan—the same determination that inspired Jimmie Doolittle and his gallant band. Yet splendid as is this personnel, a unified Air Force should have a proportion of officers whose viewpoint, moulded by four years in the Corps of Cadets, includes a full understanding of those military intangibles which are epitomized in the motto of the Corps. Here, then, is one of the most important reasons for the introduction of a flying course into the Academy's curriculum. Last Spring I insisted upon the re-arrangement of courses in order that our new Air Force should include as soon as possible a larger number of commissioned flyers imbued with the traditions and standards of West Point....

Current events remind me of questions which were put to me by members of Congress prior to December 7th, as to where American soldiers might be called upon to fight, and just what was the urgent necessity for the Army that we were endeavoring to organize and train. In reply I usually commented on the fact that we had previously fought in France, Italy, and Germany; in Africa and the Far East; in Siberia and Northern Russia. No one could tell what the future might hold for us. But one thing was clear to me, we must be prepared to fight anywhere, and with a minimum of delay. The possibilities were not overdrawn, for today we find American soldiers throughout the Pacific, in Burma, China, and India. Recently they struck at Tokio. They have wintered in Greenland and Iceland. They are landing in Northern Ireland and England, and they will land in France. We are determined that before the sun sets on this terrible struggle our flag will be recognized throughout the world as a symbol of freedom on the one hand and of overwhelming force on the other.

The state of the public mind has changed. Many of those who were in confusion have come to a clear conclusion as to what we must do. Our people, solidly behind the Army, are supporting wholeheartedly every measure for the prosecution of the war. The calm and the fortitude with which they accept the vicissitudes that are inevitable in a struggle that goes to the four corners of the earth are very reassuring. And our greatest reassurance comes from the courage and fortitude of the wives and parents of those who fought to the last ditch in the Philippines....

I express my complete confidence that you will carry, with a proud and great resolution, into this new Army of citizen-soldiers at their American best, all the traditions, all the history and background of your predecessors at West Point—and may the good Lord be with you.

Glossary

Jimmie Doolittle	General James Doolittle, aviation pioneer and leader of the "Doolittle raid" on Tokyo, Japan, in the aftermath of the Japanese attack on Pearl Harbor on December 7, 1941

WASHINGTON'S BIRTHDAY REMARKS AT PRINCETON UNIVERSITY (1947)

As you all must recognize, we are living today in a most difficult period. The war years were critical, at times alarmingly so. But I think that the present period is in many respects even more critical. The problems are different but no less vital to the national security than those during the days of active fighting. But the more serious aspect is the fact that we no longer display that intensity, that unity of purpose with which we concentrated upon the war task and achieved the victory. Now that an immediate peril is not plainly visible, there is a natural tendency to relax, and to return to business as usual, politics as usual, pleasure as usual.

Many of our people have become indifferent to what I might term the long-time dangers to the nation's security. It is natural and necessary, that there should be a relaxation of wartime tensions. But I feel that we are seriously failing in our attitude toward the international problems whose solution will largely determine our future. The public appears generally in the attitude of a spectator—interested, yes, but, whose serious thinking is directed to local, immediate matters. Spectators of life are not those who will retain their liberties nor are they likely to contribute to their country's security. There are many who deplore, but few who are willing to act, to act directly or to influence political action. Action depends upon conviction, and conviction in turn depends upon understanding—a general understanding both of the past history of man on this globe and an understanding that action is a basic necessity of man's nature. Justice Holmes said, "Man is born to act. To act is to affirm the worth of an end, and to affirm the worth of an end is to create an ideal." So I say to you as earnestly as I can that the attitude of the spectator is the culminating frustration of man's nature. We have had a cessation of hostilities, but we have no genuine peace. Here at home we are in a state of transition between a war and peace economy. In Europe and Asia fear and famine still prevail. Power relationships are in a state of flux. Order has yet to be brought out of confusion. Peace has yet to be secured. And how this is accomplished will depend very much upon the American people.

Most of the other countries of the world find themselves exhausted economically, financially and physically. If the world is to get on its feet, if the productive facilities of the world are to be restored, if democratic processes in many countries are to resume their functioning, a strong lead and definite assistance from the United States will be necessary....

Twenty-five years ago the people of this country, and of the world for that matter, had the opportunity to make vital decisions regarding their future welfare. I think we must agree that the negative course of action followed by the United States after the First World War did not achieve order or security, and that it had a direct bearing upon the recent war and its endless tragedies. There were people in those days who understood the lessons of history, who knew well what should be done in order to minimize the danger of another world disaster, but their combined voice was a feeble one and their proposals were ignored. Now this, in my opinion, is where you come into the picture. In order to take a full part in the life which is before you, I think you must in effect relive the past so that you may turn to the present with deep convictions and an understanding of what manner of country this is for which men for many generations have laid down their lives. Therefore, a deep understanding of history is necessary—not merely recent history which concerns itself with the trivia surrounding conspicuous men and events, but an understanding of that history which records the main currents of the past activities of men and which leads to an understanding of what has created and what has destroyed great civilizations. You should have an understanding of what course of action has created power and security and of the mistakes which have undermined the power and security of many nations, and above all, a clear understanding of the institutions upon which human liberty and individual freedom have depended, and the struggles to gain and maintain them....

I am therefore greatly concerned that the young men and women of this country, men like yourselves and the students in every university, college and high school in the United States, shall acquire a genuine understanding of lessons of history as they relate to governments and the characteristics of nations and peoples, and as to the causes of the wars which have destroyed so much of human life and progress. You should fully understand the special position that the United States now occupies in the world, geographically, financially, militarily, and scientifically, and the implications involved. The development of a sense of responsibility for world order and security, the development of a sense of overwhelming importance of this country's acts, and failures to act in relation to world order and security—these, in my opinion, are great "musts" for your generation.

Glossary

Justice Holmes	Oliver Wendell Holmes, Jr., associate justice of the U.S. Supreme Court (1902–1932)

Marshall Plan Speech (1947)

I need not tell you that the world situation is very serious. That must be apparent to all intelligent people. I think one difficulty is that the problem is one of such enormous complexity that the very mass of facts presented to the public by press and radio make it exceedingly difficult for the man in the street to reach a clear appraisement of the situation. Furthermore, the people of this country are distant from the troubled areas of the earth and it is hard for them to comprehend the plight and consequent reactions of the long-suffering peoples, and the effect of those reactions on their governments in connection with our efforts to promote peace in the world.

In considering the requirements for the rehabilitation of Europe, the physical loss of life, the visible destruction of cities, factories, mines, and railroads was correctly estimated, but it has become obvious during recent months that this visible destruction was probably less serious than the dislocation of the entire fabric of European economy. For the past ten years conditions have been abnormal. The feverish preparation for war and the more feverish maintenance of the war effort engulfed all aspects of national economies. Machinery has fallen into disrepair or is entirely obsolete. Under the arbitrary and destructive Nazi rule, virtually every possible enterprise was geared into the German war machine. Long-standing commercial ties, private institutions, banks, insurance companies, and shipping companies disappeared through loss of capital, absorption through nationalization, or by simple destruction. In many countries, confidence in the local currency has been severely shaken. The breakdown of the business structure of Europe during the war was complete. Recovery has been seriously retarded by the fact that two years after the close of hostilities a peace settlement with Germany and Austria has not been agreed upon. But even given a more prompt solution of these difficult problems, the rehabilitation of the economic structure of Europe quite evidently will require a much longer time and greater effort than has been foreseen....

The truth of the matter is that Europe's requirements for the next three or four years of foreign food and other essential products—principally from America—are so much greater than her present ability to pay that she must have substantial additional help or face economic, social, and political deterioration of a very grave character.

The remedy seems to lie in breaking the vicious circle and restoring the confidence of the European people in the economic future of their own countries and of Europe as a whole. The manufacturer and the farmer throughout wide areas must be able and willing to exchange their product for currencies, the continuing value of which is not open to question.

Aside from the demoralizing effect on the world at large and the possibilities of disturbances arising as a result of the ... desperation of the people concerned, the consequences to the economy of the United States should be apparent to all. It is logical that the United States should do whatever it is able to do to assist in the return of normal economic health in the world, without which there can be no political stability and no assured peace.

Our policy is directed not against any country or doctrine but against hunger, poverty, desperation, and chaos. Its purpose should be the revival of a working economy in the world so as to permit the emergence of political and social conditions in which free institutions can exist. Such assistance, I am convinced, must not be on a piecemeal basis as various crises develop. Any assistance that this Government may render in the future should provide a cure rather than a mere palliative. Any government that is willing to assist in the task of recovery will find full cooperation, I am sure, on the part of the United States Government. Any government which maneuvers to block the recovery of other countries cannot expect help from us.

Furthermore, governments, political parties or groups which seek to perpetuate human misery in order to profit therefrom politically or otherwise will encounter the opposition of the United States.

It is already evident that, before the United States Government can proceed much further in its efforts to alleviate the situation and help start the European world on its way to recovery, there must be some agreement among the countries of Europe as to the requirements of the situation and the part those countries themselves will take in order to give proper effect to whatever action might be undertaken by this Government. It would be neither fitting nor efficacious for our Government to undertake to draw up unilaterally a program designed to place Europe on its feet economically. This is the business of the Europeans. The initiative, I think, must come from Europe. The role of this country should consist of friendly aid in the drafting of a European program and of later support of such a program so far as it may be practical for us to do so. The program should be a joint one, agreed to by a number, if not all, European nations.

Nobel Peace Prize Acceptance Speech (1953)

In my country my military associates frequently tell me that we Americans have learned our lesson. I completely disagree with this contention and point to the rapid disintegration between 1945 and 1950 of our once vast power for maintaining the peace. As a direct consequence, in my opinion, there resulted the brutal invasion of South Korea, which for a time threatened the complete defeat of our hastily arranged forces in that field. I speak of this with deep feeling because in 1939 and again in the early fall of 1950 it suddenly became my duty, my responsibility, to rebuild our national military strength in the very face of the gravest emergencies.

These opening remarks may lead you to assume that my suggestions for the advancement of world peace will rest largely on military strength. For the moment the maintenance of peace in the present hazardous world situation does depend in very large measure on military power, together with Allied cohesion. But the maintenance of large armies for an indefinite period is not a practical or a promising basis for policy. We must stand together strongly for these present years, that is, in this present situation; but we must, I repeat, we must find another solution, and that is what I wish to discuss this evening.

There has been considerable comment over the awarding of the Nobel Peace Prize to a soldier. I am afraid this does not seem as remarkable to me as it quite evidently appears to others. I know a great deal of the horrors and tragedies of war. Today, as chairman of the American Battle Monuments Commission, it is my duty to supervise the construction and maintenance of military cemeteries in many countries overseas, particularly in Western Europe. The cost of war in human lives is constantly spread before me, written neatly in many ledgers whose columns are gravestones. I am deeply moved to find some means or method of avoiding another calamity of war. Almost daily I hear from the wives, or mothers, or families of the fallen. The tragedy of the aftermath is almost constantly before me.

I share with you an active concern for some practical method for avoiding war. Let me first say that I regard the present highly dangerous situation as a very special one, which naturally dominates our thinking on the subject of peace, but which should not, in my opinion, be made the principal basis for our reasoning towards the manner for securing a condition of long continued peace. A very strong military posture is vitally necessary today. How long it must continue I am not prepared to estimate, but I am sure that it is too narrow a basis on which to build a dependable, long-enduring peace. The guarantee for a long continued peace will depend on other factors in addition to a moderated military strength, and no less important. Perhaps the most important single factor will be a spiritual regeneration to develop goodwill, faith, and understanding among nations. Economic factors will undoubtedly play an important part. Agreements to secure a balance of power, however disagreeable they may seem, must likewise be considered. And with all these there must be wisdom and the will to act on that wisdom....

In this brief discussion, I can give only a very limited treatment of these great essentials to peace. However, I would like to select three more specific areas for closer attention.

The first relates to the possibilities of better education in the various factors affecting the life of peaceful security, both in terms of its development and of its disruption. Because wisdom in action in our Western democracies rests squarely upon public understanding, I have long believed that our schools have a key role to play. Peace could, I believe, be advanced through careful study of all the factors which have gone into the various incidents now historical that have marked the breakdown of peace in the past. As an initial procedure our schools, at least our colleges but preferably our senior high schools, as we call them, should have courses which not merely instruct our budding citizens in the historical sequence of events of the past, but which treat with almost scientific accuracy the circumstances which have marked the breakdown of peace and have led to the disruption of life and the horrors of war....

It is for this reason that I believe our students must first seek to understand the conditions, as far as possible without national prejudices, which have led to past tragedies and should strive to determine the great fundamentals which must govern a peaceful progression toward a constantly higher level of civilization. There are innumerable instructive lessons out of the past, but all too frequently their presentation is highly colored or distorted in the effort to present a favorable national point of view. In our school histories at home, certainly in years past, those written in the North present a strikingly different picture of our Civil War from those written in the South. In some portions it is hard to realize they are dealing with the same war. Such reactions are all too common in matters of peace and security. But we are told that we live in a highly scientific age. Now the progress of science depends on facts and not fancies or prejudice. Maybe in this age we can find a way of facing the facts and discounting the distorted records of the past....

For my second suggestion, I would like to consider the national attitudes that bear on the great problem of peace....Despite the amazing conquest of the air and its reduction of distances to a matter of hours and not days, or minutes instead of hours, the United States is remote in a general sense from the present turbulent areas of the world. I believe the measure of detachment, limited though it is, has been of help in enabling us on occasion to take an impartial stand on heated international problems....

From this fact we have acquired, I think, a feeling and a concern for the problems of other peoples. There is a deep urge to help the oppressed and to give aid to those upon whom great and sudden hardship has fallen....

The third area I would like to discuss has to do with the problem of the millions who live under subnormal conditions and who have now come to a realization that they may aspire to a fair share of the God-given rights of human beings. Their aspirations present a challenge to the more favored nations to lend assistance in bettering the lot of the poorer. This is a special problem in the present crisis, but it is of basic importance to any successful effort toward an enduring peace. The question is not merely one of self-interest arising from the fact that these people present a situation which is a seed bed for either one or the other of two greatly differing ways of life. Ours is democracy, according to our interpretation of the meaning of that word. If we act with wisdom and magnanimity, we can guide these yearnings of the poor to a richer and better life through democracy.

We must present democracy as a force holding within itself the seeds of unlimited progress by the human race. By our actions we should make it clear that such a democracy is a means to a better way of life, together with a better understanding among nations. Tyranny inevitably must retire before the tremendous moral strength of the gospel of freedom and self-respect for the individual, but we have to recognize that these democratic principles do not flourish on empty stomachs, and that people turn to false promises of dictators because they are hopeless and anything promises something better than the miserable existence that they endure. However, material assistance alone is not sufficient. The most important thing for the world today in my opinion is a spiritual regeneration which would reestablish a feeling of good faith among men generally. Discouraged people are in sore need of the inspiration of great principles. Such leadership can be the rallying point against intolerance, against distrust, against that fatal insecurity that leads to war. It is to be hoped that the democratic nations can provide the necessary leadership.

John Marshall (Library of Congress)

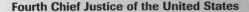
Featured Documents
- ◆ *Marbury v. Madison* (1803)
- ◆ *McCulloch v. Maryland* (1819)
- ◆ *Gibbons v. Ogden* (1824)

Overview

Serving as chief justice of the United States from 1801 to 1835, John Marshall well deserves to be known as the "Great Chief Justice." He profoundly enhanced the reputation and status of the Supreme Court, which went from being the weakest branch of the federal government to being the primary interpreter of the federal Constitution and one of the most respected legal institutions in the nation. Under his leadership, the Court made major steps in advancing the constitutional growth of the United States and in clarifying the nature of the Union, which is only tentatively outlined in the text of the Constitution itself. In addition, Marshall and his colleagues were able to shape American public and private law to facilitate economic stability and to create what modern economists term a *common market*. These constitutional changes were essential to the prosperity of the infant United States and in the enhancement of the nation's international standing in a highly competitive commercial world.

Even in ordinary times these would have been magnificent contributions to the general welfare, but Marshall accomplished them despite the adamant opposition of President Thomas Jefferson and his political party, which controlled the presidency and both houses of Congress during Marshall's thirty-four years as chief justice. At the same time, public opinion during the first four decades of the nineteenth century strongly favored states' rights and sharp limitations on the powers of the federal government. As a consequence, each of the new appointees to the Supreme Court made by Jefferson and his successors threatened to weaken the Court's efforts to provide the legal basis for effective government at the national level.

A veteran of five years' service in the Culpeper Minutemen and the Continental army, Marshall was a native of the Northern Neck of Virginia, and his family enjoyed a close friendship with General George Washington. Admitted to practice law after the American Revolution, Marshall became successful, principally in the highest courts of the state, which were in Richmond. In 1797 he was persuaded to accept a commission as one of three diplomats sent to France; when he and his two colleagues refused to pay a bribe to the French government before the French would begin talks, they returned home to receive the enthusiastic thanks of the American people. Known as the XYZ Affair, this event and the public support it generated for the

courage and patriotism of the American ministers, resulted in Marshall's winning a seat in the U.S. House of Representatives. Taking his seat in March 1799, he remained in Congress until President John Adams appointed him secretary of state in May 1800. In January 1801 Adams nominated Marshall to head the U.S. Supreme Court, and the Senate quickly confirmed the nomination. Adams would later assert that Marshall's appointment as chief justice was the most significant act of his presidency.

Marshall was a Federalist, and he lived in the shadow of his fellow Virginian George Washington, who was both his commanding general and a family friend from his childhood. This personal affinity reinforced Marshall's commitment to Federalist ideology and devoted service within the party's structure. Along with his brother-in-law, Edward Carrington, Marshall became actively involved in the electoral process in Virginia and influential in the distribution of patronage appointments within the Old Dominion. As secretary of state in the Adams administration, he was directly involved in the day-to-day administration of the federal government, particularly during Adams's increasingly frequent absences from the capital.

For Marshall, being a Federalist also involved holding a vision of America's future, based in part upon the vast treasure of land and resources that the nation had barely begun to develop and also upon a foundation of stability in property ownership and regularity in commercial relationships. Post-Revolutionary America was, in fact, similar to modern developing nations: It lacked access to capital investment, and regional and state-based diversity undermined economic relationships among the states. As chief justice, Marshall bore a faith in the nation's economic future that clearly anticipated that commercial activity would enhance and alter the agricultural basis of American prosperity. Although he had reservations about the impact of industrialization on the United States, he reluctantly accepted the need for economic growth and diversification if the new nation was to take its rightful place in the international community.

Yet Marshall's Federalist politics did not override the personal qualities that made him a successful leader of the Supreme Court. As evidenced by family tradition, contemporary anecdotes, and occasional letters and other documents, Marshall was a man who enjoyed life, valued his friends, and was eminently capable of arguing persuasively and bringing others to the acceptance of his opinions. He

Time Line

1755
- **September 24**
  John Marshall is born in the vicinity of Germantown, Fauquier County, Virginia.

1775–1779
- Marshall is engaged in active military service with the Culpeper Minutemen Battalion and Virginia Continental Line.

1780
- **May–July**
  Marshall attends George Wythe's law lectures at the College of William and Mary.
- **August 28**
  Marshall is admitted to law practice by the Fauquier County Court.

1782
- **May 25**
  Marshall is elected a member of the Virginia House of Delegates for the first of seven terms.

1782–1784
- Marshall additionally serves as a member of the Virginia Council of State.

1785–1788
- Marshall serves as recorder (judge) of the Richmond City Hustings Court.

1788
- **June**
  Marshall takes part in the Virginia convention assembled to consider the ratification of the federal Constitution.

1795
- **February 2**
  Marshall is admitted to practice before the U.S. Supreme Court.

1797–1798
- In the XYZ Affair, Marshall is as one of three U.S. ministers appointed to negotiate a treaty with France who refuse to supply a bribe.

---

was an instinctive mediator and builder of consensus. In the male-dominated politics of his day, he was accepted as a friend by all, with the exception of his distant cousin Thomas Jefferson. His gift for friendship enhanced his capacity to build agreement among the justices of the Supreme Court, just as it had made him an effective politician and leader. By 1827 Chief Justice Marshall's influence within the Supreme Court had begun to wane. In June 1835 digestive troubles drove him to consult Philadelphia physicians, and he died in that city on July 6, 1835.

Explanation and Analysis of Documents

Marbury v. Madison (1803), *McCulloch v. Maryland* (1819), and *Gibbons v. Ogden* (1824) are milestone documents in Chief Justice Marshall's career and prime examples of his work as a judge and leader of the Court. They also demonstrate the evolution of his role as Court personnel changed and new issues arose for decision. *Marbury* is perhaps the purest example of Marshall's logical processes and approach to constitutional decision and thus has become one of the first documents studied in courses on American constitutional law. Its contribution to our understanding of Marshall inheres in the great probability that it is an opinion composed by him with minimal, if any, contributions from his colleagues on the bench. *McCulloch* was decided in the February 1819 term of the Court, the point at which the Marshall Court reached its peak in power and influence. However, the other major constitutional cases at that term—*Dartmouth College v. Woodward* and *Sturges v. Crowninshield*—show that unanimity among the justices had begun to wane, particularly on issues concerning economic regulation. Although *McCulloch* did not directly raise property or trade matters, and was agreed to by all the justices, it may also have drawn upon Marshall's ability to achieve consensus among his associate justices. Despite difficult economic times and the rising spirit of states' rights, *McCulloch* is an eloquent and far-reaching manifestation of the potentiality for federal authority and of its formative role in the future growth of the American republic. Marshall's memorable phraseology rings out to give readers some appreciation of his persuasive powers in the Court's conferences.

Less monumental in a literary sense, *Gibbons* is the most encyclopedic of the chief justice's opinions for the Court. Although it was strongly influenced by the need to accommodate opposing views, Marshall's opinion nevertheless presented a carefully reasoned and precisely analyzed exposition of the commerce clause of the Constitution. Yet the opinion left important questions unanswered, causing contemporaries to misconstrue its meaning and postponing to future Supreme Courts more detailed consideration of Congress's powers over commerce. Taken together *Marbury*, *McCulloch*, and *Gibbons* are perhaps the best evidence of Marshall's leadership of the Court. They demonstrate his deep respect for the Constitution and his awareness of judicial responsibility to be cautious

---

and conscientious in interpreting that document as the preeminent source of American fundamental law. They reverberate with his confidence and pride in the American federal nation and his determination to make the federal government adequate to the great ends constitutionally assigned to it. And they reflect his ability to shape compromise and to reconcile conflicting opinions into workable decisions in constitutional law.

◆ Marbury v. Madison

Marbury v. Madison was the first case in which the U.S. Supreme Court declared an act of Congress unconstitutional. The case is also important because it represents the Marshall Court's first use of an "opinion of the Court" in a constitutional law case. This form of opinion replaced the seriatim opinion, in which each justice wrote his own reasoning and decision concerning the matters in litigation. In making this change, the Marshall Court established the practice that seniority among the justices determined who would deliver the opinion of the Court or who, alternatively, might appoint a fellow justice to deliver the opinion. Since the chief justice is considered senior in rank to all other justices, Marshall was thereafter authorized to deliver, and perhaps to write, opinions of the Court in most cases. He appears to have done so in virtually all cases before 1812 and in a majority afterward until his death.

Marbury v. Madison came before the Court on a motion asking that a mandamus writ be issued to James Madison, Thomas Jefferson's secretary of state, commanding him to deliver William Marbury's commission as a justice of the peace of the District of Columbia. A mandamus is a court order directing that a named individual perform an act required by law. On the date established for the hearing, Charles Lee, the U.S. attorney general, challenged the constitutional power of the Supreme Court to issue a mandamus. He pointed out that the Constitution gave the Court only limited power to try cases brought before it as a trial court; its original jurisdiction was limited to cases between the American states, cases involving foreign nations, and cases in which foreign ambassadors, ministers, or other diplomats were involved. On the other hand, the Judiciary Act of 1789 contained a provision that explicitly gave the Supreme Court this power. Lee's concern, then, was that if Congress could increase the Supreme Court's original jurisdiction without first obtaining a constitutional amendment, how could the Constitution remain superior to federal statutes that were supposedly valid only if enacted in accordance with the Constitution?

In his opinion Marshall elects to consider, first, the manner of appointing and commissioning officers of the federal government and then to determine whether Marbury was entitled to a commission and whether it was justifiable to deny him the document. After an exhaustive consideration, he concludes that Marbury had a property right to his office and that to deny him his commission was wrongful.

The remaining question was whether the Supreme Court is authorized to issue a writ of mandamus when acting as a trial court. Marshall looks closely at Article III of

Time Line

1799
- **April 21**
  Marshall is elected as a Virginia member of the U.S. House of Representatives.

1800
- **May 13**
  Marshall is appointed U.S. secretary of state.

1801
- **January 27**
  Marshall is confirmed by the Senate as chief justice of the United States.

1803
- **February 24**
  Marshall delivers the Supreme Court's opinion in *Marbury v. Madison*.

1807
- **August– September 1**
  In the U.S. Circuit Court for Virginia, Marshall presides over the criminal trial of Aaron Burr.

1819
- **March 6**
  Marshall delivers the U.S. Supreme Court's opinion in *McCulloch v. Maryland*.
- **April–July**
  Marshall publishes essays in defense of *McCulloch v. Maryland* signed by "A Friend of the Union."
- **June 15–July 1**
  Marshall writes "A Friend of the Constitution" essays in further defense of *McCulloch v. Maryland*.

1824
- **March 2**
  Marshall delivers the Court's opinion in *Gibbons v. Ogden*.

1835
- **July 6**
  Marshall dies in Philadelphia, Pennsylvania.

the U.S. Constitution, which spells out the powers of the various federal courts, giving special attention to the Supreme Court. The Constitution's grant of original trial jurisdiction to the Supreme Court is brief, limited, and quite specific: It covers cases involving foreign nations and their diplomats and cases in which one or more states of the Union are involved. All other cases before the Supreme Court were to be appellate cases, where the authority of all federal courts would be set by Congress through the enactment of statutes. In the Judiciary Act of 1789, however, Congress attempted to give the Supreme Court trial court authority to issue a mandamus writ. Marshall thus aims to determine which provision was controlling, that of the Constitution or the statute enacted by Congress.

For Marshall, simply phrasing the issue that way was tantamount to giving the answer: The Constitution must always be understood as controlling. He bases his conclusion on three propositions: First, the people of the United States have the authority to establish fundamental principles that are to govern the operations of the federal government; they had exercised that choice in ratifying the Constitution, which became the supreme law of the federal Union. Second, the federal government is limited in its powers by the terms of the Constitution; permitting those limits to be exceeded by the enactment of a congressional statute would jeopardize the fundamental nature of the Constitution. Third, the supremacy clause of the Constitution (Article VI, Clause 2) determines that the Constitution "and the Laws of the United States which shall be made in Pursuance thereof ... shall be the supreme Law of the Land." The wording leaves no doubt that the terms of the Constitution are superior to any and all congressional enactments and that in the case of conflict the Constitution's terms must prevail.

Marshall next asks what courts and judges should do when confronted with such a conflict and again turns to Article VI for the answer. The judges of every state as well as federal judicial officers are required to take an oath to support the Constitution. When the terms of the Constitution clash with those of a federal statute, the courts must follow their sworn obligation to support the superior law of the Constitution. That is the very essence of judicial duty.

The Supreme Court's authority to invalidate a congressional statute is held to be firmly based upon the fundamental status of the Constitution, and this status, in turn, depends upon the sovereignty of the people. The limited power of the federal government is thus maintained by judicial decisions that place constitutional requirements above the legislative powers of Congress, and the Constitution itself imposes this duty of judicial review upon all judges holding office in the United States.

By modern standards, Marshall's approach to judicial review in *Marbury* seems almost simplistic and certainly mechanical. One merely compares the Constitution's text with the statute in question and determines whether there is a significant difference between them; if so, the Constitution must prevail, and an oath-bound judge must follow the Constitution. Thus, in the present case, Marshall concludes that the Judiciary Act of 1789, being incompatible with the Constitution, is invalid and that the Supreme Court does not have the authority to issue a writ of mandamus in an original jurisdiction case. The clarity of the process set forth by Marshall makes *Marbury* a classic description of judicial review; that very precision means that the case retains utility in modern times even though the practical application of judicial review has become much more complicated.

◆ *McCulloch v. Maryland*

Prior to the American Civil War, the nature of the Union was much in debate, with the discussion being fueled by regional animosities and power struggles between the states and the national government. It was in *McCulloch v. Maryland* that the issue of federalism was first clearly presented in a constitutional case of major significance. Maryland imposed a tax on certain bank notes issued in the state, but the tax fell almost exclusively upon notes issued by the Second Bank of the United States. James McCulloch, the cashier of the Baltimore branch of the Second Bank, continued to issue untaxed notes after the effective date of the state statute and so was sued for the taxes due in an action brought by Maryland officials in the Baltimore County Court. Ordered to pay the tax despite his plea that it was invalid under the federal Constitution, McCulloch appealed to the Maryland Court of Appeals, which affirmed the trial court's judgment. A further appeal brought the case before the Supreme Court in the February 1819 term.

Marshall's opinion in *McCulloch* continues to dominate the way in which contemporary jurists understand and debate the Constitution's delegation of power to the federal government. Admitting that the framers of the Constitution carefully enumerated the legislative powers of Congress, the chief justice takes pains to note that the phraseology of the document specifically avoids the use of the word *express* in describing aspects of congressional authority. For Marshall, that indicates a rejection of the format of the Articles of Confederation, which gave the central government only that authority expressly mentioned. The Constitution for Marshall also presumes that Congress might enact measures that are implied as possible in the Constitution's grant of enumerated powers, to thus supplement those powers. Finally, Marshall broadly construes the Constitution's "necessary and proper" clause as permitting Congress to adopt those means that are suitable and appropriate to implement both enumerated and implied powers.

Although the *McCulloch* opinion does not specifically address federal supremacy, its expansive interpretation of congressional power did much to enhance the authority of the federal government. The Court was compelled to confront arguments by Maryland's counsel that the Union was created by state action rather than by the people of the United States acting in separate state ratifying conventions. At its most extreme extent, the compact theory holds that the ratifying states thus transferred only those powers included within the Constitution's express terms; in addition, the states are held to retain all aspects of sovereignty not expressly transferred to the federal government. With the application of the compact theory to the Second Bank's operations within Maryland, it was asserted that Maryland's permission was required before the federal government could operate a bank within the state. Since taxation is a concurrent power available to both state and federal governments, Maryland's counsel held that it was constitutional for the state to tax notes issued by the Second Bank within Maryland. These broader political theory issues are necessarily covered within Marshall's opinion.

Less memorable in the *McCulloch* opinion is Marshall's tentative foray into the grim battlefield of state-federal tax immunities. He asserts that a state tax that falls upon the activities of the U.S. government or its instrumentalities is unconstitutional. He supports that position with the general proposition that to permit the states to impose taxes on federal activity would be to endanger the operations of the U.S. government. More correctly, the chief justice relies upon the inequity and inherent danger in permitting such a tax to be valid. On a theoretical level, Marshall points out that any state taxation on federal government operations imposes burdens on Americans resident throughout the Union, who, because of nonresidency in Maryland, have not consented to being indirectly taxed as such and cannot retaliate at the ballot box. This is an example of taxation without representation, a chief complaint of the rebelling American colonists, but Marshall diplomatically refrains from making such a connection. Subsequent elaborations of the state-federal tax immunity question by the Supreme Court have rendered antiquated much of this portion of Marshall's opinion. However, the more general discussion concerning the impact of taxation on relationships within the Union serves to emphasize the degree to which the Court was willing to draw supremacy principles from the national electoral base upon which the Union is established.

In his opinion, Marshall draws upon the history of the Bank of the United States to support his view of its constitutionality. The First Bank of the United States was chartered in 1791 only after extensive discussion in President Washington's cabinet and a strong endorsement in Secretary of the Treasury Alexander Hamilton's report on the need for a national bank, a document upon which Marshall drew heavily in preparing the *McCulloch* opinion. After twenty years, the bank's charter lapsed, causing such difficulty during the War of 1812 that the Second Bank was chartered in 1816, likewise for a twenty-year period. This long history of serious discussion and two statutory authorizations was deemed strong evidence of constitutionality, and so the chief justice took advantage of *McCulloch* to legitimate and reinforce that record.

Marshall makes certain to refute Maryland's reliance upon the compact theory of government. Although the Constitutional Convention was populated by delegations from the various states, the Constitution was ratified not by those delegates or by the state legislatures, but rather by popularly elected state ratifying conventions. It was their favorable response—on behalf of the people of the United States and not on behalf of state governments—that gave the federal Constitution its legitimacy. As Marshall asserts, "The constitution, when thus adopted, was of complete obligation, and bound the State sovereignties." The U.S. government was thus formed as a government of the people. It emanated from them, and its powers are exercised directly upon them and for their benefit.

The next issue was originally raised by the framers' failure to include within Congress's enumerated powers the authority to charter corporations or banking institutions. Marshall points out that the power to charter corporations is an inherent aspect of sovereignty and the Constitution's failure to include those measures within specifically enumerated powers did not negate Congress's authority to charter banks or other corporations. To the contrary: The Constitution requires that Congress be able to exercise powers implied within the general grant of enumerated powers; this is essential if the enumerated powers were to be effective in achieving the great purposes of the national government. Thus, the Constitution bestows broad authority that allows Congress to adopt appropriate means to achieve the objects specified in the enumerated powers. Marshall observes, "In considering this question, then, we must never forget that it is a constitution we are expounding." The federal powers to conduct war, to impose and collect taxes, and to operate post offices all anticipated the establishment of financial institutions. The chartering of the Bank of the United States thus fell within the powers implied by the constitutional grants of enumerated power.

The Constitution also specifically sanctions the exercise of powers "necessary and proper" for the execution of enumerated powers. This gives Congress generous leeway in selecting means for implementing both enumerated and implied powers. Looking at the constitutional text, Marshall finds that in Article I, Section 10, the framers used the term "absolutely necessary" to limit state taxing powers; he asks why similar phraseology was not used to limit the word "necessary" in the "necessary and proper" clause. Deploring Maryland's attempt to apply a restrictive construction of the Constitution, he notes that if the end be constitutionally authorized and the means be "plainly adapted to that end" and not specifically prohibited by the Constitution, the congressional action in question is valid.

Even conceding that the U.S. government is a sovereignty of limited powers, Marshall insists that within those limited powers the federal government is supreme. That conceptualization of federal power permeates Marshall's consideration of the power of taxation as concurrent among the state and federal governments. In establishing a bank to conduct its financial business and by the issuance of that bank's notes, the federal government acted within all of the states to effectuate its enumerated powers. Supremacy as well as constitutional construction demand that the actions of a single state not be permitted to restrict the effectiveness of, or to impose a taxation burden upon, the operations of the Bank of the United States.

Having asserted that the Maryland tax upon bank notes issued by nonresident institutions was unconstitutional as applied to the Second Bank of the United States, Marshall concedes that a real property tax, assessed upon all real estate within Maryland, might be validly imposed on real property of the Bank of the United States. He is careful not to elaborate on this aspect of his opinion, but one may surmise that he would have specifically distinguished between a tax on federal bank operations and a tax on federal bank property holdings equally imposed on all other property interests. This was but an initial step toward the development of a detailed and complex system of constitutional law concerning federal-state tax immunities.

◆ Gibbons v. Ogden

Also known as the Steamboat Case, *Gibbons v. Ogden* (1824) arose from the New York legislature's grant of a monopoly on steamboat navigation within the state as a reward for the successful establishment of such travel on a regular basis between New York City and Albany. Originally offered to the inventor John Fitch, the grant was about to lapse when the partnership of the former New York chancellor Robert R. Livingston and the engineer Robert Fulton obtained a transfer of Fitch's rights. Their successful demonstration of compliance in 1807 gave them a New York monopoly to traverse the Hudson River, Long Island Sound, and all other navigable waters within the Empire State. In addition, in 1809 Robert Fulton's improvements upon earlier steamboat designs resulted in the grant of a U.S. patent for the partnership's steamboat. However, the value of steam navigation, particularly on the Mississippi River watershed, and interstate retaliation against New York's monopoly grant encouraged competitors to enter the steamboat business in New York Bay and Long Island Sound.

Strong antimonopoly sentiments in the Midwest and Southwest, augmented by innovative steamboat designs by and sharp competition from Henry Shreve, made it difficult for the Livingston-Fulton syndicate to defend their enterprise in western waters. After 1817 the steamboat route between Elizabeth, New Jersey, and New York City became the focus of extended litigation. Ultimately, a Livingston-Fulton licensee, Aaron Ogden, sued a competitor, Thomas Gibbons, for violation of the New York monopoly grant, and Gibbons defended himself by claiming the protection of the commerce clause and the 1793 Act for Enrolling and Licensing Ships or Vessels to be Employed in the Coasting Trade and Fisheries, and for Regulating the Same, commonly known as the Federal Coasting Licensing Act. Chancellor James Kent awarded an injunction against Gibbons and upheld the constitutionality of the New York monopoly. Gibbons's appeal to New York's Court for the Trial of Impeachments and the Correction of Errors was rejected in January 1822, and the case was carried to Marshall's Supreme Court, where it was argued in February 1824.

Even before it was argued in the Supreme Court, *Gibbons* attracted widespread attention. The navigation of the Hudson River and New York Bay involved substantial profits that could be enhanced only with the completion of the Erie Canal, which would occur in 1825. New Jersey and Connecticut, the states directly affected by the New York

monopoly, retaliated against New York steamboat operators who ventured into their territorial waters. Gibbons and his associates gained newspaper publicity and popular approval with their daring maritime challenges to the Livingston-Fulton syndicate. Human interest was sparked by the personal feud between Thomas Gibbons and Aaron Ogden, which at one point threatened to erupt into a duel. As if this background to the litigation were not sufficient to earn national attention, the parties each recruited leading members of the Supreme Court bar to argue on their behalf. Gibbons's appeal was presented by Daniel Webster and U.S. Attorney General William Wirt; Thomas J. Oakley and Thomas Addis Emmet appeared on behalf of Aaron Ogden. The Court took three weeks to deliver its March 2 opinion and enter judgment, which reversed the decision of the New York Court of Impeachments and Errors and nullified the New York monopoly.

The chief justice opens the Court's opinion with a terse rejection of the compact theory of government advocated by Ogden's counsel in support of New York's grant of a monopoly despite the existence of the commerce clause in the federal Constitution. Having settled that point once more, he proceeds to define commerce and to consider the component parts of commercial activity. Counsel for the Livingston-Fulton syndicate argued strongly that commercial activity did not include navigation but was restricted to the buying and selling of goods, the interchange of goods, and contractual aspects of traffic. Appealing to general understanding, the chief justice insists that commerce has always been understood to include navigation; this is also shown through the exceptions from Congress's authority over commerce delineated in the Constitution. Specifically, in regulating commerce, Congress is prohibited from giving a preference to one port over another. Even more pointedly, the Constitution prevents commercial regulation that would require a vessel bound for one state to enter, clear, or pay duties in another state. Marshall's use of commonly accepted meanings of words and his examination of the "four corners" of the federal Constitution for indications of meaning were hallmarks of his jurisprudential method. This approach permitted him to arrive at definitions that were both accurate and in accord with constitutional intent.

He next considers the extent of Congress's power to regulate commerce. Even before the ratification of the Constitution, Congress's authority was broadly construed to include every aspect of commercial intercourse between the United States and foreign nations. Since both foreign commerce and commerce "among the states" are grouped together in the same sentence in the Constitution, the generous interpretation of the term *commerce* established by Marshall must be applicable to interstate commerce. The word *among*, meanwhile, encompasses trade concerning more than one state while precluding congressional regulation of activity solely within the interior of a single state. Marshall asserts that the Constitution was not intended to give Congress the power to regulate commerce activities completely "within a particular State which do not affect other States, and with which it is not necessary to interfere

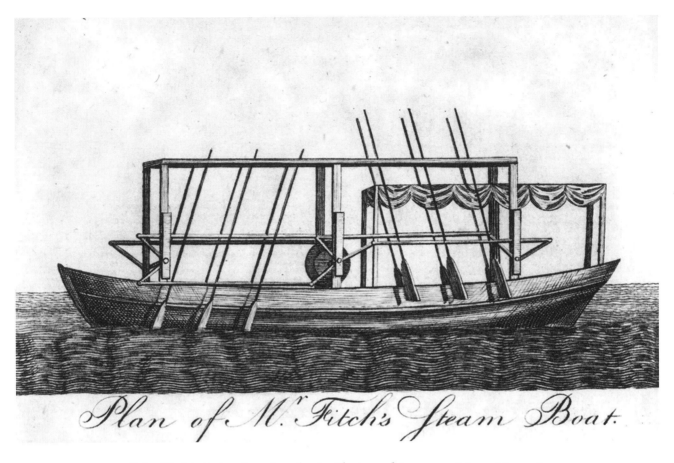

John Fitch's design for a ferry boat with steam-driven oars (Library of Congress)

for the purpose of executing some of the general powers of the [U.S.] government." In other words, Congress's regulatory power extends to commerce internal to a state only if the commerce "affects" a sister state or interferes with the execution of the general authority vested in the U.S. government. The Constitution does not apply a rigid geographic measure to what qualifies as commerce "among the states." Rather, it requires that courts examine the degree to which state economic regulations affect the general welfare of associated states and the constitutional authority of the federal government.

Marshall then examines the comprehensive nature of Congress's authority to regulate, asking whether that power is exclusive or concurrent with the states. Examining the concurrent taxing power vested in both the U.S. and state governments, he indicates that the power to tax is essential to the existence of both federal and state governments and is exercised without the danger that one government's authority might be usurped by the other. On the other hand, state regulations of foreign or interstate commerce always trespass upon the constitutional power of Congress. As such, they are invalid under the supremacy clause of the Constitution. Conceding that Congress might elect to assist the states in the execution of their reserved powers and noting that Congress might also adopt state legislation as part of the federal regulation of commerce, Marshall

nevertheless insists that these cooperative procedures between the states and the federal government do not demonstrate equal concurrency of federal and state power over foreign or interstate commerce. Quite to the contrary, these examples of intergovernmental cooperation arise from the differing sources of police power reserved to the states, on one hand, and, on the other hand, from the federal government's constitutional power over commerce. Absent any adverse impact upon the authority of the federal government, these overlapping powers might coexist. Whenever there is an adverse impact, however, the Constitution's supremacy clause invalidates the state legislation.

The chief justice finally considers counsels' contention that, by its terms alone, the Constitution prohibits the states from regulating interstate commerce. This was an assertion of what future scholars would term the "dormancy" view of the commerce clause, which states that the mere grant of the commerce power in the Constitution prohibits the states from acting in that area. In effect, this view reserves to Congress a preemptive right to legislate with regard to interstate commerce, excluding the states from any legislative authority because of the existence of this power, however unexercised. In the *Gibbons* opinion, Marshall takes refuge in the 1793 Federal Coasting Licensing Act and finds it to be a comprehensive conferral of navigation rights upon all licensees. He holds that as the possessor of such a license, Thomas Gibbons was granted the right to navigate between New York City and Elizabeth, New Jersey. The New York monopoly conflicted with those statutory federal rights and thus violated the commerce clause of the Constitution.

Gibbons is as important for what it does not decide as for what it does decide. It provides a broad and pragmatic definition of the commerce clause as it relates to both foreign commerce and trade "among the states," and it applies principles of the supremacy clause to invalidate state action that "affects" foreign and interstate commerce. In doing so, the decision establishes a firm foundation upon which future constitutional theory could be built. At the same time, its ambiguities leave much room for future judicial elaboration; this is true of Marshall's refusal to hold the commerce clause as ipso facto conferring an exclusive power upon Congress, and it also applies to the Court's unwillingness to comment upon the dormancy construction of the Constitution's grant of power. Thus, Marshall's opinion stands as but the beginning of what would be the Supreme Court's extended elaboration of the scope and applicability of the commerce clause. As such, it is perhaps the most noteworthy of Marshall's opinions when measured by its present-day impact on American economic life and social legislation.

Impact and Legacy

Two centuries of Supreme Court adjudication have served to isolate Marshall's opinions from most current issues in constitutional law. They remain "great cases" in that they form an essential background to understanding contemporary decision making, but in most circumstances they are no longer considered binding precedents. Nonetheless, Marshall is yet cited in modern times because his opinions established basic principles that have been subsequently refined and modified but which remain foundational and eminently quotable.

Marbury v. Madison remains the fundamental case that received judicial review into federal law; as such it is almost universally the first case studied in American constitutional law. Its preeminence is due to its logical exposition and its clear statement of the basic principles of American limited government and its demonstration of the role of judges in applying those rules in constitutional cases. *Marbury* is also a model for the formulation of judicial opinions, which are written to supply the reasoning and analysis by which judges arrive at their decisions. The persistent importance of *Marbury* in American law is illustrative of the degree to which Marshall's "style"—in behavior and in literary skill—has shaped both the process of judging and the persona of judgeship.

McCulloch v. Maryland is one of the foundational cases involving the supremacy clause of the Constitution. The case provided long-lasting precedents concerning the division of powers between the states and the federal government. As legitimated by Marshall's exposition of the doctrine of implied powers, the "necessary and proper" clause gives the federal legislature broad discretion in selecting the means by which the powers granted by the Constitution may be exercised. These important constitutional developments should not mask the stylistic power of Marshall's prose as he enunciates his concept of a vigorous and effective federal government providing leadership of a Union that allows due importance to the sovereignty of its component states.

Finally, *Gibbons v. Ogden* elaborated an extensive federal power to regulate both foreign and interstate commerce. As a result of the foundation laid by *Gibbons*, the vast majority of all federal economic regulatory activity finds its constitutional basis in the commerce clause of the Constitution. In response to the Great Depression, the Supreme Court began an expansion of the commerce clause's scope to include virtually all economic legislation conducive for economic recovery and regulation. The commerce clause continues to play a central role in American life and federal government.

The logic, force, and persuasiveness of John Marshall's opinions, as amplified by his continued function as the voice of the Supreme Court for most of his term as chief justice, speak strongly about his leadership of the nation's highest tribunal. He possessed a great ability to secure consensus among his colleagues, and his example introduced an atmosphere of collegiality that has persisted in the Court ever since. The transition to unitary opinions did much to give authority and clarity to the Court's reasoning, and except in cases eliciting extreme differences among the justices, majority opinions have continued to be the dominant form of decision to the present day. By his example, John Marshall set a high standard of leadership for those who have succeeded him as chief justice.

Key Sources

Marshall's papers are available in a twelve-volume definitive edition, *The Papers of John Marshall* (1974–2006), edited by Herbert A. Johnson and others. Marshall's opinions are in the *U.S. Supreme Court Reports*, vols. 5–34. The chief justice's biography of General Washington was published in five volumes, as *The Life of George Washington, Commander in Chief of the Forces during the War Which Established the Independence of His Country, and the First President of the United States* (1804–1807) A second edition, in two volumes, was published posthumously, under the same title (1836). A modern printing of the second edition, *The Life of George Washington: Special Edition for Schools* (2000), is available. Introductory material from the first volume of the first edition was published separately as *A History of the Colonies Settled by the English on the Continent of North America* (1824).

Further Reading

■ Books

Baxter, Maurice G. *The Steamboat Monopoly: Gibbons v. Ogden, 1824.* New York: Knopf, 1972.

"That the people have an original right to establish, for their future government, such principles as, in their opinion, shall most conduce to their own happiness, is the basis on which the whole American fabric has been erected."

(*Marbury v. Madison*)

"To what purpose are powers limited, and to what purpose is that limitation committed to writing, if these limits may, at any time, be passed by those intended to be restrained? The distinction between a government with limited and unlimited powers is abolished, if those limits do not confine the persons on whom they are imposed."

(*Marbury v. Madison*)

"It is emphatically the province and duty of the judicial department to say what the law is."

(*Marbury v. Madison*)

"If any one proposition could command the universal assent of mankind, we might expect it would be this—that the government of the Union, though limited in its powers, is supreme within its sphere of action."

(*McCulloch v. Maryland*)

"We must never forget that it is a constitution we are expounding."

(*McCulloch v. Maryland*)

"The genius and character of the whole government seem to be that its action is to be applied to all the external concerns of the nation, and to those internal concerns which affect the States generally, but not to those which are completely within a particular State, which do not affect other States, and with which it is not necessary to interfere for the purpose of executing some of the general powers of the government."

(*Gibbons v. Ogden*)

Clinton, Robert L. *Marbury v. Madison* and *Judicial Review*. Lawrence: University Press of Kansas, 1989.

Cox, Thomas H. "Courting Commerce, *Gibbons v. Ogden* and the Transformation of Commerce Regulation in the Early Republic." PhD dissertation, State University of New York at Albany, 2004.

Currie, David P. *The Constitution in the Supreme Court: The First Hundred Years, 1789–1888*. Chicago: University of Chicago Press, 1985.

Frankfurter, Felix. *The Commerce Clause under Marshall, Taney and Waite*. Chapel Hill: University of North Carolina Press, 1937.

Haskins, George L., and Herbert A. Johnson. *Foundations of Power: John Marshall, 1801–15*. New York: Macmillan, 1981.

Hobson, Charles F. *The Great Chief Justice: John Marshall and the Rule of Law*. Lawrence: University Press of Kansas, 1996.

Johnson, Herbert A. *The Chief Justiceship of John Marshall, 1801–1835*. Columbia: University of South Carolina Press, 1997.

Kahn, Paul W. *The Reign of Law*: Marbury v. Madison *and the Construction of America*. New Haven, Conn.: Yale University Press, 2002.

Killenbeck, Mark R. M'Culloch v. Maryland: *Securing a Nation*. Lawrence: University Press of Kansas, 2006.

Newmyer, R. Kent. *John Marshall and the Heroic Age of the Supreme Court*. Baton Rouge: Louisiana State University Press, 2001.

Snowiss, Sylvia,. *Judicial Review and the Law of the Constitution*. New Haven, Conn.: Yale University Press, 1990.

White, G. Edward. *The Marshall Court and Cultural Change, 1815–35*. New York: Macmillan, 1988.

Wolfe, Christopher. *The Rise of Modern Judicial Review: From Constitutional Interpretation to Judge-Made Law*. Lanham, Md.: Rowman & Littlefield,1994.

—Herbert A. Johnson

Questions for Further Study

1. Research and discuss Marshall's adversarial relationship with his cousin Thomas Jefferson. What differences, in political philosophy or personality or both, were at the heart of their disagreement? Explain how Marshall's life-long support of the Federalist Party might have been a major point of contention between the two. How is Marshall's federalism represented in the three Supreme Court opinions included here?

2. Discuss *Marbury v. Madison* with regard to how it fundamentally shaped the Supreme Court and its function within the federal system. How did the ruling mark a major shift in legal thinking with respect to the relative powers of the judicial and legislative branches? How much was Marshall himself responsible for this shift in thinking?

3. Address the issues approached in *McCulloch v. Maryland*, a case that centers on the supremacy clause, which defines the power of the federal government over the states. What was the controversy over the word *express* as used in the Constitution, and how does Marshall view the constitutionality of the Bank of the United States? How does Marshall's position on the bank differ from that of Andrew Jackson?

4. The events behind *Gibbons v. Ogden* have often been described as a great drama involving larger-than-life characters. Retell the story of the case, being sure to address the constitutional issues at stake here. What is the commerce clause, and what is Marshall's position on its relevance to the case at hand? How does the compact theory, also raised in *McCulloch*, come into play? What are Marshall's criticisms of that theory, as expressed here and earlier, in *McCulloch*?

MARBURY V. MADISON (1803)

At the last term,…a rule was granted in this case, requiring the secretary of state to show cause why a mandamus should not issue, directing him to deliver to William Marbury his commission as a justice of the peace for the county of Washington, in the district of Columbia.

No cause has been shown, and the present motion is for a mandamus. The peculiar delicacy of this case, the novelty of some of its circumstances, and the real difficulty attending the points which occur in it, require a complete exposition of the principles on which the opinion to be given by the court is founded.…

The following questions have been considered and decided.

1. Has the applicant a right to the commission he demands?

2. If he has a right, and that right has been violated, do the laws of his country afford him a remedy?

3. If they do afford him a remedy, is it a mandamus issuing from this court?

The first object of inquiry is, 1. Has the applicant a right to the commission he demands?

His right originates in an act of congress passed in February 1801, concerning the district of Columbia.…

The eleventh section of this law enacts, "that there shall be appointed in and for each of the said counties, such number of discreet persons to be justices of the peace as the president of the United States shall…think expedient, to continue in office for five years." It appears from the affidavits, that in compliance with this law, a commission for William Marbury as a justice of peace for the county of Washington was signed by John Adams, then president of the United States;…but the commission has never reached the person for whom it was made out.

In order to determine whether he is entitled to this commission, it becomes necessary to inquire whether he has been appointed to the office. For if he has been appointed, the law continues him in office for five years, and he is entitled to the possession of those evidences of office, which, being completed, became his property.…

Mr. Marbury, then, since his commission was signed by the president and sealed by the secretary of state, was appointed; and as the law creating the office gave the officer a right to hold for five years independent of the executive, the appointment was not revocable; but vested in the officer legal rights which are protected by the laws of his country.

To withhold the commission, therefore, is an act deemed by the court not warranted by law, but violative of a vested legal right.

This brings us to the second inquiry; which is, 2. If he has a right, and that right has been violated, do the laws of his country afford him a remedy? The very essence of civil liberty certainly consists in the right of every individual to claim the protection of the laws, whenever he receives an injury. One of the first duties of government is to afford that protection;…

The government of the United States has been emphatically termed a government of laws, and not of men. It will certainly cease to deserve this high appellation, if the laws furnish no remedy for the violation of a vested legal right.…

It is then the opinion of the court,

1. That by signing the commission of Mr. Marbury, the president of the United States appointed him a justice of peace for the county of Washington in the district of Columbia; and that the seal of the United States, affixed thereto by the secretary of state, is conclusive testimony of the verity of the signature, and of the completion of the appointment; and that the appointment conferred on him a legal right to the office for the space of five years.

2. That, having this legal title to the office, he has a consequent right to the commission; a refusal to deliver which is a plain violation of that right, for which the laws of his country afford him a remedy.

It remains to be inquired whether, 3. He is entitled to the remedy for which he applies. This depends on,

1. The nature of the writ applied for. And,

2. The power of this court.

1. The nature of the writ....

Lord Mansfield...in the case of *The King v. Baker et al.* states with much precision and explicitness the cases in which this writ may be used.

"Whenever," says that very able judge, "there is a right to execute an office, perform a service, or exercise a franchise...and a person is kept out of possession, or dispossessed of such right, and has no other specific legal remedy, this court ought to assist by mandamus, upon reasons of justice...and upon reasons of public policy, to preserve peace, order and good government."...

Still, to render the mandamus a proper remedy, the officer to whom it is to be directed, must be one to whom, on legal principles, such writ may be directed; and the person applying for it must be without any other specific and legal remedy.

1. With respect to the officer to whom it would be directed. The intimate political relation, subsisting between the president of the United States and the heads of departments,...excites some hesitation with respect to the propriety of entering into such investigation. Impressions are often received without much reflection or examination; and it is not wonderful that in such a case as this, the assertion, by an individual, of his legal claims in a court of justice, to which claims it is the duty of that court to attend, should at first view be considered by some, as an attempt to intrude into the cabinet, and to intermeddle with the prerogatives of the executive.

It is scarcely necessary for the court to disclaim all pretensions to such a jurisdiction.... The province of the court is, solely, to decide on the rights of individuals, not to inquire how the executive, or executive officers, perform duties in which they have a discretion....

But, if this be not such a question;...if it be no intermeddling with a subject, over which the executive can be considered as having exercised any control; what is there in the exalted station of the officer, which shall bar a citizen from asserting, in a court of justice, his legal rights, or shall forbid a court to listen to the claim; or to issue a mandamus, directing the performance of a duty, not depending on executive discretion, but on particular acts of congress and the general principles of law?...

It is not by the office of the person to whom the writ is directed, but the nature of the thing to be done, that the propriety or impropriety of issuing a mandamus is to be determined....

The doctrine, therefore, now advanced is by no means a novel one....

The mandamus, now moved for...is to deliver a commission; on which subjects the acts of congress are silent. This difference is not considered as affecting the case. It has already been stated that the applicant has, to that commission, a vested legal right, of which the executive cannot deprive him. He...has a right to the commission which the secretary has received from the president for his use....

This, then, is a plain case of a mandamus, either to deliver the commission, or a copy of it from the record; and it only remains to be inquired,

Whether it can issue from this court.

The act to establish the judicial courts of the United States authorizes the supreme court "to issue writs of mandamus, in cases warranted by the principles and usages of law, to any courts appointed, or persons holding office, under the authority of the United States."

The secretary of state, being a person, holding an office under the authority of the United States, is precisely within the letter of the description; and if this court is not authorized to issue a writ of mandamus to such an officer, it must be because the law is unconstitutional, and therefore absolutely incapable of conferring the authority, and assigning the duties which its words purport to confer and assign.

The constitution vests the whole judicial power of the United States in one supreme court, and such inferior courts as congress shall...ordain and establish. This power is expressly extended to all cases arising under the laws of the United States; and consequently, in some form, may be exercised over the present case; because the right claimed is given by a law of the United States....

It has been insisted at the bar, that as the original grant of jurisdiction to the supreme and inferior courts is general, and the clause, assigning original jurisdiction to the supreme court, contains no negative or restrictive words; the power remains to the legislature to assign original jurisdiction to that court in other cases than those specified in the article which has been recited; provided those cases belong to the judicial power of the United States....

When an instrument organizing fundamentally a judicial system, divides it into one supreme, and so many inferior courts...then enumerates its powers, and proceeds so far to distribute them, as to define the jurisdiction of the supreme court by declaring the cases in which it shall take original jurisdiction, and that in others it shall take appellate jurisdiction, the plain import of the words seems to be, that in one class of cases its jurisdiction is original, and not appellate; in the other it is appellate, and not original. If any other construction would render the clause inoperative, that is an additional reason for rejecting such other construction, and for adhering to the obvious meaning.

To enable this court then to issue a mandamus, it must be shown to be an exercise of appellate jurisdiction, or to be necessary to enable them to exercise appellate jurisdiction....

The authority ... given to the supreme court, by the act establishing the judicial courts of the United States, to issue writs of mandamus to public officers, appears not to be warranted by the constitution; and it becomes necessary to inquire whether a jurisdiction, so conferred, can be exercised....

That the people have an original right to establish, for their future government, such principles as, in their opinion, shall most conduce to their own happiness, is the basis on which the whole American fabric has been erected. The exercise of this original right is a very great exertion; nor can it nor ought it to be frequently repeated. The principles, therefore, so established are deemed fundamental. And as the authority, from which they proceed, is supreme, and can seldom act, they are designed to be permanent....

The powers of the legislature are defined and limited; and that those limits may not be mistaken or forgotten, the constitution is written. To what purpose are powers limited, and to what purpose is that limitation committed to writing; if these limits may, at any time, be passed by those intended to be restrained? The distinction between a government with limited and unlimited powers is abolished, if those limits do not confine the persons on whom they are imposed, and if acts prohibited and acts allowed are of equal obligation. It is a proposition too plain to be contested, that the constitution controls any legislative act repugnant to it; or, that the legislature may alter the constitution by an ordinary act.

Between these alternatives there is no middle ground. The constitution is either a superior, paramount law ... or it is on a level with ordinary legislative acts, and like other acts, is alterable when the legislature shall please to alter it.

If the former part of the alternative be true, then a legislative act contrary to the constitution is not law: if the latter part be true, then written constitutions are absurd attempts, on the part of the people, to limit a power in its own nature illimitable.

Certainly all those who have framed written constitutions contemplate them as forming the fundamental and paramount law of the nation, and consequently the theory of every such government must be, that an act of the legislature repugnant to the constitution is void....

It is emphatically the province and duty of the judicial department to say what the law is. Those who apply the rule to particular cases, must of necessity expound and interpret that rule. If two laws conflict with each other, the courts must decide on the operation of each. So if a law be in opposition to the constitution: if both the law and the constitution apply to a particular case, so that the court must either decide that case conformably to the law, disregarding the constitution; or conformably to the constitution, disregarding the law: the court must determine which of these conflicting rules governs the case. This is of the very essence of judicial duty....

The judicial power of the United States is extended to all cases arising under the constitution....

In some cases then, the constitution must be looked into by the judges. And if they can open it at all, what part of it are they forbidden to read, or to obey?...

The oath of office, too, imposed by the legislature, is completely demonstrative of the legislative opinion on this subject. It is in these words: "I do

Glossary

appellate jurisdiction	the right of a court to hear a case on appeal
Lord Mansfield	William Murray, 1st Earl of Mansfield, British jurist of the eighteenth century
original jurisdiction	the right of a court to hear a case for the first time
revocable	capable of being revoked or withdrawn
verity	truth
vested	secured, absolute, without contingencies
writ	a formal legal order

solemnly swear that I will administer justice without respect to persons, and do equal right to the poor and to the rich; and that I will faithfully and impartially discharge all the duties incumbent on me as according to the best of my abilities and understanding, agreeably to the constitution and laws of the United States."

Why does a judge swear to discharge his duties agreeably to the constitution of the United States, if that constitution forms no rule for his government?...

Thus, the particular phraseology of the constitution of the United States confirms and strengthens the principle, supposed to be essential to all written constitutions, that a law repugnant to the constitution is void, and that courts, as well as other departments, are bound by that instrument.

The rule must be discharged.

McCulloch v. Maryland (1819)

The first question made in the cause is, has Congress power to incorporate a bank?...

The power now contested was exercised by the first Congress elected under the present constitution. The bill for incorporating the Bank of the United States did not steal upon an unsuspecting legislature, and pass unobserved.... The original act was permitted to expire; but a short experience of the embarrassments to which the refusal to revive it exposed the government, convinced those who were most prejudiced against the measure of its necessity, and induced the passage of the present law....

In discussing this question, the counsel for the State of Maryland have deemed it of some importance, in the construction of the constitution, to consider that instrument, not as emanating from the people, but as the act of sovereign and independent States. The powers of the general government, it has been said, are delegated by the States, who alone are truly sovereign; and must be exercised in subordination to the States, who alone possess supreme dominion.

It would be difficult to sustain this proposition. The convention which framed the constitution was indeed elected by the State legislatures. But the instrument, when it came from their hands, was a mere proposal, without obligation..... It was reported to the then existing Congress of the United States, with a request that it might "be submitted to a convention of delegates, chosen in each State by the people thereof, ... for their assent and ratification."... They acted upon it in the only manner in which they can act safely, effectively and wisely, on such a subject, by assembling in convention....

From these conventions, the constitution derives its whole authority.... The people were at perfect liberty to accept or reject it; and their act was final. It required not the affirmance, and could not be negatived, by the State governments. The constitution, when thus adopted, was of complete obligation, and bound the State sovereignties....

This government is acknowledged by all, to be one of enumerated powers....

If any one proposition could command the universal assent of mankind, we might expect it would be this—that the government of the Union, though limited in its powers, is supreme within its sphere of action.... It is the government of all; its powers are delegated by all; it represents all, and acts for all....

Among the enumerated powers, we do not find that of establishing a bank or creating a corporation. But there is no phrase in the instrument which ... excludes incidental or implied powers; and which requires that everything granted shall be expressly and minutely described....A constitution, to contain an accurate detail of all the subdivisions of which its great powers will admit, and of all the means by which they may be carried into execution, would partake of the prolixity of a legal code, and could scarcely be embraced by the human mind.... Its nature, therefore, requires, that only its great outlines should be marked, its important objects designated, and the minor ingredients which compose those objects, be deduced from the nature of the objects themselves.... In considering this question, then, we must never forget that it is a constitution we are expounding.

Although, among the enumerated powers of government, we do not find the word "bank" or "incorporation," we find the great powers, to lay and collect taxes; to borrow money; to regulate commerce; to declare and conduct a war; and to raise and support armies and navies....

It is not denied, that the powers given to the government imply the ordinary means of execution.... But it is denied, that the government has its choice of means; or, that it may employ the most convenient means, if, to employ them, it be necessary to erect a corporation.

The government which has a right to do an act,... must ... be allowed to select the means; and those who contend that it may not select any appropriate means, that one particular mode of effecting the object is excepted, take upon themselves the burden of establishing that exception.

The creation of a corporation, it is said, appertains to sovereignty.... But to what portion of sovereignty does it appertain?...In America, the powers of sovereignty are divided between the government of the Union, and those of the States. They are each sovereign, with respect to the objects committed to it, and neither sovereign, with respect to the objects committed to the other....

But the constitution of the United States has not left the right of Congress to employ the necessary means, for the execution of the powers conferred on the government, to general reasoning. To its enumeration of powers is added, that of making "all laws which shall be necessary and proper, for carrying into execution the foregoing powers, and all other powers vested by this constitution, in the government of the United States, or in any department thereof."

The counsel for the State of Maryland have urged various arguments, to prove that this clause, though, in terms, a grant of power, is not so, in effect; but is really restrictive of the general right of selecting means for executing the enumerated powers....

The argument on which most reliance is placed, is drawn from that peculiar language of this clause. Congress is not empowered by it to make all laws, which may have relation to the powers conferred on the government, but such only as may be *"necessary and proper"* for carrying them into execution. The word *"necessary"* is considered as controlling the whole sentence, and as limiting the right to pass laws for the execution of the granted powers, to such as are indispensable....

Is it true, that this is the sense in which the word "necessary" is always used? Does it always import an absolute physical necessity, so strong, that one thing to which another may be termed necessary, cannot exist without that other? We think it does not....

The subject [of the case under consideration] is the execution of those great powers on which the welfare of a nation essentially depends. It must have been the intention of those who gave these powers, to insure, so far as human prudence could insure, their beneficial execution. To have prescribed the means by which government should, in all future time, execute its powers, would have been to change, entirely, the character of the instrument, and give it the properties of a legal code....

We admit...that the powers of the government are limited, and that its limits are not to be transcended. But we think the sound construction of the constitution must allow to the national legislature that discretion, with respect to the means by which the powers it confers are to be carried into execution, which will enable that body to perform the high duties assigned to it, in the manner most beneficial to the people. Let the end be legitimate, let it be within the scope of the constitution, and all means which are appropriate, which are plainly adapted to that end, which are not prohibited, but consist with the letter and spirit of the constitution, are constitutional....

If a corporation may be employed, indiscriminately with other means, to carry into execution the powers of the government, no particular reason can be assigned for excluding the use of a bank, if required for its fiscal operations.... That it is a convenient, a useful, and essential instrument in the prosecution of its fiscal operations, is not now a subject of controversy. All those who have been concerned in the administration of our finances, have concurred in representing its importance and necessity.... Under the confederation, Congress, justifying the measure by its necessity, transcended, perhaps, its powers, to obtain the advantage of a bank; and our own legislation attests the universal conviction of the utility of this measure. The time has passed away, when it can be necessary to enter into any discussion, in order to prove the importance of this instrument, as a means to effect the legitimate objects of the government....

No trace is to be found in the constitution, of an intention to create a dependence of the government of the Union on those of the States, for the execution of the great powers assigned to it....

After the most deliberate consideration, it is the unanimous and decided opinion of this Court, that the act to incorporate the Bank of the United States is a law made in pursuance of the constitution, and is a part of the supreme law of the land....

We proceed to inquire—

2. Whether the State of Maryland may, without violating the constitution, tax that branch?

That the power of taxation is one of vital importance; that it is retained by the States; that it is not abridged by the grant of a similar power to the government of the Union; that it is to be concurrently exercised by the two governments—are truths which have never been denied. But such is the paramount character of the constitution, that its capacity to withdraw any subject from the action of even this power, is admitted....

On this ground, the counsel for the bank place its claim to be exempted from the power of a State to tax its operations. There is no express provision for the case, but the claim has been sustained on a principle which so entirely pervades the constitution...as to be incapable of being separated from it, without rending it into shreds.

This great principle is, that the constitution and the laws made in pursuance thereof are supreme; that they control the constitution and laws of the respective States, and cannot be controlled by them....

The argument on the part of the State of Maryland, is, not that the States may directly resist a law of Congress, but that they may exercise their acknowledged powers upon it, and that the constitution leaves them this right, in the confidence that they will not abuse it....

The people of a State give to their government a right of taxing themselves and their property, and as the exigencies of government cannot be limited, they prescribe no limits to the exercise of this right, resting confidently on the interest of the legislator, and on the influence of the constituent over their representative, to guard them against its abuse. But the means employed by the government of the Union have no such security, nor is the right of a State to tax them sustained by the same theory. Those means are not given by the people of a particular State, not given by the constituents of the legislature, which claim the right to tax them, but by the people of all the States. They are given by all, for the benefit of all—and upon theory, should be subjected to that government only which belongs to all....

The sovereignty of a State extends to everything which exists by its own authority, or is introduced by its permission; but does it extend to those means which are employed by Congress to carry into execution powers conferred on that body by the people of the United States? We think it demonstrable, that it does not....

That the power to tax involves the power to destroy; that the power to destroy may defeat and render useless the power to create; that there is a plain repugnance in conferring on one government a power to control the constitutional measures of another, which other, with respect to those very measures, is declared to be supreme over that which exerts the control, are propositions not to be denied. But all inconsistencies are to be reconciled by the magic of the word CONFIDENCE. Taxation, it is said, does not necessarily and unavoidably destroy. To carry it to the excess of destruction, would be an abuse, to presume which, would banish that confidence which is essential to all government.

But is this a case of confidence? Would the people of any one State trust those of another with a power to control the most insignificant operations of their State government? We know they would not. Why, then, should we suppose, that the people of any one State should be willing to trust those of another with a power to control the operations of a government to which they have confided their most important and most valuable interests? In the legislature of the Union alone, are all represented. The legislature of the Union alone, therefore, can be trusted by the people with the power of controlling measures which concern all, in the confidence that it will not be abused. This, then, is not a case of confidence, and we must consider it is as it really is.

If we apply the principle for which the State of Maryland contends, to the constitution, generally, we shall find it capable of changing totally the character of that instrument. We shall find it capable of arresting all the measures of the government, and of prostrating it at the foot of the States. The American people have declared their constitution and the laws made in pursuance thereof, to be supreme; but this principle would transfer the supremacy, in fact, to the States.

If the States may tax one instrument, employed by the government in the execution of its powers, they may tax any and every other instrument....This was not intended by the American people. They did not design to make their government dependent on the States.

We are unanimously of opinion, that the law passed by the legislature of Maryland, imposing a tax on the Bank of the United States, is unconstitutional and void.

Glossary

affirmance	acceptance, affirmation
appertains	applies
enumerated	listed, specified
exigencies	emergencies, urgent situations
negatived	rejected, refused
prolixity	long-windedness, excess of words

GIBBONS V. OGDEN (1824)

The appellant contends that this decree is erroneous because the laws which purport to give the exclusive privilege it sustains are repugnant to the Constitution and laws of the United States.

They are said to be repugnant:

1st. To that clause in the Constitution which authorizes Congress to regulate commerce.

2d. To that which authorizes Congress to promote the progress of science and useful arts.

The State of New York maintains the Constitutionality of these laws.....

The subject to be regulated is commerce, and our Constitution being...one of enumeration, and not of definition, to ascertain the extent of the power, it becomes necessary to settle the meaning of the word. The counsel for the appellee would limit it to traffic, to buying and selling, or the interchange of commodities, and do not admit that it comprehends navigation. This would restrict a general term, applicable to many objects, to one of its significations. Commerce ... is something more: it is intercourse. It describes the commercial intercourse between nations, and parts of nations, in all its branches, and is regulated by prescribing rules for carrying on that intercourse....

If commerce does not include navigation, the government of the Union has no direct power over that subject, and can make no law prescribing what shall constitute American vessels or requiring that they shall be navigated by American seamen. Yet this power has been exercised from the commencement of the government, has been exercised with the consent of all, and has been understood by all to be a commercial regulation....

If the opinion that "commerce," as the word is used in the Constitution, comprehends navigation also, requires any additional confirmation, that additional confirmation is, we think, furnished by the words of the instrument itself.

The 9th section of the 1st article declares that "no preference shall be given, by any regulation of commerce or revenue, to the ports of one State over those of another." This clause cannot be understood as applicable to those laws only which are passed for the purposes of revenue, because it is expressly applied to commercial regulations, and the most obvious preference which can be given to one port over another in regulating commerce relates to navigation. But the subsequent part of the sentence is still more explicit. It is, "nor shall vessels bound to or from one State be obliged to enter, clear, or pay duties, in another." These words have a direct reference to navigation....

The word used in the Constitution, then, comprehends, and has been always understood to comprehend, navigation within its meaning, and a power to regulate navigation is as expressly granted as if that term had been added to the word "commerce."

To what commerce does this power extend? The Constitution informs us, to commerce "with foreign nations, and among the several States, and with the Indian tribes."

Comprehensive as the word "among" is, it may very properly be restricted to that commerce which concerns more States than one..... The genius and character of the whole government seem to be that its action is to be applied to all the external concerns of the nation, and to those internal concerns which affect the States generally, but not to those which are completely within a particular State, which do not affect other States, and with which it is not necessary to interfere for the purpose of executing some of the general powers of the government. The completely internal commerce of a State, then, may be considered as reserved for the State itself....

This principle is, if possible, still more clear, when applied to commerce "among the several States."... What is commerce "among" them, and how is it to be conducted? Can a trading expedition between two adjoining States, commence and terminate outside of each? And if the trading intercourse be between two States remote from each other, must it not commence in one, terminate in the other, and probably pass through a third?...The power of Congress, then, whatever it may be, must be exercised within the territorial jurisdiction of the several States....

We are now arrived at the inquiry—What is this power?

It is the power to regulate, that is, to prescribe the rule by which commerce is to be governed. This power, like all others vested in Congress, is complete in itself, may be exercised to its utmost extent, and acknowledges no limitations other than are prescribed in the Constitution....

But it has been urged with great earnestness that, although the power of Congress to regulate commerce with foreign nations and among the several States be coextensive with the subject itself, and have no other limits than are prescribed in the Constitution, yet the States may severally exercise the same power, within their respective jurisdictions....

When a State proceeds to regulate commerce with foreign nations, or among the several States, it is exercising the very power that is granted to Congress, and is doing the very thing which Congress is authorized to do. There is no analogy, then, between the power of taxation and the power of regulating commerce....

We must first determine whether the act of laying "duties or imposts on imports or exports" is considered in the Constitution as a branch of the taxing power, or of the power to regulate commerce. We think it very clear that it is considered as a branch of the taxing power.... The power of imposing duties on imports is classed with the power to levy taxes, and that seems to be its natural place. But the power to levy taxes could never be considered as abridging the right of the States on that subject, and they might, consequently, have exercised it by levying duties on imports or exports, had the Constitution contained no prohibition on this subject. This prohibition, then, is an exception from the acknowledged power of the States to levy taxes, not from the questionable power to regulate commerce....

So, if a State, in passing laws on subjects acknowledged to be within its control...shall adopt a measure of the same character with one which Congress may adopt, it does not derive its authority from the particular power which has been granted, but from some other, which remains with the State and may be executed by the same means....

Since, in exercising the power of regulating their own purely internal affairs the States may sometimes enact laws the validity of which depends on their interfering with, and being contrary to, an act of Congress passed in pursuance of the Constitution, the Court will enter upon the inquiry whether the laws of New York, as expounded by the highest tribunal of that State, have, in their application to this case, come into collision with an act of Congress and deprived a citizen of a right to which that act entitles him.... In one case and the other, the acts of New York must yield to the law of Congress, and the decision sustaining the privilege they confer

against a right given by a law of the Union must be erroneous....

It will at once occur that, when a Legislature attaches certain privileges and exemptions to the exercise of a right over which its control is absolute, the law must imply a power to exercise the right. The privileges are gone if the right itself be annihilated. It would be contrary to all reason, and to the course of human affairs, to say that a State is unable to strip a vessel of the particular privileges attendant on the exercise of a right, and yet may annul the right itself; that the State of New York cannot prevent an enrolled and licensed vessel, proceeding from Elizabethtown, in New Jersey, to New York, from enjoying, in her course, and on her entrance into port, all the privileges conferred by the act of Congress, but can shut her up in her own port, and prohibit altogether her entering the waters and ports of another State. To the Court, it seems very clear that the whole act on the subject of the coasting trade, according to those principles which govern the construction of statutes, implies unequivocally an authority to licensed vessels to carry on the coasting trade.

But we will proceed briefly to notice those sections which bear more directly on the subject.

The first section declares that vessels enrolled by virtue of a previous law, and certain other vessels enrolled as described in that act, and having a license in force, as is by the act required,

> and no others, shall be deemed ships or vessels of the United States, entitled to the privileges of ships or vessels employed in the coasting trade.

This section seems to the Court to contain a positive enactment that the vessels it describes shall be entitled to the privileges of ships or vessels employed in the coasting trade....

The fourth section directs the proper officer to grant to a vessel qualified to receive it, "a license for carrying on the coasting trade," and prescribes its form. After reciting the compliance of the applicant with the previous requisites of the law, the operative words of the instrument are,

> license is hereby granted for the said steamboat *Bellona* to be employed in carrying on the coasting trade for one year from the date hereof, and no longer.

The license must be understood to be what it purports to be, a legislative authority to the steamboat

Bellona "to be employed in carrying on the coasting trade, for one year from this date."

It has been denied that these words authorize a voyage from New Jersey to New York. It is true that no ports are specified, but it is equally true that the words used are perfectly intelligible, and do confer such authority as unquestionably as if the ports had been mentioned. The coasting trade is a term well understood. The law has defined it, and all know its meaning perfectly. The act describes with great minuteness the various operations of a vessel engaged in it, and it cannot...be doubted that a voyage from New Jersey to New York is one of those operations....

But if the license be a permit to carry on the coasting trade, the respondent denies that these boats were engaged in that trade, or that the decree under consideration has restrained them from prosecuting it. The boats of the appellant were, we are told, employed in the transportation of passengers, and this is no part of that commerce which Congress may regulate.

If, as our whole course of legislation on this subject shows, the power of Congress has been universally understood in America to comprehend navigation, it is a very persuasive, if not a conclusive, argument to prove that the construction is correct, and if it be correct, no clear distinction is perceived between the power to regulate vessels employed in transporting men for hire and property for hire.... A coasting vessel employed in the transportation of passengers is as much a portion of the American marine as one employed in the transportation of a cargo....

Vessels have always been employed to a greater or less extent in the transportation of passengers, and have never been supposed to be, on that account, withdrawn from the control or protection of Congress....

If, then, it were even true that the *Bellona* and the *Stoudinger* were employed exclusively in the conveyance of passengers between New York and New Jersey, it would not follow that this occupation did not constitute a part of the coasting trade of the United States, and was not protected by the license annexed to the answer.... The laws of New York, which grant the exclusive privilege set up by the respondent, take no notice of the employment of vessels, and relate only to the principle by which they are propelled. Those laws do not inquire whether vessels are engaged in transporting men or merchandise, but whether they are moved by steam or wind. If by the former, the waters of New York are closed

against them, though their cargoes be dutiable goods, which the laws of the United States permit them to enter and deliver in New York. If by the latter, those waters are free to them though they should carry passengers only....

The questions, then, whether the conveyance of passengers be a part of the coasting trade and whether a vessel can be protected in that occupation by a coasting license are not, and cannot be, raised in this case. The real and sole question seems to be whether a steam machine in actual use deprives a vessel of the privileges conferred by a license....

The first idea which presents itself is that the laws of Congress for the regulation of commerce do not look to the principle by which vessels are moved. That subject is left entirely to individual discretion, and, in that vast and complex system of legislative enactment concerning it...there is not...one word respecting the peculiar principle by which vessels are propelled through the water, except what may be found in a single act granting a particular privilege to steamboats....

But all inquiry into this subject seems to the Court to be put completely at rest by the act already mentioned, entitled, "An act for the enrolling and licensing of steamboats."

This act authorizes a steamboat employed, or intended to be employed, only in a river or bay of the United States, owned wholly or in part by an alien, resident within the United States, to be enrolled and licensed as if the same belonged to a citizen of the United States.

This act demonstrates the opinion of Congress that steamboats may be enrolled and licensed, in common with vessels using sails. They are, of course, entitled to the same privileges, and can no more be restrained from navigating waters and entering ports which are free to such vessels than if they were wafted on their voyage by the winds, instead of being propelled by the agency of fire....

Powerful and ingenious minds, taking as postulates that the powers expressly granted to the government of the Union are to be contracted by construction into the narrowest possible compass and that the original powers of the States are retained if any possible construction will retain them may, by a course of well digested but refined and metaphysical reasoning founded on these premises, explain away the Constitution of our country and leave it a magnificent structure indeed to look at, but totally unfit for use. They may so entangle and perplex the understanding as to obscure principles which were before thought quite plain, and induce doubts where, if the mind were to pursue its own course, none would be perceived. In such a case, it is peculiarly necessary to recur to safe and fundamental principles to sustain those principles, and when sustained, to make them the tests of the arguments to be examined.

Glossary

9th section of the 1st article	reference to the Records of the Federal Convention, that is, of the Constitutional Convention
appellant	the party that appeals a ruling of a lower court
appellee	the party opposed to the appellant in a court of appeals such as the Supreme Court; the respondent
coextensive	the same as, equivalent to
dutiable goods	goods on which duties or tariffs can be levied
enumeration	a listing or specification
postulates	assumptions

Thurgood Marshall (AP/Wide World Photos)

Featured Documents
- *Grayned v. City of Rockford* (1972)
- *Furman v. Georgia* (1972)
- *Regents of the University of California v. Bakke* (1978)
- *Florida v. Bostick* (1991)

Overview

Thurgood Marshall, whose grandfathers were both born slaves but became freemen, was the first African American U.S. Supreme Court justice. He was born on July 2, 1908, in Baltimore, Maryland, and his life spanned years during which segregation existed both in law and in practice. His formative experiences in Baltimore played an important role in his strong belief as an adult in the importance of the rule of law and the possibilities the U.S. Constitution held in advancing integration and protecting the rights of racial minorities. He did as much as perhaps any single American to create today's postsegregation society.

In 1925 Marshall enrolled at the historically black Lincoln University in Pennsylvania. After graduation, he hoped to attend the University of Maryland law school but was denied admission because of his race, so he enrolled in law school at Howard University, where he came under the tutelage of its highly regarded dean, Charles Hamilton Houston. Houston trained his law students in the art of legal argumentation and litigation strategy, focusing on defending the civil rights of African Americans. After graduating from Howard in 1933, Marshall moved to New York City, which was then a dynamic mecca of African American culture and politics. There he was exposed to diverse viewpoints and backgrounds and served first as a staff attorney and then as the legal director of the National Association for the Advancement of Colored People (NAACP). By 1940 Marshall had risen to become the NAACP's chief counsel.

Marshall, an ardent integrationist, was a key architect of the legal strategy behind modern American civil rights. During his years at the NAACP, he litigated dozens of important legal challenges to segregation, building a base of experience as well as court rulings that would eventually lead to the end of legal segregation. It was Marshall's life goal to overturn the "separate but equal" doctrine enshrined in *Plessy v. Ferguson* (1896), a case in which the U.S. Supreme Court ruled that racial segregation of public railroad cars was legal because, presumably, the cars occupied for blacks were "equal" to those reserved for white travelers. He worked closely with Houston in creating the legal strategy that dismantled the *Plessy* doctrine. A half century after *Plessy*, the Court issued its landmark decision in *Brown v. Board of Education of Topeka* (1954), holding that segregated public schools violated the U.S. Constitu-

tion. Marshall built the legal strategy behind *Brown* and, in a watershed moment in American history, successfully argued the case before the U.S. Supreme Court. Although the post-*Brown* years found the civil rights movement battling de facto segregation in the schools (that is, segregation that existed "in fact" rather than by law), Marshall continued to lend a guiding hand first as a justice on the U.S. Court of Appeals for the Second Circuit and later as a Supreme Court justice.

In 1967 President Lyndon B. Johnson nominated Marshall to the U.S. Supreme Court. Although his confirmation hearing was at times contentious, with conservative southern senators attempting to portray Marshall as a Communist sympathizer, his confirmation was secured with some intervention on the part of Johnson, a gifted parliamentarian and backroom dealer. As a member of the highest appeals court in the United States, he would be reviewing cases that would become the legal progeny of holdings he had played a role in as an advocate. At the same time, Marshall's tenure on the Supreme Court, which lasted until 1991, coincided with a powerful backlash against some of the legal gains made during the civil rights movement, which served to create a complex jurisprudence on race. Marshall died on January 24, 1993, in Washington, D.C.

Explanation and Analysis of Documents

Marshall's life spanned a momentous period in American history, from the entrenched segregation of the early twentieth century to the post–civil-rights movement after midcentury in which discrimination grievances had become incorporated into formal legal structures. It is noteworthy that it was Marshall, the grandchild of slaves, who played a crucial role in affording civil rights the protection of the law. As an NAACP attorney, he was a prime advocate of legal strategies that ushered in an integrated American society. As an associate Supreme Court justice, Marshall continued his passion for correcting some of the practices he viewed as systemically discriminatory. His opinions in four cases, *Grayned v. City of Rockford*, *Furman v. Georgia*, *Regents of the University of California v. Bakke*, and *Florida v. Bostick*, provide a glimpse into his thinking on civil rights and segregation issues during a period when the legal treatment of civil rights evolved significantly.

Time Line

1908
- **July 2**
  Marshall is born in Baltimore, Maryland.

1925
- Marshall enrolls at historically black Lincoln University.

1930
- Marshall enters the school of law at historically black Howard University.

1933
- Marshall graduates from Howard University and begins private practice in Baltimore.

1934
- Marshall begins work with the Baltimore branch of the National Association for the Advancement of Colored People.

1936
- Marshall is hired as assistant counsel at the New York headquarters of the National Association for the Advancement of Colored People.

1954
- **May 17**
  The Supreme Court invalidates the "separate but equal" doctrine as it applied to public schools in *Brown v. Board of Education*, a case that Marshall successfully argued.

1961
- **September 23**
  President John F. Kennedy nominates Marshall to the U.S. Court of Appeals for the Second Circuit; Marshall takes his seat on the court in October.

1965
- **July 13**
  Marshall is appointed as U.S. solicitor general by President Lyndon B. Johnson.

◆ *Grayned v. City of Rockford*

Although Marshall privately voiced doubts about the efficacy of civil disobedience in effecting civil rights gains, during his NAACP years he publicly supported groups such as the Southern Christian Leadership Conference, an organization at the forefront of civil rights protests in the 1950s and 1960s led by the Reverend Martin Luther King, Jr. In *Grayned v. City of Rockford* (1972), Marshall, writing for the majority, supported the right to demonstrate peacefully by striking down an antipicketing ordinance that had been used against civil rights demonstrators. But he held that an antinoise ordinance that was also applied against the appellant was lawful. The opinion displays jurisprudential restraint and objectivity in that each ordinance, though used against the same appellant for the same conduct, was carefully considered in terms of nuanced legal standards.

Appellant Richard Grayned was convicted of violating a local antipicketing ordinance by demonstrating in front of West High School in Rockford, Illinois. He was participating in a demonstration that arose from grievances of African American students. The antipicketing ordinance prohibited picketing or demonstrating on a public way within 150 feet of any primary or secondary school building, starting thirty minutes before school commenced until thirty minutes after school ended. However, it excepted peaceful labor picketing from the prohibition of demonstrating near schools. The Court held that the ordinance violated the Fourteenth Amendment's equal protection clause because it made an impermissible distinction between labor picketing and other peaceful picketing.

Grayned had also been convicted of violating a Rockford antinoise ordinance. In this instance, Marshall found that the ordinance did not violate the law. In his opinion Marshall states that "it is a basic principle of due process that an enactment is void for vagueness if its prohibitions are not clearly defined." He emphasizes the danger of such laws by stating that "a vague law impermissibly delegates basic policy matters to policemen, judges, and juries for resolution on an *ad hoc* and subjective basis, with the attendant dangers of arbitrary and discriminatory application." He further states that the antinoise ordinance was designed, "according to its preamble, 'for the protection of Schools,'" and "forbids deliberately noisy or diversionary activity that disrupts or is about to disrupt normal school activities." But, in a display of nuance and judicial restraint, Marshall argues that the antinoise ordinance's restrictions on noise that "disrupted" the school environment was not vague and held that it was constitutional. He elaborates by writing that "although the prohibited quantum of disturbance is not specified in the ordinance, it is apparent from the statute's announced purpose that the measure is whether normal school activity has been or is about to be disrupted."

◆ *Furman v. Georgia*

In this case, which consolidated three cases, the Supreme Court addressed the legal question of whether the imposition of the death penalty amounted to "cruel and unusual punishment" in violation of the Eighth and Fourteenth Amendments to the Constitution. This was an issue close to Marshall's heart because, as NAACP counsel, he had seen firsthand that the death penalty sentencing rate for African Americans, particularly when the victims were white, was disproportionately high. Marshall expended a significant amount of energy speaking to his colleagues on the Court about this issue and was successful in forming a majority bloc.

The petitioners were three African American men convicted for murder and rape in state courts in Georgia and Texas. The issue of federalism, which weighs the relative rights of state governments and the federal government, was important in this case because statutes in the two states mandated that juries determine whether the death sentence was to be applied. The Court took up the question, then, of whether the Eighth Amendment barring "cruel and unusual punishment" applied to the states. The Court sent the case back to the lower courts for reconsideration while holding that the death penalty did, in fact, violate the Eighth and Fourteenth Amendments. The Court's reasoning was that capital punishment was applied in a discretionary, haphazard, and discriminatory way because it was imposed in a small number of total possible cases and primarily against certain minority groups. This case resulted in the suspension of capital punishment in the United States for a period of time.

In his concurrence, Marshall clarified that his position against the death penalty was not meant to condone or mitigate the conduct for which the petitioners had been convicted. Quoting Austin Gardiner, England's lord chancellor (the head of Britain's legal profession), Marshall states that "the question then is not whether we condone rape or murder, for surely we do not; it is whether capital punishment is 'a punishment no longer consistent with our own self-respect' and, therefore, in violation of the Eighth Amendment." Marshall then argues that the Founding Fathers' original intent in the Eighth Amendment was to prohibit torture and "other cruel punishments." He provides a historical accounting of the emergence of the Eighth Amendment, its derivation from English law, and the practices (such as torture) that led to its passage. He connects the arguments made in the sixteenth century—that the Magna Carta (the English legal charter dating to 1215) prohibited the "cruel and barbarous" practice of torture by English ecclesiastical (church) courts—to what he viewed as such protections in the U.S. Constitution. Marshall notes that the language of the Eighth Amendment's prohibition on "cruel and unusual" punishment originated from the English Bill of Rights of 1689. He states that whether the English Bill of Rights prohibited cruel and unusual punishments because of excessive or illegal punishments, in reaction to barbaric forms of punishment, or both, the Founders of the United States clearly borrowed the language of the English Bill of Rights and included it in the Eighth Amendment to outlaw not only torture but also other cruel punishments. He then reviews historical precedent on the meaning and application of the Eighth Amendment's prohibition on "cruel and unusual" punishment.

Time Line

1967

■ **June 13**
President Lyndon B. Johnson nominates Marshall as the first African American U.S. Supreme Court judge; Marshall takes his seat on the Court on October 2, 1967.

1972

■ **June 26**
Marshall writes the majority Court opinion in *Grayned v. City of Rockford*.

■ **June 29**
Marshall writes a concurrence with the Court's decision in *Furman v. Georgia*.

1978

■ **June 28**
Marshall writes a separate opinion in *Regents of the University of California v. Bakke*.

1991

■ **June 20**
Marshall writes a dissent from the Court's decision in *Florida v. Bostick*.

■ **June 28**
Marshall retires from the U.S. Supreme Court.

1993

■ **January 24**
Marshall dies in Washington, D.C.

Marshall argues that the most important principle in analyzing what was "cruel and unusual" was evolving standards. Thus, a penalty that was permissible at one time in history is not necessarily permissible later. He provides precedent for this concept by arguing that though prior courts may have held that the death penalty was not cruel and unusual, they had allowed that this view could change based on contemporary public opinion. Marshall states that although prior courts and individual justices may have held that the death penalty is constitutional, the current Court was not bound by that view. He emphasizes this point by noting that "the very nature of the Eighth Amendment would dictate that unless a very recent decision existed, *stare decisis* [the obligation of courts to follow precedent] would bow to changing values, and the question of the constitutionality of capital punishment at a given moment in history would remain open." Marshall's early experience at the NAACP in defending cases involving charges of rape against African American men provided some of his motivation for ending what he perceived as an inequitably applied sentencing measure. But in his intricately written concurrence Marshall emphasizes that this was an argument based on principle, one premised on a lifelong view that the Constitution should be an arbiter of fairness.

◆ Regents of the University of California v. Bakke

In *Regents of the University of California v. Bakke*, nearly twenty-five years after his groundbreaking work in *Brown v. Board of Education*, Marshall was confronted with a growing legal challenge to integration efforts based on the view that affirmative action (policies that take race or gender into account for purposes of hiring, admission to universities, and the like) had discriminatory consequences for some whites. In this case, the appellant was a white male who had applied unsuccessfully for admission to the University of California at Davis medical school. He argued that a special admissions program that set aside a fixed number of seats for minority applicants resulted in his rejection and was therefore discriminatory, in violation of the equal protection clause of the Fourteenth Amendment.

The Court agreed, holding that the medical school admissions program had violated the equal protection clause of the Fourteenth Amendment. In particular, it held that the use of racial quotas (a fixed number of seats for racial minorities) discriminated against others and violated the Constitution. The broader legal issue here was the perception that affirmative action programs presented a conflict between group rights and individual rights. Since race is considered a "suspect category," the Court required that the University of California show that its use of race was necessary to promote a substantial state interest. The Court majority found that the school had failed to do so and that race could be considered in admissions only if it was one factor among others in a competitive process.

The *Bakke* case was controversial in that it left behind confusion for many years as to whether and in what contexts race could be used as a factor in the university admissions process. The majority opinion provided that race was an acceptable factor in admissions when it is part of a governmental interest in the educational environment's First Amendment need for the "robust exchange of ideas." Marshall's strongly worded dissent was a reflection of his alarm over what he perceived as a retrenchment of segregation in public schools as white litigants sought to challenge programs intended to bring more African Americans into schools. But from a legal standpoint it reflected his concern that the equal protection clause of the Fourteenth Amendment would be lost as a tool to remedy the present and past effects of historical discrimination against African Americans. He writes, "It must be remembered that, during most of the past 200 years, the Constitution as interpreted by this Court did not prohibit the most ingenious and pervasive forms of discrimination against the Negro." He goes on to conclude, "Now, when a State acts to remedy the effects of that legacy of discrimination, I cannot believe that this same Constitution stands as a barrier."

To recenter the issue on remedying the present effects of historical discrimination, Marshall, in his opinion, conducts a detailed review of the history of slavery and segregation and the laws that supported it. He writes that for three and a half centuries, slaves were "dragged to this country in chains to be sold into slavery." Slaves were "uprooted" from their homelands and "thrust into bondage for forced labor." A slave had no legal rights. It was against the law for anyone to teach a slave to read, and families could be broken up by the sale of slaves whenever the owner wished. Killing or injuring a slave was not regarded as unlawful. "The system of slavery brutalized and dehumanized both master and slave," Marshall concludes.

Marshall provides legislative history for his argument that using race to remedy past discrimination did not violate the Fourteenth Amendment. He states, "It is because of a legacy of unequal treatment that we now must permit the institutions of this society to give consideration to race in making decisions about who will hold the positions of influence, affluence, and prestige in America. For far too long, the doors to those positions have been shut to Negroes." Reflecting his great concern that the holding amounted to a retrenchment of segregation, he states his fear that the nation has "come full circle." Affirmative action programs began after the Civil War, but the Court "destroyed the movement toward complete equality" in such cases as the Civil Rights Cases (a group of 1883 cases in which the Court concluded that Congress did not have the authority to prohibit racial discrimination in the states and declared the Civil Rights Act of 1875 unconstitutional) and *Plessy v. Ferguson*. In the century that followed, the Court tacitly approved of the nation's failure to achieve a more just society until *Brown v. Board of Education*, the civil rights acts of the 1960s, and the emergence of affirmative action. But now, he concludes, the Court is again intruding, "this time to stop affirmative-action programs of the type used by the University of California."

Writing in a persuasive and passionate tone, Marshall states that "if we are ever to become a fully integrated society, one in which the color of a person's skin will not determine the opportunities available to him or her, we must be willing to take steps to open those doors." He goes on to say, "I do not believe that anyone can truly look into America's past and still find that a remedy for the effects of that past is impermissible." This case, however, marked the beginning of a series of legal challenges to programs intended to remedy past racial discrimination by providing affirmative action for educational access for African Americans. Today, affirmative action jurisprudence lies more in the language of the Court majority, with emphasis on the exchange of ideas and First Amendment protections, than it does in Marshall's Fourteenth Amendment–based argument for remedying past harm.

Allan Bakke is trailed by news and television reporters after attending his first day at the Medical School of the University of California at Davis on September 25, 1978. (AP/Wide World Photos)

◆ *Florida v. Bostick*

In addition to his concern over the death penalty and affirmative action, Marshall was opposed to decisions that supported arbitrary police practices, which he viewed as a civil rights issue. In an important criminal procedure case, *Florida v. Bostick* (1991), the Court did not hold it unconstitutional for police to board intercity buses and ask individual passengers to allow their bags to be searched. Marshall wrote a strongly worded dissent, joined by Justices Harry Blackmun and John Paul Stevens.

In this case, two uniformed police officers (one with a visible pistol) boarded a bus as part of a routine drug interdiction program. Without "articulable" suspicion—that is, suspicion the officers could put into words rather than a mere hunch—the officers asked the appellant to confirm his identity, which he did. The officers then informed him that they were searching for illegal drugs and requested the passenger's consent to search his baggage. The officers informed the passenger that he had the right to refuse consent. The passenger's baggage produced cocaine, and he was arrested and convicted in Florida state court. The appellant attempted but failed to suppress the evidence and appealed to the U.S. Supreme Court on the ground that the seizure of the evidence violated the Fourth Amendment.

This case involved the "free to leave" test of Fourth Amendment law as it applied to bus searches and seizures. This test considers whether a "reasonable person" would feel "free to leave" if asked by police, while a passenger on a bus, to consent to a search of baggage. The Court majority held that the "free to leave" test did not apply because the passenger's freedom of movement had been restricted not by the police conduct but by a factor independent of police conduct, specifically, by his being a passenger on a bus. The majority wrote that the appropriate inquiry is whether a reasonable person would feel free to decline the officers' requests or otherwise terminate the encounter. The Court majority struck down the holding of the Florida Supreme Court that bus searches were seizures, arguing that the bus context was just one of a set of factual considerations.

Although Marshall did not disagree with the majority's preference for the test of "free to decline," he strongly disagreed with their decision, arguing that the facts amounted to police coercion. He states that the consequences of this case had broader impact than the fate of this particular appellant, for such "dragnet"-style sweeps were a common tool of the "war on drugs." Normally, officers are allowed to conduct warrantless searches and seizures only when they have reasonable "articulable suspicion" of criminal wrong-

"A vague law impermissibly delegates basic policy matters to policemen, judges, and juries for resolution on an ad hoc and subjective basis, with the attendant dangers of arbitrary and discriminatory application."

(Grayned v. City of Rockford)

"The question then is not whether we condone rape or murder, for surely we do not; it is whether capital punishment is 'a punishment no longer consistent with our own self-respect' and, therefore, violative of the Eighth Amendment."

(Furman v. Georgia)

"It must be remembered that, during most of the past 200 years, the Constitution as interpreted by this Court did not prohibit the most ingenious and pervasive forms of discrimination against the Negro. Now, when a State acts to remedy the effects of that legacy of discrimination, I cannot believe that this same Constitution stands as a barrier."

(Regents of the University of California v. Bakke)

"It is because of a legacy of unequal treatment that we now must permit the institutions of this society to give consideration to race in making decisions about who will hold the positions of influence, affluence, and prestige in America. For far too long, the doors to those positions have been shut to Negroes."

(Regents of the University of California v. Bakke)

"In my view, the law-enforcement technique with which we are confronted in this case—the suspicionless police sweep of buses in intrastate or interstate travel—bears all of the indicia of coercion and unjustified intrusion associated with the general warrant. Because I believe that the bus sweep at issue in this case violates the core values of the Fourth Amendment, I dissent."

(Florida v. Bostick)

"It does not follow, however, that the approach of passengers during a sweep is completely random. Indeed, at least one officer who routinely confronts interstate travelers candidly admitted that race is a factor influencing his decision whom to approach,"

(Florida v. Bostick)

doing. Marshall argues that such sweeps were reminiscent of the general warrant in early English history, when searches and seizures did not require reasonable cause or specific suspicion of an individual and were often used for political reasons. He states that "the law-enforcement technique with which we are confronted in this case—the suspicionless police sweep of buses in intrastate or interstate travel—bears all of the indicia of coercion and unjustified intrusion associated with the general warrant." Marshall concludes that the bus sweep "violates the core values of the Fourth Amendment," and on this basis he dissented.

Marshall adds that such bus sweeps "occur within cramped confines, with officers typically placing themselves in between the passenger selected for an interview and the exit of the bus." Further, because the bus is close to its destination, "passengers are in no position to leave as a means of evading the officers' questioning." To Marshall, such bus sweeps were an unjust intrusion of government power, a practice that "burdens the experience of traveling by bus with a degree of governmental interference to which, until now, our society has been proudly unaccustomed."

Marshall argues that it was unlikely that most people riding on such buses would feel that they could legally refuse such a search. His work at the NAACP provided him with the recognition that working-class people and lower-income African Americans would be disproportionately affected by this type of police search, since these groups disproportionately rode on buses. He addresses the potential role of race in such sweeps, noting that they were not entirely random. He notes the candid admission of one of the officers who routinely confronts interstate travelers that race influenced his decision about whom to confront.

Impact and Legacy

Marshall's life was the product both of the times and of his own making. Born at a critical moment, he played a central role in affecting historical changes that radically altered American society. After decades of working on behalf of African American civil rights, Marshall, famous already for effectively ending legal segregation in *Brown*, went on to become the first African American U.S. solicitor general and the first African American U.S. Supreme Court justice. During his tenure on the Court he was in the odd position of ruling on cases dependent on precedent he had helped create

Questions for Further Study

1. Compare and contrast Marshall's legal reasoning with that of his less well-known mentor, Charles Hamilton Houston. In what ways did Houston, dean of the law school at Howard University, influence the future Supreme Court justice? To what degree do the two men differ, and are those differences based in substantive issues of political philosophy or merely differences of personality, experience, or perception?

2. It has been said that Marshall exhibited a great subtlety of reasoning in his *Grayned v. City of Rockford* opinion. Writing for the majority, he maintained that a municipal antipicketing ordinance used by the city of Rockford, Illinois, to shut down a demonstration by African American students was unconstitutional; on the other hand, an antinoise ordinance, Marshall held, was not. What are the reasons he gives for his distinction between the constitutionality of the two laws?

3. *Regents of the University of California v. Bakke* shows just how challenging the questions approached by the nation's highest court can be. Evaluate the merits of both sides: Which, do you think, has more justification? Why? Marshall's dissent addresses the matter of equal protection, which remained a contentious legal issue long after the passage of the Fourteenth Amendment in 1868. What views on the amendment, its equal protection clause, and their applicability in this situation does he share with his colleague William Brennan?

4. Discuss the issues raised in *Florida v. Bostick*, which concerns the question of Fourth Amendment freedoms as related to a police practice of searching passengers' bags aboard public transportation. Weigh the relative merits of the two sides in the case and then consider Marshall's dissent. How and how well does he make his points about discrimination and freedom? Whereas *Bostick* took place amid the "war on drugs," what if the police search had occurred amid the early-twenty-first-century "war on terror" and the item confiscated had been not cocaine but a bomb? Would that change your evaluation of Thomas's dissent? Why or why not?

Marshall, Thurgood

as an NAACP attorney. Although toward the end of his life he may have seen much of his work as an advocate shift in an undesired direction, it is to his credit that he was pivotal in crafting the legal framework whereby civil rights disputes can be processed. In other words, whether a party agrees with the precedent that Marshall set is not as important as the fact that he helped fashion the legal framework by which such conflicts can be addressed. His goal of creating an integrated American society was part of his broader philosophy of the importance of the rule of law. His advocacy as an NAACP attorney resulted in a civil rights framework that protects not only minority people but Americans as a whole. Precedents that Marshall helped to form, including those involving important safeguards such as due process in search and seizure, serve to protect all Americans.

Key Sources

The Thurgood Marshall Papers at the Library of Congress encompass 173,700 items (http://lcweb2.loc.gov/cgi-bin/query/h?faid/faid:@field(DOCID+ms001047). An index of selected writings relevant to Marshall prepared by Howard University's Moorland-Spingarn Research Center, Washington, D.C., can be found at http://www.founders.howard.edu/moorland-spingarn/MARSHALL.htm. Mark Tushnet is the editor of *Thurgood Marshall: His Speeches, Writings, Arguments, Opinions, and Reminiscences* (2001).

Further Reading

■ Articles

Gormley, Ken. "A Mentor's Legacy; Charles Hamilton Houston, Thurgood Marshall and the Civil Rights Movement." *American Bar Association Journal* 78 (June 1992): 62–63.

Hayes, William K. "Thurgood Marshall: Rampart against Racism, Notes." *Black Law Journal* 2 (1972): 240–247.

Hoptman, Virginia. "Principled Justice: A Personal Reflection on Justice Marshall." *Harvard Civil Rights-Civil Liberties Law Review* 27 (1992): 1–7.

Maclin, Tracey. "Justice Thurgood Marshall: Taking the Fourth Amendment Seriously." *Cornell Law Review* 77 (1992): 723–812.

■ Books

Davis, Michael D., and Hunter R. Clark. *Thurgood Marshall: Warrior at the Bar, Rebel on the Bench.* Secaucus, N.J.: Carol Publishing Group, 1992.

Goldman, Roger, and David Gallen. *Thurgood Marshall: Justice for All.* New York: Carroll and Graf, 1992.

Ogletree, Charles J., Jr. *All Deliberate Speed: Reflections on the First Half Century of* Brown v. Board of Education. New York: W. W. Norton, 2004.

Williams, Juan. *Thurgood Marshall: American Revolutionary.* New York: Times Books, 1998.

■ Web Sites

Smith, Stephen, and Kate Ellis. "Thurgood Marshall before the Court." American RadioWorks Web site.
    http://americanradioworks.publicradio.org/features/marshall.

—Michael Chang

GRAYNED V. CITY OF ROCKFORD (1972)

Appellant Richard Grayned was convicted for his part in a demonstration in front of West Senior High School in Rockford, Illinois. Negro students at the school had first presented their grievances to school administrators. When the principal took no action on crucial complaints, a more public demonstration of protest was planned. On April 25, 1969, approximately 200 people—students, their family members, and friends—gathered next to the school grounds. Appellant ... was part of this group. The demonstrators marched around on a sidewalk about 100 feet from the school building, which was set back from the street....

After warning the demonstrators, the police arrested 40 of them, including appellant. For participating in the demonstration, Grayned was tried and convicted of violating two Rockford ordinances, hereinafter referred to as the "anti-picketing" ordinance and the "anti-noise" ordinance.... We conclude that the anti-picketing ordinance is unconstitutional, but affirm the court below with respect to the anti-noise ordinance.

I

At the time of appellant's arrest and conviction, Rockford's anti-picketing ordinance provided that "A person commits disorderly conduct when he knowingly:

"(i) Pickets or demonstrates on a public way within 150 feet of any primary or secondary school building while the school is in session and one-half hour before the school is in session and one-half hour after the school session has been concluded, provided that this subsection does not prohibit the peaceful picketing of any school involved in a labor dispute...."

This ordinance is identical to the Chicago disorderly conduct ordinance we have today considered in *Police Department of Chicago v. Mosley, ante*, p. 92. For the reasons given in *Mosley*, we agree with dissenting Justice Schaefer below, and hold that §18.1 (i) violates the Equal Protection Clause of the Fourteenth Amendment. Appellant's conviction under this invalid ordinance must be reversed.

II

The antinoise ordinance reads, in pertinent part, as follows:

"No person, while on public or private grounds adjacent to any building in which a school or any class thereof is in session, shall willfully make or assist in the making of any noise or diversion which disturbs or tends to disturb the peace or good order of such school session or class thereof...."

It is a basic principle of due process that an enactment is void for vagueness if its prohibitions are not clearly defined. Vague laws offend several important values. First, because we assume that man is free to steer between lawful and unlawful conduct, we insist that laws give the person of ordinary intelligence a reasonable opportunity to know what is prohibited, so that he may act accordingly. Vague laws may trap the innocent by not providing fair warning. Second, if arbitrary and discriminatory enforcement is to be prevented, laws must provide explicit standards for those who apply them. A vague law impermissibly delegates basic policy matters to policemen, judges, and juries for resolution on an *ad hoc* and subjective basis, with the attendant dangers of arbitrary and discriminatory application. Third, but related, where a vague statute "abut[s] upon sensitive areas of basic First Amendment freedoms," it "operates to inhibit the exercise of [those] freedoms." Uncertain meanings inevitably lead citizens to "'steer far wider of the unlawful zone'...than if the boundaries of the forbidden areas were clearly marked."...

Although the question is close, we conclude that the anti-noise ordinance is not impermissibly vague....

We find no unconstitutional vagueness in the anti-noise ordinance. Condemned to the use of words, we can never expect mathematical certainty from our language. The words of the Rockford ordinance are marked by "flexibility and reasonable breadth, rather than meticulous specificity," *Esteban v. Central Missouri State College* ... (Blackmun, J.), cert. denied,...but we think it is clear what the ordinance as a whole prohibits. Designed, according to its preamble, "for the protection of Schools," the ordinance forbids deliberately noisy or diversionary activity that disrupts or is about to disrupt normal school activities. It forbids this willful activity at fixed times—when school is in session—and at a sufficiently fixed place—"adjacent" to the school....

Although the prohibited quantum of disturbance is not specified in the ordinance, it is apparent from the statute's announced purpose that the measure is whether normal school activity has been or is about to be disrupted. We do not have here a vague, general "breach of the peace" ordinance, but a statute written specifically for the school context, where the prohibited disturbances are easily measured by their impact on the normal activities of the school. Given this "particular context," the ordinance gives "fair notice to those to whom [it] is directed."...

Although appellant does not claim that, as applied to him, the anti-noise ordinance has punished protected expressive activity, he claims that the ordinance is overbroad on its face. Because overbroad laws, like vague ones, deter privileged activity, our cases firmly establish appellant's standing to raise an overbreadth challenge. The crucial question, then, is whether the ordinance sweeps within its prohibitions what may not be punished under the First and Fourteenth Amendments. Specifically, appellant contends that the Rockford ordinance unduly interferes with First and Fourteenth Amendment rights to picket on a public sidewalk near a school. We disagree....

Rockford's modest restriction on some peaceful picketing represents a considered and specific legislative judgment that some kinds of expressive activity should be restricted at a particular time and place, here in order to protect the schools. Such a reasonable regulation is not inconsistent with the First and Fourteenth Amendments. The anti-noise ordinance is not invalid on its face.

The judgment is affirmed in part and reversed in part.

Glossary

appellant	the party who appeals a case to a higher court
enactment	law, ordinance
quantum	amount, quantity

FURMAN V. GEORGIA (1972)

Marshall's Concurrence

These three cases present the question whether the death penalty is a cruel and unusual punishment prohibited by the Eighth Amendment to the United States Constitution....

The elasticity of the constitutional provision under consideration presents dangers of too little or too much self-restraint. Hence, we must proceed with caution to answer the question presented. By first examining the historical derivation of the Eighth Amendment and the construction given it in the past by this Court, and then exploring the history and attributes of capital punishment in this country, we can answer the question presented with objectivity and a proper measure of self-restraint.

Candor is critical to such an inquiry. All relevant material must be marshaled and sorted and forthrightly examined. We must not only be precise as to the standards of judgment that we are utilizing, but exacting in examining the relevant material in light of those standards.

Candor compels me to confess that I am not oblivious to the fact that this is truly a matter of life and death....

I

The Eighth Amendment's ban against cruel and unusual punishments derives from English law....

Cruel punishments were not confined to those accused of crimes, but were notoriously applied with even greater relish to those who were convicted. Blackstone described in ghastly detail the myriad of inhumane forms of punishment imposed on persons found guilty of any of a large number of offenses. Death, of course, was the usual result....

This legislative history has led at least one legal historian to conclude "that the cruel and unusual punishments clause of the Bill of Rights of 1689 was, first, an objection to the imposition of punishments that were unauthorized by statute and outside the jurisdiction of the sentencing court, and second, a reiteration of the English policy against disproportionate penalties," and not primarily a reaction to the torture of the High Commission, harsh sentences, or the assizes.

Whether the English Bill of Rights prohibition against cruel and unusual punishments is properly read as a response to excessive or illegal punishments, as a reaction to barbaric and objectionable modes of punishment, or as both, there is no doubt whatever that in borrowing the language and in including it in the Eighth Amendment, our Founding Fathers intended to outlaw torture and other cruel punishments.

The precise language used in the Eighth Amendment first appeared in America on June 12, 1776, in Virginia's "Declaration of Rights," §9 of which read: "That excessive bail ought not to be required, nor excessive fines imposed, nor cruel and unusual punishments inflicted." This language was drawn verbatim from the English Bill of Rights of 1689. Other States adopted similar clauses, and there is evidence in the debates of the various state conventions that were called upon to ratify the Constitution of great concern for the omission of any prohibition against torture or other cruel punishments.

The Virginia Convention offers some clues as to what the Founding Fathers had in mind in prohibiting cruel and unusual punishments. At one point George Mason advocated the adoption of a Bill of Rights, and Patrick Henry concurred....

"In this business of legislation, your members of Congress will loose the restriction of not imposing excessive fines, demanding excessive bail, and inflicting cruel and unusual punishments. These are prohibited by your declaration of rights. What has distinguished our ancestors?—That they would not admit of tortures, or cruel and barbarous punishment. But Congress may introduce the practice of the civil law, in preference to that of the common law. They may introduce the practice of France, Spain, and Germany—of torturing, to extort a confession of the crime. They will say that they might as well draw examples from those countries as from Great Britain, and they will tell you that there is such a necessity of strengthening the arm of government, that they must have a criminal equity, and extort confession by torture, in order to punish with still more relentless severity. We are then lost and undone."

Henry's statement indicates that he wished to insure that "relentless severity" would be prohibited by the Constitution. Other expressions with respect to the proposed Eighth Amendment by Members of the First Congress indicate that they shared Henry's view of the need for and purpose of the Cruel and Unusual Punishments Clause....

The fact, therefore, that the Court, or individual Justices, may have in the past expressed an opinion that the death penalty is constitutional is not now binding on us....There is no holding directly in point, and the very nature of the Eighth Amendment would dictate that unless a very recent decision existed, *stare decisis* would bow to changing values, and the question of the constitutionality of capital punishment at a given moment in history would remain open.

Faced with an open question, we must establish our standards for decision....

In addition, even if capital punishment is not excessive, it nonetheless violates the Eighth Amendment because it is morally unacceptable to the people of the United States at this time in their history.

In judging whether or not a given penalty is morally acceptable, most courts have said that the punishment is valid unless "it shocks the conscience and sense of justice of the people."...

No nation in the recorded history of man has a greater tradition of revering justice and fair treatment for all its citizens in times of turmoil, confusion, and tension than ours. This is a country which stands tallest in troubled times, a country that clings to fundamental principles, cherishes its constitutional heritage, and rejects simple solutions that compromise the values that lie at the roots of our democratic system.

In striking down capital punishment, this Court does not malign our system of government. On the contrary, it pays homage to it. Only in a free society could right triumph in difficult times, and could civilization record its magnificent advancement. In recognizing the humanity of our fellow beings, we pay ourselves the highest tribute. We achieve "a major milestone in the long road up from barbarism" and join the approximately 70 other jurisdictions in the world which celebrate their regard for civilization and humanity by shunning capital punishment.

Glossary

Blackstone	William Blackstone, British jurist of the eighteenth century whose *Commentaries on the Laws of England* was highly influential in jurisprudence for generations
elasticity	flexibility; susceptibility to differing interpretations
George Mason	author of the Virginia Declaration of Rights
"major milestone in the long road up from barbarism"	quotation from Attorney General Ramsey Clark in his book *Crime in America*
one legal historian	Anthony Granucci, in a 1969 article in the *California Law Review*
Patrick Henry	an enthusiastic supporter of the American Revolution, best known for his "Give me liberty, or give me death!" speech
stare decisis	the legal principle that courts are obligated to follow precedents established in earlier legal cases

REGENTS OF THE UNIVERSITY OF CALIFORNIA V. BAKKE (1978)

Marshall's Separate Opinion

I agree with the judgment of the Court only insofar as it permits a university to consider the race of an applicant in making admissions decisions. I do not agree that petitioner's admissions program violates the Constitution. For it must be remembered that, during most of the past 200 years, the Constitution as interpreted by this Court did not prohibit the most ingenious and pervasive forms of discrimination against the Negro. Now, when a State acts to remedy the effects of that legacy of discrimination, I cannot believe that this same Constitution stands as a barrier.

Three hundred and fifty years ago, the Negro was dragged to this country in chains to be sold into slavery. Uprooted from his homeland and thrust into bondage for forced labor, the slave was deprived of all legal rights. It was unlawful to teach him to read; he could be sold away from his family and friends at the whim of his master; and killing or maiming him was not a crime. The system of slavery brutalized and dehumanized both master and slave....

The denial of human rights was etched into the American Colonies' first attempts at establishing self-government....

The implicit protection of slavery embodied in the Declaration of Independence was made explicit in the Constitution, which treated a slave as being equivalent to three-fifths of a person for purposes of apportioning representatives and taxes among the States.... In their declaration of the principles that were to provide the cornerstone of the new Nation, therefore, the Framers made it plain that "we the people," for whose protection the Constitution was designed, did not include those whose skins were the wrong color....

The status of the Negro as property was officially erased by his emancipation at the end of the Civil War. But the long-awaited emancipation, while freeing the Negro from slavery, did not bring him citizenship or equality in any meaningful way....

The enforced segregation of the races continued into the middle of the 20th century. In both World Wars, Negroes were, for the most part, confined to separate military units; it was not until 1948 that an end to segregation in the military was ordered by President Truman. And the history of the exclusion of Negro children from white public schools is too well known and recent to require repeating here. That Negroes were deliberately excluded from public graduate and professional schools—and thereby denied the opportunity to become doctors, lawyers, engineers, and the like is also well established....

The position of the Negro today in America is the tragic but inevitable consequence of centuries of unequal treatment. Measured by any benchmark of comfort or achievement, meaningful equality remains a distant dream for the Negro....

In light of the sorry history of discrimination and its devastating impact on the lives of Negroes, bringing the Negro into the mainstream of American life should be a state interest of the highest order. To fail to do so is to ensure that America will forever remain a divided society....

As has been demonstrated in our joint opinion, this Court's past cases establish the constitutionality of race-conscious remedial measures. Beginning with the school desegregation cases, we recognized that, even absent a judicial or legislative finding of constitutional violation, a school board constitutionally could consider the race of students in making school assignment decisions....

While I applaud the judgment of the Court that a university may consider race in its admissions process, it is more than a little ironic that, after several hundred years of class-based discrimination against Negroes, the Court is unwilling to hold that a class-based remedy for that discrimination is permissible. In declining to so hold, today's judgment ignores the fact that for several hundred years, Negroes have been discriminated against not as individuals, but rather solely because of the color of their skins....

It is because of a legacy of unequal treatment that we now must permit the institutions of this society to give consideration to race in making decisions about who will hold the positions of influence, affluence, and prestige in America. For far too long, the doors to those positions have been shut to Negroes. If we are ever to become a fully integrated society, one in which the color of a person's skin will not determine the opportunities available to him or her, we must be willing to take steps to open those doors. I do not believe that anyone can truly look into America's past and still find that a remedy for the effects of that past is impermissible.

It has been said that this case involves only the individual, Bakke, and this University. I doubt, however, that there is a computer capable of determining the number of persons and institutions that may be affected by the decision in this case. For example, we are told by the Attorney General of the United States that at least 27 federal agencies have adopted regulations requiring recipients of federal funds to take "'*affirmative action* to overcome the effects of conditions which resulted in limiting participation ... by persons of a particular race, color, or national origin.'"...I cannot even guess the number of state and local governments that have set up affirmative-action programs, which may be affected by today's decision.

I fear that we have come full circle. After the Civil War our Government started several "affirmative action" programs. This Court in the *Civil Rights Cases* and *Plessy v. Ferguson* destroyed the movement toward complete equality. For almost a century no action was taken, and this nonaction was with the tacit approval of the courts. Then we had *Brown v. Board of Education* and the Civil Rights Acts of Congress, followed by numerous affirmative-action programs. Now, we have this Court again stepping in, this time to stop affirmative-action programs of the type used by the University of California.

Glossary

President Truman	President Harry S. Truman, who integrated the military through Executive Order 9981 in 1948

FLORIDA V. BOSTICK (1991)

Marshall's Dissent

Our Nation, we are told, is engaged in a "war on drugs." No one disputes that it is the job of law enforcement officials to devise effective weapons for fighting this war. But the effectiveness of a law enforcement technique is not proof of its constitutionality.... In my view, the law enforcement technique with which we are confronted in this case—the suspicionless police sweep of buses in intrastate or interstate travel—bears all of the indicia of coercion and unjustified intrusion associated with the general warrant. Because I believe that the bus sweep at issue in this case violates the core values of the Fourth Amendment, I dissent.

At issue in this case is a "new and increasingly common tactic in the war on drugs": the suspicionless police sweep of buses in interstate or intrastate travel.... Typically under this technique, a group of state or federal officers will board a bus while it is stopped at an intermediate point on its route. Often displaying badges, weapons or other indicia of authority, the officers identify themselves and announce their purpose to intercept drug traffickers. They proceed to approach individual passengers, requesting them to show identification, produce their tickets, and explain the purpose of their travels. Never do the officers advise the passengers that they are free not to speak with the officers. An "interview" of this type ordinarily culminates in a request for consent to search the passenger's luggage.

These sweeps are conducted in "dragnet" style. The police admittedly act without an "articulable suspicion" in deciding which buses to board and which passengers to approach for interviewing. By proceeding systematically in this fashion, the police are able to engage in a tremendously high volume of searches.... The percentage of successful drug interdictions is low....

To put it mildly, these sweeps "are inconvenient, intrusive, and intimidating."... They occur within cramped confines, with officers typically placing themselves in between the passenger selected for an interview and the exit of the bus.... Because the bus is only temporarily stationed at a point short of its destination, the passengers are in no position to leave as a means of evading the officers' questioning.

Undoubtedly, such a sweep holds up the progress of the bus.... Thus, this "new and increasingly common tactic,"... burdens the experience of traveling by bus with a degree of governmental interference to which, until now, our society has been proudly unaccustomed....

Two officers boarded the Greyhound bus on which respondent was a passenger while the bus, en route from Miami to Atlanta, was on a brief stop to pick up passengers in Fort Lauderdale. The officers made a visible display of their badges and wore bright green "raid" jackets bearing the insignia of the Broward County Sheriff's Department; one held a gun in a recognizable weapons pouch.... These facts alone constitute an intimidating "show of authority."... Once on board, the officers approached respondent, who was sitting in the back of the bus, identified themselves as narcotics officers and began to question him. One officer stood in front of respondent's seat, partially blocking the narrow aisle through which respondent would have been required to pass to reach the exit of the bus....

Even if respondent had perceived that the officers would *let* him leave the bus, moreover, he could not reasonably have been expected to resort to this means of evading their intrusive questioning. For so far as respondent knew, the bus's departure from the terminal was imminent.... The vulnerability that an intrastate or interstate traveler experiences when confronted by the police outside of his "own familiar territory" surely aggravates the coercive quality of such an encounter....

The Fourth Amendment clearly condemns the suspicionless, dragnet-style sweep of intrastate or interstate buses. Withdrawing this particular weapon from the government's drug war arsenal would hardly leave the police without any means of combatting the use of buses as instrumentalities of the drug trade. The police would remain free, for example, to approach passengers whom they have a reasonable, articulable basis to suspect of criminal wrongdoing. Alternatively, they could continue to confront passengers without suspicion so long as they took simple steps, like advising the passengers confronted of their right to decline to be questioned, to dispel the aura of coercion and intimidation that pervades such encounters. There is no reason to expect that such requirements would render the Nation's buses law enforcement–free zones.

The majority attempts to gloss over the violence that today's decision does to the Fourth Amendment with empty admonitions. "If th[e] [war on drugs] is to be fought," the majority intones, "those who fight it must respect the rights of individuals, whether or not those individuals are suspected of having committed a crime."… The majority's actions, however, speak louder than its words.

I dissent.

indicia	indications, characteristics
instrumentalities	tools
intrastate	within the state

GEORGE MASON   1725–1792

Politician and Founding Father

Featured Documents
◆ Letter to the Committee of Merchants in London (1766)
◆ Fairfax County Resolves (1774)
◆ Virginia Declaration of Rights (1776)
◆ "Objections to This Constitution of Government" (1787)

Overview

Often known as the "forgotten Founder," the Virginia planter and statesman George Mason was born on December 11, 1725, in Fairfax County, Virginia. Because his father died in a boating accident when young George was just ten years old, he spent considerable time with his uncle, John Mercer, a prominent Virginia lawyer, poring over his uncle's law books. Although he never attended college or sought political office, he was appointed to the Virginia House of Burgesses in 1758 and served until 1761.

Mason was an active opponent of the British Parliament's passage of the Stamp Act in March 1765. The Stamp Act required colonists to pay a tax on almost everything that was printed, including legal documents, pamphlets, and playing cards. By December he had devised a strategy to help colonials evade paying the taxes levied under the Stamp Act. The following June he wrote a letter to the Committee of Merchants in London that was published in the *London Public Ledger*. In addition, he also helped draft nonimportation measures as another method of avoiding taxation. With nonimportation agreements, the American colonies essentially declared a boycott of British goods.

In July 1774, Mason, with the help of George Washington, drafted the Fairfax County Resolves. In this document he outlined the actions Virginia would take after the British Parliament passed and began enforcing the Intolerable Acts to punish Massachusetts for the Boston Tea Party—the action taken by a crowd of Bostonians on December 16, 1773, when they dumped some forty-five tons of British tea from ships into Boston Harbor to protest British taxation. The Intolerable Acts, sometimes called the Coercive Acts, were a series of punitive measures the British Parliament passed in response and that many colonists regarded as infringements on their rights as British subjects. At this same time, Mason began serving on the Fairfax County Committee of Safety and headed up the local militia, the Fairfax Independent Company. In May 1775 he was appointed as a delegate to the Virginia Convention in Williamsburg. The following May, Mason was placed in charge of a committee to draft a bill of rights and a constitution for Virginia. The Virginia Convention passed the Virginia Declaration of Rights on June 12 and the Virginia constitution on June 29, 1776.

Citing poor health, Mason withdrew from politics in 1780 but returned in May 1787 when he was appointed as a Virginia delegate to the Constitutional Convention. This body was charged with revising the Articles of Confederation, the 1781 document under which the American colonies were organized as a nation—the precursor to the Constitution—and that was passed by the Second Continental Congress. Although he was instrumental in forming the Constitution, Mason refused to sign the document, instead publishing a list of objections to it. He retired from politics again in 1790 because of declining health and died at his Virginia home, Gunston Hall, on October 7, 1792.

Explanation and Analysis of Documents

George Mason's overriding concern in both his public and private life was the preservation of citizens' rights and liberties. Early in his career, he was active in Virginia politics, and in such documents as the Virginia Declaration of Rights, his focus was on the rights and liberties of Virginians. But as the British Parliament continued to infringe those rights in all the colonies and war broke out between Britain and the colonies, Mason widened his focus to include the entire nation. He wanted the new nation to be strong, but in common with many of the nation's Founders, he feared a central government that was too strong. For this reason, he defended the Articles of Confederation, generally regarded as too weak to hold the nation together, and argued that the executive and legislative branches should not exercise power not expressly granted to them by the articles. Further, although he attended the Constitutional Convention, he opposed ratification of the U.S. Constitution, primarily because it did not include a bill of rights. He was also an opponent of excess taxation and believed that both Parliament and the U.S. Congress were overstepping their bounds in imposing taxes on the citizenry without their consent.

◆ Letter to the Committee of Merchants in London

In January 1766 a group of London merchants petitioned the British Parliament to repeal the Stamp Act because American colonists, to protest the act, were boycotting British goods. The act was repealed in March. In May 1766 the *Virginia Gazette* published a letter to America from a committee of London merchants, written the previous February. The committee urged the merchants in

1725

- **December 11**
  George Mason is born on the Mason family plantation in Fairfax County, Virginia.

1748

- Mason runs unsuccessfully to be the Fairfax County representative to the Virginia House of Burgesses.

1758

- **September**
  During the French and Indian War, Mason is appointed to the Virginia House of Burgesses, where he serves until 1761.

1765

- **December 23**
  Mason develops a plan for colonial landlords to avoid the Stamp Act passed in March 1765.

1766

- **June 6**
  Mason writes a letter to the Committee of Merchants in London opposing the Stamp Act.

1774

- **July 18**
  Mason writes the Fairfax County Resolves in response to the passage of the Intolerable Acts. He is also appointed that summer to the Committee of Safety created to implement the resolves.

1775

- **July 17**
  Mason is chosen as a delegate to the Virginia Convention.

- **August 25**
  Mason is appointed to the Second Continental Congress but declines the position.

1776

- **May 20–26**
  Mason composes the Virginia Declaration of Rights, which is adopted on June 12, 1776.

New York not to gloat over the repeal of the Stamp Act and to comply with Parliament's legislation.

In response, Mason wrote a letter of his own, signing it simply "A Virginia Planter." He felt that the letter from the London merchants, though nominally addressed to New Yorkers, was in reality addressed to American colonists in general and was condescending to them. In response, Mason sought to assert the colonists' rights as British subjects. He first quotes extensively from the letter from the London merchants, who wrote an extended analogy comparing the colonists to errant schoolboys, or children whose proper role in life was to follow the dictates of their parents, in this case the British Parliament. Mason characterizes this comparison as "a little ridiculous" and asserts that the millions of men and women now living in the colonies want nothing more than their "Birth-right" as "loyal & useful Subjects" of Great Britain.

Mason goes on to acknowledge "the supreme Authority of Great Britain over her Colonys." He points out that the American colonists object to Great Britain's imposition of "arbitrary" law courts in place of the right of trial by jury and notes that if such a step can be taken in the colonies, nothing would prevent a similar step being taken in the home country. He then emphasizes the close connections that exist between Britain and the colonies, pointing out that the American colonists are in large part British by birth, outlook, and "Dispositions." Indeed, writes Mason, "We are still the same People with them, in every Respect."

Mason touches on the subject of trade. Earlier in his response, he notes that Britain prohibits the American colonies from conducting trade with other countries, forcing American to import British goods "upon extravagant terms"—that is, goods that are expensive. He picks this theme up later in his letter by noting the fruitfulness of the colonies, with their varied climate, rich soil, and a population doubling every twenty years. The result of this fruitfulness and Americans' industry was the ability to produce a surplus of goods that could be traded. If Britain were to open the channels of trade rather than suppressing them, the result would be greater wealth that Americans could use to buy more British products. The alternative, Mason asserts, is "Oppression," a return to the tyranny of the Stamp Act or similar measures, and the potential for "a general Revolt in America."

Mason then cites the historical example of the Low Countries, consisting roughly of modern Belgium and the Netherlands. In the early decades of the sixteenth century, the Low Countries were under the authority of Spain. Like the American colonies with regard to Britain, the Low Countries paid taxes to the Spanish throne, and the Spanish monarch treated the Low Countries in a generally heavy-handed manner. In the mid-sixteenth century, the Low Countries revolted, leading to the Eighty Years' War, which spanned the years 1569 to 1648. And like the American colonies, the Low Countries issued a declaration of independence from Spain, in this case, in 1581. When Mason refers to "the Part that England herself then acted," it is difficult to know exactly to what he refers, but possibly he had in mind the aid that England's queen Elizabeth gave to Dutch rebels.

Mason then returns to the theme of the close connections that have always existed between Britain and the American colonies. He acknowledges "Dependence" on Britain and asserts, "We claim Nothing but the Liberty & Privileges of Englishmen." He goes on to asserts that "our Laws, our Language, our Principles of Government, our Inter-marriages, & other Connections, our constant Intercourse, and above all our Interest, are so many Bands which hold us to Great Britain, not to be broken, but by Tyranny and Oppression." Mason then emphasizes the colonies' loyalty to Britain by affirming the Act of Settlement, a measure Parliament passed in 1701 to settle succession to the British throne on the Protestant Hanoverian line and its heirs; at the same time he rejects "Jacobiteism," a reference to the rebellious movement whose goal was to return the heirs of the Catholic Stuart family to the throne. The name came from Jacobus, the Latin version of James, referring to King James II, who was deposed as king of England in 1688. For decades thereafter, James's supporters launched uprisings to restore the Stuart line.

◆ Fairfax County Resolves

In December 1773, Boston colonists rebelled against the British tax on tea with the Boston Tea Party, throwing tea into the harbor in Boston. The following May, Parliament vowed to close down the harbor on June 1, 1774. Hearing of the impending closure, the Virginia House of Burgesses declared a day of fasting and prayer on June 1. Throughout the summer, Mason and the other members of the House of Burgesses met at the nearby Raleigh Tavern to draft a response to the British Parliament. They called for nonimportation of British goods and nonexportation of American goods and for a Continental Congress.

Mason was charged with drafting the Fairfax Resolves outlining the colonies' rights and grievances against the British government. The list of twenty-four items was presented to the group on July 18, 1774. In the first resolve, or resolution, Mason asserts a familiar theme: that the American colonies were formed under the protection of Great Britain by British subjects, who were therefore subject to all just British laws but at the same time entitled to all the "Privileges, Immunities and Advantages" of British citizens. Later, in the eighth resolve, he takes up a similar theme by acknowledging the American colonists' wish to retain ties with Britain. In the second resolve, he sounds yet another familiar theme: "the fundamental Principle of the People's being governed by no Laws, to which they have not given their Consent." This point of view would in the months before the American Revolution be expressed by the well-known phrase "No taxation without representation." The issue of taxation, which prompted the Boston Tea Party, is the subject of the fifth and sixth resolves, where Mason asserts that excessive taxation is a form of tyranny.

In the twelfth resolve, Mason examines the issue from a broader perspective. He points out that tension between Britain and its colonies would have the effect of embolden-

Time Line

1776
■ **June 8–10**
Mason drafts the Virginia constitution, which is adopted on June 29, 1776.

1787
■ **May 17**
Mason is appointed as the Virginia representative to the Federal Convention, which would meet in Philadelphia in May 1787 to revise the Articles of Confederation.

■ **September 16**
Mason writes "Objections to This Constitution of Government," outlining his reasons for refusing to sign the Constitution; the document is published in the *Virginia Journal* on November 22, 1787.

1788
■ **June 3–27**
Mason represents Stafford County, Virginia, at the state convention to ratify the Constitution. He calls for a second federal convention.

1790
■ **March 25**
Mason is appointed to the U.S. Senate but declines because of poor health.

1791
■ **December 15**
The Bill of Rights, the first ten amendments to the U.S. Constitution, is ratified.

1792
■ **October 7**
Mason dies at his Virginia home, Gunston Hall.

ing Britain's enemies, the chief one of which, though Mason does not mention it, is France. In then calling for a Continental Congress, Mason frames his proposal as one that would provide for the common defense of Britain and the American colonies. He concludes this passage with his hope for a "just, lenient, permanent, and constitutional Form of Government."

After thanking those British citizens who have supported the American colonists, Mason gets to the major proposal of the resolves. In the fifteenth and sixteenth resolves, he calls for American merchants to stop exporting goods to

The masthead for the Pennsylvania Journal and Weekly Advertiser, *showing a skull-and-crossbones representation of the official stamp required by the Stamp Act of 1765, with a statement by the publisher that the paper would not be able to bear the cost of the stamp* (Library of Congress)

Britain and importing British goods. In this regard, in the seventeenth resolve, he also calls for an end to the slave trade and urges Americans not to import slaves transported by Britain. Mason concludes by asserting Virginia's common cause with Boston, saying that any "cruel and oppressive Measure of Government" imposed on Boston would not be adhered to in Virginia. He ends on a conciliatory note, saying that the colonies should "humbly" petition the king of England (George III) for redress of their rights.

◆ Virginia Declaration of Rights

In May 1776, the Virginia Convention formed a committee to draft a declaration of rights. Mason was put in charge of composing the document, which outlined the rights of Virginians. The Virginia Declaration of Rights was formally adopted by the Virginia Convention on June 12, 1776. Drawing on the 1689 English Bill of Rights (which, in tandem with the 1701 Act of Settlement, amounts to Britain's "constitution") and the views of such English Enlightenment social philosophers as John Locke, the Virginia Declaration of Rights was the first of its kind to fully define the rights of citizens and the relationship to their

government and was the first colonial statement of individual rights. In addition, it essentially gave the colonists permission to declare independence from Great Britain.

The first nine articles discuss the principles of a free government, while the remaining seven articles deal with the rights of individual citizens. Mason begins the document by stating that all men are equally free and independent and have basic rights that cannot be denied. His statement that among these rights are "enjoyment of life and liberty, with the means of acquiring and possessing property, and pursuing and obtaining happiness and safety" would find its way, in only slightly altered form, into the Declaration of Independence. Many at the Virginia Convention did not agree with Mason's opening proclamation that all men were created free and independent, because slaves were not free or independent. The group discussed the issue of slavery for four days but eventually retained the clause as Mason wrote it.

Mason's declaration goes on to say that all power lies with the people and that government is established for their "benefit, protection, and security." As such, the people have the right to alter or abolish the government if necessary. Further, Mason's declaration was an important document in the history of American republicanism in asserting that no public office should be "hereditary." He was an early proponent of what in modern life has come to be called "term limits" for public officials, the notion that public office is a form of service and that those who serve should at some point return to private life. Mason also takes up the issue of the rights of accused criminals. In the eighth, ninth, and tenth articles, he asserts rights that would become important features of the Bill of Rights of the U.S. Constitution. Among these are the rights of an accused criminal to a speedy trial by jury, to confront witnesses, to know the charges leveled against him, and to not have to incriminate himself. Further, citizens should not be subject to excessive bail, and searches by the authorities should be carried out only with a warrant.

Because the document was discussed at the Virginia Convention during June 1776, when the nation was at war with Britain, six additional items, such as the right to a uniform government and the issue of standing armies, were included. Mason opposed standing armies as dangerous, although he also asserted the right of Virginians to maintain a militia for their defense. In addition, he calls for freedom of the press, pointing out that such a freedom is "one of the greatest bulwarks of liberty and can never be restrained but by despotic governments." He also calls for freedom of religion, saying that "all men are equally entitled to the free exercise of religion, according to the dictates of conscience"—though ironically, perhaps, he calls for "Christian forbearance" in tolerating one another's religious beliefs.

◆ "Objections to This Constitution of Government"

The Constitutional Convention took place in Philadelphia from May 25 to September 17, 1787. The purpose of the convention was to amend the Articles of Confederation. This document, which can be thought of as a precursor to the Constitution, was the one under which the United States had been operating since independence from Great Britain. The Articles of Confederation, however, proved to be a flawed document. A considerable amount of interstate conflict arose, and it was clear to the nation's leaders that the Articles of Confederation was a weak document, for it granted too much power to the individual states and not enough to the federal government. Many of the delegates to the convention, among them such prominent statesmen as Alexander Hamilton and James Madison, arrived in Philadelphia with the intention not just of amending the articles but of creating an entirely new constitution.

The convention delegates, however, were by no means of one mind. Some members of the convention left in protest before the closing ceremonies because of objections to the proposed Constitution. Three others refused to sign the new document. As the remainder returned to their states to urge ratification, they knew that no one was entirely happy with the document. George Mason was one of Virginia's delegates to the convention. Although he was instrumental in the formation of the U.S. Constitution,

believing that it would affect future generations of Americans, he ultimately was one of the three who refused to sign the document.

As the convention was nearing its end in September 1787, Mason proposed that a group be formed to develop a bill of rights that would preface the Constitution. In this effort he was supported by Elbridge Gerry from Massachusetts, who later served as vice president under James Madison and whose name would survive in the word *gerrymander*, referring to the process of drawing congressional districts in a way that helps the political party in power. The majority of the delegates to the convention, however, felt that the individual states' bills of rights would be sufficient and there was no need to draft another.

After the Constitutional Convention closed and the proposed constitution was returned to the states for ratification, debates about the merits of the new document were widespread in the press. The most famous documents examining the new constitution were the Federalist Papers, written largely by Hamilton and Madison. Taking part in the public debate, too, was Roger Sherman of Connecticut, whose "Letters of a Countryman" urged legislators not to make ratification contingent on the inclusion of a bill of rights. Mason, however, had a different view, and he wrote his reasons for objecting to the proposed Constitution on the back of a report from the convention's Committee of Style. First and foremost, the Constitution did not include a declaration of rights. Mason expresses his belief that without a bill of rights the document did not give enough consideration to the rights of citizens. He also asserts that the judicial branch of government was arranged in a way that left "justice…unattainable, by a great part of the community, as in England, and enabling the rich to oppress and ruin the poor." He feared that the government would have too much power if the Constitution remained as it was.

In addition, Mason expresses fear that the president of the United States would ultimately become a "tool of the Senate," "unsupported by proper information and advice." Moreover, he argues that the president's ability to grant pardons for treason could allow the president to "screen from punishment those whom he had secretly instigated to commit the crime, and thereby prevent a discovery of his own guilt." Likewise, he contends that federal judges should be appointed by Congress rather than the president because the relationship between the president and the judiciary would "enable them to accomplish what usurpations they please upon the rights and liberties of the people."

Mason claims that the office of vice president was unnecessary and only blurred the roles of the executive and legislative branches because the vice president became the president of the Senate. He also expresses fear that the five southern states, in the minority in both the Senate and the House of Representatives, would be ruined if a congressional majority were allowed to make all commercial and navigation legislation. Instead, he argues for a two-thirds majority in both houses. Ultimately, Mason predicts, the new government would become a "monarchy, or a corrupt, tyrannical aristocracy."

"Let our fellow-Subjects in Great Britain reflect that we are descended from the same Stock with themselves, nurtured in the same Principles of Freedom…that We are still the same People with them, in every Respect; only not yet debauched by Wealth, Luxury, Venality, & Corruption; and then they will be able to judge how the late Regulations have been relished in America."

(Letter to the Committee of Merchants in London)

"Resolved that the most important and valuable Part of the British Constitution, upon which its very Existence depends, is the fundamental Principle of the People's being governed by no Laws, to which they have not given their Consent, by Representatives freely chosen by themselves."

(Fairfax County Resolves)

"We take this Opportunity of declaring our most earnest Wishes to see an entire Stop for ever put to such a wicked cruel and unnatural [slave] Trade."

(Fairfax County Resolves)

"All men are by nature equally free and independent, and have certain inherent rights."

(Virginia Declaration of Rights)

"All power is vested in, and consequently derived from, the people."

(Virginia Declaration of Rights)

"There is no declaration of any kind, for preserving the liberty of the press, or the trial by jury in civil causes."

("Objections to This Constitution of Government")

"It is at present impossible to foresee whether [the government] will, in its operation, produce a monarchy, or a corrupt, tyrannical aristocracy."

("Objections to This Constitution of Government")

Impact and Legacy

Perhaps the most lasting legacy of George Mason is the Bill of Rights to the U.S. Constitution, which is based on Mason's Virginia Declaration of Rights. Not long after Virginia passed the document, five other colonies passed similar bills of rights. By the following year, eight additional states had composed similar documents declaring the rights of their citizens. By 1783 all of the states had some sort of bill of rights, and all were modeled extensively on the Virginia Declaration of Rights. Additionally, in drafting the Declaration of Independence, Thomas Jefferson relied heavily on Mason's Declaration of Rights. Indeed, much of the language was in the Declaration of Independence was drawn from Mason's document.

As a delegate to the Constitutional Convention, Mason argued for the inclusion of a bill of rights. Although the idea was defeated at the time, the tenets in Mason's Declaration of Rights were eventually incorporated into the first ten amendments to the Constitution. In 1789 the Virginia Declaration of Rights also became the basis for France's Declaration of the Rights of Man and of the Citizen. In addition, the United Nations modeled its 1948 Declaration of Human Rights on Mason's document.

Key Sources

The Papers of George Mason, 1725–1792 (1970), edited by Robert Allen Rutland in three volumes, is the most com-prehensive collection of Mason's writings. The George Mason Manuscript Collection at the Gunston Hall Plantation Library and Archives contains personal papers and correspondence of George Mason as well as papers written about him; it also maintains a bibliography of resources about Mason. Some of Mason's letters to Thomas Jefferson and George Washington are located in the Thomas Jefferson Papers and the George Washington Papers at the Library of Congress. Kate Mason Rowland's two-volume biography, *The Life of George Mason, 1725–1792* (1892; reprint, 1964), also includes selected speeches, papers, and correspondence.

Further Reading

■ Articles

Bernstein, Mark. "'The Necessity of Refusing My Signature.'" *American History* 41, no. 4 (October 2006): 50–55.

Horrell, Joseph. "George Mason and the Fairfax Court." *Virginia Magazine of History and Biography* 91, no. 4 (October 1983): 418–439.

Schwartz, Stephan A. "George Mason." *Smithsonian* 31, no. 2 (May 2000): 143–154.

Tarter, Brent. "George Mason and the War for Independence." *Virginia Magazine of History and Biography* 99, no. 3 (July 1991): 279–304.

Questions for Further Study

1. In his 1766 letter to the London merchants, Mason is in some ways the quintessential American responding to the perceived condescension of foreigners. Still, he exhibits great respect for England and makes it clear that he speaks as a British subject. Eight years later, however, in the Fairfax County Resolves, the admiration remains, but the loyalty has shifted from Britain to America. Discuss the ways in which Mason expresses these views and how they changed as Mason came to consider himself a citizen of an embryonic American republic rather than a subject of the Crown. What factors accounted for the shift?

2. How is the influence of the Virginia Declaration of Rights evident in the Declaration of Independence? Be sure to consider, among other things, the fact that Thomas Jefferson adapted whole phrases from the earlier document, and—far more important—built upon principles articulated in the Virginia Declaration. To what degree is the Declaration of Independence a direct descendant of the Virginia Declaration and in what regard do the two declarations differ from each other?

3. Given the fact that his work ultimately helped shape one of the greatest declarations of rights in all human history, it is ironic that Mason himself is little known, the "forgotten Father." Why do you think he has not received more attention, and how might Americans benefit by learning about him? How are some of the issues he raises relevant today—or perhaps for as long as the nation shall stand? (For example, consider Mason's discussion of the potential for abuse of power by the executive branch and its central figure, the president, in his objections to the Constitution.)

Wallenstein, Peter. "Flawed Keepers of the Flame: The Interpreters of George Mason." *Virginia Magazine of History and Biography* 102, no. 2 (April 1994): 229–270.

■ **Books**

Broadwater, Jeff. *George Mason, Forgotten Founder*. Chapel Hill: University of North Carolina Press, 2006.

Cohen, Martin B. *Federalism: The Legacy of George Mason*. Fairfax, Va.: George Mason University Press, 1988.

Copeland, Lammot du Pont, and Richard K. MacMaster. *The Five George Masons: Patriots and Planters of Virginia and Maryland*. Charlottesville: University Press of Virginia, 1975.

Davidow, Robert P. *Natural Rights and Natural Law: The Legacy of George Mason*. Fairfax, Va.: George Mason University Press, 1986.

Miller, Helen Hill. *George Mason, Gentleman Revolutionary*. Chapel Hill: University of North Carolina Press, 1975.

Pacheco, Josephine F. *The Legacy of George Mason*. Fairfax, Va.: George Mason University Press, 1983.

Senese, Donald J., and Edward W. Chester. *George Mason and the Legacy of Constitutional Liberty: An Examination of the Influence of George Mason on the American Bill of Rights*. Fairfax, Va.: Fairfax County History Commission, 1989.

Shumate, T. Daniel. *The First Amendment: The Legacy of George Mason*. Fairfax, Va.: George Mason University Press, 1985.

■ **Web Sites**

"George Mason: Life and Times." Gunston Hall Plantation Web site. http://www.gunstonhall.org/georgemason/.

—Michael J. O'Neal and Nicole Mitchell

LETTER TO THE COMMITTEE OF MERCHANTS IN LONDON (1766)

Virginia
Potomack
River June 6th 1766
To the Committee of Merchants in London

GENTLEMEN

There is a Letter of yours dated the 28th of Febry last, lately printed in the public Papers here; which tho' addressed to a particular Set of men, seems intended for the Colonys in general; and being upon a very interesting Subject, I shall, without further Preface or Apology, exercise the Right of a Freeman, in making such Remarks upon it as I think proper.

The Epithets of Parent & Child have been so long applyed to Great Britain & her Colonys, that Individuals have adopted them, and we rarely see anything, from your Side of the Water, free from the authoritative Style of a Master to a School-Boy.

"We have, with infinite Difficulty & Fatigue got you excused this one Time; pray be a good boy for the future; do what your Papa and Mamma bid you, & hasten to return them your most grateful Acknowledgements for condescending to let you keep what is your own; and then all your Acquaintance will love you, & praise you, & give you pretty things; and if you shou'd, at any Time hereafter, happen to transgress, your Friends will all beg for you, and be Security for your good Behaviour; but if you are a naughty Boy, & turn obstinate, & don't mind what your Papa & Mamma say to you, but presume to think their Commands (let them be what they will) unjust or unreasonable, or even seem to ascribe their present Indulgence to any other Motive than Excess of Moderation & Tenderness, and pretend to judge for yourselves, when you are not arrived at the Years of Discretion, or capable of distinguishing between Good & Evil; then every-body will hate you, & say you are a graceless & undutiful Child; your Parents & Masters will be obliged to whip you severely, & your Friends will be ashamed to say any thing in your Excuse: nay they will be blamed for your Faults. See your work—See what you have brought the Child to—If he had been well scourged at first for opposing our absolute Will & Pleasure, & daring to think he had any such thing as Property of his own, he wou'd not have had the Impudence to repeat the Crime."

"My dear Child, we have laid the Alternative fairly before you, you can't hesitate in the Choice, and we doubt not you will observe such a Conduct as your Friends recommend."

Is not this a little ridiculous, when applyed to three Millions of as loyal & useful Subjects as any in the British dominions, who have been only contending for their Birth-right, and have now only gained, or rather kept, what cou'd not, with common Justice, or even Policy, be denied them? But setting aside the Manner, let me seriously consider the Substance & Subject of your Letter....

We do not deny the supreme Authority of Great Britain over her Colonys.... Wou'd to God that this Distinction between us & your fellow Subjects residing in Great Britain, by depriving us of the ancient Tryal, by a Jury of our Equals, and substituting in its place an arbitrary Civil Law Court—to put it in the Power of every Sycophant & Informer.... Are the Inhabitants of Great Britain absolutely certain that, in the Ministry or Parliament of a future Day, such Incroachments will not be urged as Precedents against themselves?

Is the Indulgence of Great Britain manifested by prohibiting her Colonys from exporting to foreign Countrys such Commoditys as she does not want, & from importing such as she does not produce or manufacture & therefore can not furnish but upon extravagant Terms?...

Let our fellow-Subjects in Great Britain reflect that we are descended from the same Stock with themselves, nurtured in the same Principles of Freedom; which we have both suck'd in with our Mother's Milk: that in crossing the Atlantic Ocean, we have only changed our Climate, not our Minds, our Natures & Dispositions remain unaltered; that We are still the same People with them, in every Respect; only not yet debauched by Wealth, Luxury, Venality, & Corruption; and then they will be able to judge how the late Regulations have been relished in America....

If we are ever so unfortunate to be made Slaves; which God avert! what Matter is it to us whether our chains are forged in London, or at Constantinople? Whether the Oppression comes from a British Parliament, or a Turkish Divan?

You tell us that "our Task-Masters will probably be restored." Do You mean the Stamp-Officers, or the Stamp-Ministry? If the first, the Treatment they have already found here will hardly make them fond of returning—If the latter, we despise them too much to fear them.—They have sufficiently exposed their own Ignorance, Malice, & Impotence....

Our Land is cheap and fresh, we have more of it than we are able to employ; while we can live in Ease & Plenty upon our Farms, Tillage, & not Arts, will engage our Attention. If by opening the Channels of Trade, you afford Us a ready Market for the Produce of our Lands, and an Opportunity of purchasing cheap the Conveniencys of Life, all our superfluous Gain will sink into Your Pockets, in Return for British Manufactures. If the Trade of this Continent with the French & Spaniards, in their Sugar-Islands, had not been restrained, Great Britain would soon have undersold them, with their own Produce, in every Market of the World. Until you lay Us under a necessity of shifting for ourselves, You need not be afraid of the Manufactures of America.... There is a Passion natural to the Mind of man, especially a free Man, which renders him impatient of Restraint. Do you, does any sensible Man think that three or four Millions of People, not naturally defective in Genius, or in Courage, who have tasted the Sweets of Liberty in a Country that doubles its Inhabitants every twenty Years, in a Country abounding in such Variety of Soil & Climate, capable of producing not only the Necessarys, but the Conveniencys & Delicacys of Life, will long submit to Oppression; if unhappily for

yourselves, Oppression shou'd be offered them? Such another Experiment as the Stamp-Act wou'd produce a general Revolt in America.

Do you think that all your rival Powers in Europe wou'd sit still, & see you crush your once flourishing & thriving Colonys, unconcerned Spectators of such a Quarrel? Recollect what happened in the Low-Countrys a Century or two ago. Call to Mind the Cause of the Revolt. Call to Mind too the Part that England herself then acted. The same Causes will generally produce the same Effects; and it requires no great Degree of Penetration to foretell that what has happened, may happen again. God forbid there shou'd be Occasion, and grant that the Union, Liberty, and mutual Happiness of Great Britain, & her Colonys may continue, uninterrupted, to the latest Ages!

America has always acknowledged her Dependence upon Great Britain. It is her Interest, it is her Inclination to depend upon Great Britain. We readily own that these Colonys were first setled, not at the Expence, but under the Protection of the English Government....

We claim Nothing but the Liberty & Privileges of Englishmen, in the same Degree, as if we had still continued among our Brethren in Great Britain: these Rights have not been forfeited by any Act of ours, we can not be deprived of them without our Consent, but by Violence & Injustice; We have received them from our Ancestors and, with God's Leave, we will transmit them, unimpaired to our Posterity. Can those, who

Glossary

animadvert	criticize, express disapproval
Chimaera	chimera; in Greek mythology, a fire-breathing monster; a fantasy
Constantinople	at the time, the capital of the Turkish Ottoman Empire, now called Istanbul
Divan	an Islamic governing body, or its chief official
Epithets	words or phrases, often abusive, used to designate persons or objects
Incroachments	encroachments, or intrusions
obdt. Servt	obedient servant, a conventional closing in a letter at the time
Posterity	descendants
Sugar-Islands	islands in the West Indies where sugar was produced
Sycophant	a flatterer
Tryal	trial
Tyes	ties

have hitherto acted as our Friends, endeavour now, insidiously, to draw from Us Concessions destructive to what we hold far dearer than Life!...

Our Laws, our Language, our Principles of Government, our Inter-marriages, & other Connections, our constant Intercourse, and above all our Interest, are so many Bands which hold us to Great Britain, not to be broken, but by Tyranny and Oppression. Strange, that among the late Ministry, there shou'd not be found a Man of common Sense & common Honesty, to improve & strengthen these natural Tyes by a mild & just Government, instead of weakening, & almost dissolving them by Partiality & Injustice!...

These are the Sentiments of a Man, who spends most of his Time in Retirement, and has seldom med[d]led in public Affairs,... who tho' not born within the Verge of the British Isle, is an Englishman in his Principles; a Zealous Assertor of the Act of Settlement,... unalienably affected to his Majesty's sacred Person & Government, in the Defence of which he wou'd shed the last Drop of his Blood; who looks upon Jacobiteism as the most absurd Infatuation, the wildest Chimaera that ever entered into the Head of Man; who adores the Wisdom & Happiness of the British Constitution; and if He had his Election now to make, wou'd prefer it to any that does, or ever did exist. I am not singular in this my Political Creed; these are the general Principles of his Majesty's Subjects in America;...

If any Person shou'd think it worth his while to animadvert upon what I have written, I shall make no Reply. I have neither Abilitys nor Inclination to turn Author. If the Maxims have asserted, & the Reflections I have made, are in themselves just, they will need no Vindication; if they are erronious, I shall esteem it a Favour to have my Errors pointed out; and will, in modest Silence, kiss the Rod that corrects me.

I am, Gentlemen, Your most obdt. Servt.

A Virginia Planter.

Fairfax County Resolves (1774)

At a general Meeting of the Freeholders and Inhabitants of the County of Fairfax on Monday the 18th day of July 1774, at the Court House, George Washington Esquire Chairman, and Robert Harrison Gent. Clerk of the said Meeting—

1. Resolved that this Colony and Dominion of Virginia can not be considered as a conquered Country; and if it was, that the present Inhabitants are the Descendants not of the Conquered, but of the Conquerors.

That the same was not setled at the national Expence of England, but at the private Expence of the Adventurers, our Ancestors, by solemn Compact with, and under the Auspices and Protection of the British Crown; upon which we are in every Respect as dependant, as the People of Great Britain, and in the same Manner subject to all his Majesty's just, legal, and constitutional Prerogatives. That our Ancestors, when they left their native Land, and setled in America, brought with them (even if the same had not been confirmed by Charters) the Civil-Constitution and Form of Government of the Country they came from; and were by the Laws of Nature and Nations, entitled to all its Privileges, Immunities and Advantages; which have descended to us their Posterity, and ought of Right to be as fully enjoyed, as if we had still continued within the Realm of England.

2. Resolved that the most important and valuable Part of the British Constitution, upon which its very Existence depends, is the fundamental Principle of the People's being governed by no Laws, to which they have not given their Consent, by Representatives freely chosen by themselves; who are affected by the Laws they enact equally with their Constituents; to whom they are accountable, and whose Burthens they share; in which consists the Safety and Happiness of the Community: for if this Part of the Constitution was taken away, or materially altered, the Government must degenerate either into an absolute and despotic Monarchy, or a tyrannical Aristocracy, and the Freedom of the People be annihilated....

5. Resolved that the Claim lately assumed and exercised by the British Parliament, of making all such Laws as they think fit, to govern the People of these Colonies, and to extort from us our Money with out our Consent, is not only diametrically contrary to the first Principles of the Constitution, and the original Compacts by which we are dependant upon the British Crown and Government; but is totally incompatible with the Privileges of a free People, and the natural Rights of Mankind; will render our own Legislatures merely nominal and nugatory, and is calculated to reduce us from a State of Freedom and Happiness to Slavery and Misery.

6. Resolved that Taxation and Representation are in their Nature inseperable; that the Right of withholding, or of giving and granting their own Money is the only effectual Security to a free People, against the Incroachments of Despotism and Tyranny; and that whenever they yield the One, they must quickly fall a Prey to the other....

8. Resolved that it is our greatest Wish and Inclination, as well as Interest, to continue our Connection with, and Dependance upon the British Government; but tho' we are its Subjects, we will use every Means which Heaven hath given us to prevent our becoming its Slaves....

12. Resolved that Nothing will so much contribute to defeat the pernicious Designs of the common Enemies of Great Britain and her Colonies as a firm Union of the latter; who ought to regard every Act of Violence or Oppression inflicted upon any one of them, as aimed at all; and to effect this desireable Purpose, that a Congress shou'd be appointed, to consist of Deputies from all the Colonies, to concert a general and uniform Plan for the Defence and Preservation of our common Rights, and continueing the Connection and Dependance of the said Colonies upon Great Britain under a just,

lenient, permanent, and constitutional Form of Government.

13. Resolved that our most sincere and cordial Thanks be given to the Patrons and Friends of Liberty in Great Britain, for their spirited and patriotick Conduct in Support of our constitutional Rights and Privileges, and their generous Efforts to prevent the present Distress and Calamity of America....

15. Resolved that until American Grievances be redressed, by Restoration of our just Rights and Privileges, no Goods or Merchandize whatsoever ought to be imported into this Colony....

16. Resolved that it is the Opinion of this Meeting, that the Merchants and Venders of Goods and Merchandize within this Colony shou'd take an Oath, not to sell or dispose of any Goods or Merchandize whatsoever....

17. Resolved that it is the Opinion of this Meeting, that during our present Difficulties and Distress, no Slaves ought to be imported into any of the British Colonies on this Continent; and we take this Opportunity of declaring our most earnest Wishes to see an entire Stop for ever put to such a wicked cruel and unnatural Trade....

19. Resolved that it is the Opinion of this Meeting, if American Grievances be not redressed before the first Day of November one thousand seven hundred and seventy five, that all Exports of Produce from the several Colonies to Great Britain {or Ireland} shou'd cease....

22. Resolved that shou'd the Town of Boston be forced to submit to the late cruel and oppressive Measures of Government, that we shall not hold the same to be binding upon us, but will, notwithstanding, religiously maintain, and inviolably adhere to such Measures as shall be concerted by the general Congress, for the preservation of our Lives Liberties and Fortunes.

23. Resolved that it be recommended to the Deputies of the general Congress to draw up and transmit an humble and dutiful Petition and Remonstrance to his Majesty, asserting with decent Firmness our just and constitutional Rights and Privileg[es,] lamenting the fatal Necessity of being compelled to enter into Measur[es] disgusting to his Majesty and his Parliament, or injurious to our fellow Subjects in Great Britain; declaring, in the strongest Terms, ou[r] Duty and Affection to his Majesty's Person, Family [an]d Government, and our Desire to continue our Dependance upon Great Bri[tai]n; and most humbly conjuring and besecching his Majesty, not to reduce his faithful Subjects of America to a State of desperation, and to reflect, that from our Sovereign there can be but one Appeal. And it is the Opinion of this Meeting, that after such Petition and Remonstrance shall have been presented to his Majesty, the same shou'd be printed in the public Papers, in all the principal Towns in Great Britain.

Glossary

Burthens	antique spelling of "burdens"
freeholders	property owners
Incroachments	encroachments, or intrusions
pernicious	tending toward evil
Posterity	descendants
Prerogatives	privileges

Virginia Declaration of Rights (1776)

A DECLARATION OF RIGHTS made by the Representatives of the good people of VIRGINIA, assembled in full and free Convention; which rights do pertain to them and their posterity, as the basis and foundation of Government.

Article 1

That all men are by nature equally free and independent, and have certain inherent rights, of which, when they enter into a state of society, they cannot, by any compact, deprive or divest their posterity; namely, the enjoyment of life and liberty, with the means of acquiring and possessing property, and pursuing and obtaining happiness and safety.

Article 2

That all power is vested in, and consequently derived from, the people; that magistrates are their trustees and servants, and at all times amenable to them.

Article 3

That government is, or ought to be, instituted for the common benefit, protection, and security of the people, nation or community; of all the various modes and forms of government that is best, which is capable of producing the greatest degree of happiness and safety and is most effectually secured against the danger of maladministration; and that, whenever any government shall be found inadequate or contrary to these purposes, a majority of the community hath an indubitable, unalienable, and indefeasible right to reform, alter or abolish it, in such manner as shall be judged most conducive to the public weal.

Article 4

That no man, or set of men, are entitled to exclusive or separate emoluments or privileges from the community, but in consideration of public services; which, not being descendible, neither ought the offices of magistrate, legislator, or judge be hereditary.

Article 5

That the legislative and executive powers of the state should be separate and distinct from the judicative; and, that the members of the two first may be restrained from oppression by feeling and participating the burthens of the people, they should, at fixed periods, be reduced to a private station, return into that body from which they were originally taken, and the vacancies be supplied by frequent, certain, and regular elections in which all, or any part of the former members, to be again eligible, or ineligible, as the laws shall direct.

Article 6

That elections of members to serve as representatives of the people in assembly ought to be free; and that all men, having sufficient evidence of permanent common interest with, and attachment to, the community have the right of suffrage and cannot be taxed or deprived of their property for public uses without their own consent or that of their representatives so elected, nor bound by any law to which they have not, in like manner, assented, for the public good.

Article 7

That all power of suspending laws, or the execution of laws, by any authority without consent of the representatives of the people is injurious to their rights and ought not to be exercised.

Article 8

That in all capital or criminal prosecutions a man hath a right to demand the cause and nature of his accusation to be confronted with the accusers and witnesses, to call for evidence in his favor, and to a speedy trial by an impartial jury of his vicinage, without whose unanimous consent he cannot be found guilty, nor can he be compelled to give evidence against himself; that no man be deprived of his liberty except by the law of the land or the judgement of his peers.

Article 9

That excessive bail ought not to be required, nor excessive fines imposed; nor cruel and unusual punishments inflicted.

Article 10

That general warrants, whereby any officer or messenger may be commanded to search suspected places without evidence of a fact committed, or to seize any person or persons not named, or whose offense is not particularly described and supported by evidence, are grievous and oppressive and ought not to be granted.

Article 11

That in controversies respecting property and in suits between man and man, the ancient trial by jury is preferable to any other and ought to be held sacred.

Article 12

That the freedom of the press is one of the greatest bulwarks of liberty and can never be restrained but by despotic governments.

Article 13

That a well regulated militia, composed of the body of the people, trained to arms, is the proper, natural, and safe defense of a free state; that standing armies, in time of peace, should be avoided as dangerous to liberty; and that, in all cases, the military should be under strict subordination to, and be governed by, the civil power.

Article 14

That the people have a right to uniform government; and therefore, that no government separate from, or independent of, the government of Virginia, ought to be erected or established within the limits thereof.

Article 15

That no free government, or the blessings of liberty, can be preserved to any people but by a firm adherence to justice, moderation, temperance, frugality, and virtue and by frequent recurrence to fundamental principles.

Article 16

That religion, or the duty which we owe to our Creator and the manner of discharging it, can be directed by reason and conviction, not by force or violence; and therefore, all men are equally entitled to the free exercise of religion, according to the dictates of conscience; and that it is the mutual duty of all to practice Christian forbearance, love, and charity towards each other.

Adopted unanimously June 12, 1776
Virginia Convention of Delegates

Glossary

burthens	antique spelling of "burdens"
emoluments	salaries and other benefits of employment
indefeasible	incapable of being undone or defeated
indubitable	undoubted
vicinage	vicinity, locality

"OBJECTIONS TO THIS CONSTITUTION OF GOVERNMENT" (1787)

There is no Declaration of Rights, and the laws of the general government being paramount to the laws and constitution of the several States, the Declarations of Rights in the separate States are no security. Nor are the people secured even in the enjoyment of the benefit of the common law.

In the House of Representatives there is not the substance but the shadow only of representation; which can never produce proper information in the legislature, or inspire confidence in the people; the laws will therefore be generally made by men little concerned in, and unacquainted with their effects and consequences.

The Senate have the power of altering all money bills, and of originating appropriations of money, and the salaries of the officers of their own appointment, in conjunction with the president of the United States, although they are not the representatives of the people or amenable to them.

These with their other great powers, viz.: their power in the appointment of ambassadors and all public officers, in making treaties, and in trying all impeachments, their influence upon and connection with the supreme Executive from these causes, their duration of office and their being a constantly existing body, almost continually sitting, joined with their being one complete branch of the legislature, will destroy any balance in the government, and enable them to accomplish what usurpations they please upon the rights and liberties of the people.

The Judiciary of the United States is so constructed and extended, as to absorb and destroy the judiciaries of the several States; thereby rendering law as tedious, intricate and expensive, and justice as unattainable, by a great part of the community, as in England, and enabling the rich to oppress and ruin the poor.

The President of the United States has no Constitutional Council, a thing unknown in any safe and regular government. He will therefore be unsupported by proper information and advice, and will generally be directed by minions and favorites; or he will become a tool to the Senate—or a Council of State will grow out of the principal officers of the great departments; the worst and most dangerous of all ingredients for such a Council in a free country; From this fatal defect has arisen the improper power of the Senate in the appointment of public officers, and the alarming dependence and connection between that branch of the legislature and the supreme Executive.

Hence also sprung that unnecessary officer the Vice-President, who for want of other employment is made president of the Senate, thereby dangerously blending the executive and legislative powers, besides always giving to some one of the States an unnecessary and unjust pre-eminence over the others.

The President of the United States has the unrestrained power of granting pardons for treason, which may be sometimes exercised to screen from punishment those whom he had secretly instigated to commit the crime, and thereby prevent a discovery of his own guilt.

By declaring all treaties supreme laws of the land, the Executive and the Senate have, in many cases, an exclusive power of legislation; which might have been avoided by proper distinctions with respect to treaties, and requiring the assent of the House of Representatives, where it could be done with safety.

By requiring only a majority to make all commercial and navigation laws, the five Southern States, whose produce and circumstances are totally different from that of the eight Northern and Eastern States, may be ruined, for such rigid and premature regulations may be made as will enable the merchants of the Northern and Eastern States not only to demand an exorbitant freight, but to monopolize the purchase of the commodities at their own price, for many years, to the great injury of the landed interest, and impoverishment of the people; and the danger is the greater as the gain on one side will be in proportion to the loss on the other. Whereas requiring two-thirds of the members present in both Houses would have produced mutual moderation, promoted the general interest, and removed an insuperable objection to the adoption of this government.

Under their own construction of the general clause, at the end of the enumerated powers, the Congress may grant monopolies in trade and commerce, constitute new crimes, inflict unusual and severe punishments, and extend their powers as far as they shall think proper; so that the State legislatures have no security for the powers now presumed to remain to them, or the people for their rights.

There is no declaration of any kind, for preserving the liberty of the press, or the trial by jury in civil causes; nor against the danger of standing armies in time of peace.

The State legislatures are restrained from laying export duties on their own produce.

Both the general legislature and the State legislature are expressly prohibited making ex post facto laws; though there never was nor can be a legislature but must and will make such laws, when necessity and the public safety require them; which will hereafter be a breach of all the constitutions in the Union, and afford precedents for other innovations.

This government will set out a moderate aristocracy: it is at present impossible to foresee whether it will, in its operation, produce a monarchy, or a corrupt, tyrannical aristocracy; it will most probably vibrate some years between the two, and then terminate in the one or the other.

The general legislature is restrained from prohibiting the further importation of slaves for twenty odd years; though such importations render the United States weaker, more vulnerable, and less capable of defence.

Glossary

viz.	abbreviation of the Latin *videlicet*, meaning "such as" or "that is to say"

Joseph McCarthy (AP/Wide World Photos)

JOSEPH MCCARTHY 1908–1957

U.S. Senator

Featured Documents
- "Enemies from Within" Speech (1950)
- Telegram to President Harry S. Truman (1950)
- Letter to President Dwight Eisenhower (1953)

Overview

Joseph Raymond McCarthy was born on November 14, 1908, in Grand Chute, Wisconsin, and died on May 2, 1957, in Bethesda, Maryland. The product of a rural midwestern background, McCarthy was an ambitious young man who studied law and became a circuit judge in 1940. He served in the Marines during World War II and fabricated his heroism as "Tailgunner Joe." He was first elected to the U.S. Senate in 1946, but his fame resulted from his adoption of the anti-Communist cause in early 1950. A bold and uncompromising partisan, he fiercely attacked the administrations of both President Harry S. Truman and President Dwight D. Eisenhower for harboring Communists and Communist sympathizers within the federal government. He easily won reelection in 1952 on an anti-Communist platform and became a national figure notorious for hectoring witnesses at the Senate hearings he chaired and implying that they were hiding their own Communist leanings or protecting other members of the Communist Party.

McCarthy's technique was to get witnesses condemned in the court of public opinion by showing—or implying—that they associated with suspected or known Communists and Communist sympathizers. So deep was McCarthy's impact on the country that his strategy for fighting Communism became known as *McCarthyism*, a shorthand way of describing anyone who leveled strident and, some would say, rash charges of un-Americanism (disloyalty) against an individual. McCarthyism has become a political tactic in which an opponent's reputation is smeared with guilt by association.

Outside the Senate chambers, McCarthy used speeches to attack not only Communists and Communist sympathizers (or *fellow travelers*) but also his own political opponents—Democrats and, later, anyone in the Republican administration of President Eisenhower who criticized McCarthy. Until 1954 many Republican politicians considered McCarthy an asset and invited him to speak in support of their campaigns. McCarthy often alluded to evidence about specific individuals without actually naming them. His speeches and writings were full of innuendo and foreboding. Indeed, nearly all of his public speaking after the election of 1952 presented a view of an America besieged—internationally by the Soviet Union and internally by a Communist Party and its sympathizers that had penetrated the highest levels of the federal government in Washington. McCarthy spoke as if his own country were in imminent danger. If the president and nation did not act quickly, the battle against Communism would be lost. His sense of urgency made it seem as if each day the United States was falling further behind the Soviet Union and other Communist powers that were determined to rule the world and to destroy American-style democracy.

Even McCarthy's staunchest supporters had to admit that his attacks on such outstanding American officials as George C. Marshall (founder of the Marshall Plan that helped to restore Western Europe to prosperity after World War II) were disgraceful and preposterous. McCarthy's downfall came about when he challenged the U.S. Army itself and was taken to task by its attorney Joseph Welch on nationwide television. Welch's reprimand was combined with increasingly adverse treatment of McCarthy in the media, most significantly by Edward R. Murrow on CBS television, which eventually led to his censure by the U.S. Senate. As a man of great excesses, McCarthy was never able to curb his alcoholism, and he died from alcohol-related causes.

Explanation and Analysis of Documents

McCarthy's anti-Communist speeches and writings occurred in an American postwar world shocked that the Soviet Union was able to explode its own atomic bomb so soon after the United States developed an advanced technology deemed far greater than anything its rivals could produce. The prosecution of spies such as Klaus Fuchs and Julius and Ethel Rosenberg confirmed public suspicion that the Soviet Union had stolen the knowledge necessary to create its nuclear weapons. McCarthy began to speak out about government officeholders who had colluded with Communist agents to steal U.S. government secrets and skew American foreign policy when the United States became involved in the Korean War.

Although other politicians had leveled similar charges, none of them claimed to have the kind of specific information about Communist subversion that McCarthy said he had obtained. Far more ruthless and outspoken than any of his contemporaries, McCarthy attacked the highest officials in the Truman and Eisenhower administrations and insinuated that they had tolerated a climate of disloyalty. McCarthy also went far beyond other Republicans in criti-

Time Line

1908
- **November 14**
  McCarthy is born in Grand Chute, Wisconsin.

1939
- McCarthy is elected to public office as a circuit judge.

1942
- **June 4**
  McCarthy enlists in the U.S. Marines but never sees combat.

1945
- McCarthy is reelected as circuit court judge.

1946
- McCarthy is elected to the U.S. Senate.

1950
- **February 9**
  McCarthy delivers his famous anti-Communism speech in Wheeling, West Virginia.
- **February 11**
  McCarthy sends a telegram to President Harry S. Truman reiterating key points made in the Wheeling speech.
- **July 17**
  The Tydings Committee (named for Democratic Senator Millard Tydings of Maryland) in the U.S. Senate, which had opened hearings in early March to investigate McCarthy's charges, concludes by denouncing McCarthy's methods.

1951
- **June 14**
  McCarthy attacks George C. Marshall as an instrument of a Communist conspiracy.

1953
- **February 3**
  McCarthy sends a letter to President Dwight D. Eisenhower questioning the loyalty of one of Eisenhower's nominees for a federal position.

cizing his own party and president. He spoke as a force unto himself, disregarding the niceties of party loyalty and Senate decorum. He used his public speeches to endow himself with an aura of authority and menace that he used to intimidate the executive branch as well as his Senate colleagues and witnesses at his hearings.

◆ **"Enemies from Within" Speech**

Senator McCarthy made his famous anti-Communist speech on February 9, 1950, at a celebration of the anniversary of Abraham Lincoln's birth. His first paragraph marks the occasion by expressing a wish that this could be a peaceful, disarmed world of the kind Lincoln had desired. McCarthy is implying that conditions are not what could be hoped for.

The second short paragraph baldly describes a "cold war" world and an arms race—not what Americans expected to experience five years after victory in World War II. The third paragraph quickly picks up momentum by alluding not only to the division of Europe into the Soviet-dominated East and the pro-American West but also to tensions over Communist China and Formosa (Taiwan), the island on which Chiang Kai-shek established a government after the Communists defeated him. Moreover, Indochina, once dominated by the French, is now the target of Communist infiltration.

It is not too late, however, to establish peace, McCarthy suggests, if the United States deals openly with a new kind of war—a war between the two ideologies represented by the United States and the Soviet Union. McCarthy implies that the reality of this struggle has not been named for what it actually is: a moral battle between a Christian culture and an atheistic Communist state. In other words, the new struggle is not merely between different political systems but is really a battle over the very way the world should be organized, with the Communist imposition of government ownership of resources and the one-party state representing, in McCarthy's words, a "momentous" turn in history.

Joseph Stalin built on Vladimir Lenin's legacy, McCarthy notes in paragraph 6, but Communist ideology in itself is not the problem. Coexistence of different ideologies would be possible if Lenin and Stalin had not been intent on spreading their "religion of immoralism" to half the world already. If Communism should triumph—and McCarthy fears that it might—it would "wound and damage mankind" more deeply than any other political system. Noting the continuity of ideas from Karl Marx to Lenin to Stalin, McCarthy concludes that Communists do not believe they can prevail without destroying Christian civilization.

McCarthy's two-sentence statement in paragraph 10 combines a biblical, apocalyptic, prophetic tone with a down-to-earth American way of describing a crisis, a defining moment in history: "Today we are engaged in a final, all-out battle between communistic atheism and Christianity. The modern champions of communism have selected this as the time, and ladies and gentlemen, the chips are down—they are truly down." The metaphor of a poker game, in which there is a showdown, so to speak, a revealing of the cards that have been dealt and the determination of a winner, accentuates the urgency of McCarthy's message. In six years, McCarthy reports, Communism has spread while "our side" has shrunk, changing the odds from 9 to 1 in our favor to "8 to 5 against us." What is worse, our side has collaborated in its own defeat: "As one of our outstanding historical figures once said, 'When a great democracy is destroyed, it will not be from enemies from without, but rather because of enemies from within.'"

McCarthy then sounds a theme that would be repeated often in his hearings and by other anti-Communists supporting him: America has been betrayed by its best-educated and most privileged citizens. McCarthy's audience would have in mind Alger Hiss, an Ivy League–educated State Department official who had been convicted of perjury in a trial relating to conspiracy to spy against the U.S. government for the Soviet Union. In a copy of the speech delivered to the press before he spoke, McCarthy claimed to have a list of 205 State Department employees known to be Communist Party members. Some days later he reduced his claim to a list of fifty-seven names. The number is not important except insofar as McCarthy was claiming he had evidence (never released to the public) that the secretary of state, Dean Acheson, had done nothing to rectify the problem. In effect, McCarthy was accusing the secretary of state of colluding with Communists by allowing them to remain in positions that could shape U.S. foreign policy according to the dictates of the Soviet Union. Indeed, McCarthy directly links Acheson to Communists by noting that Acheson has "proclaimed his loyalty to a man [Alger Hiss] guilty of what has always been considered as the most abominable of all crimes—being a traitor to the people who gave him a position of great trust—high treason."

McCarthy's concluding paragraph casts his anti-Communist program in broader terms. He calls not only for expelling Communists from government positions but also, in a larger sense, working for "a new birth of honesty and decency in government." This ending fits well with his notion that the anti-Communist movement is a moral crusade, a heroic calling to save America from its disloyal and highly privileged upper class. Joe McCarthy, "Tailgunner Joe," is making himself the spokesman for the democratic majority whose values have been subverted by a traitorous elite.

◆ **Telegram to President Harry S. Truman**

McCarthy followed up his speech in Wheeling with a telegram to President Truman reiterating his charges that a "nest of Communists and Communist sympathizers" was shaping American foreign policy. Although a State Department official had denied McCarthy's allegations, McCarthy reminds Truman of Truman's own loyalty program aimed precisely at "weeding out fellow travelers." Making it difficult for the president to deflect the thrust of the Wheeling speech, McCarthy compliments the Truman program's identification of hundreds who were security risks. McCarthy understood that Truman, a Democrat, would be especially concerned about the charges of a Republican senator intent on amplifying the anti-Communist cause and

Time Line

1954

■ **April 22**
Thirty-six days of hearings on Communist infiltration of the U.S. Army begin.

■ **March 9**
Edward R. Murrow's broadcast questioning the integrity of McCarthy's investigation of alleged Communists airs.

■ **December 2**
U.S. Senate censures McCarthy.

1957

■ **May 2**
McCarthy dies in Bethesda, Maryland.

questioning the executive branch's will to rid itself of subversive employees. What makes McCarthy's indictment of the federal government especially disturbing is the apparent specificity of his evidence—the fifty-seven names, now part of an effort to suggest the U.S. State Department has not carried through on the purge of the disloyal that Truman's own loyalty program had been devised to accomplish.

McCarthy's second paragraph strikes directly at Dean Acheson, noting that of three hundred "certified to the Secretary for discharge because of Communism," only eighty had been fired. McCarthy's language at this point, however, is vague. What does "because of Communism" mean? Were those certified to be discharged Communists, fellow travelers, or linked in some other way to Communists and Communist causes? The sweeping nature of McCarthy's words makes it impossible to understand the actual nature of the threat he believes Communism poses while at the same time making the threat seem widespread—indeed so pervasive that Acheson, McCarthy implies, has deliberately debilitated Truman's own loyalty program. Even worse, McCarthy alleges that Acheson had vetted the list of three hundred with Alger Hiss's help, which, if true, would mean that a former State Department official convicted of perjury related to charges of conspiracy to commit espionage had been consulted on others like himself who were disloyal to the American government. So McCarthy proposes that Truman call his secretary of state and ask him about the Communists he failed to discharge.

The last sentence in paragraph 2 is an implied attack on Truman's order forbidding the State Department to release information to Congress about employees with "communistic connections," because in paragraph 3 McCarthy notes he has been able to obtain information in spite of this order. While McCarthy's number is "57" he suggests that Secretary of State Acheson can provide the president with a longer list. In effect, McCarthy is accusing the president of hampering investigations into Communists in govern-

H. A. Smith and Representative J. Parnell Thomas stand with hands upraised on October 20, 1947, as Smith, committee investigator, is sworn in as the first witness at a House Un-American Activities Committee hearing in Washington, D.C. (AP/Wide World Photos)

ment, or rather he is saying that President Truman will be responsible for delaying investigations if he does not immediately consult with Secretary Acheson and direct him to provide fuller lists of subversives. That McCarthy was putting the president on notice and claiming leadership of the anti-Communist cause is clear from his list of demands, which include a demand for a detailed accounting to Congress of the State Department employees that Alger Hiss had placed and a demand that Truman's order to government departments directing them not to disclose information to congressional committees be revoked.

The political nature of McCarthy's attack is apparent in the last paragraph of his telegram: "Failure on your part will label the Democratic Party of being the bedfellow of international communism." Attempting to turn Truman against his secretary of state as well as to ratify his charges, McCarthy implies there will be a tremendous political price to pay if Truman does not meet his demands. Moreover, Truman will be putting in jeopardy the many Demo-

crats who are, in McCarthy's words, loyal and hardly deserving of being connected to those who protect Communists and fellow travelers.

No matter what course Truman might take, McCarthy's telegram cunningly enhances McCarthy's own position. If Truman were to agree to McCarthy's demands, he would be conceding the point about Communist infiltration. If he were to reject McCarthy's demands, the president could be accused of ignoring or—worse—obstructing investigations of the Communist threat to American institutions and indeed to the country itself.

◆ **Letter to President Dwight D. Eisenhower**
With the election of the Republican Party presidential candidate, Dwight Eisenhower, many assumed that Senator McCarthy would tone down, if not cease, his attacks on Communist subversion of the federal government. After all, an even more important anti-Communist figure, Richard Nixon, who had been instrumental in compiling the evi-

dence against Alger Hiss, had been elected as Eisenhower's vice president. But McCarthy hardly diminished his assault on the security lapses of the federal government, even though Vice President Nixon was able to persuade McCarthy not to make a public show of his opposition to James Conant, president of Harvard University and Eisenhower's nominee for High Commissioner in West Germany. Robert Taft, the reigning Republican conservative in the Senate, also succeeded in cajoling McCarthy not to deliver a speech against Conant. But McCarthy could not resist challenging the nomination in a letter to the new president.

McCarthy begins politely enough by telling Eisenhower that as a courtesy McCarthy is writing to explain his position on Conant, whose nomination the Senate would consider shortly. Beginning with the first of four principal objections, McCarthy notes the Conant speech on October 7, 1944, supporting the Morgenthau Plan, which advocated reducing West Germany to an agricultural state. Although the plan was not implemented, in retrospect, at least, it could be seen as a maneuver that would benefit the Soviet Union, since the latter controlled and could industrialize and militarize East Germany. Under the Morgenthau Plan, in other words, the part of Germany controlled by the United States and its allies would not have the capacity to resist an aggressive Soviet-backed East Germany. Even worse, Harry Dexter White, a Treasury Department official accused of espionage by Whittaker Chambers, Elizabeth Bentley, and other former Communists in hearings McCarthy had conducted in the Senate, had been largely responsible for the Morgenthau Plan. This is why McCarthy writes to Eisenhower that the plan "played directly into the hands of our enemy." McCarthy reminds Eisenhower of his own characterization of the plan as "silly and tragic." Although McCarthy notes that he is not positing a direct connection between Conant and White, Conant was an unwitting collaborator, nevertheless, in efforts to undermine Western strength.

Then McCarthy takes issue with Conant's *Atlantic Monthly* article advocating a redistribution of wealth, power, and privilege after each generation. If Conant did not advocate a violent Communist-led expropriation of private wealth and corporations, nonetheless his beliefs would lead to the "complete socialization of any country." McCarthy does not elaborate on the term *socialization*, but he clearly intends the term as the opposite of a free, capitalist economy and political structure. In effect, he is arguing that Conant stands for ideas that are inimical to American interests and, specifically, to the way America has prospered.

McCarthy's third concern is that Conant's opposition to parochial schools will cause problems for a high commissioner of Germany. Because most Germans are Catholics or Lutherans and believe strongly in education in their faith, Conant's views could only cause "ill feeling toward America and furnish ammunition for the Communist propaganda guns." McCarthy is obviously alluding to the U.S. interest in bolstering West Germany as a strong ally opposed not only to East Germany but also to the Soviet-led political movements that were very active in Italy, France, Greece, and other countries. In this global per-

Senator Joseph McCarthy consults two of his aides, Roy Cohn (left) and Don Surine (right), during the afternoon session of the Army-McCarthy hearing in Washington, D.C., on April 26, 1954. (AP/Wide World Photos)

spective, in the cold war in which the two sides were seeking to bring converts and countries to their side, public opinion in Germany had to remain favorable to the United States. So appointing Conant simply made it more difficult to foster the West German–U.S. alliance.

McCarthy's fourth concern strikes at the very heart of his own political program. Conant, it seems, does not have the proper attitude toward rooting out Communists in higher education. It troubles McCarthy that even though Conant approved of expelling Communists from institutions of higher learning, Conant cautioned that should an investigation discover only a few Communists, then the damage caused by removing them would be greater than the benefit of retaining them. McCarthy disputes Conant's judgment, especially his claim that there were no Communists at Harvard. Prominent professors like Harlow Shapley and F. O. Matthiessen (who had committed suicide in 1951), known for their leftist politics, leads a skeptical McCarthy to suppose that at the very least more investigation is needed, since these professors had been "doing the work of the Communist Party." The prominent intellectuals had worked in behalf of Communist causes, and in McCarthy's view, anyone aligned with such causes is, by definition, a security threat, someone giving aid and comfort to the enemy. This, in fact, is for McCarthy the very meaning of the cold war: One has to choose sides and be careful not to abet Communist propaganda. Conant moreover seemed blind to this understanding of the Communist menace. McCarthy allows his customary sarcasm to show only once by suggesting that everyone except Conant understood that men like Shapley and Matthiessen were pro-Communist.

If Conant himself is not Communist or pro-Communist—and McCarthy sees no reason to make that charge—he is something just as disturbing, an "innocent" apparently unaware of the brutality of the Communist conspiracy against democratic institutions. How could such a man deal with Communist influence in West Germany? In other words, it is Conant's ignorance and blindness as much as his actual views that disturb McCarthy. To McCarthy, Conant's stance is a good example of the naive fellow-traveling views of academics, government officials, and other intellectuals who do not see that their tolerant views have real-world consequences that would injure the interests of the United States. How could men such as Conant defend America if they do not see the threat Communism poses?

McCarthy does not dispute Conant's integrity, intelligence, or honesty. But he does quote Conant's words against him: Conant's view was that a professor who believed in the betterment of civilization might very well prove a poor choice to represent a government that had to negotiate with another nation. The implications of McCarthy's words are clear: Conant is such a professor—that is, a man devoted to peace and world comity who does not understand the hard truths of national rivalries and, specifically, of the cold war. Conant was just fine as president of Harvard, in other words, but not suitable as a high commissioner of Germany. Yet because McCarthy did not believe he could successfully oppose Conant's nomination, and because he saw that many senators wanted to defer to the new president, he had decided not to put up an "all-out fight" against approval of Conant's nomination. In alluding to Eisenhower's recent and sizable election victory, McCarthy is also clearly unwilling to challenge the new president's popularity.

Essential Quotes

> "Today we are engaged in a final, all-out battle between communistic atheism and Christianity. The modern champions of communism have selected this as the time, and ladies and gentlemen, the chips are down—they are truly down."
>
> ("Enemies from Within" Speech)

> "As one of our outstanding historical figures once said, 'When a great democracy is destroyed, it will not be from enemies from without, but rather because of enemies from within.'"
>
> ("Enemies from Within" Speech)

> "Despite this State Department black-out, we have been able to compile a list of 57 Communists in the State Department. This list is available to you but you can get a much longer list by ordering Secretary Acheson to give you a list of those whom your own board listed as being disloyal and who are still working in the State Department."
>
> (Telegram to President Harry S. Truman)

> "Let me make it clear that I do not accuse Mr. Conant of being either Communist or pro-Communist. However, I strongly feel that his innocent statements about Communist activities in education and about the presence of communism in his own faculty indicate a woeful lack of knowledge of the vicious and intricate Communist conspiracy."
>
> (Letter to President Dwight Eisenhower)

In his final paragraph McCarthy implies that making public his letter to Eisenhower and carrying on the fight against Conant will only damage the anti-Communist cause. He wishes to do nothing that might aid Communist propaganda. Consequently, he is choosing the lesser of two evils, voting against Conant but also refraining from making public statements about the matter.

One of McCarthy's biographers, Thomas C. Reeves, suggests that McCarthy's letter also served as a warning to the new president—in effect, reserving the right to object to other nominees if Eisenhower exercised poor judgment. This interpretation of McCarthy's letter seems sound, in view of McCarthy's subsequent attack on government institutions—notably the U.S. Army. Even though Eisenhower himself had been leader of the Allied Forces in World War II and had enormous prestige, McCarthy continued his anti-Communist campaign very much along the lines expressed in his private letter to the president.

Impact and Legacy

For many Joseph McCarthy remains America's most hated senator. Even fervent anti-Communists deplored his rough treatment of suspected Communists and fellow travelers. He was too quick to impugn reputations and destroy careers. He fomented an atmosphere of paranoia and vindictiveness. He abused his privileged position as a U.S. senator to bully witnesses at his hearings. The Senate resolution censuring him specified that he had abused his colleagues and the constitutional process. He had dishonored the Senate by questioning the motives of his fellow senators and had violated Senate ethics.

Still, McCarthy has had his defenders, especially conservatives like William F. Buckley, Jr., founder of the *National Review*. In *The Redhunter: A Novel Based on the Life of Senator Joe McCarthy* (1999), Buckley presents a hero—flawed, to be sure, but nevertheless a man motivated by conviction, not opportunism. Similarly, Arthur Herman believes that McCarthy understood the massive threat Communist subversion posed for a free society easily infiltrated by covert agents and their enablers. A good deal of what became known as McCarthyism was unfairly attributed to McCarthy, Herman argues, emphasizing that the senator had nothing to do with blacklisting Communists or with the tactics of the House Committee on Un-American Activities.

Key Sources

For McCarthy's Senate speeches and debates, see the *Congressional Record*, vols. 93–102, covering the years 1947–1956. The State Historical Society of Wisconsin holds a number of papers relating to McCarthy's career (including his scrapbooks) and to his relationships and background in Wisconsin as well as the files of his biographers Richard Rovere and Thomas C. Reeves. Material on McCarthy can also be found in the presidential libraries of Harry S. Truman, Dwight D. Eisenhower, and Lyndon Baines Johnson. McCarthy wrote *McCarthyism, the Fight*

Questions for Further Study

1. McCarthy's name has become a virtual watchword for political behaviors completely at odds with the American traditions of fairness and the rule of law, and his writings and speeches provide ample illustrations of the bullying and intimidation that made him infamous. Examine his "enemies from within" speech and his communications with presidents Harry Truman and Dwight Eisenhower with an eye for the tactics he uses, including false claims, logical fallacies, unfounded accusations, and veiled threats. Give specific examples.

2. Compare McCarthy's actions with those of Andrei Zhdanov, a man who might be regarded as a Soviet counterpart. Zhdanov presided over one of Joseph Stalin's last major purges, this one primarily among artists and intellectuals, who came under suspicion for not being loyal enough to the dictator or the Communist system. What are the similarities between McCarthy and Zhdanov, and what are some important differences? What do the two men's careers say about their respective nations' political systems?

3. Discuss the actual degree of influence Communism enjoyed in America before McCarthy's time. Consider, for instance, the favorable response of many intellectuals (and some workers) to the Russian Revolution, the heightened appeal of Stalinism during the Great Depression, and the increased activities of Soviet spies both during and after World War II. What was the ultimate effect of McCarthy's career on the influence of Communism in the United States? Could a case be made that McCarthy was one of the best things that ever happened to Communists?

for America in response to "questions asked by friend and foe," as the subtitle states.

Further Reading

■ Books

Feuerlicht, Roberta Strauss. *Joe McCarthy and McCarthyism: The Hate That Haunts America*. New York: McGraw Hill, 1972.

Fried, Albert, ed. *McCarthyism, the Great American Red Scare: A Documentary History*. New York: Oxford University Press, 1996.

Herman, Arthur. *Joseph McCarthy: Reexamining the Life and Legacy of America's Most Hated Senator*. New York: Free Press, 1999.

Oshinsky, David M. *A Conspiracy So Immense: The World of Joe McCarthy*. New York: Free Press, 1983.

Reeves, Thomas C. *The Life and Times of Joe McCarthy: A Biography*. New York: Stein and Day, 1982.

Rovere, Richard. *Senator Joe McCarthy*. New York: Harcourt, Brace, Jovanovich, 1959.

Thomas, Lately. *When Even Angels Wept: The Senator Joseph McCarthy Affair—A Story without a Hero*. New York: William Morrow, 1973.

Wicker, Tom. *Shooting Star: The Brief Arc of Joe McCarthy*. Orlando, Fla.: Harcourt, 2006.

—Carl Rollyson

"Enemies from Within" Speech (1950)

Ladies and gentlemen, tonight as we celebrate the one hundred forty-first birthday of one of the greatest men in American history, I would like to be able to talk about what a glorious day today is in the history of the world. As we celebrate the birth of this man who with his whole heart and soul hated war, I would like to be able to speak of peace in our time—of war being outlawed—and of world-wide disarmament. These would be truly appropriate things to be able to mention as we celebrate the birthday of Abraham Lincoln.

Five years after a world war has been won, men's hearts should anticipate a long peace—and men's minds should be free from the heavy weight that comes with war. But this is not such a period—for this is not a period of peace. This is a time of "the cold war." This is a time when all the world is split into two vast, increasingly hostile armed camps—a time of a great armament race.

Today we can almost physically hear the mutterings and rumblings of an invigorated god of war. You can see it, feel it, and hear it all the way from the Indochina hills, from the shores of Formosa, right over into the very heart of Europe itself.

The one encouraging thing is that the "mad moment" has not yet arrived for the firing of the gun or the exploding of the bomb which will set civilization about the final task of destroying itself. There is still a hope for peace if we finally decide that no longer can we safely blind our eyes and close our ears to those facts which are shaping up more and more clearly… and that is that we are now engaged in a show-down fight … not the usual war between nations for land areas or other material gains, but a war between two diametrically opposed ideologies.

The great difference between our western Christian world and the atheistic Communist world is not political, gentlemen, it is moral. For instance, the Marxian idea of confiscating the land and factories and running the entire economy as a single enterprise is momentous. Likewise, Lenin's invention of the one-party police state as a way to make Marx's idea work is hardly less momentous.

Stalin's resolute putting across of these two ideas, of course, did much to divide the world. With only these differences, however, the east and the west could most certainly still live in peace.

The real, basic difference, however, lies in the religion of immoralism…invented by Marx, preached feverishly by Lenin, and carried to unimaginable extremes by Stalin. This religion of immoralism, if the Red half of the world triumphs—and well it may, gentlemen—this religion of immoralism will more deeply wound and damage mankind than any conceivable economic or political system.

Karl Marx dismissed God as a hoax, and Lenin and Stalin have added in clear-cut, unmistakable language their resolve that no nation, no people who believe in a god, can exist side by side with their communistic state.

Karl Marx, for example, expelled people from his Communist Party for mentioning such things as love, justice, humanity or morality. He called this "soulful ravings" and "sloppy sentimentality."…

Today we are engaged in a final, all-out battle between communistic atheism and Christianity. The modern champions of communism have selected this as the time, and ladies and gentlemen, the chips are down—they are truly down.

Lest there be any doubt that the time has been chosen, let us go directly to the leader of communism today—Joseph Stalin. Here is what he said—not back in 1928, not before the war, not during the war—but 2 years after the last war was ended: "To think that the Communist revolution can be carried out peacefully, within the framework of a Christian democracy, means one has either gone out of one's mind and lost all normal understanding, or has grossly and openly repudiated the Communist revolution."…

Ladies and gentlemen, can there be anyone tonight who is so blind as to say that the war is not on? Can there by anyone who fails to realize that the Communist world has said the time is now?… that this is the time for the show-down between the democratic Christian world and the communistic atheistic world?

Unless we face this fact, we shall pay the price that must be paid by those who wait too long.

Six years ago,… there was within the Soviet orbit, 180,000,000 people. Lined up on the antitotalitarian side there were in the world at that time, roughly 1,625,000,000 people. Today, only six years later, there are 800,000,000 people under the absolute domination of Soviet Russia—an increase of over

400 percent. On our side, the figure has shrunk to around 500,000,000. In other words, in less than six years, the odds have changed from 9 to 1 in our favor to 8 to 5 against us.

This indicates the swiftness of the tempo of Communist victories and American defeats in the cold war. As one of our outstanding historical figures once said, "When a great democracy is destroyed, it will not be from enemies from without, but rather because of enemies from within."…

The reason why we find ourselves in a position of impotency is not because our only powerful potential enemy has sent men to invade our shores…but rather because of the traitorous actions of those who have been treated so well by this Nation. It has not been the less fortunate, or members of minority groups who have been traitorous to this Nation, but rather those who have had all the benefits that the wealthiest Nation on earth has had to offer … the finest homes, the finest college education and the finest jobs in government we can give.

This is glaringly true in the State Department. There the bright young men who are born with silver spoons in their mouths are the ones who have been most traitorous.…

I have here in my hand a list of 205 … a list of names that were made known to the Secretary of State as being members of the Communist Party and who nevertheless are still working and shaping policy in the State Department.…

As you know, very recently the Secretary of State proclaimed his loyalty to a man guilty of what has always been considered as the most abominable of all crimes—being a traitor to the people who gave him a position of great trust—high treason.…

He has lighted the spark which is resulting in a moral uprising and will end only when the whole sorry mess of twisted, warped thinkers are swept from the national scene so that we may have a new birth of honesty and decency in government.

Glossary

antitotalitarian	in opposition to political systems characterized by total control over every aspect of life and society (for example, Nazism and Communism)
ideologies	political belief systems; often used in reference to the most rigid or extreme of such systems
Red	Communist

TELEGRAM TO PRESIDENT HARRY S. TRUMAN (1950)

In the Lincoln Day speech at Wheeling Thursday night I stated that the State Department harbors a nest of Communists and Communist sympathizers who are helping to shape our foreign policy. I further stated that I have in my possession the names of 57 Communists who are in the State Department at present. A State Department spokesman promptly denied this, claiming that there is not a single Communist in the Department. You can convince yourself of the falsity of the State Department claim very easily. You will recall that you personally appointed a board to screen State Department employees for the purpose of weeding out fellow travelers—men whom the board considered dangerous to the security of this Nation. Your board did a painstaking job, and named hundreds which had been listed as dangerous to the security of the Nation, because of communistic connections.

While the records are not available to me, I know absolutely of one group of approximately 300 certified to the Secretary for discharge because of communism. He actually only discharged approximately 80. I understand that this was done after lengthy consultation with the now-convicted traitor, Alger Hiss. I would suggest, therefore, Mr. President, that you simply pick up your phone and ask Mr. Acheson how many of those whom your board had labeled as dangerous Communists he failed to discharge. The day the House Un-American Activities Committee exposed Alger Hiss as an important link in an international Communist spy ring you signed an order forbidding the State Department's giving any information in regard to the disloyalty or the communistic connections of anyone in that Department to the Congress.

Despite this State Department black-out, we have been able to compile a list of 57 Communists in the State Department. This list is available to you but you can get a much longer list by ordering Secretary Acheson to give you a list of those whom your own board listed as being disloyal and who are still working in the State Department. I believe the following is the minimum which can be expected of you in this case.

1. That you demand that Acheson give you and the proper congressional committee the names and a complete report on all of those who were placed in the Department by Alger Hiss, and all of those still working in the State Department who were listed by your board as bad security risks because of their communistic connections.

2. That you promptly revoke the order in which you provided under no circumstances could a congressional committee obtain any information or help in exposing Communists.

Failure on your part will label the Democratic Party of being the bedfellow of international communism. Certainly this label is not deserved by the hundreds of thousands of loyal American Democrats throughout the Nation, and by the sizable number of able loyal Democrats in both the Senate and the House.

Glossary

fellow travelers	people who do not belong to Communist organizations but nevertheless support or sympathize with the aims of Communists

Letter to President Dwight Eisenhower (1953)

February 3, 1953
The President
The White House

Dear Mr. President:

I understand that the matter of the confirmation of James B. Conant as High Commissioner in Germany will come before the Senate within the next few days. I feel as a courtesy to you, that I should inform you of the position which I shall take when this matter comes to the Senate floor.

I am strongly opposed to Mr. Conant's confirmation on the following four principal grounds:

1. His speech made in New York City on October 7, 1944, which, in my opinion, can be interpreted only as advocating the destruction of all industry in Western Germany, as shortly thereafter advocated in the Morgenthau Plan, which, as you know, was to a great extent prepared by Harry Dexter White. I feel that the Morgenthau plan was completely unrealistic and played directly into the hands of our enemy. In fact, I believe Mr. Cordell Hull referred to it as a plan of "blind vengeance" and that you referred to the plan as "silly and tragic." You understand, of course, that I am not taking the position that Mr. Conant collaborated with Morgenthau or Harry Dexter White, but his plan covered in his speech was the same in its essential aspect, namely the destruction of industry in Western Germany.

2. His article in May of 1940 in the *Atlantic Monthly*, entitled "Education for Classless Society". Therein he states:

   "If the American ideal is not to be an illusion the citizens of this republic must not shrink from drastic action. The requirement, however, is not a radical expropriation of wealth at any given innocent, it is rather a continuous process by which power and privilege may be automatically redistributed at the end of each generation".

It will be noted here that he opposes the Communist idea of a "radical expropriation of wealth at any given moment", but that he does favor a process by which the wealth will be automatically distributed at the end of each generation. This can mean only one thing, namely one hundred percent inheritance tax, which, of course, would ultimately result in the complete socialization of any country.

3. His opposition to parochial schools. He obviously has a right to oppose parochial schools and is undoubtedly honest in his opposition. However, as you know, most of the Germans are either Catholic or Lutheran and the parochial school subject is one upon which they feel very strongly. It would, therefore, seem that to appoint a man as High Commissioner of Germany who opposes the type of school system which is the heart of the educational system of Germany and about which those people feel so strongly will create a great deal of ill feeling toward America and furnish ammunition for the Communist propaganda guns.

4. His recent speech in which he first states that if there are Communists in colleges they should be rooted out by the Government, but then states that if an investigation were made and a few Communists found, the damage done would be greater than the harm in their remaining as educators. At the same time, you will recall, he stated there are no Communists at Harvard. It may be that Harlow Shapley, Kirtley Mather, and the late F. O. Matthiessen are not and were not Communists, but the surprise would lie in finding that out. They have been up early every morning doing the work of the Communist causes on occasion after occasion. The reasonable presumption is that if they teach at Harvard they are intelligent men. If they are intelligent men and work sedulously in behalf of Communist causes, then the most reasonable inference is that they are doing so because they are either Communist or pro-Communist. They apparently are so recognized by everyone except Mr. Conant.

Let me make it clear that I do not accuse Mr. Conant of being either Communist or pro-Communist. However, I strongly feel that his innocent statement about Communist activities in education and about the presence of communism in his own faculty indicate a woeful lack of knowledge of the vicious and intricate Communist conspiracy. Certainly it does not show any qualifications for the task of safeguarding the American Embassy at Bonn against Communist penetration, nor with the task of meeting the Communist threat in Western Germany.

Let me make it clear that I feel that undoubtedly Mr. Conant is a fine gentleman. He also is apparently intelligent—intelligent enough to have said on one occasion when addressing a Convocation of the University of New York in 1947, that he was greatly concerned by the fact that many temperamentally unsuited persons were making their way into universities.

And he added: After all, "I can imagine a native scientist or philosopher, with strong loyalties to the advancement of civilization, and the unity of the world, who would be a questionable asset to a government department charged with negotiations with another nation. The same men, on the other hand, because of their professional competence, might make excellent professors."

Feeling as strongly as I do that Mr. Conant is not qualified for the job in Germany, normally I would put up an all-out fight on the Senate floor in an attempt to prevent his confirmation. I frankly would do that now if I thought there were any possibility of defeating him. However, I am convinced that many Senators who might normally question Conant's fitness will go along with the new President, who has received such an overwhelming vote of confidence from the American people.

This presents a very serious question of what would be gained or lost for this country and the peace of the world by greatly publicizing what I consider Mr. Conant's shortcoming for this job. I greatly fear that an all-out fight on my part against Conant, which I normally would feel compelled to make, would not accomplish his defeat and would furnish the Communists in Europe a vast amount of ammunition for their guns. For that reason, I have very reluctantly decided that while I shall vote against Mr. Conant, I shall not make any public statements in regard to him at this time, nor is this letter being made public by me. I might add that this is one of the most difficult decisions I have ever made. I feel that whichever course I take damage is being done. I am choosing what I consider the lesser of the two evils.

Wishing you good luck and good health, I remain

Very sincerely yours,
JOE McCARTHY

Glossary

Bonn	capital of West Germany from 1949 to 1990
Cordell Hull	U.S. Secretary of State from 1933 to 1944
Kirtley Mather	American geologist at Harvard University, most famous for providing evidence on behalf of evolutionary teaching in the 1926 Scopes Monkey Trial
Morgenthau Plan	a program, named after Secretary of the Treasury Henry Morgenthau, Jr., for occupying and disarming Germany after World War II
parochial schools	religious schools

William McKinley (Library of Congress)

WILLIAM MCKINLEY 1843–1901

Twenty-fifth President of the United States

Featured Documents

◆ Message to Congress about Intervention in Cuba (1898)
◆ "Benevolent Assimilation" Proclamation (1898)
◆ Home Market Club Speech (1899)
◆ Last Speech (1901)

Overview

William McKinley was born in Ohio in 1843. He fought in the Civil War and then was elected to the House of Representatives, where he served from 1876 to 1890. From 1892 to 1896 he was governor of Ohio. Nominated by the Republicans for the presidency in 1896, McKinley was elected and served from 1897 until he was assassinated in 1901. During his four and a half years in office, a dispute with Spain over the rebellion of Cuba against the Spanish led to war in 1898. That conflict, in turn, resulted in an American victory and the negotiation of a peace treaty in Paris. The outcome of the war led to America's acquisition of Guam, the Philippines, and Puerto Rico. McKinley was reelected to the presidency in 1900. He was shot by an anarchist sympathizer on September 6, 1901, and died on September 14, 1901.

McKinley was the first modern president. Although he had been elected largely on domestic issues in the campaign of 1896, he became a significant chief executive in the area of foreign policy. During his administration the United States fought the Spanish-American War over the fate of the island of Cuba. McKinley used his power as commander in chief to direct the war effort, govern the possessions that were added from the peace treaty with Spain, and prosecute a war in the Philippines. The administration also sought to penetrate the Far East for American trade through the policy of the Open Door with China, a concept developed in the mid-nineteenth century and stating that all nations, in principle, should have equal trading rights in China. These developments accelerated the process by which the United States became a world power.

McKinley's importance also stemmed from his impact on the office of the presidency itself. In forging closer relationships with the press, traveling extensively to promote his programs, and working closely with Congress, McKinley set precedents that subsequent executives emulated during the twentieth century. By the start of his second term, there were complaints in some quarters that McKinley had accumulated too much power and was stretching the authority of the presidency in directions the framers of the Constitution had not anticipated. Such criticisms attest to the significant impact McKinley's policies and his public articulation of the goals of his administration had in reshaping the way Americans saw their presidents.

In domestic affairs, McKinley's presidency witnessed an economic rebound from the depression of the 1890s. The enactment of the Dingley Act (1897) and the Gold Standard Act (1900) were key elements in the Republican program of a protective tariff and a sound, reliable currency, respectively. As businesses consolidated during the years of returning prosperity, the issue of "the trusts" (monopolies) became an important one in American politics. McKinley was assassinated before he could fully engage the issue, but there were indications as his second term began that he intended to regulate the trusts along the lines that Theodore Roosevelt later followed in his first term as president. Even though he had been an advocate of a protective tariff early in his career, McKinley endorsed liberalizing of American trade and planned to make that a hallmark of his second term. His last speech, delivered in September 1901 in Buffalo, New York, was a significant indication of the direction in which he, as president, wanted to take the country.

Explanation and Analysis of Documents

McKinley was president of the United States during the period of overseas expansion that grew out of the war with Spain in 1898. A popular speaker as a campaigner, McKinley wrote presidential messages and delivered addresses that proved significant in persuading Americans to adopt this expanded world role at the end of the nineteenth century. At a time when radio did not yet exist, the president had to make his case through the prose that his constituents read in their newspapers or in pamphlet form. McKinley proved quite adept at framing arguments that would convince citizens of the wisdom of the course he was proposing. Four public documents demonstrate McKinley's technique as a molder of opinion and the person who set priorities for the nation: his message to Congress asking for authority to intervene in Cuba, his proclamation of a policy of "benevolent assimilation" in the Philippines, his speech about imperialism to the Home Market Club in Boston, and his last speech, given in Buffalo, New York.

◆ Message to Congress about Intervention in Cuba

By late March 1898 the United States was in a confrontation with Spain over the fate of the island of Cuba, the last Spanish possession in the Western Hemisphere.

1843
- **January 29**
  William McKinley is born in Niles, Ohio.

1861
- **June 11**
  McKinley is mustered into the Union Army.

1876
- McKinley is elected to the House of Representatives.

1890
- McKinley is defeated for another term in the House.

1892
- **January 11**
  McKinley is inaugurated as governor of Ohio.

1894
- **January 8**
  McKinley is inaugurated for a second term as governor.

1896
- **November 3**
  McKinley is elected president of the United States.

1898
- **April 11**
  McKinley asks Congress for authority to intervene in Cuba.

- **December 21**
  McKinley orders "benevolent assimilation" in the Philippines.

1899
- **February 16**
  McKinley delivers a speech on imperialism to the Home Market Club in Boston.

1900
- **November 6**
  McKinley is reelected as president.

1901
- **September 5**
  McKinley delivers a speech on trade in Buffalo, New York.

Diplomatic efforts to induce Spain to leave Cuba in a peaceful manner had failed. The United States believed that the continuing violence in Cuba threatened American commerce; required expenditures of money to enforce neutrality laws; and, according to the president, "caused irritation, annoyance, and disturbance among our citizens." The Spanish would not relinquish what they called their "Ever Faithful" island without a military struggle. To break the impasse, McKinley submitted his message to Congress about Cuban intervention on April 11, 1898. In this written exposition of the situation the United States faced in Cuba, the president shaped the alternatives that the lawmakers would have to consider in debating intervention.

The first portion of McKinley's message examines the background of events in Cuba before he took office in March 1897. He reviews the involvement of the United States in the affairs of the island and the periodic uprisings against Spanish rule that disturbed the peace in the Caribbean. These paragraphs reflect the ongoing concern of the United States about the presence of a European power and its colonial possession in the Western Hemisphere. Then the president states that there is little likelihood that either the Spanish or the Cuban rebels could achieve a military victory on the battlefield. His diplomacy, especially in March 1898, looked toward negotiations with Spain to bring about a peaceful resolution of the conflict. It was implicit in McKinley's offer to the Spanish that the government in Madrid must recognize independence for Cuba and withdraw Spanish forces. As the president notes in his message, the Spanish response did not meet the American demands. Instead of negotiations, the Spanish reserved final judgment about the fate of Cuba to itself; the most it would concede was a suspension of hostilities. That would leave control of the situation to the Spanish military commander, who would determine how long the pause in the fighting would endure.

McKinley then decided that the United States must intervene to end the fighting. He made his decision on the grounds of humanity, the American duty to the citizens of Cuba, and the adverse effects of continued fighting on American trade. But his main reason for intervention was the demands the war made on the United States itself, resulting in what he calls in his message "a constant menace to our peace." As an example, he cites the destruction of the battleship *Maine*, which had blown up in Havana harbor on February 15, 1898. The vessel had been sent there to show American interest in lessening the fighting on the island. For all these reasons, the president concludes that "the war in Cuba must stop."

The reaction to the message itself was mixed in Congress, but lawmakers did grant the president the authority to intervene in Cuba. That decision, in turn, moved Spain to declare war on the United States, and hostilities between the two nations were under way by the end of April. The fighting went on in Cuba and the Philippines. Spain's Asian possessions were attacked as part of a war plan to force Madrid to negotiate a peace settlement.

At the battle of Manila Bay, on May 1, 1898, the American squadron, commanded by Commodore George Dewey, defeated the Spanish vessels defending the islands. Soon McKinley sent troops to complete the occupation of the Philippines. Meanwhile, in Cuba the army gained possession of the strategic heights overlooking Santiago Harbor and forced the Spanish army to sue for an end to the fighting in mid-July. By mid-August an armistice between Spain and the United States brought the military phase of the conflict to an end.

The large question for the McKinley administration became the fate of the Philippines. During the peace negotiations that went on in Paris during the autumn of 1898, the American delegation received instructions from the president that the United States should insist on the acquisition of the Philippines as part of the final settlement of the war. The Treaty of Paris, signed on December 10, 1898, ceded the Philippines to the United States in exchange for a payment of $20 million. By that time the question of overseas expansion had become a hot political issue in the United States. Republicans generally favored holding the Philippines. Democrats in Congress and out were predominantly opposed to this strategy. With the peace treaty to be considered in the Senate in early 1899, the way in which the administration dealt with the Philippines had large consequences for the president and his party.

◆ "Benevolent Assimilation" Proclamation

McKinley was determined to govern the Philippines under his power as commander in chief until Congress established a civil government for the islands. By late 1898 tensions rose between American forces on the ground and Filipinos who resented the presence of the United States in their country. The prospect of an armed conflict was very much on the minds of American policy makers at the time. When McKinley took steps to establish a framework for the military government in the Philippines, he thus spoke both to the residents of the islands and to the political controversy at home.

On December 21, 1898, McKinley issued an executive proclamation setting out how government should operate in the Philippines. His reference to "benevolent assimilation" gave the document its name in history. Notice that the president assumes that the peace treaty is in operation, even though Congress had not yet acted to approve it. From that premise, he then asserts that American sovereignty and military control should at once be extended throughout the archipelago. McKinley lays out the duties of the military commander to reassure the inhabitants of the islands that "all their private rights and relations" would be safeguarded. He also announces the friendly purpose of the United States and the goal of protecting "their personal and religious rights." The president then argues for an approach that would return the Philippines to normal life as rapidly as possible. Those residents who were willing to accept the supremacy of the United States would be protected. Those who did not would be treated "with firmness if need be, but without severity, so far as possible."

The key phrase in this document and the one that has established its historical significance for an understanding of

Time Line

1901

■ **September 6**
An anarchist sympathizer shoots McKinley at the Temple of Music in Buffalo.

■ **September 14**
McKinley dies in Buffalo.

McKinley as president relates to the use of the term *benevolent assimilation*. The racial and ethnic overtones of the phrase are immediately evident to the modern reader. During the late nineteenth century, Americans were convinced that their form of government was the best in the world. Asian, Latin American, and African peoples were, in the popular mind of the day, not as far advanced as were the Anglo-Saxon civilizations. It was the duty, some imperialists argued, to spread the blessings of civilization to areas where backwardness persisted. That there was ample bigotry and condescension in this point of view now seems clear. But for McKinley and the leaders of his generation, the honest and moral purposes of the United States were self-evident. He believed that he had a mission to provide "the blessings of good and stable government" to the people of the Philippines.

During the month and a half that followed, the Senate debated the Treaty of Paris. At the same time, in the Philippines, the tense military situation continued. In early February fighting broke out between the U.S. Army and Filipino insurgents. The senators approved the treaty by one more vote than the two-thirds necessary, and the United States could now claim full legal possession of the Philippines as a result of the war with Spain. But the country was waging an imperial war to subjugate the Philippine people and make good on its claims of sovereignty over the islands. Meanwhile, full-scale debate raged in the United States about the merits of overseas expansion. The Democrats, led by William Jennings Bryan, challenged the assumptions of American foreign policy that acquiring possessions overseas was a good result of the recent war.

◆ Home Market Club Speech

It was in this context that McKinley prepared to deliver a major address in Boston. He was to speak on February 16, 1899, at a dinner of the Home Market Club, a lobbying organization for the policy of tariff protection that was at the heart of Republican economic doctrine. The president was thus assured of a friendly audience that would be receptive to his message. He began working on his speech in early February even before the Treaty of Paris was approved and refined it as events dictated during the two weeks that followed. As he did with all his speeches, McKinley tried out lines and themes with his personal secretaries as they transcribed his words.

In his remarks, McKinley makes several central arguments. He notes at the outset that many Democrats had favored war with Spain in the spring of 1898 but now that the conflict had produced unexpected results "are the first

A United States Army surgeon attending wounded soldiers in a field hospital during the Spanish-American War. The Red Cross emblem appears on the sleeve of one man. (Library of Congress)

to cry out against the far-reaching consequences of their own act." The president traces the war and its outcome, the acquisition of the Philippines. He predicts that the American commanders in the islands "will have the support of the country in upholding our flag where it now floats, the symbol and assurance of liberty and justice." McKinley goes on to say that the chief executive "cannot anticipate or avoid the consequences" of the war, "but he must meet them."

The president then frames the issues that the nation confronted in the Philippines. He notes "universal agreement that the Philippines shall not be turned back to Spain." Once that had been decided, he says, "there was but one alternative, and that was either Spain or the United States in the Philippines." He rejects the idea of allowing the Filipinos to establish their own government, one that, in his mind, would have soon faced conditions of anarchy and the threat of foreign occupation. A protectorate also seemed out of the question, since it provided the responsibility of sovereignty without the power to enforce the demands of governing.

In approaching what to do in the newly acquired possession, McKinley asserts that the United States always considered "the welfare and happiness and the rights of the inhabitants of the Philippine Islands." He does not believe that Americans should have asked the consent of the Fil-

ipinos in conducting war in the Philippines. The existence of armed resistance made such a strategy impractical. "It is not a good time for the liberator to submit important questions concerning liberty and government to the liberated while they are engaged in shooting down their rescuers."

With the treaty ratified in Congress, McKinley states that the decision about the government of the Philippines now lay with the lawmakers. In February 1899 they would not reconvene again until the following December. During that period, McKinley would use the power of the executive branch as commander in chief to ensure a stable government in the islands. He scoffs at the idea that his policies implied imperialism. "No imperial designs lurk in the American mind. They are alien to American sentiment, thought, and purpose. Our priceless principles undergo no change under a tropical sun. They go with the flag."

In his conclusion, he asks his audiences to look beyond the "blood-stained trenches around Manila" into the future, when prosperity would have returned to the Philippines. At that time, the president says, Filipino children and their descendants "shall for ages hence bless the American republic because it emancipated and redeemed their fatherland, and set them in the pathway of the world's best civilization."

The passage of time and changed assumptions regarding imperialism and ruling other peoples without their consent would render McKinley's words archaic and out of step with modern attitudes. At the time, however, his speech to the Home Market Club proved to be a powerful statement of the purposes and goals of his administration. It did not silence his anti-imperialist critics, but it did announce priorities that a majority of Americans shared. While the people did not favor further expansion, neither did they wish in 1899–1900 to relinquish the gains of the war with Spain.

◆ **Last Speech**

The last speech that McKinley ever delivered came on September 5, 1901, at the Pan-American Exposition in Buffalo, New York. For that reason, it has become known as "McKinley's Last Speech," and copies of the address usually carry that title. Of course, McKinley did not know at that time that he would be shot the next day. His comments were part of a campaign he was launching as he began his second term. He had been reelected in November 1900 over William Jennings Bryan and believed that his policies had been endorsed as well. Although McKinley had been identified with the doctrine of the protective tariff from the start of his political career, he had come to think that it was time for the United States to liberalize its trade relations with other countries. His administration had negotiated reciprocal trade agreements with several countries, and the United States Senate was to take those up when Congress met for its regular session in December 1901.

The Republicans in the Senate did not share McKinley's view of trade policy, and so the president intended to build public support for his new program through a series of speeches during the fall of 1901. After McKinley's death, Theodore Roosevelt as his successor abandoned the trade treaties and pursued attacks on large corporations or "trusts" instead. McKinley's speech at Buffalo thus represented not the start of a presidential campaign for his program but a punctuation point for McKinley's life and presidency. Read in the context of what he hoped to accomplish during his second term, it is a document that says much about McKinley's vision of the future for the United States. In his remarks, for example, he notes in the third paragraph that "isolation is no longer possible or desirable." His comments in the third and fourth paragraphs describe a crude form of early-twentieth-century globalization and the changes that technology was making in people's lives. For that reason, the president adds, "no nation can longer be indifferent to any other." Having outlined these elements, McKinley then comes to the point of his address. "By sensible trade arrangements which will not interrupt our home production, we shall extend the outlets for our increasing surplus" of products.

The message of trade reciprocity then becomes clear: "We must not repose in fancied security that we can forever sell everything and buy little or nothing." As a result, "reciprocity is the natural outgrowth of our wonderful industrial development under the domestic policy now firmly established." McKinley argues that "reciprocity

treaties are in harmony with the spirit of the times; measures of retaliation are not." He then lists the policies that the nation should follow—promotion of the merchant marine, the building of a canal across Central America, and telegraph cable service to the Pacific. Praise came in the newspaper accounts the next day (September 6) for what McKinley had said. That same afternoon, McKinley was shot; he died eight days later. People remembered his speech for a time. As the dynamic personality of Theodore Roosevelt took over the presidency, the import of McKinley's words receded, however, and his themes became indistinct and eventually disappeared.

Impact and Legacy

The impact of McKinley's words in his own time and in the present could not offer a more striking contrast. When he was in office, he articulated the views of a majority of Americans with great effectiveness. The message about Cuba, the Home Market Club speech, and the Buffalo address represented a president framing alternatives and setting priorities in a decisive manner. He led public opinion in shaping how the war with Spain would be waged and how the occupation of the Philippines should be conducted and in providing a road map for broadening trade relations. McKinley strengthened the power of his office and used his authority as commander in chief to govern the overseas empire that had come out of the Spanish-American War.

McKinley's ability to capture the mood of the people in his prose made his reputation dependent on how history viewed what he said and did as president. In the decades that have elapsed since McKinley died, the war with Spain and the imperial adventures that followed have come to be seen as mistaken examples of national overreaching in the world. Subjugating other countries and ruling people against their will are repudiated policies. The words that McKinley used to justify what the nation was doing now seem either insincere or hypocritical. When he says that "the war in Cuba must stop" or that "benevolent assimilation" must occur in the Philippines, he speaks in language that grates on the modern ear. The next step is to assume that McKinley must have known better and thus employed these phrases knowing that they concealed sinister motives. Many historians take that position toward McKinley as a national leader.

In analyzing McKinley's language in these documents, it is important to recognize that McKinley and Americans of his generation believed in the purposes that the president espoused. Steeped in notions of Anglo-Saxon superiority and the innate benevolence of the United States, Americans responded when McKinley set forth the ideas of a national duty to uplift peoples who came from different cultures and backgrounds. These attitudes, though somewhat diminished in the modern-day United States, still exist. A study of McKinley's language thus provides insights into how the United States became a world power and into the reasons that Americans gave in the late nineteenth century to explain why that key historical development took place.

"In the name of humanity, in the name of civilization, in behalf of endangered American interests which gives us the right and the duty to speak and to act, the war in Cuba must stop."

(Message to Congress about Intervention in Cuba)

"The mission of the United States is one of benevolent assimilation substituting the mild sway of justice and right for arbitrary rule."

("Benevolent Assimilation" Proclamation)

"It is not a good time for the liberator to submit important questions concerning liberty and government to the liberated while they are engaged in shooting down their rescuers."

(Home Market Club Speech)

"No imperial designs lurk in the American mind. They are alien to American sentiment, thought, and purpose. Our priceless principles undergo no change under a tropical sun. They go with the flag."

(Home Market Club Speech)

"Expositions are the timekeepers of progress."

(Last Speech)

"We must not repose in fancied security that we can forever sell everything and buy little or nothing."

(Last Speech)

"Reciprocity treaties are in harmony with the spirit of the age; measures of retaliation are not."

(Last Speech)

Key Sources

The William McKinley Papers at the Library of Congress are available on microfilm at major research libraries. The George B. Cortelyou Papers at the Library of Congress contain documents on McKinley that were once part of the president's papers. *Speeches and Addresses of William McKinley, from March 1, 1897 to May 30, 1900* (1900), has most of the president's major public speeches while he was in office. *Speeches and Addresses of William McKinley, from His Election to Congress to the Present Time* (1893), is a basic collection of McKinley's speeches in Congress and

Questions for Further Study

1. Three documents—the message to Congress about intervention in Cuba, the "benevolent assimilation" proclamation, and the Home Market Club speech—serve to present McKinley's case for the war against Spain and for the occupation of the Philippines that followed. Compare the means by which he addresses various audiences in these documents: first Congress, where he faced opposition from Democrats; then the secretary of war, a member of his own executive branch; and, finally, the supportive group assembled at the Home Market Club. Consider similarities and differences in the ways he communicates with each. What themes remain consistent and in what ways does McKinley alter his approach for a particular audience? Evaluate his overall effectiveness in presenting a rationale for intervention and occupation.

2. As a result of the Spanish-American War, the United States gained control over three former Spanish possessions: Cuba, the Philippines, and Puerto Rico. U.S. administrations, beginning with McKinley's, would deal quite differently with these entities: Cuba gained official independence soon after the conclusion of hostilities, but a strong U.S. influence there continued until 1959, whereas the Philippines did not achieve sovereignty until 1946 and Puerto Rico remains a U.S. possession. In what ways do McKinley's statements, particularly with regard to Cuba and the Philippines, prefigure this differing treatment? Evaluate the relative success or failure of the U.S. government to maintain continued good relations with each entity and its citizenry. Consider those instances that highlight the strategic value of and America's ongoing interest in the former Spanish possessions.

3. Although McKinley is remembered as an effective communicator within the political landscape of his era, in many cases his use of language makes comprehension difficult for a modern reader. For example, the second paragraph of his message to Congress about Cuba is a single lengthy sentence with a number of clauses that collectively seem to hinder rather than enhance communication. How might McKinley, were he alive at the beginning of the twenty-first century, present his ideas? Consider particular passages and examples of his wording, and restate them in contemporary language. Pay special attention to his use of terminology unfamiliar to the modern ear as well as words and phrases likely to be deemed inappropriate by the standards of our own time.

4. In his final speech, delivered at the Pan-American Exposition in Buffalo, New York, McKinley addresses issues, such as international trade and the influence of developing technologies, that continue to dominate headlines in our own time. Globalization, one of the leading concerns in the contemporary political landscape, was then in its infancy, yet McKinley observed numerous challenges and opportunities likely to arise in the wake of increased international trade and communication. In what ways is this speech forward-looking and relevant to our own time? How might McKinley, if he were alive today, regard the contemporary global environment and its contradictions— for example, the fact that U.S. products continue to be enormously popular, yet manufacturing jobs have shifted away from the United States? Underlying many of his comments on technology is the "idea of progress": the belief, common in his time, that humanity was on the path to greater and greater success and well-being, thanks to technology. In what ways does such a standpoint seem naive or outdated today and in what ways is the "idea of progress" still relevant?

from his first term as governor of Ohio. *McKinley's Speeches in September* (1896) provides a record of what McKinley said as a presidential candidate in September 1896. Finally, George Raywood Devitt, *A Supplement to a Compilation of the Messages and Papers of the Presidents, 1789–1902* (1903), prints McKinley's official messages and speeches while he was president. The Web sites of the William McKinley Presidential Library & Museum (http://www.mckinleymuseum.org/) and the Miller Center of Public Affairs "American President: An Online Reference Resource" (http://millercenter.org/academic/americanpresident/mckinley) offer information on McKinley and his administration.

Further Reading

■ **Books**

Armstrong, William H. *Major McKinley: William McKinley and the Civil War*. Kent, Ohio: Kent State University Press, 2000.

Gould, Lewis L. *The Presidency of William McKinley*. Lawrence: University Press of Kansas, 1980.

———. *The Spanish-American War and President McKinley*. Lawrence: University Press of Kansas, 1982.

Leech, Margaret. *In the Days of McKinley* New York: Harper & Bros., 1959.

Morgan, H. Wayne. *William McKinley and His America*. Rev. ed. Kent, Ohio: Kent State University Press, 2003.

Phillips, Kevin P. *William McKinley* New York: Henry Holt, 2003.

—Lewis L. Gould

MESSAGE TO CONGRESS ABOUT INTERVENTION IN CUBA (1898)

To the Congress of the United States:

Obedient to that precept of the Constitution which commands the President to give from time to time to the congress information of the state of Union and to recommend to their consideration such measures as he shall judge necessary and expedient, it becomes my duty now to address your body with regard to the grave crisis that has arisen in the relations of the United States to Spain by reason of the warfare that for more than three years has raged in the neighboring island of Cuba.

I do so because of the intimate connection of the Cuban question with the state of our own Union and the grave relation the course which it is now incumbent upon the nation to adopt must needs bear to the traditional policy of our Government if it is to accord with the precepts laid down by the founders of the Republic and religiously observed by succeeding Administrations to the present day.

The present revolution is but the successor of other similar insurrections which have occurred in Cuba against the dominion of Spain, extending over a period of nearly half a century, each of which, during its progress, has subjected the United States to great effort and expense in enforcing its neutrality laws, caused enormous losses to American trade and commerce, caused irritation, annoyance, and disturbance among our citizens, and by the exercise of cruel, barbarous, and uncivilized practices of warfare, shocked the sensibilities and offended the humane sympathies of our people.

Since the present revolution began in February, 1895, this country has seen the fertile domain at our threshold ravaged by fire and sword in the course of a struggle unequaled in the history of the island and rarely paralleled as to the numbers of the combatants and the bitterness of the contest by any revolution of modern times where dependent people striving to be free have been opposed by the power of the sovereign state.

Our people have beheld a once prosperous community reduced to comparative want, its lucrative commerce virtually paralyzed, its exceptional productiveness diminished, its fields laid waste, its mills in ruins, and its people perishing by tens of thousands from hunger and destitution. We have found ourselves constrained, in the observance of that strict neutrality which our laws enjoin, and which the law of nations commands, to police our own waters and watch our own seaports in prevention of any unlawful act in aid of the Cubans.

Our trade has suffered; the capital invested by our citizens in Cuba has been largely lost, and the temper and forbearance of our people have been so sorely tried as to beget a perilous unrest among our own citizens which has inevitably found its expression from time to time in the National Legislature, so that issues wholly external to our own body politic engross attention and stand in the way of the close devotion to domestic advancement that becomes a self-contained commonwealth whose primal maxim has been the avoidance of all foreign entanglements. All this must need awaken, and has, indeed, aroused the utmost concern on the part of this Government, as well during my predecessor's term as in my own....

In this state of affairs my Administration found itself confronted with the grave problem of its duty. My message of last December reviewed the situation and narrated the steps taken with a view to relieving its acuteness and opening the way to some form of honorable settlement. The assassination of the Prime Minister, Canovas, led to a change of government in Spain. The former administration, pledged to subjugation without concession, gave place to that of a more liberal party, committed long in advance to a policy of reform, involving the wider principle of home rule for Cuba and Puerto Rico....

The war in Cuba is of such a nature that short of subjugation or extermination a final military victory for either side seems impracticable. The alternative lies in the physical exhaustion of the one or the other party, or perhaps of both—a condition which in effect ended the ten year's war by the truce of Zanjon. The prospect of such a protraction and conclusion of the present strife is a contingency hardly to be contemplated with equanimity by the civilized world, and least of all by the United States, affected and injured as we are, deeply and intimately, by its very existence.

Realizing this, it appeared to be my duty, in a spirit of true friendliness, no less to Spain than the Cubans who have so much to lose by the prolongation of the struggle, to seek to bring about an immediate termination of the war....

The forcible intervention of the United States as a neutral to stop the war, according to the large dictates of humanity and following many historical precedents where neighboring States have interfered to check the hopeless sacrifices of life by internecine conflicts beyond their borders, is justifiable on rational grounds. It involves, however, hostile constraint upon both the parties to the contest as well to enforce a truce as to guide the eventual settlement.

The grounds for such intervention may be briefly summarized as, follows:

First. In the cause of humanity and to put an end to the barbarities, bloodshed, starvation, and horrible miseries now existing there, and which the parties to the conflict are either unable or unwilling to stop or mitigate. It is no answer to say this is all in another country, belonging to another nation, and is therefore none of our business. It is specially our duty, for it is right at our door.

Second. We owe it to our citizens in Cuba to afford them that protection and indemnity for life and property which no government there can or will afford, and to that end to terminate the conditions that deprive them of legal protection.

Third. The right to intervene may be justified by the very serious injury to the commerce, trade, and business of our people, and by the wanton destruction of property and devastation of the island.

Fourth, and which is of the utmost importance. The present condition of affairs in Cuba is a constant menace to our peace, and entails upon this Government an enormous expense. With such a conflict waged for years in an island so near us and with which our people have such trade and business relations; when the lives and liberty of our citizens are in constant danger and their property destroyed and themselves ruined; where our trading vessels are liable to seizure and are seized at our very door by war ships of a foreign nation, the expeditions of filibustering that we are powerless to prevent altogether, and the irritating questions and entanglements thus arising—all these and others that I need not mention, with the resulting strained relations, are constant menace to our peace, and compel us to keep on a semiwar footing with a nation with which we are at peace.

These elements of danger and disorder already pointed out have been strikingly illustrated by a tragic event which has deeply and justly moved the American people. I have already transmitted to Congress the report of the naval court of inquiry on the destruction of the battle ship Maine in the harbor of Havana during the night of the 15th of February. The destruction of that noble vessel has filled the national heart with inexpressible horror. Two hundred and fifty-eight brave sailors and marines and two officers of our Navy, reposing in the fancied security of a friendly harbor, have been hurled to death, grief and want brought to their homes, and sorrow to the nation.

The naval court of inquiry, which it is needless to say, commands the unqualified confidence of the Government, was unanimous in its conclusion that the destruction of the Maine was caused by an exterior explosion, that of a submarine mine. It did not assume to place the responsibility. That remains to be fixed.

In any event the destruction of the Maine, by whatever exterior cause, is a patent and impressive proof of a state of things in Cuba that is intolerable. That condition is thus shown to be such that the Spanish Government can not assure safety and security to a vessel of the American Navy in the harbor of Havana on a mission of peace, and rightfully there....

The long trail has proved that the object for which Spain has waged the war can not be attained. The fire of insurrection may flame or may smolder with varying seasons, but it has not been and it is plain that it can not be extinguished by present methods. The only hope of relief and repose from a condition which can no longer be endured is the enforced pacification of Cuba. In the name of humanity, in the name of civilization, in behalf of endangered American interests which gives us the right and the duty to speak and to act, the war in Cuba must stop.

In view of these facts and of these considerations, I ask the Congress to authorize and empower the President to take measure to secure a full and final termination of hostilities between the Government of Spain and the people of Cuba, and to secure in the island the establishment of a stable government, capable of maintaining order and observing its international obligations, insuring peace and tranquility and the security of its citizens as well as our own, and to use the military and naval forces of the United States as may be necessary for these purposes.

And in the interest of humanity and to aid in preserving the lives of the starving people of the island I recommend that the distribution of food and supplies be continued, and that an appropriation be made out of the public Treasury to supplement the charity of our citizens.

The issue is now with the Congress. It is a solemn responsibility. I have exhausted every effort to relieve the intolerable condition of affairs which is at our doors. Prepared to execute every obligation imposed upon me by the Constitution and the law, I await your action.

Yesterday, and since the preparation of the foregoing message, official information was received by me that the latest decree of the Queen Regent of Spain directs General Blanco, in order to prepare and facilitate peace, to proclaim a suspension of hostilities, the duration and details of which have not yet been communicated to me.

This fact with every other pertinent consideration will, I am sure, have your just and careful attention in the solemn deliberations upon which you are about to enter. If this measure attains a successful result, then our aspirations as a Christian, peace-loving people will be realized. If it fails, it will be only another justification for our contemplated action.

William McKinley

Executive Mansion, April 11, 1898.

Glossary

body politic	the total political organization of a group or nation
Canovas	Antonio Cánovas del Castille, nineteenth-century Spanish political leader
expeditions of filibustering	attacks by freebooters, or pirates
fertile domain at threshold	Cuba
General Blanco	Ramón Blanco y Erenas, nineteenth- and early-twentieth-century Spanish military leader and colonial administrator, captain-general (governor) of Cuba at the time
hostile constraint	armed action to prevent something from happening
National Legislature	Congress
primal maxim	first principle, or guiding idea
Queen Regent of Spain	Maria Christina of Austria, queen consort to King Alfonso XII of Spain, who ruled from 1885 to 1902 on behalf of her young son, Alfonso XIII
Truce of Zanjon	an 1878 agreement, also known as the Pact of Zanjón, that ended the Ten Years' War, one of several unsuccessful efforts by Cubans to gain independence from Spain

"BENEVOLENT ASSIMILATION" PROCLAMATION (1898)

EXECUTIVE MANSION,
Washington, December 21, 1898.

To the Secretary of War.

Sir: The destruction of the Spanish fleet in the harbor of Manila by the United States naval squadron commanded by Rear-Admiral Dewey, followed by the reduction of the city and the surrender of the Spanish forces, practically effected the conquest of the Philippine Islands and the suspension of the Spanish sovereignty therein. With the signature of the treaty of peace between the United States and Spain by their respective plenipotentiaries at Paris on the 10th instant, and as a result of the victories of American arms, the future control, disposition, and government of the Philippine Islands are ceded to the United States. In the fulfillment of the rights of sovereignty thus acquired, and the responsible obligations of government thus assumed, the actual occupation and administration of the entire group of the Philippine Islands becomes immediately necessary, and the military government heretofore maintained by the United States in the city, harbor, and bay of Manila is to be extended with all possible dispatch to the whole of the ceded territory.

In performing this duty the military commander of the United States is enjoined to make known to the inhabitants of the Philippine Islands that in succeeding to the sovereignty of Spain, in severing the former political relations, and in establishing a new political power, the authority of the United States is to be exerted for the securing of the persons and property of the people of the islands and for the confirmation of all their private rights and relations. It will be the duty of the commander of the forces of occupation to announce and proclaim in the most public manner that we come not as invaders or conquerors, but as friends, to protect the natives in their homes, in their employments, and in their personal and religious rights. All persons who, either by active aid or by honest submission, co-operate with the Government of the United States to give effect to these beneficent purposes will receive the reward of its support and protection. All others will be brought within the lawful rule we have assumed, with firmness if need be, but without severity, so far as possible.

Within the absolute domain of military authority, which necessarily is and must remain supreme in the ceded territory until the legislation of the United States shall otherwise provide, the municipal laws of the territory in respect to private rights and property and the repression of crime are to be considered as continuing in force, and to be administered by the ordinary tribunals, so far as practicable. The operations of civil and municipal government are to be performed by such officers as may accept the supremacy of the United States by taking the oath of allegiance, or by officers chosen, as far as practicable, from the inhabitants of the islands.

While the control of all the public property and the revenues of the state passes with the cession, and while the use and management of all public means of transportation are necessarily reserved to the authority of the United States, private property, whether belonging to individuals or corporations, is to be respected except for cause duly established. The taxes and duties heretofore payable by the inhabitants to the late government become payable to the authorities of the United States unless it be seen fit to substitute for them other reasonable rates or modes of contribution to the expenses of government, whether general or local. If private property be taken for military use, it shall be paid for when possible in cash, at a fair valuation, and when payment in cash is not practicable, receipts are to be given.

All ports and places in the Philippine Islands in the actual possession of the land and naval forces of the United States will be opened to the commerce of all friendly nations. All goods and wares not prohibited for military reasons by due announcement of the military authority will be admitted upon payment of such duties and other charges as shall be in force at the time of their importation.

Finally, it should be the earnest wish and paramount aim of the military administration to win the confidence, respect, and affection of the inhabitants of the Philippines by assuring them in every possible way that full measure of individual rights and liberties which is the heritage of free peoples, and by proving to them that the mission of the United States is one of benevolent assimilation, substituting the mild sway of justice and right for arbitrary rule. In the fulfillment of this high mission, supporting the temperate administration of affairs for the greatest good of the governed, there must be sedulously maintained the strong arm of authority, to repress disturbance and to overcome all obstacles to the bestowal of the blessings of good and stable government upon the people of the Philippine Islands under the free flag of the United States.

William McKinley

Glossary

duties	fines
instant	of the current month
plenipotentiaries	authorized representatives
receipts	IOUs, or documents certifying that a repayment is to be made at a later date

HOME MARKET CLUB SPEECH (1899)

My fellow-citizens, the years go quickly. It seems not so long, but it is, in fact, six years, since it was my honor to be a guest of the Home Market Club. Much has happened in the intervening time.... We had four long years of adversity, which taught us some lessons that will never be unlearned, and which will be valuable in guiding our future action. We have not only been successful in our financial and business affairs, but in a war with a foreign power which has added great glory to American arms and a new chapter to American history....

Many who were impatient for the conflict a year ago, apparently heedless of its larger results, are the first to cry out against the far-reaching consequences of their own act. Those of us who dreaded war most, and whose every effort was directed to prevent it, had fears of new and grave problems which might follow its inauguration.

The evolution of events, which no man could control, has brought these problems upon us. Certain it is that they have not come through any fault on our own part, but as a high obligation; and we meet them with clear conscience and unselfish purpose, and with good heart resolve to undertake their solution....

The Philippines, like Cuba and Porto Rico, were intrusted to our hands by the war, and to that great trust, under the providence of God and in the name of human progress and civilization, we are committed. It is a trust we have not sought; it is a trust from which we will not flinch. The American people will hold up the hands of their servants at home to whom they commit its execution, while Dewey and Otis and the brave men whom they command will have the support of the country in upholding our flag where it now floats, the symbol and assurance of liberty and justice.

What nation was ever able to write an accurate program of the war upon which it was entering, much less decree in advance the scope of its results? Congress can declare war, but a higher Power decrees its bounds and fixes its relations and responsibilities. The President can direct the movements of soldiers in the field and fleets upon the sea, but he cannot foresee the close of such movements or prescribe their limits. He cannot anticipate or avoid the consequences, but he must meet them....

We hear no complaint of the relations created by the war between this government and the islands of Cuba and Porto Rico. There are some, however, who regard the Philippines as in a different relation; but whatever variety of views there may be on this phase of the question, there is universal agreement that the Philippines shall not be turned back to Spain. No true American consents to that. Even if unwilling to accept them ourselves, it would have been a weak evasion of duty to require Spain to transfer them to some other power or powers, and thus shirk our own responsibility.... We could not discharge the responsibilities upon us until these islands became ours either by conquest or treaty. There was but one alternative, and that was either Spain or the United States in the Philippines. The other suggestions—first, that they should be tossed into the arena of contention for the strife of nations; or, second, be left to the anarchy and chaos of no protectorate at all—were too shameful to be considered. The treaty gave them to the United States....

Our concern was not for territory or trade or empire, but for the people whose interests and destiny, without our willing it, had been put in our hands. It was with this feeling that, from the first day to the last, not one word or line went from the Executive in Washington to our military and naval commanders at Manila, or to our peace commissioners at Paris, that did not put as the sole purpose to be kept in mind, first after the success of our arms and the maintenance of our own honor, the welfare and happiness and the rights of the inhabitants of the Philippine Islands. Did we need their consent to perform a great act for humanity? We had it in every aspiration of their minds, in every hope of their hearts.... Every present obligation has been met and fulfilled in the expulsion of Spanish sovereignty from their islands; and while the war that destroyed it was in progress we could not ask their views. Nor can we now ask their consent. Indeed, can any one tell me in what form it could be marshaled and ascertained until peace and order, so necessary to the reign of reason, shall be secured and established? A reign of terror is not the kind of rule under which right action and deliberate judgment are possible. It is not a good time for the liberator to submit important questions concerning liberty and government to the liberated while they are engaged in shooting down their rescuers....

The future of the Philippine Islands is now in the hands of the American people. Until the treaty was ratified or rejected, the Executive Department of this government could only preserve the peace and protect life and property. That treaty now commits the free and enfranchised Filipinos to the guiding hand and the liberalizing influences, the generous sympathies, the uplifting education, not of their American masters, but of their American emancipators....

That the inhabitants of the Philippines will be benefited by this republic is my unshaken belief. That they will have a kindlier government under our guidance, and that they will be aided in every possible way to be a self-respecting and self-governing people, is as true as that the American people love liberty and have an abiding faith in their own government and in their own institutions. No imperial designs lurk in the American mind. They are alien to American sentiment, thought, and purpose. Our priceless principles undergo no change under a tropical sun. They go with the flag....

If we can benefit these remote peoples, who will object! If, in the years of the future, they are estab-lished in government under law and liberty, who will regret our perils and sacrifices? Who will not rejoice in our heroism and humanity?...

I have no light or knowledge not common to my countrymen. I do not prophesy. The present is all-absorbing to me. But I cannot bound my vision by the blood-stained trenches around Manila,—where every red drop, whether from the veins of an American soldier or a misguided Filipino, is anguish to my heart,—but by the broad range of future years, when that group of islands, under the impulse of the year just past, shall have become the gems and glories of those tropical seas—a land of plenty and of increasing possibilities; a people redeemed from savage indolence and habits, devoted to the arts of peace, in touch with the commerce and trade of all nations, enjoying the blessings of freedom, of civil and religious liberty, of education, and of homes, and whose children and children's children shall for ages hence bless the American republic because it emancipated and redeemed their fatherland, and set them in the pathway of the world's best civilization.

Glossary

bound	limit
Dewey	George Dewey, U.S. Navy admiral famous for his 1898 victory in the Battle of Manila Bay
enfranchised	permitted to engage in the political process, for instance, by voting
Executive	the president and the executive branch of the U.S. government
Otis	Elwell Stephen Otis, commander of U.S. troops in the Philippines from 1898 to 1900
Porto Rico	Puerto Rico
protectorate	a guarantee of safety by one government over another, less powerful one
savage	uneducated

Last Speech (1901)

I am glad again to be in the city of Buffalo and exchange greetings with her people, to whose generous hospitality I am not a stranger, and with whose good will I have been repeatedly and signally honored. To-day I have additional satisfaction in meeting and giving welcome to the foreign representatives assembled here, whose presence and participation in this Exposition have contributed in so marked a degree to its interest and success....

Expositions are the timekeepers of progress. They record the world's advancement. They stimulate the energy, enterprise and intellect of the people, and quicken human genius. They go into the home. They broaden and brighten the daily life of the people. They open mighty storehouses of information to the student. Every exposition, great or small, has helped to some onward step.

Comparison of ideas is always educational and, as such, instructs the brain and hand of man. Friendly rivalry follows, which is the spur to industrial improvement, the inspiration to useful invention and to high endeavor in all departments of human activity. It exacts a study of the wants, comforts, and even the whims of the people, and recognizes the efficacy of high quality and low prices to win their favor. The quest for trade is an incentive to men of business to devise, invent, improve and economize in the cost of production. Business life, whether among ourselves, or with other peoples, is ever a sharp struggle for success. It will be none the less in the future.

Without competition we would be clinging to the clumsy and antiquated process of farming and manufacture and the methods of business of long ago, and the twentieth would be no further advanced than the eighteenth century. But though commercial competitors we are, commercial enemies we must not be. The Pan-American Exposition has done its work thoroughly, presenting in its exhibits evidences of the highest skill and illustrating the progress of the human family in the Western Hemisphere. This portion of the earth has no cause for humiliation for the part it has performed in the march of civilization. It has not accomplished everything; far from it. It has simply done its best, and without vanity or boastfulness, and recognizing the manifold achievements of others it invites the friendly rivalry of all the powers in the peaceful pursuits of trade and commerce, and will cooperate with all in advancing the highest and best interests of humanity. The wisdom and energy of all the nations are none too great for the world work. The success of art, science, industry and invention is an international asset and a common glory.

After all, how near one to the other is every part of the world. Modern inventions have brought into close relation widely separated peoples and make them better acquainted. Geographic and political divisions will continue to exist, but distances have been effaced. Swift ships and fast trains are becoming cosmopolitan. They invade fields which a few years ago were impenetrable. The world's products are exchanged as never before and with increasing transportation facilities come increasing knowledge and larger trade. Prices are fixed with mathematical precision by supply and demand. The world's selling prices are regulated by market and crop reports. We travel greater distances in a shorter space of time and with more ease than was ever dreamed of by the fathers. Isolation is no longer possible or desirable. The same important news is read, though in different languages, the same day in all Christendom.

The telegraph keeps us advised of what is occurring everywhere, and the Press foreshadows, with more or less accuracy, the plans and purposes of the nations. Market prices of products and of securities are hourly known in every commercial mart, and the investments of the people extend beyond their own national boundaries into the remotest parts of the earth. Vast transactions are conducted and international exchanges are made by the tick of the cable. Every event of interest is immediately bulletined. The quick gathering and transmission of news, like rapid transit, are of recent origin, and are only made possible by the genius of the inventor and the courage of the investor. It took a special messenger of the government, with every facility known at the time for rapid travel, nineteen days to go from the City of Washington to New Orleans with a message to General Jackson that the war with England had ceased and a treaty of peace had been signed. How different now!...

At the beginning of the nineteenth century there was not a mile of steam railroad on the globe; now there are enough miles to make its circuit many times. Then there was not a line of electric telegraph; now we have a vast mileage traversing all lands and seas. God and man have linked the nations together. No nation can longer be indifferent to any other. And as we are brought more and more in touch with each other, the less occasion is there for misunderstandings, and the stronger the disposition, when we have differences, to adjust them in the court of arbitration, which is the noblest forum for the settlement of international disputes....

We have a vast and intricate business, built up through years of toil and struggle in which every part of the country has its stake, which will not permit of either neglect or of undue selfishness. No narrow, sordid policy will subserve it. The greatest skill and wisdom on the part of manufacturers and producers will be required to hold and increase it. Our industrial enterprises, which have grown to such great proportions, affect the homes and occupations of the people and the welfare of the country. Our capacity to produce has developed so enormously and our products have so multiplied that the problem of more markets requires our urgent and immediate attention. Only a broad and enlightened policy will keep what we have. No other policy will get more. In these times of marvelous business energy and gain we ought to be looking to the future, strengthening the weak places in our industrial and commercial systems, that we may be ready for any storm or strain.

By sensible trade arrangements which will not interrupt our home production we shall extend the outlets for our increasing surplus. A system which provides a mutual exchange of commodities is manifestly essential to the continued and healthful growth of our export trade. We must not repose in the fancied security that we can for ever sell everything and buy little or nothing. If such a thing were possible it would not be best for us or for those with whom we deal. We should take from our customers such of their products as we can use without harm to our industries and labor. Reciprocity is the natural outgrowth of our wonderful industrial development under the domestic policy now firmly established.

What we produce beyond our domestic consumption must have a vent abroad. The excess must be relieved through a foreign outlet, and we should sell everywhere we can and buy wherever the buying will enlarge our sales and productions, and thereby make a greater demand for home labor.

The period of exclusiveness is past. The expansion of our trade and commerce is the pressing problem. Commercial wars are unprofitable. A policy of good will and friendly trade relations will prevent reprisals. Reciprocity treaties are in harmony with the spirit of the times; measures of retaliation are not....

Who can tell the new thoughts that have been awakened, the ambitions fired and the high achievements that will be wrought through this Exposition?

Gentlemen, let us ever remember that our interest is in concord, not conflict; and that our real eminence rests in the victories of peace, not those of war. We hope that all who are represented here may be moved to higher and nobler efforts for their own and the world's good, and that out of this city may come not only greater commerce and trade for us all, but, more essential than these, relations of mutual respect, confidence and friendship which will deepen and endure. Our earnest prayer is that God will graciously vouchsafe prosperity, happiness and peace to all our neighbors, and like blessings to all the peoples and powers of earth.

Glossary

bulletined	recorded in written form
Christendom	the entire Christianized world, comprising primarily Europe and nations founded elsewhere by descendants of Europeans
Exposition	a public exhibition, displaying technological and other achievements of a given place and time
quicken	encourage
reciprocity treaties	agreements beneficial to all participants
tick of the cable	the transmission of messages in Morse code over telegraph wires

James Monroe (Library of Congress)

JAMES MONROE   1758–1831

Fifth President of the United States

Featured Documents
- ◆ Address to the National Convention of France (1794)
- ◆ Second Annual Message to Congress (1818)
- ◆ Second Inaugural Address (1821)
- ◆ Seventh Annual Message to Congress (1823)
- ◆ Special Message to the Senate on the Slave Trade Convention with Great Britain (1824)

Overview

James Monroe, the nation's fifth president (1817–1825), was a complex thinker whose reasoning tended to be dense. As a consequence, his public writings—as a U.S. senator, governor of Virginia, ambassador to France and Great Britain, U.S. secretary of war and secretary of state, and president—require careful reading. His thoughts on the Constitution were typical. He attended the Constitutional Convention, and he was unhappy with the way some of its deliberations had gone. At the time, he was identified as an Antifederalist—that is, as someone who objected to a national government with powers stronger than those of the individual states. But as was typical for him, he did not fit in very well with all the Antifederalist views, and he eventually played an important role in persuading Virginia to ratify the Constitution. Deeply troubling for him was the absence of a bill of rights; he wanted the Constitution to specifically protect the civil liberties of individual citizens. Further, he thought that by giving each state an identical number of senators, the Senate would too often deadlock the government. He wanted the number of senators to be apportioned by population, somewhat like the House of Representatives. He objected to senators being chosen by state legislatures; instead, he wanted senators to be elected by a direct vote of the people to make them more beholden to the best interests of the people of their states. In addition, he thought that the president of the United States should be chosen by a direct popular vote.

On the other hand, Monroe disagreed with most Antifederalists about the power of the presidency. Whereas most Antifederalists wanted a weak chief executive, Monroe approved of giving the president veto power. He hoped that a strong chief executive would be able to mediate among the nation's opposing factions and thereby prevent paralysis of the government. Most Antifederalists would have disagreed with his belief that control of state militias should be given to the federal government. He thought that the United States would better respond to crises if the militias could be universally mobilized and coordinated in national defense.

Subtleties in his wording when discussing America and Americans might escape many modern readers, but they would have been noticed by most of his audience in his own day. He was careful to refer to the United States of America as a "compact" and to use plural verbs and pronouns when referring to the United States, as in the "United States are." The word *compact*, in particular, was associated with states' rights advocates, who opposed the supremacy of federal laws over the laws of individual states; states' rights advocates usually wanted to protect the institution of slavery. But it would be an error to believe that Monroe was of a mind with his secretary of war, John C. Calhoun. Calhoun was a strong supporter of states' rights and slavery who made the word *compact* the essence of his argument that the United States could be broken apart anytime a state violated the Constitution, because the Constitution represented a compact that became invalid whenever a state did not abide by it. To Calhoun's thinking, the compact was violated whenever free states refused to return escaped slaves to slave states.

Monroe was not party to that thinking. He found slavery distressing, even calling the trading of slaves a crime. As governor of Virginia, he put down a slave rebellion and was saddened when some of the rebellious slaves were executed. He joined many others in searching for a way to remove dangerous slaves without executing them. One idea was to send slaves to western territories to settle them as emancipated people. Another was to sell rebellious slaves to Caribbean islands, where slavery was practiced. One plan that Monroe seemed to favor was to emancipate all slaves by having the federal government buy them. During his presidency, Monroe entertained the idea of pushing for emancipation but let the idea die because America could not afford to pay the owners for their slaves. In any case, he lent much of his public influence to the freeing of slaves and their resettling in Africa in what became the nation of Liberia.

Explanation and Analysis of Documents

Monroe devoted his life to finding practical solutions to political and social problems. His writing reflects this: It is much more focused on solving and anticipating problems than it is on political theory. During the Revolutionary War, both George Washington and Thomas Jefferson valued

Time Line

1758
- **April 28**
  James Monroe was born in Westmoreland County, Virginia.

1783–1786
- Monroe serves in the Continental Congress, representing Virginia.

1790
- **November 9**
  Monroe is elected to the U.S. Senate and serves until 1794.

1794
- **July 31**
  Monroe becomes ambassador to France, a post he holds until 1796.
- **August 14**
  Monroe delivers his momentous address to the National Convention of France, in which he assures the French that the United States is an ally.

1799
- **December 19**
  Monroe becomes governor of Virginia, serving until 1802.

1803
- **July 18**
  Monroe is named ambassador to Great Britain, a post he fills until 1807.

1811
- **January 16**
  Monroe is again elected governor of Virginia but resigns in April of that year.
- **April 2**
  Monroe is named U.S. secretary of state.

1814
- **September 27**
  Monroe becomes secretary of war; he serves as acting secretary of state until March 1815 and then resumes position as actual secretary of state until 1817.

Monroe for his levelheadedness and his ability to keep his composure under stress. At the same time, he was an idealist. He believed that the American experiment in democracy would succeed where other such efforts had failed and that one of America's great gifts to the world would be its example of rule deriving from the public rather than from overlords. Thus he was a statesman who combined idealism about human liberty with a devotion to making his ideals succeed in the real world. For him, his writings served this practical purpose.

◆ Address to the National Convention of France

On August 14, 1794, Monroe addressed the National Convention, the French legislative body. This was a momentous event, when the representative of one fledgling democracy spoke to the leaders of a nation that, like America, had just thrown off monarchal rule. When Monroe arrived in France as America's new minister plenipotentiary (ambassador), he faced significant dangers. The previous American ambassador had alienated French leaders, and Americans' criticisms of the French Revolution were well known to the French. Maximilien de Robespierre had been deposed from leadership of the French government only recently. President George Washington had gone through a number of choices for ambassador, all of whom had refused the appointment to France. Washington was looking for someone who would not rock the boat of American diplomacy. Eventually he and State Department secretary Edmund Jennings Randolph settled on Monroe because they thought Monroe was a moderate who would not be a controversial choice and because he was known to like the French and therefore might be favorably received by them. His instructions from Randolph, however, were vague and contradictory, so Monroe defined his mission as that of renewing an alliance between France and the United States. When the executive branch of the French government refused to recognize him as America's ambassador, he asked to speak to the French legislature, the National Convention. He was outspokenly in favor of the French Revolution, and a crowd outside the National Convention's meeting welcomed him warmly.

With limited time to write his speech, Monroe offered a direct statement of principles that plainly established his own views on liberty, the French Revolution, and the relationship between France and America. He opens by pressing the point that he was the ambassador of the United States and, by implication, that he should be accepted as such. His phrase "their ally, the United States of America," is carefully chosen and conveys the premise that will underlie his dealings with France—that the two nations are properly to be thought of as diplomatic and economic allies, sharing the "same interest" and the "same principles." It was one of his cherished beliefs that democracies should join together to protect and even promote democratic revolutions, and he makes the point that as liberated nations, France and the United States should bind themselves to each other, for both were based on the principle of the "equal and unalienable rights of men." This principle was fundamental to Monroe's thinking on foreign policy throughout his life and would give rise to the Monroe Doctrine, which derived in part from Monroe's belief that the newly liberated former colonies of Spain and Portugal in Latin America were themselves natural allies of the United States.

Monroe goes on to emphasize the "affection" of the people of the United States for France, which aided America in its own recent revolution. Then, in the final paragraph, he illustrates the thinking that got him into trouble at home and nearly resulted in his disgrace. In it, he asserts his personal approval of the French Republic. The U.S. government had an ambassador in London, negotiating a complex treaty intended to end British seizure of American sailors and protect American trade with Great Britain. Monroe's remarks seemed likely to antagonize the British, who were vehement enemies of the new French government. Monroe had not been fully informed about the negotiations in London and had no way of knowing that he was saying anything contrary to national policy.

The result, however, was that he was welcomed in France and became a celebrity there. He was able to persuade the French government to lift most of it restrictions on American trade and to allow American merchant ships to carry on trade between France and Great Britain. He expresses the wish that in the steps he is taking he will "merit the approbation" of both France and his home country. In the United States, however, he seemed to many people to have disobeyed the State Department. Monroe's speech, though, was an extraordinary step that had far-reaching repercussions. It helped end a stalemate in the diplomatic relations between France and the United States and almost ended Monroe's political career.

◆ **Second Annual Message to Congress**

Most of Monroe's second annual message to Congress, distributed on November 16, 1818, focuses on one of the major controversies of Monroe's presidency, the invasion and occupation of Florida by American forces led by Major General Andrew Jackson. It was an uncomfortable problem for Monroe, who preferred to be viewed as a peacemaker but who saw Jackson's situation as similar to the one he himself had been in when he was ambassador to France. Many American politicians considered Jackson's invasion of East Florida (at the time the area consisted of East and West Florida) as a violation of international law, and Jackson was accused by some of having exceeded his orders. Others thought that Monroe had given Jackson orders to invade East Florida and should admit it. Jackson himself was angry at Monroe because Monroe's orders had been vaguely worded: They seemed to imply that Jackson was to invade and occupy East Florida while giving Monroe the leeway to claim that he had never said outright that Jackson was to do so. The focus of Monroe's second annual message to Congress is on the Florida affair. Monroe had rejected Great Britain's offer to mediate between Spain and the United States, and in his message to Congress he explains why.

Monroe's message is one of his most artfully phrased documents. It lays out the danger in allowing the Floridas

Time Line

1817	■ **March 4** Monroe becomes president of the United States, serving until 1825.
1818	■ **November 16** Monroe's second annual message is distributed to Congress.
1821	■ **March 4** Monroe delivers his second inaugural address.
1823	■ Monroe begins a policy of recognizing the governments of former Spanish colonies in the Americas. ■ **December 2** Monroe sends his seventh annual message to Congress; it contains the Principles of 1823, which later became known as the Monroe Doctrine.
1824	■ **May 21** Monroe sends a special message to the Senate on the slave trade convention with Great Britain.
1831	■ **July 4** Monroe dies in New York City.

to be used by "adventurers," "fugitives," and pirates and suggests that the Seminole Indians were encouraged to wage war on the United States by outsiders hoping to profit from the Seminoles' actions. He writes: "It is to the interference of some of these adventurers, in misrepresenting the claims and titles of the Indians to land and in practicing on their savage propensities, that the Seminole war is principally to be traced." He characterizes Florida as a "theater of every species of lawless adventure." He states that an entire island had been given over to pirates. He makes reference to Amelia Island, which lies along the east coast of Florida and was used by smugglers and slave traders as an unofficial port. In 1817 an army of adventurers assembled to invade the island and use it as a launching pad for an invasion of Florida; while the latter invasion came to naught, Amelia Island was, in fact, overrun by a band of pirates.

Monroe expresses indignation that Spain failed to make "indemnity to our citizens" for the "spoliation" suffered at the hands of the criminals Spain had been unable to control and, indeed, tolerated. At the same time, Monroe manages to make Spain look only partly responsible for the problems in the Floridas, noting that "throughout the whole of those Provinces to which the Spanish title extends the Government of Spain has scarcely been felt." He speaks as though Spain were a victim of evil forces and says that America was doing Spain a favor by invading East Florida. His phrase "imaginary line which separates Florida from the United States" is difficult to justify, given that the line was a national border. For an army to cross such lines would be an act of war; Monroe insists, however, that acts of war occurred when the Seminoles and adventurers began crossing into the United States to raid and loot. The border was "imaginary" because the Seminoles did not recognize it as a limit on their territory and because it was constantly being crossed by people who lived in East Florida.

In the final paragraph, Monroe deftly deals with the issue of Jackson's behavior and the nature of the orders Monroe had issued to Jackson. He subtly shifts the blame back onto Spain and its officers in Florida, who, in Monroe's view, had inflamed the situation. He accuses the Spanish of violating the terms of a 1795 treaty and then argues that Jackson, in effect, had no choice but to carry out an invasion of Florida. Monroe then dismisses the matter by promising Congress that all documents related to the affair will be laid before it.

◆ Second Inaugural Address

Monroe's second inaugural address is important for the light it casts on Monroe's thinking midway through his presidency. He had managed to maneuver the United States through a minefield of foreign problems, especially the Florida affair, which could have brought war between the United States and European countries. Great Britain loomed as a potential antagonist, and Monroe was alert to the possibility of Great Britain's launching a war against the United States if the United States appeared to be aiding rebellious Spanish and Portuguese colonies. Great Britain would do so to secure for itself trade advantages that could be lost if the United States became an ally of the former colonies. Monroe was not yet ready to publicly assert America's dominance in the New World, so he focuses in his address mostly on domestic matters.

The excerpt begins with Monroe's comments on Native Americans, which were among the most sympathetic of those of American leaders of his era. Like most Americans of the time, he assumed that the imposition of American rule would make Native American lives better, and he looked forward, he says, to a time when the nation could provide the Indians with "civil government," "education of their children," and "instruction in the arts of husbandry." He reveals an unusually acute understanding of their difficult position, caught between their own aspirations and those of Americans migrating westward, and he acknowledges that the "dense population" of settlers "has constantly driven them back, with almost the total sacrifice of the

lands which they have been compelled to abandon." His identification of the pressures on Native Americans is a significant statement in the history of relations between the United States and Native American tribes. He goes on to urge the Congress to devise some plan that will work to the benefit of Native Americans.

Monroe goes on to function partly as a cheerleader: He wanted Americans to realize that their lives were improving, and he calls attention to how well the American experiment in republican rule was working. He states that the nation had grown in strength and that "self-government" had enabled the young nation to solve internal problems. He celebrates America's representative democracy, which had allowed the nation to avoid the "defects" that undermined earlier republics, particularly by creating one social order—the people—that controlled the reins of government. He observes that the federal and state governments had largely avoided conflict, and he looks forward to a time when "our system will...attain the highest degree of perfection of which human institutions are capable." In the final paragraph of the excerpt, he takes note of the nation's extraordinary growth, both geographically (through, for example, the Louisiana Purchase, made during the administration of Thomas Jefferson, and the accession of Florida) and in population. He congratulates the nation for simultaneously being a "great power" and one "with an utter incapacity to oppress the people."

◆ Seventh Annual Message to Congress

Monroe's statements on the new nations of the Americas are those for which he is presently best known, and he takes up the issue in his seventh annual message to Congress in 1823. He had been working on the ideas he presented in this message to Congress at least as far back as when he was secretary of state. He believed that freely elected governments should unite to help one another. He envisioned a world in which everybody would eventually benefit from the civil liberties that were fundamental to the United States. Almost from the moment he took office as president, he began working with his cabinet on what should be done to aid the former colonies of the Americas as they emerged as independent nations. In this, his next-to-last annual message to Congress, he hoped to clarify relations between the powers of the Old World and the nations of the New World and to point to the direction he believed America should take in the future.

In the excerpt presented here, Monroe begins by striking a conciliatory note. He makes reference to the governments of Russia and Great Britain and indicates that the United States wanted to maintain "amicable" negotiations and "friendly" proceedings with regard to territories in the Americas controlled by those nations—in the case of Russia, the West Coast down from Alaska, and in the case of Britain, the Oregon Territory. These territories, he believed, would inevitably form part of the nation's westward expansion, and Monroe did not want foreign influence to stand in the way of that expansion. He makes his position on the matter clear when he says, "that the American continents, by the free and independent condition which they have assumed and maintain, are henceforth not to be considered as subjects for future colonization by any European powers."

In the next paragraph, Monroe adopts a similar rhetorical tactic. He begins with a conciliatory note, mentioning the close ties of blood and history that linked Europe with the United States, and he makes reference to the fact that Americans took great interest in developments in Europe. Europe, with its complex ties of alliance, was in an unsettled state and continued to try to extend its colonial reach to the Americas. Monroe again shifts gears to make his position clear: "We should consider any attempt on their part to extend their system to any portion of this hemisphere as dangerous to our peace and safety." In the final paragraph of the excerpt, Monroe reassures the European powers that America had no wish to interfere with their internal affairs and that it was America's goal "to cultivate friendly relations" with the nation's of Europe "and to preserve those relations by a frank, firm, and manly policy, meeting in all instances the just claims of every power, submitting to injuries from none."

The matter was a tricky one because a diplomatic misstep could bring war with Great Britain, France, or Spain, each of which wanted to control the riches that trade with the new nations would bring. Of particular concern to Monroe was the possibility that some European powers would try to press the new nations back into colonial status. Monroe wanted to use America's power to shield the new nations of the New World from the military aggression of overseas powers.

In the matter of new Latin American nations, Monroe was prepared to display American military power. He makes clear in his address that the America of 1823 was not the same as that of 1812, when Great Britain had invaded the United States, burning down villages and looting Washington, D.C. He suggests that America was now an even greater power than the one that ultimately drove the British from American soil. In 1823 Monroe believed he could fearlessly state America's intention to protect the new nations of his hemisphere and persuade the European colonial powers to take him and America seriously. His blunt declaration that the United States would not allow any new colonies to be established in the Americas was called the Principles of 1823 at the time and for many years after. It is now known as the Monroe Doctrine.

◆ **Special Message to the Senate on the Slave Trade Convention with Great Britain**

Slavery was the nation's foremost social issue and one with which every early American president had to deal. For most of his life, Monroe was in an acutely uncomfortable position on the issue: He came from Virginia, a state where slavery was viewed by many as essential to their economic and political prosperity. On the other hand, Monroe's views on slavery were severe: If he could end slavery in the United States, he would. But his best hope of ending slavery—by having the government buy slaves from their owners—was too expensive. Besides, he and many others worried that some states would become entirely black if slaves were freed. Moreover, violent conflict between the black states and other states would result. He took a view more hopeful than realistic—that slave owning would become diffused through the nation, lose its centers of support in the slave states, and die out because of lack of interest.

As president Monroe could take decisive action through foreign diplomacy. The goal was not to end slavery per se but to outlaw the trading in slaves, which would allow slavery to die a natural death. Monroe begins his message by rejecting the methods advocated by the European nations that had already outlawed the slave trade. This method consisted of allowing the crews of ships to board and search vessels suspected of being used to transport slaves. Guilty parties would then be tried by special tribunals. Monroe argues, however, that this method is "repugnant to the feelings of the nation and a dangerous tendency." In time of peace, no nation should be allowed to interdict the vessels of another nation.

Monroe, then offers a different solution. He proposes that engaging in the slave trade should be regarded as an act of piracy and therefore a violation of the law. He made this proposal to Great Britain and reports with pleasure that Great Britain accepted it. He is also pleased to report that the British Parliament had taken a step similar to that which the U.S. Congress has taken—declaring the slave trade an act of piracy—and he expresses hope that Great Britain would press a similar proposal on the other nations of Europe. Monroe concludes, then, that "the crime will then be universally proscribed as piracy, and the traffic be suppressed forever."

The Slave Trade Convention with Great Britain was an action Monroe apparently regarded with pride. As he points out, there were already a few treaties among European nations limiting the international trade in Africans taken to become slaves, but he tried for a solution that would pragmatically end the trade altogether. He believed this required a treaty to which the signatories could commit themselves without qualms. His purpose in this document is not only to report the progress of negotiations with Great Britain but also to urge the U.S. Congress to ratify the convention. Despite his well-reasoned explanation of his rationale for the convention, Congress refused to ratify it.

Impact and Legacy

By the time Monroe became president, he was a legendary figure, regarded by many Americans as one of the titans who led America out of oppression and into a new kind of society in which power came from the bottom up rather than the top down, from average citizens instead of potentates or dictators. He was one of America's most practical political thinkers. He was not a genius in many fields—as were Thomas Jefferson and Benjamin Franklin—but he was brilliant in his own realm of political give-and-take. As a political leader, he was a conscientious worker who took the day-to-day operations of his offices seriously. For this

"*I well know that whilst I pursue the dictates of my own heart in wishing the liberty and happiness of the French nation, and which I most sincerely do, I speak the sentiments of my own Country; and that by doing everything in my power to preserve and perpetuate the harmony so happily subsisting at present between the two Republics, I shall promote the interest of both.*"

(Address to the National Convention)

"*The right of self defense never ceases. It is among the most sacred, and alike necessary to nations and to individuals, and whether the attack be made by Spain herself or by those who abuse her power, its obligation is not the less strong.*"

(Second Annual Message to Congress)

"*In this great nation there is but one order, that of the people, whose power, by a peculiarly happy improvement of the representative principle, is transferred from them, without impairing in the slightest degree their sovereignty, to bodies of their own creation, and to persons elected by themselves, in the full extent necessary for all the purposes of free, enlightened and efficient government. The whole system is elective, the complete sovereignty being in the people, and every officer in every department deriving his authority from and being responsible to them for his conduct.*"

(Second Inaugural Address)

"*The American continents, by the free and independent condition which they have assumed and maintain, are henceforth not to be considered as subjects for future colonization by any European powers.*"

(Seventh Annual Message to Congress)

"*The crime [the slave trade] will then be universally proscribed as piracy, and the traffic be suppressed forever.*"

(Special Message to the Senate on the Slave Trade Convention with Great Britain) reason, he transformed both the State Department and War Department into agencies that were more efficient than before he led them and more answerable to Congress and the president. Where political infighting had ruled, he tried to infuse a sense of professionalism and a devotion to the good of the nation.

Monroe managed to create an era of cooperation among politicians of differing social views and give the nation a sense of direction into a future as he saw it: one of limitless possibilities for Americans and for the world. He put an end to the warfare with East Florida and secured America's southern border, in the process opening up new avenues for trade. During his administration, the Mississippi River became America's river, creating a powerful source of trade within the states and territories. He helped secure a western passage for the United States to the Pacific Coast and averted war with Great Britain over western territories. He may always be remembered for his Monroe Doctrine, which has become a fundamental part of American law and foreign policy. Monroe intended it to be a forthright "hands off" declaration with regard to the new nations of the Americas, most of which were experimenting with popular rule. It would be no exaggeration to state that it was under the administration of James Monroe that the United States began its journey, which culminated in the twentieth century, from a small, fledgling nation to a world power.

Key Sources

Most of the most informative of Monroe's writings are gathered in *The Political Writings of James Monroe*, edited by James P. Lucier (2001); its texts and much of the commentary on individual works are taken from Alexander Hamilton's edition of Monroe's writings. The standard edition of Monroe's works is still the seven-volume *The Writings of James Monroe*, edited by Stanislaus Hamilton (1898–1903); volumes 2 through 7 are available online (http://www.archive.org/search.php?query=Stanislaus%20Hamilton). Monroe's presidential inaugural addresses and his seventh message to Congress are available online at the Web site of the Miller Center of Public Affairs of the University of Virginia (http://millercenter.org/scripps/archive/speeches/detail).

Further Reading

■ Articles

Ammon, Harry. "Agricola versus Aristides: James Monroe, John Marshall, and the Genet Affair in Virginia." *Virginia Magazine of History and Biography* 74 (July 1966): 312–320.

Schoenherr, Steven E., and Iris H. W. Engelstrand. "James Monroe, Friend of the West." *Journal of the West* 31 (July 1992): 20–26.

Questions for Further Study

1. In the decades following the American Revolution, the United States maintained a wary relationship with Europe—in particular, with England, France, and to a lesser extent Spain. Trace the development of this relationship, using Monroe's address to the Convention of France, his seventh annual message to Congress, and the special message to the Senate on the slave trade convention with Great Britain, along with Andrew Jackson's Proclamation Regarding the Opening of U.S. Ports to British Vessels, Alexander Hamilton's "Against an Alliance with France" and his letter to Harrison Otis Gray on westward expansion, and John Jay's draft of the Proclamation of Neutrality.

2. Similarly, trace the development of America's attitudes to Native Americans in the early decades of the nation as they are reflected in documents from Thomas Jefferson (second inaugural address), Andrew Jackson (second annual message to Congress), Sam Houston (his inaugural address to the Texas Congress and his speech opposing the Kansas-Nebraska Act), and Monroe (second annual message to Congress and second inaugural address).

3. Historians regard James Monroe as more of a practical problem solver than as a deep political thinker interested in the theory of government. To what extent do the documents suggest that Monroe was a practical problem solver? Cite specific examples.

4. Early American leaders had to deal with the possibilities and challenges involved in the westward expansion of the United States. How did Monroe in his seventh annual message to Congress, Thomas Jefferson in his second inaugural address, Andrew Jackson in his second annual message to Congress, and Hamilton in his letter to Harrison Otis Gray on westward expansion deal with those possibilities and challenges?

■ Books

Ammon, Harry. *James Monroe: The Quest for National Identity.* Charlottesville: University of Virginia Press, 1990.

Cunningham, Noble E., Jr. *The Presidency of James Monroe.* Lawrence: University Press of Kansas, 1996.

Howe, Daniel Walker. *What Hath God Wrought: The Transformation of America, 1815–1848.* New York: Oxford University Press, 2007.

■ Web Sites

"Biography of James Monroe." The White House Web site.
   http://www.whitehouse.gov/history/presidents/jm5.html.

"Monroe, James." Biographical Directory of the United States Congress Web site.
   http://bioguide.congress.gov/scripts/biodisplay.pl?index=M000 858.

—Kirk H. Beetz and Michael J. O'Neal

ADDRESS TO THE NATIONAL CONVENTION OF FRANCE (1794)

Citizens, President and Representatives of the French People: My admission into this Assembly, in the presence of the French Nation (for all the citizens of France are represented here) to be recognized as the Representative of the American Republic, impresses me with a degree of sensibility which I cannot express. I consider it as a new proof of that friendship and regard which the French Nation has always shewn to their ally, the United States of America.

Republics should approach near to each other. In many respects they all have the same interest. But this is more especially the case with the American and French Republics: their governments are similar; they both cherish the same principles and rest on the same basis, the equal and unalienable rights of men. The recollection too of common dangers and difficulties will increase their harmony, and cement their union. America had her day of oppression, difficulty and war, but her sons were virtuous and brave and the storm which long clouded her political horizon has passed and left them in the enjoyment of peace, liberty and independence. France our ally and our friend and who aided in the contest, has now embarked in the same noble career; and I am happy to add that whilst the fortitude, magnanimity and heroic valor of her troops, command the admiration and applause of the astonished world, the wisdom and firmness of her councils unite equally in securing the happiest result.

America is not an unfeeling spectator of your affairs in the present crisis. I lay before you in the declarations of every department of our Government, declarations which are founded in the affection of the citizens at large, the most decided proof of her sincere attachment to the liberty, prosperity and happiness of the French Republic. Each branch of Congress, according to the course of proceedings there, has requested the president to make this known to you in its behalf; and in fulfilling the desires of those branches I am instructed to declare to you that he has expressed his own.

In discharging the duties of the office which I am now called on to execute, I promise myself the highest satisfaction; because I well know that whilst I pursue the dictates of my own heart in wishing the liberty and happiness of the French nation, and which I most sincerely do, I speak the sentiments of my own Country; and that by doing everything in my power to preserve and perpetuate the harmony so happily subsisting at present between the two Republics, I shall promote the interest of both. To this great object therefore all my efforts will be directed. If I shall be so fortunate as to succeed in such manner as to merit the approbation of both Republics I shall deem it the happiest event of my life, and return hereafter with a consolation, which those who mean well and have served the cause of liberty alone can feel.

Glossary

shewn	antique spelling of "shown"
unalienable	not alienable; incapable of being taken away

SECOND ANNUAL MESSAGE TO CONGRESS (1818)

Events have occurred which clearly prove the ill effect of the policy which that Government has so long pursued on the friendly relations of the two countries, which it is presumed is at least of as much importance to Spain as to the United States to maintain. A state of things has existed in the Floridas the tendency of which has been obvious to all who have paid the slightest attention to the progress of affairs in that quarter. Throughout the whole of those Provinces to which the Spanish title extends the Government of Spain has scarcely been felt. Its authority has been confined almost exclusively to the walls of Pensacola and St. Augustine, within which only small garrisons have been maintained. Adventurers from every country, fugitives from justice, and absconding slaves have found an asylum there. Several tribes of Indians, strong in the numbers of their warriors, remarkable for their ferocity, and whose settlements extend to our limits, inhabit those Provinces. These different hordes of people, connected together, disregarding on the one side the authority of Spain, and protected on the other by an imaginary line which separates Florida from the United States, have violated our laws prohibiting the introduction of slaves, have practiced various frauds on our revenue, and committed every kind of outrage on our peaceable citizens which their proximity to us enabled them to perpetrate. The invasion of Amelia Island last year by a small band of adventurers, not exceeding 150 in number, who wrested it from the inconsiderable Spanish force stationed there, and held it several months, during which a single feeble effort only was made to recover it, which failed, clearly proves how completely extinct the Spanish authority had become, as the conduct of those adventurers while in possession of the island as distinctly shows the pernicious purposes for which their combination had been formed.

This country had, in fact, become the theater of every species of lawless adventure. With little population of its own, the Spanish authority almost extinct, and the colonial governments in a state of revolution, having no pretension to it, and sufficiently employed in their own concerns, it was in great measure derelict, and the object of cupidity to every adventurer. A system of buccaneering was rapidly organizing over it which menaced in its consequences the lawful commerce of every nation, and

particularly the United States, while it presented a temptation to every people, on whose seduction its success principally depended. In regard to the United States, the pernicious effect of this unlawful combination was not confined to the ocean; the Indian tribes have constituted the effective force in Florida. With these tribes these adventurers had formed at an early period a connection with a view to avail themselves of that force to promote their own projects of accumulation and aggrandizement. It is to the interference of some of these adventurers, in misrepresenting the claims and titles of the Indians to land and in practicing on their savage propensities, that the Seminole war is principally to be traced. Men who thus connect themselves with savage communities and stimulate them to war, which is always attended on their part with acts of barbarity the most shocking, deserve to be viewed in a worse light than the savages. They would certainly have no claim to an immunity from the punishment which, according to the rules of warfare practiced by the savages, might justly be inflicted on the savages themselves.

If the embarrassments of Spain prevented her from making an indemnity to our citizens for so long a time from her treasury for their losses by spoliation and otherwise, it was always in her power to have provided it by the cession of this territory. Of this her Government has been repeatedly apprised, and the cession was the more to have been anticipated as Spain must have known that in ceding it she would likewise relieve herself from the important obligation secured by the treaty of 1795 and all other compromitments respecting it. If the United States, from consideration of these embarrassments, declined pressing their claims in a spirit of hostility, the motive ought at least to have been duly appreciated by the Government of Spain. It is well known to her Government that other powers have made to the United States an indemnity for like losses sustained by their citizens at the same epoch.

There is nevertheless a limit beyond which this spirit of amity and forbearance can in no instance be justified. If it was proper to rely on amicable negotiation for an indemnity for losses, it would not have been so to have permitted the inability of Spain to fulfill her engagements and to sustain her authority in the Floridas to be perverted by foreign adventurers and savages to purposes so destructive to the lives of our fellow citizens and the highest interests of the United States. The right of self defense never ceases. It is among the most sacred, and alike necessary to nations and to individuals, and whether the attack be made by Spain herself or by those who abuse her power, its obligation is not the less strong. The invaders of Amelia Island had assumed a popular and respected title under which they might approach and wound us. As their object was distinctly seen, and the duty imposed on the Executive by an existing law was profoundly felt, that mask was not permitted to protect them. It was thought incumbent on the United States to suppress the establishment, and it was accordingly done. The combination in Florida for the unlawful purposes stated, the acts perpetrated by that combination, and, above all, the incitement of the Indians to massacre our fellow citizens of every age and of both sexes, merited a like treatment and received it. In pursuing these savages to an imaginary line in the woods it would have been the height of folly to have suffered that line to protect them. Had that been done the war could never cease. Even if the territory had been exclusively that of Spain and her power complete over it, we had a right by the law of nations to follow the enemy on it and to subdue him there. But the territory belonged, in a certain sense at least, to the savage enemy who inhabited it; the power of Spain had ceased to exist over it, and protection was sought under her title by those who had committed on our citizens hostilities which she was bound by treaty to have prevented, but had not the power to prevent. To have stopped at that line would have given new encouragement to these savages and new vigor to the whole combination existing there in the prosecution of all its pernicious purposes....

In authorizing Major-General Jackson to enter Florida in pursuit of the Seminoles care was taken not to encroach on the rights of Spain. I regret to have to add that in executing this order facts were disclosed respecting the conduct of the officers of Spain in authority there in encouraging the war, furnishing munitions of war and other supplies to carry it on, and in other acts not less marked which evinced their participation in the hostile purposes of that combination and justified the confidence with which it inspired the savages that by those officers they would be protected. A conduct so incompatible with the friendly relations existing between the two countries, particularly with the positive obligations of the 5th article of the treaty of 1795, by which Spain was bound to restrain, even by force, those savages from acts of hostility against the United States, could not fail to excite surprise. The commanding general was convinced that he should fail in his object, that he should in effect accomplish nothing, if he did not deprive those savages of the resource on which they had calculated and of the protection on which they had relied in making the war. As all the documents relating to this occurrence will be laid before Congress, it is not necessary to enter into further detail respecting it.

Glossary

absconding	escaping
aggrandizement	the act of increasing prestige, power, or wealth
cession	the act of ceding, relinquishing, or giving up
compromitments	acts of abiding by the decision of a judge or arbiter
indemnity	recompense, repayment
Major-General ackson	General Andrew Jackson, leader of U.S. forces during the Seminole War, military governor of Florida, and later president of the United States
Seminole war	conflict between U.S. forces and the Seminole Indian tribe from 1817 to 1818, usually called the First Seminole War to distinguish it from later conflicts
treaty of 1795	variously called Pinckney's Treaty, the Treaty of San Lorenzo, and the Treaty of Madrid, signed on October 27 that year to establish relations between Spain and the United States

SECOND INAUGURAL ADDRESS (1821)

The care of the Indian tribes within our limits has long been an essential part of our system, but, unfortunately, it has not been executed in a manner to accomplish all the objects intended by it. We have treated them as independent nations, without their having any substantial pretensions to that rank. The distinction has flattered their pride, retarded their improvement, and in many instances paved the way to their destruction. The progress of our settlements westward, supported as they are by a dense population, has constantly driven them back, with almost the total sacrifice of the lands which they have been compelled to abandon. They have claims on the magnanimity and, I may add, on the justice of this nation which we must all feel. We should become their real benefactors; we should perform the office of their Great Father, the endearing title which they emphatically give to the Chief Magistrate of our Union. Their sovereignty over vast territories should cease, in lieu of which the right of soil should be secured to each individual and his posterity in competent portions; and for the territory thus ceded by each tribe some reasonable equivalent should be granted, to be vested in permanent funds for the support of civil government over them and for the education of their children, for their instruction in the arts of husbandry, and to provide sustenance for them until they could provide it for themselves. My earnest hope is that Congress will digest some plan, founded on these principles, with such improvements as their wisdom may suggest, and carry it into effect as soon as it may be practicable....

If we turn our attention, fellow-citizens, more immediately to the internal concerns of our country, and more especially to those on which its future welfare depends, we have every reason to anticipate the happiest results. It is now rather more than forty-four years since we declared our independence, and thirty-seven since it was acknowledged. The talents and virtues which were displayed in that great struggle were a sure presage of all that has since followed. A people who were able to surmount in their infant state such great perils would be more competent as they rose into manhood to repel any which they might meet in their progress. Their physical strength would be more adequate to foreign danger, and the practice of self-government, aided by the light of experience, could not fail to produce an effect equal-

ly salutary on all those questions connected with the internal organization. These favorable anticipations have been realized.

In our whole system, national and State, we have shunned all the defects which unceasingly preyed on the vitals and destroyed the ancient Republics. In them there were distinct orders, a nobility and a people, or the people governed in one assembly. Thus, in the one instance there was a perpetual conflict between the orders in society for the ascendency, in which the victory of either terminated in the overthrow of the government and the ruin of the state; in the other, in which the people governed in a body, and whose dominions seldom exceeded the dimensions of a county in one of our States, a tumultuous and disorderly movement permitted only a transitory existence. In this great nation there is but one order, that of the people, whose power, by a peculiarly happy improvement of the representative principle, is transferred from them, without impairing in the slightest degree their sovereignty, to bodies of their own creation, and to persons elected by themselves, in the full extent necessary for all the purposes of free, enlightened and efficient government. The whole system is elective, the complete sovereignty being in the people, and every officer in every department deriving his authority from and being responsible to them for his conduct.

Our career has corresponded with this great outline. Perfection in our organization could not have been expected in the outset either in the National or State Governments or in tracing the line between their respective powers. But no serious conflict has arisen, nor any contest but such as are managed by argument and by a fair appeal to the good sense of the people, and many of the defects which experience had clearly demonstrated in both Governments have been remedied. By steadily pursuing this course in this spirit there is every reason to believe that our system will soon attain the highest degree of perfection of which human institutions are capable, and that the movement in all its branches will exhibit such a degree of order and harmony as to command the admiration and respect of the civilized world.

Our physical attainments have not been less eminent. Twenty-five years ago the river Mississippi was shut up and our Western brethren had no outlet for their commerce. What has been the progress since that time? The river has not only become the property of the United States from its source to the ocean, with all its tributary streams (with the exception of the upper part of the Red River only), but Louisiana, with a fair and liberal boundary on the western side and the Floridas on the eastern, have been ceded to us. The United States now enjoy the complete and uninterrupted sovereignty over the whole territory from St. Croix to the Sabine. New States, settled from among ourselves in this and in other parts, have been admitted into our Union in equal participation in the national sovereignty with the original States. Our population has augmented in an astonishing degree and extended in every direction. We now, fellow-citizens, comprise within our limits the dimensions and faculties of a great power under a Government possessing all the energies of any government ever known to the Old World, with an utter incapacity to oppress the people.

Glossary

Chief Magistrate of our Union	the president
husbandry	farming
presage	an omen, or foretelling
Sabine	a river in Texas and Louisiana that, along a portion of its length, forms the boundary between what would become the two states
St. Croix	a city in the Virgin Islands

SEVENTH ANNUAL MESSAGE TO CONGRESS (1823)

At the proposal of the Russian Imperial Government, made through the minister of the Emperor residing here, a full power and instructions have been transmitted to the minister of the United States at St. Petersburg to arrange by amicable negotiation the respective rights and interests of the two nations on the northwest coast of this continent. A similar proposal had been made by His Imperial Majesty to the Government of Great Britain, which has likewise been acceded to. The Government of the United States has been desirous by this friendly proceeding of manifesting the great value which they have invariably attached to the friendship of the Emperor and their solicitude to cultivate the best understanding with his Government. In the discussions to which this interest has given rise and in the arrangements by which they may terminate the occasion has been judged proper for asserting, as a principle in which the rights and interests of the United States are involved, that the American continents, by the free and independent condition which they have assumed and maintain, are henceforth not to be considered as subjects for future colonization by any European powers....

It was stated at the commencement of the last session that a great effort was then making in Spain and Portugal to improve the condition of the people of those countries, and that it appeared to be conducted with extraordinary moderation. It need scarcely be remarked that the result has been so far very different from what was then anticipated. Of events in that quarter of the globe, with which we have so much intercourse and from which we derive our origin, we have always been anxious and interested spectators. The citizens of the United States cherish sentiments the most friendly in favor of the liberty and happiness of their fellow-men on that side of the Atlantic. In the wars of the European powers in matters relating to themselves we have never taken any part, nor does it comport with our policy so to do. It is only when our rights are invaded or seriously menaced that we resent injuries or make preparation for our defense. With the movements in this hemisphere we are of necessity more immediately connected, and by causes which must be obvious to all enlightened and impartial observers. The political system of the allied powers is essentially different in this respect from that of America. This difference proceeds from that which exists in their respective Governments; and to the defense of our own, which has been achieved by the loss of so much blood and treasure, and matured by the wisdom of their most enlightened citizens, and under which we have enjoyed unexampled felicity, this whole nation is devoted. We owe it, therefore, to candor and to the amicable relations existing between the United States and those powers to declare that we should consider any attempt on their part to extend their system to any portion of this hemisphere as dangerous to our peace and safety. With the existing colonies or dependencies of any European power we have not interfered and shall not interfere. But with the Governments who have declared their independence and maintained it, and whose independence we have, on great consideration and on just principles, acknowledged, we could not view any interposition for the purpose of oppressing them, or controlling in any other manner their destiny, by any European power in any other light than as the manifestation of an unfriendly disposition toward the United States. In the war between those new Governments and Spain we declared our neutrality at the time of their recognition, and to this we have adhered, and shall continue to adhere, provided no change shall occur which, in the judgment of the competent authorities of this Government, shall make a corresponding change on the part of the United States indispensable to their security.

The late events in Spain and Portugal shew that Europe is still unsettled. Of this important fact no stronger proof can be adduced than that the allied powers should have thought it proper, on any principle satisfactory to themselves, to have interposed by force in the internal concerns of Spain. To what extent such interposition may be carried, on the same principle, is a question in which all independent powers whose governments differ from theirs are interested, even those most remote, and surely none more so than the United States. Our policy in regard to Europe, which was adopted at an early stage of the wars which have so long agitated that quarter of the globe, nevertheless remains the same, which is, not to interfere in the internal concerns of any of its powers; to consider the government de facto as the legitimate government for us; to cultivate friendly relations with it, and to preserve those relations by a frank, firm, and manly policy, meeting in all instances the just claims of every power, submitting to injuries from none. But in regard to those continents circumstances are eminently and conspicuously different. It is impossible that the allied powers should extend their political system to any portion of either continent without endangering our peace and happiness; nor can anyone believe that our southern brethren, if left to themselves, would adopt it of their own accord. It is equally impossible, therefore, that we should behold such interposition in any form with indifference. If we look to the comparative strength and resources of Spain and those new Governments, and their distance from each other, it must be obvious that she can never subdue them. It is still the true policy of the United States to leave the parties to themselves, in the hope that other powers will pursue the same course.

Glossary

acceded to	agreed to
comport	be consistent with
de facto	in fact
interposition	intervention
shew	antique spelling of "show"
St. Petersburg	at the time, the capital city of the Russian Empire

SPECIAL MESSAGE TO THE SENATE ON THE SLAVE TRADE CONVENTION WITH GREAT BRITAIN (1824)

Great Britain in her negotiations with other powers had concluded treaties with Spain, Portugal, and the Netherlands, in which, without constituting the crime as piracy or classing it with crimes of that denomination, the parties had conceded to the naval officers of each other the right of search and capture of the vessels of either that might be engaged in the slave trade, and had instituted courts consisting of judges, subjects of both parties, for the trial of the vessels so captured.

In the negotiations with the United States Great Britain had earnestly and repeatedly pressed on them the adoption of similar provisions. They had been resisted by the Executive on two grounds: One, that the constitution of mixed tribunals was incompatible with their Constitution; and the other, that the concession of the right of search in time of peace for an offense not piratical would be repugnant to the feelings of the nation and a dangerous tendency. The right of search is the right of war of the belligerent toward the neutral. To extend it in time of peace to any object whatever might establish a precedent which might lead to others with some powers, and which, even if confined to the instance specified, might be subject to great abuse.

Animated by an ardent desire to suppress this trade, the United States took stronger ground by making it, by the act above referred to, piratical, a measure more adequate to the end and free from many of the objects applicable to the plan which had been proposed to them. It is this alternative which the Executive, under the sanction and injunctions above stated, offered to the British Government, and which that government has accepted. By making the crime piracy the right of search attaches to the crime, and which when adopted by all nations will be common to all; and that it will be so adopted may fairly be presumed if steadily persevered in by the parties to the present convention. In the meantime, and with a view to a fair experiment, the obvious course seems to be to carry into effect with every power such treaty as may be made with each in succession.

In presenting this alternative to the British Government it was made an indispensable condition that the trade should be made piratical by act of Parliament, as it had been by an act of Congress. This was provided for in the convention, and has since been complied with. In this respect, therefore, the nations rest on the same ground. Suitable provisions have also been adopted to protect each party from abuse of the power granted to the public ships of the other. Instead of subjecting the persons detected in the slave [trade] to trial by the courts of the captors, as would be the case if such trade was piracy by the laws of nations, it is stipulated that until that event they shall be tried by the courts of their own country only. Hence there could be no motive for an abuse of the right of search, since such abuse could not fail to terminate to the injury of the captor.

Should this convention be adopted, there is every reason to believe that it will be the commencement of a system destined to accomplish the entire abolition of the slave trade. Great Britain, by making it her own, confessedly adopted at the suggestion of the United States, and being pledged to propose and urge its adoption by other nations in concert with the United States, will find it for her interest to abandon the less-effective system of her previous treaties with Spain, Portugal, and the Netherlands, and to urge on those and other powers their accession to this. The crime will then be universally proscribed as piracy, and the traffic be suppressed forever....

It must be obvious that the restriction of search for pirates to the African coast is incompatible with the idea of such a crime. It is not doubted also if the

Glossary

convention	treaty or agreement
extirpate	eliminate
proscribed	forbidden

convention is adopted that no example of the commission of that crime by the citizens or subjects of either power will ever occur again. It is believed, therefore, that this right as applicable to piracy would not only extirpate the trade, but prove altogether innocent in its operation.

Richard M. Nixon (Library of Congress)

RICHARD M. NIXON   1913–1994

Thirty-seventh President of the United States

Featured Documents
- ◆ "Checkers" Speech (1952)
- ◆ "Kitchen" Debate with Nikita Khrushchev (1959)
- ◆ Resignation Address to the Nation (1974)

Overview

Richard Milhous Nixon was born on January 9, 1913, in Yorba Linda, California. Although the family was poor and suffered during the depression, he did further his education. Nixon excelled in his studies at Whittier College and Duke University School of Law. After serving as a lieutenant commander in the U.S. Navy during World War II, Nixon went into politics, defeating a veteran congressman and quickly establishing himself as a rising star in the Republican Party. Nixon gained fame and respect as a fierce anti-Communist. His investigation of the U.S. State Department official Alger Hiss eventually led to a trial in which Hiss was convicted for conspiracy to commit espionage on behalf of the Soviet Union. Although Nixon became the subject of controversy because he was accused of campaigning using secret funds and had to allay his party's anxiety in his famous "Checkers" speech, he remained as Eisenhower's vice president for a full two terms. Indeed, he became a stalwart leader of the Republican Party, holding his own in the "kitchen" debate with Nikita Khruschev over the respective merits of the United States and USSR's political systems. He was chosen as his party's nominee for president in 1960.

Nixon appeared to be the favorite to win the presidency going into the 1960 election. His Democratic opponent, John Kennedy, was attempting to become the first Catholic to be elected president, and it was thought that the more experienced Nixon would best Kennedy in a series of debates. But Kennedy's wit, steadfastness, and fresh appeal resulted in a narrow victory for the Democrat. Although Nixon's political career seemed to be over after a second defeat in 1962 as a gubernatorial candidate in California, he solidified his ties to the Republican Party, campaigning vigorously for its candidates, becoming the party's standard-bearer in 1968, and winning the presidential election over Hubert Humphrey and a divided Democratic Party.

Nixon had always been a target of the political left, which despised his aggressive and, some thought, unscrupulous tactics of smearing opponents with the Communist label. His contentious presidency ran aground in his second term in his efforts to gather intelligence on his political enemies. He attempted to cover up what he knew about the Watergate break-in into the Democratic Party offices. This incident involved several members on the payroll of the Republican Party who were looking for material that could

be used against the Democrats during Nixon's reelection campaign in 1972. Even after Nixon's legal counsel, John Dean, warned the president that he was becoming involved in covering up a crime and obstructing justice, Nixon continued to withhold information about the break-in from Congress and the American people. Evidence in the form of tape recordings exposed his crimes (all related to his obstruction of justice), and he was forced to resign from office in August 1974, the only president ever to do so.

Explanation and Analysis of Documents

Nixon had earned a reputation as a hard-nosed politician with a gift for seeking publicity. He had been put on the presidential ticket with Dwight Eisenhower, even though Eisenhower seemed to have no rapport with Nixon and did little to support his running mate when Nixon found himself in trouble during the 1952 presidential campaign and had to deal with accusations that he had used a secret political fund for his personal benefit. To save himself—there were calls for Nixon's resignation—the vice presidential candidate turned to the relatively new medium of television to deliver his famous "Checkers" speech. Nixon's gamble was that he could address the American people directly, explain himself, and return to the good graces of the Republican Party and their presidential candidate. His strategy worked well.

In later years Nixon continued to rely on radio and television to mold his image. His famous "kitchen" debate with Khrushchev showed that Nixon could remain cool under pressure, especially when a world leader tried to bully him. Instead of responding to Khrushchev's provocations, Nixon remained calm, firm, and even charming. By the beginning of Nixon's second term, however, the years of political battles seemed to have soured him as well as induced a strain of self-pity. His resignation speech represents a rather sentimental defense of his actions in an effort to shore up his persona during a period of failure and shame.

◆ "Checkers" Speech

In September 1952 during the presidential campaign, news broke that Richard Nixon had been supported with a secret fund put together by his influential California backers. Nixon had done nothing illegal, and he was hardly the only politician to cover his expenses with undisclosed con-

1913

- **January 9**
  Richard Milhous Nixon is born in Yorba Linda, California.

1937

- Nixon graduates from Duke University School of Law.

1942–1946

- Nixon serves as a lieutenant commander in the U.S. Navy during World War II.

1947–1950

- Nixon is elected twice to the U.S. House of Representatives.

1950–1952

- Nixon serves in the U.S. Senate, becoming the Republican Party's point man in the cold war against Communism.

1952–1960

- As vice president in the Eisenhower administration, Nixon becomes involved in foreign policy issues and tours South America.

1952

- **September 23**
  In the "Checkers" speech, Nixon defends his integrity and explains his use of campaign funds while attacking the Democratic Party and emerging as one of the Republican Party's most forceful campaigners.

1959

- **July 24**
  While touring a model American kitchen at the American exhibition in Moscow, Nixon engages Soviet premier Nikita Khrushchev in a dialogue (informally known as the "kitchen" debate) over the respective merits of their two governments.

1960

- Nixon is defeated by the Democrat John F. Kennedy in the presidential election.

tributions to his campaign, but his running mate, General Dwight Eisenhower, had criticized corruption in the administration of Harry S. Truman, and the Republicans had vowed to reform political life in Washington, D.C. As a young and relatively inexperienced senator, Nixon was especially vulnerable. He had no particular rapport with Eisenhower, who did not come immediately to his running mate's defense. Concerned that this scandal might be enough to remove him from the Republican Party ticket, Nixon decided to address a national television audience. That this was indeed a crisis became apparent when Eisenhower proposed that Nixon should offer his resignation after the speech. Only then would Eisenhower decide the vice presidential nominee's fate. Nixon ignored Eisenhower's request, staking his political future on his television performance. In this event Nixon provided a compelling defense and attack on his political opponents so deftly worded that Eisenhower sent for Nixon to appear with him as he campaigned in West Virginia, affirming that Nixon was indeed his "boy."

Nixon opens his thirty-minute speech without a preamble, stating in his first sentence that his honesty and integrity have been challenged. By his second sentence, he is attacking the current administration as much as he is defending himself, observing that unlike those now in power he would neither ignore nor simply deny the accusations against him. In the next several paragraphs, Nixon suggests that he is setting a high moral standard for himself and that it is not enough to say he has done nothing illegal. He has not used any of the $18,235 contributed to his campaign for personal expenses. The money is not a secret fund, and it has not been used to grant special favors to contributors. Indeed, public records would show that Nixon had not attempted to influence any government organ on behalf of his supporters. Nixon then provides a specific accounting of his senator's salary, how his staff is funded, and why additional campaign funding is necessary. As he gives such information, he responds as if to an inquiry—asking himself the hard questions he supposes the public would wish answered. This self-interrogation projects the persona of an honest, forthright man with nothing to hide.

Nixon next shifts to a series of questions he puts to the public. Should the public have to pay for political publications, speeches, broadcasts, and trips? He could confidently answer for the public: It would not approve of charging such expenses to the taxpayers. So how would a senator fund his political activities? This would not be a problem, Nixon notes, if he were rich. But, Nixon says, he is not rich. Nixon also rejects the ploy of putting his wife on the payroll, noting that the Democratic nominee for vice president does have his wife on the payroll. Nixon claims he is not offering a criticism but merely asking the public to decide what is right. In effect, however, Nixon transforms his crisis and his need to defend himself into an indictment of his Democratic rivals.

There are plenty of people in Washington, D.C., who could be employed as staff members, Nixon points out, so that he does not think it proper to give his wife a job. At this point in the speech, Nixon gestured to his wife, Pat, who was seated on camera near him. By including his wife and referring directly to her, Nixon personalizes a political issue, implying that he ought to be judged, in part, by the family story he proceeds to tell. Even though his wife is highly skilled, having taught shorthand and stenography in high school, and is capable of working in his office, Nixon notes that he has never employed her. He has also done without other sources of income—a legal practice, for example—because he is so committed to his public work and because he wants to avoid conflicts of interest that might arise in his cases as a lawyer should his clients have government business. This is why, in short, Nixon claims he needs a campaign fund—to avoid the pitfalls he outlines in his speech. How else could he have the resources to expose the Communists that are part of a corrupt federal government? Thus Nixon associates his fund-raising with a public good and with the success he had with the Alger Hiss case.

Continuing to question himself, Nixon offers the proof he is sure the public would demand from him. Thus he could report that his campaign fund has been independently audited, proving he has not used money for personal purposes or to perform favors for others. No taxpayer money was involved, Nixon is proud to say. At this point, Nixon moves beyond defending himself and even beyond attacking his opponents in order to focus on his own probity. Here is a man who felt entitled to congratulate himself on his ethical behavior. Saying he had the audit in his hand, he reports that he is sending it to General Eisenhower. The audit conducted by a nationally recognized firm and supervised by a prominent law firm served to bolster Nixon's proclamation of his rectitude. And yet there would be more questions and more smears, Nixon informs his audience, thus ensuring that he has anticipated the political attacks on his television address to the nation. To those who still might suppose he is hiding money from public scrutiny, Nixon now vows to disclose his entire financial history.

Such a declaration of openness was startling and unprecedented, especially in a television speech. In effect, Nixon presents a highly condensed autobiography, beginning with his birth in 1913 in a modest family that owned a grocery store. Like his brothers, Nixon had worked in the store and had worked his way through school. Marrying his wife, Pat, in 1940 was the best thing that ever happened to him, he says, even though early on they, like so many couples listening to his address, had a difficult time making ends meet. Again, the personal, direct nature of Nixon's words emphasizes his down-to-earth plainspoken persona.

Nixon speaks quickly of his war record, his modest savings after the war, and his decision to enter political life. In addition to a salaried income, he and Pat have a small inheritance, fees for speeches, and some income from his law practice. He lists the rent he pays in Washington, D.C.; the cost of their homes in Whittier, California, and Washington, D.C.; a small life insurance policy; and a 1950 Oldsmobile. He also has debts (mortgages and a loan from his parents and another on his life insurance). As Nixon

Time Line

1962
- Nixon is defeated in the California governor's race.

1968
- Nixon is elected president of the United States for the first of two terms.

1973
- **January 23**
  Nixon announces an accord with North Vietnam to end America's involvement in Indochina.

1974
- **August 8**
  Nixon tenders his resignation in an address to the nation.

1994
- **April 22**
  Nixon dies in New York City.

says, it is not much, but what they have has been honestly earned. In a famous line, he notes: "Pat doesn't have a mink coat. But she does have a respectable Republican cloth coat, and I always tell her she would look good in anything." It was a touching moment: the honest man still in love with his wife. Nixon does admit to receiving one gift: a spotted cocker spaniel that his daughter Tricia named Checkers. With some endearing humor, Nixon vows he will not give up the dog.

Nixon presents his speech as a trial—one that most Americans would find hard to endure. Like the rest of his speech, this statement was calculated to evoke considerable empathy for his vulnerable position. Who would want to disclose so much? Now in a position of considerable authority, having revealed his own finances, Nixon attacks the Democratic Party's chairman, who, according to Nixon, has suggested that a poor man ought not to run for public office. Neither Nixon nor the Republican Party believed in this proposition. Nixon emphasizes his point by noting that Adlai Stevenson, the Democratic nominee for president, has a family fortune to rely on. Abraham Lincoln, on the other hand, presents another model for a politician—a model of someone who believed in the common people. It was time, Nixon argues, for Stevenson to make a detailed accounting of his political funding and of those who support him. Moreover, he says, Senator John Sparkman (the Democratic vice presidential nominee) needed to explain why his wife was on the payroll. To do anything less is to fail the test of openness that Nixon has just set up.

Nixon invokes the Hiss case, suggesting that during the course of his investigation there were attempts to silence him. With the country in such peril, Nixon was willing to

Soviet Premier Nikita Khrushchev, left, and Vice President Richard M. Nixon shake hands at the start of a meeting in the Kremlin in Russia on July 24, 1959.
(AP/Wide World Photos)

confront and refute the smears against him. He then repeats the classic Republican charge against the Truman administration and Democratic control of Congress: "Seven years of the Truman-Acheson administration, and what's happened? Six hundred million people lost to Communists." He also attributes the American lives lost and injured in war with Korea to Truman's failed leadership.

Because Nixon loves his country and because Dwight Eisenhower swore to clean up the corruption in Washington, Nixon says that he will persevere, especially since men like Stevenson called the Hiss case a "red herring." It is men like Hiss, Nixon implies, who are responsible for the espionage that gave the Soviet Union the secret of the atomic bomb. Stevenson is soft on Communism, Nixon suggests, and not fit to be president. After reading a letter from one of his supporters that demonstrates how the common people support him, Nixon vows not to quit. His wife, Pat, will not quit. The Irish do not quit, Nixon reminds his audience. But Nixon would leave the decision to the public and ask that it contact the Republican National Committee with its verdict. Nixon ends not with speaking about himself but with a plea that people vote for Eisenhower. This is more important than his own fate, Nixon implies, since a vote for Eisenhower is "good for America."

◆ **"Kitchen" Debate with Nikita Khrushchev**

On July 23, 1959, Vice President Nixon flew to Moscow as part of what was called a cultural exchange between the two world superpowers. The stated goal of Nixon's eleven-day visit was the development of a mutual understanding between rival nations competing for international approval and influence. The exchange also provided an opportunity for each country to present its case to the world. The pro-

paganda could be significant for both sides. This exchange was to be the first high-level meeting between a U.S. and a Soviet leader since the Geneva Summit of 1955.

On a visit to the American National Exhibition the next day, Nixon met Soviet Premier Nikita Khrushchev for the first time. They faced each other in a model American kitchen designed for a suburban home. It was equipped with all the modern conveniences that any American family could afford, the manufacturer claimed. Such an exhibition posed a challenge to Premier Khrushchev, since the Soviet economy lagged far behind the United States in providing domestic, labor-saving devices for its population.

That the two men engaged in an intense impromptu debate reflected the eagerness of both leaders to score points for their side of the cold war. The Soviet Union had taken the lead in exploring space with the launch of its *Sputnik* satellite in 1957, challenging U.S. dominance in technology. Khrushchev was determined to build on this coup even as Nixon extolled the superior merits of American innovation and a capitalist economy. His dogged and cheerful defense of U.S. ingenuity and productivity received good press and enhanced his political standing.

Khrushchev begins their discussion by proclaiming his country's desire for peace, especially in an atomic age when no leader could hope to prevail by means of war. But he quickly shifts to boasting that in a mere seven years the Soviet economy would surpass that of the United States. Communism, he implies, was the future, and capitalism was an outmoded system Americans could cling to if they so wished. In effect, he is here twitting Nixon, the famous anti-Communist who warned against Soviet subversions of U.S. institutions. The Soviet Union has no need, in other words, to attack the United States. According to him, Khrushchev simply needs to concentrate on perfecting his superior system.

Although Khrushchev's comments are provocative, Nixon's response is mild and rather sly, suggesting that he has come to expect exaggerations from Khrushchev. There would be an opportunity later, he notes, to respond to the Soviet premier's "sweeping and extemporaneous" remarks. But Nixon's reference to American color television makes the point that the United States has the superior technology. He is also alluding to the fact that the debate is being recorded on another new American invention: color videotape. Competition is good for everyone, Nixon states, and then adds more sharply: "After all, you don't know everything."

Khrushchev attacks Nixon for his ignorance of Communism and his fear of it, but Nixon refuses to be baited and even concedes that the Soviets are ahead of the United States in some respects, such as rocket technology. When Khrushchev refuses to acknowledge the U.S. advantage in color television, Nixon points out that Khrushchev will concede nothing. While the Soviet leader takes pride in never giving up, Nixon switches the argument to a call for more openness and more communication between the two rivals. Although Khrushchev approves of Nixon's plea for each side to fully acknowledge each other's ideas, not to fear them, Khrushchev insists this is exactly the message the Soviet Union has been sending to the United States. To

Khrushchev's effort to co-opt his argument, Nixon replies that the Soviet premier is a good lawyer—a point Khrushchev deflects by noting they are both good lawyers for capitalism and Communism, respectively.

Nixon then uses the kitchen as an example of how affordable life is for an American worker and how such a kitchen makes life easier for housewives. But Khrushchev dismisses most of this technology as useless gadgets or machines his own nation has also developed. Nevertheless, Nixon and Khrushchev are eager not to seem too contentious, a point Nixon reinforces by saying the debate has been in good humor. While Khrushchev remains adamant that the Soviet domestic economy includes the kinds of devices found in the model American kitchen, Nixon shifts the argument to the basis of U.S. and Soviet competition, expressing a hope that the two countries would no longer have to compete for military supremacy. But it is American generals who insist on an arms race, Khrushchev retorts. With respect to the Soviet premier's claim to military superiority, Nixon merely notes that neither side can win a war with modern weapons. In reply to a skeptical Khrushchev who points out the threat of American bases in foreign lands, Nixon wonders aloud whether the two nations can settle their differences at another Geneva conference.

◆ **Resignation Address to the Nation**

With the House of Representatives preparing to impeach Nixon, the Supreme Court ruled unanimously on July 24, 1974, that the president had to surrender all of his tape-recorded meetings to the House Judiciary Committee. Thus Nixon would have to disclose a meeting that clearly established he had taken part in covering up the crimes associated with the Watergate break-in (when men in the employ of the Republican National Committee burglarized the Democratic National Committee's headquarters in the Watergate Hotel). At this point, the president and important members of his staff began to consider his resignation from office.

Although he was still popular with many Republicans, the president's national poll ratings had dropped to less than 30 percent, and by July 27 the House Judiciary Committee had voted its first article of impeachment by a vote of 27 to 11. The article charged that the president had obstructed the investigation of the Watergate break-in. On July 29 the committee approved a second article, charging Nixon with abusing the power of the presidency and violating his oath of office (to faithfully execute the country's laws). The committee specified instances when the president had misused government agencies, such as the Internal Revenue Service, and had used illegal wiretaps. This abuse of power article passed 28 to 10. On July 30 the committee approved a third article, holding Nixon in contempt of Congress. This third article was adopted 21 to 17.

Even so, President Nixon hesitated to resign. Then, with the release of more tape recordings showing the president's involvement in a cover-up, Nixon lost most of his support, even that of staunch Republicans. Distraught and behaving in an unstable fashion, prone to rages and rambling conversations, suffering from insomnia and drinking too much

alcohol, Nixon was confronted with a delegation of Republican leaders from the House and Senate who explained why he could no longer govern. Nixon and his aides finished preparing his resignation speech, which he delivered on August 8, 1974.

Nixon begins his speech by reminding his audience of how many times he has addressed them from the Oval Office about decisions that would shape the nation's history. He has always done so to the best of his ability, he says, putting the nation's welfare first. By the second paragraph it is clear that Nixon is resigning, but he has to explain why he has decided to do so rather than face a House vote on the articles of impeachment and a trial in the Senate. He has been determined to follow the constitutional process, but he has lost his political base. There is no point in prolonging the process, since he cannot govern effectively. Indeed, this is precisely what his fellow Republicans have come to the White House to tell him.

Nixon's family has urged him to continue in office, no matter what personal agony such a decision might entail. But the president notes that he cannot take action on difficult decisions without political support. A president, no matter how powerful, cannot act on his own. What the resignation cost Nixon personally is evident in one sentence: "I have never been a quitter." He is resigning only because he is putting the nation's interests first, he notes in the next two paragraphs. Having to defend himself would mean that the country would not have a full-time president concerned with peace and prosperity. In another one-sentence statement Nixon announces his intention to resign from office the next day and says that Vice President Ford will take the oath of office as president at the same time. Although he is sad at not being able to complete his second term, he assures the nation that it will be in good hands with President Ford and that Ford deserves the nation's support as part of the healing process, the overcoming of bitterness that the Watergate affair has occasioned. Not until paragraph 11 does Nixon make any illusion to the articles of impeachment. But even his admission of guilt is couched in the notion of selfless devotion to the nation. In other words, he has not been trying merely to save himself: "If some of my judgments were wrong—and some were wrong—they were made in what I believed at the time to be the best interests of the nation."

Nixon claims to be leaving office without bitterness and with gratitude to his supporters. He says that his opponents want only the good of the country, no matter how much their judgments differ from his. It is this spirit of reconciliation that governs his concluding paragraphs as well as Nixon's desire to emphasize his administration's accomplishments: ending the Vietnam War, establishing a cooperative relationship with China, making progress toward peace in the Middle East, and effecting détente with the Soviet Union, which would lead, Nixon hopes, not only to limitations in the production of atomic bombs but also eventually to their elimination.

Whatever his failures might be, Nixon emphasizes that he has taken Theodore Roosevelt's injunction to heart and "dared greatly." Nixon intends to continue working for world peace, for "prosperity, justice and opportunity for all of our people." Because of his efforts, Nixon believes the world is a safer place. The presidency has made him feel closer to individual Americans, and he ends his speech praying for God's grace for his fellow Americans. Nixon fails to address exactly what he has done and why it justifies his resignation, taking refuge instead in the reiteration of his good intentions for the American people and the world.

Impact and Legacy

On the one hand, Nixon's standing in American history is high. Although his anti-Communist investigations were controversial, in retrospect his view of Alger Hiss and the threat of Communist subversion has proved to have had considerable merit. Similarly, his foreign policy, chiefly his overtures to Communist China and the opening up of that country to the West seem wise and innovative. He brought an end to the war in Vietnam, although many critics still feel his aggressive tactics prolonged the war unnecessarily. On balance, his stature as a world leader remains high. Of course, Nixon's resignation from office colors his legacy. His attempt to subvert the institutions of government to undermine his political enemies severely limits any effort to recast his presidency in a more favorable light. He attempted to cover up the crimes of his subordinates, so that in effect he violated his oath of office—to preserve and protect the Constitution.

Key Sources

The Richard Nixon Presidential Library and Museum holds his pre- and post-presidential papers, files from his early political career and his vice presidency, foreign correspondence (1947–1968), correspondence with such important figures as John F. Kennedy and Martin Luther King, Jr., and files relating to travel and personal appearances. Rick Perlstein edited the collection *Richard Nixon: Speeches, Writings, Documents* (2008). The collection also includes photographs, films, and other records and documents. Nixon's personal narrative is presented in *RN: Memoirs of Richard Nixon* (1978).

Further Reading

■ Books

Ambrose, Stephen E. *Nixon: The Education of a Politician 1913–1962*. New York: Simon and Schuster, 1987.

———. *Nixon: The Triumph of a Politician 1962–1972*. New York: Simon and Schuster, 1989.

———. *Nixon: Ruin and Recovery 1973–1990*. New York: Simon and Schuster, 1991.

Black, Conrad. *Richard Nixon: A Life in Full*. New York: Public Affairs, 2007.

Drew, Elizabeth. *Richard M. Nixon: The American Presidents Series: The 37th President, 1969–1974*. New York: Times Books, 2007.

Morris, Roger. *Richard Milhous Nixon: The Rise of an American Politician*. New York: Henry Holt and Company, 1990.

Wicker, Tom. *One of Us: Richard Nixon and the American Dream*. New York: Random House, 1991.

Wills, Garry. *Nixon Agonistes: The Crisis of the Self-Made Man*. Boston: Houghton Mifflin, 1970.

—Carl Rollyson

Questions for Further Study

1. Examine the "Checkers" speech in light of its success in achieving what Nixon set out to do with it: respond to accusations and defend his actions. What are the principal elements of its effectiveness as a political speech? Consider, for instance, the humble and down-home tone Nixon employs, his use of anecdotes, and his apparent lack of defensiveness. (The last is particularly interesting, in that defensiveness was one of the defining attitudes of Nixon during the Watergate years.)

2. Discuss the arguments and argument styles employed by Nixon and Khrushchev in the "kitchen debate." What are the best and worst arguments each man puts forth for his political system?

3. Compare and contrast Nixon's resignation speech and the "Checkers" speech. How does the man in the 1974 speech seem different from the one who made the other address twenty-two years earlier? How are they the same? Pay particular attention to the fact that both speeches are about wrongdoing or alleged wrongs, though, of course, the events surrounding Watergate were far more serious than the 1952 financial scandal.

4. Much has been made about the Watergate scandal, and rightly so. As time has gone on, however, Nixon's stature has risen in light of his successes. Discuss some of those successes, including implementation of civil rights laws held over from the Johnson era and the establishment of diplomatic relations with China. Contrast these successes with his less positive economic record, exemplified by the disastrous effect of his wage and price controls.

"CHECKERS" SPEECH (1952)

My Fellow Americans,

I come before you tonight as a candidate for the Vice-presidency and as a man whose honesty and integrity has been questioned....

I am sure that you have read the charges, and you have heard it, that I, Senator Nixon, took $18,000 from a group of my supporters....

It was not a secret fund....Well, then, some of you will say, and rightly, "Well, what did you use the fund for, Senator?...

Do you think that when I or any other Senator makes a political speech, has it printed, [we] should charge the printing of that speech and the mailing of that speech to the taxpayers?

Do you think, for example, when I or any other Senator makes a trip to his home state to make a purely political speech that the cost of that trip should be charged to the taxpayers?

Do you think when a Senator makes political broadcasts or political television broadcasts, radio or television, that the expense of those broadcasts should be charged to the taxpayers?

I know what your answer is. It is the same answer that audiences give me whenever I discuss this particular problem.

The answer is no. The taxpayers should not be required to finance items which are not official business but which are primarily political business....

Then the question arises, you say, "Well, how do you pay for these and how can you do it legally?"...The first way is to be a rich man. So I couldn't use that.

Another way that is used is to put your wife on the payroll....You will have to pass judgment on that particular point, but I have never done that.... I just didn't feel it was right to put my wife on the payroll— My wife sitting over there....

She used to teach stenography and she used to teach shorthand in high school.... I am proud to say tonight that in the six years I have been in the Senate of the United States, Pat Nixon has never been on the government payroll.

What are the other ways that these finances can be taken care of? Some who are lawyers, and I happen to be a lawyer, continue to practice law, but I haven't been able to do that....

And so I felt that the best way to handle these necessary political expenses...was to accept the aid which people in my home state of California, who contributed to my campaign and who continued to make these contributions after I was elected, were glad to make....

I am proud to report to you tonight...the opinion that was prepared by Gibson, Dunn, & Crutcher, based on all the pertinent laws, and statutes, together with the audit report prepared by the certified public accountants.

"It is our conclusion that Senator Nixon...did not violate any federal or state law by reason of the operation of the fund."...

And so now, what I am going to do—and incidentally this is unprecedented in the history of American politics—I am going at this time to give to this television and radio audience, a complete financial history, everything I have earned, everything I have spent and everything I own, and I want you to know the facts....

Pat and I have the satisfaction that every dime that we have got is honestly ours....

Pat doesn't have a mink coat. But she does have a respectable Republican cloth coat, and I always tell her she would look good in anything.

One other thing I probably should tell you, because if I don't they will probably be saying this about me, too. We did get something, a gift, after the election.

A man down in Texas heard Pat on the radio mention the fact that our two youngsters would like to have a dog, and, believe it or not, the day before we left on this campaign trip we got a message from Union Station in Baltimore, saying they had a package for us. We went down to get it. You know what it was?

It was a little cocker spaniel dog, in a crate that he had sent all the way from Texas, black and white, spotted, and our little girl Tricia, the six year old, named it Checkers.

And you know, the kids, like all kids, loved the dog, and I just want to say this, right now, that regardless of what they say about it, we are going to keep it.

It isn't easy to come before a nation-wide audience and bare your life, as I have done. But I want to say some things before I conclude, that I think most of you will agree on.

Mr. Mitchell, the Chairman of the Democratic National Committee, made this statement that if a man couldn't afford to be in the United States Senate, he shouldn't run for senate. And I just want to make my position clear.

I don't agree with Mr. Mitchell when he says that only a rich man should serve his government in the United States Senate or Congress. I don't believe that represents the thinking of the Democratic Party, and I know it doesn't represent the thinking of the Republican Party.

I believe that it's fine that a man like Governor Stevenson, who inherited a fortune from his father, can run for President. But I also feel that it is essential in this country of ours that a man of modest means can also run for President, because, you know—remember Abraham Lincoln—you remember what he said—"God must have loved the common people, he made so many of them."

And now I'm going to suggest some courses of conduct.

First of all, you have read in the papers about other funds, now, Mr. Stevenson apparently had a couple.... I think that what Mr. Stevenson should do should be to come before the American people, as I have, give the names of the people that contributed to that fund,... and see what favors, if any, they gave out for that....

And as far as Mr. Sparkman is concerned, I would suggest... he should come before the American people and indicate what outside sources of income he has had....

I know this is not the last of the smears.... And the purpose of the smears, I know, is this, to silence me, to make me let up.

Well, they just don't know who they are dealing with.... I remember in the dark days of the Hiss trial some of the same columnists, some of the same radio commentators who are attacking me now and misrepresenting my position, were violently opposing me at the time I was after Alger Hiss. But I continued to fight because I knew I was right, and I can say to this great television and radio audience that I have no apologies to the American people for my part in putting Alger Hiss where he is today.... I intend to continue to fight.

Why do I feel so deeply?... Because, you see, I love my country. And I think my country is in danger. And I think the only man that can save America at this time is the man that's running for President, on my ticket, Dwight Eisenhower....

Seven years of the Truman-Acheson administration, and what's happened? Six hundred million people lost to Communists.

And a war in Korea in which we have lost 117,000 American casualties, and I say that those in the State Department that made the mistakes which caused that war and which resulted in those losses should be kicked out of the State Department just as fast as we can get them out of there....

You have read about the mess in Washington. Mr. Stevenson can't clean it up because he was picked by the man, Truman, under whose Administration the mess was made....

Take Communism.... Mr. Stevenson, has pooh-poohed and ridiculed the Communist threat in the United States—he has accused us ... of looking for Communists in the Bureau of Fisheries and Wildlife. I say that a man who says that isn't qualified to be President of the United States.

And I say that the only man who can lead us into this fight to rid the government of both those who are Communists and those who have corrupted this government is Eisenhower, because General Eisenhower, you can be sure, recognizes the problem, and knows how to handle it....

This evening I want to read to you just briefly excerpts from a letter that I received, a letter, which after all this is over, no one can take away from us....:

"Dear Senator Nixon,

"Since I am only 19 years of age, I can't vote in this presidential election, but believe me if I could, you and General Eisenhower would certainly get my vote. My husband is in the Fleet Marines in Korea. He is in the front lines. And we have a two month old son he has never seen. And I feel confident that with great Americans like you and General Eisenhower in the White House, lonely Americans like myself will be united with their loved ones now in Korea. I only pray to God that you won't be too late. Enclosed is a small check to help you with your campaign. Living on $85 a month it is all I can do."

Folks, it is a check for $10, and it is one that I shall never cash.... We hear a lot about prosperity these days, but I say why can't we have prosperity built on peace, rather than prosperity built on war? Why can't we have prosperity and an honest government in Washington D.C. at the same time?

Believe me, we can. And Eisenhower is the man that can lead the crusade to bring us that kind of prosperity.

And now, finally, I know that you wonder whether or not I am going to stay on the Republican ticket or resign.... I don't believe that I ought to quit, because I am not a quitter. And, incidentally, Pat is not a quitter. After all, her name is Patricia Ryan and she was born on St. Patrick's day, and you know the Irish never quit.

But the decision, my friends, is not mine. I would do nothing that would harm the possibilities of

Dwight Eisenhower to become President of the United States. And for that reason I am submitting to the Republican National Committee tonight through this television broadcast the decision which it is theirs to make. Let them decide whether my position on the ticket will help or hurt. And I am going to ask you to help them decide. Wire and write the Republican National Committee whether you think I should stay on or whether I should get off. And whatever their decision, I will abide by it....

Regardless of what happens, I am going to continue this fight. I am going to campaign up and down America until we drive the crooks and the Communists and those that defend them out of Washington, and remember folks, Eisenhower is a great man. Folks, he is a great man, and a vote for Eisenhower is a vote for what is good for America.

Glossary

audit	a systematic review of financial records
Gibson, Dunn & Crutcher	a large and influential law firm, founded in the late nineteenth century and still in operation at the beginning of the twenty-first
shorthand	a system of abbreviated handwriting used for rapidly recording spoken words
stenography	the art of shorthand
wire	send a telegram

"KITCHEN" DEBATE WITH NIKITA KHRUSHCHEV (1959)

Khrushchev: "We want to live in peace and friendship with Americans because we are the two most powerful countries and if we live in friendship then other countries will also live in friendship.... How long has America existed? Three hundred years?"

Nixon: "One hundred and fifty years."

Khrushchev:...We have existed not quite 42 years and in another seven years we will be on the same level as America.... Plainly speaking, if you want capitalism you can live that way. That is your own affair and doesn't concern us.... We are all glad to be here at the exhibition with Vice President Nixon. I personally, and on behalf of my colleagues, express my thanks for the president's message. I have not as yet read it but I know beforehand that it contains good wishes. I think you will be satisfied with your visit and if I cannot go on without saying it—if you would not take such a decision [proclamation by the United States Government of Captive Nations Week, a week of prayer for peoples enslaved by the Soviet Union] which has not been thought out thoroughly, as was approved by Congress, your trip would be excellent. But you have churned the water yourselves—why this was necessary God only knows."...

[Wrapping his arms about a Soviet workman] "Does this man look like a slave laborer?" [Waving at others] "With men with such spirit how can we lose?"

Nixon: [pointing to American workmen] "With men like that we are strong. But these men, Soviet and American, work together well for peace, even as they have worked together in building this exhibition. This is the way it should be. Your remarks are in the tradition of what we have come to expect—sweeping and extemporaneous. Later on we will both have an opportunity to speak and consequently I will not comment on the various points that you raised, except to say this—this color television is one of the most advanced developments in communication that we have.

"I can only say that if this competition in which you plan to outstrip us is to do the best for both of our peoples and for peoples everywhere, there must be a free exchange of ideas. After all, you don't know everything."

Khrushchev: "If I don't know everything you don't know anything about communism except fear of it."

Nixon: "There are some instances where you may be ahead of us, for example in the development of the thrust of your rockets for the investigation of outer space; there may be some instances in which we are ahead of you—in color television, for instance."

Khrushchev: "No, we are up with you on this, too."...

Nixon: "You see, you never concede anything."

Khrushchev: "I do not give up."

Nixon: "Wait till you see the picture. Let's have far more communication and exchange in this very area that we speak of. We should hear you more on our televisions. You should hear us more on yours."

Khrushchev: "That's a good idea. Let's do it like this. You appear before our people. We will appear before your people. People will see and appreciate this."

Nixon: "There is not a day in the United States when we cannot read what you say. When Kozlov was speaking in California about peace, you were talking here in somewhat different terms. This was reported extensively in the American press. Never make a statement here if you don't want it to be read in the United States. I can promise you every word you say will be translated into English."

Khrushchev: "I doubt it. I want you to give your word that this speech of mine will be heard by the American people."

Nixon [shaking hands on it]: "By the same token, everything I say will be translated and heard all over the Soviet Union?"

Khrushchev: "That's agreed."

Nixon: "You must not be afraid of ideas."

Khrushchev: "We are telling you not to be afraid of ideas. We have no reason to be afraid."...

Nixon: "...We are all agreed on that. All right? All right?"

Khrushchev: "Fine.... But I want to stress what I am in agreement with. I know that I am dealing with a very good lawyer.... You are a lawyer for capitalism and I am a lawyer for communism. Let's compare."

Nixon: "The way you dominate the conversation you would make a good lawyer yourself. If you were in the United States Senate you would be accused of filibustering." [Halting Khrushchev at model kitchen in model house]: "You had a very nice house in your exhibition in New York. My wife and I saw and enjoyed it very much. I want to show you this kitchen. It is like those of our houses in California."

Khrushchev: [after Nixon called attention to a built-in panel-controlled washing machine]: "We have such things."

Nixon: "This is the newest model.... Let me give you an example you can appreciate. Our steelworkers, as you know, are on strike. But any steelworker could buy this house. They earn $3 an hour. This house costs about $100 a month to buy on a contract running 25 to 30 years."

Khrushchev: "We have steel workers and we have peasants who also can afford to spend $14,000 for a house....

"Many things you've shown us are interesting but they are not needed in life.... They are merely gadgets....

"The Americans have created their own image of the Soviet man and think he is as you want him to be. But he is not as you think. You think the Russian people will be dumbfounded to see these things, but the fact is that newly built Russian houses have all this equipment right now. Moreover, all you have to do to get a house is to be born in the Soviet Union. You are entitled to housing. I was born in the Soviet Union. So I have a right to a house. In America, if you don't have a dollar—you have the right to choose between sleeping in a house or on the pavement. Yet you say that we are slaves of communism."...

Nixon: "You can learn from us and we can learn from you. There must be a free exchange. Let the people choose the kind of house, the kind of soup, the kind of ideas they want....

"We do not claim to astonish the Russian people. We hope to show our diversity and our right to choose. We do not wish to have decisions made at the top by government officials who say that all homes should be built in the same way. Would it not be better to compete in the relative merits of washing machines than in the strength of rockets? Is this the kind of competition you want?"

Khrushchev: "Yes that's the kind of competition we want. But your generals say: 'Let's compete in rockets. We are strong and we can beat you.' But in this respect we can also show you something."

Nixon: "To me you are strong and we are strong. In some ways, you are stronger. In others, we are stronger. We are both strong not only from the standpoint of weapons but from the standpoint of will and spirit. Neither should use that strength to put the other in a position where he in effect has an ultimatum. In this day and age that misses the point. With modern weapons it does not make any difference if war comes. We both have had it."

We want peace too and I believe that you do also."

Khrushchev: "Yes, I believe that....We want to liquidate all bases from foreign lands. Until that happens, we will speak different languages. One who is for putting an end to bases on foreign lands is for peace. One who is against it is for war. We have liquidated our forces and offered to make a peace treaty and eliminate the point of friction in Berlin. Until we settle that question, we will talk different languages."

Nixon: "Do you think it can be settled at Geneva?"

Khrushchev: "If we considered it otherwise, we would not have incurred the expense of sending our foreign minister to Geneva....It does not depend on us."

Nixon: "It takes two to make an agreement. You cannot have it all your own way."

Khrushchev: "These are questions that have the same aim. To put an end to the vestiges of war, to make a peace treaty with Germany—that is what we want. It is very bad that we quarrel over the question of war and peace."

Nixon: "There is no question but that your people and you want the government of the United States being for peace; anyone who thinks that it is not for peace is not an accurate observer of America. In order to have peace, Mr. Prime Minister, even in an argument between friends, there must be sitting down around a table. There must be discussion. Each side must find areas where it looks at the other's point of view. The world looks to you today with regard to Geneva. I believe it would be a grave mistake and a blow to peace if it were allowed to fail."

Khrushchev: "The two sides must seek ways of agreement."

Glossary

filibustering	speaking at great length as a means of avoiding a genuine discussion or debate
Kozlov	Soviet statesman Frol Kozlov, a key figure in Khrushchev's regime
we are up with you	we have caught up with you

RESIGNATION ADDRESS TO THE NATION (1974)

Good evening:

This is the 37th time I have spoken to you from this office, where so many decisions have been made that shape the history of this nation. Each time I have done so to discuss with you some matter that I believe affected the national interest. In all the decisions I have made in my public life I have always tried to do what was best for the nation.

Throughout the long and difficult period of Watergate, I have felt it was my duty to persevere—to make every possible effort to complete the term of office to which you elected me. In the past few days, however, it has become evident to me that I no longer have a strong enough political base in the Congress to justify continuing that effort. As long as there was such a base, I felt strongly that it was necessary to see the constitutional process through to its conclusion; that to do otherwise would be unfaithful to the spirit of that deliberately difficult process, and a dangerously destabilizing precedent for the future. But with the disappearance of that base, I now believe that the constitutional purpose has been served. And there is no longer a need for the process to be prolonged.

I would have preferred to carry through to the finish whatever the personal agony it would have involved, and my family unanimously urged me to do so. But the interests of the nation must always come before any personal considerations. From the discussions I have had with Congressional and other leaders I have concluded that because of the Watergate matter I might not have the support of the Congress that I would consider necessary to back the very difficult decisions and carry out the duties of this office in the way the interests of the nation will require.

I have never been a quitter....

But as President, I must put the interests of America first.... Therefore, I shall resign the Presidency effective at noon tomorrow.

Vice President Ford will be sworn in as President at that hour in this office.

As I recall the high hopes for America with which we began this second term, I feel a great sadness that I will not be here in this office working on your behalf to achieve those hopes in the next two and a half years. But in turning over direction of the Government to Vice President Ford I know, as I told the nation when I nominated him for that office ten months ago, that the leadership of America would be in good hands....

As he assumes that responsibility he will deserve the help and the support of all of us. As we look to the future, the first essential is to begin healing the wounds of this nation. To put the bitterness and divisions of the recent past behind us and to rediscover those shared ideals that lie at the heart of our strength and unity as a great and as a free people....

I regret deeply any injuries that may have been done in the course of the events that led to this decision. I would say only that if some of my judgments were wrong—and some were wrong—they were made in what I believed at the time to be the best interests of the nation.

To those who have stood with me during these past difficult months, to my family, my friends, the many others who joined in supporting my cause because they believed it was right, I will be eternally grateful for your support. And to those who have not felt able to give me your support, let me say I leave with no bitterness toward those who have opposed me, because all of us in the final analysis have been concerned with the good of the country, however our judgments might differ....

These years have been a momentous time in the history of our nation and the world. They have been a time of achievement in which we can all be proud, achievements that represent the shared efforts of the administration, the Congress and the people. But the challenges ahead are equally great. And they, too, will require the support and the efforts of the Congress and the people, working in cooperation with the new Administration.

We have ended America's longest war. But in the work of securing a lasting peace in the world, the goals ahead are even more far-reaching and more difficult. We must complete a structure of peace, so that it will be said of this generation—our generation of Americans—by the people of all nations, not only that we ended one war but that we prevented future wars.

We have unlocked the doors that for a quarter of a century stood between the United States and the People's Republic of China. We must now insure that the one-quarter of the world's people who live in the People's Republic of China will be and remain, not our enemies, but our friends.

In the Middle East, 100 million people in the Arab countries, many of whom have considered us their enemy for nearly 20 years, now look on us as their friends. We must continue to build on that friendship so that peace can settle at last over the Middle East and so that the cradle of civilization will not become its grave. Together with the Soviet Union we have made the crucial breakthroughs that have begun the process of limiting nuclear arms. But, we must set as our goal, not just limiting, but reducing and finally destroying these terrible weapons, so that they cannot destroy civilization. And so that the threat of nuclear war will no longer hang over the world and the people. We have opened a new relation with the Soviet Union. We must continue to develop and expand that new relationship, so that the two strongest nations of the world will live together in cooperation rather than confrontation.

Around the world—in Asia, in Africa, in Latin America, in the Middle East—there are millions of people who live in terrible poverty, even starvation. We must keep as our goal turning away from production for war and expanding production for peace so that people everywhere on this earth can at last look forward, in their children's time, if not in our own time, to having the necessities for a decent life....

We must press on, however, toward a goal not only of more and better jobs but of full opportunity for every American, and of what we are striving so hard right now to achieve—prosperity without inflation.

For more than a quarter of a century in public life, I have shared in the turbulent history of this evening. I have fought for what I believe in. I have tried, to the best of my ability, to discharge those duties and meet those responsibilities that were entrusted to me. Sometimes I have succeeded. And sometimes I have failed. But always I have taken heart from what Theodore Roosevelt once said about the man in the arena, whose face is marred by dust and sweat and blood, who strives valiantly, who errs and comes short again and again because there is not effort without error and shortcoming, but who does actually strive to do the deed, who knows the great enthusiasms, the great devotions, who spends himself in a worthy cause, who at the best knows in the end the triumphs of high achievements and with the worst if he fails, at least fails while daring greatly.

I pledge to you tonight that as long as I have a breath of life in my body, I shall continue in that spirit. I shall continue to work for the great causes to which I have been dedicated throughout my years as a Congressman, a Senator, Vice President and President, the cause of peace—not just for America but among all nations—prosperity, justice and opportunity for all of our people.

There is one cause above all to which I have been devoted and to which I shall always be devoted for as long as I live.

When I first took the oath of office as President five and a half years ago, I made this sacred commitment: to consecrate my office, my energies, and all the wisdom I can summon to the cause of peace among nations. I've done my very best in all the days since to be true to that pledge. As a result of these efforts, I am confident that the world is a safer place today, not only for the people of America but for the people of all nations, and that all of our children have a better chance than before of living in peace rather than dying in war.

This, more than anything, is what I hoped to achieve when I sought the Presidency.

This, more than anything, is what I hope will be my legacy to you, to our country, as I leave the Presidency.

To have served in this office is to have felt a very personal sense of kinship with each and every American.

In leaving it, I do so with this prayer: May God's grace be with you in all the days ahead.

Sandra Day O'Connor (Library of Congress)

SANDRA DAY O'CONNOR

Supreme Court Justice

Featured Documents

◆ *Webster v. Reproductive Health Services* (1989)

◆ *Metro Broadcasting, Inc. v. Federal Communications Commission* (1990)

◆ *Zelman v. Simmons-Harris* (2002)

◆ *Grutter v. Bollinger* (2003)

Overview

Sandra Day O'Connor holds the distinction of being the first woman to serve on the U.S. Supreme Court. She was born into a ranching family on March 26, 1930, in El Paso, Texas, though she grew up in Arizona, which would be her home state throughout most of her life. She received a bachelor's degree in economics from Stanford University, in California, in 1950 and remained at Stanford to complete a law degree in 1952—taking two years rather than the normal three. Coincidentally, the U.S. chief justice under whom she would serve, William Rehnquist, was a classmate at Stanford, and the two even briefly dated.

After completing her law degree, O'Connor was unable to find work as a lawyer in California because of her gender. Although she graduated near the top of her class, the only job she was offered was that of legal secretary. Accordingly, she turned to the public sector. Her first job was as a deputy county attorney in California. She then accompanied her husband to Frankfurt, Germany, to work as a civilian attorney for the military. Returning to the United States, she opened her own law firm near Phoenix, Arizona, and then served four years as the state's assistant attorney general. She entered the legislative branch of government in 1969 when she was appointed to the Arizona State Senate, to subsequently win two additional terms and serve as the senate's majority leader. She joined Arizona's judiciary when she was elected judge of the Maricopa County Superior Court, and she was later appointed to the state's court of appeals.

On July 7, 1981, President Ronald Reagan nominated O'Connor to the Supreme Court to replace Justice Potter Stewart. Her nomination initially met with some skepticism. Conservatives were concerned that she did not have enough judicial experience, while liberals were concerned that, as a member of the Republican Party, she was not committed to protecting abortion rights. Nonetheless, after being unanimously confirmed by the U.S. Senate, O'Connor took her seat on September 25, 1981. During her years on the Supreme Court, she proved moderately conservative, frequently voting with the more conservative Rehnquist. In such cases as *Webster v. Reproductive Health Services* (1989) and *Metro Broadcasting, Inc. v. Federal Communications Commission* (1990), she carved out pragmatic decisions, examining issues on a case-by-case basis. She was frequently the conservative swing vote on the nine-member Court in closely divided five-to-four decisions.

Unlike most Supreme Court justices, who enjoy lifetime appointments and often do not retire until age and ill health force them to, O'Connor retired from the bench in good health on January 31, 2006, primarily to spend more time with her husband, who was afflicted with Alzheimer's disease. In the years following her retirement, she became active as a public speaker, focusing on educating the public about the independence of the judiciary.

Explanation and Analysis of Documents

During her quarter century on the U.S. Supreme Court, O'Connor, in common with other justices, wrote numerous and various decisions on cases that appeared before the Court. In some instances she was responsible for writing the majority opinion; in others, she dissented from the majority; and in still others, she voted with the majority but felt compelled to write her own concurrence, expanding on the views of the majority or agreeing with the majority's conclusion but for her own reasons.

In her Court opinions, O'Connor generally charted a moderately conservative course. She tended to approach each case as narrowly as possible, showing a reluctance to issue sweeping decisions that would change the legal landscape in the United States. Thus, for example, she resisted efforts to overturn *Roe v. Wade*, the landmark 1973 case prohibiting the states from outlawing abortion, but at the same time she was willing to support the legality of certain restrictions on abortions, as she did in *Webster v. Reproductive Health Services*. Similarly, she supported affirmative action programs and race-based admissions policies to universities, yet at the same time she took more conservative positions on the death penalty as it involved African Americans, desegregation of schools, and gerrymandering (the process of strategically redrawing congressional district boundaries, such as to boost the chances of minorities winning elections in affected districts). Overall, she often served as the swing vote in close decisions.

◆ Webster v. Reproductive Health Services

Since 1973, when the Supreme Court issued its ruling in the landmark case *Roe v. Wade*, abortion has persisted

Time Line

1930

- **March 26**
  Sandra Day is born in El Paso, Texas.

1950

- Day graduates with a bachelor's degree in economics from Stanford University.

1952

- Now married, Sandra Day O'Connor graduates from Stanford Law School.

- O'Connor is appointed deputy attorney for San Mateo County, California.

1954

- O'Connor begins a four-year stint as a civilian attorney for the U.S. military in Frankfurt, Germany.

1965

- O'Connor becomes assistant attorney general for Arizona.

1969

- O'Connor is named to the Arizona State Senate, to be reelected twice and named majority leader in 1972.

1974

- O'Connor is elected judge of the Maricopa County Superior Court, in Arizona.

1979

- **December 4**
  O'Connor is sworn in as a justice on the Arizona Court of Appeals.

1981

- **July 7**
  President Ronald Reagan nominates O'Connor for a seat on the U.S. Supreme Court, which she assumes on September 25.

1989

- **July 3**
  O'Connor issues her concurrence in *Webster v. Reproductive Health Services*.

as a highly contentious issue in the United States. Indeed, the fortunes of a nominee for a seat on the Supreme Court, who must be approved by the U.S. Senate, can often turn on perceptions of how the nominee might rule on abortion cases. Some Americans fear that a highly conservative Court could potentially overturn *Roe*, while others continue to hope that the Court will do exactly that.

Many abortion cases that appear before the Supreme Court, however, do not bear directly on the constitutionality of the essentials of *Roe*. Rather, they turn on questions involving the right of states to place restrictions on abortion, by, for example, specifying when in the life of the unborn fetus abortions can be obtained or prohibiting the use of state funds or facilities to perform abortions. Arguments continue to rage over whether an unborn fetus enjoys rights, whether a fetus that is potentially viable (able to sustain life) outside the womb is entitled to state protection, and such tangential issues as whether a minor needs the consent of a parent or guardian to have an abortion. In the eyes of many, any restriction on abortion rights lies on a slippery slope leading to an overturning of *Roe v. Wade*.

Webster v. Reproductive Health Services (1989) was a case revolving around just such arguments. It grew out of a Missouri law, referred to in the document as §188.029, that placed a number of restrictions on abortion in the state. To begin with, a preamble to the law stated that "unborn children have protectable interests in life, health, and well-being." The law went on to require the Missouri legal code to extend the same rights to unborn children as it does to other persons and to prohibit any doctor employed by the government from aborting any fetus believed by the doctor to be viable. Further, the law banned doctors from using state facilities or the assistance of state employees to perform abortions and also prohibited the use of state employees, facilities, or funds to counsel women to have abortions—though these two restrictions would not apply if the mother's life was in danger. A U.S. district court in Missouri struck down these last provisions of the law. The U.S. Court of Appeals for the Eighth Circuit affirmed the district court's ruling, holding that the provisions of the Missouri law were inconsistent with *Roe v. Wade* and were therefore unconstitutional. The state's attorney general, William Webster, appealed the case to the U.S. Supreme Court, where it was argued on April 26, 1989. The Court issued its decision on July 3 of that year.

Chief Justice William Rehnquist wrote the decision for the majority, but the Court's decision was a complicated one, with various justices writing dissents or concurrences—and in some cases both—with respect to various portions of the majority opinion. Essentially, however, the Supreme Court reversed the appeals court decision, ruling that the Missouri law did not violate the due process clause of the Fourteenth Amendment to the Constitution and was therefore valid. Specifically, the majority ruled that the law's preamble was not unconstitutional because it was not used to justify any universal regulations or restrictions on abortions. Further, prohibiting the use of state facilities, funds, or employees was not inconsistent with any of the

Court's previous abortion rulings because no one has a documented "affirmative right" to state aid to have an abortion. Finally, the Court ruled that the law's provisions requiring doctors to perform tests to determine the viability of a fetus after twenty weeks of pregnancy were constitutional. The Court did, however, rule that limits on abortion that encompassed the entire second trimester of pregnancy violated constitutional rights.

O'Connor voted with the majority, but in addition to Rehnquist's opinion for the Court she wrote her own concurrence, aligning with various portions of the decision. Her concurrence in *Webster* provides an example of her closely reasoned opinions and, perhaps more important, her painstaking efforts to square any given decision with previous Court rulings. In the section of her concurrence reproduced here, she takes up the issue of the viability of a fetus and the question of whether "the State may…directly promote its interest in potential life when viability is possible." Put simply, the Missouri law under examination in this case placed restrictions on abortion by requiring physicians to perform tests to determine whether a fetus could survive outside the womb; if it could, then physicians could not legally abort it. The parties who contested the law argued that such a requirement places an undue burden on a woman seeking an abortion, principally by increasing the cost because of the additional tests. O'Connor contends that this burden is not excessive.

O'Connor first takes up the presumption of the Missouri law that a twenty-week-old fetus may be viable. She notes that the law's requirement that tests for viability be performed from that point onward by any woman seeking an abortion is not intended to substitute state regulation for a physician's judgment, as the court of appeals held. Rather, the provision in the Missouri law, O'Connor maintains, is merely a means to enable the presumption of viability at twenty weeks to be overcome. O'Connor goes on to argue that the Missouri law and the Court's upholding of it are not in any way inconsistent with prior Court rulings. In this discussion, she cites two important cases in the history of abortion rights: *Thornburgh v. American College of Obstetricians and Gynecologists* (1986) and *Planned Parenthood Assn. of Kansas City, Mo., Inc. v. Ashcroft* (1983). O'Connor points out that in these cases, the Court upheld the principle that a state has a legitimate interest in "potential life" when "viability is certain"; she notes that in *Thornburgh* the Court struck down a Pennsylvania law only because the law failed to take into account emergency circumstances, not because the Court rejected the principle.

O'Connor proceeds to cite *Colautti v. Franklin*, a 1979 case that overturned a state law attempting to discourage abortion, one of a number of such laws passed in the wake of *Roe v. Wade*. Quoting the Court's decision in *Colautti*, O'Connor affirms that "Missouri has not substituted any of the 'elements entering into the ascertainment of viability' as 'the determinant of when the State has a compelling interest in the life or health of the fetus.'" In other words, viability—and thus the legality of a possible abortion—are still determined by the doctor rather than the state, and as

such the Court's present ruling is consistent with the *Colautti* ruling.

A key issue in the abortion debate concerned the question of whether a state could burden a pregnant woman's decision to have an abortion by, for example, increasing its cost or requiring a hospital stay. With respect to the Missouri law, O'Connor dismisses the objection to the added cost of testing as invalid: "Requiring the performance of examinations and tests useful to determining whether a fetus is viable, when viability is possible, and when it would not be medically imprudent to do so, does not impose an undue burden on a woman's abortion decision." She distinguishes *Webster* from an earlier case, *Akron v. Akron Center for Reproductive Health, Inc.*, by noting that the latter case dealt with a requirement that a woman having an abortion at any time during the second trimester had to be hospitalized. This, in O'Connor's view, was an unreasonable burden. In contrast, the Missouri law, requiring "examinations and tests that could usefully and prudently be performed when a woman is 20–24 weeks pregnant to determine whether the fetus is viable would only marginally, if at all, increase the cost of an abortion." Thus, the law does not unduly burden the pregnant woman.

O'Connor further notes that a fetus is not viable during much of the second trimester of pregnancy. (Conventionally, pregnancy is divided into three stages. The first is from conception to twelve weeks, when a fetus is clearly not viable. The second stage extends from the thirteenth through the twenty-eighth week. It is during the second trimester, generally between the twentieth and twenty-fourth weeks, that a fetus becomes viable.) Thus, requiring tests for viability in weeks twenty through twenty-four is not the same as requiring a hospital stay at any time during the second trimester. On the basis of these arguments,

O'Connor concludes that the Court's decision in *Webster*, contrary to the findings of the lower courts, is consistent with the Court's rulings in earlier cases. It is on this basis that she voted to reverse the judgment of the court of appeals and uphold the Missouri law.

◆ *Metro Broadcasting, Inc. v. Federal Communications Commission*

On March 28, 1990, the Supreme Court heard arguments in *Metro Broadcasting, Inc. v. Federal Communications Commission*. The Court issued its five-to-four decision on June 27 of that year. The Federal Communications Commission (FCC) is the federal agency that regulates broadcasting in the United States under the Communications Act of 1934. Because the airwaves are believed to be a finite resource that belongs to the public (in contrast to broadcasts disseminated through cable or satellite), the federal government has historically regulated them. A key component of this regulation is the granting of broadcast licenses. These licenses are scarce and coveted, as the FCC limits their number so that the airwaves do not become too "crowded," so that powerful stations in major cities do not drown out smaller and weaker stations in rural areas and small towns, and so that large corporations cannot own so many stations that they would effectively control broadcasting in large swaths of the country.

At issue in the *Metro* case was the constitutionality of two of the FCC's minority preference policies. The first, challenged by Metro Broadcasting, was that the FCC could give preference to minority applicants for broadcast licenses, all other factors being roughly equal. The second had to do with what are called "distress sales." If a company was about to lose its license, perhaps because of financial difficulties, it could sell the license to a minority buyer before the FCC had a chance to rule on the future of the troubled station. This provision was challenged by a company called Shurberg Broadcasting in a separate case. The Supreme Court consolidated the two cases in *Metro* because both dealt with the overarching issue of minority preferences.

The constitutional issue—all Supreme Court cases at bottom deal with constitutional issues—was whether the FCC's policies violated the equal protection clause of the Fifth Amendment. The Court majority, in an opinion written by William J. Brennan, Jr., ruled that they did not, holding that by granting minority preferences, the FCC was providing an appropriate remedy for past discrimination and promoting Congress's goal of encouraging more programming diversity. The Court reasoned that Congress had a legitimate interest in encouraging diversity in broadcasts and a range of programming options. Further, the Court concluded that such diversity serves the best interests of the entire viewing public, not just minority groups, and that the FCC's policies did not unduly burden nonminorities. The Court also ruled that distress sales were allowable when there were no other competing bids for the license.

O'Connor wrote the dissent for the four members of the Court who disagreed with the majority opinion. She opens her dissent by appealing to fundamental constitutional principles: that the government is to treat people as individuals, not as members of classes, including racial classes; that the government is not to allocate burdens or benefits based on the presumption that all members of a class think or act in a certain way; and that the government can classify people on the basis of race only if such classifications are "necessary and narrowly tailored to achieve a compelling interest."

O'Connor then turns to the issue of the standard of scrutiny that the Court is to use in ruling on matters such as those at hand. In her discussion, she uses terms that have particular meanings in jurisprudence. One of these terms is "strict scrutiny," a standard that obligates the Court to determine whether a state has a "compelling" interest to legitimize its regulation of behavior. This is the highest standard of scrutiny, which the Court applies to matters of fundamental rights. In more routine matters, the Court applies a lower standard of scrutiny, often referred to as the "rational basis standard." This standard, which applies to matters that do not involve fundamental rights, asks whether the state has an "important" or "rational" interest in regulating behavior. O'Connor argues that the Court majority incorrectly based its *Metro* opinion on this lower standard of review. Because the matter is one involving fundamental rights, she reasons, the Court should have applied the strict scrutiny standard. In failing to do so, O'Connor asserts, the Court arrived at an incorrect decision.

O'Connor proceeds to fully explicate her reasoning. She notes that the FCC provides benefits. Under the Constitution, it should do so to individuals as individuals, not to individuals as members of a racial or other group. To give preference to any group is to deny others equal protection under the law. Decisions such as that of the majority, she contends, encourage "race-based reasoning" and divide the nation into "racial blocs." They have a tendency to stigmatize the group that is singled out and are inconsistent with the nation's principle that people should be evaluated on the basis of individual merit. In making this argument, O'Connor cites the 1978 case *Regents of the University of California v. Bakke*, in which a white man argued that the university's quota system for minority applicants to medical school was unconstitutional and the Supreme Court agreed.

O'Connor then frames her analysis around the reverse situation and cites key Supreme Court cases of the 1950s, *Brown v. Board of Education* and its companion case, *Bolling v. Sharpe*. In those 1954 desegregation cases, the Court rejected the use of racial classifications in segregated public schools. O'Connor clarifies the constitutional issues involved when she cites the Fifth Amendment, with its due process clause, and the Fourteenth Amendment, which extended the reach of due process and equal protection to the states.

O'Connor continues by launching into an extended analysis of the relationship between the judiciary and Congress. She argues that any law passed by Congress is subject to the same level of scrutiny as any other law: "The respect due a coordinate branch yields neither less vigilance in defense of equal protection principles nor any corresponding diminution of the standard of review." If, she says, the Supreme Court invokes the Fourteenth Amendment to extend equal protection and due process to individuals in the states, then the federal government's actions are subject to the same strict scrutiny under the Fifth Amendment. O'Connor rejects the notion that the policies of the FCC, because they are "benign," are somehow exempt from this requirement. She mentions two earlier cases, *Fullilove v. Klutznick* (1980) and *City of Richmond v. J. A. Croson Co.* (1989), that the Court cited as precedents in reaching its decision in *Metro*. She maintains that those cases are actually distinguishable from *Metro*, principally because the federal action at issue in the latter case, unlike those in the two others, is not "remedial." That is, it is not intended to directly provide present remedies for past discrimination. O'Connor contends that it is legitimate for Congress to craft laws that provide specific remedial measures to counteract specific instances of discrimination. It is not legitimate, however, for Congress to pass broad measures that might serve a social good but that are not intended to undo the ongoing effects of past discrimination.

O'Connor next expands on her objection to the notion of "benign" racial classifications. Even if the intention behind the classification is praiseworthy, she says, "governmental distinctions among citizens based on race or ethnicity, even in the rare circumstances permitted by our cases, exact costs and carry with them substantial dangers." She notes that "the right to equal protection of the laws is a personal right." The Court's assumption that it can tell which racial classifications are benign is dangerous; even the word *benign* "carries with it no independent meaning, but reflects only acceptance of the current generation's conclusion that a politically acceptable burden, imposed on particular citizens on the basis of race, is reasonable." She concludes by asserting that "we are a Nation not of black and white alone, but one teeming with divergent communities knitted together by various traditions and carried forth, above all, by individuals." Because the FCC has not met its burden of proof as to whether its interest is compelling, and because the Court failed to apply what O'Connor regards as the appropriate standard of review, she dissents from the Court's decision.

◆ Zelman v. Simmons-Harris

At the heart of the *Zelman* case was the contentious issue of school vouchers. Normally, the residents of a city or county pay property taxes, some of which are used to fund public schools. Affluent parents can afford to pay the taxes but also pay to send their children to private schools if they wish. Thus, affluent parents have a choice that is generally denied to parents who are poor or of modest means. Under a school voucher plan, these parents are given a voucher, which represents a sum of money that they can use to exercise choice in the schooling of their children. Generally, the amount of the voucher is tied to the parents' income, with higher amounts provided for the poorest parents and lesser amounts for parents who are less poor. In effect, the voucher amounts to a refund of tax money that is thus not being spent for the benefit of children in public schools. School voucher plans often are put in place because of perceptions that local public schools are failing in their mission and that parents would like to find alternatives for their children. In many instances, the alternative to a public school is a school with a religious affiliation. Catholic schools are commonplace, but there are also Lutheran schools, Jewish schools, and schools conducted by evangelical Christians, Muslims, and other religious groups. And there are private schools that have no religious affiliation.

At issue in *Zelman* was whether a program in Cleveland, Ohio—the Pilot Project Scholarship Program—violated the establishment clause of the U.S. Constitution. The establishment clause is found in the First Amendment to the Constitution and reads, "Congress shall make no law respecting an establishment of religion." In Ohio a taxpayer group filed suit to halt the voucher program, arguing that it violated the establishment clause because 82 percent of the schools participating in the program had a religious affiliation and 96 percent of the participating children were students in religiously affiliated schools. Thus, these students were providing indirect aid to religious institutions through their voucher dollars. The district court agreed with the taxpayer group and ruled in its favor. The U.S. Sixth Circuit Court of Appeals affirmed the district court's ruling.

The U.S. Supreme Court, however, in a five-to-four decision, overturned the decision of the lower courts and held that the program did not violate the establishment clause. Writing for the majority, Chief Justice William Rehnquist argued that the program was neutral with regard to religion. Its goal was simply to provide choices for poorer parents seeking educational opportunities for their children. In particular, some 60 percent of the students enrolled under the program were poor. That a portion of the money went to religiously affiliated schools did not mean that the government was in any way either "establishing" a particular religion or promoting religion in general.

O'Connor voted with the majority, but in a separate concurrence she outlined her reasons for doing so in more detail, particularly because she was troubled by the dissenting justices' reliance on partial and misleading data. In the portion of her concurrence excerpted here, she focuses on the core issue of whether the Cleveland program violated the establishment clause. She first makes reference to the so-called *Lemon* test, taken from the 1971 Court decision in *Lemon v. Kurtzman*. This is a three-pronged test that the Court uses to determine whether a law or statue violates the establishment clause. The Court first asks whether a law or statute has a "secular legislative purpose." If it does, then the Court asks a second question, whether its "principal or primary effect" is one that neither advances nor inhibits religion. The third prong of the test is to ensure that the law or statute does "not foster an excessive government entanglement with religion."

O'Connor argues that the Cleveland program passes the *Lemon* test. She first maintains that the program "is neutral as between religious schools and nonreligious schools." She rejects the arguments of fellow justice David Souter,

Barbara Grutter, left, talks to reporters outside the Supreme Court in Washington, D.C., on April 1, 2003. (AP/Wide World Photos)

who wrote a dissent contending that the program's structure encourages attendance at religiously affiliated schools. O'Connor points out, for example, that parents had nonreligious options under the program and that these nonreligious schools were able to compete with religious schools in terms of quality. The mere fact that many parents selected religious schools does not indicate that religious schools were prioritized by the government as options. She takes the lower courts and Souter to task for failing to take into account this range of options, which included magnet schools (schools with specialized courses or curricula, such as in art, music, or science), charter schools (taxpayer-supported public schools with curricula and goals different from those of surrounding public schools), and public schools in neighboring suburbs.

It is on this basis that O'Connor concludes that Cleveland's program advances a secular purpose, does not advance religion, and does not excessively entangle government with religion. It should be noted that in other portions of her concurrence, she provides extensive evidence of government benefits that accrue to religious institutions (for example, that churches are exempt from paying local property taxes and that former soldiers spend GI Bill tuition money at colleges with religious affiliations), using these data to support the assertion that government benefits to religion alone do not necessarily violate the *Lemon* test. She concludes that for the Cleveland program

> the goal of the Court's Establishment Clause jurisprudence is to determine whether ... parents were free to direct state educational aid in either a nonreligious or religious direction. That inquiry requires an evaluation of all reasonable educational options Ohio provides the Cleveland school system, regardless of whether they are formally made available in the same section of the Ohio Code as the voucher program.

◆ Grutter v. Bollinger

The genesis of *Grutter v. Bollinger* was in 1997, when Barbara Grutter, a white woman, applied for admission to the University of Michigan Law School. Despite having excellent credentials, she was denied admission. She sued certain persons, including Lee Bollinger, who was the university's president at the time but was formerly dean of the law school, on the ground that the law school used race as a factor in admissions with the goal of achieving diversity in the student body. The result, Grutter argued, was that highly qualified white students were unfairly denied admission in favor of possibly less-qualified minority students. Initially, Grutter won, with the district court ruling that the law school could not use race as a factor in admissions decisions. However, the U.S. Court of Appeals for the Sixth Circuit reversed the judgment of the district court. The Supreme Court affirmed the decision of the court of appeals, holding that the law school's use of racial preferences did not violate the equal protection clause of the Fourteenth Amendment, nor did it violate the 1964 Civil Rights Act. O'Connor wrote the opinion for the five-to-four majority.

Grutter has particular interest because, superficially, O'Connor's views might seem to contradict those she expressed in *Metro Broadcasting, Inc. v. FCC*. In that case she argued that the FCC's minority preferences for broadcasting licenses violated the equal protection clause of the Fifth Amendment to the Constitution. The basis for her argument was that the state did not have a compelling interest in establishing a racial category with regard to broadcasting. Here, she took a different but not inconsistent view, recognizing "a compelling state interest in student body diversity" in "the context of higher education."

O'Connor's decision in *Grutter* illustrates the importance of legal precedent in Court rulings. In her decision she makes frequent reference to the *Bakke* case. *Regents of the University of California v. Bakke* was the 1978 case, also involving higher education, in which the Court ruled that rigid quota systems for the admission of minority applicants were impermissible. O'Connor further notes that in rulings over the next three decades, the Court found the use of racial categories permissible only for the purpose of "remedying past discrimination." O'Connor asserts, though, that this is not the only legitimate reason to permit race-based government action. Another relevant goal is diversity in high education, and this is a goal whose legitimacy O'Connor recognizes. The law school's use of race as one factor in admissions is thus considered a narrowly tailored solution to a problem that the state has a compelling interest in solving.

O'Connor, in this opinion, recognizes the law school's distinction between a quota and what it called a "critical mass." The problem in *Bakke* was that the University of California maintained a rigid quota system, whereby a specific number of enrollment slots were set aside for underrepresented minority students. The admissions decisions of the University of Michigan Law School were considered permissible because they were not based on quotas. Rather, they were based on ensuring a diverse student body that promoted racial understanding and lively debate, which could be achieved not with token numbers of minorities but with meaningful, if unspecified, numbers.

A further point is that race at the University of Michigan Law School was just one of numerous "soft" factors used in admissions decisions, along with letters of recommendation, the applicant's admissions essay, the reputation of the applicant's undergraduate school, and leadership and work experience. These factors contrasted with "hard" factors, principally the applicant's undergraduate grade point average and score on the Law School Admission Test. O'Connor affirms that by using race as one factor in admissions, the university could better prepare a diverse array of students for professional careers and leadership positions, and she cites the large numbers of governors, members of the Senate and House of Representatives, and judges who have law degrees. On several occasions, O'Connor refers to "amici." This is a plural form of *amicus*, or more formally, *amicus curiae*, a Latin phrase that means "friend of the court" and refers to legal briefs submitted by experts supporting one side or the other. O'Connor takes note of the case's numerous amici briefs arguing for the educational benefits of racial diversity.

In summarizing this portion of her decision, O'Connor states that in order for the nation's leaders to have "legitimacy," the paths to leadership must be "visibly open to talented and qualified individuals of every race and ethnicity." America is a "heterogeneous society," and the duty of higher education is to prepare all students for the individuals and institutions with which they will interact as active citizens in and potential civic leaders of that society.

Impact and Legacy

The ascension of Sandra Day O'Connor to the Supreme Court had one immediate practical effect. Traditionally, the members of the Court addressed one another as "Mr. Justice"; the appearance of a woman required a change in that tradition. The justices now address each other simply as "Justice." More significant, O'Connor provided an unequaled role model for many women. Despite compiling an enviable record at a prestigious university, she was unable to practice her chosen profession in the private sector because of sexism. However, she continued to work within the system, assembling an extensive résumé in all three branches of government: the executive (as a state attorney general), the legislative (as a state senator), and the judicial. Especially early in her tenure on the Supreme Court, she was the focus of intense scrutiny. Observers from both sides of the political aisle closely examined her every vote, her every decision, to determine whether the "woman" justice would advance or impede their causes. In the eyes of some observers, it was as though O'Connor were being required to single-handedly carry the weight of all women's aspirations on her shoulders.

O'Connor's effects on American jurisprudence were not transformative. Indeed, her goal was never to create sweeping changes in the law, nor was it to use the bench to forward a personal agenda. She became known for arriving at pragmatic solutions to problems in decisions that deferred to precedent while recognizing the nation's changing social landscape. In matters involving abortion rights, for example, some women's groups initially regarded her as a traitor because she allowed some state regulation of abortion. In time, however, women recognized that her willingness to compromise in some areas of the abortion debate allowed her to protect the essential ability of women to obtain abortions. Further, on such contentious issues as school vouchers and affirmative action, she charted a middle course that conservatives could recognize as consistent with constitutional principles and liberals could welcome as important reflections of new social realities.

Key Sources

The Sandra Day O'Connor Papers, encompassing the years 1963 to 1988, are housed at the Library of Congress Manuscript Division, with a catalog listing available online (http://memory.loc.gov/ammem/awhhtml/awmss5/judg_atty. html). All of O'Connor's Supreme Court decisions can be found through online legal sources. O'Connor is also the author of two autobiographical books: *The Majesty of the Law: Reflections of a Supreme Court Justice* (2004) and, with her brother, H. Alan Day, *Lazy B: Growing Up on a Cattle Ranch in the American Southwest* (2002). In her retirement, O'Connor has published a number of articles and editorial opinion columns, including "Fair and Independent Court" in *Daedalus* (Fall 2008) and "The Threat to Judicial Independence" in the *Wall Street Journal* (September 27, 2006).

Further Reading

■ Articles

Bales, Scott. "Justice Sandra Day O'Connor: No Insurmountable Hurdles." *Stanford Law Review* 58, no. 6 (2006): 1705–1712.

Chemerinsky, Erwin. "The O'Connor Legacy." *Trial* 41, no. 9 (September 1, 2005): 68–69.

Rosen, Jeffrey. "Light Footprint: On Affirmative Action, Justice Sandra Day O'Connor Finally Puts Society's Needs above Her Own." *New Republic* (July 7, 2003): 16–17.

"Sandra Day O'Connor Leaves a Legacy of Powerful Pragmatism and Key Swing Votes." *Time* (July 11, 2005): 30–33.

■ Books

Biskupic, Joan. *Sandra Day O'Connor: How the First Woman on the Supreme Court Became Its Most Influential Justice*. New York: HarperCollins, 2006.

Maveety, Nancy. *Justice Sandra Day O'Connor: Strategist on the Supreme Court*. Lanham, Md.: Rowman & Littlefield, 1996.

"No decision of this Court has held that the State may not directly promote its interest in potential life when viability is possible."

(*Webster v. Reproductive Health Services*)

"It is clear to me that requiring the performance of examinations and tests useful to determining whether a fetus is viable, when viability is possible, and when it would not be medically imprudent to do so, does not impose an undue burden on a woman's abortion decision."

(*Webster v. Reproductive Health Services*)

"The Constitution provides that the Government may not allocate benefits and burdens among individuals based on the assumption that race or ethnicity determines how they act or think."

(*Metro Broadcasting, Inc. v. Federal Communications Commission*)

"We are a Nation not of black and white alone, but one teeming with divergent communities knitted together by various traditions and carried forth, above all, by individuals. Upon that basis, we are governed by one Constitution, providing a single guarantee of equal protection, one that extends equally to all citizens."

(*Metro Broadcasting, Inc. v. Federal Communications Commission*)

"Courts are instructed to consider two factors: first, whether the program administers aid in a neutral fashion, without differentiation based on the religious status of beneficiaries or providers of services; second, and more importantly, whether beneficiaries of indirect aid have a genuine choice among religious and nonreligious organizations when determining the organization to which they will direct that aid."

(*Zelman v. Simmons-Harris*)

"In order to cultivate a set of leaders with legitimacy in the eyes of the citizenry, it is necessary that the path to leadership be visibly open to talented and qualified individuals of every race and ethnicity. All members of our heterogeneous society must have confidence in the openness and integrity of the educational institutions that provide this training."

(*Grutter v. Bollinger*)

McFeatters, Ann Carey. *Sandra Day O'Connor: Justice in the Balance*. Albuquerque: University of New Mexico Press, 2006.

Urofsky, Melvin I. *Biographical Encyclopedia of the Supreme Court: The Lives and Legal Philosophies of the Justices*. Washington, D.C.: CQ Press, 2006.

Van Sickel, Robert W. *Not a Particularly Different Voice: The Jurisprudence of Sandra Day O'Connor*. 2nd ed. New York: Peter Lang, 2002.

■ **Web Sites**

Hamilton, Marci. "The Remarkable Legacy of Justice Sandra Day O'Connor." July 14, 2005. FindLaw Web site.
  http://writ.news.findlaw.com/hamilton/20050714.html.

"Sandra Day O'Connor." Oyez Web site.
  http://www.oyez.org/justices/sandra_day_oconnor/.

—Michael J. O'Neal

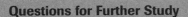

Questions for Further Study

1. Discuss O'Connor's significance as the first female Supreme Court justice, as well as her impact as a role model for women. How did her early experiences shape her later views on equal rights? Is there a conflict between her politically conservative views on some social issues and her status as a symbol of equal rights for women? Why or why not?

2. Examine the logic O'Connor applies in her *Webster v. Reproductive Health Services* opinion, particularly her argument on viability. How does *Webster*, in her judgment, differ from the earlier *Akron v. Akron Center for Reproductive Health, Inc.* in terms of the "unreasonable burden" factor?

3. The Supreme Court's five-to-four split on *Metro Broadcasting, Inc. v. Federal Communications Commission* shows that the issue at hand—a challenge to minority preferences by the FCC based on Fifth Amendment equal protection rights—was not an easy one to settle. Discuss the relative merits of the Court's ruling compared with the dissent, written by O'Connor. Which, in your opinion, is more convincing and why?

4. Consider the similarities and differences between *Metro* and *Grutter v. Bollinger*, both of which involved the equal protection clause of the Fifth Amendment. As evidenced from her written opinions in each case, did O'Connor maintain a position that was consistent and fair? Why or why not? Contrast her views with those of Thurgood Marshall in *Regents of the University of California v. Bakke*.

5. Discuss the facts and constitutional issues involved in *Zelman v. Simmons-Harris*, a challenge over school vouchers grounded in the establishment clause of the First Amendment. What logic does the majority apply to show that the scholarship program in question is neutral with regard to religion? How does O'Connor extend this idea with her concurrence, particularly its application of "the *Lemon* test"? And finally, in your opinion, what does government neutrality on the subject of religion mean? What is religious neutrality, as opposed to, on the one hand, a preference for a particular religion and, on the other, an undue hostility toward religion and its practitioners?

WEBSTER V. REPRODUCTIVE HEALTH SERVICES (1989)

O'Connor's Concurrence

The time when viability is achieved may vary with each pregnancy, and the determination of whether a particular fetus is viable is, and must be, a matter for the judgment of the responsible attending physician.

The 20-week presumption of viability in the first sentence of § 188.029, it could be argued (though, I would think, unsuccessfully), restricts "the judgment of the responsible attending physician," by imposing on that physician the burden of overcoming the presumption. This presumption may be a "superimpos[ition] [of] state regulation on the medical determination whether a particular fetus is viable," but, if so, it is a restriction on the physician's judgment that is not before us. As the plurality properly interprets the second sentence of § 188.029, it does nothing more than delineate means by which the unchallenged 20-week presumption of viability may be overcome if those means are useful in doing so and can be prudently employed. Contrary to the plurality's suggestion, the District Court did not think the second sentence of § 188.029 unconstitutional for this reason. Rather, both the District Court and the Court of Appeals thought the second sentence to be unconstitutional precisely because they interpreted that sentence to impose state regulation on the determination of viability that it does not impose....

I do not think the second sentence of § 188.029, as interpreted by the Court, imposes a degree of state regulation on the medical determination of viability that in any way conflicts with prior decisions of this Court. As the plurality recognizes, the requirement that, where not imprudent, physicians perform examinations and tests useful to making subsidiary findings to determine viability "promot[es] the State's interest in potential human life, rather than in maternal health." No decision of this Court has held that the State may not directly promote its interest in potential life when viability is possible. Quite the contrary. In *Thornburgh v. American College of Obstetricians and Gynecologists*, the Court considered a constitutional challenge to a Pennsylvania statute requiring that a second physician be present during an abortion performed "when viability is possible." For guidance, the Court looked to the earlier decision in *Planned Parenthood Assn. of Kansas City, Mo., Inc. v.*

Ashcroft, upholding a Missouri statute requiring the presence of a second physician during an abortion performed after viability. The *Thornburgh* majority struck down the Pennsylvania statute merely because the statute had no exception for emergency situations, and not because it found a constitutional difference between the State's promotion of its interest in potential life when viability is possible and when viability is certain. Despite the clear recognition by the *Thornburgh* majority that the Pennsylvania and Missouri statutes differed in this respect, there is no hint in the opinion of the *Thornburgh* Court that the State's interest in potential life differs depending on whether it seeks to further that interest postviability or when viability is possible. Thus, all nine Members of the *Thornburgh* Court appear to have agreed that it is not constitutionally impermissible for the State to enact regulations designed to protect the State's interest in potential life when viability is possible. That is exactly what Missouri has done in § 188.029.

Similarly, the basis for reliance by the District Court and the Court of Appeals below on *Colautti v. Franklin* disappears when § 188.029 is properly interpreted. In *Colautti*, the Court observed:

Because this point [of viability] may differ with each pregnancy, neither the legislature nor the courts may proclaim one of the elements entering into the ascertainment of viability—be it weeks of gestation or fetal weight or any other single factor—as the determinant of when the State has a compelling interest in the life or health of the fetus. Viability is the critical point.

The courts below, on the interpretation of §188.029 rejected here, found the second sentence of that provision at odds with this passage from *Colautti*. On this Court's interpretation of § 188.029, it is clear that Missouri has not substituted any of the "elements entering into the ascertainment of viability" as "the determinant of when the State has a compelling interest in the life or health of the fetus." All the second sentence of § 188.029 does is to require, when not imprudent, the performance of "those tests that are useful to making *subsidiary* findings as to viability." Thus, consistent with *Colautti*, viability remains the "critical point" under § 188.029.

Finally, and rather half-heartedly, the plurality suggests that the marginal increase in the cost of an abortion created by Missouri's viability testing provision may make § 188.029, even as interpreted, suspect under this Court's decision in *Akron v. Akron Center for Reproductive Health, Inc.*, striking down a second-trimester hospitalization requirement. I dissented from the Court's opinion in *Akron* because it was my view that, even apart from *Roe*'s trimester framework, which I continue to consider problematic, the *Akron* majority had distorted and misapplied its own standard for evaluating state regulation of abortion which the Court had applied with fair consistency in the past: that, previability, "a regulation imposed on a lawful abortion is not unconstitutional unless it unduly burdens the right to seek an abortion."

It is clear to me that requiring the performance of examinations and tests useful to determining whether a fetus is viable, when viability is possible, and when it would not be medically imprudent to do so, does not impose an undue burden on a woman's abortion decision. On this ground alone, I would reject the suggestion that § 188.029 as interpreted is unconstitutional. More to the point, however, just as I see no conflict between § 188.029 and *Colautti* or any decision of this Court concerning a State's ability to give effect to its interest in potential life, I see no conflict between § 188.029 and the Court's opinion in *Akron*. The second-trimester hospitalization requirement struck down in *Akron* imposed, in the majority's view, "a heavy, and unnecessary, burden," more than doubling the cost of "women's

access to a relatively inexpensive, otherwise accessible, and safe abortion procedure." By contrast, the cost of examinations and tests that could usefully and prudently be performed when a woman is 20–24 weeks pregnant to determine whether the fetus is viable would only marginally, if at all, increase the cost of an abortion....

Moreover, the examinations and tests required by § 188.029 are to be performed when viability is possible. This feature of § 188.029 distinguishes it from the second-trimester hospitalization requirement struck down by the *Akron* majority. As the Court recognized in *Thornburgh*, the State's compelling interest in potential life postviability renders its interest in determining the critical point of viability equally compelling. Under the Court's precedents, the same cannot be said for the *Akron* second-trimester hospitalization requirement. As I understand the Court's opinion in *Akron*, therefore, the plurality's suggestion today that *Akron* casts doubt on the validity of § 188.029, even as the Court has interpreted it, is without foundation, and cannot provide a basis for reevaluating *Roe*. Accordingly, because the Court of Appeals misinterpreted § 188.029, and because, properly interpreted, § 188.029 is not inconsistent with any of this Court's prior precedents, I would reverse the decision of the Court of Appeals.

In sum, I concur in Parts I, II-A, II-B, and II-C of the Court's opinion and concur in the judgment as to Part II-D.

Glossary

gestation	the period of conception to the birth of a baby
plurality	a Supreme Court decision in which a majority of the justices agree on the outcome but offer different rationales for their decision
second trimester	the middle third of a pregnancy
superimposition	to place before or in front of
viability	the ability of a fetus to live outside the womb

O'Connor, Sandra Day

METRO BROADCASTING, INC. V. FEDERAL COMMUNICATIONS COMMISSION (1990)

O'Connor's Dissent

At the heart of the Constitution's guarantee of equal protection lies the simple command that the Government must treat citizens "as individuals, not 'as simply components of a racial, religious, sexual or national class.'" Social scientists may debate how peoples' thoughts and behavior reflect their background, but the Constitution provides that the Government may not allocate benefits and burdens among individuals based on the assumption that race or ethnicity determines how they act or think. To uphold the challenged programs, the Court departs from these fundamental principles and from our traditional requirement that racial classifications are permissible only if necessary and narrowly tailored to achieve a compelling interest. This departure marks a renewed toleration of racial classifications and a repudiation of our recent affirmation that the Constitution's equal protection guarantees extend equally to all citizens. The Court's application of a lessened equal protection standard to congressional actions finds no support in our cases or in the Constitution. I respectfully dissent.

I

As we recognized last Term, the Constitution requires that the Court apply a strict standard of scrutiny to evaluate racial classifications such as those contained in the challenged FCC distress sale and comparative licensing policies. "Strict scrutiny" requires that, to be upheld, racial classifications must be determined to be necessary and narrowly tailored to achieve a compelling state interest. The Court abandons this traditional safeguard against discrimination for a lower standard of review, and in practice applies a standard like that applicable to routine legislation. Yet the Government's different treatment of citizens according to race is no routine concern. This Court's precedents in no way justify the Court's marked departure from our traditional treatment of race classifications and its conclusion that different equal protection principles apply to these federal actions.

In both the challenged policies, the FCC provides benefits to some members of our society and denies benefits to others based on race or ethnicity. Except in the narrowest of circumstances, the Constitution bars such racial classifications as a denial to particular individuals, of any race or ethnicity, of "the equal protection of the laws." The dangers of such classifications are clear. They endorse race-based reasoning and the conception of a Nation divided into racial blocs, thus contributing to an escalation of racial hostility and conflict. Such policies may embody stereotypes that treat individuals as the product of their race, evaluating their thoughts and efforts—their very worth as citizens—according to a criterion barred to the Government by history and the Constitution. Racial classifications, whether providing benefits to or burdening particular racial or ethnic groups, may stigmatize those groups singled out for different treatment and may create considerable tension with the Nation's widely shared commitment to evaluating individuals upon their individual merit. Cf. *Regents of University of Calif v. Bakke* (1978) "Because racial characteristics so seldom provide a relevant basis for disparate treatment, and because classifications based on race are potentially so harmful to the entire body politic, it is especially important that the reasons for any such classifications be clearly identified and unquestionably legitimate."

The Constitution's guarantee of equal protection binds the Federal Government as it does the States, and no lower level of scrutiny applies to the Federal Government's use of race classifications. In *Bolling v. Sharpe*, the companion case to *Brown v. Board of Education* (1954), the Court held that equal protection principles embedded in the Fifth Amendment's Due Process Clause prohibited the Federal Government from maintaining racially segregated schools in the District of Columbia: "[I]t would be unthinkable that the same Constitution would impose a lesser duty on the Federal Government." Consistent with this view, the Court has repeatedly indicated that "the reach of the equal protection guarantee of the Fifth Amendment is coextensive with that of the Fourteenth."

Nor does the congressional role in prolonging the FCC's policies justify any lower level of scrutiny. As with all instances of judicial review of federal legislation, the Court does not lightly set aside the considered judgment of a coordinate branch. Nonetheless, the respect due a coordinate branch yields neither less vigilance in defense of equal protection principles nor any corresponding diminution of the standard of review. In *Weinberger v. Wiesenfeld*, for example, the Court upheld a widower's equal protection challenge to a provision of the Social Security Act, found the assertedly benign congressional purpose to be illegitimate, and noted that [t]his Court's approach to Fifth Amendment equal protection claims has always been precisely the same as to equal protection claims under the Fourteenth Amendment.

The Court has not varied its standard of review when entertaining other equal protection challenges to congressional measures. And *Bolling v. Sharpe*, supra, itself involved extensive congressional regulation of the segregated District of Columbia public schools.

Congress has considerable latitude, presenting special concerns for judicial review, when it exercises its "unique remedial powers…under section 5 of the Fourteenth Amendment," but this case does not implicate those powers. Section 5 empowers Congress to act respecting the States, and of course this case concerns only the administration of federal programs by federal officials. Section 5 provides to Congress the "power to enforce, by appropriate legislation, the provisions of this article," which in part provides that "[n]o State shall … deny to any person within its jurisdiction the equal protection of the laws." Reflecting the Fourteenth Amendment's "dramatic change in the balance between congressional and state power over matters of race," that section provides to Congress a particular structural role in the oversight of certain of the States' actions.

The Court asserts that *Fullilove* supports its novel application of intermediate scrutiny to "benign" race-conscious measures adopted by Congress. Three reasons defeat this claim. First, *Fullilove* concerned an exercise of Congress' powers under 5 of the Fourteenth Amendment. In *Fullilove*, the Court reviewed an act of Congress that had required States to set aside a percentage of federal construction funds for certain minority-owned businesses to remedy past discrimination in the award of construction contracts. Although the various opinions in *Fullilove* referred to several sources of congressional authority, the opinions make clear that it was 5 that led the Court to apply a different form of review to the challenged program. Last Term, *Croson* resolved any doubt that might remain regarding this point. In *Croson*, we invalidated a local set-aside for minority contractors. We distinguished *Fullilove*, in which we upheld a similar set-aside enacted by Congress, on the ground that, in *Fullilove* "Congress was exercis-

ing its powers under 5 of the Fourteenth Amendment." *Croson* indicated that the decision in *Fullilove* turned on "the unique remedial powers of Congress under 5," and that the latitude afforded Congress in identifying and redressing past discrimination rested on 5's "specific constitutional mandate to enforce the dictates of the Fourteenth Amendment." JUSTICE KENNEDY's concurrence in *Croson* likewise provides the majority with no support, for it questioned whether the Court should, as it had in *Fullilove*, afford any particular latitude even to measures undertaken pursuant to 5.

Second, *Fullilove* applies at most only to congressional measures that seek to remedy identified past discrimination. The Court upheld the challenged measures in *Fullilove* only because Congress had identified discrimination that had particularly affected the construction industry, and had carefully constructed corresponding remedial measures. *Fullilove* indicated that careful review was essential to ensure that Congress acted solely for remedial, rather than other, illegitimate purposes. The FCC and Congress are clearly not acting for any remedial purpose, and the Court today expressly extends its standard to racial classifications that are not remedial in any sense. This case does not present "a considered decision of the Congress and the President," nor does it present a remedial effort or exercise of 5 powers.

Finally, even if *Fullilove* applied outside a remedial exercise of Congress' 5 powers, it would not support today's adoption of the intermediate standard of review proffered by JUSTICE MARSHALL but rejected in *Fullilove*. Under his suggested standard, the Government's use of racial classifications need only be "'substantially related to achievement'" of important governmental interests. Although the Court correctly observes that a majority did not apply strict scrutiny, six Members of the Court rejected intermediate scrutiny in favor of some more stringent form of review. Three Members of the Court applied strict scrutiny. Chief Justice Burger's opinion, joined by JUSTICE WHITE and Justice Powell, declined to adopt a particular standard of review, but indicated that the Court must conduct "a most searching examination," and that courts must ensure that any congressional program that employs racial or ethnic criteria to accomplish the objective of remedying the present effects of past discrimination is narrowly tailored to the achievement of that goal. JUSTICE STEVENS indicated that "[r]acial classifications are simply too pernicious to permit any but the most exact connection between justification and classification." Even JUSTICE MARSHALL's opinion, joined by JUSTICE BRENNAN and JUSTICE BLACKMUN, undermines the Court's course today: that opinion expressly drew its lower standard of review from the plurality opinion in *Regents of University of Calif. v. Bakke* (1978), a case that did not involve congressional action, and stated that the appropriate standard of review for the congressional measure challenged in *Fullilove* "is the same as that under the Fourteenth Amendment." And, of course, *Fullilove* preceded our determination in *Croson* that strict scrutiny applies to preferences that favor members of minority groups, including challenges considered under the Fourteenth Amendment.

The guarantee of equal protection extends to each citizen, regardless of race: the Federal Government, like the States, may not "deny to any person within its jurisdiction the equal protection of the laws." As we observed only last Term in *Croson*, "[a]bsent searching judicial inquiry into the justification for such race-based measures, there is simply no way of determining what classifications are "benign" or "remedial" and what classifications are in fact motivated by illegitimate notions of racial inferiority or simple racial politics."

The Court's reliance on "benign racial classifications," is particularly troubling. "'Benign' racial classification" is a contradiction in terms. Governmental distinctions among citizens based on race or ethnicity, even in the rare circumstances permitted by our cases, exact costs and carry with them substantial dangers. To the person denied an opportunity or right based on race, the classification is hardly benign. The right to equal protection of the laws is a personal right, securing to each individual an immunity from treatment predicated simply on membership in a particular racial or ethnic group. The Court's emphasis on "benign racial classifications" suggests confidence in its ability to distinguish good from harmful governmental uses of racial criteria. History should teach greater humility. Untethered to narrowly confined remedial notions, "benign" carries with it no independent meaning, but reflects only acceptance of the current generation's conclusion that a politically acceptable burden, imposed on particular citizens on the basis of race, is reasonable. The Court provides no basis for determining when a racial classification fails to be "benevolent." By expressly distinguishing "benign" from remedial race-conscious measures, the Court leaves the distinct possibility that any racial measure found to be substantially related to an important governmental objective is also, by definition, "benign." Depending on the preference of the moment, those racial distinctions might be directed expressly or in practice at any racial or ethnic group. We are a Nation not of black and white alone, but one teeming with divergent communities knitted together by various traditions and carried forth, above all, by individuals. Upon that basis, we are governed by one Constitution, providing a single guarantee of equal protection, one that extends equally to all citizens.

This dispute regarding the appropriate standard of review may strike some as a lawyers' quibble over words, but it is not. The standard of review establishes whether and when the Court and Constitution

Glossary

Croson	*City of Richmond v. J. A. Croson Co.*, a 1989 U.S. Supreme Court case
Fullilove	*Fullilove v. Klutznick*, a 1980 U.S. Supreme Court case
Justice Blackmun	Harry Blackmun, associate justice of the Supreme Court
Justice Brennan	William J. Brennan, associate justice of the Supreme Court
Justice Burger	Warren Burger, chief justice of the United States
Justice Kennedy	Anthony Kennedy, associate justice of the Supreme Court
Justice Marshall	Thurgood Marshall, associate justice of the Supreme Court
Justice Stevens	John Paul Stevens, associate justice of the Supreme Court
Justice White	Byron White, associate justice of the Supreme Court
supra	often used in legal cases to refer "above" to a law or case cited earlier in the document
untethered	unconnected

allow the Government to employ racial classifications. A lower standard signals that the Government may resort to racial distinctions more readily. The Court's departure from our cases is disturbing enough, but more disturbing still is the renewed toleration of racial classifications that its new standard of review embodies....

In sum, the Government has not met its burden even under the Court's test that approves of racial classifications that are substantially related to an important governmental objective. Of course, the programs even more clearly fail the strict scrutiny that should be applied. The Court has determined, in essence, that Congress and all federal agencies are exempted, to some ill-defined but significant degree, from the Constitution's equal protection requirements. This break with our precedents greatly undermines equal protection guarantees, and permits distinctions among citizens based on race and ethnicity which the Constitution clearly forbids. I respectfully dissent.

ZELMAN V. SIMMONS-HARRIS (2002)

O'Connor's Concurrence

Today's decision [does not] signal a major departure from this Court's prior Establishment Clause jurisprudence. A central tool in our analysis of cases in this area has been the *Lemon* test. As originally formulated, a statute passed this test only if it had "a secular legislative purpose," if its "principal or primary effect" was one that "neither advance[d] nor inhibit[ed] religion," and if it did "not foster an excessive government entanglement with religion." In *Agostini v. Felton*, we folded the entanglement inquiry into the primary effect inquiry. This made sense because both inquiries rely on the same evidence, and the degree of entanglement has implications for whether a statute advances or inhibits religion....

The Court's opinion in these cases focuses on a narrow question related to the *Lemon* test: how to apply the primary effects prong in indirect aid cases? Specifically, it clarifies the basic inquiry when trying to determine whether a program that distributes aid to beneficiaries, rather than directly to service providers, has the primary effect of advancing or inhibiting religion, or, as I have put it, of "endors[ing] or disapprov[ing] ... religion." Courts are instructed to consider two factors: first, whether the program administers aid in a neutral fashion, without differentiation based on the religious status of beneficiaries or providers of services; second, and more importantly, whether beneficiaries of indirect aid have a genuine choice among religious and nonreligious organizations when determining the organization to which they will direct that aid. If the answer to either query is "no," the program should be struck down under the Establishment Clause....

III

There is little question in my mind that the Cleveland voucher program is neutral as between religious schools and nonreligious schools. *Justice Souter* rejects the Court's notion of neutrality, proposing that the neutrality of a program should be gauged not by the opportunities it presents but rather by its effects. In particular, a "neutrality test ... [should] focus on a category of aid that may be directed to religious as well as secular schools, and ask whether the scheme favors a religious direction." *Justice Souter* doubts that the Cleveland program is neutral under this view. He surmises that the cap on tuition that voucher schools may charge low-income students encourages these students to attend religious rather than nonreligious private voucher schools. But *Justice Souter's* notion of neutrality is inconsistent with that in our case law. As we put it in *Agostini*, government aid must be "made available to both religious and secular beneficiaries on a nondiscriminatory basis."

I do not agree that the nonreligious schools have failed to provide Cleveland parents reasonable alternatives to religious schools in the voucher program. For nonreligious schools to qualify as genuine options for parents, they need not be superior to religious schools in every respect. They need only be adequate substitutes for religious schools in the eyes of parents. The District Court record demonstrates that nonreligious schools were able to compete effectively with Catholic and other religious schools in the Cleveland voucher program. The best evidence of this is that many parents with vouchers selected nonreligious private schools over religious alternatives and an even larger number of parents send their children to community and magnet schools rather than seeking vouchers at all. Moreover, there is no record evidence that any voucher-eligible student was turned away from a nonreligious private school in the voucher program, let alone a community or magnet school.

To support his hunch about the effect of the cap on tuition under the voucher program, *Justice Souter* cites national data to suggest that, on average, Catholic schools have a cost advantage over other types of schools. Even if national statistics were relevant for evaluating the Cleveland program, *Justice Souter* ignores evidence which suggests that, at a national level, nonreligious private schools may target a market for different, if not higher, quality of education. For example, nonreligious private schools are smaller; have smaller class sizes; have more highly educated teachers; and have principals with longer job tenure than Catholic schools.

Additionally, *Justice Souter's* theory that the Cleveland voucher program's cap on the tuition encourages low-income students to attend religious schools ignores that these students receive nearly double the amount of tuition assistance under the community schools program than under the voucher program and that none of the community schools is religious.

In my view the more significant finding in these cases is that Cleveland parents who use vouchers to send their children to religious private schools do so as a result of true private choice. The Court rejects, correctly, the notion that the high percentage of voucher recipients who enroll in religious private schools necessarily demonstrates that parents do not actually have the option to send their children to nonreligious schools. Likewise, the mere fact that some parents enrolled their children in religious schools associated with a different faith than their own says little about whether these parents had reasonable nonreligious options. Indeed, no voucher student has been known to be turned away from a nonreligious private school participating in the voucher program. This is impressive given evidence in the record that the present litigation has discouraged the entry of some nonreligious private schools into the voucher program. Finally, as demonstrated above, the Cleveland program does not establish financial incentives to undertake a religious education.

I find the Court's answer to the question whether parents of students eligible for vouchers have a genuine choice between religious and nonreligious schools persuasive. In looking at the voucher program, all the choices available to potential beneficiaries of the government program should be considered. In these cases, parents who were eligible to apply for a voucher also had the option, at a minimum, to send their children to community schools. Yet the Court of Appeals chose not to look at community schools, let alone magnet schools, when evaluating the Cleveland voucher program. That decision was incorrect. Focusing in these cases only on the program challenged by respondents ignores how the educational system in Cleveland actually functions. The record indicates that, in 1999, two nonreligious private schools that had previously served 15 percent of the students in the voucher program were prompted to convert to community schools because parents were concerned about the litigation surrounding the program, and because a new community schools program provided more per-pupil financial aid. Many of the students that enrolled in the two schools under the voucher program transferred to the community schools program and continued to attend these schools. This incident provides strong evidence that both parents and nonreligious schools view the voucher program and the community schools program as reasonable alternatives.

Considering all the educational options available to parents whose children are eligible for vouchers, including community and magnet schools, the Court finds that parents in the Cleveland schools have an array of nonreligious options. Not surprisingly, respondents present no evidence that any students who were candidates for a voucher were denied slots in a community school or a magnet school. Indeed, the record suggests the opposite with respect to community schools....

Ultimately, *Justice Souter* relies on very narrow data to draw rather broad conclusions. One year of poor test scores at four community schools targeted at the most challenged students from the inner city says little about the value of those schools, let alone the quality of the 6 other community schools and 24 magnet schools in Cleveland. *Justice Souter*'s use of statistics confirms the Court's wisdom in refusing to consider them when assessing the Cleveland program's constitutionality. What appears to motivate *Justice Souter*'s analysis is a desire for a limiting principle to rule out certain nonreligious schools as alternatives to religious schools in the voucher program. But the goal of the Court's Establishment Clause jurisprudence is to determine whether, after the Cleveland voucher program was enacted, parents were free to direct state educational aid in either a nonreligious or religious direction. That inquiry requires an evaluation of all reasonable educational options Ohio provides the Cleveland school system, regardless of whether they are formally made available in the same section of the Ohio Code as the voucher program.

Based on the reasoning in the Court's opinion, which is consistent with the realities of the Cleveland educational system, I am persuaded that the Cleveland voucher program affords parents of eligible children genuine nonreligious options and is consistent with the Establishment Clause.

Glossary

jurisprudence	the theory and philosophy of law
Justice Souter	David Souter, associate justice of the U.S. Supreme Court

GRUTTER V. BOLLINGER (2003)

With these principles in mind, we turn to the question whether the Law School's use of race is justified by a compelling state interest. Before this Court, as they have throughout this litigation, respondents assert only one justification for their use of race in the admissions process: obtaining "the educational benefits that flow from a diverse student body." In other words, the Law School asks us to recognize, in the context of higher education, a compelling state interest in student body diversity.

We first wish to dispel the notion that the Law School's argument has been foreclosed, either expressly or implicitly, by our affirmative-action cases decided since *Bakke*. It is true that some language in those opinions might be read to suggest that remedying past discrimination is the only permissible justification for race-based governmental action. But we have never held that the only governmental use of race that can survive strict scrutiny is remedying past discrimination. Nor, since *Bakke*, have we directly addressed the use of race in the context of public higher education. Today, we hold that the Law School has a compelling interest in attaining a diverse student body.

The Law School's educational judgment that such diversity is essential to its educational mission is one to which we defer. The Law School's assessment that diversity will, in fact, yield educational benefits is substantiated by respondents and their *amici*. Our scrutiny of the interest asserted by the Law School is no less strict for taking into account complex educational judgments in an area that lies primarily within the expertise of the university. Our holding today is in keeping with our tradition of giving a degree of deference to a university's academic decisions, within constitutionally prescribed limits.

We have long recognized that, given the important purpose of public education and the expansive freedoms of speech and thought associated with the university environment, universities occupy a special niche in our constitutional tradition. In announcing the principle of student body diversity as a compelling state interest, Justice Powell [in *Bakke*] invoked our cases recognizing a constitutional dimension, grounded in the First Amendment, of educational autonomy: "The freedom of a university to make its own judgments as to education includes the selection of its student body." From this premise,

Justice Powell reasoned that by claiming "the right to select those students who will contribute the most to the 'robust exchange of ideas,'" a university "seek[s] to achieve a goal that is of paramount importance in the fulfillment of its mission." Our conclusion that the Law School has a compelling interest in a diverse student body is informed by our view that attaining a diverse student body is at the heart of the Law School's proper institutional mission, and that "good faith" on the part of a university is "presumed" absent "a showing to the contrary."

As part of its goal of "assembling a class that is both exceptionally academically qualified and broadly diverse," the Law School seeks to "enroll a 'critical mass' of minority students." The Law School's interest is not simply "to assure within its student body some specified percentage of a particular group merely because of its race or ethnic origin." That would amount to outright racial balancing, which is patently unconstitutional. Rather, the Law School's concept of critical mass is defined by reference to the educational benefits that diversity is designed to produce.

These benefits are substantial. As the District Court emphasized, the Law School's admissions policy promotes "cross-racial understanding," helps to break down racial stereotypes, and "enables [students] to better understand persons of different races." These benefits are "important and laudable," because "classroom discussion is livelier, more spirited, and simply more enlightening and interesting" when the students have "the greatest possible variety of backgrounds."

The Law School's claim of a compelling interest is further bolstered by its *amici*, who point to the educational benefits that flow from student body diversity. In addition to the expert studies and reports entered into evidence at trial, numerous studies show that student body diversity promotes learning outcomes, and "better prepares students for an increasingly diverse workforce and society, and better prepares them as professionals."

These benefits are not theoretical but real, as major American businesses have made clear that the skills needed in today's increasingly global marketplace can only be developed through exposure to widely diverse people, cultures, ideas, and viewpoints. What is more, high-ranking retired officers and civilian leaders of the United States military assert that, "[b]ased on [their] decades of experience," a "highly qualified, racially diverse officer corps…is essential to the military's ability to fulfill its principle mission to provide national security." The primary sources for the Nation's officer corps are the service academies and the Reserve Officers Training Corps (ROTC), the latter comprising students already admitted to participating colleges and universities. At present, "the military cannot achieve an officer corps that is *both* highly qualified *and* racially diverse unless the service academies and the ROTC used limited race-conscious recruiting and admissions policies." To fulfill its mission, the military "must be selective in admissions for training and education for the officer corps, *and* it must train and educate a highly qualified, racially diverse officer corps in a racially diverse setting." We agree that "[i]t requires only a small step from this analysis to conclude that our country's other most selective institutions must remain both diverse and selective."

We have repeatedly acknowledged the overriding importance of preparing students for work and citizenship, describing education as pivotal to "sustaining our political and cultural heritage" with a fundamental role in maintaining the fabric of society. This Court has long recognized that "education … is the very foundation of good citizenship." For this reason, the diffusion of knowledge and opportunity through public institutions of higher education must be accessible to all individuals regardless of race or ethnicity. The United States, as *amicus curiae*, affirms that "[e]nsuring that public institutions are open and available to all segments of American society, including people of all races and ethnicities, represents a paramount government objective." And, "[n]owhere is the importance of such openness more acute than in the context of higher education." Effective participation by members of all racial and ethnic groups in the civic life of our Nation is essential if the dream of one Nation, indivisible, is to be realized.

Moreover, universities, and in particular, law schools, represent the training ground for a large number of our Nation's leaders. Individuals with law degrees occupy roughly half the state governorships, more than half the seats in the United States Senate, and more than a third of the seats in the United States House of Representatives. The pattern is even more striking when it comes to highly selective law schools. A handful of these schools accounts for 25 of the 100 United States Senators, 74 United States Courts of Appeals judges, and nearly 200 of the more than 600 United States District Court judges.

In order to cultivate a set of leaders with legitimacy in the eyes of the citizenry, it is necessary that the path to leadership be visibly open to talented and qualified individuals of every race and ethnicity. All members of our heterogeneous society must have confidence in the openness and integrity of the educational institutions that provide this training. As we have recognized, law schools "cannot be effective in isolation from the individuals and institutions with which the law interacts." Access to legal education (and thus the legal profession) must be inclusive of talented and qualified individuals of every race and ethnicity, so that all members of our heterogeneous society may participate in the educational institutions that provide the training and education necessary to succeed in America.

The Law School does not premise its need for critical mass on "any belief that minority students always (or even consistently) express some characteristic minority viewpoint on any issue." To the contrary, diminishing the force of such stereotypes is both a crucial part of the Law School's mission, and one that it cannot accomplish with only token numbers of minority students. Just as growing up in a particular region or having particular professional experiences is likely to affect an individual's views, so too is one's own, unique experience of being a racial minority in a society, like our own, in which race unfortunately still matters. The Law School has

Glossary

heterogeneous	varied, diverse
holding	a term referring to the legal principle that a court asserts and uses as the basis for issuing a ruling
Justice Powell	Lewis F. Powell, associate justice of the Supreme Court
laudable	praiseworthy

determined, based on its experience and expertise, that a "critical mass" of underrepresented minorities is necessary to further its compelling interest in securing the educational benefits of a diverse student body.

J. Robert Oppenheimer (AP/Wide World Photos)

J. ROBERT OPPENHEIMER   1904–1967

Physicist and Government Adviser

Featured Documents
◆ **Memorandum to Brigadier General Thomas Farrell on the Radiological Dangers of a Nuclear Detonation (1945)**
◆ **A Report on the International Control of Atomic Energy (1946)**
◆ **General Advisory Committee's Report on the Building of the H-Bomb (1949)**

Overview

J. Robert Oppenheimer was born in New York City to Ella and Julius Oppenheimer on April 22, 1904. He was educated at the private Ethical Culture School. This institution had been founded by Felix Adler, a strong advocate of modern liberal humanism, who argued in the disastrous wake of World War I that the only way to avoid such catastrophes in the future was to create a single world government. These ideas deeply influenced Oppenheimer's later political thought. In 1925 Oppenheimer completed an undergraduate degree in chemistry at Harvard in just three years. He also developed an intense interest in experimental physics and decided to pursue further study in that field. Since there was at that time no world-class department of physics in the United States, he enrolled at Cambridge University in England. After a year, however, it became obvious that he did not have the painstaking technique necessary to become a great laboratory experimenter, and he switched to the study of theoretical physics at Göttingen in Germany, completing his PhD in 1927. He took his advanced degree in German and lectured the following year in Dutch (a language he learned in only a few weeks) during an academic appointment in the Netherlands. Oppenheimer had a remarkable facility with language; he not only was proficient in Greek, Latin, and French (all commonly taught in the universities of the time) but also learned Sanskrit simply for his own reading interests.

Oppenheimer is considered the father of mathematical theoretical physics in the United States. In the 1920s and 1930s he did fundamental work on both relativity and quantum mechanics (whose relationship has still not been resolved) and was the first to predict the existence of black holes. His most important theoretical work is considered to be the publication in 1928, in collaboration with Max Born, of the Born-Oppenheimer approximation, which makes possible mathematical computations concerning the wavefunction of molecules in quantum chemistry. As an academic, he built the Department of Physics at the University of California at Berkeley from scratch (while simultaneously working in the more established department at Caltech to stay in touch with the physics community). In 1947 he took over Albert Einstein's position as director of the Institute for Advanced Study in Princeton, New Jersey, where he began for the first time to incorporate humanities into the program. For almost any physicist those accomplishments alone would have made a brilliant career, but in Oppenheimer's case they hardly approach the significance of his work as scientific chief of the Manhattan Project—the U.S. government's program to develop nuclear weapons during World War II—and his subsequent role in national politics.

In 1941 Oppenheimer was invited by the government to begin work on the calculations necessary to design an atomic bomb, and in 1942 he was made director of the secret laboratory at Los Alamos, New Mexico, under the military command of General Leslie Groves. In this capacity he oversaw a team of America's leading physicists, chemists, and engineers working to design and build an atomic bomb based on the newly discovered principle of nuclear fission, using the enormous energies released when atoms of heavy elements such as uranium-235 or plutonium are split apart. Oppenheimer's team produced three weapons—the first one exploded in the Trinity Test near Alamogordo, New Mexico, on July 16, 1945, and two more that were dropped on the Japanese cities of Hiroshima and Nagasaki in August to end World War II.

After the war Oppenheimer served as chairman of the General Advisory Committee to the U.S. Atomic Energy Commission, one of the most important positions in developing government policy on nuclear weapons and nuclear energy. After his attempts to internationalize control of nuclear weapons and prevent the arms race between the United States and Soviet Union failed, Oppenheimer was attacked by his political enemies over his links to radical politics in the 1930s and was denied his security clearance in an infamous McCarthy-era hearing in 1954. Having lost all influence with the government, Oppenheimer concentrated on his academic work at the Institute for Advanced Study and engaged in a career as a public lecturer, speaking against the dangers of nuclear war. His public reputation was rehabilitated to a degree by the John F. Kennedy administration in 1963, with the grant of the Enrico Fermi Award for achievements in physics (ironically named after a scientist who had worked under Oppenheimer at Los Alamos). He died from cancer on February 18, 1967.

Explanation and Analysis of Documents

Oppenheimer gained prominence as a physicist and academic because of his success in publishing research in the highly specialized language of the physical sciences and

1904

■ **April 22**
J. Robert Oppenheimer is born in New York City.

1925

■ Oppenheimer completes his undergraduate degree at Harvard University.

1925–1926

■ Oppenheimer studies experimental physics at Cambridge University, England.

1927

■ Oppenheimer take his PhD in theoretical physics from the University of Göttingen in Germany.

1929

■ Oppenheimer takes a joint appointment at California Institute of Technology, Pasadena, and the University of California, Berkeley, building the latter into the first major physics program in the United States during his residence there through 1947.

1943

■ Oppenheimer is put in charge of designing and building the atomic bomb as director of the Los Alamos Scientific Laboratory in New Mexico, continuing as director of the facility until 1946.

1945

■ **May 11**
Oppenheimer sends a memorandum to Brigadier General Thomas Farrell describing the radiological dangers of a nuclear detonation.

■ **July 16**
Oppenheimer oversees the Trinity Test, the first detonation of a nuclear weapon.

1946

■ **March 16**
Oppenheimer and four other consultants submit a report on the international control of atomic energy to the secretary of state's Committee on Atomic Energy.

through his abilities in the seminar room, though he was a somewhat shaky lecturer. During the war his success at Los Alamos depended on his skill at mediating among the very different worlds of the soldiers, scientists, and engineers assigned to the project and persuading them to work together in the face of personal and political suspicions and rivalries. After the war, as an important adviser to the U.S. government on nuclear issues, he had to communicate in the bureaucratic language of government work, in documents of the type represented here. After the failure of his bureaucratic career, he turned to public lectures—some delivered on the then-new medium of television—and to publishing less-formal essays to convince the world of the dangers of the arms race between the United States and Soviet Union.

◆ **Memorandum to Brigadier General Thomas Farrell on the Radiological Dangers of a Nuclear Detonation**

Thomas Farrell, chief of staff to General Leslie Groves, was the second-ranking military officer in the command chain of the Manhattan Project (the project's name reflecting the fact that its headquarters had once been in New York City). This memo from Oppenheimer seeks to inform Farrell about possible dangers to military personnel from direct radiation and from radioactive fallout in the vicinity of a detonation of the "special bomb." Oppenheimer also notes the importance of "meteorological effects," such as temperature, wind, and especially rain in determining where and how soon the radioactive cloud rising from the explosion would return to the ground.

Likened at the time to gas warfare, which had recently been internationally outlawed because its use was considered immoral, the dropping of bombs on Japan created fallout that killed more than one hundred and fifty thousand people in the immediate aftermath and, in the ensuing years, was responsible for deaths from cancer and for birth defects among the descendants of the people exposed to it. The radioactivity of the heavy metals used in the bombs also took a toll on the scientists working on nuclear weapons at Los Alamos and elsewhere. Although Oppenheimer's own throat cancer might well have been associated with smoking, Enrico Fermi and many other scientists would eventually die of cancers that were thought to be directly related to their exposure to radiation.

In discussions of the moral issues of the atomic bombings of Japan, this memo from Oppenheimer to Farrell is often cited as evidence that the scientists working on the bombs did not understand the nature, extent, and effects of radioactive fallout. For example, Oppenheimer concludes his memo by stating that the "probable results of monitoring will be that it will be quite safe to enter" the test area. However, he applied that statement only to entry "some weeks" after the detonation. The document also makes it clear that Oppenheimer and his team had a quite accurate understanding of how deadly the weapon would be. The memo states that the bomb itself contained "about 109 times as much toxic material ... as is needed for a single lethal dose"—in other words, it contained enough radioactive material to kill a billion people. Moreover, apart from this lingering fallout, direct radiation from the nuclear blast would be "lethal within a radius of about six-tenths of a mile." Oppenheimer does observe that little was known about how radioactive fallout would move through the atmosphere, but considerable knowledge in this area was soon gained from the Trinity Test.

Oppenheimer's memo is a purely technical document that was not directed to a lay audience. It simply states the radiation effects predicted for a nuclear detonation and the dangers those effects might pose to personnel in the vicinity. Yet even this brief factual presentation makes it abundantly clear that he and his team had created a new kind of weapon, one that could destroy an entire city and poison its hinterland. Moreover, precisely because of this new kind and scale of destructive power, the bomb obviously would be most effective when used against cities, not against traditional military targets that might be spread over many square miles in the field. It is fair to ask, then, why men like Oppenheimer and Fermi and many others, dedicated to pacifism and internationalism, worked to create such a terrible weapon. On the one hand, Nazi Germany seemed such a threat to the most basic institutions of civilization that it was easy to justify going to almost any lengths to defeat it. Indeed, although the bombs were actually used against Germany's ally Japan (because Germany had, in the meantime, been overcome by conventional means), the rationale for the development of the atomic bomb was the defeat of Germany and especially the fear that, since most of the basic research supporting nuclear fission had been done by German scientists before the war, Germany might develop its own bomb.

◆   **A Report on the International Control of Atomic Energy**

In late 1945, after World War II had ended, the government created a new body to give advice about the development of atomic energy and atomic weapons, the secretary of state's Committee on Atomic Energy. It was headed by the then undersecretary of state Dean Acheson and included many of the same people who had worked on the Manhattan Project, including Oppenheimer's old military partner, General Leslie Groves. In order to garner scientific advice, the General Advisory Committee was created under David Lilienthal. Lilienthal was a bureaucrat who had had a successful tenure at the Tennessee Valley Authority, which had brought electrical power to much of the rural South during the Great Depression and the war. Oppenheimer was chief among the scientists whom Lilienthal appointed to give technical advice. This made Oppenheimer a very influential figure in the future development of nuclear energy. It also involved him in the internal political struggles of the U.S. government.

In order to understand Oppenheimer's views on arms control, one needs to appreciate that, like many veterans of the Manhattan Project, he had been profoundly affected by the destructive power of the weapons he had helped to cre-

Time Line

1946
- Oppenheimer is appointed as chairman of the General Advisory Committee to the U.S. Atomic Energy Commission, serving until 1952.
- Oppenheimer is appointed as a member of the Research and Development Board's Committee on Atomic Energy, serving until 1954.

1947
- Oppenheimer takes over Albert Einstein's position as director and professor of physics at the Institute for Advanced Study in Princeton, New Jersey, posts he held until he retired in 1966.

1949
- **October 30**
Oppenheimer, as chairman of the U.S. Atomic Energy Commission's General Advisory Committee, transmits his committee's report on building the hydrogen bomb to the commission's head.

1954
- **May 27**
Oppenheimer's security clearance is revoked by the Personnel Security Board of the U.S. Atomic Energy Commission.

1962
- **May 3**
Oppenheimer is elected as a Fellow of the Royal Society in Great Britain.

1963
- President John F. Kennedy gives Oppenheimer the Enrico Fermi Award as a token of political rehabilitation.

1967
- **February 18**
Oppenheimer dies at his home in Princeton, New Jersey.

A giant column of dark smoke rises more than twenty thousand feet into the air, after the second atomic bomb ever used in warfare explodes over Nagasaki, Japan. (AP/Wide World Photos)

ate. He held a strongly religious outlook on life, although he was not an adherent of one of the common American faith traditions. The greatest influence on his moral philosophy was the Bhagavad Gita, an ancient Hindu work of spirituality and poetry. (It was to read this book in its original language that he had learned Sanskrit.) He saw the conversion of matter to energy in a nuclear explosion as the human unshackling of one of the fundamental processes of the universe, a phenomenon to him akin to the revelation of a god. Through his work, he believed, the human race had acquired the ability to exterminate itself. His was a deeply pessimistic reaction to the tasks that, in his view, had fallen to him by fate. He feared that the weapons he had made, and the more powerful ones to follow, would not lead to peace but, through an international arms race, would eventually threaten an even more destructive war than the one he had helped to end.

Oppenheimer took his positions based on his own internal moral compass and his beliefs in what he considered to be necessary. He was probably chosen for the General Advisory Committee because it was known that he supported the internationalist beliefs of Acheson—as did other officials, such as Secretary of War Henry Stimson. The main idea of the portion of the report included here, and a fundamental basis of the report as a whole, is one that Oppenheimer shared with Acheson and Stimson: namely, that nuclear weapons were too terrible to use in future conflicts

and that therefore the control of nuclear energy should be internationalized, so that no individual country would ever have the resources necessary to manufacture and use them. Even though this would entail surrendering America's nuclear monopoly (which, since all that was at issue were scientific facts, would be short-lived anyway), the effective elimination of nuclear weapons from any nation's arsenal seemed a better guarantee of security. Other figures, like Secretary of State James Burns, felt that it would be foolish to give up such a military advantage and did not trust the Soviet Union (America's main rival in the developing cold war) to act rationally in its own interest.

In the short term the internationalist view taken by Oppenheimer and embodied in what became known as the Acheson-Lilienthal Report triumphed. In 1946 it became the official policy of the administration of President Harry S. Truman. The section of the report quoted here touches on the essential feature of this policy, although without giving the details. That policy envisioned the creation of a new United Nations Atomic Development Authority (ADA). This international body would own all nuclear resources everywhere in the world, from uranium mines through processed heavy metals. Nuclear power plants would continue in the hands of national governments, but the ADA would give them only enough fissile material to operate, without any surplus for weapons use. Thus no nation in the world would have nuclear weapons. (Those already created by the United States would be handed over to the ADA.)

Oppenheimer and his fellow consultants deal mainly here with the issue of disclosing nuclear information held as secret by the United States. They state at the outset that this technical "knowledge" is "one of the elements of the present monopoly of the United States" in the field of nuclear weapons, and they concede that providing some of this knowledge to others might "provide the basis for an acceleration of a rival effort" to make such weapons. On the other hand, they argue that sharing of some of this information is necessary because without it, the United Nations' nuclear commission "cannot even begin the task that has been assigned to it."

Oppenheimer's consulting team proposes releasing secret nuclear data in three stages. The first stage would involve the basic knowledge the UN commission's members and their technical advisers need merely to set up the ADA. These personnel "must be in a position to understand what the prospects for constructive applications of atomic energy are," "to appreciate the nature of the safeguards which the plan we here propose affords," and "to evaluate alternatives which may arise." Most important, "they must have a sound enough overall knowledge of the field as a whole to recognize that no relevant or significant matters have been withheld." The consultants note that "much of the information" needed for these purposes "is already widely known" but that "there are further items now held by us as secret without which the necessary insight will be difficult to obtain." However, these additional items "are of a theoretical and descriptive nature" and "are largely qualitative," involving "almost nothing of know-how." In essence, the consultants recommend that information of this kind be shared, since "the process of reaching common agreement on measures of international control presupposes an adequate community of knowledge of fact."

A second stage of information sharing would be needed, the team says, once the ADA "is in existence and undertakes operations in a given field," such as constructing nuclear reactors. At that point, "it must have made available to it all information bearing on that field—practical as well as theoretical." A third stage might be necessary if "at a late date" the ADA, when fully established as a worldwide regulatory authority, were to engage in "research and development in the field of atomic explosives." The consultants emphasize that the release of information at each stage must be fixed by international agreement, but they warn that "a too cautious release of information to the Atomic Development Authority might in fact have the effect of preventing it from ever coming to life." They conclude that "one of the decisive responsibilities of the Authority is the establishment and maintenance of the security of the world against atomic warfare. It must be encouraged to exercise that responsibility, and to obtain for itself the technical mastery that is essential."

Despite the quick adoption by the Truman administration of the plan outlined in the Acheson-Lilienthal Report, in the longer run the hopes of Oppenheimer and his colleagues were disappointed. When Truman's special ambassador Bernard Baruch presented the plan in the United Nations, the Soviet Union ultimately made its implementation impossible. The USSR, with its own nuclear program under way, did not react well to additional requirements insisted upon by Truman and Baruch. In particular, the Soviets objected to submitting themselves to the authority of the United Nations to impose sanctions for violations of the proposed accord, to allowing unlimited inspection by UN officials, and to the proclamation by the United States that it would keep its own nuclear arsenal until it and it alone decided that sufficient safeguards were in place to justify abandoning it. The failure of the international approach supported by Oppenheimer in the Acheson-Lilienthal Report meant that there would be no curb in the growth of nuclear weapons. This was the start of the arms race as the Soviet Union rushed to design and test its own atomic bomb.

◆ General Advisory Committee's Report on the Building of the H-Bomb

The first detonation of an atomic bomb by the Soviet Union took place on August 29, 1949. The signature of its radioactive fallout was immediately detected by the American military. The U.S. government commissioned a report from a panel of nuclear experts headed by Oppenheimer. Their report considered various options available to the United States in response to the new Soviet threat. One potential American response was to consider building a new kind of weapon referred to as the "super" in the jargon of atomic scientists and generally known as the hydrogen bomb. This device would not split heavy atoms apart, as did the fission process of the atomic bomb, but would combine together atoms of hydrogen (specifically the heavy isotope

deuterium) into helium, re-creating the process that powers the sun. Oppenheimer's report makes it clear that a "characteristic of the super bomb is that once the problem of initiation" of the fusion reaction was solved, there would be "no limit to the explosive power of the bomb itself except that imposed by requirements of delivery."

The atomic bombs dropped on Japan produced blasts equivalent to those of a few thousand tons of a conventional explosive like TNT. The explosive force produced by a hydrogen bomb is virtually unlimited. In practice, the largest explosive yield from such a device came in a Soviet test of a bomb whose force was equivalent to fifty million tons of TNT, more than all the conventional explosives that have ever been detonated in human history. Such an explosion could kill human beings sixty miles from its center and produce an enormous amount of radioactive fallout. Oppenheimer's report clearly anticipated the proposed bomb's power, stating that "it has generally been estimated that the weapon would have an explosive effect some hundreds of times that of present fission bombs. This would correspond to a damage area of the order of hundreds of square miles, to thermal radiation effects extending over a comparable area, and to very grave contamination problems." The possession of such a weapon would seem to counter any threat posed by Soviet atomic weapons.

Oppenheimer, however, opposed production of the "super"—in the first instance, on moral grounds. Such a weapon could not be targeted exclusively on "installations of military or semi-military purposes." As Oppenheimer's report phrases it, "Its use therefore carries much further than the atomic bomb itself the policy of exterminating civilian populations." In his view even the possession of such a weapon constituted a threat of genocide, a morally unacceptable position to hold or to offer in the contest with the Soviets for the allegiance of other countries around the world. The committee's majority opinion, which Oppenheimer supported, warned that the use of a hydrogen bomb "would involve a decision to slaughter a vast number of civilians," going on to voice alarm "as to the possible global effects of the radioactivity." Thus "a super bomb might become a weapon of genocide." Moreover, the mere "existence of such a weapon in our armory would have far-reaching effects on world opinion; reasonable people the world over would realize that the existence of a weapon of this type … represents a threat to the future of the human race which is intolerable." For this reason, "the psychological effect of the weapon in our hands would be adverse to our interest."

On the other hand, when this report was produced in 1949 it was not at all clear that the "super" was technically feasible. But it was certain that efforts to develop and test such a weapon would take resources away from the production of fission weapons whose destructive potential would be a credible deterrent against the Soviets even in the seemingly unlikely event that they developed a hydrogen bomb. Oppenheimer suggested that a better alternative would be to negotiate a ban, binding on both superpowers, on research into such weapons.

Other members of the General Advisory Committee, including the respected Enrico Fermi, took a much stronger stand than Oppenheimer, suggesting that the idea of making and using or threatening to use such a weapon was so morally evil that the United States should never pursue it, regardless of its technical feasibility or what the Soviets might do. In fact, once the work of the physicist Edward Teller in 1951 made it clear that a hydrogen bomb could be built, Oppenheimer reversed the position he had taken in the 1949 report, largely because he considered it inevitable that the Soviets (who showed no inclination to negotiate the matter) would eventually make one. Against the advice of the General Advisory Committee, work on the "super" went ahead. The first American hydrogen bomb was tested in 1952; the Soviets tested their first hydrogen bomb in 1955.

Impact and Legacy

Oppenheimer's statements of his best moral and scientific judgment on large issues—for example, his desire to internationalize the control of nuclear development and his advocacy of building tactical fission weapons rather than hydrogen bombs—came back to haunt him in the 1950s, as did the political causes adopted by some of his relatives and associates. It was the time of the great red scare in America, when anything involving Communism was widely regarded with fear and suspicion. The U.S. senator Joseph McCarthy and the director of the Federal Bureau of Investigation, J. Edgar Hoover, had compiled certain evidence against Oppenheimer. Among other things, his wife, Katherine, and his brother, Frank, had been members of the Communist Party in the 1930s (an era in which a number of Americans thought Communism might offer potential solutions to the Great Depression and to the threat of another world war). Moreover, while he was working at Los Alamos during the war, he had been contacted by a Soviet agent. He had reported this contact immediately to military security officers, but in the charged political atmosphere of the 1950s the slightest suspicion could and did end careers. In this volatile environment even Oppenheimer's concerns about the spread of nuclear weapons could be regarded as somehow disloyal. Oppenheimer was grilled before McCarthy's Senate committee in 1953, and political enemies of his on the Atomic Energy Commission and in Congress demanded that President Dwight D. Eisenhower revoke his security clearance. It was revoked the following year shortly before its expiration.

The loss of his security clearance meant the end of Oppenheimer's career in government. He continued to make his case against the arms race to the public, but to little effect. Over the ensuing decades the United States and the Soviet Union each deployed thousands of nuclear warheads on long-range missiles. Oppenheimer's achievement in creating nuclear weapons and yet having the moral fortitude to argue for restraint in their use and even their abo-

lition remains without parallel. In particular, his hounding from public life stands as one of the darkest examples of the excesses of the red scare of the 1950s, which threatened the freedoms of speech and conscience enshrined in the U.S. Constitution. His real crime had been to oppose the arms race with the Soviet Union, which various factions of the government had decided would best assure the security of the United States as well as their own control of American policy.

Key Sources

The Library of Congress houses a collection of Oppenheimer's papers amounting to seventy-four thousand items. The catalog of these papers was originally published as a separate monograph: Carolyn H. Sung and David Mathisen, *J. Robert Oppenheimer: A Register of His Papers in the Library of Congress* (1974) and is now updated in an electronic form on the Library of Congress Web site (http://lcweb2.loc.gov/service/mss/eadxmlmss/eadpdfmss/1998/ms998007.pdf). These papers include all of his official correspondence and reports related to his position in various government projects and agencies, an annotated collection of his own published documents prepared in connection with his hearing before the Personnel Security Board of the Atomic Energy Commission, his personal correspondence with the world's leading scientists and intellectuals, and a lifetime of lecture notes. *Robert Oppenheimer: Letters and Recollections*, a collection of Oppenheimer's more personal correspondence and reminiscences of him by his friends and colleagues, was published in 1980 under the editorship of Alice Kimball Smith and Charles Weiner. The final decisions in Oppenheimer's security-clearance hearing in 1954 has been placed online by Yale University (http://www.yale.edu/lawweb/avalon/abomb/oppmenu.htm). Shortly after Oppenheimer lost his security clearance in 1954, Edward R. Murrow interviewed him on the television program *See It Now*. A clip from this show has been placed online by the Atomic Archive (http://www.atomicarchive.com/Movies/Movie8.shtml). Oppenheimer wrote a series of books aimed at informing and shaping public opinion about nuclear issues. These works include *Science and Common Understanding* (1954), the text of which is available online at the Internet Archive (http://www.archive.org/details/scienceandthecom007308mbp), and a collection of essays entitled *The Open Mind* and which is available online (http://www.theatlantic.com/doc/194902/oppenheimer-mind). In 1962 Oppenheimer gave the Whiden Lectures at McMaster University in Canada; the lectures were published in 1964 as *The Flying Trapeze: Three Crises for Physicists*.

Further Reading

■ Articles

Bernstein, Barton. "The Oppenheimer Loyalty-Security Case Reconsidered." *Stanford Law Review* 42 (1990): 1383–1484.

Oppenheimer, J. Robert

"*The active material of the bomb itself is toxic. There is about 109 times as much toxic material initially in the bomb itself as is needed for a single lethal dose.*"

(Memorandum to Brigadier General Thomas Farrell on the Radiological Dangers of a Nuclear Detonation)

"*When fully in operation the plan herein proposed can provide a great measure of security against surprise attack. It can do much more than that. It can create deterrents to the initiation of schemes of aggression, and it can establish patterns of cooperation among nations, the extension of which may even contribute to the solution of the problem of war itself.*"

(A Report on the International Control of Atomic Energy)

"*A second characteristic of the super bomb is that once the problem of initiation has been solved, there is no limit to the explosive power of the bomb itself except that imposed by requirements of delivery.*"

(General Advisory Committee's Report on the Building of the H-Bomb)

"*We base our recommendation on our belief that the extreme dangers to mankind inherent in the proposal wholly outweigh any military advantage that could come from this development. Let it be clearly realized that this is a super weapon; it is in a totally different category from an atomic bomb.... Its use would involve a decision to slaughter a vast number of civilians.*"

(General Advisory Committee's Report on the Building of the H-Bomb)

"*In determining not to proceed to develop the super bomb, we see a unique opportunity of providing by example some limitations on the totality of war and thus of limiting the fear and arousing the hopes of mankind.*"

(General Advisory Committee's Report on the Building of the H-Bomb)

Day, Michael A. "Oppenheimer on the Nature of Science." *Centaurus* 43 (2001): 73–112.

■ **Books**

Bethe, Hans A. *The Road from Los Alamos*. New York: Simon and Schuster, 1991.

Cassidy, David C. *J. Robert Oppenheimer and the American Century*. Upper Saddle River, N.J.: Pi Press, 2005.

Herken, Gregg. *Brotherhood of the Bomb: The Tangled Lives and Loyalties of Robert Oppenheimer, Ernest Lawrence, and Edward Teller*. New York: Henry Holt, 2002.

Mason, Richard. *Oppenheimer's Choice: Reflections from Moral Philosophy*. Albany: State University of New York Press, 2006.

Polenberg, Richard, ed. *In the Matter of J. Robert Oppenheimer: The Security Clearance Hearing*. Ithaca, N.Y.: Cornell University Press, 2002.

Thorpe, Charles. *Oppenheimer: The Tragic Intellect*. Chicago: University of Chicago Press, 2006.

—Bradley A. Skeen

Questions for Further Study

1. Discuss the development of Oppenheimer's political thinking—in particular, his relationship with political leftism, from the childhood influence of Felix Adler's one-world government movement to allegations of Communist involvement during the 1950s. How justified was the concern over his political loyalties as they might affect his role in matters of international security? Was Senator Joseph McCarthy the only person who expressed these concerns or did others of less odious reputation and more genuine motives?

2. How much of Oppenheimer's importance to history is primarily as a scientist and how much more relates to his role as an administrator? How well did he manage interactions with several worlds—those of soldiers, scientists, and government figures and the world at large? How did his abilities as a manager of others affect the success of the Manhattan Project and thus of the United States itself in World War II?

3. As director of the Manhattan Project, Oppenheimer was among the most prominent critics of nuclear warfare, yet he was far from the only person who expressed concerns about the future of a world in which humankind possessed the power to annihilate itself. Others, however, argued just as convincingly that the bombing of Hiroshima and Nagasaki, by rendering a land invasion of Japan unnecessary, actually saved lives in the long run and that the possession of a nuclear arsenal by the United States guaranteed ultimate peace. In your opinion, was the dropping of atomic bombs on Japan in August 1945 justifiable, or did this create more problems than it solved? Does it matter that the bomb was originally built for use against Germany rather than Japan? How might the cold war have played out differently if America had not developed and employed nuclear weaponry? Would the Soviets have managed to build their own bomb anyway, and would this have given them a decisive advantage?

Memorandum to Brigadier General Thomas Farrell on the Radiological Dangers of a Nuclear Detonation (1945)

In accordance with our discussions May 10th I am submitting the following brief summary of the radiological effects to be expected from the special bomb. This may be of use to the services concerned in the operations, and should probably be brought to their attention.

A. The bomb under consideration differs from normal explosive bombs in that its detonation involves the production of radiation and of radioactive substances.

1. The active material of the bomb itself is toxic. There is about 10^9 times as much toxic material initially in the bomb itself as is needed for a single lethal dose.

2. During the detonation, radiations are emitted which (unless personnel is shielded) are expected to be injurious within a radius of a mile and lethal within a radius of about six-tenths of a mile.

3. After detonation, highly radioactive materials are produced. The activity decreases inversely with the time. One second after detonation there will be the equivalent of about 10^{12} curies of radium. After a day this will fall to about 10 million curies.

B. The circumstances of delivery of the bomb should not normally lead to the deposition of a large fraction of either the initial active material or the radioactive products in the immediate vicinity of the target; but the radiations emitted during detonation will, of course, have an effect on exposed personnel in the target area. The actual physical distribution of the radioactive products is not known to us, since it depends in detail on meteorological conditions as well as on the specific air mass motions induced by the explosion; these latter have not been experimentally studied. It is, however, likely that most of the activity will rise to a considerable height above the target and will remain as a fairly compact cloud for a period of hours after the detonation. The subsequent history depends essentially on temperature and wind conditions. If the bomb is delivered during rain, or under conditions of such high humidity that it itself causes rain, it may be expected that most of the active material will be brought down by the rain in the vicinity of the target area.

C. In practice, the following three precautions will have to be observed:

1. Aircraft must maintain a minimum distance from the detonation in order to avoid radiation. Taking into account the dilution of the atmosphere, this minimum distance is about two and one-half miles. Operations should be conducted so that this distance is exceeded if the operations proceed according to plan.

2. Following aircraft must avoid coming close to the cloud of active material, and monitoring to determine the extent and disposition of the activity will be necessary if aircraft are to enter the area within hours of the primary detonation.

3. Certainly if there has been rain, and conceivably without this, some activity may reach the ground in the neighborhood of the target area. Monitoring will be necessary if this area is to be entered within some weeks of the primary detonation. The probable results of monitoring will be that it is quite safe to enter.

J. R. Oppenheimer

Glossary

curies	units of measurement for radioactive material, with one curie equal to the radioactive decay of 37 billion atoms per second; named after French physicist Marie Curie
special bomb	the phrase used by its developers to refer to the atomic bomb

A Report on the International Control of Atomic Energy (1946)

Washington, D. C., March 16, 1946
DEPARTMENT OF STATE PUBLICATION 2498
Disclosure of Information as an Essential of International Action

One of the elements in the present monopoly of the United States is knowledge. This ranges all the way from purely theoretical matters to the intimate practical details of know-how. It is generally recognized that the transmission of any part, or all, of this knowledge to another nation could provide the basis for an acceleration of a rival effort to make atomic weapons. Even that part of our knowledge which is theoretical, which can be transmitted by word of mouth, by formula, or by written note is of value in this context. If such knowledge were available to a rival undertaking it would shorten the time needed for the solution of the practical problems of making atomic weapons, by eliminating certain unworkable alternatives, by fixing more definitely design features which depend on this theoretical knowledge, and by making it possible to undertake the various steps of the program more nearly in parallel, rather than in sequence. It is not…possible to give a reliable estimate of how much such revelation would shorten the time needed for a successful rival effort. It is conceivable that it would not be significantly shortened. It is conceivable that it might be shortened by a year or so. For an evaluation on this point depends on information, which is not available to us, on the detailed plans and policies of such a rival undertaking, as well as on their present state of knowledge. It is, of course, clear that even with all such theoretical knowledge available, a major program, surely lasting many years, is required for the actual production of atomic weapons.

Our monopoly on knowledge cannot be, and should not be, lost at once. Here again there are limitations on the scheduling inherent in the nature of our proposals, and in the nature of the deliberations necessary for their acceptance. But even with the recognition of these limitations, there is a rather wide freedom of choice in the actual scheduling of disclosures. Here considerations of acceptability and of general political background will make a decisive contribution.

It is clear that the information, which this country alone has, can be divided more or less roughly into categories. The acceptance and operation of the plan will require divulging certain categories of this information at successive times. A schedule can outline the point at which this must occur. In particular, there is a limited category of information which should be divulged in the early meetings of the United Nations Commission discussing these problems. There is a more extensive category which must be divulged some years hence after a charter has been adopted and the Atomic Development Authority is ready to start its operations; and there are other categories that may be reserved until the Authority later undertakes some of the subsequent stages of its operations, for instance, those that involve research on weapons. We are convinced that under the plan proposed in this report such scheduling is possible, though it is clear … that many factors beyond the scope of this report, and involving the highest considerations of international policy, will be involved in such schedules. We wish to emphasize that it will involve an initial divulging of information, which is justifiable in view of the importance of early progress on the path of international cooperation.

It is true, as the Secretary of State has said, that there is nothing in the Resolution setting up the Atomic Energy Commission that compels the United States to produce information for the use of the United Nations Commission. But the point that needs to be emphasized is that unless we are prepared to provide the information essential to an understanding of the problem, the Commission itself cannot even begin the task that has been assigned to it.

Let us examine in a little more detail the nature of the information which is required in the early stages. What is important for the discussions in the United Nations Organization Commission is that the Members and their technical advisors have an understanding of the problem of the international control of atomic energy and of the elements of the proposals that the United States member will put forward. They must be in a position to understand what the prospects for constructive applications of atomic energy are and to appreciate the nature of the safeguards which the plan we here propose affords. They must be in a position to evaluate alternatives which may arise, and to have insight into the rather complex interrelations of the various activities in this

Document Text

field. Above all they must have a sound enough overall knowledge of the field as a whole to recognize that no relevant or significant matters have been withheld. For the process of reaching common agreement on measures of international control presupposes an adequate community of knowledge of fact. Much of the information which is required for this purpose is already widely known. We are convinced, however, that there are further items now held by us as secret without which the necessary insight will be difficult to obtain. These items are of a theoretical and descriptive nature and have in large part to do with the constructive applications of atomic energy. In our opinion, they are largely qualitative; and they involve almost nothing of know-how.

On the other hand, when the Atomic Development Authority is in existence and undertakes operations in a given field, it must have made available to it all information bearing on that field—practical as well as theoretical. Thus, if the Authority, as its first major undertaking, attempts to obtain control of raw materials, we must be prepared to make available to it all knowledge bearing on this problem. This will, of course, be a common obligation on all participating nations. Conversely, should it by charter agreement be determined that research and development in the field of atomic explosives will be undertaken by the Authority only at a late date, the specific technological information relating to such developments would not be required by it in the earlier phases. It is important to bear in mind that before the Authority can undertake some of its functions, such as the construction of reactors or the development of power, it will have to spend some time in planning these activities and in research directed toward them, and that information must be made available early enough to make such planning and research effective.

These are examples of requirements for information by the Atomic Development Authority at certain stages of its progress. In accepting the plan here recommended for international control, the United States will be committed to making available this information at the time, and in the full measure required by the operating necessities. Once the sequence and timing of stages has been fixed by negotiation and agreement between the nations, a minimum rate of disclosure of information will have been fixed by the agreement as well. A too cautious release of information to the Atomic Development Authority might in fact have the effect of preventing it from ever coming to life. For one of the decisive responsibilities of the Authority is the establishment and maintenance of the security of the world against atomic warfare. It must be encouraged to exercise that responsibility, and to obtain for itself the technical mastery that is essential.

We may further clarify the nature of the disclosures required by this board's proposals by a reference to a report. We have had the opportunity to examine in detail a report of December, 1945, prepared for the Manhattan District by its Committee on Declassification, a committee of seven scientists, including the wartime heads of all the major laboratories of the Project. This Committee was directed to report on a policy of declassification—that is disclosure—of scientific and technical material now classified as Secret, a policy which would best promote the national welfare, and protect the national security. In interpreting its directive the Committee limited itself to a consideration of these objectives in the absence of any system of international control. It recommended against declassification at the present time of a very considerable body of technical, technological, industrial, and ordnance information that is information bearing directly on the manufacture of weapons and the design and operation of production plants. But it recommended the prompt declassification of a large body of scientific fact and of technical information of noncritical nature and wide applicability. It expressed the view that the further declassification of critical items of basic theoretical knowledge would conduce, not only to the national welfare, but to the long-term national security as well—no doubt because of the damaging effect which continued secrecy in these matters could have on our own scientific and technical progress. Corresponding to these distinctions, the Committee divided our secret scientific and technical information into three categories, the first of which it recommended for immediate declassification; the second of which it recommended for eventual declassification in the interests of long-term, national security of the United States; and for the third of which it recommended against declassification in the absence of effective international control. We have tried to see what technical information this board would find essential for the sort of understanding that must be established as a basis for discussion in the UNO Commission, and to compare this with the items listed in the report of the Committee on Declassification. Many of the facts needed are already public; many are included in Class One; the remainder are all in Class Two, and comprise perhaps one-third of the items there listed. It is important again to emphasize that the Declassification Committee's recommendation was aimed at furthering our own long-term national security in the absence of international measures.

Oppenheimer, J. Robert

MILESTONE DOCUMENTS OF AMERICAN LEADERS

1619

We wish to emphasize that the initial disclosures will place in the hands of a nation (should it be acting in bad faith) information which could lead to an acceleration of an atomic armament program. We do not regard this circumstance as in any way peculiar to the plan recommended in this report. It is inherent in the concept of international control. The adoption of any workable scheme of international control may shorten the time during which the United States has a position as favorable as it has today. We cannot be sure of this, but we must be prepared for it.

In this section we have been discussing the problem of transition to international control as it affects the security of the United States. During this transition the United States' present position of monopoly may be lost somewhat more rapidly than would be the case without international action. But without such action the monopoly would in time disappear in any event. Should the worst happen and, during the transition period, the entire effort collapse, the United States will at all times be in a favorable position with regard to atomic weapons. This favorable position will depend upon material things; less and less will it rest upon keeping nations and individuals ignorant.

When fully in operation the plan herein proposed can provide a great measure of security against surprise attack. It can do much more than that. It can create deterrents to the initiation of schemes of aggression, and it can establish patterns of cooperation among nations, the extension of which may even contribute to the solution of the problem of war itself. When the plan is in full operation there will no longer be secrets about atomic energy. We believe that this is the firmest basis of security; for in the long term there can be no international control and no international cooperation which does not presuppose an international community of knowledge.

Chester I. Barnard
Dr. J. R. Oppenheimer
Dr. Charles A. Thomas
Harry A. Winne
David E. Lilienthal, Chairman

Manhattan District	a military district under the supervision of the U.S. Army Corps of Engineers, the source of the term *Manhattan Project*, the program that developed the atomic bomb
ordnance	munitions, military supplies
Secretary of State	James Francis Byrnes

GENERAL ADVISORY COMMITTEE'S REPORT ON THE BUILDING OF THE H-BOMB (1949)

PART I

(1) PRODUCTION. With regard to the present scale of production of fissionable material, the General Advisory Committee has a recommendation to make the Commission. We are not satisfied that the present scale represents either the maximum or the optimum scale. We recognize the statutory and appropriate role of the National Military Establishment in helping to determine that. We believe, however, that before this issue can be settled, it will be desirable to have from the Commission a careful analysis of what the capacities are which are not now being employed. We have in mind that further plants, both separation and reactor, might be built, more rapidly to convert raw material into fissionable material. It would seem that some notion of the costs, yields and time scales for such undertakings would have to precede any realistic evaluation of what we should do. We recommend that the Commission undertake such studies at high priority. We further recommend that projects should not be dismissed because they are expensive but that their expense be estimated.

(2) TACTICAL DELIVERY. The General Advisory Committee recommends to the Commission an intensification of efforts to make atomic weapons available for tactical purposes, and to give attention to the problem of integration of bomb and carrier design in this field.

(3) NEUTRON PRODUCTION. The General Advisory Committee recommends to the Commission the prompt initiation of a project for the production of freely absorbable neutrons. With regard to the scale of this project the figure per day may give a reasonable notion. Unless obstacles appear, we suggest that the expediting of design be assigned to the Argonne National Laboratory.

With regard to the purposes for which these neutrons may be required, we need to make more explicit statements. The principal purposes are the following:

(a) The production of U-233.

(b) The production of radiological warfare agents.

(c) Supplemental facilities for the test of reactor components.

(d) The conversion of U-235 to plutonium.

(e) A secondary facility for plutonium production.

(f) The production of tritium (1) for boosters, (2) for super bombs.

We view these varied objectives in a quite different light. We have a great interest in the U-233 program, both for military and for civil purposes. We strongly favor, subject to favorable outcome of the 1951 Eniwetok tests, the booster program. With regard to radiological warfare, we would not wish to alter the position previously taken by our Committee. With regard to the conversion to plutonium, we would hardly believe that this alone could justify the construction of these reactors, though it may be important should unanticipated difficulties appear in the U-233 and booster programs. With regard to the use of tritium in the super bomb, it is our unanimous hope that this will not prove necessary. It is the opinion of the majority that the super program itself should not be undertaken and that the Commission and its contractors understand that construction of neutron producing reactors is not intended as a step in the super program.

PART II

SUPER BOMBS

The General Advisory Committee has considered at great length the question of whether to pursue with high priority the development of the super bomb. No member of the Committee was willing to endorse this proposal. The reasons for our views leading to this conclusion stem in large part from the technical nature of the super and of the work necessary to establish it as a weapon. We therefore here transmit *an elementary* account of these matters.

The basic principle of design of the super bomb is the ignition of the thermo-nuclear DD reaction by the use of a fission bomb, and of high temperatures, pressure, and neutron densities which accompany it. In overwhelming probability, tritium is required as an intermediary, more easily ignited than the deuterium itself and, in turn, capable of igniting the deuterium.

The steps which need to be taken if the super bomb is to become a reality include:

(1) The provision of tritium in amounts perhaps of several per unit.

(2) Further theoretical studies and criticisms aimed at reducing the very great uncertainties still inherent in the behavior of this weapon under extreme conditions of temperature, pressure and flow.

(3) The engineering of designs which may on theoretical grounds appear hopeful, particularly with regard to the problems presented.

(4) Carefully instrumented test programs to determine whether the deuterium-tritium mixture will be ignited by the fission bomb.

It is notable that there appears to be no experimental approach short of actual test which will substantially add to our conviction that a given model will or will not work, and it is also notable that because of the unsymmetric and extremely unfamiliar conditions obtaining, some considerable doubt will surely remain as to the soundness of theoretical anticipation. Thus we are faced with a development which cannot be carried to the point of conviction without the actual construction and demonstration of the essential elements of the weapon in question. This does not mean that further theoretical studies would be without avail. It does mean that they could not be decisive. A final point that needs to be stressed is that many tests may be required before a workable model has been evolved or before it has been established beyond reasonable doubt that no such model can be evolved. Although we are not able to give a specific probability rating for any given model, we believe that an imaginative and concerted attack on the problem has a better than even chance of producing the weapon within five years.

A second characteristic of the super bomb is that once the problem of initiation has been solved, there is no limit to the explosive power of the bomb itself except that imposed by requirements of delivery. This is because one can continue to add deuterium—an essentially cheap material—to make larger and larger explosions, the energy release and radioactive products of which are both proportional to the amount of deuterium itself. Taking into account the probable limitations of carries likely to be available for the delivery of such a weapon, it has generally been estimated that the weapon would have an explosive effect some hundreds of times that of present fission bombs. This would correspond to a damage area of the order of hundreds of square miles, to thermal radiation effects extending over a comparable area, and to very grave contamination problems which can easily be made more acute, and may possibly be rendered less acute, by surrounding the deuterium with uranium or other material. It needs to be borne in mind that for delivery by ship, submarine or other such carrier, the limitations here outlined no longer apply and that the weapon is from a technical point of view without limitations with regard to the damage that it can inflict.

It is clear that the use of this weapon would bring about the destruction of innumerable human lives; it is not a weapon which can be used exclusively for the destruction of material installations of military or semi-military purposes. Its use therefore carries much further than the atomic bomb itself the policy of exterminating civilian populations. It is of course true that super bombs which are not as big as those here contemplated could be made, provided the initiating mechanism works. In this case, however, there appears to be no chance of their being an economical alternative to the fission weapons themselves. It is clearly impossible with the vagueness of design and the uncertainty as to performance as we have them at present to give anything like a cost estimate of the super. If one uses the strict criteria of damage area per dollar and if one accepts the limitations on air carrier capacity likely to obtain in the years immediately ahead, it appears uncertain to us whether the super will be cheaper or more expensive that the fission bomb.

PART III

Although the members of the Advisory Committee are not unanimous in their proposals as to what should be done with regard to the super bomb, there are certain elements of unanimity among us. We all hope that by one means or another, the development of these weapons can be avoided. We are all reluctant to see the United States take the initiative in precipitating this development. We are all agreed that it would be wrong at the present moment to commit ourselves to an all-out effort toward its development.

We are somewhat divided as to the nature of the commitment not to develop the weapon. The majority feel that this should be an unqualified commitment. Others feel that it should be made conditional on the response of the Soviet government to a proposal to renounce such development. The Committee recommends that enough be declassified about the super bomb so that a public statement of policy can be made at this time. Such a statement might in our opinion point to the use of deuterium as the principal source of energy. It need not discuss initiating mechanisms nor the role which we believe tritium will play. It should explain that the weapon cannon be explored without developing it and proof-firing it. In one form or another, the statement should express our desire not to make this development. It should explain the scale and general nature of the destruction which its use would entail. It should make clear that there are no known or foreseen non-military applications of this development. The separate views of the members of the Committee are attached to this report for your use.

J. R. Oppenheimer

MAJORITY ANNEX
October 30, 1949
We have been asked by the Commission whether or not they should immediately initiate an "all-out" effort to develop a weapon whose energy release is 100 to 1000 times greater and whose destructive power in terms of area of damage is 20 to 100 times greater than those of the present atomic bomb. We recommend strongly against such action.

We base our recommendation on our belief that the extreme dangers to mankind inherent in the proposal wholly outweigh any military advantage that could come from this development. Let it be clearly realized that this is a super weapon; it is in a totally different category from an atomic bomb. The reason for developing such super bombs would be to have the capacity to devastate a vast area with a single bomb. Its use would involve a decision to slaughter a vast number of civilians. We are alarmed as to the possible global effects of the radioactivity generated by the explosion of a few super bombs of conceivable magnitude. If super bombs will work at all, there is no inherent limit in the destructive power that may be attained with them. Therefore, a super bomb might become a weapon of genocide.

The existence of such a weapon in our armory would have far-reaching effects on world opinion; reasonable people the world over would realize that the existence of a weapon of this type whose power of destruction is essentially unlimited represents a threat to the future of the human race which is intolerable. Thus we believe that the psychological effect of the weapon in our hands would be adverse to our interest.

Glossary

1951 Eniwetok tests	tests of nuclear bombs conducted by the United States at Eniwetok, an atoll in the Marshall Islands
Argonne National Laboratory	one of the nation's oldest and largest scientific research facilities, located about twenty-five miles southwest of Chicago
fissionable	capable of undergoing nuclear fission, or a chain reaction
further plants, both separation and reactor	reference to the two types of facilities needed to produce nuclear materials, one that separates the fissionable material from other materials, the other that produces the nuclear chain reaction
neutron	the subatomic particle in the nucleus of an atom that carries no electrical charge
plutonium	a radioactive element
thermo-nuclear DD reaction	a nuclear reaction, such as in a hydrogen bomb, that yields charged particles of deuterium, a hydrogen isotope
tritium	a radioactive isotope of hydrogen
U-233	an isotope of the uranium atom
U-235	an isotope of the uranium atom

We believe a super bomb should never be produced. Mankind would be far better off not to have a demonstration of the feasibility of such a weapon, until the present climate of world opinion changes.

It is by no means certain that the weapon can be developed at all and by no means certain that the Russians will produce one within a decade. To the argument that the Russians may succeed in developing this weapon, we would reply that our undertaking it will not prove a deterrent to them. Should they use the weapon against us, reprisals by our large stock of atomic bombs would be comparably effective to the use of a super.

In determining not to proceed to develop the super bomb, we see a unique opportunity of providing by example some limitations on the totality of war and thus of limiting the fear and arousing the hopes of mankind.

James B. Conant
Hartley Rowe
Cyril Stanley Smith
L. A. DuBridge
Oliver E. Buckley
J. R. Oppenheimer

Thomas Paine (Library of Congress)

THOMAS PAINE   1737–1809

Writer and Philosopher

Featured Documents
♦ *The Crisis*, No. 1 (1776)
♦ *The Crisis*, No. 4 (1777)

Overview

Thomas Paine was born in England in 1737. He attended the competitive Thetford Grammar School and, like any student of that time, studied Latin and rhetoric together with mathematics. At age thirteen he began to work in the family business of corset making (a fact that was later used against him in British political cartoons), but he was not successful at it. Beginning in 1761 Paine worked in a number of civil service jobs, mostly as an excise officer, collecting taxes on manufactured goods. This work also proved unsteady, and he had to supplement his income by working in other professions—as a privateer (a crewman on a ship granted the right by the British government to attack and confiscate the merchant shipping of enemy nations), as a schoolteacher, and as the manager of a tobacco shop. He succeeded in none of these ventures and in 1774 declared bankruptcy. His first venture into political propaganda was a pamphlet he sent to members of parliament titled *The Case of the Officers of Excise*, arguing for improved working conditions for that class of civil servants. This apparently had little effect at the time. A few weeks after his bankruptcy, Paine met the American statesman Benjamin Franklin in London. Paine impressed him enough that Franklin wrote letters of introduction on Paine's behalf to contacts in Philadelphia, and Paine immigrated to America, arriving on November 30, 1774.

In Franklin's political circles Paine became part of the most radical movement, one that was calling for the independence of the American colonies from Great Britain. In January 1776 Paine published *Common Sense*, a book that changed the course of American history. It convinced thousands of Americans, including George Washington and John Adams, that there was no choice left, other than open rebellion, to correct what was viewed as the British misadministration of the colonies. In doing so, it laid the immediate groundwork for the Declaration of Independence, written six months later. It also made Paine one of the most successful authors in American history. At a time when the population of the colonies was about two million free adults, the book sold 120,000 copies in a few months and half a million before the end of the Revolution. *Common Sense* also became a best seller in France. Yet Paine dedicated the work to the cause of American freedom and never derived any income from it. He followed the same practice with all of his propagandistic writings and, for this reason, teetered on the brink of personal financial ruin throughout the Revolutionary War.

In the first years of the Revolution, Paine was given a series of minor bureaucratic jobs in the civil service meant to support his efforts at writing propaganda. He was with Washington's army through the campaigning season of 1776 and witnessed its disastrous rout at the hands of the British from New York to the outskirts of the American capital at Philadelphia. In response, Paine wrote the first issue of the pamphlet series known as *The Crisis*, or *The American Crisis*, in late December 1776, when it seemed as though the Revolution might actually fail if, as many thought likely, the British captured Philadelphia. Washington thought well enough of this tract to have it read out to his troops hours before his raid across the Delaware River. Paine published thirteen issues of *The Crisis* over the course of the Revolutionary War.

After the American Revolution, Paine became increasingly interested in the French Revolution, publishing *The Rights of Man* in 1791 to explain and justify its aim and accomplishments to the English-speaking world in both Great Britain and America. Until the dictatorship of Napoléon, he also became deeply involved in French radical politics. In 1802 he retired on grants and land provided by the states of Pennsylvania and New York as well as by the new United States (a name Paine himself coined). Paine died on June 8, 1809, in New York City.

Explanation and Analysis of Documents

After the phenomenal success of *Common Sense* in aligning popular American opinion with the cause of the Revolution, Paine became the unofficial propagandist of the new nation. He spent the campaigning season of 1776 with George Washington's army in New York and New Jersey, writing articles meant to prop up public support for the rebellion despite the series of unmitigated military disasters Washington suffered that year. At what seemed the lowest point of American military fortunes, Paine published the first issue of *The Crisis*, also known as *The American Crisis*, a pamphlet that was read out to Washington's army prior to the crossing of the Delaware and the vital American success at the Battle of Trenton. The next year Paine was employed writing the correspondence between the Continental Congress and Benjamin Franklin, who was serving as American ambassador in Paris. On September 11, 1777, the British won the Battle of the Brandywine south of Philadelphia, and Paine

Time Line

1737

- **January 29**
  Thomas Paine is born in Thetford, England.

1774

- **November 30**
  Paine immigrates to Philadelphia in the then British Colonies in North America.

1776–1781

- Paine is given a series of minor bureaucratic jobs with the civil service of the new American government.

1776

- **January 10**
  Paine anonymously publishes *Common Sense*.

- **December 23**
  Paine publishes the first issue of *The American Crisis*.

1777

- **September 12**
  Paine publishes the fourth issue of *The American Crisis*.

1791

- **March 13**
  Paine publishes *The Rights of Man*, supporting the French Revolution.

1792–1793

- Paine becomes a representative to the National Convention in France.

1793

- Paine begins to write *The Age of Reason*.

- **December 28**
  Paine is arrested as part of the Terror, a period of violence following the onset of the French Revolution.

1802

- Paine retires to an estate in New Rochelle, New York, granted him as a reward for his work in the American Revolution.

1809

- **June 8**
  Paine dies in Greenwich Village, New York.

worked through the night to bring out the fourth issue of *The Crisis* to buoy up the American spirit and advise Americans not to abandon the Revolution in the face of the inevitable capture of the capital. After this early stage of the war, the American military position was never again so grim, but Paine produced thirteen issues of *The Crisis* throughout the war years. These pamphlets were published at irregular intervals and supplemented and highlighted his regular journalistic writing.

◆ *The Crisis*, No. 1

The term *crisis* derives from the Hippocratic medical terminology of ancient Greece. In Paine's day, Greek medicine was still the dominant paradigm of medicine, though it was beginning to be overturned by the scientific approaches propagated at institutions such as the Pennsylvania Hospital co-founded by Benjamin Franklin in 1751. Such a crisis was considered to be the point in the progression of an illness at which the physician could accurately determine whether the patient would recover or die. Paine tells his readers in the first installment of *The Crisis* (December 23, 1776) that the Revolution had reached such a point. He gives an impressionistic description of military actions in the fall of 1776 but took for granted his reader's own knowledge of recent events.

The military phase of the Revolution had been sparked in the spring of 1775 when British troops in Boston tried to seize the arms of local militias, the so-called Minutemen, stored in the villages of Lexington and Concord outside the city. They were surprised and overcome by the militias' resistance. This left a small British army bottled up on the Charleston peninsula in Boston Harbor. These forces were obliged to evacuate by sea when guns seized from the dilapidated Fort Ticonderoga were brought to bear on the British garrison. A British force of about twenty-two thousand men started to build up on Staten Island with the aim of seizing New York. George Washington concentrated twenty thousand men, the largest force he would ever command, on Long Island. Washington was soundly defeated in the field and was forced to withdraw through a series of field fortifications, first at Brooklyn Heights, then Harlem Heights on Manhattan (today known as Washington Heights), and finally Fort Lee in New Jersey. Although Washington effectively harassed and slowed the advance of the British, it was evident that he could not stand up to them in open battle.

By the middle of December, Washington had been pushed back over the Delaware River into Pennsylvania on the outskirts of the American capital of Philadelphia. He had barely five thousand troops left and would be reduced to a mere fifteen hundred after enlistments ended at New Year's. The British, on the other hand, had more than ten thousand troops in southern New Jersey. Disregarding Washington as a military threat, they had retired into winter quarters (the normal practice of eighteenth-century armies, to avoid the difficulties of campaigning in bad weather). The professional officers of the British army, at least, seem to have agreed with Paine that the crisis of the

Revolution had been reached, but they concluded that its failure was now inevitable.

Washington had other ideas. Having been deeply inspired by Paine's *Common Sense*, he dispatched the author to Philadelphia. (Paine had been with the army for months, reporting on its campaign for his newspaper, the *Pennsylvania Journal*, which he edited without pay.) Washington hoped that Paine could make use of the idle printing presses in the city, which was quickly being abandoned by its inhabitants in the face of its seemingly inevitable capture by the British. Even Congress had decamped to Baltimore. After walking from Trenton to Philadelphia, Paine immediately began to write the first issue of *The Crisis*, using notes he had taken during the previous weeks and finishing it overnight. It was published on December 23 and immediately dispatched throughout the colonies to be reprinted and distributed. Washington had it read out to his troops on the afternoon of December 26, just hours before he successfully went on the offensive with his famous crossing of the Delaware. He caught the Hessian garrison (the subject of xenophobic attacks by Paine) of Trenton off guard, defeated it, and retook the city, capturing one thousand Hessian troops as prisoners. Similar small-scale actions throughout the winter, mostly conducted by the New Jersey militia, drove the British out of that colony in a few months, reversing the effect of their earlier victories. So, indeed, the war had reached a crisis, but one in line with Paine's favorable expectations.

Paine concedes the difficulties Americans find themselves in and the hard choices they demand with one of the most famous lines in American literature: "These are the times that try men's souls." But he reminds his readers that the war began because of Britain's intolerable tyranny and that this tyranny would not end if Britain achieved a military victory; rather it would grow worse. He reminds them, too, that Britain's victories had been overturned earlier, by as unlikely an agent as Joan of Arc. In analyzing the military situation, Paine finds his true genius. He describes Washington's army being driven across New Jersey (as he himself witnessed), without fabrication or exaggeration though with a great deal of optimism. He makes it clear that Washington made the British advance very costly and that in the long run Britain would not be able to keep up with that cost of waging war and so must eventually withdraw. For this reason, even if the British should capture Philadelphia and win more victories in the field, America would nevertheless triumph.

In a *Pennsylvania Journal* issue of the following January, Paine would compare Washington to the ancient Roman dictator Fabius Maximus, who—realizing that the Romans could not defeat in battle the army of Hannibal after he invaded Italy—devised the successful strategy of containing his army and wearing it down. This Fabian strategy is often very effective in warfare, but since it does not aim at glorious victory and often allows for defeat in battle, it is very hard for politicians and members of the general public to accept. Using examples of its effectiveness, Paine

makes this difficult-to-grasp kind of warfare comprehensible to his readers in language that is at one and the same time simple and profound.

> Howe [the British Commander], it is probable, will make an attempt on this city [Philadelphia]; should he fail on this side the Delaware, he is ruined. If he succeeds, our cause is not ruined. He stakes all on his side against a part on ours; admitting he succeeds, the consequence will be, that armies from both ends of the continent will march to assist their suffering friends in the middle states; for he cannot go everywhere, it is impossible.

Paine discusses at length the position of the Tories (about a quarter to a third of the adult male population), Americans who wished to remain loyal to Great Britain and who opposed the Revolution. They were on his mind no doubt in part because of his immediate circumstances. Tories were most common in the middle colonies, such as New Jersey and Pennsylvania: Paine had feared being attacked by Tory gangs on his walk from Trenton to Philadelphia. By the time he arrived, the capital itself had already been abandoned by anyone who could afford to leave, except for Tories, who looked forward to welcoming the British army. Paine's hostility to Tories was not exceptional. Already, and increasingly so, British Loyalists were fleeing their homes, forced out by their Revolutionary neighbors, and making their way either to British-held areas like Long Island or to other British possessions in North America such as Canada or the Bahamas. Those who spoke up in favor of the king could easily find themselves tarred and feathered. This meant having boiling tar poured over one's whole body, a procedure that would lead at least to disfigurement and more often to death, and then being rolled in goose feathers to add humiliation to the injury. Abandoned Tory property was being confiscated by the states and used to pay for the war. This was no mere fancy of Paine's, but a growing reality.

Paine makes use of a great deal of religious rhetoric in his pamphlet, hoping to enlist the sympathies of his devout readers. But he begins setting this tone with a somewhat misleading statement: "I have as little superstition in me as any man living." The pious reader might be inclined to take this as Paine vouching for his own orthodoxy. A comparison of this statement with Paine's own later writings, however, makes it clear that he is soft-peddling his own deist views. There can be no question that Paine was a radical deist, since he devoted whole books, such as *The Age of Reason*, to disproving that Christianity is a revealed religion. Deism was the religious philosophy of the Enlightenment, which held that some unknowable omnipotent creator must be responsible for the creation and functioning of the universe and perhaps for ensuring its justice. It rejected specific religious mythologies, including those of Christianity. Deism was the most common belief of the Founders, who were educated inheritors of the Enlightenment, but it was still a difficult concept for the more popular audience Paine was

Cartoon showing Thomas Paine being hanged (Library of Congress)

addressing, as it would be even today. Throughout *The Crisis*, Paine makes many statements along these lines: "God Almighty will not give up a people to military destruction" or "I am as confident, as I am that God governs the world." He is careful to say nothing to compromise his own deistic philosophy, but at the same time he also says nothing that Christian readers could not endorse once they had supplied the context of their own faith.

In a footnote to his text, Paine advises the American people, "The present winter is worth an age, if rightly employed; but, if lost or neglected, the whole continent will partake of the evil." Americans employed their winter well. The people of New Jersey drove the British out of their state, and the Congress organized two new armies: Washington's to protect Philadelphia and another, commanded by Horatio Gates and Benedict Arnold, to fight in Upstate New York. The latter army eventually defeated the invading British force from Canada at Saratoga, New York—a victory that not only embarrassed the British but also brought France, along with Britain's other Continental enemies, into the war, making British defeat certain. The national will to fight, rather than surrender to the British army just outside the capital of Philadelphia, and the will of Washington's men to carry out a successful offensive at Trenton after months of defeat and retreat, were bolstered by Paine's common sense in *The Crisis*.

◆ *The Crisis,* **No. 4**

Writing nine months after the first issue of *The Crisis*, on September 11, 1777, Paine again leads off the fourth issue with a summary of the year's fighting. He makes no

mention of the Saratoga campaign that was even at the time of his writing unfolding in Upstate New York. The British army in Canada had intended to march south down the Hudson Valley to link up with the other major British force stationed in New York City. Instead, a smaller American force was able to delay it, break it up with raids and diversions, and eventually (by October 17) defeat it and capture its remnant. This victory was the decisive event of 1777. It resulted in the declaration of war by France and other European powers against Britain on America's behalf.

Paine, however, had uppermost in his mind the fighting around Philadelphia, with which he was more directly concerned since he was working in the city at his newspaper and helping to prepare the correspondence of the Continental Congress. In late August the main British army from New York began to be transshipped to the mouth of the Delaware River (eschewing another march through New Jersey) south of the American capital. On September 11, 1777, the British defeated and nearly destroyed Washington's army at the Battle of the Brandywine. (Paine's rather fantastic description of the American defeat may charitably be called confused rather than fabricated, owing to lack of definite information.) The British again moved directly on Philadelphia. When Paine realized what had happened—initially from hearing cannon fire through his office window—he immediately set to work on the fourth issue of *The Crisis*, writing through the night and handing it to the publisher the next morning. This, too, would eventually become a widely circulated pamphlet, but it had little immediate effect on the flight of almost the entire Patriot population from Philadelphia. Paine tried to organize a militia to resist the British in house-to-house street fighting, but with almost no one except Loyalists left in the city this proved impossible. The British entered Philadelphia on September 26, and Paine fled the next night to Trenton, knowing that if he fell into the hands of British authorities he would be executed for treason.

Facing nearly the same situation he had at the beginning of the previous winter, Paine renews his crisis metaphor, in more explicitly medical terms. "The nearer any disease approaches to a crisis, the nearer it is to a cure. Danger and deliverance make their advances together, and it is only the last push, in which one or the other takes the lead." Paine's readers would know that a physician of the period might well expect a disease to go through a series of crises before it was finally resolved.

Paine likewise renews his Fabian analysis of the military situation, hammering home to his audience the very difficult-to-accept message that momentary military defeat was irrelevant in the long run. The military and political situation he is explaining to his readers here (especially in his apparent lack of detailed knowledge about events in Upstate New York) was in many respects similar to that which existed at the time of his writing the first *Crisis* essay, as Paine is himself well aware: "[The British Commander] Howe has been once on the banks of the Delaware, and from thence driven back with loss and disgrace: and why not be again driven from the Schuylkill?" referring to the different river obstacles that separated the British army from Philadelphia in 1776 and 1777. The new part of Paine's message in this pamphlet is his call to the people of Philadelphia to resist the impending effort of the British to occupy the city:

> You are more immediately interested than any other part of the continent: your all is at stake; it is not so with the general cause; you are devoted by the enemy to plunder and destruction: it is the encouragement which Howe, the chief of plunderers, has promised his army. Thus circumstanced, you may save your- selves by a manly resistance, but you can have no hope in any other conduct.

Paine spells it out very plainly to the citizens of Philadel- phia that they risked losing their property and even their very lives to the British if the army occupied the city unop- posed, so it was in their best interest to resist the British sol- diers step by step through the city. He is overly optimistic about the prospect of help from Washington's badly disor- ganized army to the south and also from the American army in the north (in New York), since it was heavily (and victori- ously) engaged in maneuvering between Saratoga and the Canadian border and could do nothing for Philadelphia. In the event, the Patriots of Philadelphia chose to flee rather than to fight, and the British did not sack the city but instead occupied it to strengthen the support of its remain- ing Loyalist population. After London, Philadelphia was the largest and richest city in the British Empire, hardly a place to be destroyed lightly by the British army.

Paine was more prophetic in his closing address to Howe, the British commander. His fleeting success in tak- ing the American capital would make no difference in the long run. British victories did little to defeat the American military strength, as dispersed and great as it was, springing up everywhere in the form of militias and new recruits (with over a quarter million Americans seeing some form of mili- tary service during the Revolution). In contrast, the British projection of military power, which depended on transat- lantic supply lines, was too fragile to sustain even the loss- es of victory. Anticipating Howe's capture of Philadelphia, Paine tells him, "What you now enjoy is only a respite from ruin; an invitation to destruction; something that will lead on to our deliverance at your expense." The declaration of war on England by France and other European powers after Saratoga would make the British position untenable.

Impact and Legacy

Paine was an anomaly. When he was thirty-nine, with no background in politics or writing, his propaganda galva- nized a political movement that would turn the world upside down. This movement dealt the greatest blow to the British Empire that it would feel until the end of colonial- ism following World War II and created a new nation that would dominate the twentieth century. Paine subsequently

played midwife to the United States during its difficult labor. He wrote newspaper articles and pamphlets aimed at convincing the American people that military success was irrelevant; that the inherent rightness of their cause, as much as the strength of their strategic situation, must inevitably triumph; and that—so long as rebellious forces operated in the field—the British could not hope to subdue an entire continent, no matter what their temporary suc- cesses. Paine was remarkably successful at presenting these basically sound military doctrines to a relatively unso- phisticated audience. There is no way to calculate the effect he had in keeping support for the Revolution alive at its lowest points. Paine had intended to write a history of the Revolutionary War, and no one would have been better placed to do so than he was. Still, in the immediate after- math of the Revolution, the new nation was in such dire economic straits that Congress could not even grant Paine an allowance to permit him to write full time.

Paine moved on to become a great apologist for the French Revolution, risking and very nearly losing his own life again in his quest to promote freedom. (Arrested during the Terror, he was saved from the guillotine when the chalk mark singling him out for execution was put by accident on the back rather than the front of his prison cell door, so that it was not noticed when the condemned were taken away.) Having advanced the Enlightenment political philosophy of democracy as far as any one man could have done, Paine spent the last years of his life in an effort to overturn revealed religion—as he had helped to overturn monarchy— and replace it with the Enlightenment concept of deism, although this work was far less successful in effecting wide- spread radical social change. Even Napoléon Bonaparte, in an audience with Paine in 1800, acknowledged the profound impact *The Rights of Man* had had on his own political thought. But Paine left France in 1802, after growing dis- gusted with Napoléon's autocracy. He returned to the Unit- ed States, where the government was finally in a position to reward him for his efforts on behalf of the Revolution.

Key Sources

Thomas Paine's complete works have never been repub- lished in a modern edition. Three separate collections exist that each contain the bulk of his writing, but each makes different omissions, and each contains different works that are probably spurious. These collections are Moncure Con- way's *Writings of Thomas Paine* (1894–1896) in four vol- umes, William M. Van der Weyde's *Life and Works of Thomas Paine* (1925) in nine volumes, and Philip S. Foner's *Complete Writings of Thomas Paine* (1994) in two volumes. These writings have been digitized and put on the Internet by the Thomas Paine National Historical Association based at his estate in New Rochelle, New York (http://www.thomas paine.org/contents.html). Gordon S. Wood has edited an extensive, but far from complete anthology of Paine's most important works as a handbook for quick reference: *Com- mon Sense and Other Writings* (2003).

"These are the times that try men's souls. The summer soldier and the sunshine patriot will, in this crisis, shrink from the service of their country; but he that stands it now, deserves the love and thanks of man and woman."

(*The Crisis*, No. 1)

"Tyranny, like hell, is not easily conquered."

(*The Crisis*, No. 1)

"If there must be trouble, let it be in my day, that my child may have peace."

(*The Crisis*, No. 1)

"By perseverance and fortitude we have the prospect of a glorious issue; by cowardice and submission, the sad choice of a variety of evils—a ravaged country—a depopulated city—habitations without safety, and slavery without hope—our homes turned into barracks and bawdy-houses for Hessians, and a future race to provide for, whose fathers we shall doubt of."

(*The Crisis*, No. 1)

"Those who expect to reap the blessings of freedom, must, like men, undergo the fatigues of supporting it."

(*The Crisis*, No. 4)

"The nearer any disease approaches to a crisis, the nearer it is to a cure."

(*The Crisis*, No. 4)

"We are not moved by the gloomy smile of a worthless king, but by the ardent glow of generous patriotism."

(*The Crisis*, No. 4)

"We fight not to enslave, but to set a country free."

(*The Crisis*, No. 4)

Further Reading

■ Books

Conway, Moncure D. *The Life of Thomas Paine with a History of His Literary, Political, and Religious Career in America, France, and England.* New York: G. P. Putnam's Sons, 1909.

Esposito, Vincent J., ed. *The West Point Atlas of American Wars,* Vol. 1: *1689–1900.* New York: Praeger, 1959.

Keane, John. *Tom Paine: A Political Life.* Boston: Little, Brown, 1995.

Kuklick, Bruce, ed. *Thomas Paine.* Aldershot, England: Ashgate, 2006.

Larkin, Edward. *Thomas Paine and the Literature of Revolution.* New York: Cambridge University Press, 2005.

Vickers, Vikki J. *"My Pen and My Soul Have Ever Gone Together": Thomas Paine and the American Revolution.* New York: Routledge, 2006.

—Bradley A. Skeen

Questions for Further Study

1. "These are the times that try men's souls," the first sentence of *The Crisis,* No. 1, is perhaps the most frequently quoted statement from Thomas Paine's writings. How do this sentence and, indeed, the entire first paragraph convey the author's intent in writing the piece?

2. Paine frequently refers to God in *The Crisis,* No. 1. Some readers might find this surprising, given that Paine wrote during a time when many philosophers and political thinkers were skeptical of traditional religious beliefs. What purpose did Paine's references to God serve in this document?

3. Compare and contrast the nature of Paine's rhetoric with that of other fiery revolutionary thinkers in American history. You might, for example, focus on César Chávez's "wrath of grapes" speech or Jesse Jackson's speech at the 1988 Democratic National Convention, "The Struggle Continues." What tactics do these writers use to foster a sense of unity of purpose in their audiences as it pertains to the issue of freedom and rights?

THE CRISIS, NO. 1 (1776)

THESE are the times that try men's souls. The summer soldier and the sunshine patriot will, in this crisis, shrink from the service of their country; but he that stands it now, deserves the love and thanks of man and woman. Tyranny, like hell, is not easily conquered; yet we have this consolation with us, that the harder the conflict, the more glorious the triumph. What we obtain too cheap, we esteem too lightly: it is dearness only that gives every thing its value. Heaven knows how to put a proper price upon its goods; and it would be strange indeed if so celestial an article as FREEDOM should not be highly rated. Britain, with an army to enforce her tyranny, has declared that she has a right (not only to TAX) but "to BIND us in ALL CASES WHATSOEVER," and if being bound in that manner, is not slavery, then is there not such a thing as slavery upon earth. Even the expression is impious; for so unlimited a power can belong only to God.

Whether the independence of the continent was declared too soon, or delayed too long, I will not now enter into as an argument; my own simple opinion is, that had it been eight months earlier, it would have been much better. We did not make a proper use of last winter, neither could we, while we were in a dependent state. However, the fault, if it were one, was all our own; we have none to blame but ourselves. But no great deal is lost yet. All that Howe has been doing for this month past, is rather a ravage than a conquest, which the spirit of the Jerseys, a year ago, would have quickly repulsed, and which time and a little resolution will soon recover.

I have as little superstition in me as any man living, but my secret opinion has ever been, and still is, that God Almighty will not give up a people to military destruction, or leave them unsupportedly to perish, who have so earnestly and so repeatedly sought to avoid the calamities of war, by every decent method which wisdom could invent. Neither have I so much of the infidel in me, as to suppose that He has relinquished the government of the world, and given us up to the care of devils; and as I do not, I cannot see on what grounds the king of Britain can look up to heaven for help against us: a common murderer, a highwayman, or a house-breaker, has as good a pretence as he.

'Tis surprising to see how rapidly a panic will sometimes run through a country. All nations and ages have been subject to them. Britain has trembled like an ague at the report of a French fleet of flat-bottomed boats; and in the fourteenth [fifteenth] century the whole English army, after ravaging the kingdom of France, was driven back like men petrified with fear; and this brave exploit was performed by a few broken forces collected and headed by a woman, Joan of Arc. Would that heaven might inspire some Jersey maid to spirit up her countrymen, and save her fair fellow sufferers from ravage and ravishment! Yet panics, in some cases, have their uses; they produce as much good as hurt. Their duration is always short; the mind soon grows through them, and acquires a firmer habit than before. But their peculiar advantage is, that they are the touchstones of sincerity and hypocrisy, and bring things and men to light, which might otherwise have lain forever undiscovered. In fact, they have the same effect on secret traitors, which an imaginary apparition would have upon a private murderer. They sift out the hidden thoughts of man, and hold them up in public to the world. Many a disguised Tory has lately shown his head, that shall penitentially solemnize with curses the day on which Howe arrived upon the Delaware.

As I was with the troops at Fort Lee, and marched with them to the edge of Pennsylvania, I am well acquainted with many circumstances, which those who live at a distance know but little or nothing of. Our situation there was exceedingly cramped, the place being a narrow neck of land between the North River and the Hackensack. Our force was inconsiderable, being not one-fourth so great as Howe could bring against us. We had no army at hand to have relieved the garrison, had we shut ourselves up and stood on our defence. Our ammunition, light artillery, and the best part of our stores, had been removed, on the apprehension that Howe would endeavor to penetrate the Jerseys, in which case Fort Lee could be of no use to us; for it must occur to every thinking man, whether in the army or not, that these kind of field forts are only for temporary purposes, and last in use no longer than the enemy directs his force against the particular object which such forts are raised to defend. Such was our situation and condition at Fort Lee on the morning of the 20th of November, when an officer arrived with information that the enemy with 200 boats had landed about seven miles above; Major General [Nathanael] Green, who commanded the garrison, immediately ordered them under arms, and sent express to General Washington at the town of Hackensack, distant by the way of the ferry = six miles. Our first object was to secure the bridge over the Hackensack, which laid up the river between the enemy and us, about six miles from us, and three from them. General Washington arrived in about three-quarters of an hour, and marched at the head of the troops towards the bridge, which place I expected we should have a brush for; however, they did not choose to dispute it with us, and the greatest part of our troops went over the bridge, the rest over the ferry, except some which passed at a mill on a small creek, between the bridge and the ferry, and made their way through some marshy grounds up to the town of Hackensack, and there passed the river. We brought off as much baggage as the wagons could contain, the rest was lost. The simple object was to bring off the garrison, and march them on till they could be strengthened by the Jersey or Pennsylvania militia, so as to be enabled to make a stand. We staid four days at Newark, collected our out-posts with some of the Jersey militia, and marched out twice to meet the enemy, on being informed that they were advancing, though our numbers were greatly inferior to theirs. Howe, in my little opinion, committed a great error in generalship in not throwing a body of forces off from Staten Island through Amboy, by which means he might have seized all our stores at Brunswick, and intercepted our march into Pennsylvania; but if we believe the power of hell to be limited, we must likewise believe that their agents are under some providential control.

I shall not now attempt to give all the particulars of our retreat to the Delaware; suffice it for the present to say, that both officers and men, though greatly harassed and fatigued, frequently without rest, covering, or provision, the inevitable consequences of a long retreat, bore it with a manly and martial spirit. All their wishes centred in one, which was, that the country would turn out and help them to drive the enemy back. Voltaire has remarked that King William never appeared to full advantage but in difficulties and in action; the same remark may be made on General Washington, for the character fits him. There is a natural firmness in some minds which cannot be unlocked by trifles, but which, when unlocked, discovers a cabinet of fortitude; and I reckon it among those kind of public blessings, which we do not immediately see, that God hath blessed him with uninterrupted health, and given him a mind that can even flourish upon care.

I shall conclude this paper with some miscellaneous remarks on the state of our affairs; and shall begin with asking the following question, Why is it that the enemy have left the New England provinces, and made these middle ones the seat of war? The answer is easy: New England is not infested with Tories, and we are. I have been tender in raising the cry against these men, and used numberless arguments to show them their danger, but it will not do to sacrifice a world either to their folly or their baseness. The period is now arrived, in which either they or we must change our sentiments, or one or both must fall. And what is a Tory? Good God! what is he? I should not be afraid to go with a hundred Whigs against a thousand Tories, were they to attempt to get into arms. Every Tory is a coward; for servile, slavish, self-interested fear is the foundation of Toryism; and a man under such influence, though he may be cruel, never can be brave.

But, before the line of irrecoverable separation be drawn between us, let us reason the matter together: Your conduct is an invitation to the enemy, yet not one in a thousand of you has heart enough to join him. Howe is as much deceived by you as the American cause is injured by you. He expects you will all take up arms, and flock to his standard, with muskets on your shoulders. Your opinions are of no use to him, unless you support him personally, for 'tis soldiers, and not Tories, that he wants.

I once felt all that kind of anger, which a man ought to feel, against the mean principles that are held by the Tories: a noted one, who kept a tavern at Amboy, was standing at his door, with as pretty a child in his hand, about eight or nine years old, as I ever saw, and after speaking his mind as freely as he thought was prudent, finished with this unfatherly expression, "Well! give me peace in my day." Not a man lives on the continent but fully believes that a separation must some time or other finally take place, and a generous parent should have said, "If there must be trouble, let it be in my day, that my child may have peace;" and this single reflection, well applied, is sufficient to awaken every man to duty. Not a place upon earth might be so happy as America. Her situation is remote from all the wrangling world, and she has nothing to do but to trade with them. A man can distinguish himself between temper and principle, and I am as confident, as I am that God governs the world, that America will never be happy till she gets clear of foreign dominion. Wars, without ceasing, will break out till that period arrives, and the continent must in the end be conqueror; for though the flame of liberty may sometimes cease to shine, the coal can never expire.

America did not, nor does not want force; but she wanted a proper application of that force. Wisdom is not the purchase of a day, and it is no wonder that we should err at the first setting off. From an excess of tenderness, we were unwilling to raise an army, and trusted our cause to the temporary defence of a well-meaning militia. A summer's experience has now taught us better; yet with those troops, while they were collected, we were able to set bounds to the progress of the enemy, and, thank God! they are again assembling. I always considered militia as the best troops in the world for a sudden exertion, but they will not do for a long campaign. Howe, it is probable, will make an attempt on this city [Philadelphia]; should he fail on this side the Delaware, he is ruined. If he succeeds, our cause is not ruined. He stakes all on his side against a part on ours; admitting he succeeds, the consequence will be, that armies from both ends of the continent will march to assist their suffering friends in the middle states; for he cannot go everywhere, it is impossible. I consider Howe as the greatest enemy the Tories have; he is bringing a war into their country, which, had it not been for him and partly for themselves, they had been clear of. Should he now be expelled, I wish with all the devotion of a Christian, that the names of Whig and Tory may never more be mentioned; but should the Tories give him encouragement to come, or assistance if he come, I as sincerely wish that our next year's arms may expel them from the continent, and the Congress appropriate their possessions to the relief of those who have suffered in well-doing. A single successful battle next year will settle the whole. America could carry on a two years' war by the confiscation of the property of disaffected persons, and be made happy by their expulsion. Say not that this is revenge, call it rather the soft resentment of a suffering people, who, having no object in view but the good of all, have staked their own all upon a seemingly doubtful event. Yet it is folly to argue against determined hardness; eloquence may strike the ear, and the language of sorrow draw forth the tear of compassion, but nothing can reach the heart that is steeled with prejudice.

Quitting this class of men, I turn with the warm ardor of a friend to those who have nobly stood, and are yet determined to stand the matter out: I call not upon a few, but upon all: not on this state or that state, but on every state: up and help us; lay your shoulders to the wheel; better have too much force than too little, when so great an object is at stake. Let it be told to the future world, that in the depth of winter, when nothing but hope and virtue could survive, that the city and the country, alarmed at one common danger, came forth to meet and to repulse

it. Say not that thousands are gone, turn out your tens of thousands; throw not the burden of the day upon Providence, but "show your faith by your works," that God may bless you. It matters not where you live, or what rank of life you hold, the evil or the blessing will reach you all. The far and the near, the home counties and the back, the rich and the poor, will suffer or rejoice alike. The heart that feels not now is dead; the blood of his children will curse his cowardice, who shrinks back at a time when a little might have saved the whole, and made them happy. I love the man that can smile in trouble, that can gather strength from distress, and grow brave by reflection. 'Tis the business of little minds to shrink; but he whose heart is firm, and whose conscience approves his conduct, will pursue his principles unto death. My own line of reasoning is to myself as straight and clear as a ray of light. Not all the treasures of the world, so far as I believe, could have induced me to support an offensive war, for I think it murder; but if a thief breaks into my house, burns and destroys my property, and kills or threatens to kill me, or those that are in it, and to "bind me in all cases whatsoever" to his absolute will, am I to suffer it? What signifies it to me, whether he who does it is a king or a common man; my countryman or not my countryman; whether it be done by an individual villain, or an army of them? If we reason to the root of things we shall find no difference; neither can any just cause be assigned why we should punish in the one case and pardon in the other. Let them call me rebel and welcome, I feel no concern from it; but I should suffer the misery of devils, were I to make a whore of my soul by swearing allegiance to one whose character is that of a sottish, stupid, stubborn, worthless, brutish man. I conceive likewise a horrid idea in receiving mercy from a being, who at the last day shall be shrieking to the rocks and mountains to cover him, and fleeing with terror from the orphan, the widow, and the slain of America.

There are cases which cannot be overdone by language, and this is one. There are persons, too, who see not the full extent of the evil which threatens them; they solace themselves with hopes that the enemy, if he succeed, will be merciful. It is the madness of folly, to expect mercy from those who have refused to do justice; and even mercy, where conquest is the object, is only a trick of war; the cunning of the fox is as murderous as the violence of the wolf, and we ought to guard equally against both. Howe's first object is, partly by threats and partly by promises, to terrify or seduce the people to deliver up their arms and receive mercy. The ministry recommended the same plan to Gage, and this is what the Tories call making their peace, "a peace which passeth all understanding" indeed! A peace which would be the immediate forerunner of a worse ruin than any we have yet thought of. Ye men of Pennsylvania, do reason upon these things! Were the back counties to give up their arms, they would fall an easy prey to the Indians, who are all armed: this perhaps is what some Tories would not be sorry for. Were the home counties to deliver up their arms, they would be exposed to the resentment of the back counties who would then have it in their power to chastise their defection at pleasure. And were any one state to give up its arms, that state must be garrisoned by all Howe's army of Britons and Hessians to preserve it from the anger of the rest. Mutual fear is the principal link in the chain of mutual love, and woe be to that state that breaks the compact. Howe is mercifully inviting you to barbarous destruction, and men must be either rogues or fools that will not see it. I dwell not upon the vapors of imagination; I bring reason to your ears, and, in language as plain as A, B, C, hold up truth to your eyes.

I thank God, that I fear not. I see no real cause for fear. I know our situation well, and can see the way out of it. While our army was collected, Howe dared not risk a battle; and it is no credit to him that he decamped from the White Plains, and waited a mean opportunity to ravage the defenceless Jerseys; but it is great credit to us, that, with a handful of men, we sustained an orderly retreat for near an hundred miles, brought off our ammunition, all our field pieces, the greatest part of our stores, and had four rivers to pass. None can say that our retreat was precipitate, for we were near three weeks in performing it, that the country might have time to come in. Twice we marched back to meet the enemy, and remained out till dark. The sign of fear was not seen

Glossary

ague	chills and fever
bawdy-houses	houses of prostitution
dearness	the quality of being expensive
Gage	General Thomas Gage, commander in chief of the British army in America from 1763 to 1775
Hessians	German soldiers who fought for Britain during the Revolutionary War
Howe	British general William Howe, commander in chief of the British army in America from 1775 to 1778
impious	lacking respect or reverence
Jerseys	New Jersey, at the time divided into East and West New Jersey
Joan of Arc	fifteenth-century French military heroine and Catholic saint
King William	eleventh-century British king William the Conqueror
Major General Nathanael Green	a general in the Continental army
"peace which passeth all understanding"	a loose quotation from the biblical book of Philippians, chapter 4
sottish	drunken
Tory	in America, a British Loyalist
Voltaire	the pen name of the eighteenth-century French author François-Marie Arouet
Whigs	in America, supporters of the revolution against Britain

in our camp, and had not some of the cowardly and disaffected inhabitants spread false alarms through the country, the Jerseys had never been ravaged. Once more we are again collected and collecting; our new army at both ends of the continent is recruiting fast, and we shall be able to open the next campaign with sixty thousand men, well armed and clothed. This is our situation, and who will may know it. By perseverance and fortitude we have the prospect of a glorious issue; by cowardice and submission, the sad choice of a variety of evils—a ravaged country—a depopulated city—habitations without safety, and slavery without hope—our homes turned into barracks and bawdy-houses for Hessians, and a future race to provide for, whose fathers we shall doubt of. Look on this picture and weep over it! and if there yet remains one thoughtless wretch who believes it not, let him suffer it unlamented.

COMMON SENSE.

December 23, 1776.

THE CRISIS, NO. 4 (1777)

THOSE who expect to reap the blessings of freedom, must, like men, undergo the fatigues of supporting it. The event of yesterday was one of those kind of alarms which is just sufficient to rouse us to duty, without being of consequence enough to depress our fortitude. It is not a field of a few acres of ground, but a cause, that we are defending, and whether we defeat the enemy in one battle, or by degrees, the consequences will be the same.

Look back at the events of last winter and the present year, there you will find that the enemy's successes always contributed to reduce them. What they have gained in ground, they paid so dearly for in numbers, that their victories have in the end amounted to defeats. We have always been masters at the last push, and always shall be while we do our duty. Howe has been once on the banks of the Delaware, and from thence driven back with loss and disgrace: and why not be again driven from the Schuylkill? His condition and ours are very different. He has everybody to fight, we have only his one army to cope with, and which wastes away at every engagement: we can not only reinforce, but can redouble our numbers; he is cut off from all supplies, and must sooner or later inevitably fall into our hands.

Shall a band of ten or twelve thousand robbers, who are this day fifteen hundred or two thousand men less in strength than they were yesterday, conquer America, or subdue even a single state? The thing cannot be, unless we sit down and suffer them to do it. Another such a brush, notwithstanding we lost the ground, would, by still reducing the enemy, put them in a condition to be afterwards totally defeated. Could our whole army have come up to the attack at one time, the consequences had probably been otherwise; but our having different parts of the Brandywine creek to guard, and the uncertainty which road to Philadelphia the enemy would attempt to take, naturally afforded them an opportunity of passing with their main body at a place where only a part of ours could be posted; for it must strike every thinking man with conviction, that it requires a much greater force to oppose an enemy in several places, than is sufficient to defeat him in any one place.

Men who are sincere in defending their freedom, will always feel concern at every circumstance which seems to make against them; it is the natural and honest consequence of all affectionate attachments, and the want of it is a vice. But the dejection lasts only for a moment; they soon rise out of it with additional vigor; the glow of hope, courage and fortitude, will, in a little time, supply the place of every inferior passion, and kindle the whole heart into heroism.

There is a mystery in the countenance of some causes, which we have not always present judgment enough to explain. It is distressing to see an enemy advancing into a country, but it is the only place in which we can beat them, and in which we have always beaten them, whenever they made the attempt. The nearer any disease approaches to a crisis, the nearer it is to a cure. Danger and deliverance make their advances together, and it is only the last push, in which one or the other takes the lead.

There are many men who will do their duty when it is not wanted; but a genuine public spirit always appears most when there is most occasion for it. Thank God! our army, though fatigued, is yet entire. The attack made by us yesterday, was under many disadvantages, naturally arising from the uncertainty of knowing which route the enemy would take; and, from that circumstance, the whole of our force could not be brought up together time enough to engage all at once. Our strength is yet reserved; and it is evident that Howe does not think himself a gainer by the affair, otherwise he would this morning have moved down and attacked General Washington.

Gentlemen of the city and country, it is in your power, by a spirited improvement of the present circumstance, to turn it to a real advantage. Howe is now weaker than before, and every shot will contribute to reduce him. You are more immediately interested than any other part of the continent: your all is at stake; it is not so with the general cause; you are devoted by the enemy to plunder and destruction: it is the encouragement which Howe, the chief of plunderers, has promised his army. Thus circumstanced, you may save yourselves by a manly resistance, but you can have no hope in any other conduct. I never yet knew our brave general, or any part of the army, officers or men, out of heart, and I have seen them in circumstances a thousand times more trying than the present. It is only those that are not in action, that feel languor and heaviness, and the best way to rub it off is to turn out, and make sure work of it.

Our army must undoubtedly feel fatigue, and want a reinforcement of rest though not of valor. Our own interest and happiness call upon us to give them every support in our power, and make the burden of the day, on which the safety of this city depends, as light as possible. Remember, gentlemen, that we have forces both to the northward and southward of Philadelphia, and if the enemy be but stopped till those can arrive, this city will be saved, and the enemy finally routed. You have too much at stake to hesitate. You ought not to think an hour upon the matter, but to spring to action at once. Other states have been invaded, have likewise driven off the invaders. Now our time and turn is come, and perhaps the finishing stroke is reserved for us. When we look back on the dangers we have been saved from, and reflect on the success we have been blessed with, it would be sinful either to be idle or to despair.

I close this paper with a short address to General Howe. You, sir, are only lingering out the period that shall bring with it your defeat. You have yet scarce began upon the war, and the further you enter, the faster will your troubles thicken. What you now enjoy is only a respite from ruin; an invitation to destruction; something that will lead on to our deliverance at your expense. We know the cause which we are engaged in, and though a passionate fondness for it may make us grieve at every injury which threatens it, yet, when the moment of concern is over, the determination to duty returns. We are not moved by the gloomy smile of a worthless king, but by the ardent glow of generous patriotism. We fight not to enslave, but to set a country free, and to make room upon the earth for honest men to live in. In such a case we are sure that we are right; and we leave to you the despairing reflection of being the tool of a miserable tyrant.

COMMON SENSE.

PHILADELPHIA, Sept. 12, 1777.

Glossary

Howe	British general William Howe, commander in chief of the British army in America from 1775 to 1778

ELY PARKER

1828–1895

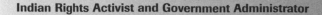

Indian Rights Activist and Government Administrator

Featured Documents
◆ Report on Indian Affairs to the War Department (1867)
◆ Annual Report of the Commissioner of Indian Affairs (1869)
◆ Letter of Resignation as Commissioner of Indian Affairs (1871)
◆ Letter to Harriet Maxwell Converse about Indian Policy Reform (1885)

Overview

Ely Samuel Parker, or Hasanoanda ("Leading Name"), was born in 1828 at Indian Falls, on the Tonawanda (Seneca) Reservation in western New York State. He descended from a politically powerful family, and his mother belonged to the Wolf Clan, the same clan as the famed Seneca orator Red Jacket. In 1851 the Seneca formally acknowledged Parker's role as a community leader and "raised" him to a position as one of the fifty sachems of the Iroquois Confederacy. He was just twenty-three years old. Along with his new status in the community came a new name: Donehogawa, or "Open Door." This was the customary name bestowed upon the Iroquois sachem who guarded the western door of both the physical and symbolic longhouse against outsiders.

In 1857 Parker negotiated a treaty that ended the decades-long land dispute with the Ogden Land Company, an important victory for the Seneca leader. In 1861 he alleviated some of the community tensions unleashed by the legacy of the land dispute and, in his first attempt at political reform, reshaped the reservation government by instituting a system of elective offices and legislative mandates. In 1863, during the Civil War, Parker was granted a commission in the Union Army at the rank of captain and joined General Ulysses S. Grant at the battle of Vicksburg. After the war ended, Parker worked as Grant's aide-de-camp and personal adviser on Indian affairs. In this capacity Parker developed a four-point program of reform for the Bureau of Indian Affairs (BIA) and submitted it to the War Department in 1867. This document served, at least in part, as the foundation of Grant's peace policy, an important reform movement in post–Civil War Indian affairs. After his inauguration as president, Grant appointed Parker as the first Indian commissioner of the BIA, a post that he accepted, optimistically convinced that his experience working with legislators and policy makers would allow him to implement the reform agenda reflected in his 1867 plan. In his first annual report as commissioner in 1869, Parker wrote about the various ways his reform program had begun to be executed. This report focused closely on developments related to congressional funding, education, and the establishment of an oversight board, all issues that would continue to hold much significance in Indian affairs. It did not reflect, however, the

fierce opposition he faced from a group of conservative, Christian, elitist, non-Native reformers.

In 1870 one of these men, William Welsh, filed formal charges against Parker, alleging that Parker had committed fraud and had willfully mismanaged the BIA. Although a House of Representatives investigation exonerated Parker in 1871, he resigned from his position. His resignation letter stated that congressional legislation and the actions of the Board of Indian Commissioners had removed all the power and influence of his office and that therefore he could no longer hold the position. Following his career as a public servant, Parker became close friends with Harriet Maxwell Converse, a poet and Indian political activist, and aided her as an informant and confidant. In 1885 he wrote a very insightful and powerful letter to her, in which he reflected upon the history of federal Indian policy and reform. This letter revealed the frustrations and anger that many Indian policy reformers felt about the direction of Indian policy in the nineteenth century.

Explanation and Analysis of Documents

Parker rose to prominence as a federal policy maker during the Reconstruction era, a moment of potential optimism for a reconfiguration of racial politics in the United States. He was an eloquent writer and orator, and although he based his arguments for Indian policy reform on historical evidence and first-hand observation, Parker perhaps misjudged the level to which legislators and other interested parties would be willing to reshape the BIA, a notoriously corrupt and graft-ridden agency in the nineteenth century. Four documents—a report on Indian affairs to the War Department, his annual report as commissioner, his letter of resignation from the post of commissioner, and a letter to Harriet Maxwell Converse—demonstrate Parker's initial optimism and resolve to reform Indian policy as well as the ways in which he became frustrated with the system and resentful toward public servants who stood in the way of reform.

◆ Report on Indian Affairs to the War Department
In 1867, responding to several tragedies in Indian affairs during the Civil War, including the 1862 Dakota War and the 1864 Sand Creek Massacre, General Grant asked Parker, who had served informally as his adviser on

1828

- Ely S. Parker, or Hasanoanda ("Leading Name"), is born at Indian Falls, on the Tonawanda Reservation in western New York State.

1851

- **September 19**
  At the age of twenty-three, Parker is "raised" to the position of sachem of the Six Nations. He is given the customary name Donehogawa, or "Open Door."

1857

- **November 5**
  Parker negotiates a treaty with the Office of Indian Affairs to end the decades-long land dispute between his Tonawanda Seneca community and the Ogden Land Company, allowing the Seneca to maintain a portion of their homeland.

1861

- Parker reforms Tonawanda Reservation governance.

1863

- **May 25**
  A commission, endorsed by Ulysses S. Grant, is issued for Ely Parker. He enters the army as an assistant adjutant general of volunteers at the rank of captain but quickly becomes Grant's military secretary.

1865

- **April 9**
  Parker drafts the official copy of the surrender agreement between Ulysses S. Grant and Robert E. Lee that ends the Civil War.

1867

- **January 24**
  Parker, acting as Grant's informal adviser on Indian affairs, submits a letter to the War Department proposing a four-point program of reform.

Indian matters since the war ended, to develop an agenda for the reform of the BIA. In response, Parker proposed a four-point plan for "the establishment of a permanent and perpetual peace, and for the settling of all matters of differences between the United States and the various Indian tribes." This lofty statement represented the idea shared by many non-Native policy makers and officials at the time—that such a goal not only was possible but also could be achieved expeditiously.

In his reform agenda, Parker focused on providing public oversight of policy administration by both Native and non-Native individuals and sought to establish and protect specific land rights for Native communities. Finally, he wanted to develop BIA bureaucracy by transferring it back to the War Department in an effort to end corruption and to protect it from the influence of land speculators and business interests outside the government. Parker also believed that the government should provide money, goods, services, and new opportunities—particularly educational opportunities—for Native people, to compensate for dispossession and colonization.

◆ **Annual Report of the Commissioner of Indian Affairs**

In 1868 President Grant appointed Parker as commissioner of Indian affairs. Parker accepted the position optimistically and believed that his experiences as a leader among the Tonawanda Seneca and within the federal bureaucracy would serve him well in his attempt to reform the bureau and help Indian people. Several months into his term, Parker submitted his first annual report to the secretary of the interior.

In his report Parker argues that the successes experienced in relations between Indians and whites during the previous months were the direct result of "the concentration of the Indians upon suitable reservations, and the supplying them with the means for engaging in agricultural and mechanical pursuits, and for their education and moral training." He also refers to increased federal appropriations and the creation of a board of Indian commissioners, both suggestions Parker had made in his 1867 report on Indian affairs to the War Department. Between the time that Parker's report was delivered and legislative action was taken, however, the character and foundation of the oversight commission changed considerably. Congress established the Board of Indian Commissioners (BIC) on April 10, 1869, and called for the selection of "men eminent for their intelligence and philanthropy, to serve without pecuniary compensation" but left out any mention that the group should be composed of Native and non-Native people alike. Furthermore, the fact that the men were not to be paid ensured that only elite members of society—those with the leisure time to devote to philanthropic causes—would agree to participate in such a committee. Although this was clearly not the oversight committee he had initially envisioned—which should have demonstrated that perhaps his reform agenda would face stiffer criticism and create more controversy than he had supposed—Parker

nonetheless considered the BIC's suggestions very important to the development of Indian policy.

It is also important to note that Parker suggests in this report that the treaty-making relationship between Indian nations and the federal government be ended. Parker's critics often cite this fact as evidence that he betrayed Indian people as he sought fame and notoriety in mainstream society. If his words are read closely, however, it becomes clear that, according to Parker's experience, this measure would protect Indian communities from the almost fatal factionalism he had witnessed among the Seneca during the Ogden Land Controversy.

◆ Letter of Resignation as Commissioner of Indian Affairs

No matter how optimistic Parker was about the possibilities for reform in Indian affairs, conflicts and controversies with the BIC emerged almost immediately. In particular, William Welsh, the first president of the BIC, believed that the BIC should hold a central position in the Department of the Interior, with powers and responsibilities equal or superior to those of the commissioner. He and all of the other members of the BIC were conservative, elitist, zealously Christian, and connected to manufacturing, transportation, and mineral-extraction interests that stood to benefit from Indian dispossession. The BIC worked to monitor Indian appropriations, but it also lobbied legislators, especially during the period 1869–1874, to dispossess Indians of their lands and undermine their sovereignty. Members of the BIC also saw Parker as a potential stumbling block and vowed to have him removed from his position.

In December 1870 Welsh published an open letter to the secretary of the interior, suggesting that Parker was guilty of fraud and mismanagement. The House of Representatives soon resolved to investigate these charges, and a public hearing began on January 16, 1871. Following two months of investigations and hearings, the House Committee on Appropriations exonerated Parker; they found no evidence of fraud or misconduct. Still, they noted that testimony revealed irregularities, incompetence, and neglect—comments that described a healthy number of Grant's historically inept administration. After the investigation, however, Parker realized that he would be unable to make headway among reformers and legislators who expected Indians to be the subjects of federal policy but never its creators. On August 1, 1871, Parker resigned his commission. In his resignation letter of June 29 Parker states that he believes in the reform efforts of the current administration but says that the BIC's "operating wholly outside of and almost independent of the Indian Bureau" had rendered the commissioner's office impotent and made his position ambiguous. He left public service at that point.

◆ Letter to Harriet Maxwell Converse about Indian Policy Reform

Following his years in public service, Parker moved to Fairfield, Connecticut, and entered into various business enterprises. He won and then lost a fortune in the stock

Time Line

1869

- **April 13**
  Parker is nominated for the position of commissioner of Indian affairs by newly elected President Grant.

- **December 23**
  Parker issues the annual report of the commissioner of Indian affairs.

1871

- **June 29**
  Parker submits his resignation as commissioner of Indian affairs following a House of Representatives investigation into the conduct of his administration.

1885

- Parker writes to Harriet Maxwell Converse about Indian policy reform.

1895

- **August 30**
  After suffering a series of strokes and other complications related to diabetes, Parker dies in Fairfield, Connecticut.

market. In 1876 he moved to New York City and became a clerk in the New York City Police Department, where he became close friends with Harriet Maxwell Converse, a poet, magazine writer, ethnographer, and political activist, and aided her as an informant and confidant. Born in 1836, in Elmira, New York, Harriet Maxwell Converse had learned about Indian culture and society first from her father and grandfather. When she and Parker met, probably in 1881, Converse was an established poet and writer, and although she had some interest in Indian history and folklore, she had yet to explore these topics at length. Through their collaboration, however, she became increasingly interested in and politically active on behalf of New York State's Indian population and helped to defeat several potentially damaging federal bills in the 1890s and early 1900s.

Despite his personal and public struggles in the 1870s, Parker remained actively engaged in Indian political issues. He frequently corresponded with Seneca leaders and traveled to Tonawanda as often as his health and other responsibilities would allow. His friendship with Converse aided these efforts; because she was also an activist who shared Parker's political agenda, she represented a sounding board for his ideas. In 1885, as part of an ongoing discussion about federal Indian policy with Converse, Parker expressed great dissatisfaction with the history of Indian policy reform. His missive to Converse demonstrates the frustrations that many post–Civil War reformers felt by the end of the century. This letter is particularly interesting, because in it Parker comments on the support for the allotment program, a federal policy of dispossession that would be established in the 1887 General Allotment Act. While its supporters argued in the campaign leading up to its passage that Indian communities were calling for an allotment program, Parker asserted that the "Indians, as a body, are deadly opposed to the scheme, for they see in it too plainly the certain and speedy dissolution of their tribal and national organizations." Although his letter strongly criticizes most Indian policy reformers, it ends on a positive note, with Parker's personal maxim and solution to the "Indian Problem"—"Education to be made first above all. Other good things will follow."

Impact and Legacy

Although Parker probably did not realize it during his life, his reform agenda on the federal level represented a significant break with previous traditions in Indian policy and was a forerunner to larger, later trends in social policy making. By attempting to effect public oversight of policy administration by concerned citizens with no vested interests beyond philanthropy, Parker initiated techniques that would rise to prominence in the larger efforts of social policy reformers in the Progressive era. In his assertion that one of the most important responsibilities of the BIA was to provide supplies, goods, money, and educational opportunities to Native peoples and that rather than breaking up tribal groups, the BIA should work to maintain Indian community coherence, he applied a framework based on compensatory legislation that intended to ease the disruptions caused by dispossession and colonial action while allowing Native people to assimilate into mainstream American society on their own terms and in their own time. This framework was very similar to that which would be used by later reformers who worked among urban immigrant groups at the turn of the twentieth century. Finally, by working for the transfer of the BIA back to the War Department, with its efficient, impartial, and expanded bureaucratic capacity, Parker started a movement that, though unsuccessful in the transfer debate, would result in the increasing bureaucratization of Indian affairs and the ultimate confinement of Indian peoples through the General Allotment Act of 1887 and its accompanying coercive assimilation programs.

Although Parker did not play an active role in federal policy making after 1871, his notions of an efficient and impartial bureaucracy and compensatory legislation appealed to later activists and thinkers, and they built upon the reform framework that he had established. One of these men, Thomas A. Bland, an Indiana physician, writer, and activist in the late 1870s and 1880s, also opposed the movement toward land allotment and coercive assimilation policies. Bland's organization, the National Indian Defense Association, confronted the politically powerful Indian Rights Asso-

ciation, led by Herbert Welsh, William Welsh's nephew. Bland and his organization questioned the goals and methods of the disruptive allotment policies as well as the implications of such policies for the role and responsibilities of the state. In doing so, they encouraged policy makers to pause and consider Indian voices, thus slowing the legislative process significantly in the mid-1880s. In 1887, however, Welsh, the Indian Rights Association, and their political allies succeeded in pushing the allotment program through Congress and ushered in an era of dispossession, poverty, and despair for Indian communities across the nation.

The Indian-centered opposition that Parker had created—with its notions of compensatory and protective legislation—did not disappear, however. In 1933 President Franklin D. Roosevelt appointed a reform-minded Indian advocate named John Collier as commissioner of Indian affairs, and his administration created and implemented a system of compensatory legislation that reflected Roosevelt's broader social and economic policy reform agenda. In his Indian New Deal, Collier reversed the policies of the allotment era, restored surplus land at various reservations, and provided funding for Native communities to purchase additional lands. Collier sought to reshape the ideologies of policy makers and reformers by changing the overtly hostile attitude many of these people held toward customary Native American cultures and practices. In doing so, he drew heavily from Parker's earlier, Indian-centered ideas, so much so, in fact, that it could be argued that Parker himself was the harbinger of the Indian New Deal.

Key Sources

The New York State Library in Albany; the Buffalo and Erie County Historical Society Research Library in Buffalo, New York; the American Philosophical Society in Philadelphia; and the Rush Rhees Library at the University of Rochester, in Rochester, New York, hold collections of Parker's papers relating to his education, his career, and his correspondence with friends, family, and colleagues. Additional materials are held at the Newberry Library in Chicago; the Henry E. Huntington Library in San Marino, California; and the State Historical Society of Wisconsin. The National Archives and Records Administration keeps documents concerning Parker's career in the federal government. In 2004 the Public Broadcasting Service aired an original documentary about Ely S. Parker entitled *Warrior in Two Worlds* and maintains a corresponding Web site at http://www.pbs.org/warrior/indexf.html.

Further Reading

■ Articles

Genetin-Pilawa, C. Joseph. "'All Intent on Seeing the White Woman Married to the Red Man': The Parker/Sackett Affair and the Public Spectacle of Intermarriage." *Journal of Women's History* 20, no. 2 (2008): 57–85.

"*The expense of this entire plan for establishing peace, saving lives, making every route of travel across the continent entirely safe, civilizing and perpetuating the Indian race, and developing immense tracts of country now held by hostile bands of Indians, would be but a mere tithe to the amount now annually paid by the government for these purposes.*"

(Report on Indian Affairs to the War Department)

"*By the timely supplies of subsistence and clothing furnished, and the adoption of measures intended for their benefit, the tribes from whom the greatest trouble was apprehended have been kept comparatively quiet, and some advance it is to be hoped, made in the direction of their permanent settlement in the localities assigned to them, and their entering upon a new course of life.*"

(Annual Report of the Commissioner of Indian Affairs)

"*The effect of the Congressional legislation, since I have had the honor to hold the position of Commissioner of Indian Affairs, has been to almost wholly divest the Indian Bureau of all its original importance, duties, and proper responsibilities.*"

(Letter of Resignation as Commissioner of Indian Affairs)

"*I have little or no faith in the American Christian civilization methods of healing...the Indians of this country. It has not been honest, pure or sincere. Black deception, damnable frauds and persistent oppression has been its characteristics, and its religion today is, that the only good Indian is a dead one.*"

(Letter to Harriet Maxwell Converse about Indian Policy Reform)

"*All schemes, to apparently serve the Indians, are only plausible pleas put out to hoodwink the civilized world that everything possible has been done to save this race from total annihilation, and to wipe out the stain on the American name for its treatment of the aboriginal population.*"

(Letter to Harriet Maxwell Converse about Indian Policy Reform)

"*Education to be made first above all. Other good things will follow.*"

(Letter to Harriet Maxwell Converse about Indian Policy Reform)

Michaelsen, Scott. "Ely S. Parker and Amerindian Voices in Ethnography." *American Literary History* 8, no. 4 (1996): 615–638.

■ **Books**

Armstrong, William H. *Warrior in Two Camps: Ely S. Parker, Union General and Seneca Chief*. Syracuse, N.Y.: Syracuse University Press, 1978.

Conable, Mary H. "A Steady Enemy: The Ogden Land Company and the Seneca Indians." PhD diss., University of Rochester, 1994.

Deloria, Philip J. *Playing Indian*. New Haven, Conn.: Yale University Press, 2001.

Konkle, Maureen. *Writing Indian Nations: Native Intellectuals and the Politics of Historiography, 1827–1863*. Chapel Hill: University of North Carolina Press, 2004.

Michaelsen, Scott. *The Limits of Multiculturalism: Interrogating the Origins of American Anthropology*. Minneapolis: University of Minnesota Press, 1999.

Morgan, Lewis Henry. *The League of the Ho-dé-no-sau-nee, or Iroquois*. New York: Mark H. Newman & Co., 1851.

Parker, Arthur Caswell. *The Life of General Ely S. Parker: Last Grand Sachem of the Iroquois and General Grant's Military Secretary*. Buffalo, N.Y.: Buffalo Historical Society, 1919.

Tooker, Elisabeth. "Ely S. Parker." In *American Indian Intellectuals: of the Nineteenth and Early Twentieth Centuries*, ed. Margot Liberty. Norman: University Press of Oklahoma, 2002.

Waltmann, Henry G. "Ely Samuel Parker 1869–71." In *The Commissioners of Indian Affairs, 1824–1977*, ed. Robert M. Kvasnicka and Herman J. Viola. Lincoln: University of Nebraska Press, 1979.

—Joseph Genetin-Pilawa

Questions for Further Study

1. There is much controversy over the question of whether Parker—regardless of his intentions—ultimately helped or hurt the cause of Native Americans. Discuss this question from both sides. Consider such specifics as his opposition to native treaty making with the federal government, his attitude with regard to the expansion of bureaucracy, and his influence on the "Indian New Deal" of the 1930s.

2. Evaluate the specifics of Parker's report and recommendations to the War Department, including his plans for the concentration of tribes and the appointment of a commission to oversee Indian affairs as well as his argument in favor of continued military authority in negotiations with Indians.

3. Parker argues eloquently, in his reports to the War Department and later to the Commissioner of Indian Affairs, for the idea that Native Americans should organize along modern lines so as to preserve their way of life. He repeatedly recommends "civilization," by which he means an organized society as opposed to the tribal and often nomadic system that prevailed among native peoples. Was he right or wrong in his position? The answer may not be as simple as it seems: One might argue, for instance, that organization and modernization would have protected the Indians against white aggression even as it had the ironic effect of eroding native culture.

REPORT ON INDIAN AFFAIRS TO THE WAR DEPARTMENT (1867)

HEADQUARTERS ARMIES OF THE UNITED STATES
Washington City, January 25, 1867

General: In compliance with your request, I have the honor to submit the following proposed plan for the establishment of a permanent and perpetual peace, and for settling all matters of differences between the United States and the various Indian tribes.

I am, very respectfully, your obedient servant,
E.S. PARKER
Colonel and Aide-de-Camp
General U.S. Grant
Commanding armies of the United States.

First. The retransfer of the Indian bureau from the Interior Department back to the War Department, or military branch of the government, where it originally belonged, until within the last few years.

The condition and disposition of all the Indians west of the Mississippi river, as developed in consequence of the great and rapid influx of immigration by reason of the discovery of the precious metals throughout the entire west, renders it of the utmost importance that military supervision should be extended over the Indians. Treaties have been made with a very large number of the tribes, and generally reservations have been provided as homes for them. Agents appointed from civil life have generally been provided to protect their lives and property, and to attend to the prompt and faithful observance of treaty stipulations. But as the hardy pioneer and adventurous miner advanced into the inhospitable regions occupied by the Indians, in search of the precious metals, they found no rights possessed by the Indians that they were bound to respect. The faith of treaties solemnly entered into were totally disregarded, and Indian territory wantonly violated. If any tribe remonstrated against the violation of their natural and treaty rights, members of the tribe were inhumanely shot down and the whole treated as mere dogs. Retaliation generally followed, and bloody Indian wars have been the consequence, costing many lives and much treasure. In all troubles arising in this manner the civil agents have been totally powerless to avert the consequences, and, when too late, the military have been called in to pro-

tect the whites and punish the Indians, when if, in the beginning, the military had had the supervision of the Indians, their rights would not have been improperly molested, or if disturbed in their quietude by any lawless whites, a prompt and summary check to any further aggressions could have been given. In cases where the government promises the Indians the peaceable and quiet possession of a reservation, and precious metals are discovered or found to exist upon it, the military alone can give the Indians the needed protection and keep the adventurous miner from encroaching upon the Indians until the government has come to some understanding with them. In such cases, the civil agent is absolutely powerless.

Most of Indian treaties contain stipulations for the payment annually to Indians of annuities, either in money or goods or both, and agents are appointed to make these payments whenever government furnishes them the means. I know of no reason why officers of the army could not make all these payments as well as civilians. The expense of agencies would be saved, and I think, the Indians would be honestly dealt by. An officer's honor and interest is at stake, and impels him to discharge his duty honestly and faithfully, while civil agents have none of those incentives, the ruling passion with them being generally to avoid all trouble and responsibility, and to make as much money as possible out of their offices.

In the retransfer of this bureau I would provide for the complete abolishment of the system of Indian traders which in my opinion, is a great evil to Indian communities. I would make government the purchaser of all articles usually brought in by Indians, giving them a fair equivalent for the same in money or goods at cost prices. In this way it would be an easier matter to regulate the sale or issue of arms and ammunition to Indians a question which of late has agitated the minds of the civil and military authorities. If the entry of large numbers of Indians to any military post is objectionable, it can easily be arranged that only limited numbers shall be admitted daily....

Many other reasons might be suggested why the Indian department should altogether be under military control, but a familiar knowledge of the practical workings of the present system would seem to be the most convincing proofs of the propriety of the measure. It is pretty generally advocated by those most familiar with our Indian relations, and so far as I know, the Indians themselves desire it. Civil officers are not usually respected by the tribes, but they fear and regard the military, and will submit to their counsels, advice, and dictation, when they would not listen to a civil agent.

Second. The next measure I would suggest is the passage by Congress of a plan of territorial government for the Indians, as was submitted last winter, or a similar one. When once passed, it should remain upon the stature books as the permanent and settled policy of the government. The boundaries of the Indian territory or territories should be well defined by metes and bounds, and should remain inviolate from settlement by any except Indians and government employees.

The subject of the improvement and civilization of the Indians, and the maintenance of peaceful relations with them, has engaged the serious consideration of every administration since the birth of the American republic; and, if I recollect aright, President Jefferson was the first to inaugurate the policy of the removal of the Indians from the States to the country west of the Mississippi; and President Monroe, in furtherance of this policy, recommended that the Indians be concentrated, as far as was practicable, and civil governments established for them, with schools for every branch of instruction in literature and the arts of civilized life…. It is presumed that humanity dictated the original policy of the removal and concentration of the Indians in the west to save them from threatened extinction. But to-day, by reason of the immense augmentation of the American population, and the extension of their settlements throughout the entire west, covering both slopes of the Rocky mountains, the Indian races are more seriously threatened with a speedy extermination than ever before in the history of the country. And, however much such a deplorable result might be wished for by some, it seems to me that the honor of a Christian nation and every sentiment of humanity dictate that no pains be spared to avert such an appalling calamity befalling a portion of the human race. The establishment of all the Indians upon any one territory is perhaps impracticable, but numbers of them can, without doubt, be consolidated in separate districts of country, and the same system of government be made to apply to each. By the concentration of tribes, although in several and separate districts, government can more readily control them and more economically press and carry out plans for their improvement and civilization, and a better field be

offered for philanthropic aid and Christian instruction. Some system of this kind has, at different periods in the history of our government, been put forward, but never successfully put into execution. A renewal of the attempt, with proper aids, it seems to me cannot fail of success.

Third. The passage by Congress of an act authorizing the appointment of an inspection board, or commission, to hold office during good behavior, or until the necessity for their services is terminated by the completion of the retransfer of the Indian bureau to the War Department. It shall be the duty of their board to examine the accounts of the several agencies, see that every cent due the Indians is paid to them promptly as may be promised in treaties, and that proper and suitable goods and implements of agriculture are delivered to them, when such articles are due; to make semi-annual reports, with such suggestions as, in their judgment, might seem necessary to the perfect establishment of a permanent and friendly feeling between the people of the United States and the Indians.

This commissioner could undoubtedly be dispensed within a few years, but the results of their labors might be very important and beneficial, not only in supervising and promptly checking the delinquencies of incompetent and dishonest agents, but it would be a most convincing proof to the Indians' mind that the government was disposed to deal honestly and fairly by them. Such a commission might, indeed, be rendered wholly unnecessary if Congress would consent to the next and fourth proposition which I submit in this plan.

Fourth. The passage of an act authorizing the appointment of a permanent Indian commission, to be a mixed commission, composed of such white men as possessed in a large degree the confidence of their country, and a number of the most reputable educated Indians, selected from different tribes. The entire commission might be composed of ten members, and, if deemed advisable, might be divided so that five could operate north and five south of a given line, but both to be governed by the same general instructions, and impressing upon the Indians the same line of governmental policy. It shall be made their duty to visit all the Indian tribes within the limits of the United States, whether, to do this, it requires three, five, or ten years. They shall hold talks with them, setting forth the great benefits that would result to them from a permanent peace with the whites, from the abandonment of their nomadic mode of life, and adopting agricultural and pastoral pursuits, and the habits and modes of civilized communities. Under the directions of the President the commission shall explain to the various tribes the advantages of their consolidation upon some common territory, over which Congress shall have extended the aegis of good, wise, and wholesome laws for their protection and perpetuation....

The commission shall assure the tribes that the white man does not want the Indian exterminated from the face of the earth, but will live with him as good neighbors, in peace and quiet. The value of maintaining friendly and brotherly relations among themselves is to be urged upon the tribes, and its continual discussion to be made one of the permanent duties of the commission. They are also to urge constantly the propriety, necessity, and benefit to result from their concentration in certain districts of the country, there to live peaceably as members of the same family, as brothers and friends having the same interests and the same destiny. I am free to admit that the most difficult task for the commission would be to obtain the consent of the Indians to consolidate, by removing certain defined districts. But by constantly keeping the subject before them, and by yearly visitations, the wisdom and humanity of the policy would gradually develop in the Indian mind, and one by one the tribes would come into the measure, and the whole policy be adopted. There would be very many prejudices to combat and overcome. As members of the great human family, they know and feel that they are endowed with certain rights. They possess fair intellectual faculties. They entertain the most ardent love for the largest liberty and independence. Originally their greatest desire was to be left undisturbed by the overflowing white population that was quietly but surely pressing to overwhelm them, and they have been powerless to divert or stem the current of events. They saw their hunting grounds and fisheries disappear before them. They have been reduced to limits too narrow for the hunter state, and naturally many of them at times have sought by violence the redress of what they conceived to be great and heinous wrongs against their natural rights. Though ignorant, in the common acceptation of the term, they are a proud people, and quickly resent the least suspicion of dictation in the government of their actions, come from what quarter it may. Most of the tribes are eminently subject to the influence and control of interested, unprincipled, and crafty individuals, who, to retain their influence and power, would oppose the idea of a consolidation of tribes, because now they are something, while under the new order of things they might be nothing. They will pander to the prejudices of their

people by preaching the sanctimoniousness of their separate creation, nationality, and customs, and claim that as their Creator made them, so they must ever remain. They flatter the pride of the Indian mind. Their reasoning is so specious, but yet it is all sophistry....

The appointment of a number of reputable educated Indians upon this commission is suggested because they are familiar with the best modes of communicating with the tribes, whether friendly or unfriendly; they are familiar with the peculiarities of the Indian mind, and know how to make the desired impression upon it, and it would add greatly to the confidence of the tribes in the earnestness, sincerity, and humanity of the government,...

This project, at first blush, may seem to be devised on too extensive a scale, and involving too much expense for an experiment. I cannot so regard it. On the contrary, I believe it to be more economical than any other plan that could be suggested. A whole army of Indian agents, traders, contractors, jobbers, and hangers-on would be dispensed with, and from them would come the strongest opposition to the adoption of this plan, as it would effectually close to them the corrupt sources of their wealth.

In 1865, the Secretary of the Interior estimated the cost to the government of maintaining each regiment of troops operating against the Indians on the frontier at two millions of dollars per annum, and that only a few hundred Indians had been killed. By a recent publication in the newspapers (but whether true I cannot say) it was stated that the cost of operations against the Indians during the past year was thirty millions of dollars; that a certain number only of Indians had been killed, each life costing the government sixty thousand dollars. Though the cost of carrying on a war is now pretty well understood in this country, the expense of an Indian war extending along a frontier of thousands of miles cannot be safely estimated. The expense of the Florida Indian war, against a few Indians, who long refused to leave a country hardly inhabitable by civilized man, it is known, cost millions of treasure and many valuable lives.

The expense of this entire plan for establishing peace, saving lives, making every route of travel across the continent entirely safe, civilizing and perpetuating the Indian race, and developing immense tracts of country now held by hostile bands of Indians, would be but a mere tithe to the amount now annually paid by the government for these purposes. There are plenty of troops already in the Indian country, and after the commission has commenced its labors hostilities would very soon cease. Yet the military would have to be maintained in the country until the labors of the commission were fairly and fully developed, and, if successful, the troops could be moved into or contiguous to the Indian districts, to protect them from frauds and impositions, to maintain them in their just and legal rights, and to act as the magisterial agents of the government. The benefits to result from even a partial success of this plan would, to my mind, justify the government in attempting it, especially as it seems so much more economical than the prosecution of the present Indian policy.

E.S. PARKER

Glossary

agents … from civil life	civilian representatives
annuities	annual payments
dispensed	removed from office
humanity	the desire to provide humane treatment
in the common acceptation of the term	as the term is generally understood
jobbers	middlemen between manufacturers and retailers
magisterial agents	judicial representatives
pastoral pursuits	raising cattle or other pastured animals
sophistry	argument for the sake of winning an argument rather than actually being right
specious	appearing to be true but in fact false
they have been reduced to limits too narrow for the hunter state	they no longer possess the natural resources necessary to survive as hunter-gatherers
tithe	a tenth; usually referring to a tenth part of one's income, given over to a church or charitable organization either voluntarily or in the form of a tax
War Department	the pre-1947 name for what is now the U.S. Department of Defense

ANNUAL REPORT OF THE COMMISSIONER OF INDIAN AFFAIRS (1869)

DEPARTMENT OF THE INTERIOR,
OFFICE OF INDIAN AFFAIRS,
Washington City, D.C., December 23, 1869.

Sir: As required by law, I have the honor to submit this, my first annual report of our Indian affairs and relations during the past year, with accompanying documents.

Among the reports of the superintendents and agents herewith, there will be found information, with views and suggestions of much practical value, which should command the earnest attention of our legislators, and all others who are concerned for the future welfare and destiny of the remaining original inhabitants of our country. The question is still one of deepest interest, "What shall be done for the amelioration and civilization of the race?" For a long period in the past, great and commendable efforts were made by the government and the philanthropist, and large sums of money expended to accomplish these desirable ends, but the success never was commensurate with the means employed. Of late years a change of policy was seen to be required, as the cause of failure, the difficulties to be encountered, and the best means of overcoming them, became better understood. The measures to which we are indebted for an improved condition of affairs are, the concentration of the Indians upon suitable reservations, and the supplying them with the means for engaging in agricultural and mechanical pursuits, and for their education and moral training. As a result, the clouds of ignorance and superstition in which many of this people were so long enveloped have disappeared, and the light of a Christian civilization seems to have dawned upon their moral darkness, and opened up a brighter future. Much however, remains to be done for the multitude yet in their savage state, and I can but earnestly invite the serious consideration of those whose duty it is to legislate in their behalf, to the justice and importance of promptly fulfilling all treaty obligations, and the wisdom of placing at the disposal of the department adequate funds for the purpose, and investing it with the powers to adopt the requisite measures for the settlement of all the tribes, when practicable, upon tracts of land to be set apart for their use and occupancy....

Before entering upon a *resume* of the affairs of the respective superintendencies and agencies for the past year, I will here briefly notice several matters of interest which, in their bearing upon the management of our Indian relations, are likely to work out, judging from what has been the effect so far, the most beneficial results.

Under an act of Congress approved April 10, 1868, two millions of dollars were appropriated to enable the President to maintain peace among and with various tribes, bands, and parties of Indians; to promote their civilization; bring them, when practicable, upon reservations, and to relieve their necessities, and encourage their efforts at self-support. The Executive is also authorized to organize a board of commissioners, to consist of not more than ten persons, selected from among men eminent for their intelligence and philanthropy, to serve without pecuniary compensation, and who, under his direction, shall exercise joint control with the Secretary of the Interior over the disbursement of this large fund. The commissioner selected in accordance with this provision of the law … met in this city in May last, and after deliberating upon the points suggested for their consideration…involving the legal status of the Indians, their rights, and the obligations of the government toward them; the propriety of any further treaties being made; the expediency of a change in the mode of annuity payments, and other points of special interest, they decided as preliminary to future operations, and for the more convenient and speedy discharge of their duties, upon dividing the territory inhabited by Indians into three sections, and appointed sub-committees out of their number to visit each, and examine into the affairs of the tribes therein, and to report at a meeting to be held in Washington prior to the coming session of Congress.

In regard to the fund of two million dollars referred to, it may be remarked that it has enabled the department to a great extent to carry out the purposes for which it was appropriated. There can be no question but that mischief has been prevented, and suffering either relieved or warded off from numbers who otherwise, by force of circumstances, would have been led into difficulties and extreme want. By the timely supplies of subsistence and clothing furnished, and the adoption of measures intended for their benefit, the tribes from whom the greatest trouble was apprehended have been kept comparatively quiet, and some advance it is to be hoped, made in the direction of their permanent settlement in the localities assigned to them, and their entering upon a new course of life. The subsistence they receive is furnished through the agency of the commissary department of the army, with, it is believed, greater economy and more satisfaction than could have resulted had the mode heretofore observed been followed. In this connection I desire to call attention to the fact that the number of wild Indians and others, also not provided for by treaty stipulations, whose precarious condition requires that something should be done for their relief, and who are thrown under the immediate charge of the department, is increasing. It is, therefore, a matter of serious consideration and urgent necessity that means be afforded to properly care for them. For this purpose, in my judgment, there should be annually appropriated by Congress a large contingent fund, similar to that in question, and subject to the same control....

With a view to more efficiency in the management of affairs of the respective superintendencies and agencies, the Executive has inaugurated a change of policy whereby a different class of men from those heretofore selected have been appointed to duty as superintendents and agents. There was doubtless just ground for it, as great and frequent complaints have been made for years past, of either the dishonesty or inefficiency of many of these officers. Members of the Society of Friends, recommended by the society, now hold these positions in the Northern Superintendency, embracing all Indians in Nebraska; and in the Central, embracing tribes residing in Kansas, together with the Kiowas, Comanches, and other tribes in the Indian country. The other superintendencies and agencies, excepting that of Oregon and two agencies there, are filled by army officers detailed for such duty. The experiment has not been sufficiently tested to enable me to say definitely that it is a success, for but a short time has elapsed since these Friends and officers entered upon duty; but so far as I can learn the plan works advantageously, and will probably prove a positive benefit to the service, and the indications are that the interests of the government and the Indians will be subserved by an honest and faithful discharge of duty, fully answering the expectations entertained by those who regard the measure as wise and proper.

I am pleased to have it to remark that there is now a perfect understanding between the officers of this department and those of the military, with respect to their relative duties and responsibilities in reference to Indian affairs. In this matter, with the approbation of the President and yourself, a circular letter was addressed by this office in June last to all superintendents and agents defining the policy of the government in its treatment of the Indians; as comprehended in these general terms, viz: that they should be secured in their legal rights; located, when practicable, upon reservations; assisted in agricultural pursuits and the arts of civilized life; and that Indians who should fail or refuse to come in and locate in permanent abodes provided for them, would be subject wholly to the control and supervision of military authorities, to be treated as friendly or hostile as circumstances might justify. The War Department concurring, issued orders upon the subject for the information and guidance of the proper military officers and the result has been harmony of action between the two departments, no conflict of opinion having arisen as to the duty, power and responsibility of either.

Arrangements now, as heretofore, will doubtless be required with tribes desiring to be settled upon reservations for the relinquishment of their rights to the lands claimed by them and for assistance in sustaining themselves in a new position, but I am of the opinion that *they should not be of a treaty nature*. It has become a matter of serious import whether the treaty system in use ought longer to be continued. In my judgment it should not. A treaty involves the idea of a compact between two or more sovereign powers, each possessing sufficient authority and force to compel a compliance with the obligations incurred. The Indian tribes of the United States are not sovereign nations, capable of making treaties, as none of them have an organized government of such inherent strength as would secure a faithful obedience of its people in the observance of compacts of this character. They are held to be the wards of the government, and the only title the law concedes to them to the lands they occupy or claim is a mere possessory one. But, because treaties have been made with them, generally for the extinguishment of their supposed absolute title to land inhabited by them, or over which they roam, they have become falsely impressed with the notion of national independence. It is time that this idea should be dispelled, and the government cease the cruel farce of thus dealing with its helpless and ignorant wards. Many good men, looking at this matter only from a Christian point of view, will perhaps say that the poor Indian has been greatly wronged and ill treated; that this whole country was once his, of which he has been despoiled, and that he has been driven from place to place until he has hardly left to him a spot to lay his head. This indeed may be philanthropic and humane, but the stern letter of the law admits no such conclusion, and great injury has been done by the government in deluding this people into the belief of their being independent sovereignties, while they were at the same time recognized only as its dependents and wards. As civilization advances and their possessions of land are required for settlement, such legislation should be granted to them as a wise, liberal, and just government ought to extend to subjects holding their dependent relation. In regard to treaties now in force, justice and humanity require that they be promptly and faithfully executed, so that the Indians may not have cause of complaint, or reason to violate their obligations by acts of violence and robbery.

Glossary

civilization	a value-neutral term referring to a society possessing certain attributes, such as a non-nomadic way of life and written language
commissary	supply
letter of the law	the exact provisions of the law, without any allowance for mitigating circumstances
savage	a term indicating (without implying judgment) the opposite of *civilized*—nomadic, with a subsistence way of life
Society of Friends	the Quakers, a peaceful religious group who enjoyed generally good relations with Native Americans
subserved	served, attended to
success never was commensurate with the means employed	the results did not justify the costs
viz.	abbreviation for the Latin *videlicet* meaning "for example"
wards of	persons under the protection and care of
wild	a term synonymous with *savage* but not used here derogatorily

LETTER OF RESIGNATION AS COMMISSIONER OF INDIAN AFFAIRS (1871)

Washington, D.C., June 29

To the President:

The effect of the Congressional legislation, since I have had the honor to hold the position of Commissioner of Indian Affairs, has been to almost wholly divest the Indian Bureau of all its original importance, duties, and proper responsibilities. The Commissioner of Indian Affairs, under the present arrangements, is merely a supernumerary officer of the Government, his principal duties being simply those of a clerk to a Board of Indian Commissioners, operating wholly outside of and almost independent of the Indian Bureau. I would gladly and willingly do anything in my power to aid in forwarding and promoting to a successful issue the President's wise and beneficent Indian policy, but I cannot, in justice to myself, longer continue to hold the ambiguous position of Commissioner of Indian Affairs.

I therefore most respectfully but firmly tender my resignation of said office, to take effect the 1st day of August, 1871. Sincerely thanking you, Mr. President, for the kindness and consideration you have always shown me, I have the honor to be, and shall ever remain, your obedient servant.

(Signed,)

ELY S. PARKER.

Glossary

issue	result
supernumerary	extra
tender	present, hand over

LETTER TO HARRIET MAXWELL CONVERSE ABOUT INDIAN POLICY REFORM (1885)

To you though I will confess, and you must not abuse or betray my confidence, that I have little or no faith in the American Christian civilization methods of healing the Indians of this country. It has not been honest, pure or sincere. Black deception, damnable frauds and persistent oppression has been its characteristics, and its religion today is, that the only good Indian is a dead one. Guns stand, loaded to the muzzle, ready to prove this lie. Another creed under which the Indian is daily sinking deeper into the quagmire of oppression is, that "might makes right," and on it is based the fallacy transferred or transposed from the Negro to the Indian "that the Indian has no rights which the white man is bound to respect." The matter of Indian civilization is assuming the character of Joseph's coat—of many colors—the most conspicuous and prominent just now, being the compulsory allotment of lands and enforced citizenship, nolens volens. All other methods of dispossessing the Indian of every vested and hereditary right having failed, compulsion must now be resorted to, a sure, certain death to the poor Indians. Misguided Indian philanthropists tell us that absorption of the aboriginal race into the great body politic is their only hope of salvation. I see nothing in the experiment but an accelerated motor for the absorption of the Indian race back into the bosom of Mother Earth. The only salvation for the Indians, and the only solution of the great Indian problem is to give them secular and industrial schools in abundance. This alone will perpetuate their life. There is land enough on this portion of God's footstool called America for the Indian and the white man to live upon side by side without jostling and exemplifying the Kilkenny cat game. The Indian wishes to be let alone in his wigwam. His good life is bound up and interwoven with his law, his women and his children.

Our wise legislators at Washington, the Indian Aid and the Indian Rights Associations are all advocating with a red hot zeal, the allotment and civilization schemes. Lastly come the Board of Indian Commissioners adding fuel to the existing fires, by telling us that the Indians are "fast accepting the policy" that would make them responsible citizens. They say that 6000 Indians already hold allotments of lands in severalty and that not less than 75,000 more are asking for the same privilege. I do not believe in the sanctity or truth of the statement. The Indians, as a body, are deadly opposed to the scheme, for they see in it too plainly the certain and

Glossary

aboriginal	native
an accelerated motor ... Mother Earth	a means of hastening the complete destruction of Native Americans
black	a term that at the time had no racial meaning but was used to imply spiritual darkness
body politic	the totality of the people within a politically organized entity (for example, a country)
in severalty	separately or independently
Joseph's coat of many colors	a reference to a story in Genesis 37 but, in Parker's use, having the implication of something pieced together willy-nilly
the Kilkenny cat game	a fight to the death
nolens volens	from the Latin, meaning "willing or not"
vested	legally given or assigned

speedy dissolution of their tribal and national organizations. It is very evident to my mind that all schemes, to apparently serve the Indians, are only plausible pleas put out to hoodwink the civilized world that everything possible has been done to save this race from total annihilation, and to wipe out the stain on the American name for its treatment of the aboriginal population....But I am writing an uncalled for thesis on Indian rights and wrongs, an almost inexhaustible theme, so I drop it since no good can result to continue it.—Education to be made first above all. Other good things will follow.

Alice Paul (Library of Congress)

ALICE PAUL

1885–1977

Woman's Rights Activist

Featured Documents
- Testimony before the House Judiciary Committee (1915)
- Equal Rights Amendment (1921)
- "Conversations with Alice Paul: Woman Suffrage and the Equal Rights Amendment" (1972–1973)

Overview

Alice Paul, one of the nation's most outspoken suffragists and feminists in the early twentieth century and beyond, was born to a Quaker family at their Paulsdale estate in Mount Laurel, New Jersey, on January 11, 1885. Her religious background is relevant because the Hicksite Quakerism the family practiced placed a great deal of emphasis on gender equality. She came from a prominent family, with ancestors who included William Penn on her mother's side and the Massachusetts Winthrops on her father's. Her maternal grandfather was one of the founders of Swarthmore College, where Paul earned a bachelor's degree in biology in 1905. After attending the New York School of Philanthropy, she earned a master's degree from the University of Pennsylvania in 1907 and then went on to study at England's University of Birmingham and the London School of Economics before returning to the University of Pennsylvania, where she earned a PhD in sociology in 1912.

Her years in England, 1907 to 1910, were eventful. It was there that she served her apprenticeship in the struggle for women's rights. She came under the influence of the militant feminists Emmeline Pankhurst and her daughters, Christabel and Sylvia, and during those years she earned her stripes as an activist through demonstrations, arrests, imprisonment, hunger strikes, and force-feeding. On her return to the United States, she enlisted in the suffrage movement, first with the National American Woman Suffrage Association, though she and the young women she attracted to the movement were impatient with the association's conservative tactics. Accordingly, she broke with the association to found the Congressional Union for Woman Suffrage in 1913. The purpose of the new organization was to seek a federal constitutional amendment granting women the right to vote. In 1915 she appeared before the Judiciary Committee of the U.S. House of Representatives to testify on behalf of the proposed amendment.

In 1916 the Congressional Union evolved into the National Woman's Party. Paul and her followers, dubbed the Silent Sentinels, gained notoriety by launching a two-and-a-half-year picket (with Sundays off) of the White House, urging President Woodrow Wilson to support a suffrage amendment. After the United States entered World War I in 1917, few people believed that the picketers would continue. They did, often writing such incendiary phrases as "Kaiser Wilson" on placards, leading many people to conclude that the

women were unpatriotic. (The reference was to Kaiser Wilhelm, ruler of Germany, America's enemy in the war.) Public opinion began to sway in favor of the suffragists when it was learned that more than 150 picketers had been arrested and sentenced to jail, usually on thin charges of obstructing traffic, and that the conditions the jailed women endured were often brutal. Paul, in particular, was subjected to inhuman treatment and launched a hunger strike in protest until she and the other protestors were released after a court of appeals ruled the arrests illegal. Meanwhile, the National Woman's Party continued to campaign against U.S. legislators who opposed the suffrage amendment.

After the passage by Congress (1919) and successful ratification (1920) of the Nineteenth Amendment recognizing the right of women to vote, Paul remained active in the woman's rights movement. In 1921 she wrote an equal rights amendment in the face of opposition from more conservative women's groups, who feared that such an amendment might strip women of protective legislation—in such areas as labor conditions—that had been passed during the Progressive Era. Nevertheless, she campaigned to make an equal rights amendment a plank in the platforms of both major political parties, which she succeeded in doing by 1944. In November 1972 and May 1973 she shared her reflections on the women's movement with an interviewer as part of an oral history project conducted by the University of California, Berkeley. She lived long enough to see Congress approve the Equal Rights Amendment in 1972, though the amendment was not ratified by enough states to allow it to become part of the Constitution. Paul died on July 9, 1977.

Explanation and Analysis of Documents

Alice Paul did not produce a large body of written documents. Modern students of the woman's suffrage and early feminist movements can gain insight into Paul's values and beliefs from oral sources, including her 1915 testimony to the House Judiciary Committee and an interview she granted in 1972–1973, near the end of her life. Also crucial is her hand in writing an equal rights amendment for women.

◆ Testimony before the House Judiciary Committee

The suffrage movement at the end of the nineteenth century and during the first two decades of the twentieth

1885

- **January 11**
  Paul is born at her family's Paulsdale estate in Mount Laurel, New Jersey.

1905

- Paul earns a bachelor's degree from Swarthmore College.

1907

- Paul earns a master's degree from the University of Pennsylvania.

- Paul travels to England, where she remains until 1910; in addition to continuing her studies, she becomes associated with the Women's Social and Political Union and the activists Emmeline, Christabel, and Sylvia Pankhurst.

1912

- Paul earns a PhD from the University of Pennsylvania, joins the National American Woman Suffrage Association, and is appointed chair of the organization's Congressional Committee.

1913

- Paul breaks with the National American Woman Suffrage Association and cofounds the Congressional Union for Woman Suffrage.

1915

- **December 16**
  Paul testifies before the House Judiciary Committee.

1916

- Paul founds the National Woman's Party.

1917

- **January**
  Paul is a key leader as women begin picketing the White House and urging President Woodrow Wilson to support a suffrage amendment to the Constitution; in the following months she is among those arrested and imprisoned for this effort.

century was an amalgam of high ideals of justice and equality and more practical, mundane politics. Throughout these years, various organizations were formed, re-formed, and combined to pursue the right to vote through a variety of methods.

The mainstream suffrage organization was the National American Woman Suffrage Association, formed in 1890 by the combination of two predecessor organizations, the National Woman Suffrage Association and the American Woman Suffrage Association. The leaders of this group included such towering figures as Susan B. Anthony, Carrie Chapman Catt, Elizabeth Cady Stanton, and Frances Willard. Many of these women, however, had been fighting in the trenches for decades—Susan B. Anthony, for example, died in 1906 at the age of eighty-six—and a new generation of suffragists was growing impatient with the slow pace of progress. Among them was Alice Paul, who had absorbed the more radical tactics of militant feminists during the years she lived and studied in England, where she joined the Women's Social and Political Union. As a member, Paul urged the National American Woman Suffrage Association to adopt more militant tactics, but the more conservative organization resisted her pleas and forced her and her protégées out. Accordingly, Paul joined forces with such women as Lucy Burns, Olympia Brown, Mabel Vernon, Belle La Follette, Mary Ritter Beard, Maria Montessori, Doris Stevens, and Crystal Eastman to form the Congressional Union for Woman Suffrage (CUWS) in 1913.

During these years one of the principal issues faced by the suffragist movement was whether to pursue voting rights on a state-by-state basis or to seek an amendment to the Constitution. Already a number of states, led by Colorado, Idaho, Utah, and Wyoming and followed by Washington, California, Kansas, Oregon, Arizona, Montana, Nevada, and the Alaska Territory, had granted suffrage to women not only in municipal and state elections but in federal elections as well. Various other states had considered suffrage amendments to their state constitutions at different times. Approaching the matter one state at a time, though, was exhausting work, and it was generally believed that extending the franchise to women in the states of the highly conservative South would be next to impossible, particularly because of fears among many southerners that doing so would give black women the vote. For this reason, the new generation of suffragists focused on an amendment to the national Constitution.

One of the tactics the CUWS pursued was to target and defeat members of Congress who were up for reelection in 1914. Since1878 the so-called Anthony Amendment had been proposed in every session of Congress. This was the original suffrage amendment formulated by Susan B. Anthony and other suffrage leaders in that year and which in 1920 would be ratified as the Nineteenth Amendment to the Constitution. In the intervening years, however, the amendment had been blocked, primarily by members of the Democratic Party, a party that was particularly strong in the South. In such states as Alabama, Georgia, and Louisiana every senator and congressman was a Democrat. Although Democrats also represented states in which suffrage had been granted, the CUWS targeted them in the 1914 election because, according to Paul, they had stood with the party in blocking efforts to bring a national amendment up for a vote on the floor of the Senate and House. The CUWS wanted to demonstrate that in states where women had the vote, they could use that power to chastise their congressional representatives and to demonstrate support for a national amendment.

It was in this context that Paul testified before the House Judiciary Committee on the suffrage question on December 16, 1915. In her remarks she summarizes the position of the CUWS—simply that its members wanted the House Judiciary Committee to refer the Anthony Amendment to the floor of the House of Representatives for a vote. (Congressional procedure dictates that any bill has to be referred by an appropriate committee for consideration on the floor.) Paul adds that her organization was "absolutely non-partisan," even though it had targeted Democrats in the previous year's election. She emphasizes that women of all political parties supported the goal of suffrage.

At this point the Democrat William Ezra Williams of Illinois interrupted the proceedings and asked Paul about the issue of pursuing suffrage through the states rather than nationally. Paul makes clear in her remarks that the goal of the Congressional Union was to pursue an amendment to the federal Constitution, noting that the western states, where suffrage was a reality, gave women a power base from which to urge a national amendment. She emphasizes the same point in a brief exchange with the Democratic Representative Warren Gard of Ohio.

Then the Democrat Joseph Taggart of Kansas asked Paul a pointed question—why the group opposed Democrats in the last election. In her reply Paul puts forward the position of the CUWS. The organization, she says, tried repeatedly, "again and again, week after week, and month after month," to bring the matter of suffrage to a vote in Congress. Repeatedly the effort was blocked. The culprits, in Paul's view, were congressional Democrats on the Rules Committee who refused to vote the measure out of committee and onto the floor of the House. These Democrats argued that the matter was one for the individual states to decide. Accordingly, the CUWS took a bold step: The organization went to the women of the West—the states where suffrage had been granted were all in the Midwest, the Rocky Mountain region, and the West Coast—and persuaded them that they could use their votes to defeat Democrats. The campaign was successful in defeating twenty-four of the forty-three Democratic candidates who were up for reelection in those states. This campaign, Paul notes, had the desired effect. When Congress reconvened, the Rules Committee, claiming that it had been "misunderstood," voted to bring the suffrage amendment to the floor of the House, and Democratic opposition to the measure "melted away."

The remainder of the committee's proceedings betrayed a certain level of irritation on the part of some members of the committee—irritation that Paul met with clear, measured responses. When asked about the CUWS's plans for

Time Line

1919

- **June 4**
  The Nineteenth Amendment, recognizing the right of women to vote, is passed by the U.S. Senate, having already passed in the House of Representatives.

1920

- **August 24**
  Tennessee becomes the thirty-sixth state to ratify the Nineteenth Amendment, giving it the three-quarters majority required for its addition to the Constitution.

1921

- Paul writes an equal rights amendment.

1923

- The Equal Rights Amendment is introduced in Congress for the first time; it has been reintroduced in every session of Congress since then.

1972

- The Equal Rights Amendment passes Congress but is not ratified by the necessary thirty-eight states by the deadline of July 1982.

- **November 24–26**
  Paul takes part in an interview for the oral history project conducted by the University of California, Berkeley.

1973

- **May 10–12**
  A second and final session of the oral history interview takes place.

1977

- **July 9**
  Paul dies in Moorestown, New Jersey.

the next election, Paul says that the answer to that depended on the actions of Congress and on the Democratic Party's platform in 1916. The Democrat Edwin Webb of North Carolina flatly gave his opinion that the platform would not include a suffrage amendment. In reply, Paul pointedly mentions that one-fifth of the vote in the next year's presidential election would come from states with woman's suffrage and says that "what we shall do in that election depends upon what you do." Congressman Gard questioned why the suffrage issue should come up for a vote in states that already had a suffrage amendment. Paul replies that those states "had never voted on the question of a National Amendment." Congressman Taggart suggested that the best way for the CUWS to proceed was to increase its power base by getting suffrage amendments passed in more states. Paul answers that the organization had repeatedly been given this advice, proving "beyond all cavil" that the organization was "on the right track." Taggart then raised the question of whether it was fair to target men from the party who had supported women's suffrage; Paul replies that in every case these men had stood by their party in blocking efforts to bring the amendment to a vote.

After the committee's chairman, Minnesota Republican Andrew Volstead, expressed the view that the inquiry was improper, Taggart and the Indiana Democrat Ralph Moss attempted to pin Paul down on her motives and future plans, including the question of whether the CUWS had a "blacklist." Paul, a slender, delicate woman who on this occasion appeared in a violet dress, refused to buckle under this interrogation and insisted that her only motive was to win the vote for women.

◆ Equal Rights Amendment

After ratification of the Nineteenth Amendment in 1920, many women drifted away from the movement, feeling that its major goal, suffrage for women, had been achieved. Doubtless adding to this flagging interest in feminist issues was the prosperity of the 1920s, a prosperity that, combined with fatigue brought on by the privations of World War I, produced the so-called Roaring Twenties. This was a decade of relief characterized by loosened moral strictures and a belief that new technologies (the automobile, the radio, and the refrigerator, among many others) could solve social and economic problems and create a better life for Americans.

Alice Paul and the members of the National Woman's Party, which numbered about ten thousand members at its apogee, disagreed. Paul believed that while the Nineteenth Amendment was a major step, full equality for women could not be achieved without an equal rights amendment. Accordingly, in 1921 she wrote the first version of the Equal Rights Amendment that nearly a half century later Congress would approve and submit to the states for ratification. The amendment she wrote, which she called the Lucretia Mott Amendment to honor the prominent nineteenth-century abolitionist and feminist, consisted of a single statement: "Men and women shall have equal rights throughout the United States and every place subject to its jurisdiction." She presented the amendment at a convention in Seneca Falls, New York, held to commemorate the 1848 Seneca Falls Convention that essentially launched the suffrage movement.

Paul's Equal Rights Amendment was first submitted to Congress in 1923. It was submitted to every session of Congress until it was passed in 1972. By 1944 both the Democratic and Republican parties included the amendment in their platforms. The amendment was revised in 1943 to read, "Equality of rights under the law shall not be denied or abridged by the United States or by any state on account of sex," and by this time it was referred to as the Alice Paul Amendment.

◆ "Conversations with Alice Paul: Woman Suffrage and the Equal Rights Amendment"

In these interview sessions in late 1972 and the spring of 1973, Paul looks back on her six decades of feminist activism, with particular focus on the Equal Rights Amendment. She begins by laughingly noting that the suffrage campaign had generated heavy expenses and that the bills had to be paid. She mentions "Mrs. Belmont." Alva Belmont, though hardly a familiar name today, was a prominent and wealthy socialite who donated large amounts of money to suffrage organizations. She herself founded one of these organizations, the Political Equality League, in 1909, and she was a member of the National American Woman Suffrage Association. In an effort to broaden support among immigrants, African Americans, and working-class women, she established a "suffrage settlement house" in Harlem, New York. Later she merged her organization with Paul's Congressional Union for Woman Suffrage, and she was instrumental in helping Paul found the National Woman's Party. Using her own money, she purchased the party's headquarters building in Washington, D.C., now the Sewall-Belmont House and Museum.

Paul goes on to discuss her uncertainties about legal matters surrounding an equal rights amendment. Characteristically, in the face of her own perceived lack of knowledge, she went back to school and earned bachelor's, master's, and doctoral degrees in law from the American University. Armed with solid academic credentials, she was able to persuade the Republican and Democratic parties to include support for an equal rights amendment in their platforms. Interestingly, she notes that some of the strongest opposition she encountered came not from men but from women—a pattern that would continue for the next half century. Many women, women's groups, and labor organizations, including the League of Women Voters, the Women's Bureau of the U.S. Department of Labor, the National Consumers' League, and the American Federation of Labor, opposed such an amendment at some point. They feared that it would nullify protective legislation that had been passed to improve working conditions for women in factories and that it could deny women rights to alimony in cases of divorce.

One of the most prominent organizations that opposed Paul's efforts was the National Women's Trade Union League, which argued that an equal rights amendment would benefit primarily educated women who wanted to enter professions but would not benefit working-class women, who labored for wages and who had fought hard for laws that shortened their working hours and bettered the conditions under which they worked. The league feared that an equal rights amendment could bring into question the constitutionality of labor laws that recognized the distinctive experiences of men and women in the labor force, thereby forcing women to work

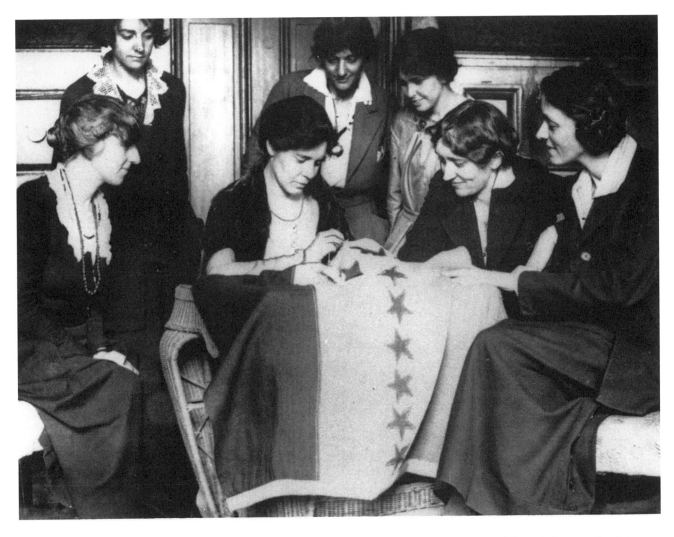

Celebrating ratification of the women's suffrage amendment, Alice Paul, seated second from left, sews the thirty-sixth star on a banner in August 1920. The star represented Tennessee, whose ratification completed the number of states needed to put the amendment in the Constitution. (AP/Wide World Photos)

under the same conditions as men. In later decades some women opposed an equal rights amendment in the belief that it could require women to, among other things, register for the draft, serve in the military, and use unisex restrooms, and that it would preclude the existence of exclusively women's (and men's) organizations.

In her discussion of efforts to gain support for an equal rights amendment as part of the Democratic Party platform, Paul makes reference to Emma Guffey Miller, who played a prominent role in this effort. Miller campaigned for Democrats as early as 1920. In 1924, after seconding the nomination of Al Smith for president at the Democratic National Convention, she earned the distinction of being the first woman in the party's history to receive a vote (though actually it was a half vote) for the presidential nomination. Later she served as chair of the National Woman's Party (1960–1965) and as the party's life president (1965–1970). Throughout her career she was a vigorous supporter of an equal rights amendment.

Paul goes on to discuss the mechanics of the proposed amendment. She and her supporters received advice from a number of people, including members of the Senate Judiciary Committee. In particular, she discusses the change in the wording of the amendment. It was feared that the original wording—"Men and women shall have equal rights throughout the United States and every place subject to its jurisdiction"—allowed too much interference in personal issues, which would endanger support for the amendment. Accordingly, the amendment was reworded to focus more on the action of government: "Equality of rights under the law shall not be denied or abridged by the United States or by any state on account of sex."

Impact and Legacy

Compared with such towering figures as Susan B. Anthony, Alice Paul is not as widely remembered as a leader in the movements for women's suffrage and an equal rights amendment, except among students of these movements. She produced little in the way of ringing eloquence that is still quoted today. Yet it is fair to say that without her efforts and those of hundreds of her colleagues, the success of the campaign for a suffrage amendment would have been considerably delayed. Arguably, the pressure she and the "Silent Sentinels" exerted on President Woodrow Wilson induced him to change his position on the suffrage amendment, and the pressure she brought to bear on Congress moved the glacially slow process along. Additionally, her militancy brought the issue to the attention of the American public, so that by the end of the 1910s growing numbers of both women and men were willing to accept woman's suffrage.

Paul's campaign for an equal rights amendment was, in the final analysis, not successful. Thirty-eight states had to ratify the amendment for it to become part of the Constitution. After an initial flurry of ratifications, the pace slowed, and only thirty-five states ratified it—and five of those states rescinded their ratifications. The campaign did, however, succeed in putting equal rights on the national agenda and making it a topic of discussion. The amendment failed, but in the minds of many legal scholars and members of the public, it had its desired effect in a more roundabout way, for numerous pieces of legislation were passed that took into account the status of women. One prominent example is the 1964 Civil Rights Act; Paul led a coalition that succeeded in getting a sexual discrimination clause added to the bill. In 1938 Paul helped found the World Woman's Party, with headquarters in Geneva, Switzerland. The organization later worked to include gender equality as part of the United Nations Charter and to establish the United Nations Commission on the Status of Women.

Although she was certainly a feminist hero, Paul has been the subject of scholarly debate over two issues. One was the attitude of her organizations toward African Americans. The other was her position on abortion. Paul and her colleagues have been accused of a subtle form of racism, given that the movement she spearheaded consisted almost entirely of white middle- and upper-class women, typically to the exclusion of working-class and African American women. It has been argued that the movement excluded African Americans out of fear that including them in any visible way would alienate the southern states, diminishing the ratification prospects of a suffrage amendment. Additionally, Paul appears to have opposed any effort to link the Equal Rights Amendment to abortion rights. Some observers have claimed that this opposition was a political decision based on a desire not to muddy the waters with the volatile and divisive issue of abortion. Others, however, have argued that throughout her life Paul explicitly opposed abortion and is reputed to have said that abortion rights exploited women, given that half the babies aborted were female.

Key Sources

There is no collection of Alice Paul's papers. She wrote articles for the *Suffragist*, a journal she helped found. Additional resources can be located through the Alice Paul

Institute's Web site at (http://www.alicepaul.org/index.htm). The Rutgers University library in New Brunswick, New Jersey, maintains a microfilm collection of the *Suffragist* magazine.

Further Reading

■ Books

Adams, Katherine H., and Michael L. Keene. *Alice Paul and the American Suffrage Campaign*. Urbana: University of Illinois Press, 2007.

Baker, Jean H. *Votes for Women: The Struggle for Suffrage Revisited*. New York: Oxford University Press, 2002.

———. *Sisters: The Lives of America's Suffragists*. New York: Hill and Wang, 2006.

Butler, Amy E. *Two Paths to Equality: Alice Paul and Ethel M. Smith in the ERA Debate, 1921–1929*. Albany: State University of New York Press, 2002.

DuBois, Ellen Carol. *Woman Suffrage and Women's Rights*. New York: New York University Press, 1998.

Flexner, Eleanor, and Ellen Fitzpatrick. *Century of Struggle: The Women's Rights Movement in the United States*. Cambridge, Mass.: Harvard University Press, 1996.

Ford, Linda G. "Alice Paul and the Triumph of Militancy." In *One Woman, One Vote: Rediscovering the Woman Suffrage Movement*, ed. Marjorie Spruill Wheeler. Troutdale, Ore.: NewSage Press, 1995.

Irwin, Inez Haynes. *The Story of the Woman's Party*. New York: Harcourt, Brace, 1921.

Kraditor, Aileen S. *The Ideas of the Woman Suffrage Movement, 1890–1920*. New York: W. W. Norton, 1981.

Lunardini, Christine A. *From Equal Suffrage to Equal Rights: Alice Paul and the National Woman's Party, 1910–1928*. New York: New York University Press, 1986.

Stevens, Doris. *Jailed for Freedom: American Women Win the Vote*. Troutdale, Ore.: NewSage Press, 1995.

—Michael J. O'Neal

Questions for Further Study

1. Compare and contrast Alice Paul's approach to pursuing equal rights for women as she explained it in her testimony before the House Judiciary Committee with the approach to black civil rights detailed by Ella Baker in "Ella Baker: Organizing for Civil Rights." Similarly, compare and contrast Paul's approach to suffrage and equal rights legislation to that of Susan B. Anthony, particularly as reflected in Anthony's "Is It a Crime for a Citizen of the United States to Vote?" and "The Status of Woman, Past, Present, and Future."

2. In 1970, Representative Shirley Chisholm delivered her "Speech in Favor of the Equal Rights Amendment." How did the arguments presented in her speech represent a natural historical progression of the concerns raised by Alice Paul in her efforts to get an equal rights amendment passed?

3. In 1928, Eleanor Roosevelt published her article "Women Must Learn to Play the Game as Men Do." To what extent did Alice Paul "play the game as men did," as reflected in her testimony before the House Judiciary Committee?

Testimony before the House Judiciary Committee (1915)

In closing the argument before this committee, may I summarize our position? We have come here to ask one simple thing: that the Judiciary Committee refer this Suffrage Amendment, known as the Susan B. Anthony Amendment, to the House of Representatives. We are simply asking you to do what you can do—that you let the House of Representatives decide this question. We have tried to bring people to this hearing from all over the United States to show the desire of women that this should be done.

I want to emphasize just one point, in addition, that we are absolutely non-partisan. We are made up of women who are strong Democrats, women who are strong Republicans, women who are Socialists, Progressives—every type of women. We are all united on this one thing—that we put Suffrage before everything else. In every election, if we ever go into any future elections, we simply pledge ourselves to this—that we will consider the furtherance of Suffrage and not our party affiliations in deciding what action we shall take.

Mr. Williams, of Illinois: Is it your policy to fight this question out only as a national issue? Do you make any attempt to secure relief through the States?

Miss Paul: The Congressional Union is organized to work for an Amendment to the National Constitution. We feel that the time has come, because of the winning of so many Suffrage States in the West, to use the votes of women to get Suffrage nationally. In the earlier days in this country, all the Suffrage work was done in the States, but the winning of the Western States has given us a power which we did not have before, so we have now turned from State work to national work. We are concentrating on the national government.

Mr. Gard: Miss Paul, is it true that you prefer to approach this through the State legislatures than to approach it directly through the people?

Miss Paul: We prefer the quickest way, which we believe is by Congressional action.

Mr. Taggart: Why did you oppose the Democrats in the last election?

Miss Paul: We came into existence when the administration of President Wilson first came in. We appealed to all members of Congress to have this Amendment put through at once. We did get that measure out upon the floor of the House and Senate, but when it came to getting a vote in the House we found we were absolutely blocked. We went again and again, week after week, and month after month to the Democratic members of the Rules Committee, who controlled the apportioning of the time of the House, and asked them to give us five or ten minutes for the discussion of Suffrage. Every time they refused. They told us that they were powerless to act because the Democrats had met in caucus and decided that Suffrage was a matter to be decided in the States and should not be brought up in Congress. (Here Miss Paul, moving the papers in front of her, deftly extracted a letter.) I have here a letter from Mr. Henry, Chairman of the Rules Committee, in which he says: "It would give me great pleasure to report the Resolution to the House, except for the fact that the Democratic caucus, by its direct action, has tied my hands and placed me in a position where I will not be authorized to do so unless the caucus is reconvened and changes its decision. I am sure your good judgment will cause you to thoroughly understand my attitude."…

After we had been met for months with the statement that the Democratic Party had decided in caucus not to let Suffrage come up in Congress, we said, "We will go out to the women voters in the West and tell them how we are blocked in Washington, and ask them if they will use their vote for the very highest purpose for which they can use it—to help get votes for other women."

We campaigned against every one of the forty-three men who were running for Congress on the Democratic ticket in any of the Suffrage States; and only nineteen of those we campaigned against came back to Washington. In December, at the close of the election, we went back to the Rules Committee. They told us then that they had no greater desire in the world than to bring the Suffrage Amendment out. They told us that we had misunderstood them in thinking that they were opposed to having Suffrage come up in Congress. They voted at once to bring Suffrage upon the floor for the first time in history. The whole opposition of the Democratic Party melted away and the decision of the party caucus was reversed.

The part we played in the last election was simply to tell the women voters of the West of the way the Democratic Party had blocked us at Washington and of the way the individual members of the Party, from the West, had supported their Party in blocking us. As soon as we told this record they ceased blocking us and we trust they will never block us again.

Question: But what about next time?

Miss Paul: We hope we will never have to go into another election. We are appealing to all Parties and to all men to put this Amendment through this Congress and send it on to the State Legislatures. What we are doing is giving the Democrats their opportunity. We did pursue a certain policy which we have outlined to you as you requested. As to what we may do we cannot say. It depends upon the future situation.

Question: But we want to know what you will do in the 1916 election?

Miss Paul: Can you possibly tell us what will be in the platform of the Democratic Party in 1916?

Mr. Webb: I can tell one plank that will not be there, and that is a plank in favor of Woman Suffrage.

Question: If conditions are the same, do you not propose to fight Democrats just the same as you did a year ago?

Miss Paul: We have come to ask your help in this Congress. But in asking it we have ventured to remind you that in the next election one-fifth of the vote for President comes from Suffrage States. What we shall do in that election depends upon what you do.

Mr. Webb: We would know better what to do if we knew what you were going to do.

Mr. Gard: We should not approach this bearing in any partisan sense. What I would like is to be informed about some facts. I asked Mrs. Field what reason your organization had for asking Congress to submit this question to States that have already acted upon it. Why should there be a resubmission to the voters by national action in States which have either voted for or against it, when the machinery exists in these same States to vote for it again?

Miss Paul: They have never voted on the question of a National Amendment.

Mr. Gard: The States can only ratify it. You would prefer that course to having it taken directly to the people?

Miss Paul: Simply because we have the power of women's votes to back up this method.

Mr. Gard: You are using this method because you think you have power to enforce it?

Miss Paul: Because we know we have power.

Mr. Taggart: The women who have the vote in the West are not worrying about what women are doing in the East. You will have to get more States before you try this nationally.

Miss Paul: We think that this repeated advice to go back to the States proves beyond all cavil that we are on the right track.

Mr. Taggart: Suppose you get fewer votes this time? Do you think it is fair to those members of Congress who voted for Woman Suffrage and have stood for Woman Suffrage, to oppose them merely because a majority of their Party were not in favor of Woman Suffrage?

Miss Paul: Every man that we opposed stood by his Party caucus in its opposition to Suffrage.

Mr. Volstead: This inquiry is absolutely unfair and improper. It is cheap politics, and I have gotten awfully tired listening to it.

Mr. Taggart: Have your services been bespoken by the Republican committee of Kansas for the next campaign?

Miss Paul: We are greatly gratified by this tribute to our value.

Mr. Moss: State just whether or not it is a fact that the question is, What is right? and not, What will be the reward or punishment of the members of

Glossary

bring the Suffrage Amendment out	the act whereby legislators vote a bill, in this case the one on woman suffrage, out of committee for a vote
caucus	any group of members in the House of Representatives who meet to pursue common legislative interests
Congressional Union	the Congressional Union for Woman Suffrage, founded in 1913 by Alice Paul and her associates
Mrs. Field	Sara Bard Field, prominent suffragist and feminist orator
plank	a figure of speech referring to a goal expressed in a political party's platform, or agenda

this committee? Is not that the only question that is pending before this committee?

Miss Paul: Yes, as we have said over and over today. We have come simply to ask that this committee report this measure to the House, that the House may consider the question.

Mr. Moss: Can you explain to the committee what the question of what you are going to do to a member of this committee or a Congressman in regard to his vote has to do with the question of what we should do as our duty?

Miss Paul: As I have said, we don't see any reason for discussing that.

Mr. Webb: You have no blacklist, have you, Miss Paul?

Miss Paul: No.

Mr. Taggart: You are organized, are you not, for the chastisement of political Parties that do not do your bidding at once?

Miss Paul: We are organized to win votes for women and our method of doing this is to organize the women who have the vote to help other women to get it.

EQUAL RIGHTS AMENDMENT (1921)

Equal Rights Amendment, Original

Men and women shall have equal rights throughout the United States and every place subject to its jurisdiction.

Congress shall have power to enforce this article by appropriate legislation.

Equal Rights Amendment, Revised

Section 1. Equality of rights under the law shall not be denied or abridged by the United States or by any state on account of sex.

Section 2. The Congress shall have the power to enforce, by appropriate legislation, the provisions of this article.

Section 3. This amendment shall take effect two years after the date of ratification.

Glossary

abridged	lessened, diminished

Paul, Alice

"CONVERSATIONS WITH ALICE PAUL: WOMAN SUFFRAGE AND THE EQUAL RIGHTS AMENDMENT" (1972–1973)

[Amelia] Fry: ... You had another meeting at Seneca Falls like the original one [in July of 1923].

[Alice] Paul: No, that Seneca Falls meeting was just to commemorate Seneca Falls. It was the seventy-fifth anniversary.

Fry: But you did submit an equal rights amendment wording.

Paul: Yes by that time I think I had gotten all my awful bills out of the way and paid.... I always sympathize at the end of these Republican campaigns, Democrat campaigns, because I know that somebody is being left with these awful bills. Because you really would have thought, with wealthy women like Mrs. Belmont and so on that, while certainly one couldn't be too grateful for all she did, after all they all sailed away on their own lives. Suffrage was won and now the thing is over. We certainly had a hard time then.

But I would end up, it seems to me, by saying that when the ratification was over, we celebrated by putting in the Capitol the statues of the great pioneers who in large measure had started the modern campaign at Seneca Falls [in 1848]. It was one of the really big things we did, because it was starting women to have a feeling of respect for women and by putting statues of women in the Capitol when it had always been a Capitol of men. Until Jeannette Rankin no woman was venturing into the...Cosmos Club....Then when we had a convention on and presented the statue to the Capitol, the last thing that we did in the suffrage campaign was that we voted to go on. Elsie Hill was very gallant and courageous and took the leadership....

By the end of two years..., we sort of, I guess, gathered up some more strength. And this was a really very wonderful meeting up at Seneca Falls. There we proposed not only would we work for equality but we would work for an equal rights amendment to the Constitution. And we started on that campaign. That's enough to finish up with.

Fry: And you did submit a wording of the amendment, which is in that issue of the *Suffragist* (or I guess maybe it was called the *Equal Rights* by that time).

Paul: ...I made the speech, you know, presenting this [amendment]. Of course, by this time I had recovered enough strength I think to feel convinced that we ought to go ahead with the campaign and we

ought to do it in the form of another amendment to have *complete* emancipation as our goal.... I said, "This is just a tentative proposal because we have asked a good many lawyers to work on the form and so on, and the wording doesn't make much difference if we agree on what we want." So I presented this:

"Men and women shall have equal rights throughout the United States and every place subject to its jurisdiction."

That said it all, and I said, "That's what we want, let's say what we want...."

That's when I started in to study law because I thought, "I can't do anything without knowing as much as the people who will be our opponents. I don't know anything whatsoever about law."

So I then went up and lived at the headquarters and early morning about six I went to the American University and enrolled in the law department, and I got my bachelor's degree in law.

And then I thought, "I really don't know much, I must say, still about law, as far as being able to cope with the people who say you can't have any such amendment as that." So you see we went around from person to person who was supposed to be a great authority. I went up myself to see Dean Pound at Harvard, who was supposed to be the greatest authority on constitutional law in the country, and Mrs. Lewis had her son work on it, and Elsie Hill met her husband when she and I went down to see him in the George Washington University law school to ask him to work on some kind of an amendment to the Constitution.

Fry: You mean, a man she later married?

Paul: Yes, her later husband. That's where she met him. Everybody drew up things, and we knew they wouldn't do. But I thought I wasn't very well-equipped to be making judgments on this subject, so then I went on and took a master's degree in law at the American University. And then I thought, "Still, I really don't know very much about this—it is such a vast subject"—we had to study Roman law and all kinds of laws..., things like that, quite a lot to do. So I then took the doctor of law. By that time I felt really I could talk to people on this subject, because I knew that they didn't know very much either. My feeling of complete ignorance they seemed pretty much to share.

So then the Judiciary Committee of the Senate paid no attention to us at all. We went to all the national conventions of the Republican party and the Democratic party that intervened...but 1923 was the first hearing on the subject of the new amendment, and the amendment was "Men and women shall have equal rights throughout the United States and every place subject to its jurisdiction."

Well, at that hearing—and this seems almost impossible to believe—all the women's organizations that came, with the votes in their hands so they counted for something (while before nobody paid much attention to us or to anybody else when we went to hearings because we were all voteless), now became a great power, even more power in the minds of the congressmen and the senators than they really had, because they didn't have back of themselves any united, strong group that would always stand together on this subject. But they got up and spoke and the congressmen certainly felt they had power then. All of them spoke, I think, *against* the Equal Rights Amendment. And if they didn't speak against us they remained silent. They didn't speak for us. So we were the only group that spoke for the Equal Rights Amendment when it was first put in.

Then we saw just what Lucy Burns and all these people thought we would find. Our problem would not be the Senate and Congress and the President, because now we were voters and had this power; but it would be changing the thought of American women, because more than half the country were now new voters. And if the new voters through their own organizations went up and said, "Please don't have a thing to do with this. We don't want women working at night. We don't want women standing up to work, and we don't want women to lose their alimony, and we don't want married women working when their husbands are working," and all these things that they said.... Well, we said, "Now we have a wholly different task, which is to change the thought of American women, really."

So we started then to one convention after another after another and kept it up until this year. We are still keeping it up, the last one being the League of Women Voters and the one before that the AAUW [American Association of University Women]. I have told you all this, I think, before.

Fry: Well, yes, and I remember myself taking long lists of women's organizations to use with congressmen for you. By 1971 huge numbers had gotten behind the Amendment.

Paul: I know, but you see our task through these years was this monotonous one of getting these women to change their minds to make them see what this principle meant and so on. So that's what has taken, more or less, all these years to do. Well now, we went to convention after convention of the political parties. It was in 1940....

Well, in 1940 for the first time we got in the Republican platform. Then in 1944 we got it in the Democratic one. That was a very hard-fought fight. Then we had it in both. Well, by that time Congress began to—

Fry: When did Republicans—?

Paul: 1940. 1944—Democrats. And that's when we finally began to work with Mrs. Emma Guffey Miller because she was so prominent in the Democratic party. She came in and joined us then and laid our fight before the Democratic National Convention to put it in the platform, and we got it in.

Well, then Congress began to pay more attention to us. It was in the political party platforms, and the Judiciary Committee of the Senate began seriously to consider the wording....

While I was not national chairman, I went down whenever I could to try to help—I went in to see Senator Burton, I remember, from Ohio, who was on the Supreme Court later. At that time he was on the Senate Judiciary Committee. I went to talk about how it could be worded. I remember him saying, "Well, Senator Austin of Vermont, who is perhaps the most concerned man on the Judiciary Committee, and I have worked and worked and worked and worked and we still cannot find the wording that we think will express what you want."

So this went on. We had asked Dean Pound, and the versions that everybody had given us we knew enough at least about law to know we didn't want it. A great deal of this responsibility fell on me because I was now beginning to know a little bit about law, you see. So I think it was in 1943 that finally we took a draft to—Mrs. Broy went with me; she didn't know very much about it but she was our political chairman so she went with me—to see Senator Austin. We handed him a draft, "Equality of rights under the law shall not be denied or abridged"

The Amendment read, "Equality of rights under the law shall not be denied or abridged by the United States or by any state on account of sex. Congress and the several states shall have the power, within their respective jurisdictions, to enforce this article by appropriate legislation...." It was to take effect five years after ratification.—what we now have, you see, the one that is now through Congress. So he studied it for a time and then he said, "Well, I really think perhaps this is just exactly right. I don't see anything the matter with it. And I think it will probably give you just what we all have in mind. But I wouldn't want to do it without Senator [Joseph Christopher] O'Mahoney of Wyoming who, on the Democratic side, is the chief person working for this measure."

So Mrs Broy and I then went up to Senator O'Mahoney's office. He was just departing for Wyoming where he lived, but he studied it and he said, "Well, you can go back and tell the senator that you just left that I will be, anyway, the second senator and I will support it, so you will have probably the man who is most concerned on the Republican side and the man who is the most concerned on the Democratic side." So we did.

Then we were asked to make sure that the women of the country who had already (in a few cases, not many, but a few organizations had) endorsed the old amendment, "Men and women shall have equal rights," these two men said, "We don't want to put this in and then find that the women won't stand back of us. So will you get the signature of the responsible person in every woman's organization that has endorsed the old amendment ('Men and women shall have equal rights') saying that they approve of the new amendment." So that's what we started and did.

We drew up a paper with the new proposed amendment addressed to the Senate Judiciary and called up each women's organization or had them come to see us, or in some form or other had them consider it, and we got a page of signatures of all these different women's groups. None of them knew enough to have any objection! Especially when we said we thought we could get the Senate Judiciary to support this. You see, the difference was, the old one said, "Men and women shall have equal rights throughout the United States and every place subject to its jurisdiction." They took the position that while they personally were for equal rights throughout the United States, they didn't think Congress had the right to interfere so much in the lives of *individual* people; they thought it ought to deal with the *government*; the *government* should not deny equal rights. So when we changed it to saying, "Equality of rights under the law shall not be denied or abridged *by the United States or any state* on account of sex," then they all signed, they all signed their approval of the new one.

Glossary

Cosmos Club	a private social club in Washington, D.C., for people distinguished in the arts, literature, and science and which first admitted women in 1988
Elsie Hill	a leading feminist and officer of the National Woman's Party and the Congressional Union for Woman Suffrage
Emma Guffey Miller	prominent Pennsylvania Democrat, active as a member of the state's Democratic National Committee and delegate to the Democratic National Convention
Jeannette Rankin	the first woman to be elected to the U.S. House of Representatives
Lucy Burns	one of the founders of the National Woman's Party
Mrs. Broy	Cecil Norton Broy, well-known member of the National Woman's Party
Mrs. Lewis	Dora Lewis, one of the leaders of the National Woman's Party who served several stints in jail for participating in suffrage demonstrations and pickets
Senator Austin	Senator Warren Austin
Senator Burton	Harold H. Burton
Seneca Falls	a city in New York that was the site of a pivotal women's rights convention in 1848

Frances Perkins (Library of Congress)

FRANCES PERKINS

1880–1965

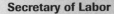

Secretary of Labor

Featured Documents
- "Social Insurance for U.S." Radio Address (1935)
- "What You Really Want Is an Autopsy": Opening Remarks to the Tristate Silicosis Conference (1940)
- "City Diets and Democracy" (1941)
- "Three Decades: A History of the Department of Labor" (1943)

Overview

As secretary of labor during Franklin Delano Roosevelt's administration, Frances Perkins was a tireless advocate for New Deal social reforms. The first woman to hold a cabinet position, she restructured and refocused the Department of Labor and was instrumental in crafting the Social Security Act of 1935 and the Fair Labor Standards Act of 1938. A passionate speaker, Perkins developed her oratory skills as a spokesperson for women's suffrage and social reforms in the early 1900s. Early in her career, she persuaded politicians to pass legislation to improve conditions for women and children before women had the right to vote. As a voice for working Americans, she negotiated with unions during a period of labor unrest and spoke eloquently about the plight of the average American during the Great Depression. Always concerned with social justice, Perkins was a leader not only as a woman cabinet member but also as a champion of reform.

Fanny Perkins was born on April 10, 1880, in Boston, Massachusetts, but spent most of her youth in Worcester, where her father established a successful stationery business. She attended Mount Holyoke College, where she learned of the growing settlement movement, a network of college graduates who would "settle" in poor urban areas and work with residents to reform their neighborhoods. Perkins volunteered at two settlement houses while she worked as a teacher in Lake Forest, Chicago, including the well-known Hull House started by Jane Addams. The experience was life changing; Fanny changed her name to Frances, earned a master's degree in social economics from Columbia University, and embarked on a career in social reform. Before receiving her degree, she took a position as secretary of the New York City Consumers' League, one of the most prominent organizations in the American reform movement.

Perkins's visibility eventually earned her an appointment to the state's Factory Investigating Commission following the Triangle Shirtwaist Factory fire of 1911, in which 146 workers died, many of whom were women. The commission's recommendations resulted in enactment of more than thirty new laws regulating fire prevention, work hours for women and children, and sanitary conditions in the workplace. In 1913 Perkins married Paul C. Wilson, who was involved in city government. She worried that her visibility would embarrass her husband; she retained her maiden name in part to distance herself from him publicly. In 1929 newly elected Governor Franklin Roosevelt appointed her as industrial commissioner of New York. In this role she continued to pursue issues of social justice and reform through legislative lobbying and public speaking. She was a vocal proponent of unemployment insurance and old-age assistance, foreshadowing her role in developing the federal system of Social Security. Perkins adopted a consensus style of management, involving workers, management, and the general public in developing solutions to labor problems.

Roosevelt tapped Perkins as secretary of labor when he became president in 1933. Her appointment met with resentment by many who felt that the position belonged to a union man rather than a woman reformer. As the nation faced the worst years of the depression, she actively embraced Roosevelt's New Deal reforms and instituted some of her own. She reorganized the Department of Labor, establishing a merit system and emphasizing workers' rights rather than the larger interests of the business community. Unlike previous secretaries, Perkins regularly pushed for new legislation to aid workers. She was instrumental in the creation of the Civilian Conservation Corps and held public meetings throughout the country to give workers a voice in developing the National Recovery Administration codes of fair competition. Her management style was at times a point of contention; when she refused to deport a striker during the San Francisco longshoremen's strike, she faced impeachment charges, which were dismissed following a House committee investigation. Roosevelt appointed Perkins head of the Committee on Economic Security, the body responsible for developing the Social Security Act, which established the first national system of unemployment insurance and old-age assistance. She oversaw the drafting of the Fair Labor Standards Act of 1938, which outlawed child labor in factories and set minimum wages and maximum working hours. She resigned in 1945 after serving for twelve years.

During her brief retirement, Perkins published *The Roosevelt I Knew* (1946), a personal account of her working relationship with Roosevelt before and during his presidency. In September of the same year, President Harry S. Truman appointed Perkins to the U.S. Civil Service Commission, which made decisions regarding the hiring and retention of government employees. She resigned in 1953, returning to teaching in her later years. She taught at Cor-

1880

- **April 10**
  Fanny Coralie Perkins is born in Boston, Massachusetts.

1902

- **June**
  Perkins graduates from Mount Holyoke College with a degree in science.

1904–1907

- Perkins teaches at Ferry Hall in Lake Forest, Illinois, while volunteering at Hull House and Chicago Commons.

1905

- **June 11**
  Changing her first name, Perkins is confirmed and enrolled in the Church of the Holy Spirit, Lake Forest, Illinois, as Frances C. Perkins.

1910

- **June 10**
  Perkins receives a master's degree in social economics from Columbia University.

1911

- Perkins serves as expert witness and investigator for the New York State Factory Investigating Commission.

1919

- **January 13**
  Governor Al Smith appoints Perkins as a member of New York State's Industrial Commission.

1929

- **January 14**
  Perkins is sworn in as industrial commissioner of New York, having been appointed by Governor Franklin Delano Roosevelt.

1933

- **February 28**
  President Franklin Roosevelt announces Perkins's appointment as secretary of labor.

nell University's School of Industrial and Labor Relations for eight years. Vigorous well into her eighties, her health deteriorated late in 1964. In the spring of 1965 Perkins suffered several strokes and died on May 14, 1965.

Explanation and Analysis of Documents

Frances Perkins dramatically changed the role of the Department of Labor during her tenure as secretary of labor under President Franklin Delano Roosevelt. From her work in the settlement house movement to her pioneering service as the first woman cabinet member, she championed the interests of working Americans through public speeches, legislative action, and deft political negotiations. Her ability to form persuasive arguments and moderate among various interest groups is shown in four key documents: her radio address on social insurance, her comments at a conference on worker safety, an article on public nutrition, and an article on the history of the Department of Labor.

◆ "Social Insurance for U.S." Radio Address

On January 17, 1935, President Roosevelt sent the Senate his draft Economic Security Bill. Nearly a month later, Perkins addressed the nation in a radio broadcast to explain the details of that proposed legislation. She had been intimately involved in developing the bill; in fact, she had come to Washington with the goal of implementing some type of national unemployment insurance. As industrial commissioner in New York, Perkins had studied the causes of unemployment in search of a cure, canvassing the state and talking to employers and workers. She had traveled to England to study that country's system of unemployment insurance. After her extensive research, she came to the conclusion that the solution to unemployment required a combination of public works programs and unemployment insurance and convinced Roosevelt that this remedy would work on a national basis.

The Senate Finance Committee debated the bill, and several of the committee members—conservative southerners—found fault with the proposed legislation for various reasons. Although the public initially supported the bill, press coverage was increasingly negative; editorials criticized the legislation's details and the way in which it was developed. Much of the negative press centered on Perkins, who, as a woman with a history as a social reformer, was disliked by many in the political establishment. As one of the chief architects of social insurance, and to combat this negative publicity, Perkins became the primary spokesperson in favor of the bill, making numerous speeches on radio and before groups. One of the earliest such speeches is her radio address of February 25, 1935, which shows her style of persuasive argument through the use of evidence based on careful research.

Perkins sets the tone for her speech in the first paragraph. She emphasizes the role that research and prudent discussion played in the development of this legislation.

Perkins was the chair of the Committee on Economic Security, the group that had designed the social security system. By using words such as "conscientious," "thorough," and "better-ordered," she counters the criticism that her committee was made up of bureaucrats rather than competent experts.

Although Perkins was not a particularly charismatic speaker, she here conveys much of the same message of trust and hope that Roosevelt did in his public speeches. A deeply religious woman, she rooted her faith in making a difference on earth rather than merely focusing on the afterlife. Although she rarely uses fiery rhetoric, she does call people to action, yet with a language grounded in reality. Her audience needed some kind of hope; by the end of 1934, close to one quarter of the nation's workforce was unemployed. She offers "sanity and wisdom" based on sound judgment and experience rather than more emotional appeals.

Perkins ties herself to Roosevelt by quoting an important speech of his. On June 8, 1934, Roosevelt announced to Congress his plans to pursue a national program for social unemployment and old-age insurance. By referencing that speech, Perkins gives the background of the bill currently before the Senate and points out that the proposed legislation is a key component of Roosevelt's agenda for his term in office. Her discussion of industrialization driving the need for social insurance echoes Roosevelt's earlier speeches, including his messages to Congress and his Fireside Chats. Both she and Roosevelt had to address the objection that social insurance would stifle American individualism; Roosevelt was adamant that the program not simply be a government handout. By casting social insurance as a means to protect the health of the overall American economy rather than just a humanitarian act, Perkins shows that the bill before Congress is not a government dole program but a way to shore up an ailing economy faced with the new realities of industrialization. Drawing on her own research in England, she uses the British system of social insurance as an example, pointing out that America is not alone among the industrialized nations in facing the negative impacts of economic cycles.

One of the challenges Perkins faced was that she had to explain a complicated and technical bill to the general public. In order to cover the proposed legislation in adequate detail but without overwhelming her audience, she focuses on the two most important components of the social insurance bill: unemployment relief and care for the aged.

Perkins begins with a brief discussion of what would become the Works Progress Administration (WPA). This was, as she points out, a separate piece of legislation from the social insurance bill. The WPA was a jobs-creation program in which the government provided work for the unemployed in a wide variety of tasks, such as road and bridge building, rural improvements, and other infrastructure projects. There were also special programs under the WPA, including the Federal Arts Project, in which the government paid artists and musicians to produce murals and concerts, and the Federal Writers Project, which resulted

Time Line

1934

- **February 14–15**
  Perkins convenes first National Conference for Labor Legislation in Washington, D.C.

- **June 29**
  Roosevelt names Perkins as chairman of the Committee on Economic Security.

1935

- **February 25**
  Perkins delivers a radio address, "Social Insurance for U.S."

1938

- **June 25**
  Roosevelt signs the Fair Labor Standards Act, originated by Perkins in 1936.

1940

- **April 23**
  Perkins delivers the opening address to Tristate Silicosis Conference in Joplin, Missouri.

1941

- **July**
  Perkins's article "City Diets and Democracy" appears in *Survey Graphic*.

1943

- **March**
  American Federationist, the official magazine for the American Federation of Labor, publishes Perkins's article "Three Decades: A History of the Department of Labor."

1945

- **June 30**
  Perkins resigns as secretary of labor.

1946

- **September 12**
  President Harry S. Truman appoints Perkins to U.S. Civil Service Commission.

1957

- Perkins joins the faculty of Cornell University's School of Industrial and Labor Relations.

1965

- **May 14**
  Perkins dies in New York City.

in the collection and cataloguing of a vast array of historical and sociological material. Perkins emphasizes the morale-building role of this program, indicating that participants in the program would be earning support rather than receiving a government handout. This message of human dignity in the face of dire poverty and hopelessness is a theme in many of Perkins's and Roosevelt's speeches. There was a stigma associated with being poor and unemployed in her era; poverty was typically equated with moral failure rather than a failure in the system itself. In her writings and speeches, however, there is always a clear message that industrialization is responsible for many of society's ills and that it is government's responsibility to counteract the effects of modernity. At the same time, she advocates a system whereby people earn their benefits, upholding the American values of hard work and individual responsibility.

Next Perkins discusses the plan for unemployment compensation. She notes that by providing income to workers laid off for short periods of time, unemployment insurance maintains stability to the overall economy by keeping consumer spending flowing and allowing businesses flexibility in terms of their labor force. Because unemployment benefits were designed for the short term, Perkins mentions the WPA "employment assurance" program; the government provides, in her words, a "first and second line of defense" against long-term unemployment.

Perkins then provides an explanation of the unemployment insurance program. Before the depression, there had been little support for unemployment assistance outside academic circles. As job losses swelled during the 1930s, however, both political parties publicly supported unemployment insurance, as did major labor unions. The concept of a national program of unemployment assistance was another issue. Many senators opposed such a plan, arguing that the variability of unemployment rates in different industries negated the possibility of a single federal program. In order to get the bill passed, Perkins and the Committee on Economic Security created the unemployment compensation system as a combined federal and state program. Funded by a federal tax, unemployment insurance is administered by each individual state, allowing for flexibility in program design. She highlights this aspect of the unemployment assistance plan in order to assuage the concerns of employers who might resist a federal program.

After explaining the federal/state nature of unemployment insurance, Perkins discusses the plan for old-age assistance. She begins by sketching the current situation with respect to the aged. Many states had some form of aid for the elderly in need, but the depression had bankrupted most of these plans. Perkins refers to the public outcry for a solution and mentions "hare-brained schemes" that have attracted "misguided supporters." She is referring to the mélange of proposals that came from both the public and private sectors for aiding the elderly. These included Senator Huey Long's "Share Our Wealth" clubs and the very popular Townsend Plan, which promised a monthly government stipend of $200 to everyone over the age of sixty. While only a few states had developed unemployment programs, most had old-age pension programs, and the public wholeheartedly supported the concept of aid to the elderly. Perkins, therefore, did not need to persuade the public of the need for such a program. Rather, she needed to explain how the government would pay for the plan.

As she does for the unemployment program, Perkins emphasizes the flexibility of the states in determining the details of their pension systems. The federal government would provide grants to the states, but the states would make decisions about the size of pensions. This takes care of those already retired. However, for those who are employed, she describes the contributory system of social insurance in which both employees and employers pay into the trust fund. She does not go into much detail, but her comments reflect two important realities of social insurance legislation. One was the concern that the Supreme Court would rule the legislation unconstitutional; it was not at all clear that the federal government had the authority to implement such broad social insurance programs. However, by using the taxing power of the federal government, Perkins and the committee ensured that the legislation would pass the Court's scrutiny. Another concern was how the government would pay pensions for all Americans under the plan. After wrestling with this problem, the compromise was to exclude a number of workers from Social Security, including state and federal employees, those working for nonprofit organizations, and agricultural and domestic workers. The voluntary annuity program was designed to cover these workers. Although Perkins reassures the commercial insurance companies that the annuity program would not compete with their business, Congress struck this element from the bill because of insurance industry opposition.

Perkins ends her speech by once again quoting Roosevelt. Although the speech is her own, she adroitly presents herself as the spokesperson for the president, both at the beginning and the end of her remarks. As a woman in a powerful position, Perkins was the object of considerable scrutiny, and some of her unorthodox methods aroused suspicions. Her refusal to deport Harry Bridges, a radical alien, following a violent longshoremen's strike he had helped plan in San Francisco gave rise to rumors in 1934 that Perkins was a Communist. She had also "cleaned house" when she took over the Department of Labor in 1933, replacing many employees who had been hired for political reasons rather than their qualifications. Roosevelt, too, faced critics in 1934, on both the political left and right. Perkins's speech presents the Roosevelt administration as a unified front in the face of difficult times. By using direct quotes from the president, she makes it clear that she is the spokesperson for the administration. Still, her personal style is apparent, from the emphasis on evidence and research to the reformer's call for thoughtful, moral action.

Perkins gave more than one hundred speeches on social insurance and orchestrated a campaign to help ensure the bill's passage. A skillful politician, she anticipated virtually every possible objection the legislation might encounter and armed herself with research to counter all of them. Her efforts paid off; the bill passed in August 1935, establishing the basic system of Social Security that we have today.

◆ "What You Really Want Is an Autopsy": Opening Remarks to the Tristate Silicosis Conference

One of the hallmarks of Perkins's tenure as labor secretary was her emphasis on improving the working conditions for industrial employees. From her years as industrial commissioner in New York to her role in the Roosevelt administration, she fought constantly to ameliorate workplace hazards, child labor, uncontrolled work hours, and other factors that threatened the well-being of American workers.

Perkins was particularly concerned with occupational disease. As America continued to industrialize in the early twentieth century, workers were increasingly exposed to a host of chemicals, and employers had no idea whether these materials might pose a hazard to their employees. She became well acquainted with silicosis, a lung disease caused by prolonged exposure to dust containing silica particles, which are commonly found in sand and rock. Workers engaged in mining, construction, and other activities that involve dusty environments are at risk for this potentially fatal disease. Perkins actively sought to control the disease; while on the Industrial Commission in New York, she ran a contest to see who could design the best method for preventing worker exposure to silica dust. The winner's device was used during excavation for Rockefeller Center, and tests conducted on the workers before and after the excavation work showed that the device effectively protected them from silica exposure.

Silicosis became a national concern during the 1930s, as increasing numbers of workers became gravely ill. One particular incident, the construction of Hawks Nest Tunnel, brought the issue to the forefront of public attention. In 1931 a private contractor hired some five thousand workers to bore through a mountain in West Virginia as part of a hydroelectric power project for Union Carbide. Unprotected from the silica dust, workers became ill, and an estimated seven hundred men eventually died. The incident prompted a congressional investigation in 1936, and Perkins convened a national silicosis conference in Washington, D.C., in 1939. Communities centered on mining were particularly affected by silicosis, as proportionately large numbers of men wasted away and left their families behind. Joplin, Missouri, was one such mining community. In April 1940 Perkins held a conference on the silicosis crisis in Joplin to address the concerns of the mining communities in Kansas, Missouri, and Oklahoma.

Her opening remarks show her oratorical skills at their finest. In this speech she invokes the voice of the reformer that she was, driven by deeply held religious and moral beliefs. At the same time, Perkins functions as a politician in this address: She must balance the various interests of the participants in the conference and bring them together in the service of a unified purpose. Much as she did in her address on social insurance, she anticipates objections in this speech and calls opposing parties to work together for a greater cause.

Perkins opens with the Department of Labor's mission statement, establishing both the authority of her position and the department's focus on the American worker. The conference attendees included representatives of the mining industry, mining workers, and the public health service, parties that could potentially be at odds with one another. She thus sets the tone and agenda of the conference, making it clear that the goal is to find "specific and practical" solutions to the problem.

Once she sets the tone, Perkins briefly discusses the history of silicosis and then turns to the core message of her address, which is that all of the parties in attendance must cooperate to find a solution. She repeatedly uses the phrase "moral responsibility" to drive home this point. This responsibility binds the mine owners and operators, the mine workers, the communities surrounding the mines, organized religion, and government. Perkins creates a bond among these interests by pointing out their joint obligation and by stating that the solution cannot come from the outside. She effectively forges a community by contrasting these parties with the "scientists and technicians" who have no vested moral and social interest in the problem of silicosis. Just as the health of the nation and the preservation of the consumer served as the means for overcoming objections to social security, "moral responsibility" is the glue that holds together a diverse group of interests in combating silicosis.

Perkins convened the silicosis conference in response to public outcry over the disease. Despite the fact that most states modified their workers' compensation laws to recognize silicosis claims following the investigation of the Hawks Nest Tunnel disaster, the occupational disease remained a concern. Her public speeches on the subject, including her opening address to the Tristate Silicosis Conference, illustrate her commitment to worker safety and industrial reform. Thanks to Perkins's efforts, public awareness of silicosis increased, and research into methods of prevention resulted in improved occupational safety.

◆ "City Diets and Democracy"

Survey Graphic was a journal that covered topics related to social reform. The publication grew out of the late-nineteenth-century urban reform movement that shaped Perkins's background in New York and Chicago. During the 1930s, *Survey Graphic* carried articles that explained many of the New Deal programs and served as a vehicle for those who called for additional reforms.

Perkins's article is interesting in that it was published at a time when Americans' thoughts were turning toward war and away from social issues. Congress passed the Lend-Lease Act in March of 1941, giving the president authority to funnel military aid to any nation deemed vital to the defense of the United States. Lend-Lease effectively placed America on the side of Great Britain in the brewing global conflict. As the nation nervously shifted away from neutrality, employment increased in anticipation of war produc-

Men of the Civilian Conservation Corps plant trees across the wastelands of southern Mississippi on April 11, 1940—part of the U.S. Forest Service plan to reestablish forests destroyed by logging and lumbering operations.
(AP/Wide World Photos)

tion. Nevertheless, the economy was far from robust, and Perkins, although busy managing labor disputes, published this article calling for urban reforms in the American diet.

Perkins opens the article with a question that points out the disparity between rural and urban Americans. Many New Deal programs targeted people who lived in the country; during the 1930s the government sent "home demonstration agents" to help teach marketable and domestic skills, such as canning and sewing. Farmers with land were encouraged to plant gardens and were provided with seed and other supplies to grow food. Perkins notes that city wage earners do not have land to plant gardens, nor do they have government agents coming to them to illustrate how to grow and preserve healthy food. This opening question sets up her article, which calls for the extension of government programs to the urban worker.

As she does in most of her speeches and articles, Perkins makes her case with statistics gleaned from research. She notes that although Americans have a high standard of living in terms of diet, economic conditions still

prevent many from receiving adequate nutrition. She cites statistics gathered by her own department to show the burden on wage-earning families.

Once she has made her case with data, Perkins presents her solutions, arguing that even in the face of war such efforts are important. Note that she advocates government intervention in the distribution of agricultural products. Her attitude with respect to private industry comes through clearly in her recommendations; her early experience with the Triangle Shirtwaist Factory fire and subsequent investigations of industries in New York led her to lean toward the belief that business could not necessarily be trusted to do the right thing. Government, armed with the proper information and expertise, could find the solutions.

Perkins discusses "food consumption subsidies," which we know as food stamps. Early in the depression, the government instituted a number of programs to attempt to stabilize food prices, including a program to buy surplus food and distribute it to relief agencies. The formal Food Stamp Program began in 1939, and, as she notes, its goal was to eliminate agricultural surpluses while also providing urban families with proper nutrition. Perkins argues that the program should be continued; in fact, the Food Stamp Program remains part of what is now called Temporary Assistance for Needy Families, formerly known as welfare.

Perkins also calls for a continuation of the school lunch program. Early federal support for school lunch programs derived from the same concerns about agricultural overproduction as did the Food Stamp Program. Schools received surplus products, and the number of children receiving lunches grew steadily. By 1940 the government had assigned a representative to each state to work with school districts to expand the lunch program. Signed by President Truman after Perkins had left her position, the 1946 National School Lunch Act made her vision a reality.

As in her address on social insurance and her remarks to the silicosis conference, Perkins places importance on building coalitions to solve problems. She closes this article with a plea for a "delicate balance" of interests in the cause of democracy. This recognition of various interest groups is a hallmark of her political and rhetorical style. While other social reformers were more confrontational and challenging in the language they employed, Perkins was keenly aware of the need to negotiate among often diametrically opposed parties. Although her audience for this piece was primarily kindred social reformers, she still uses the language of a skilled negotiator in making her case.

◆ "Three Decades: A History of the Department of Labor"

Perkins wrote this article in recognition of the thirtieth anniversary of the Department of Labor and her tenth anniversary as secretary. Although she downplays her achievements in this piece, she relates several changes that she made in the department. Her massive overhaul of what was a rather corrupt government agency is one of her primary accomplishments. The piece was published in the *American Federationist*, the official magazine for the American Federation of Labor; thus her audience would have welcomed her overall theme of the importance of protecting the well-being of American workers.

In many respects, this is a straightforward history of a government department. But it is clear that Perkins's message is that the mission of the Department of Labor was, from the beginning, to serve the interests of the working American, specifically the union laborer. She states this forcefully in the first paragraph and reiterates it by quoting from the 1913 act that created the department. Although she states that the department has "steadfastly kept in mind the main purpose" described in its founding document, she points out that the actual functions have reflected the "changing concept of the nation's responsibility for the welfare of its workers." Here Perkins subtly signals that her administration differs markedly from those in the past. Although it is a fact-filled recitation of the department's activities, the rest of the article reflects the way she transformed not only the role of secretary of labor but also the department itself.

Perkins's focus as secretary differed dramatically from her predecessors. Most of the previous secretaries had emphasized immigration problems. The Bureau of Immigration and the Bureau of Naturalization employed a number of corrupt individuals, and the flurry of immigration laws passed in the 1910s and 1920s had effectively slowed the tide of immigration to the country by the time Perkins took the helm. As she says, she combined the two bureaus in 1933; this seemingly minor administrative move actually constituted a major change in the focus of the department and resulted in the forced retirement of several staff members. She also increased immigration agent oversight, reining in mass deportations and curbing abuses.

Perkins reoriented the Department of Labor toward the needs of the worker. Coming from a background as a reformer, she redefined the role of the department, advocating unemployment and old-age insurance, a minimum wage and limitations to work hours, improved working conditions, and the end of child labor. The expansion of the Children's Bureau reflected this reform agenda. Perkins also states that, in recent years, the department has consulted regularly with labor unions, seeking its advice not just on conditions that affect workers but also on "broad social problems confronting the people." She was renowned for soliciting the input of industrial workers as both a state and federal reformer. In one famous incident, she led thousands of steelworkers to the U.S. Post Office in Homestead, Pennsylvania, after state and company representatives denied the workers the right to meet at their workplace. A photo of the petite Perkins marching a large group of men to a neutral site made national headlines.

Perkins discusses the reorganization of the U.S. Employment Service under the Wagner-Peyser Act. What she does not say is that the revamping of this agency earned her a number of enemies. When she took over the Department of Labor, she instituted a merit system for filling positions, meaning that each job applicant had to meet certain qualifications in terms of education and experience. Her predecessors had filled many positions based on political favoritism; Perkins required a minimum of a high school diploma for the top positions, which disqualified many of the labor leaders and political figures who were in those positions. The rejected applicants were, not surprisingly, angry, but the net effect was that many more unemployed people were placed in jobs, as Perkins deftly notes.

Perkins mentions several other accomplishments of her tenure as secretary. One is the establishment of the Division of Labor Standards in 1934. This entity was the predecessor of today's Occupational Safety and Health Administration, which establishes and enforces workplace health and safety codes. Another is the Fair Labor Standards Act, which abolished child labor and established a minimum wage and guaranteed overtime pay. Perkins was instrumental in ensuring the passage of this legislation. Previous labor protections under the National Recovery Act had been eliminated when the Supreme Court ruled the National Recovery Administration unconstitutional, and she was determined to pass a law that would provide permanent protection for workers.

Although Perkins wrote a thirty-year history, she clearly emphasizes the accomplishments of her ten-year service. For her, the Department of Labor was responsible not only for "administering" benefits but also for "promoting social legislation." She was the first secretary to have such a vision and to pursue her agenda with such success and vigor.

Impact and Legacy

Historians and Perkins's contemporaries alike portray her as a private person devoted to her job, driven by a sense of moral and social obligation. Her professionalism and uneasiness with the press at times conveyed a somewhat unflattering demeanor; one *Saturday Evening Post* article characterized Perkins as "earnest, rather humorless, briskly official, and full of that eager little executive air which is the earmark of the old-fashioned feminist and social worker" (qtd. in Schiff, p. 168). Her biographer, however, argues that Perkins was driven by a strong religious motivation and deeply disliked personal publicity (Martin, pp. vii–ix). Those qualities, coupled with the fact that her husband suffered from what appears to have been bipolar disorder, added to the already stressful position of being a highly visible woman in American politics. Eleanor Roosevelt once commented that Perkins "never really learned to handle the press" (qtd. in Schiff, p. 168); as an intensely private woman in an extremely public position, it is hardly surprising that Perkins's speeches and writings are more formal and invoke a sense of moral responsibility.

She was, however, extremely effective at developing a persuasive argument using evidence. Trained in science and economics, Perkins was analytical, possessing a keen ability to distill and retain volumes of technical information as well as conveying that material in a coherent fashion. As the public voice of the Social Security Act, she adroitly explained to average Americans key elements of a complex piece of legislation. As a reformer in New York, she artfully negotiated with seasoned politicians to secure the passage of laws. Methodical and thorough, her approach succeeded in instituting myriad reforms as well as communicating those changes to the American public.

Perkins's legacy is visible in many of the laws and institutions that we have today. Without her vision, our system of Social Security would quite likely not exist, nor would the Occupational Safety and Health Administration. Under her leadership, the Department of Labor's entire focus shifted toward the protection of the rights and well-being of American workers, something we take for granted today. She championed the minimum wage, the right to collectively organize, protection from occupational diseases and hazards, a system of unemployment assistance and old-age pension, control over work hours, universal access to affordable healthy food, and the eradication of child labor. Her ideas were radical at the time, and that she succeeded in implementing so many of them is a testament to her perseverance, moral beliefs, and acuity as a negotiator. Although she is lauded as the first female cabinet member, it is her accomplishments as a reformer and advocate for labor legislation that make Perkins an exceptional figure.

Key Sources

Perkins's records are located in several libraries. The National Archives holds records of the Department of Labor, including documents generated during Perkins's term as secretary. Columbia University's Rare Book and Manuscript Library, Special Collections, holds a large collection of her papers. Her oral history is located at Columbia's Oral History Research Office, both in text and in audio formats. The interviews took place over several years and contain a wealth of information on Perkins's private as well as professional life. There are also Perkins documents in the Schlesinger Library at Radcliffe Institute for Advanced Study, Mount Holyoke College, the American Woman's Collection of Connecticut College, and Cornell University (New York State School of Industrial and Labor Relations, Martin P. Catherwood Library). In 1946 Perkins published *The Roosevelt I Knew*, a memoir of her years as industrial commissioner of New York and as secretary of labor. There is a 1987 documentary on Perkins, titled *You May Call Her Madam Secretary* (Vineyard Video Productions).

Further Reading

■ Books

Colman, Penny. *A Woman Unafraid: The Achievements of Frances Perkins*. New York: Atheneum, 1993.

Felbinger, Claire L., and Wendy A. Haynes, eds. *Outstanding Women in Public Administration*. Armonk, N.Y.: M. E. Sharpe, 2004.

Martin, George. *Madam Secretary: Frances Perkins*. Boston: Houghton Mifflin, 1976.

Mohr, Lillian Holmen. *Frances Perkins: That Woman in FDR's Cabinet!* Croton-on-Hudson, N.Y.: North River Press, 1979.

Pasachoff, Naomi. *Frances Perkins: Champion of the New Deal*. New York: Oxford University Press, 1999.

Schiff, Karenna Gore. *Lighting the Way: Nine Women Who Changed Modern America*. New York: Hyperion, 2005.

Severn, Bill. *Frances Perkins: A Member of the Cabinet*. New York: Hawthorn Books, 1976.

■ Web Sites

"Frances Perkins." U.S. Department of Labor Web site.
   http://www.dol.gov/oasam/programs/history/perkins.htm.

"Social Security Pioneers: Frances Perkins." Social Security Administration Web site.
   http://www.ssa.gov/history/fperkins.html.

"*The heedless optimism of the boom years is past. We now stand ready to build the future with sanity and wisdom.*"

("Social Insurance for U.S." Radio Address)

"*We have come to learn that the large majority of our citizens must have protection against the loss of income due to unemployment, old age, death of the breadwinners and disabling accident and illness, not only on humanitarian grounds, but in the interest of our National welfare.*"

("Social Insurance for U.S." Radio Address)

"*All of us here today have a social responsibility, a moral responsibility, and perhaps that lesser degree of responsibility which I call legal responsibility. For the latter is not as important as the social and moral responsibility which those who know of a problem have regard to it.*"

("What You Really Want Is an Autopsy": Opening Remarks to the Tristate Silicosis Conference)

"*The political forces, the economic forces, the moral forces, and the scientific knowledge and the social knowledge which we have, should, in a conference like this, crystallize into a program. In the next 10 years that program should bring about direct results in the lives of the men who are exposed to this hazard, and in the lives of the families who suffer economic disaster when [the] problem is not solved.*"

("What You Really Want Is an Autopsy": Opening Remarks to the Tristate Silicosis Conference)

"*What about wage earners without gardens, and without home demonstration agents such as rural folks have?*"

("City Diets and Democracy")

"*On March 4, 1913, when the President approved the act creating the present Department of Labor, the dream of workers for nearly half a century for a separate department to promote the welfare of workers and a Secretary in the Cabinet to speak for them became a reality.*"

("Three Decades: A History of the Department of Labor")

"Francis Perkins (1880–1965)." AFL-CIO Web site.
http://www.aflcio.org/aboutus/history/history/perkins.cfm.

"Frances Perkins: Profile." Columbia University Libraries Oral
History Research Office Web site.
http://www.columbia.edu/cu/lweb/digital/collections/nny/perk
insf/profile.html.

—Karen Linkletter

Questions for Further Study

1. Discuss some of the challenges Perkins faced as the first woman to hold a cabinet position, and compare her performance with that of Elizabeth Dole, Madeline Albright, Condoleezza Rice, and other women who served in later presidential cabinets.

2. Consider changing views of poverty reflected in Perkins's social insurance address. In earlier times, poor people were typically held to blame for their circumstances, whereas Perkins—taking a view more common today—cites external causes over which individuals have little control. Which of these viewpoints do you consider more valid, or do you think the truth lies somewhere between?

3. Perkins clearly believed that government could play a significant and positive role in solving economic problems, but she took a more skeptical attitude toward business. Do you think she was correct in this response? Give examples to support your viewpoint, and be sure to cite actual comments made by Perkins herself.

"SOCIAL INSURANCE FOR U.S." RADIO ADDRESS (1935)

I have been asked to speak to you tonight on the administration's program for economic security which is now, as you know, before Congress. It seems to me that few legislative proposals have had as careful study, as thorough and conscientious deliberation as went into the preparation of these measures. The program now under consideration represents, I believe, a most significant step in our National development, a milestone in our progress toward the better-ordered society.

As I look back on the tragic years since 1929, it seems to me that we as a Nation, not unlike some individuals, have been able to pass through a bitter experience to emerge with a newfound insight and maturity. We have had the courage to face our problems and find a way out. The heedless optimism of the boom years is past. We now stand ready to build the future with sanity and wisdom.

The process of recovery is not a simple one. We cannot be satisfied merely with makeshift arrangements which will tide us over the present emergencies. We must devise plans that will not merely alleviate the ills of today, but will prevent, as far as it is humanly possible to do so, their recurrence in the future. The task of recovery is inseparable from the fundamental task of social reconstruction.

Among the objectives of that reconstruction, President Roosevelt in his message of June 8, 1934, to the Congress placed "the security of the men, women and children of the Nation first." He went on to suggest the social insurances with which European countries have had a long and favorable experience as one means of providing safeguards against "misfortunes which cannot be wholly eliminated in this man-made world of ours."

Subsequent to this message he created the Committee on Economic Security, of which I have the honor to be the chairman, to make recommendations to him with regard to these problems. The recommendations of that committee are embodied in the economic security bill, now pending in Congress. The measures we propose do not by any means provide a complete and permanent solution of our difficulties. If put into effect, however, they will provide a greater degree of security for the American citizen and his family than he has heretofore known. The bill is, I believe, a sound beginning on which we can build by degrees to our ultimate goal.

We cannot hope to accomplish all in one bold stroke. To begin too ambitiously in the program of social security might very well result in errors which would entirely discredit this very necessary type of legislation. It is not amiss to note here that social legislation in European countries, begun some 25 years ago, is still in a developmental state and has been subjected to numerous changes as experience and changing conditions dictated.

It may come as a surprise to many of us that we in this country should be so far behind Europe in providing our citizens with those safeguards which assure a decent standard of living in both good times and bad, but the reasons are not far to seek. We are much younger than our European neighbors. Our abundant pioneer days are not very far behind us. With unlimited opportunities, in those days, for the individual who wished to take advantage of them, dependency seemed a reflection on the individual himself, rather than the result of social or economic conditions. There seemed little need for any systematic organized plan, such as has now become necessary.

It has taken the rapid industrialization of the last few decades, with its mass-production methods, to teach us that a man might become a victim of circumstances far beyond his control, and finally it "took a depression to dramatize for us the appalling insecurity of the great mass of the population, and to stimulate interest in social insurance in the United States." We have come to learn that the large majority of our citizens must have protection against the loss of income due to unemployment, old age, death of the breadwinners and disabling accident and illness, not only on humanitarian grounds, but in the interest of our National welfare. If we are to maintain a healthy economy and thriving production, we need to maintain the standard of living of the lower income groups in our population who constitute 90 per cent of our purchasing power.

England, with its earlier industrialization, learned this lesson earlier, as well. The world depression caught up with Great Britain sooner than it did with us. She has known the haunting fear of insecurity as well as we. The foresight of nearly three decades has, however, found her somewhat better prepared with the basic framework of a social insurance system. Social insurance in Great Britain has proceeded progressively since the first decade of the century. Championed by the liberal Lloyd George and beginning with the old age pension act of 1908, it has known many revisions and extensions. Since its inception, however, it has gradually overcome the opposition of its critics, and there has never been any thought of abandoning the system. It is today in a healthy state of growth.

Practically all the other industrial countries of Europe have had similar experiences. In the trial and error procedure of Europe's quarter century of social legislation—in that concrete experience—is contained sound truths as well as mistakes from which we can learn much.

But we cannot build solely on European experience. We, with our particular kind of State-Federal Government, our wide, expansive country, with its varying economic and social standards, have many needs different from those of the more closely knit, homogeneous European countries.

The American program for economic security now before our Congress follows no single pattern. It is broader than social insurance, and does not attempt merely to copy a European model. Where other measures seemed more appropriate to our background or present situation, we have not hesitated to deviate from strict social insurance principles. In doing so we feel that we have recommended the measures which at this time seemed best calculated under our American conditions to protect individuals in the years immediately ahead from the hazards which might otherwise plunge them into destitution and dependency.

Our program deals with safeguards against unemployment, with old-age security, with maternal aid and aid to crippled and dependent children and public health services. Another major subject—health insurance—is dealt with briefly in the report of the Committee on Economic Security, but without any definite recommendations. Fortunate in having secured the cooperation of the medical and other professions directly concerned, the committee is working on a plan for health insurance which will be reported later in the year. Our present program calls for the extension of existing public health services to meet conditions accentuated by the depression. Similarly, the provisions for maternal aid and aid to dependent and crippled children are not new departures, but rather the extension and amplification of safeguards which for a number of years have been a recognized part of public responsibility.

Let me briefly describe the other measures now under consideration which do represent something of a departure from our usual course.

Recognizing unemployment as the greatest of all hazards, the committee gave primary emphasis to provisions for unemployment—employment assurance. This measure is embodied in the $4,800,000,000 public works resolution, which is separate from, but complementary to, the economic security bill itself. Employment assurance, the stimulation of private employment and the provision of public employment for those able-bodied workers whom private industry cannot yet absorb is to be solely a responsibility of the Federal Government and its major contribution in providing safeguards against unemployment. It should be noted that this is the largest employment program ever considered in any country. As outlined by the President, it will furnish employment for able-bodied men now on relief, and enable them to earn their support in a decent and socially useful way. It will uphold morale, as well as purchasing power, and directly provide jobs for many in private industry who would otherwise have none.

For the 80 per cent of our industrial workers who are employed, we propose a system of unemployment compensation, or insurance, as it is usually called. In our concern for the unemployed, we must not overlook this much larger group who also need protection.

No one who is now employed can feel secure while so many of his fellows anxiously seek work. Unemployment compensation, while it has distinct limitations which are not always clearly understood, is particularly valuable for the ordinarily regularly employed industrial worker who is laid off for short periods because of seasonal demands or other minor industrial disturbances. He can, during this period when he has a reasonable expectation of returning to work within a short time, receive compensation for his loss of income for a limited period as a definite, contractual right. His standard of living need not be undermined, he is not forced on relief nor must he accept other work unsuited to his skill and training.

Unemployment insurance, wherever it has been tried, has demonstrated its value in maintaining purchasing power and stabilizing business conditions. It is very valuable at the onset of a depression, and even in the later stages will serve to carry a part of the burden of providing for the unemployed. For those who have exhausted their rights to unemployment benefits and for those who, in any case, must be excluded from its provisions, we suggest that they be given employment opportunities on public work projects. In these two measures, employment assurance and unemployment compensation, we have a first and second line of defense which together should form a better safeguard than either standing alone.

The unemployment compensation system has been designed to remove an obstacle which has long prevented progressive industrial States from enacting unemployment insurance laws—fear of interstate competition with States not having such laws. Having removed that obstacle, the law allows the States full latitude to develop the kind of unemployment compensation systems best suited to their individual needs.

The bill provides for a Federal tax on pay rolls against which credit is allowed the employer for contributions to an approved State unemployment compensation fund. By this Federal tax every employer will be placed on the same competitive basis from a National standpoint, and at the same time, aside from compliance with a few minimum Federal standards, every State will be free to adopt the kind of law it wants.

One of the most important of the Federal requirements is that all unemployment compensation funds shall be deposited with the Federal Treasury in Washington, so as to assure their availability when needed and make it possible to utilize the reserves which will accumulate in conformity with the credit policy of the Nation.

We feel that this is a most fortunate time for the Government to take action on unemployment insurance. There has been a rapidly growing enthusiasm for it in the States for years. Many States have already prepared excellent legislation of this kind or are studying the subject, and they are but waiting word from Washington, so that they may proceed with the plans which have been so long under consideration.

I come now to the other major phase of our program. The plan for providing against need and dependency in old age is divided into three separate and distinct parts. We advocate, first, free Federally-aided pensions for those now old and in need; second, a system of compulsory contributory old-age insurance for workers in the lower income brackets, and third, a voluntary system of low-cost annuities purchasable by those who do not come under the compulsory system.

Enlightened opinion has long since discarded the old poor-house method of caring for the indigent aged, and 28 States already have old-age pension laws. Due to financial difficulties, many of these laws are now far less effective than they were intended to be. Public sentiment in this country is strongly in favor of providing these old people with a decent and dignified subsistence in their declining years. Exploiting that very creditable sentiment, impossible, hare-brained schemes for providing for the aged have sprung into existence and attracted misguided supporters. But the administration is confident that its plan for meeting the situation is both humane and practical and will receive the enthusiastic support of the people.

We propose that the Federal Government shall come to the aid of the State pension systems already in existence and stimulate the enactment of similar legislation elsewhere by grants-in-aid equal to one-half the State expenditures for such purposes but not exceeding $15 per month. This does not necessarily mean that State pensions would not anywhere exceed $30 per month. Progressive States may find it possible to grant more than $15 per month as their share. The size of the pension would, of course, be proportionate to the need of the applicant and would quite likely vary with conditions in different States. A larger pension would, for example, be necessary in certain industrial States than in communities where living conditions are easier.

For those now young or even middle-aged, a system of compulsory old-age insurance will enable them to build up, with matching contributions from their employers, an annuity from which they can draw as a right upon reaching old age. These workers will be able to care for themselves in their old age, not merely on a subsistence basis, which is all that gratuitous pensions have anywhere provided, but with a modest comfort and security. Such a system will greatly lessen the hazards of old age to the many workers who could not, unaided, provide for themselves and would greatly lessen the enormous burden of caring for the aged of future generations from public funds. The voluntary system of old-age annuities is designed to cover the same income groups as does the compulsory system, but will afford those who for many reasons cannot be included in a compulsory system an opportunity to provide for themselves.

Many of you will be interested to know that the two proposed annuity systems in no way infringe on the commercial annuity markets. Officials of insurance companies have themselves remarked that these measures would touch a strata of our population for whom commercial annuities are prohibitively expensive. These officials feel that the measures we propose will prove advantageous to their companies rather than the reverse, in so far as they promote public interest in the insurance movement.

This, in broad outlines, is the program now before us. We feel that it is a sound and reasonable plan and framed with due regard for the present state of economic recovery. I can do no better than to pass on to you the words with which President Roosevelt closed

Perkins, Frances

his letter submitting these recommendations to the Congress now in session:

The establishment of sound means toward a greater future economic security of the American people is dictated by a prudent consideration of the hazards involved in our national life. No one can guarantee this country against the dangers of future depressions, but we can reduce these dangers. We can eliminate many of the factors that cause economic depressions, and we can provide the means of mitigating their results. This plan for economic security is at once a measure of prevention and a method of alleviation.

We pay now for the dreadful consequence of economic insecurity—and dearly. This plan presents a more equitable and infinitely less expensive means of meeting these costs. We cannot afford to neglect the plain duty before us. I strongly recommend action to attain the objectives sought in this report.

Glossary

annuities	annual payments on money invested
homogeneous	composed of parts that are alike—here referring to the fact that European countries at that time were not as ethnically diverse as the United States
Lloyd George	David Lloyd George, British statesman and prime minister (1916–1922)

"WHAT YOU REALLY WANT IS AN AUTOPSY": OPENING REMARKS TO THE TRISTATE SILICOSIS CONFERENCE (1940)

First of all I want to say how glad I am that so many of you have shown interest in this problem, which we in the United States Department of Labor believe to be a part of one of the great problems of the United States—the prevention of industrial and occupational diseases. There is nothing unique about your situation, except that you have here at your gates one of the most difficult industrial diseases and one for which it is most difficult to find a cure.

We in the Department of Labor have a mandate which we received from the Congress of the United States in the basic act which creates the Department of Labor and the office of Secretary of Labor, in those words: "It shall be the duty of this Department and of the Secretary to foster, promote, and develop the welfare of the wage earners of the United States of America, to improve their working conditions, and to advance their opportunities for profitable employment." So it becomes the duty of the Department of Labor to inquire into anything that hinders the welfare of the wage earners of the United States, and to be as specific and practical as possible with regard to each situation.

One great problem is the exposure of workers to industrial and occupational diseases. Silicosis is not the only industrial disease; there are many others. Some of them take greater ravages in life and in continuing disability.

Silicosis is newly important to us because we have newly discovered it. Lead poisoning, chrome poisoning, nickel poisoning, these are some of the industrial diseases which everybody 25 and 30 years ago know something about. But it was only about 20 years ago that we in the United States began to realize what silicosis was, and to differentiate it from the old diseases that used to be called "grinder's rot" and "miner's consumption" and "miner's asthma."

The first basic medical literature on the subject came from South Africa. There they had long recognized this disease as one of the hazards of workers in the diamond mines.

In the past 25 years we have become conscious of silicosis, not only in mines and tunnels and open-cut foundations, but also in factories and mills where people work upon substances of with substances which generate a silica dust or have a silica basis. So, having become conscious of this disease and its extent, it is our duty in the Department of Labor of the United States to see if we can find ways to prevent it....

This morning I spoke with a group of women here in the mining area. They told me in their own simple words that they and their children and their husbands, many of them, had what they regarded as "the lung disease." Some of them spoke with bitterness, and some with question, and some with resignation. There was only one thing I could say for slight comfort to women who have lost their husbands, or whose little children are infected. It was that by cooperating with the doctor and the county health nurse and the State medical society and the State tuberculosis society, perhaps they could make it possible not only for their own children to be cured, but for others whom they did not know, whom they had never seen, who perhaps were yet to be born, to be protected from the ravages of this disease.

So I say to you that although some of you may not like the idea of this Tri-State area being used as a laboratory, can you not think of it perhaps as a great privilege? You may work out here the methods by which thousands of others, millions of others perhaps yet unborn, may be protected from the hazards which I know all of you—employers, taxpayers, labor people—regret as much as we in the Department of Labor do. Perhaps by the use of this area as a laboratory you may contribute more to the welfare of this community, and of the whole United States, than anyone has yet thought.

All of us here today have a social responsibility, a moral responsibility, and perhaps that lesser degree of responsibility which I call legal responsibility. For the latter is not as important as the social and moral responsibility which those who know of a problem have with regard to it.

The owners and operators of these properties have a great moral responsibility, and many of them have acknowledged it. That is one of the things that gives us courage to come here and ask them to cooperate in making a laboratory of their area, to find a way to prevent not only this but similar situations everywhere.

The people who work in those mines and those who represent the organized labor of the community generally, who take upon themselves the duty of speaking up for those who work in the mines, also have a moral responsibility to cooperate with every technical and economic effort to relieve the situation and to find the means of preventing silicosis and tuberculosis.

So too the community here, in Joplin and in all the towns down the line, have, as you have acknowledged by being here today, a moral and a social responsibility, because the problem is at your door. You didn't make it, but it is there.

The presence in this audience of a number of the ministers of religion reminds us, too, of the duty to bring about that kingdom of heaven on earth to which we all give lip service, to bring about better conditions for all the people of the United States.

Then we have here the representatives of government—of the local government, of county government, of State government, of the Federal Government. To me they are symbols of an order to which all of us in America have subscribed; an order and a pattern of society in which each individual, no matter how poor, still has tremendous worth and value; and in which the disaster of one is the concern of all.

The officers of Government, be they State or county or Federal, came as the symbols of that great enterprise which we call government in a democracy. It is a government which does not rule, but expresses and gives reality to the desire of the people that everybody in America should have a chance. The men who are crushed by material burdens may still look to their government to find a way for them to contribute their moral worth to the building of our democratic society.

That is why it is much more important that the answer to this problem of silicosis in the Tri-State area should come from the understanding and moral force of the people of the community—the people who are affected by it, taxpayers, owners, workers in the mines—than that we should come from the outside with suggestions. I don't mean that we haven't got suggestions; we have, but they take secondary place on the program. What you do yourselves is more important than the most highly specialized contributions of scientists and technicians....

This is a joint problem. No one factor can solve it alone. It requires cooperation of every intelligence that comes to bear upon the problem. And so this conference is a conscious effort to focus all the knowledge and all the forces which can take necessary and practical action to overcome this hazard.

The political forces—the agencies of government, the governors of the States who have sent their representatives here today, the commissioners of labor of the States, the health commissioners of the States, the county commissioners—all of them must answer to the people of this community in some way for what they do in the solution of this problem.

The political forces, the economic forces, the moral forces, and the scientific knowledge and the social knowledge which we have, should, in a conference like this, crystallize into a program. In the next 10 years that program should bring about direct results in the lives of the men who are exposed to this hazard, and in the lives of the families who suffer economic disaster when the problem is not solved.

Glossary

making a laboratory of their area	allowing their region to serve as a test case
mandate	authorization
Tri-State area	Kansas, Missouri (Perkins was speaking in the town of Joplin), and Oklahoma

"City Diets and Democracy" (1941)

What about wage earners without gardens, and without home demonstration agents such as rural folks have?...

1. One of the hopes of this generation is to be able to make available to all our people the goods they need for satisfactory living. The most indispensable of these goods is food. American workers have always been among the best fed in the world. According to the data compiled by the International Labor Office in the late 1930's, only in the Scandinavian countries, Great Britain and the British Dominions were average diets as high as in the United States.

2. But this average is in some respects below the standard which scientific research has set for optimum growth and health. And there are many families living below the average—families with a disproportionately large number of children....

3. In my opinion, however, the fundamental problem is economic. More than one quarter of the families surveyed by the Bureau of Labor Statistics in 1934–36 did not spend enough to secure the Bureau of Home Economics' adequate diet at minimum cost. The literature abounds with examples of the connection between economic status and health. A Children's Bureau study of six- and seven-year-old school girls indicated an inverse relationship between poor economic status and gain in weight, need for medical and dental care, number of school absences.

4. The Milbank Memorial Fund has recently been making an extensive medical evaluation of the nutritional status of high school students in New York City. It has found striking differences between the vitamin-C status between the children in high and low income groups.

5. Studies of gain in weight and its association with economic status by the Children's Bureau and a study of Pittsburgh school children provide further evidence of the relationship between poor health and poor diet.

6. Indirect evidence of the results of improper diet is provided on a large scale by the beneficial effect of school lunches. The WPA reports that nourishing hot lunches fed to school children have improved not only general health but the quality of their school work.

7. The proportion of our children who are found in families without adequate nutrition should be a matter of grave concern to all of us. A Bureau of Labor Statistics study of employed wage earners and clerical workers shows that more than 40 percent of the children in this relatively favored group live in families whose incomes are below the level necessary to provide adequate food, as well as suitable housing, clothing, medical care, personal care, union dues, carfare, newspapers, and the other sorts of recreation for which city families must pay in dollars and cents. It is a great mistake to think that a family can budget for a nutritionally adequate diet and fall far below the maintenance level in all the other goods which make up urban living. Large-city families of average size with incomes below $1,400 presumably distribute their funds to all categories of family needs without obtaining the best standards in any one.

8. In my opinion, even while we are in the midst of the national defense program, we should be considering economic measures which will bring about improvements in the American diet. These plans should be of two types: those for cutting the cost of bringing food from the farm to the urban consumer, and plans for certain consumer subsidies.

9. Processing and distribution costs bulk large in the nation's food bill. Studies of the Bureau of Agricultural Economics show that in 1940 American consumers spent about $14,800,000,000 for foods grown in this country. Of this amount the farmer got about $6,200,000,000. The remaining amount went to pay the various charges for transportation, processing, and marketing. The latter costs cover services

which are as real and as important as those rendered by the farmer. The charges for these services, however, may be unduly large either through inefficiency or monopoly control. The government should continue to take whatever measures are necessary to safeguard economy of distribution. Grading and labeling regulations which encourage efficient distribution and efficient buying by the housewife should be encouraged. There are other regulations, however, taxes and license fees which unduly raise food costs, and they should be abolished in the interest of a sound nutrition policy....

10. Food consumption subsidies became part of public policy in the United States in the years of the last depression when they seemed the best answer to the dilemma of farm surpluses of food products, on the one hand, and the many urban families without proper food on the other. The surplus marketing program was at first developed as a temporary measure, but there is much to be said for incorporating some of its best features into a national policy on nutrition.

11. The school-lunch program seems a particularly valuable addition to American institutions. More than 4,000,000 children in our schools have received free lunches during the current fiscal year. There are about 27,000,000 school children in the entire country. If all the children who now have inadequate diets were to be reached by the school-lunch program, it is unlikely that there would be many schools without some children having a free lunch. It thus seems clear that the extension of this program to all school children would have, in addition to its other advantages a very sound

psychological basis. It would also provide for children whose parents have not taught them sound food habits, and give practical lessons in what constitutes a nutritionally adequate noon meal.

12. Provision for additional adult education in nutrition for city mothers, and very likely for city fathers, too, should be part of a national nutrition policy. We need to make available to the adults of today the newer knowledge of nutrition which was not taught when they were in school. We should make it as easy as possible to translate human needs for calories, proteins, minerals, and vitamins into terms of breakfast, lunch and supper menus. We must make it easy for average men and women to protect themselves from the unscrupulous who wish to exploit the current interest in what constitutes an adequate diet.

13. Many suggestions have been made for the extension of the Food Stamp Plan to all families which have been certified for public assistance and, in addition, to independent families with incomes under $1,000. Such an increase in the program would require careful planning and a considerable increase in agricultural production, but it might yield such substantial dividends in morale as well as in health that it should be incorporated as part of a national policy on nutrition.

14. Planning for improved nutrition should also include improvement of proper nutrition standard meals in factory lunchrooms and canteens. Arrangements should be made to provide nutritionally adequate and palatable meals at cost to men and women at their

Glossary

British Dominions	former British possessions that still acknowledged the British monarch as head of state—Canada, Australia, New Zealand, and others
canteens	eating places
inverse relationship	a relationship in which one side increases as the other decreases and vice versa—as, for example, the more poverty, the greater the need for adequate health care
the last depression	the 1918–1921 U.S. economic slump, which followed World War I
WPA	the Works Progress Administration, a New Deal program that existed from 1935 to 1943

place of work with due regard for the preferences and the food consumption habits of the group to be served. Too often factory workers find it difficult to secure digestible and attractive meals near their work without paying excessive prices. This proper food will greatly increase their working efficiency as well as personal appearance.

15. Developing a national nutrition policy for the United States is not a simple task. It involves a delicate balance of the interests of producers, distributors, and consumers; of farmers and urban workers. Labor, whether agricultural labor, factory labor, labor in mines, on trains, or on waterfronts has a great stake in a nutrition program, because good nutrition is fundamental to good health, and the cooperation of healthy workers is fundamental to the development of any important national policy. The problem is one that involves individual action and social action and I believe that we may look forward with confidence to finding its solution on a democratic basis.

"THREE DECADES: A HISTORY OF THE DEPARTMENT OF LABOR" (1943)

On March 4, 1913, when the President approved the act creating the present Department of Labor, the dream of workers for nearly half a century for a separate department to promote the welfare of workers and a Secretary in the Cabinet to speak for them became a reality. Under the act all the activities relating to labor of the former Department of Commerce and Labor were transferred to the new Department of Labor. The Bureau of Labor became the Bureau of Labor Statistics, the Bureau of Immigration was divided into two bureaus, the Bureau of Immigration and the Bureau of Naturalization, and the Children's Bureau retained its original title. The Bureau of Labor Statistics was charged with the collection of "statistics of the conditions of labor and the products and distribution of the products of the same."

The Department of Labor was created in the interest of the wage-earners of the United States, the organic act expressly declaring that "the purpose of the Department of Labor shall be to foster, promote, and develop the welfare of the wage-earners of the United States, to improve their working conditions, and to advance their opportunities for profitable employment."...

During the thirty years since its creation the Department of Labor has steadfastly kept in mind the main purpose of the Department, that of service to the wage-earners of the United States. In the years following World War I the people of the nation enjoyed a period of great prosperity, emerged from a great depression and are now carrying on a greater war. The functions of the Department during these periods have developed according to the changing concept of the nation's responsibility for the welfare of its workers....

The Department's service to immigrants, which on its organization was centered in two bureaus, the Bureau of Immigration and the Bureau of Naturalization, underwent radical changes during the years.... In 1933 the two bureaus were consolidated for greater efficiency and called the Immigration and Naturalization Service....

The Children's Bureau expanded its field so that its work covers every phase of child welfare, from prenatal care to protection of the child worker. It also administers the provisions of the Social Security Act under which federal grants-in-aid are made available to the states for maternal and child-welfare services, and also the federal funds granted for crippled children's services, and cooperates with the states in establishing services for protection and care of homeless, dependent and neglected children and children in danger of becoming delinquent in areas of special need....

As early as 1918 the principle of collective bargaining was recognized by the President's Mediation Commission, of which the Secretary of Labor was chairman, and under the NRA [National Recovery Administration] in 1933–35 the principle was accepted as a policy and administrative machinery provided through the creation of the National Labor Relations Board. In recent years it has become the established policy of the government to consult with trade unions and industrial management in matters affecting their interests. The advice of labor is sought on questions of wages and working conditions and also on the broad social problems confronting the people.

The Employment Service after the war carried on its activities through cooperation with state and municipal offices, but its main service was placement of seasonal and general farmhands through the harvest season and junior placement work....In 1933 the United States Employment Service was reorganized upon the terms of the Wagner-Peyser Act, and the special facilities for veterans and farm placement incorporated therein. Under this act USES supervises and coordinates a series of affiliated state employment services providing complete, public, free employment-office facilities to workers. In 1939 the Employment Service was transferred to the Social Security Board. In the six years the Employment Service operated under the Wagner-Peyser Act in the Department of Labor, it made over 26,000,000 placements, thus bringing together workers in search of jobs and employers in search of workers....

The Division of Labor Standards was established in the Department of Labor in November, 1934, to encourage greater uniformity in state labor legislation and to provide facilities for research and advice available to states on matters pertaining to labor legislation, safety codes and the improvement of labor conditions. The Division has worked for improvement of labor standards through conferences and advisory committees. It promotes apprenticeship standards and encourages training a limited supply of apprentices. It also promotes safety in industry and industrial-disease prevention.

Important new functions were granted to the Department of Labor by the Public Contracts Act and the Fair Labor Standards Act, both of which were measures designed to reduce unemployment and better working conditions. The first act requires not over 40 hours and a fair minimum pay on government contracts in manufacturing, while the second establishes on a federal basis a floor to wages and a ceiling to hours, affecting an estimated 12,300,000 persons....

In the thirty years in which the United States Department of Labor has striven to be of service to the wage-earners of the nation, it has been instrumental not only in administering ever-increasing functions of benefit to workers but in promoting social legislation and programs of inestimable service to all working people.

Glossary

after the war	after World War I
collective bargaining	organized negotiation between workers and employers
organic act	fundamental governing law
Wagner-Peyser Act	a law passed in 1933 that created a network of public employment offices nationwide

Wendell Phillips (Library of Congress)

WENDELL PHILLIPS   1811–1884

Abolitionist, Orator, and Philanthropist

Featured Documents
- "The Murder of Lovejoy" (1837)
- "The Philosophy of the Abolition Movement" (1853)
- "Crispus Attucks" (1858)
- "The Puritan Principle and John Brown" (1859)
- "Under the Flag" (1861)
- "The Foundation of the Labor Movement" (1871)

Overview

Born in Boston in 1811, Wendell Phillips joined the American Anti-Slavery Society in 1837, associating thereafter with the abolitionist William Lloyd Garrison, that movement's most visible and divisive leader. Endowed with exceptional rhetorical gifts, Phillips became a highly sought-after public speaker despite his controversial advocacy of immediate emancipation, racial equality, women's rights, and antislavery violence and his denunciations of American politics as irredeemably pro-slavery. Within the American Anti-Slavery Society, Phillips became the abolitionists' resident intellectual by developing sophisticated justifications for the role of radical agitators in refreshing America's democracy. He also became the Garrisonians' leading legal controversialist by attacking the movement's opponents with unmatched vitriol and by developing widely debated claims that the United States Constitution was a pro-slavery document.

As conflict deepened between North and South during the 1850s, Phillips became a proponent of violent resistance, and when the insurrectionist John Brown invaded Harpers Ferry, Virginia, in 1859, Phillips defended him. He embraced the Civil War as a crusade for black equality and took a prominent role in efforts to achieve these goals during the reconstruction of the postwar South from 1865 to 1870. After the dissolution of the American Anti-Slavery Society in 1870, Phillips continued demanding black equality but also expanded his advocacy to include the labor movement, temperance, women's suffrage, and equal rights for Native Americans and Chinese immigrants. He died on February 2, 1884.

Phillips's importance involved his unique ability to make ordinary Americans respond substantively to the egalitarianism of an otherwise highly unpopular radical abolitionist movement. His extraordinary oratory explains this result, but only when it is recalled that Phillips was steeped in a nationalistic version of American history that touched the memories, fears, and aspirations of his ever-expanding Yankee audiences. He also became an acute analyst of democracy's responses to the power of public opinion, knowledge that allowed him to become one of the nation's first media stars. Phillips's speeches became highly orchestrated

events involving extended tours, heavy advance publicity, press conferences and private interviews, huge audiences, autographed photos, and ongoing editorial commentary. Thus did the media-conscious Phillips invent the role of the political "opinion maker" while multiplying his listeners' resentments against the slaveholding South.

Phillips's importance also stemmed from his empowering presence within the abolitionist movement. Possessing two degrees from Harvard, he continued reading deeply in history, the classics, law, literature, and political economy. As radical abolitionism's most deeply feared polemicist, he was noted as much for his impressive learning as for his use of extraordinarily personal invective and his mesmerizing rhetoric. His vehement attacks on pro-slavery politicians and clerics, his justifications of violence on behalf of emancipation, and his arguments in favor of overthrowing the U.S. Constitution significantly amplified the abolitionist movement's political influence as the Civil War drew closer. During that war and during Reconstruction, Phillips's leadership secured for the abolitionists a central political role in struggles to gain equality for the emancipated slaves. During the 1870s Phillips also played a prominent role in the labor movement.

Finally, Phillips's importance derives from his career as one of the nation's most generous philanthropists. Upon marrying the abolitionist and heiress Anne Terry Greene, the extraordinarily wealthy Phillips united his fortune with a second, even larger, fortune, and his speaking fees eventually earned him a third. Over nearly four decades this childless couple quietly dispersed one of the antebellum era's largest private estates, almost all of it to needy individuals.

Explanation and Analysis of Documents

Phillips's calling was that of the political agitator, and his gifts were those of a compelling public speaker and intellectual. Since his speeches circulated widely in print, his audiences of readers were even more numerous and far-flung than those that heard him in person. Six documents convey how Phillips communicated with his audiences at particularly critical junctures in his career and in the nation's history: his speech announcing his commitment to

1811	■ **November 29** Phillips is born in Boston, Massachusetts.
1831	■ Phillips graduates from Harvard University.
1833	■ Phillips graduates from Harvard University with a law degree.
1837	■ **December 8** Phillips joins the abolitionists when denouncing the murder of Elijah Lovejoy in a speech delivered in Boston.
1853	■ **January 27** Phillips delivers an address to the American Anti-Slavery Society entitled "The Philosophy of the Abolition Movement. "
1858	■ **March 5** Phillips delivers the eulogy of Crispus Attucks, the black patriot and martyr.
1859	■ **December 18** Phillips defends the slave insurrectionist John Brown in a speech entitled "The Puritan Principle and John Brown."
1861	■ **April 21** As the war begins, Phillips delivers his speech "Under the Flag." ■ **December** Phillips recants northern disunion in favor of emancipation through civil war.
1865	■ **December** Phillips assumes the presidency of the American Anti-Slavery Society, replacing the retiring William Lloyd Garrison.

immediate abolitionism, "The Murder of Lovejoy" (1837); his justification of abolitionism as essential to perpetuating American democracy, "The Philosophy of the Abolition Movement" (1853); his vision of the struggle for racial equality in American history, "Crispus Attucks" (1858); his defense of slave insurrection, "The Puritan Principle and John Brown" (1859); his embrace of civil war as a means to annihilate slavery, "Under the Flag" (1861); and his defense of the Workingman's Party and the rights of labor, "The Foundation of the Labor Movement" (1871).

◆ **"The Murder of Lovejoy"**

By late 1837 the abolitionist movement had endured four years of pro-slavery violence and political repression, culminating in the murder of the newspaper editor Elijah Lovejoy by a pro-slavery mob in Alton, Illinois. Until that moment, Phillips had remained uncommitted to the cause, but news of the murder moved him to action when he delivered an impromptu speech in Lovejoy's defense during a protest meeting in Boston's Faneuil Hall. Lovejoy's conduct was particularly controversial among the largely pacifist abolitionists because he had armed himself in his own defense and among anti-abolitionists who condemned him as a violent firebrand. A vocal proponent of the latter position was Massachusetts Attorney General James T. Austin, who praised Lovejoy's killers in the Faneuil Hall meeting as patriotic resisters who had faced down the menacing abolitionists. Although he was unprepared, Phillips rose, strenuously rebutted Austin's contentions, and eloquently defended Lovejoy's conduct.

Phillips's remarks demonstrate his compelling personal identification with New England's Revolutionary past and his lifelong desire to defend its legacies against impending pro-slavery tyranny, violently if necessary. Acutely conscious that he was descended from one of Massachusetts's most illustrious Puritan families, Phillips would often draw dramatic analogies such as the one in this speech between the Bostonian James Otis's resistance to British taxation in 1765 and Lovejoy's attempts to sustain press freedom. Henceforth, Phillips would expatiate powerfully on such historical parallels, challenging Bostonians specifically and Americans in general to base their opposition to slavery on ideals of Revolutionary patriotism.

The speech also highlights Phillips's Yankee nationalism, that is, his lifelong conviction that the expanding republic must develop in conformity with New England customs and traditions. This he made clear when asserting in this speech that settlers in far-off Alton had "forgotten the blood-tried principles of their fathers the moment they lost sight of our New England hills." Lovejoy's conduct, in Phillips's view, was heroic precisely because he attempted to uphold Yankee values against mob tyranny. Throughout his life Phillips believed that the unlimited violence that masters deployed against their slaves, abominable in its own right, also threatened the liberties of all Americans, black and white alike. Abolition, in his view, always meant the replacement of slavery's dangerously chaotic power with predictable republican liberty and Christian moral order. In this manner, one of antebellum America's most radical activists always regarded his cause as profoundly conservative.

This inaugural speech displays the elements that explain Phillips's exceptional impact as an orator. Although his beliefs were certainly radical, he promoted them by appealing to widely accepted historical myths that Americans instinctively embraced. No matter how extreme his doctrines, he enunciated them in ideological contexts that heightened his listeners' receptivity and invited their trust. Phillips's nonthreatening rhetorical style—calm, informal, sincere, epigrammatic, humorously sarcastic, and seemingly spontaneous—further magnified these effects. Never did his listeners feel that he was hectoring, manipulating, intimidating, or talking down to them.

Most crucial to explaining Phillips's appeal, however, was the rapidly spreading impression within the North that, just as he was claiming, slavery was destroying republican liberties. His overall warnings seemed to explain and even prophesy the course of political events. Mobs throughout the 1830s were indeed destroying abolitionists' presses, invading abolitionist meetings, burning black neighborhoods, and entering U.S. post offices in search of antislavery mailings. In 1838 Congress had begun denying the abolitionists' right to petition the government regarding slavery. Citing the U.S Constitution, slaveholders were forcing northerners to aid in the recapture of fugitive slaves. Increasing southern demands for slavery's westward expansion into newly opening states during the 1840s and 1850s seemed to be leading to the nationalization of the "peculiar institution."

This powerful counterpoint between Phillips's ideas and the development of the conflict between North and South put him in the unique position of speaking as a celebrity. The public wanted to know his views simply because he offered them, whether agreeing with them or not. In short, he made himself into the nation's first political pundit, which explains why so many times his speech titles read simply "The Lessons of the Hour" or "Our Duties at the Present Moment." These nonspecific rubrics allowed Phillips to adjust quickly the content of his speeches in order to respond to the most recent headlines, much in the manner of media commentators today.

◆ "The Philosophy of the Abolition Movement"

In addition to orations for the multitudes, Phillips also directed his eloquence to his abolitionist colleagues. In this personalized setting he acted as the movement's most compelling ideologist and its most sophisticated strategic thinker. An excellent example of his work in this regard is his address to the American Anti-Slavery Society in 1853 titled "The Philosophy of the Abolition Movement." In it he offers comprehensive justifications for the abolitionists' disdain for moderate approaches and their harsh verbal assaults on their opponents. In Phillips's view, it was precisely the abolitionists' extremism that justified their actions and guaranteed their ultimate success.

When Phillips delivered this speech, his weary abolitionist co-workers were much in need of ideological reinforce-

Time Line

1870

- **December**
  Phillips dissolves the American-Anti-Slavery Society after passage of the Fifteenth Amendment.

- Phillips runs as the Workingman's Party candidate for Massachusetts governor.

1871

- **September 4**
  Phillips addresses the Workingman's Party convention with his speech entitled "The Foundation of the Labor Movement."

1884

- **February 2**
  Phillips dies in Boston.

ment. Their three decades of agitation had not led to slavery's obliteration; instead, the South's "peculiar institution" had become greatly entrenched. Since Phillips had entered the movement in 1837, the enslaved population had increased from two million to three million, new slave states had been added to the Union, and Congress had approved a harsh new law to ensure the return of fugitives. Judged against the abolitionists' high initial expectations, their three decades of effort seemed to have yielded little, precisely the impression that Phillips's speech sought to counter.

Phillips's remarks demonstrate why he was considered by his critics to be abolitionism's master of vituperation or, by his beleaguered co-workers, a vital source of inspiration. His startling declaration that the "South is one great brothel, where half a million of women are flogged to prostitution, or, worse still, are degraded to believe it honorable" is typical of the extraordinarily polemical statements that he so frequently wove throughout his speeches. Reading excerpts of this speech one can begin to sense how Phillips built the remarkable ideological indictments of slavery that so dismayed his opponents and so energized his fellow abolitionists.

To accompany its electrifying language, Phillips's speech builds a defense of the abolitionist movement around a wholesale indictment of the custodians of the nation's most powerful institutions—clerics, politicians, legal authorities, and newspaper editors. According to Phillips, these shapers of public opinion had so thoroughly corrupted the nation's prevailing values with defenses of slavery that abolitionists were left no choice but full-throated denunciation. In a nation governed by a tyranny of the majority, moderate approaches and compromising tactics were simply not possible. Abolitionist duty instead demanded that corrupted opinion makers be individually named and unabashedly exposed, for only then did it become possible for public opinion to change. Thus, Phillips argued, the abolitionists' extreme language and uncompromising demands were anything but unreasonable. Instead, they constituted the highest statesmanship, marking their movement as one that displayed "sound judgment, unerring foresight, [and] the most sagacious adaptation of means to ends."

Apart from encouraging his fellow immediatists, the strategies recommended by Phillips in this speech also proved of crucial importance as political disagreements between North and South grew ever more intense in the 1850s. As northern resistance to slavery's westward expansion led to the rise of the Republican Party, abolitionists acted boldly on Phillips's admonition never to "throw away any weapon which ever broke up the crust of an ignorant prejudice." Since Republicans opposed only slavery's westward expansion while repudiating emancipation for the slaves themselves, it remained to the abolitionists alone to challenge politicians such as Abraham Lincoln and the public opinion they courted with uncompromised demands for emancipation and equality.

◆ "Crispus Attucks"

Phillips delivered his eulogy on the black Patriot and martyr of 1775, Crispus Attucks, just when many in Boston saw themselves preparing for a second American Revolution, this time against what they took to be the expanding tyranny of the Slave Power. By 1858 opinion in the city had grown extremely hostile to the South, thanks primarily to determined citizens' resistance to efforts by outside authorities to enforce the highly unpopular 1850 Fugitive Slave Law. Boston's remarkable black abolitionists took the lead in forming vigilance committees that protected individual escapees, exposed privately commissioned slave catchers, and undermined federal marshals deployed to enforce the law. Prominent white abolitionists in Boston, such as William Lloyd Garrison, Samuel Gridley Howe, Theodore Parker, and Thomas Wentworth Higginson, joined Phillips in organizing angry protest meetings and mounting legal maneuvers to aid blacks prosecuted under the law. That three of these militants—Higginson, Howe, and Parker—had already become financial backers of the slave insurrectionist John Brown measures well the depth of many abolitionists' desires for confrontation. In this context, Phillips's celebration of the African American Attucks as "the emblem of Revolutionary violence in its dawn" was a call to arms as much for whites as for blacks.

Phillips's speech offers a stunning recasting of American history because of its wholesale rejection of prevailing white supremacist assumptions, its insistence on the central historical roles of African-descended people in securing democracy, and its embrace of black revolutionary violence. When so arguing, Phillips became the first white public intellectual to advance interpretations that such talented black investigators of the American past as William Nell, Frederick Douglass, and Martin Delaney had been developing for at least a decade. In this manner, Phillips was the first notable white to integrate his understandings of the past with those of the black founders of African American history.

Phillips's strong demurrals in this oration against Theodore Parker's assertion that "Caucasians" were inherently more courageous than blacks also confirm Phillips's strenuous rejection of prevailing racial assumptions. His forthright endorsement of the Atlantic world's largest and most successful slave insurrection, the Haiti–Santo Domingo Revolution of 1792, and his claim of Egypt as the cradle of black culture document his cosmopolitan vision. ("I summon Egypt with the arts; I summon St. Domingo with the sword.") At the same time, his references to "Saxon" and "Slavonic" races underscore how far removed Phillips's thinking was historically from modern ideas of race.

Phillips's paean to Crispus Attucks also constituted one aspect of his personal campaign to remake the city of Boston and the Commonwealth of Massachusetts into racial democracies. He was, for example, heavily involved in black abolitionists' efforts to erect a statue commemorating Attucks that was to join the many other monuments to Revolutionary heroes scattered throughout the city. With similar goals in view, Phillips defied segregated seating whenever he boarded public transportation, testified before the state legislature against laws (finally repealed) banning racial intermarriage, and contributed his eloquence and legal expertise in successful efforts to desegregate public schools. Extended involvement in these local struggles clearly forecast the approach Phillips would adopt post-1865, after the South had been defeated and the slaveholders separated from their "human property." In his view, the defeated South must be completely remade in the image of Massachusetts, with the franchise extended to all men: equal civil rights for black and white alike, plantation lands redistributed to black farmers, and integrated schools open to all. The reconstruction of Massachusetts symbolized by his speech on Crispus Attucks ultimately furnished Phillips's blueprint for reconstructing the postwar nation.

◆ "The Puritan Principle and John Brown"

After John Brown attempted to incite slave insurrection by invading Harpers Ferry, Virginia, in December 1859 and was captured, tried, and hanged, Phillips became his most uninhibited defender, turning him into a powerful symbol of revolutionary abolitionism. He offered tributes to Brown in several highly publicized speeches, including a widely read eulogy he delivered at Brown's funeral. While the vast majority of white northerners vehemently condemned Brown's actions, Phillips welcomed them as opening a new age of "insurrection" that was transforming public opinion in the North and heralding doom for slavery. Nearly as unsettled by Phillips's prophecies as by Brown's actions, whites in the South moved closer to leaving the Union.

Phillips's declaration that "the lesson of the hour is insurrection" illuminates much beyond his belief in the slaves' right to rebel and the duty of whites to assist them (Redpath, p. 284). In addition, it reveals how profoundly Phillips's Puritan heritage inspired his abolitionism and how deeply he believed that the acts of charismatic rebels inspired by individual conscience accelerated the triumph of freedom. Phillips's ancestors had been leaders in English

Protestantism's seventeenth-century wars against kingship and religious "tyranny" and they also became opponents of British "oppression" during the American Revolution. Believing the overthrow of tyrants to be the highest expression of patriotism, Phillips embraced his family's history to anchor Brown's actions in the mythic origins of American liberty. In this manner, Phillips represented Brown's actions as consistent with the noblest elements of New England's Anglo-Saxon past, an ideology with enormous potential for mobilizing Yankees for civil war.

Phillips's speech also mounted a powerful rebuttal to widely repeated claims that Brown's actions were those of an isolated madman. To reassure terrified slaveholders that they held no brief for insurrection, Republican Party leaders, Abraham Lincoln prominent among them, condemned Brown's act as that of an isolated fanatic who was in no sense representative of prevailing northern opinion. To the contrary, Republicans insisted, their party upheld slavery's legality in the states in which it already existed and they were as eager to suppress insurrection as any white southerner. To counter these characterizations, Phillips uses every rhetorical device at his command to characterize Harpers Ferry as no "spasmodic act" on Brown's part but instead as the fulfillment of God's providential design, a sacred gift equal to "that divine sacrifice" made by the crucified Jesus "two thousand years ago." Brown's actions, according to Phillips, represented not only the "flowering of sixty years" of righteous living but also a supreme act of selflessness that should inspire every Christian American to "go...and do likewise."

Although Phillips's justifications of Brown repelled northern politicians, they amplified desires for violent confrontation that by 1860 had all but eroded many abolitionists' long-held commitments to pacifism. Black abolitionists joined with Phillips in public meetings that endorsed Brown's actions unanimously—so did the nation's most prominent white abolitionist and Phillips's closest associate, the longtime nonresistant William Lloyd Garrison. When a congressional investigation of the Harpers Ferry raid revealed that six of abolitionism's most prominent leaders had been Brown's financial backers, it also became clear that much of the movement was transforming itself into a revolutionary vanguard. In this respect, Phillips's celebrations of Brown's heroism reinforced abolitionists' inclinations toward violence at least as much as they inspired them while reverberating powerfully across his sprawling national network of listeners and readers.

◆ **"Under the Flag"**
Phillips delivered this speech just as sectional crisis was merging with the Civil War. Following Lincoln's election, nearly all of the slave states seceded. Confederates then fired on U.S. forces attempting to provision Fort Sumter, the federal installation located in Charleston Harbor in South Carolina. This hostile act led Lincoln's call for seventy-five thousand troops to prevent seceding states from leaving the Union. Lincoln's appeal to arms placed Phillips in a difficult position.

For nearly two decades Phillips had been the abolitionists' premier advocate of northern disunion, the doctrine that slavery could be abolished only if the free states dissolved their constitutional ties with the South. Arguing that in 1787 the Founding Fathers had built protections for slavery throughout the Constitution, Phillips had insisted that the institution's survival depended entirely on northern legal and political support. Were this support withdrawn, slavery would collapse either through insurrection or as a result of planters' demoralization. Throughout the crisis of 1861, Phillips had deployed these arguments to urge that the seceding states be allowed to depart in peace. Now, however, Lincoln had declared a war against the slave system that Phillips so hated in order to preserve the Union that Phillips had so long condemned. In this speech Phillips resolves this obvious contradiction by abandoning his northern disunionism while welcoming civil war as the means for forging a new and radically egalitarian American state.

Phillips demonstrates throughout this speech the enormous differences that always distinguished his understanding of the Civil War from the views of those who prosecuted it, Lincoln and the Republican Party. For Lincoln and for most Republicans, warfare aimed to reassemble the Union as it had existed prior to 1861, not to remake the nation through social and political revolution. Even when Lincoln issued the Emancipation Proclamation, he made clear that his primary motive was to restore the Union. In this fundamental respect, the "union" to which Phillips swore his allegiance in 1861 was worlds apart from the Constitution that Lincoln maintained. So although it seems on first reading of "Under the Flag" that Phillips was recanting his northern secessionism, in truth he remained as opposed as he had ever been to the Union as it had always existed. Instead, he now sought to transform that tyrannous arrangement through the force of arms.

In this address Phillips makes the revolutionary nature of his expectations clear in his dramatic contrasts between a South mired in the "barbarism" of the "thirteenth and fourteenth century" and a North that "thinks" and is fully involved in the egalitarian "nineteenth century." Warfare between two such antithetical civilizations, "Civilization against Barbarism" must, in Phillips's view, lead to the destruction of the latter and to the complete transformation of the entire nation to lift up "all tongues, all creeds, all races—one brotherhood." Implicit in this prediction are all the specific measures that Phillips and other radical abolitionists demanded during the war and in its immediate aftermath. For Phillips and the other radicals for whom he spoke, final victory would be assured only when the emancipated slaves possessed complete civil rights, occupation of lands confiscated from rebel planters, access to education, and unqualified male suffrage. In this respect, Phillips's "Under the Flag" oration clearly anticipated the epochal struggles for racial equality in the South after emancipation.

◆ **The Foundation of the Labor Movement**
After the passage of the Fifteenth Amendment in 1870 that mandated equal suffrage for black men, Phillips dis-

"What is the denunciation with which we are charged? It is endeavoring, in our faltering human speech, to declare the enormity of the sin of making merchandise of men.—of separating husband and wife,—taking the infant from its mother, and selling the daughter to prostitution,—of a professedly Christian nation denying, by statute, the Bible to every sixth man and woman of its population, and making it illegal for 'two or three' to meet together, except a white man be present!"

("The Philosophy of the Abolition Movement")

"I place, therefore, this Crispus Attucks in the foremost rank of the men that dared. When we talk of courage, he rises, with his dark face, in his clothes of the laborer, his head uncovered, his arm raised above him defying bayonets,—the emblem of Revolutionary violence in its dawn; and when the proper symbols are placed around the base of the statue of Washington, one corner will be filled by the colored man defying the British muskets."

("Crispus Attucks")

"What has John Brown done for us? The world doubted over the horrid word 'insurrection,' whether the victim had a right to arrest the course of his master, and even at any expense of blood, to vindicate his rights; and Brown said to his neighbors in the old school-house at North Elba, sitting among the snow, where nothing grows but men, and even wheat freezes: 'I can go South, and show the world that he has a right to rise and can rise.'"

("The Puritan Principle and John Brown")

"Years hence, when the smoke of this conflict clears away, the world will see under our banner all tongues, all creeds, all races,—one brotherhood,—and on the banks of the Potomac, the Genius of Liberty, robed in light, four and thirty stars for her diadem, broken chains under feet, and an olive-branch in her right hand."

("Under the Flag")

banded the American Anti-Slavery Society, only to embrace the rapidly developing labor movement. In that year he ran unsuccessfully for governor of Massachusetts as the Workingman's Party candidate, and the following year found him at that party's state convention, where he helped draft that party's platform before delivering this speech.

For Phillips, this transition from abolitionism to labor reform seemed logical and necessary. His long-beloved Massachusetts increasingly featured drab factory towns and demoralized wage workers, not the democratic society of educated, independent laborers he had always celebrated. At the same time, labor violence had begun erupting in several northern states and also in England and France. "Wage slavery" for whites now seemed to Phillips to constitute democracy's most threatening source of oppression and social instability. To combat it, Phillips demanded that laborers be placed on a level of parity with capitalists by securing an eight-hour workday, equal pay for workers of both genders, and laws requiring cooperative investments by workers in the incorporation of all new companies. Hardly a Marxist, Phillips clearly sought to harmonize the interests of labor and capital, not to seek the overthrow of the latter by the former.

The resolutions introducing Phillips's speech make clear how compelling the analogy seemed to be between the now-abolished system of chattel slavery in the South and the emerging system of wage slavery. Warnings that the nation was being captured by an "aristocracy of capital" clearly echoed Phillips's earlier warnings about the dangers posed by all-powerful slaveholders. At the same time, the specific remedies proposed for labor's benefit illustrate how fundamentally different abolitionism and labor reform

actually were and how drastically Phillips's role had changed when moving from one to the other. Instead of demanding revolutionary measures such as northern disunion, Phillips now advocated piecemeal legislative actions. Rather than seeking the wholesale transformation of public opinion while condemning all forms of politics, Phillips now courted the voters.

The speech itself, however, also demonstrates that deep continuities united Phillips's abolitionist past with his advocacy of labor's cause. First, he clearly regarded the latter cause as arising as the logical consequence of the former. Once the masses had "claimed emancipation from actual chains" and had successfully "claimed the ballot," equal labor rights became, in his view, the "last movement" required for securing American democracy. Further continuities can be identified in Phillips's defense of the labor movement, even in its most violent forms, as a means for securing social order. Clearly echoing his strenuous defenses of armed abolitionist resisters such as Elijah Lovejoy and John Brown, Phillips praised the revolutionaries of France's First International for attempting to seize Paris and bring revolution through force of arms. To him, as always, such violence represented not lawless anarchy, but instead patriotic resistance to corrupt disorder spawned by tyrants—necessary preludes to peaceful democracy ruled by an enlightened public through the ballot box.

Impact and Legacy

Thanks to his extraordinary gifts as a public speaker and his fundamental insights into the workings of the media of

---

Questions for Further Study

1. In "The Murder of Lovejoy," what does Phillips mean when he says that the people of Illinois had "forgotten the blood-tried principles of their fathers the moment they lost sight of our New England hills"? To what principles is Phillips referring?

2. Compare "The Murder of Lovejoy" with William Lloyd Garrison's "The Triumph of Mobocracy in Boston." How are the events detailed in these documents similar? Summarize the two authors' responses to these events. Similarly, compare Phillips's "The Puritan Principle and John Brown" with Garrison's speech relating to the execution of John Brown. How are the two authors' responses to the John Brown raid similar? Do they differ in any fundamental way?

3. To what extent would Salmon Chase, in his "Reclamation of Fugitives from Service," have agreed with the arguments Phillips presented in "The Philosophy of the Abolition Movement"?

4. What similarities does Phillips see between the slave system prior to the Civil War and the wage system in effect during America's industrial expansion in the post–Civil War era, as expressed in "The Foundation of the Labor Movement"?

---

his day, no advocate of black emancipation and racial equality had a more profound impact on American public opinion than did Phillips. For good or ill, for better than two decades Phillips's rhetoric terrified slaveholders, enraged his northern critics, inspired his fellow abolitionists, and challenged northerners to rethink their support of slavery. By achieving these goals, Phillips also became the first nationally recognized opinion maker, one whose role clearly anticipated the celebrities and pundits who dominate so much of today's political discourse.

Key Sources

The major collections of Phillips's private papers are the Crawford Blagden Papers, Houghton Library, Harvard University, and the many letters scattered throughout the Anti-Slavery Collection, the Boston Public Library. Phillips's work has been collected in *Speeches, Lectures, and Letters* (1878) and *Speeches, Lectures, and Letters*, 2nd series (1891).

Further Reading

■ Books

Bartlett, Irving. *Wendell Phillips: Brahmin Radical*. Boston: Beacon Press, 1961.

Redpath, James, ed. *Speeches, Lectures and Letters*. Boston: J. Redpath, 1863.

Stewart, James Brewer. *Wendell Phillips: Liberty's Hero*, Baton Rouge: Louisiana State University Press, 1986.

———. *Holy Warriors: The Abolitionists and American Slavery*. New York: Hill & Wang, 1996.

—James Stewart

"The Murder of Lovejoy" (1837)

Some persons seem to imagine that anarchy existed at Alton from the commencement of these disputes. Not at all. "No one of us," says an eyewitness and a comrade of Lovejoy, "has taken up arms during these disturbances but at the command of the Mayor." Anarchy did not settle down on that devoted city till Lovejoy breathed his last. Till then the law, represented in his person, sustained itself against its foes. When he fell, civil authority was trampled under foot. He had "planted himself on his constitutional rights,"—appealed to the laws,—claimed the protection of the civil authority,—taken refuge under "the broad shield of the Constitution. When through that he was pierced and fell, he fell but one sufferer in a common catastrophe." He took refuge under the banner of liberty,—amid its folds; and when he fell, its glorious stars and stripes, the emblem of free institutions, around which cluster so many heart-stirring memories, were blotted out in the martyr's blood....

Presumptuous to assert the freedom of the press on American ground! Is the assertion of such freedom before the age? So much before the age as to leave one no right to make it because it displeases the community? Who invents this libel on his country? It is this very thing which entitles Lovejoy to greater praise. The disputed right which provoked the Revolution—taxation without representation—is far beneath that for which he died. One word, gentlemen. As much as *thought* is better than money, so much is the cause in which Lovejoy died nobler than a mere question of taxes. James Otis thundered in this Hall when the King did but touch his *pocket*. Imagine, if you can, his indignant eloquence, had England offered to put a gag upon his lips....

Mr. Chairman, from the bottom of my heart I thank that brave little band at Alton for resisting. We must remember that Lovejoy had fled from city to city,—suffered the destruction of three presses patiently. At length he took counsel with friends, men of character, of tried integrity, of wide views, of Christian principle. They thought the crisis had come: it was full time to assert the laws. They saw around them, not a community like our own, of fixed habits, of character moulded and settled, but one "in the gristle, not yet hardened into the bone of manhood." The people there, children of our older States, seem to have forgotten the blood-tried principles of their fathers the moment they lost sight of our New England hills. Something was to be done to show them the priceless value of the freedom of the press, to bring back and set right their wandering and confused ideas. He and his advisers looked out on a community, staggering like a drunken man, indifferent to their rights and confused in their feelings. Deaf to argument, haply they might be stunned into sobriety. They saw that of which we cannot judge, the *necessity* of resistance. Insulted law called for it. Public opinion, fast hastening on the downward course, must be arrested.

Glossary

James Otis	American Revolutionist

"The Philosophy of the Abolition Movement" (1853)

I wish, Mr. Chairman, to notice some objections that have been made to our course ever since Mr. Garrison began his career, and which have been lately urged again....

The charges to which I refer are these: that, in dealing with slaveholders and their apologists, we indulge in fierce denunciations, instead of appealing to their reason and common sense by plain statements and fair argument;—that we might have won the sympathies and support of the nation, if we would have submitted to argue this question with a manly patience; but, instead of this, we have outraged the feelings of the community by attacks, unjust and unnecessarily severe, on its most valued institutions, and gratified our spleen by indiscriminate abuse of leading men....

[On the contrary,] I claim, before you who know the true state of the case,—I claim for the antislavery movement with which this society is identified, that, looking back over its whole course, and considering the men connected with it in the mass, it has been marked by sound judgment, unerring foresight, the most sagacious adaptation of means to ends, the strictest self-discipline, the most thorough research, and an amount of patient and manly argument addressed to the conscience and intellect of the nation, such as no other cause of the kind, in England or this country, has ever offered....

What is the denunciation with which we are charged? It is endeavoring, in our faltering human speech, to declare the enormity of the sin of making merchandise of men,—of separating husband and wife,—taking the infant from its mother, and selling the daughter to prostitution,—of a professedly Christian nation denying, by statute, the Bible to every sixth man and woman of its population, and making it illegal for "two or three" to meet together, except a white man be present! What is this harsh criticism of motives with which we are charged? It is simply holding the intelligent and deliberate actor responsible for the character and consequences of his acts....All that we ask the world and thoughtful men to note are the principles and deeds on which the American pulpit and American public men plume themselves. We always allow our opponents to paint their own pictures. Our humble duty is to stand by and assure the spectators that what they would take for a knave or a hypocrite is really, in American estimation, a Doctor of Divinity or Secretary of State.

The South is one great brothel, where half a million of women are flogged to prostitution, or, worse still, are degraded to believe it honorable. The public squares of half our great cities echo to the wail of families torn asunder at the auction-block; no one of our fair rivers that has not closed over the negro seeking in death a refuge from a life too wretched to bear; thousands of fugitives skulk along our highways, afraid to tell their names, and trembling at the sight of a human being; free men are kidnapped in our streets, to be plunged into that hell of slavery; and now and then one, as if by miracle, after long years, returns to make men aghast with his tale. The press says, "It is all right"; and the pulpit cries, "Amen." They print the Bible in every tongue in which man utters his prayers; and get the money to do so by agreeing never to give the book, in the language our mothers taught us, to any negro, free or bond south of Mason and Dixon's line. The press says, "It is all right"; and the pulpit cries, "Amen." The slave lifts up his imploring eyes, and sees in every face but ours the face of an enemy. Prove to me now that harsh rebuke, indignant denunciation, scathing sarcasm, and pitiless ridicule are wholly and always unjustifiable; else we dare not, in so desperate a case, throw away any weapon which ever broke up the crust of an ignorant prejudice, roused a slumbering conscience, shamed a proud sinner, or changed, in any way, the conduct of a human being. Our aim is to alter public opinion. Did we live in a market, our talk should be of dollars and cents, and we would seek to prove only that slavery was an unprofitable investment. Were the nation one great, pure church, we would sit down and reason of "righteousness, temperance, and judgment to come." Had slavery fortified itself in a college, we would load our cannons with cold facts, and wing our arrows with arguments. But we happen to live in the world,—the world made up of thought and impulse, of self-conceit and self-interest, of weak men and wicked. To conquer, we must reach all. Our object is not to make every man a Christian or a philosopher, but to induce every one to aid in the abolition of slavery. We expect to accomplish our object long before the nation is made over into saints or elevated into philosophers. To change public opinion, we use the very tools by which it was formed.

Glossary

Mason and Dixon's line	a surveyor's line established in the eighteenth century by Charles Mason and Jeremiah Dixon to resolve a border dispute in colonial America; popularly used to refer to the division between the northern and southern United States
Mr. Garrison	William Lloyd Garrison, prominent abolitionist best known as editor of the abolitionist newspaper the *Liberator*.

"CRISPUS ATTUCKS" (1858)

I am very glad to stand here in an hour when we come together to do honor to one of the first martyrs in our Revolution. I think we sometimes tell the story of what he did with too little appreciation of how much it takes to make the first move in the cold streets of a revolutionary epoch. It is a very easy thing to sit down and read the history; it is a very easy thing to imagine what we would have done,—it is a very different thing to strike the first blow....

Revolution always begins with the populace, never with the leaders. They argue, they resolve, they organize; it is the populace that, like the edge of the cloud, shows the lightning first. This was the lightning. I hail the 5th of March as the baptism of the Revolution into forcible resistance; without that it would have been simply a discussion of rights. I place, therefore, this Crispus Attucks in the foremost rank of the men that dared. When we talk of courage, he rises, with his dark face, in his clothes of the laborer, his head uncovered, his arm raised above him defying bayonets,—the emblem of Revolutionary violence in its dawn; and when the proper symbols are placed around the base of the statue of Washington, one corner will be filled by the colored man defying the British muskets....

I do not believe in the argument which my learned and eloquent friend Theodore Parker has stated in regard even to the *courage* of colored blood. It is a hazardous thing to dare to differ with so profound a scholar, with so careful a thinker as Theodore Parker; but I cannot accept his argument and for this reason,—he says the Caucasian race, each man of it, would kill twenty men and enslave twenty more rather than be a slave; and thence he deduces that the colored race, which suffers slavery

here, is not emphatically distinguished for courage. I take issue on that statement. There is no race in the world that has not been enslaved at one period. This very Saxon blood we boast, was enslaved for five centuries in Europe. We were slaves,—we *white* people. This very English blood of ours—Saxon—was the peculiar mark of slavery for five or six hundred years. The Slavonic race, of which we are a branch, is enslaved by millions to-day in Russia. The French race has been enslaved for centuries. Then add this fact,—no race, *not one*, ever vindicated its freedom from slavery by the sword; we did not win freedom by the sword; we did not resist, we Saxons. If you go to the catalogue of races that have actually abolished slavery by the sword, the colored race is the only one that has ever yet afforded an instance, and that is St. Domingo.... The only race in history that ever took the sword into their hands, and cut their chains, is the black race of St. Domingo. Let that fact go for what it is worth. The villeinage of France and England wore out by the progress of commerce, by the growth of free cities, by the education of the people, by the advancement of Christianity. So I think the slavery of the blacks will wear out. I think, therefore, that the simple and limited experiment of three centuries of black slavery is not basis enough for the argument. No; the black man may well scorn it, and say, "I summon before the jury, Africa, with her savage millions, that has maintained her independence for two or three thousand years; I summon Egypt with the arts; I summon St. Domingo with the sword,—and I choose to be tried in the great company, not alone!" And in that company, he may claim to have shown as much courage as any other race—full as much.

Glossary

Saxon	a reference to the Germanic tribe that invaded England in the fifth century
St. Domingo	a reference to the slave revolt in Haiti from 1791 to 1804
Theodore Parker	a prominent reformer, abolitionist, and minister
villeinage	the status of being a villein, or serf

"THE PURITAN PRINCIPLE AND JOHN BROWN" (1859)

The revelation of despotism is the great lesson which the Puritan of one month ago [John Brown] has taught us. He has flung himself, under the instinct of a great idea, against the institutions beneath which we sit, and he says, practically, to the world, as the Puritan did: "If I am a felon, bury me with curses. I will trust to a future age to judge between you and me. Posterity will summon the State to judgment, and will admit my principle. I can wait." Men say it is anarchy, that this right of the individual to sit in judgment cannot be trusted. It is the lesson of Puritanism. If the individual criticising law cannot be trusted, then Puritanism is a mistake, for the sanctity of individual judgment is the lesson of Massachusetts history in 1620 and '30....

I affirm that this is the lesson of our history,— that the world is fluid; that we are on the ocean: that we cannot get rid of the people, and we do not want to; that the millions are our basis; and that God has set us this task: "If you want good institutions, do not try to bulwark out the ocean of popular thought, educate it. If you want good laws, earn them." Conservatism says: "I can make my own hearthstone safe; I can build a bulwark of gold and bayonets about it high as heaven and deep as hell, and nobody can touch me, and that is enough." Puritanism says: "It is a delusion; it is a refuge of lies; it is not safe; the waters of popular instinct will carry it away. If you want your own cradle safe, make the cradle of every other man safe and pure. Educate the people up to the law you want." How? They cannot stop for books. Show them manhood. Show them a brave act. What has John Brown done for us? The world doubted over the horrid word "insurrection," whether the victim had a right to arrest the course of his master, and even at any expense of blood, to vindicate his rights; and Brown said to his neighbors in the old school-house at North Elba, sitting among the snow, where nothing grows but men, and even wheat freezes: "I can go South, and show the world that he has a right to rise and can rise." He went, girded about by his household, carrying his sons with him. Proof of a life devoted to an idea! Not a single spasmodic act of greatness, coming out with no back-ground, but the flowering of sixty years. The proof of it, that everything around him grouped itself harmoniously, like the planets around the central sun. He went down to Virginia, took possession of a town, and held it. He says: "You thought this was strength; I demonstrate it is weakness. You thought this was civil society; I show you it is a den of pirates." Then he turned around in his sublimity, with his Puritan devotional heart, and said to the millions, "Learn!" And God lifted a million hearts to his gibbet, as the Roman cross lifted a million of hearts to it in that divine sacrifice of two thousand years ago. To-day, more than a statesman could have taught in seventy years, one act of a week has taught these eighteen millions of people. That is the Puritan principle.

What shall it teach us? "Go thou and do likewise." Do it by a resolute life; do it by a fearless rebuke; do it by preaching the sermon of which this act is the text; do it by standing by the great example which God has given us; do it by tearing asunder the veil of respectability which covers brutality calling itself law.

Glossary

gibbet	a pillory or gallows
girded about	prepared for a confrontation
North Elba	a town in New York

"UNDER THE FLAG" (1861)

MANY times this winter, here and elsewhere, I have counselled peace,—urged, as well as I knew how, the expediency of acknowledging a Southern Confederacy, and the peaceful separation of these thirty-four States. One of the journals announces to you that I come here this morning to retract those opinions. No, not one of them! I need them all,—every word I have spoken this winter,—every act of twenty-five years of my life, to make the welcome I give this war hearty and hot....

All winter long, I have acted with that party which cried for peace. The antislavery enterprise to which I belong started with peace written on its banner. We imagined that the age of bullets was over; that the age of ideas had come; that thirty millions of people were able to take a great question, and decide it by the conflict of opinions; that, without letting the ship of state founder, we could lift four millions of men into Liberty and Justice. We thought that if your statesmen would throw away personal ambition and party watchwords, and devote themselves to the great issue, this might be accomplished. To a certain extent it has been. The North has answered to the call. Year after year, event by event, has indicated the rising education of the people,—the readiness for a higher moral life, the calm, self-poised confidence in our own convictions that patiently waits—like master for a pupil—for a neighbor's conversion. The North has responded to the call of that peaceful, moral, intellectual agitation which the antislavery idea has initiated. Our mistake, if any, has been that we counted too much on the intelligence of the masses, on the honesty and wisdom of statesmen as a class. Perhaps we did not give weight enough to the fact we saw, that this nation is made up of different ages; not homogeneous, but a mixed mass of different centuries. The North *thinks*,—can appreciate argument,—is the nineteenth century,—hardly any struggle left in it but that between the working class and the money-kings. The South *dreams*,—it is the thirteenth and fourteenth century,—baron and serf,—noble and slave. Jack Cade and Wat Tyler loom over its horizon, and the serf, rising, calls for another Thierry to record his struggle. There the fagot still burns which the Doctors of the Sorbonne called, ages ago, "the best light to guide the erring." There men are tortured for opinions, the only punishment the Jesuits were willing their pupils should look on. This is, perhaps, too flattering a picture of the South. Better call her, as Sum-

Glossary

diadem	crown
Fort Sumter	the U.S. fort on the coast of South Carolina, site of the first hostilities in the Civil War
Jack Cade	the leader of a revolt in England in 1450
Jesuits	an order of Catholic priests, known historically for their efforts to expose and eliminate heresy, or false church doctrine
olive-branch	a traditional symbol of peace
Potomac	the Potomac River, often used as a figure of speech to refer to the area surrounding Washington, D.C., and the seat of government
Sumner	Charles Sumner, U.S. senator, abolitionist, and one of the leaders of the Radical Republicans during Reconstruction
Thermopylae	the Greek site of the Battle of Thermopylae in 480 BCE
Thierry	nineteenth-century liberal French historian Augustin Thierry
Wat Tyler	leader of the English Peasants' Revolt of 1381

ner does, "the Barbarous States." Our struggle, therefore, is between barbarism and civilization. Such can only be settled by arms. The government has waited until its best friends almost suspected its courage or its integrity; but the cannon shot against Fort Sumter has opened the only door out of this hour. There were but two. One was compromise; the other was battle. The integrity of the North closed the first; the generous forbearance of nineteen States closed the other. The South opened this with cannon-shot, and Lincoln shows himself at the door. The war, then, is not aggressive, but in self defence, and Washington has become the Thermopylae at Liberty and Justice. Rather than surrender that Capital, cover every square feet of it with a living body; crowd it with a million of men, and empty every bank vault at the North to pay the cost. Teach the would once for all, that North America belongs to the Stars and Stripes, and under them no man shall wear a chain. In the whole of this conflict, I have looked only at Liberty,—only at the slave....

The noise and dust of the conflict may hide the real question at issue. Europe may think, some of us may, that we are fighting for forms and parchments, for sovereignty and a flag. But really the war is one of opinions: it is Civilization against Barbarism: it is Freedom against Slavery. The cannon-shot against Fort Sumter was the yell of pirates against the DECLARATION OF INDEPENDENCE, the war-cry of the North is the echo of that sublime pledge. The South, defying Christianity, clutches its victim. The North offers its wealth and blood in glad atonement for the selfishness of seventy years. The result is as sure as the throne of God. I believe in the possibility of justice, in the certainty of union. Years hence, when the smoke of this conflict clears away, the world will see under our banner all tongues, all creeds, all races,—one brotherhood,—and on the banks of the Potomac, the Genius of Liberty, robed in light, four and thirty stars for her diadem, broken chains under feet, and an olive-branch in her right hand.

"THE FOUNDATION OF THE LABOR MOVEMENT" (1871)

PLATFORM.

We affirm, as a fundamental principle, that labor, the creator of wealth, is entitled to all it creates.

Affirming this, we avow ourselves willing to accept the final results of the operation of a principle so radical,—such as the overthrow of the whole profit-making system, the extinction of all monopolies, the abolition of privileged classes, universal education and fraternity, perfect freedom of exchange, and, best and grandest of all, the final obliteration of that foul stigma upon our so-called Christian civilization,—the poverty of the masses. Holding principles as radical as these, and having before our minds an ideal condition so noble, we are still aware that our goal cannot be reached at a single leap. We take into account the ignorance, selfishness, prejudice, corruption, and demoralization of the leaders of the people, and to a large extent, of the people themselves; but still, we demand that some steps be taken in this direction: therefore,—

Resolved,—That we declare war with the wages system, which demoralizes alike the hirer and the hired, cheats both, and enslaves the working-man; war with the present system of finance, which robs labor, and gorges capital, makes the rich richer, and the poor poorer, and turns a republic into an aristocracy of capital; war with these lavish grants of the public lands to speculating companies, and whenever in power, we pledge ourselves to use every just and legal means to resume all such grants heretofore made; war with the system of enriching capitalists by the creation and increase of public interest-bearing debts. We demand that every facility, and all encouragement, shall be given by law to co-operation in all branches of industry and trade, and that the same aid be given to co-operative efforts that has heretofore been given to railroads and other enterprises. We demand a ten-hour day for factory-work, as a first step, and that eight hours be the working-day of all persons thus employed hereafter. We demand that, whenever women are employed at public expense to do the same kind and amount of work as men perform, they shall receive the same wages. We demand that all public debts be paid at once in accordance with the terms of the contract, and that no more debts be created. Viewing the contract importation of coolies as only another form of the slave-trade, we demand that all contracts made relative thereto be void in this country; and that no public ship, and no steamship which receives public subsidy, shall aid in such importation.

I regard the movement with which this convention is connected as the grandest and most comprehensive movement of the age. And I choose my epithets deliberately; for I can hardly name the idea in which humanity is interested, which I do not consider locked up in the success of this movement of the people to take possession of their own.

All over the world, in every civilized land, every man can see, no matter how thoughtless, that the great movement of the masses, in some shape or other, has begun. Humanity goes by logical steps, and centuries ago the masses claimed emancipation from actual chains. It was citizenship, nothing else. When that was gained, they claimed the ballot; and when our fathers won that, then the road was opened, the field was clear for this last movement, toward which the age cannot be said to grope, as we used to phrase it, but toward which the age lifts itself all over the world.

If there is any one feature which we can distinguish in all Christendom, under different names,—trades-unions, co-operation, Crispins, and Internationals,—under all flags, there is one great movement. It is for the people peaceably to take possession of their own. No more riots in the streets; no more disorder and revolution; no more arming of different bands; no cannon loaded to the lips. To-day the people have chosen a wiser method,—they have got the ballot in their right hands, and they say, "We come to take possession of the governments of the earth." In the interests of peace, I welcome this movement,—the peaceable marshalling of all voters toward remodelling the industrial and political civilization of the day. I have not a word to utter,—far be it from me!—against the grandest declaration of popular indignation which Paris wrote on the pages of history in fire and blood. I honor Paris as the vanguard of the Internationals of the world. When kings wake at night, startled and aghast, they do not dream of Germany and its orderly array or forces. Aristocracy wakes up aghast at the memory of France; and when I want to find the vanguard of the people, I look to the uneasy dreams of an aristocracy, and find what they dread most. And today the conspiracy of emperors is to put down—what? Not the Czar, not the Emperor William, not the armies of United Germany; but, when the emperors come together in the centre of Europe, what plot do they lay? To annihilate the Internationals, and France is the soul of the Internationals. I, for one, honor Paris; but in the name of Heaven, and with the ballot in our right hands, we shall not need to write our record in fire and blood; we write it in the orderly majorities at the ballot-box.

Glossary

coolies	an offensive term referring to unskilled Asian workers
Crispins	the Knights of St. Crispin, a shoemakers union
Czar	the ruler of the Russian empire, at the time, Alexander II
Emperor William	Wilhelm I, the first emperor of Germany
Internationals	a general reference to internationally organized trade and labor unions

James Polk (Library of Congress)

JAMES POLK   1795–1849

Eleventh President of the United States

Featured Documents
- ◆ **Inaugural Address (1845)**
- ◆ **Message to Congress on War with Mexico (1846)**
- ◆ **Farewell Message to Congress (1848)**

Overview

James Knox Polk—congressional representative, governor of Tennessee, and eleventh president of the United States—was born in 1795 in North Carolina. During his youth, he suffered from poor health, so his formal education did not begin until he was well into his teenage years. Nevertheless, his academic achievements were such that he was given advanced placement at the University of North Carolina. There he joined the Dialectic Society, a debating group, giving him experience in public speaking. He turned his oratorical skills to good use in 1819, when his exquisitely worded arguments helped him win election as the clerk of the Tennessee state senate. Then, in 1824, Polk was elected to the U.S. House of Representatives, an office he held for fourteen years, culminating with four years as Speaker of the House from 1835 to 1839. During these years he was a Jacksonian Democrat and a firm advocate of states' rights. When the Democratic Party in Tennessee asked him to run for governor in 1839, he did so, and he won by arguing for states' rights. Nationally, though, the Democratic Party was in decline, so when he ran for reelection in 1841 and again in 1843, he fell victim to that decline and lost. His political career seemed to be at an end.

By 1844 Polk was a wealthy man. He had built on his father's land speculations and expanded his family's holdings in property, including slaves. His thinking about slavery and its place in American life was complex and at times seemingly contradictory. On the one hand, as president he opposed the Wilmot Proviso, which would have outlawed slavery in all the new territories west of Texas, because he believed the proviso was unnecessarily inflammatory. It was his view that the climate in lands west of Texas would make slavery impractical. Therefore, it would never take hold in any of the new additions to the United States. On the other hand, he proposed extension of the Missouri Compromise, which would have outlawed slavery above the 36°30' line west of Missouri but permitted it below the line. Such an extension would have given Texas and the Southwest the option of becoming slave states if they so wished.

Polk won the presidential election partly because he favored annexation of Texas. His election gave the outgoing president, John Tyler, the justification he needed to push the annexation of Texas through Congress during the last weeks of his administration. This left Polk with four objectives for his own administration: settle the dispute with Great Britain over the Oregon Territory; acquire California from Mexico; reduce protective tariffs to produce just enough revenues to pay for the federal government, making foreign goods more affordable to most Americans; and establish a national treasury for holding government funds rather than putting the people's money in private banks, which had led to corruption. He raised these issues in his inaugural address and farewell address, and war with Mexico was the topic of his 1846 message to Congress

Polk was an independent thinker, which made him a maverick even in his own party. For instance, his ideas on states' rights evolved during his presidency and differed from those of many other states' rights advocates, to the point where Polk regarded states' rights as a matter of secondary importance. While others held that the states were the most important protectors of the rights of minorities, Polk believed that it was the federal government—not states—that was the protector of minority rights, even of people who were minorities within a given state. Furthermore, many politicians in slave states, taking an extreme view of states' rights, believed that any state had the right to secede from the Union if its rights seemed to be denied by a majority of other states. Polk rejected this view, believing that no state had the right to secede once it was part of the Union. In his major writings, Polk repeatedly insisted that the federal government represented the will of the people, even to the point of outlawing slavery. Even so, he was a master of political compromise. His presidential documents are carefully phrased to allow most sides of a dispute to believe their desires had been satisfied.

Polk was also a leader who knew how to maneuver other political leaders into doing what he wanted. His 1846 message to Congress about war against Mexico and his 1848 annual message to Congress both show how his thinking led him to the conclusion that the presidency had to be equal in power to Congress because the president was elected by a vote of all American citizens. Therefore, the president was the only figure who could speak to the needs and desires of all Americans. In these documents, he shifts the balance of power between Congress and the president, giving the president control over the military as well as the prosecution of a war and making Congress more of an adviser to the president in military matters than the controller of military affairs. He did this by making anyone in Congress who opposed him appear to be unpatriotic. In the process, he advocated a view of the United States as an

1795
- **November 2**
  James Knox Polk is born in Mecklenburg County, near Charlotte, North Carolina.

1818
- **May**
  Polk graduates from the University of North Carolina.

1820
- **June**
  Polk is admitted to the Tennessee bar.

1823
- **August**
  Polk is elected to the Tennessee legislature.

1825
- **August 4**
  Polk is elected to the U.S. House of Representatives.

1835
- **December 7**
  Polk is elected Speaker of the U.S. House of Representatives.

1839
- **August 1**
  Polk is elected governor of Tennessee.

1841
- **August 5**
  Polk loses reelection as governor to James Chamberlain Jones.

1843
- **August 5**
  Polk is again defeated by Jones for the governorship of Tennessee.

1844
- **May 29**
  Polk is nominated for president of the United States at the Democratic National Convention in Baltimore.

- **November**
  Different states hold the presidential election on different days, ending with Polk's election to the presidency of the United States.

expansionist power that should help the peoples of the world to become free. In Polk's view, the United States should be an advocate of democracy for all peoples.

Explanation and Analysis of Documents

In his own day, Polk was noted for his skills as a debater; his written works are usually intended to convert his audience to his point of view. Before becoming president, he was an ardent advocate of states' rights and of limiting the federal government only to the powers specifically given it by the Constitution. As president, he believed it was his duty to forsake his personal biases and be the representative of all the American people. He expanded the powers of the presidency, especially to wage war. In the course of his life, he developed a vision of the United States as a place where the liberties of minorities were protected by the government, where all disputes would be worked out according to the Constitution, and where secession of states was impossible. He also believed that the United States was a great power with an important role to play in international affairs.

Polk worked extremely hard on his writings, which were the result of intense research and great care in phrasing, making him one of the most quotable politicians of his era. He created sharp, concise phrases that summed up the points he wished to make. As a visionary, he tried to stir in Americans a belief that the United States had a great destiny, and he was a patriot who encouraged Americans to revere the Constitution and to reject all notions of secession by any state.

◆ Inaugural Address

Polk was a master at coining phrases that would stick in the memory of his audience, and his presidential inaugural address of March 4, 1845, represents the pinnacle of his abilities; it became a classic American document by combining unabashed patriotism with a pragmatic statement of principles. In it Polk is both cheerleader and statesman. In the first portion of the excerpts from his address, he carves out a position with regard to states' rights. He vows that he will "assume no powers not expressly granted or clearly implied" in the Constitution. He promises that he will avoid "substituting the mere discretion and caprice of the Executive or of majorities in the legislative department of the Government for powers which have been withheld from the Federal Government by the Constitution." At the same time, he urges the states not to claim powers that the Constitution does not grant them: "While the General Government should abstain from the exercise of authority not clearly delegated to it, the States should be equally careful that in the maintenance of their rights they do not overstep the limits of powers reserved to them." He then makes a glancing reference to slavery, though he does not use the word:

It is a source of deep regret that in some sections of our country misguided persons have occasionally indulged in schemes and agitations whose object is the destruction of domestic institutions existing in other sections—institutions which existed at the adoption of the Constitution and were recognized and protected by it.

Polk then turns his attention to Texas. At the time, there was much fear that Great Britain and France might intervene in U.S. affairs with their armies and navies. Thus, Polk's focus on Texas is not only a matter of laying the political groundwork for war against Mexico but also a warning to outside powers that their intervention in Texas would be met by U.S. force. During the last weeks of his presidency, John Tyler, Polk's predecessor, had pushed the annexation of Texas through Congress, and Polk wished to move quickly to resolve all issues that might slow Texas's admission as a full state rather than as a territory. The admission of Texas as a state would eliminate the Republic of Texas as a potential rival to the United States, would enable the United States to better defend its southern territories, and would open avenues to territories west of Texas. Polk's remarks that Texas chose to join the Union freely, without bloodshed, were intended to put his government in a posture of wanting peace and only reluctantly going to war if it had to. His desire to acquire territory in Oregon and Mexico was well known, and he wanted to be able to claim that the United States would settle its claims against other governments peacefully if it could, instead of first resorting to war. Polk makes his position clear:

> Foreign powers should therefore look on the annexation of Texas to the United States not as the conquest of a nation seeking to extend her dominions by arms and violence, but as the peaceful acquisition of a territory once her own, by adding another member to our confederation, with the consent of that member, thereby diminishing the chances of war and opening to them new and ever-increasing markets for their products.

Modern historians have the advantage of knowing that Mexico was nearly bankrupt and could not match the advanced military technology of the United States. Although Mexico had accepted the notion that Texas might become an independent nation, it had threatened war if Texas were annexed by the United States. In 1845 it seemed likely that both Great Britain and France would actively intervene to support Mexico if Mexico tried to reclaim Texas to gain territory in the Southwest for itself, with Great Britain perhaps trying to claim California as well. These seemed to be real possibilities to Americans, and Polk wants all concerned to know where the blame will lie if war breaks out.

By treaty, the United States and Great Britain jointly occupied the Oregon Territory. In Congress, Polk needed the votes of Democrats from the northwestern states of the Union if his plans to acquire California were to succeed, and those Democrats were very interested in having the United States acquire all the Oregon Territory. Thus, from

Time Line

1845

■ **March 4**
Polk is sworn in as president and delivers his inaugural address.

■ **December 29**
Texas is admitted as a state to the United States.

1846

■ **January 13**
Polk orders Zachary Taylor to advance his military forces to the Rio Grande.

■ **May 10**
Polk learns of an attack on American forces by Mexico, near the Rio Grande.

■ **May 11**
Polk sends an official message to Congress asking for a declaration of war against Mexico.

■ **June 15**
The Oregon Treaty is agreed to by the United States and Great Britain.

1848

■ **February 2**
The Treaty of Guadalupe Hidalgo is agreed to by the United States and Mexico.

■ **December 5**
Polk delivers his farewell message to Congress.

1849

■ **June 15**
Polk dies in Nashville, Tennessee.

this opening moment of his administration, Polk begins a delicate tightrope walk. It is unlikely that Polk ever intended to try to acquire all the Oregon Territory, which could have started a war with Great Britain and left the United States to fight on two fronts, one in Oregon and the other in Texas. Still, Polk tries to please northern Democrats by noting the U.S. claims against Great Britain, even while setting in motion negotiations to divide the Oregon Territory, thereby securing U.S. borders north of California. Thus, Polk states that it is his "duty to assert and maintain by all constitutional means the right of the United States to that portion of our territory which lies beyond the Rocky Mountains. Our title to the country of the Oregon is 'clear and unquestionable.'"

Foreseeing the challenges that a truly continent-spanning nation would have, Polk in other sections of his address lays out other plans, grand in their conception and pragmatic in their purpose, that he hopes the United States will follow, such as the creation of overland mail routes from east to west to help bind the country together. He foresaw that swift communications could prove crucial during war. Perhaps of greatest importance in the address is Polk's reiteration of the Monroe Doctrine. What came to be called the Monroe Doctrine was a statement of principle made by James Monroe that from the time of his presidency onward all of the Americas were off-limits to new colonization by powers outside the Americas. After Monroe's era, the doctrine had been almost forgotten. In his address, Polk revives the doctrine and gives it new emphasis, making it into a fundamental doctrine of U.S. foreign policy from his time on.

Much of the rest of the address is devoted to economic matters. Protective tariffs had long been an area of contention between industrialists and farmers. Southerners, in particular, hoped that Polk would ease such tariffs to make imported goods more affordable. Although some saw Polk as appeasing southerners with his desire to lower tariffs, his wanting lower tariffs actually stemmed from two principles he held dear. One was that the federal government had a duty to protect the weak and poor. Lowering tariffs meant improving the standard of living for ordinary Americans, something that Polk saw as his moral duty as the guardian of the rights and lives of average Americans. The other principle was that government should be conservative with money. In 1845 the federal government depended on tariffs to pay for its functions, and Polk wanted the government to take in no more money than necessary to pay its debts and to avoid deficit spending.

In his inaugural address, Polk accomplished what few other presidents succeeded in doing by laying out a clear, specific agenda. In the ensuing four years, he would consult with Congress and other political leaders and work tirelessly to find ways to accomplish that agenda. More to the point, he did, in fact, largely accomplish the goals he set out for the nation in his inaugural address.

◆ Message to Congress on War with Mexico

Polk begins his war message of May 11, 1846, by summarizing the diplomatic steps that had been taken in recent months to deal with the "unredressed wrongs and injuries committed by the Mexican Government on citizens of the United States in their persons and property." He notes that Mexico refused to receive the American envoy and emphasizes the efforts of American diplomats to adjust the nation's differences with Mexico. Their work was unavailing and Mexico "after a long-continued series of menaces [had] at last invaded our territory and shed the blood of our fellow-citizens on our own soil." War with Mexico was thus already a fact.

Polk then provides Congress with details about U.S. war preparations. He lays out specifics about the boundary between Texas and Mexico, and he declares that he has given General Zachary Taylor orders to prosecute a war if Mexico invades Texas, justifying his orders as being pru-

dent and intended to give Mexico ample opportunity to negotiate rather than wage war. Additionally, he details the actions of Mexican forces along the border and encounters between U.S. and Mexican forces. He sums up his discussion of these activities by asserting that "the grievous wrongs perpetrated by Mexico upon our citizens throughout a long period of years remain unredressed, and solemn treaties pledging her public faith for this redress have been disregarded." He asserts that "we have tried every effort at reconciliation" and again emphasizes that Texas had willingly decided to cast its lot with the United States.

Perhaps the most important aspect of Polk's message asking Congress to declare war on Mexico is its subtle shifting of the responsibility of making war from Congress to the president. When the message was presented to Congress, the ascendancy of the president to preeminence in the decision to wage war was emphasized by the fact that Polk's supporters limited debate to two hours and then took up all but half an hour with reading Polk's documents. Members of Congress found themselves in the unpleasant position of either approving a war that they had not discussed or of appearing to be unpatriotic. Some members of the Whig Party tried to separate the issue of the war itself from the financial and political support of the war, perhaps hoping to provide themselves with time to counter Polk's arguments. Their effort failed, and Congress followed Polk's lead by declaring war. This marked a major shift in power between the president and Congress that was not to be more fully exploited until the next strong president, Abraham Lincoln, came along.

Initially, Polk's willingness to go to war with Mexico badly divided the nation. Some members of Congress resisted what they regarded as Polk's seizure of constitutional authority to wage war, and abolitionists saw the war as part of a conspiracy to extend slavery. Nevertheless, the war itself was popular. It was fought largely with volunteers, giving it a democratic feel, and many Americans regarded it as a romantic, swashbuckling affair that extended republicanism to a beleaguered people.

◆ Farewell Message to Congress

Today this message would be called a State of the Union address, but in Polk's era, presidents did not deliver their annual message as a speech to Congress. Instead, the message was printed and distributed to members of Congress for them to read. Polk's annual message to Congress of December 5, 1848—his farewell message—is one of his most complex writings. In it, he recounts the achievements of his administration, urges the nation and Congress not to allow the issue of slavery to divide them, exhorts Congress not to undo his economic initiatives, and defends his use of the veto as part of his duty to protect the American people from bad legislation.

Polk opens by praising the United States, where "peace, plenty, and contentment reign throughout our borders." He congratulates the nation for its internal peace, in contrast to the turmoil taking place in Europe; in 1848 the countries of Europe were rocked by revolution, with rioting in

American troops storm Chapultepec, an ancient fortress in the suburbs of Mexico City. This battle, fought on September 13, 1847, was the last important conflict of the Mexican-American War. (AP/Wide World Photos)

the streets of Paris, France; Vienna, Austria; and Berlin and Frankfurt in Germany. In the United States, by contrast, "we settle all our political controversies by the peaceful exercise of the rights of freemen at the ballot box."

Polk's account of U.S. relations with Mexico was predictable. The United States had won the war so overwhelmingly that Polk could afford to speak of Mexico no longer as a tyrannical enemy but as a newfound friend. Of greater concern was the matter of slavery in the territories the United States had acquired. He tries to defuse the slavery issue, which he notes could divide the United States. Personally, he believed that the nature of the land in the Southwest would make slavery untenable, but he here adopts a moderate states' rights position by reminding his audience that "the question, involving, as it does, a principle of equality of rights of the separate and several States as equal copartners in the Confederacy, should not be disregarded." He foresees the issue of slavery dividing the nation, and in this message he pleads with both sides to allow the constitutional institutions of the United States—reflecting the will of the people—to work out whether slavery survives. He hopes that whatever happens, all sides accept, however unwillingly, the result of the democratic process.

Much of the central portion of Polk's farewell address, which is not excerpted here, is taken up by sta-

tistics and similar details of the everyday management of government. It is typical of Polk to cite statistical data in his writings. This was in part a legacy of his days in college, when he achieved much success by researching topics in minute detail and then overwhelming his audiences with the facts he had accumulated. It was also in part because he believed it was his duty to put in the public record a careful accounting of what statistics indicated about the nature of the U.S. population and about the expenditure of U.S. wealth. He deemed it important that his administration improve the economic lot of average Americans, and through his statistics he hoped to guide Congress to focus on the economic welfare of average Americans.

In the final portion of his message, Polk pleads with Congress not to undo the changes in the nation's economy created by his administration and defends his use of the veto. He asserts that it is the constitutional duty of the president to exercise veto power when necessary:

It is not alone hasty and inconsiderate legislation that he is required to check; but if at any time Congress shall, after apparently full deliberation, resolve on measures which he deems subversive of the Constitution or of the vital interests of the

"*The Constitution itself, plainly written as it is, the safeguard of our federative compact, the offspring of concession and compromise, binding together in the bonds of peace and union this great and increasing family of free and independent States, will be the chart by which I shall be directed.*"

(Inaugural Address)

"*One great object of the Constitution was to restrain majorities from oppressing minorities or encroaching upon their just rights. Minorities have a right to appeal to the Constitution as a shield against such oppression.*"

(Inaugural Address)

"*But now, after reiterated menaces, Mexico has passed the boundary of the United States, has invaded our territory and shed American blood upon the American soil.*"

(Message to Congress on War with Mexico)

"*A volunteer force is beyond question more efficient than any other description of citizen soldiers, and it is not to be doubted that a number far beyond that required would readily rush to the field upon the call of their country.*"

(Message to Congress on War with Mexico)

"*We are the most favored people on the face of the earth.*"

(Farewell Message to Congress)

"*The war with Mexico has thus fully developed the capacity of republican governments to prosecute successfully a just and necessary foreign war with all the vigor usually attributed to more arbitrary forms of government.*"

(Farewell Message to Congress)

"*The preservation of the Constitution from infraction is the President's highest duty.*"

(Farewell Message to Congress)

country, it is his solemn duty to stand in the breach and resist them.

In each case, he insists that he has fulfilled his constitutional duty as president. He had used the veto as a weapon to sink proposals he deemed to be economically unsound or as oppressive to minorities. In effect, Polk transmutes his discussion of constitutionally granted veto power into a celebration of the chief executive as a representative of all the people and as a defender of the rights of minority interests.

Impact and Legacy

Modern historians often see in Polk's presidency a turning point in American history, because through the veto as well as his extraordinary political skills, Polk made the office of president at least equal in power to Congress. During his presidency, Polk alienated both ardent abolitionists and advocates of slavery. On the one hand, his opposition to the Wilmot Proviso angered abolitionists, who castigated him long after his death. On the other hand, he wanted the new states of the West to choose for themselves whether to allow slavery (while believing that they would not), which made

many slave-state leaders regard him as a traitor. He pursued what at the time was a moderate course in order to avoid generating unnecessary and fruitless conflict that would distract the nation from what Polk believed needed to be done. Many historians vilified him for the war against Mexico, because they believed the war had been unjust; they regarded Polk as an imperialist, a view that Polk would probably have agreed with. He openly wanted the United States to extend clear across North America, from ocean to ocean, and he had plainly wanted to acquire the California ports of San Francisco, Monterey, and San Diego. To this day, many historians believe the war against Mexico was morally unjustified, even though the results were of great benefit to the United States.

After the Civil War, Polk fell into the background as a supposedly embarrassing president because he had led the United States into a perhaps immoral war and had not resolved the issue of slavery, allowing it to fester for future generations. During the twentieth century, however, Polk's reputation in the views of historians rose; many rank him among the United States' ten best presidents. Polk accomplished everything he set out to do, and he also helped Americans view themselves as a unified people. He took the power to wage war out of the hands of Congress and put it in the hands of the president. His policies greatly

Questions for Further Study

1. Throughout his single term as president, Polk walked a fine line with regard to the issue of slavery. On the one hand, he was a slave owner himself and saw slavery as a necessary evil. On the other, he resisted siding with any faction in the debate over slavery. Outline Polk's public views on slavery as hinted at in his inaugural address and in his farewell message to Congress. Then, suggest why you believe Polk took these positions in public, given the intense debate over slavery that was taking place before, during, and after his administration.

2. Compare Polk's first inaugural address with the first inaugural address of Abraham Lincoln. How are the views of the two presidents about slavery similar? Do you detect any differences in their positions on the slavery issue?

3. According to Polk, what was the role of the federal government with respect to minority rights and interests as expressed in his inaugural address and his farewell message to Congress? What does Polk mean by "minorities," and why do you believe that he was concerned about these rights, given the tension between the federal government and the states during these years?

4. On what basis did Polk justify going to war with Mexico over Texas in his message to congress on war with Mexico? Some of Polk's contemporaries believed that the war was a pretense to extend slavery to the Southwest. How would Polk have responded to this charge?

5. Throughout American history, the balance of power between the chief executive and Congress has changed; sometimes the president asserts powers, and at other times Congress reins in the power of the president. How did Polk help assert the power of the presidency in his message to Congress on war with Mexico and in his farewell message to Congress?

expanded the United States and made it a power on both the Atlantic and Pacific oceans. He placed the government on a secure financial foundation. His redefinition of the Treasury Department and his creation of the Department of the Interior continue to affect national policy. It is difficult to say whether his moderation on the issue of slavery benefited or harmed the nation; like many others in his time, he believed economic forces would quietly end slavery only a few generations after his. As matters turned out, the issue of slavery polarized the country even more than it had before Polk became president, and his leaving the issue for future generations to decide may have contributed to the festering resentment on both sides that eventually resulted in war. It is possible that Polk prevented the outbreak of civil war during his own presidency.

Key Sources

The Diary of James K. Polk during His Presidency, 1845–1849, edited by Milo Milton Quaife (1910), abridged as *Polk: The Diary of a President, 1845–1849*, edited by Allan Nevins (1929), focuses on Polk's years as president and was written by Polk for publication. The standard edition of Polk's letters is *Correspondence of James K. Polk*, 10 vols, edited by Herbert Weaver (four volumes) and Wayne Cutler (six volumes) (1969–2004).

Further Reading

■ Books

Bergeron, Paul H. *The Presidency of James K. Polk*. Lawrence: University Press of Kansas, 1987.

Borneman, Walter R. *Polk: The Man Who Transformed the Presidency and America*. New York: Random House, 2008.

Haynes, Sam W. *James K. Polk and the Expansionist Impulse*. New York: Longman, 1997.

Howe, Daniel Walker. *What Hath God Wrought: The Transformation of America, 1815–1848*. New York: Oxford University Press, 2007.

Leonard, Thomas M. *James K. Polk: A Clear and Unquestionable Destiny*. Wilmington, Del.: S. R. Books, 2001.

McCormac, Eugene Irving. *James K. Polk: A Political Biography*. Berkeley: University of California Press, 1922.

McCoy, Charles A. *Polk and the Presidency*. Austin: University of Texas Press, 1960.

Seigenthaler, John. *James K. Polk*. New York: Times Books, 2004.

■ Web Sites

"American Presidents: James Knox Polk." Miller Center of Public Affairs: American President: An Online Resource Web site.
    http://millercenter.org/index.php/academic/americanpresident/polk.

—Kirk H. Beetz and Michael J. O'Neal

INAUGURAL ADDRESS (1845)

Fellow-Citizens:...

The Constitution itself, plainly written as it is, the safeguard of our federative compact, the offspring of concession and compromise, binding together in the bonds of peace and union this great and increasing family of free and independent States, will be the chart by which I shall be directed.

It will be my first care to administer the Government in the true spirit of that instrument, and to assume no powers not expressly granted or clearly implied in its terms. The Government of the United States is one of delegated and limited powers, and it is by a strict adherence to the clearly granted powers and by abstaining from the exercise of doubtful or unauthorized implied powers that we have the only sure guaranty against the recurrence of those unfortunate collisions between the Federal and State authorities which have occasionally so much disturbed the harmony of our system and even threatened the perpetuity of our glorious Union.

"To the States, respectively, or to the people" have been reserved "the powers not delegated to the United States by the Constitution nor prohibited by it to the States." Each State is a complete sovereignty within the sphere of its reserved powers. The Government of the Union, acting within the sphere of its delegated authority, is also a complete sovereignty. While the General Government should abstain from the exercise of authority not clearly delegated to it, the States should be equally careful that in the maintenance of their rights they do not overstep the limits of powers reserved to them. One of the most distinguished of my predecessors attached deserved importance to "the support of the State governments in all their rights, as the most competent administration for our domestic concerns and the surest bulwark against antirepublican tendencies," and to the "preservation of the General Government in its whole constitutional vigor, as the sheet anchor of our peace at home and safety abroad."...

This most admirable and wisest system of well-regulated self-government among men ever devised by human minds has been tested by its successful operation for more than half a century, and if preserved from the usurpations of the Federal Government on the one hand and the exercise by the States of powers not reserved to them on the other, will, I fervently hope and believe, endure for ages to come and dispense the blessings of civil and religious liberty to distant generations. To effect objects so dear to every patriot I shall devote myself with anxious solicitude. It will be my desire to guard against that most fruitful source of danger to the harmonious action of our system which consists in substituting the mere discretion and caprice of the Executive or of majorities in the legislative department of the Government for powers which have been withheld from the Federal Government by the Constitution. By the theory of our Government majorities rule, but this right is not an arbitrary or unlimited one. It is a right to be exercised in subordination to the Constitution and in conformity to it. One great object of the Constitution was to restrain majorities from oppressing minorities or encroaching upon their just rights. Minorities have a right to appeal to the Constitution as a shield against such oppression.

That the blessings of liberty which our Constitution secures may be enjoyed alike by minorities and majorities, the Executive has been wisely invested with a qualified veto upon the acts of the Legislature. It is a negative power, and is conservative in its character. It arrests for the time hasty, inconsiderate, or unconstitutional legislation, invites reconsideration, and transfers questions at issue between the legislative and executive departments to the tribunal of the people. Like all other powers, it is subject to be abused. When judiciously and properly exercised, the Constitution itself may be saved from infraction and the rights of all preserved and protected....

It is a source of deep regret that in some sections of our country misguided persons have occasionally indulged in schemes and agitations whose object is the destruction of domestic institutions existing in other sections—institutions which existed at the adoption of the Constitution and were recognized and protected by it. All must see that if it were possible for them to be successful in attaining their object the dissolution of the Union and the consequent destruction of our happy form of government must speedily follow....

The Republic of Texas has made known her desire to come into our Union, to form a part of our Confederacy and enjoy with us the blessings of liberty secured and guaranteed by our Constitution. Texas was once a part of our country—was unwisely ceded away to a foreign power—is now independent, and possesses an undoubted right to dispose of a part or the whole of her territory and to merge her sovereignty as a separate and independent state in ours. I congratulate my country that by an act of the late Congress of the United States the assent of this Government has been given to the reunion, and it only remains for the two countries to agree upon the terms to consummate an object so important to both.

I regard the question of annexation as belonging exclusively to the United States and Texas. They are independent powers competent to contract, and foreign nations have no right to interfere with them or to take exceptions to their reunion. Foreign powers do not seem to appreciate the true character of our Government. Our Union is a confederation of independent States, whose policy is peace with each other and all the world. To enlarge its limits is to extend the dominions of peace over additional territories and increasing millions. The world has nothing to fear from military ambition in our Government. While the Chief Magistrate and the popular branch of Congress are elected for short terms by the suffrages of those millions who must in their own persons bear all the burdens and miseries of war, our Government can not be otherwise than pacific. Foreign powers should therefore look on the annexation of Texas to the United States not as the conquest of a nation seeking to extend her dominions by arms and violence, but as the peaceful acquisition of a territory once her own, by adding another member to our confederation, with the consent of that member, thereby diminishing the chances of war and opening to them new and ever-increasing markets for their products....

Nor will it become in a less degree my duty to assert and maintain by all constitutional means the right of the United States to that portion of our territory which lies beyond the Rocky Mountains. Our title to the country of the Oregon is "clear and unquestionable," and already are our people preparing to perfect that title by occupying it with their wives and children. But eighty years ago our population was confined on the west by the ridge of the Alleghenies. Within that period—within the lifetime, I might say, of some of my hearers—our people, increasing to many millions, have filled the eastern valley of the Mississippi, adventurously ascended the Missouri to its headsprings, and are already engaged in establishing the blessings of self-government in valleys of which the rivers flow to the Pacific. The world beholds the peaceful triumphs of the industry of our emigrants. To us belongs the duty of protecting them adequately wherever they may be upon our soil. The jurisdiction of our laws and the benefits of our republican institutions should be extended over

Glossary

Alleghenies	part of the Appalachian Mountain Range, in the eastern United States and in the early nineteenth century an informal boundary with the West
Chief Magistrate	the president of the United States
Confederacy	here, the confederation, or union, of the American states (as opposed to the Confederacy of southern states during the Civil War)
consummate	fulfill, complete
federative compact	the union of the states into a federation, with partially self-governing states united under a federal government
pacific	peaceful
"the support of the State governments in all their rights..."	quotation from Thomas Jefferson's first inaugural address
"To the States, respectively, or to the people"	quotation from the Tenth Amendment to the U.S. Constitution
usurpations	trespasses, seizures of power

them in the distant regions which they have selected for their homes. The increasing facilities of intercourse will easily bring the States, of which the formation in that part of our territory can not be long delayed, within the sphere of our federative Union. In the meantime every obligation imposed by treaty or conventional stipulations should be sacredly respected....

Although in our country the Chief Magistrate [president] must almost of necessity be chosen by a party and stand pledged to its principles and measures, yet in his official action he should not be the President of a part only, but of the whole people of the United States. While he executes the laws with an impartial hand, shrinks from no proper responsibility, and faithfully carries out in the executive department of the Government the principles and policy of those who have chosen him, he should not be unmindful that our fellow-citizens who have differed with him in opinion are entitled to the full and free exercise of their opinions and judgments, and that the rights of all are entitled to respect and regard.

MESSAGE TO CONGRESS ON WAR WITH MEXICO (1846)

To the Senate and House of Representatives:

The existing state of the relations between the United States and Mexico renders it proper that I should bring the subject to the consideration of Congress. In my message at the commencement of your present session the state of these relations; the causes which led to the suspension of diplomatic intercourse between the two countries in March, 1845, and the long-continued and unredressed wrongs and injuries committed by the Mexican Government on citizens of the United States in their persons and property were briefly set forth....

The strong desire to establish peace with Mexico on liberal and honorable terms, and the readiness of this Government to regulate and adjust our boundary and other causes of difference with that power on such fair and equitable principles as would lead to permanent relations of the most friendly nature, induced me in September last to seek the reopening of diplomatic relations between the two countries. Every measure adopted on our part had for its object the furtherance of these desired results. In communicating to Congress a succinct statement of the injuries which we had suffered from Mexico, and which have been accumulating during a period of more than twenty years, every expression that could tend to inflame the people of Mexico or defeat or delay a pacific result was carefully avoided. An envoy of the United States repaired to Mexico with full powers to adjust every existing difference. But though present on the Mexican soil by agreement between the two Governments, invested with full powers, and bearing evidence of the most friendly dispositions, his mission has been unavailing. The Mexican Government not only refused to receive him or listen to his propositions, but after a long-continued series of menaces have at last invaded our territory and shed the blood of our fellow-citizens on our own soil....

Thus the Government of Mexico, though solemnly pledged by official acts in October last to receive and accredit an American envoy, violated their plighted faith and refused the offer of a peaceful adjustment of our difficulties. Not only was the offer rejected, but the indignity of its rejection was enhanced by the manifest breach of faith in refusing to admit the envoy who came because they had bound themselves to receive him. Nor can it be said that the offer was fruitless from the want of opportunity of discussing it; our envoy was present on their own soil. Nor can it be ascribed to a want of sufficient powers; our envoy had full powers to adjust every question of difference. Nor was there room for complaint that our propositions for settlement were unreasonable; permission was not even given our envoy to make any proposition whatever. Nor can it be objected that we, on our part, would not listen to any reasonable terms of their suggestion; the Mexican Government refused all negotiation, and have made no proposition of any kind. In my message at the commencement of the present session I informed you that upon the earnest appeal both of the Congress and convention of Texas I had ordered an efficient military force to take a position between the Nueces and the Del Norte. This had become necessary to meet a threatened invasion of Texas by the Mexican forces, for which extensive military preparations had been made. The invasion was threatened solely because Texas had determined, in accordance with a solemn resolution of the Congress of the United States, to annex herself to our Union, and under these circumstances it was plainly our duty to extend our protection over her citizens and soil.

This force was concentrated at Corpus Christi, and remained there until after I had received such information from Mexico as rendered it probable, if not certain, that the Mexican Government would refuse to receive our envoy. Meantime Texas, by the final action of our Congress, had become an integral part of our Union. The Congress of Texas, by its act of December 19, 1836, had declared the Rio del Norte to be the boundary of that Republic. Its jurisdiction had been extended and exercised beyond the Nueces. The country between that river and the Del Norte had been represented in the Congress and in the convention of Texas, had thus taken part in the act of annexation itself, and is now included within one of our Congressional districts. Our own Congress had, moreover, with great unanimity, by the act approved December 31, 1845, recognized the country beyond the Nueces as a part of our territory by including it within our own revenue system, and a revenue officer to reside within that district has been appointed by and with the advice and consent of the Senate. It became, therefore, of urgent necessity to provide for the defense of that portion of our country. Accordingly, on the 13th of January last instructions were issued to the general in command of these troops to occupy the left bank of the Del Norte. This river, which is the southwestern boundary of the State of Texas, is an exposed frontier.

From this quarter invasion was threatened; upon it and in its immediate vicinity, in the judgment of high military experience, are the proper stations for the protecting forces of the Government. In addition to this important consideration, several others occurred to induce this movement. Among these are the facilities afforded by the ports at Brazos Santiago and the mouth of the Del Norte for the reception of supplies by sea, the stronger and more healthful military positions, the convenience for obtaining a ready and a more abundant supply of provisions, water, fuel, and forage, and the advantages which are afforded by the Del Norte in forwarding supplies to such posts as may be established in the interior and upon the Indian frontier....

The Mexican forces at Matamoras assumed a belligerent attitude, and on the 12th of April General Ampudia, then in command, notified General Taylor to break up his camp within twenty-four hours and to retire beyond the Nueces River, and in the event of his failure to comply with these demands announced that arms, and arms alone, must decide the question. But no open act of hostility was committed until the 14th of April. On that day General Arista, who had succeeded to the command of the Mexican forces, communicated to General Taylor that he considered hostilities commenced and should prosecute them. A party of dragoons of 63 men and officers were on the same day dispatched from the American camp up the Rio del Norte, on its left bank, to ascertain whether the Mexican troops had crossed or were preparing to cross the river, became engaged with a large body of these troops, and after a short affair, in which some 16 were killed and wounded, appear to have been surrounded and compelled to surrender. The grievous wrongs perpetrated by Mexico upon our citizens throughout a long period of years remain unredressed, and solemn treaties pledging her public faith for this redress have been disregarded. A government either unable or unwilling to enforce the execution of such treaties fails to perform one of its plainest duties....

We have been exerting our best efforts to propitiate her [Mexico's] good will. Upon the pretext that Texas, a nation as independent as herself, thought proper to unite its destinies with our own she has affected to believe that we have severed her rightful territory, and in official proclamations and manifestoes has repeatedly threatened to make war upon us for the purpose of reconquering Texas. In the meantime we have tried every effort at reconciliation. The cup of forbearance had been exhausted even before the recent information from the frontier of the Del Norte. But now, after reiterated menaces, Mexico has passed the boundary of the United States, has invaded our territory and shed American

Glossary

Brazos Santiago	a port city on Brazos Island, off the coast of Texas
Corpus Christi	a city in southern Texas on the Gulf of Mexico
Del Norte	more formally, the Rio Bravo Del Norte, the Mexican name of the Rio Grande, which forms the border between Texas and Mexico
dragoons	cavalrymen who dismount and fight on foot
General Ampudia	Pedro de Ampudia
General Arista	Mariano Arista
General Taylor	Zachary Taylor, Polk's successor as U.S. president
Matamoras	a town at the eastern border between Mexico and Texas
Nueces	a river in Texas
pacific	peaceful
plighted	pledged

blood upon the American soil. She has proclaimed that hostilities have commenced, and that the two nations are now at war....

In further vindication of our rights and defense of our territory, I involve the prompt action of Congress to recognize the existence of the war, and to place at the disposition of the Executive the means of prosecuting the war with vigor, and thus hastening the restoration of peace. To this end I recommend that authority should be given to call into the public service a large body of volunteers to serve for not less than six or twelve months unless sooner discharged. A volunteer force is beyond question more efficient than any other description of citizen soldiers, and it is not to be doubted that a number far beyond that required would readily rush to the field upon the call of their country. I further recommend that a liberal provision be made for sustaining our entire military force and furnishing it with supplies and munitions of war.

The most energetic and prompt measures and the immediate appearance in arms of a large and overpowering force are recommended to Congress as the most certain and efficient means of bringing the existing collision with Mexico to a speedy and successful termination.

Farewell Message to Congress (1848)

Fellow-Citizens of the Senate and of the House of Representatives:...

Peace, plenty, and contentment reign throughout our borders, and our beloved country presents a sublime moral spectacle to the world....

In reviewing the great events of the past year and contrasting the agitated and disturbed state of other countries with our own tranquil and happy condition, we may congratulate ourselves that we are the most favored people on the face of the earth. While the people of other countries are struggling to establish free institutions, under which man may govern himself, we are in the actual enjoyment of them—a rich inheritance from our fathers. While enlightened nations of Europe are convulsed and distracted by civil war or intestine strife, we settle all our political controversies by the peaceful exercise of the rights of freemen at the ballot box.

The great republican maxim, so deeply engraven on the hearts of our people, that the will of the majority, constitutionally expressed, shall prevail, is our sure safeguard against force and violence. It is a subject of just pride that our fame and character as a nation continue rapidly to advance in the estimation of the civilized world....

The war with Mexico has thus fully developed the capacity of republican governments to prosecute successfully a just and necessary foreign war with all the vigor usually attributed to more arbitrary forms of government. It has been usual for writers on public law to impute to republics a want of that unity, concentration of purpose, and vigor of execution which are generally admitted to belong to the monarchical and aristocratic forms; and this feature of popular government has been supposed to display itself more particularly in the conduct of a war carried on in an enemy's territory. The war with Great Britain in 1812 was to a great extent confined within our own limits, and shed but little light on this subject; but the war which we have just closed by an honorable peace evinces beyond all doubt that a popular representative government is equal to any emergency which is likely to arise in the affairs of a nation....

The acquisition of California and New Mexico, the settlement of the Oregon boundary, and the annexation of Texas, extending to the Rio Grande, are results which, combined, are of greater conse-quence and will add more to the strength and wealth of the nation than any which have preceded them since the adoption of the Constitution....

The question is believed to be rather abstract than practical whether slavery ever can or would exist in any portion of the acquired territory even if it were left to the option of the slaveholding States themselves. From the nature of the climate and productions in much the larger portion of it it is certain it could never exist, and in the remainder the probabilities are it would not. But however this may be, the question, involving, as it does, a principle of equality of rights of the separate and several States as equal copartners in the Confederacy, should not be disregarded....

A well-digested cheap-postage system is the best means of diffusing intelligence among the people, and is of so much importance in a country so extensive as that of the United States that I recommend to your favorable consideration the suggestions of the Postmaster-General for its improvement.

Nothing can retard the onward progress of our country and prevent us from assuming and maintaining the first rank among nations but a disregard of the experience of the past and a recurrence to an unwise public policy. We have just closed a foreign war by an honorable peace—a war rendered necessary and unavoidable in vindication of the national rights and honor. The present condition of the country is similar in some respects to that which existed immediately after the close of the war with Great Britain in 1815, and the occasion is deemed to be a proper one to take a retrospect of the measures of public policy which followed that war. There was at that period of our history a departure from our earlier policy. The enlargement of the powers of the Federal Government by construction, which obtained, was not warranted by any just interpretation of the Constitution. A few years after the close of that war a series of measures was adopted which, united and combined, constituted what was termed by their authors and advocates the "American system."...

It was not possible to reconstruct society in the United States upon the European plan. Here there was a written Constitution, by which orders and titles were not recognized or tolerated. A system of measures was therefore devised, calculated, if not intended, to withdraw power gradually and silently from the States and the mass of the people, and by construction to approximate our Government to the European models, substituting an aristocracy of wealth for that of orders and titles....

The Constitution provides that—

Every bill which shall have passed the House of Representatives and the Senate shall, before it become a law, be presented to the President of the United States. If he approve he shall sign it, but if not he shall return it with his objections to that House in which it shall have originated, who shall enter the objections at large on their Journal and proceed to reconsider it.

The preservation of the Constitution from infraction is the President's highest duty. He is bound to discharge that duty at whatever hazard of incurring the displeasure of those who may differ with him in opinion. He is bound to discharge it as well by his obligations to the people who have clothed him with his exalted trust as by his oath of office, which he may not disregard. Nor are the obligations of the President in any degree lessened by the prevalence of views different from his own in one or both Houses of Congress. It is not alone hasty and inconsiderate legislation that he is required to check; but if at any time Congress shall, after apparently full deliberation, resolve on measures which he deems subversive of the Constitution or of the vital interests of the country, it is his solemn duty to stand in the breach and resist them. The President is bound to approve or disapprove every bill which passes Congress and is presented to him for his signature. The Constitution makes this his duty, and he can not escape it if he would. He has no election. In deciding upon any bill presented to him he must exercise his own best judgment. If he can not approve, the Constitution commands him to return the bill to the House in which it originated with his objections, and if he fail to do this within ten days (Sundays excepted) it shall become a law without his signature. Right or wrong, he may be overruled by a vote of two-thirds of each House, and in that event the bill becomes a law without his sanction. If his objections be not thus overruled, the subject is only post-poned, and is referred to the States and the people for their consideration and decision. The President's power is negative merely, and not affirmative. He can enact no law. The only effect, therefore, of his withholding his approval of a bill passed by Congress is to suffer the existing laws to remain unchanged, and the delay occasioned is only that required to enable the States and the people to consider and act upon the subject in the election of public agents who will carry out their wishes and instructions. Any attempt to coerce the President to yield his sanction to measures which he can not approve would be a violation of the spirit of the Constitution, palpable and flagrant, and if successful would break down the independence of the executive department and make the President, elected by the people and clothed by the Constitution with power to defend their rights, the mere instrument of a majority of Congress. A surrender on his part of the powers with which the Constitution has invested his office would effect a practical alteration of that instrument without resorting to the prescribed process of amendment....

If it be said that the Representatives in the popular branch of Congress are chosen directly by the people, it is answered, the people elect the President. If both Houses represent the States and the people, so does the President. The President represents in the executive department the whole people of the United States, as each member of the legislative department represents portions of them....

One great object of the Constitution in conferring upon the President a qualified negative upon the legislation of Congress was to protect minorities from injustice and oppression by majorities. The equality of their representation in the Senate and the veto power of the President are the constitutional guaranties which the smaller States have that their rights will be respected. Without these guaranties all their interests would be at the mercy of majorities in Congress representing the larger States. To the smaller and weaker States, therefore, the preservation of this power and its exercise upon proper occasions demanding it is of vital importance.

Glossary

American system	a plan for strengthening the United States, so called first by Henry Clay in 1824
intestine	having to do with a country's internal affairs
Oregon	in 1848, a territory that encompassed the later states of Oregon, Washington, Idaho, and small parts of Montana and Wyoming